Greek comedy flourished in the fifth and fou
beyond Athens. Aristophanes and Menander a1_
work is in part extant, but many other dramatists are known from surviving
fragments of their plays. This sophisticated yet accessible introduction explores
the genre as a whole, integrating literary questions (such as characterization,
dramatic technique or diction) with contextual ones (for example, audience
response, festival context, interface with ritual or political frames). In addition,
it also discusses relevant historical issues (political, socio-economic and legal)
as well as the artistic and archaeological evidence. The result provides a unique
panorama of this challenging area of Greek literature which will be of help to
students at all levels and from a variety of disciplines but which will also provide
stimulus for further research.

A complete list of books in the series is at the back of the book.

THE CAMBRIDGE
COMPANION TO
GREEK COMEDY

EDITED BY
MARTIN REVERMANN

CAMBRIDGE
UNIVERSITY PRESS

CAMBRIDGE
UNIVERSITY PRESS

University Printing House, Cambridge CB2 8BS, United Kingdom

Cambridge University Press is part of the University of Cambridge.

It furthers the University's mission by disseminating knowledge in the pursuit of
education, learning and research at the highest international levels of excellence.

www.cambridge.org
Information on this title: www.cambridge.org/9780521747400

First published 2014

A catalogue record for this publication is available from the British Library

Library of Congress Cataloguing in Publication data
The Cambridge Companion to Greek Comedy / edited by Martin Revermann.
pages   cm. – (Cambridge Companions to Literature)
Includes bibliographical references and index.
ISBN 978-0-521-76028-7 (hardback)
1. Greek drama (Comedy) – History and criticism.   I. Revermann, Martin,
editor of compilation.
PA3161.C27   2014
882′.0109 – dc23   2013050037

ISBN 978-0-521-76028-7 Hardback
ISBN 978-0-521-74740-0 Paperback

To the memory of Colin Austin and Kathryn Bosher

CONTENTS

CONTENTS

CONTENTS

ILLUSTRATIONS

CONTRIBUTORS

ZACHARY P. BILES is Associate Professor of Classics at Franklin&Marshall College. He is the author of *Aristophanes and the Poetics of Competition* (Cambridge, 2011), and is working on a commentary on Aristophanes' *Wasps*.

KATHRYN BOSHER was Assistant Professor of Classics at Northwestern University. She was the editor of *Theater Outside Athens: Drama in Greek South Italy and Sicily* (Cambridge, 2012).

ERIC CSAPO is Professor of Classics at the University of Sydney. He is author of *Actors and Icons of the Ancient Theater* (2010) and *Theories of Mythology* (2005), and co-author of *The Context of Ancient Drama* (1995). Together with Peter Wilson he is currently working on a multi-volume social and economic history of the ancient theatre.

HELENE P. FOLEY is Professor of Classics, Barnard College, Columbia University. She is the author of books and articles on Greek epic and drama, on women and gender in antiquity, and on modern performance and adaptation of Greek drama. She is the author of *Ritual Irony: Poetry and Sacrifice in Euripides* (1985), *The Homeric Hymn to Demeter* (1994), *Female Acts in Greek Tragedy* (2001), *Reimagining Greek Tragedy on the American Stage* (2012) and co-author (with Elaine Fantham, Natalie Kampen, Sarah Pomeroy and Alan Shapiro) of *Women in the Classical World: Image and Text* (1984). She edited *Reflections of Women in Antiquity* (1981) and co-edited *Visualizing the Tragic: Drama, Myth and Ritual in Greek Art and Literature* (2007) as well as *Antigone on the Contemporary World Stage* (2011).

MICHAEL FONTAINE is Associate Professor of Classics at Cornell University. He is the author of *Funny Words in Plautine Comedy* (2010) and other articles on Roman comedy and Latin literature. He has also co-edited *The Oxford Handbook of Greek and Roman Comedy* (2014).

EDITH HALL is Professor of Classics at King's College London. She has published extensively on ancient Greek literature, especially Greek drama, with particular emphasis on ethnicity, gender and class as well as reception. Her many books include *Inventing the Barbarian: Greek Self-Definition through Tragedy* (1989), *Greek Tragedy and the British Theatre 1660–1914* (co-authored with Fiona Macintosh) (2005), *The Theatrical Cast of Athens: Interactions between Ancient Greek Drama and Society* (2006) and *Adventures with Iphigenia in Tauris: A Cultural History of Euripides' Black Sea Tragedy* (2013). She has co-edited *Aristophanes in Performance 421BC–AD 2007* (2007). Her major King's College London Research Project on *Classics and Class 1789–1939* was launched in 2013.

STEPHEN HALLIWELL is Professor of Greek at the University of St Andrews, Scotland. His books include *Aristotle's Poetics* (1986), *Plato Republic 10* (1988), *Plato Republic 5* (1993), *The Aesthetics of Mimesis: Ancient Texts and Modern Problems* (2002), *Greek Laughter: A Study of Cultural Psychology from Homer to Early Christianity* (Cambridge, 2008) and *Between Ecstasy and Truth: Values and Problems in Greek Poetics from Homer to Longinus* (2011).

RICHARD HUNTER is Regius Professor of Greek at the University of Cambridge and a Fellow of Trinity College. His research interests include Hellenistic poetry and its reception in Rome, ancient literary criticism, and the ancient novel. His most recent books are *The Hesiodic Catalogue of Women: Constructions and Reconstructions* (Cambridge, 2005), *The Shadow of Callimachus* (Cambridge, 2006), (with Ian Rutherford) *Wandering Poets in Ancient Greek Culture* (Cambridge, 2009), *Critical Moments in Classical Literature* (Cambridge, 2009), (with Donald Russell) *Plutarch, How to Study Poetry (De audiendis poetis)* (Cambridge, 2011), *Plato and the Traditions of Ancient Literature* (Cambridge, 2012) and *Hesiodic Voices: Studies in the Ancient Reception of the Works and Days* (Cambridge, 2014). Many of his essays have been collected in *On Coming After: Studies in Post-Classical Greek Literature and its Reception* (2008).

DAVID KONSTAN is the John Rowe Workman Distinguished Emeritus Professor of Classics and the Humanistic Tradition, and Emeritus Professor of Comparative Literature, at Brown University; he is also Professor of Classics at New York University. Among his publications are *Roman Comedy* (1983), *Sexual Symmetry: Love in the Ancient Novel and Related Genres* (1994), *Greek Comedy and Ideology* (Oxford, 1995), *Friendship in the Classical World* (Cambridge, 1997), *Pity Transformed* (2001), *The Emotions of the Ancient Greeks* (Toronto, 2006), *'A Life Worthy of the Gods': The Materialist Psychology of Epicurus* (2008) and *Before Forgiveness: The Origins of a Moral Idea* (Cambridge, 2010). He is also one of the editors of *The Birth of Comedy: Texts, Documents, and Art from Athenian Comic Competitions, 486–280* (2011). He is a past president of the American Philological Association, and a member of the American Academy of Arts and Sciences.

SUSAN LAPE is Professor of Classics at the University of Southern California. She is the author of *Reproducing Athens: Menander's Comedy, Democratic Culture, and the Hellenistic City* (Princeton, 2004) and of *Race and Citizen Identity in the Classical Athenian Democracy* (Cambridge, 2010).

C. W. MARSHALL is Professor of Greek and Roman Theatre at the University of British Columbia. He is the author of *The Stagecraft and Performance of Roman Comedy* (Cambridge, 2006) and the co-editor (with George Kovacs) of *Classics and Comics* (2011) and *No Laughing Matter: Studies in Athenian Comedy* (2012).

ALFONSO MORENO is Andrew and Randall Crawley Fellow and Tutor in Ancient History at Magdalen College, Oxford. He works on Athenian social and economic history and is the author of *Feeding the Democracy* (2007).

SEBASTIANA NERVEGNA is a Postdoctoral Fellow at the University of Sydney, funded by the Australian Research Council. She is a member of the Department of Classics and Ancient History, working in the University's Centre for Classical and Near Eastern Studies of Australia (CCANESA). She is the author of *Menander in Antiquity: The Contexts of Reception* (Cambridge, 2013), and has published articles in the *Zeitschrift für Papyrologie und Epigraphik* and in the *American Journal of Philology*.

MARTIN REVERMANN is Professor of Classics and Theatre Studies at the University of Toronto. His research interests lie in the area of ancient Greek drama (production, reception, iconography, sociology), Brecht, theatre theory and the history of playgoing. He is the author of *Comic Business: Theatricality, Dramatic Technique and Performance Contexts of Aristophanic Comedy* (2006). He also co-edited (with P. Wilson) *Performance, Iconography, Reception: Studies in Honour of Oliver Taplin* (2008) and (with I. Gildenhard) *Beyond the Fifth Century: Interactions with Greek Tragedy from the Fourth Century BCE to the Middle Ages* (2010). In addition, he is the author of articles on Greek comedy and tragedy, Brecht, Homer, theatre-related vase paintings and theatre theory.

DAVID KAWALKO ROSELLI is Associate Professor of Classics at Scripps College in Claremont, California. He is the author of *Theater of the People: Spectators and Society in Ancient Athens* (2011) and several articles and essays on the drama, social history and culture of ancient Greece. He is currently completing a book on subaltern representations and the formation of minority discourse in ancient Greece.

RALPH M. ROSEN is Rose Family Endowed Term Professor of Classical Studies at the University of Pennsylvania. His scholarly interests and publications lie broadly in Greek and Roman literature and intellectual history, with particular focus on ancient comic and satirical poetic genres. His most recent book is *Making Mockery:*

The Poetics of Ancient Satire (2007). Other interests include ancient medicine and philosophy, and much of his current work concerns the Hippocratic tradition and Galen.

IAN RUFFELL is Lecturer in Classics at the University of Glasgow. He is the author of *Politics and Anti-Realism in Athenian Old Comedy* (2011) and has published extensively on Greek comedy (with particular emphasis on formal and political questions and the nature of audience response) as well as on Roman comedy and Roman satire.

KEITH SIDWELL, Emeritus Professor of Latin and Greek at University College Cork and formerly Head of the Department of Classics, has been since 2008 Adjunct Professor in the Department of Greek and Roman Studies in the University of Calgary. His interests include Greek drama, Lucian and his reception, Medieval Latin and Neo-Latin, as well as Greek and Latin pedagogy. His most recent books are *Aristophanes the Democrat: The Politics of Satirical Comedy during the Peloponnesian War* (Cambridge, 2009) and (with Jason Harris) *Making Ireland Roman: Irish Neo-Latin Writers and the Republic of Letters* (2009).

ALAN SOMMERSTEIN is Professor of Greek at the University of Nottingham. He has published editions with translations of all the comedies of Aristophanes (1980–2002), of the plays and fragments of Aeschylus (2008) and (with three collaborators) of selected fragmentary plays of Sophocles (2006–2011). He has just completed, together with five collaborators, a two-volume study of the oath in archaic and classical Greece.

GONDA VAN STEEN is the Cassas Chair in Greek Studies at the University of Florida. Her research interests include classical drama and its reception history, especially in the nineteenth and twentieth centuries. She is the author of *Venom in Verse: Aristophanes in Modern Greece* (2000), *Liberating Hellenism from the Ottoman Empire: Comte de Marcellus and the Last of the Classics* (2011) and of *Theatre of the Condemned: Classical Tragedy on Greek Prison Islands* (2011).

ANDREAS WILLI is Diebold Professor of Comparative Philology at the University of Oxford. He is the author of *The Languages of Aristophanes: Aspects of Linguistic Variation in Classical Attic Greek* (2003) and *Sikelismos: Sprache, Literatur und Gesellschaft im griechischen Sizilien* (2008), and he has edited, among other things, *The Language of Greek Comedy* (2002). His research interests also include Greek, Latin and Indo-European historical and comparative linguistics, Greek dialectology, and ancient sociolinguistics.

NIGEL WILSON was, until his retirement in 2002, a Fellow of Classics at Lincoln College, Oxford. He has published the *Oxford Classical Text* of Aristophanes together with the volume *Aristophanea: Studies on the Text of Aristophanes* (both 2007). He is also one of the authors of *The Archimedes Palimpsest* (Cambridge, 2011).

VICTORIA WOHL is Professor of Classics at the University of Toronto. She is the author of *Intimate Commerce: Exchange, Gender, and Subjectivity in Greek Tragedy* (1998), *Love Among the Ruins: The Erotics of Democracy in Classical Athens* (2002) and *Law's Cosmos: Juridical Discourse in Athenian Forensic Oratory* (2010).

ACKNOWLEDGEMENTS

First, I would like to thank all contributors for their willingness to share their expertise within the format of a *Cambridge Companion*. A special word of thanks is due to Dr Michael Sharp, Elizabeth Hanlon and Christina Sarigiannidou of Cambridge University Press and copy-editor Elizabeth Davison for their professionalism and commitment. Adriana Brook, Patrick Hadley, Alysse Rich and Donald Sells provided helpful criticism at various points.

This volume is dedicated, with great sadness, to the memory of two late colleagues, Colin Austin and Kathryn Bosher, in grateful recognition of the contributions they have made to the study of Greek comedy.

MARTIN REVERMANN

Introduction

Greek comedy: some basics

The only fully intact textual evidence from fifth-century and (very) early fourth-century comedy are the eleven completely preserved comedies by Aristophanes, who was born, in all likelihood, shortly after 450 BCE and died after 388 BCE.[1] This is, in fact, not as thin a basis as one might initially think. For not only is the number of completely preserved Aristophanic comedies actually quite high: it amounts, after all, to about a quarter of Aristophanes' total output of around forty comedies (contrast this with the seven plays we have by Sophocles and the six or seven we have by Aeschylus, both of whom wrote considerably more plays in total than Aristophanes). What is perhaps more is the fact that those eleven comedies are datable (in most cases very precisely), and that they happen to span the entire duration of Aristophanes' artistic career, from the earlier part (*Acharnians* [425], *Knights* [424], *Clouds* [423], *Wasps* [422] and *Peace* [421]) via mid-career plays (*Birds* [414], *Lysistrata* [411], *Women at the Thesmophoria* [411] and *Frogs* [405]) to the early fourth-century plays (*Assembly Women* [393, 392 or 391?] and *Wealth* [388]).

For the remainder of the fourth century, however, the textual evidence is largely fragmentary. There is one virtually complete comedy, preserved on papyrus, the *Dyscolus* by Menander (who lived from 342/1 BCE to 292/1 BCE or thereabouts). This comedy, which has been known only since the publication of the Bodmer papyrus codex in 1959, was performed in 316 BCE (when it won first prize in Athens at the Lenaean festival). It is therefore quite an early Menander play. There are substantial parts of several other Menandrian comedies (*Aspis, Samia, Men at Arbitration* and

---

[1] On the life of Aristophanes and the chronology of his works see Gelzer (1971) 1391–1419 (the most detailed account); Easterling/Knox (1985) 775–7; Halliwell (1997) ix–xvii; von Möllendorff (2002) 58–62.

Perikeiromenê), known from the Bodmer codex just mentioned and the Cairo Codex published in 1907.[2] A few more plays, notably *The Sicyonian(s)*, we have some idea of. Apart from the *Dyscolus*, however, none of the plays just mentioned is currently datable with any confidence. Given that Menander's total output is known to have exceeded 100 comedies, what we are left to work with is therefore a fairly meagre sample.

In addition, there is a large amount of fragmentary textual evidence from both fifth- and fourth-century comedy, collected in the landmark edition by Rudolf Kassel and one of the dedicatees of this volume, the late Colin Austin (eight volumes were published between 1983 and 2001; note that in this Companion all quotations of comic fragments are from this edition). This includes remains from Sicilian playwrights, especially Epicharmus, who wrote not in the Attic dialect (which all other comedy we have was composed in) but in their local Doric dialect. Produced in the very late sixth and early fifth centuries, Epicharmus' work pre-dates anything we have of Attic comedy by decades. Unfortunately, the fragments and play titles currently known offer only a few tantalizing glimpses. Even as basic a question as to whether Epicharmus' plays, and Sicilian comedy in general, had a chorus at all remains controversial. Last but certainly not least there is rich visual evidence, especially terracotta figurines and comedy-related vase paintings, although most of these vases are not from fifth-century Athens but from South Italy in the fourth century. Their systematic collection and, even more so, their rigorous use for the understanding of comedy is a more recent phenomenon in the study of Greek comedy (associated in particular with the names of Thomas Webster and Oliver Taplin). The evidence for comedy tends to be much easier to handle methodologically than artifacts related to tragedy, and provides invaluable information about costume, masks, props and plots in particular.

A Companion to Greek Comedy

At least two general conclusions present themselves as a result of this very brief survey. First, our views on fifth- and fourth-century comedy are by default somewhat 'Aristophanocentric' and 'Menandrocentric', respectively. This cannot change fundamentally without substantial new papyrus discoveries. Having said that, this Companion makes a serious and sustained effort to widen the scope of analysis beyond Aristophanes and Menander wherever possible (most overtly so in the chapter by Biles on the rivals of Aristophanes

[2] For the history of the Menander text and its restoration see Blume (2010) and Handley (2011).

and Menander, and in Sidwell's discussion of fourth-century comedy before Menander).

Secondly, and as a corollary to the first point, the study of Greek comedy is bound to have an Athenocentric bias. Again, this Companion counteracts this inbuilt feature of studying Greek comedy as much as possible by dedicating a separate chapter to Sicilian comedy (Bosher) and by featuring three chapters which discuss the ways in which Greek comedy was received and appropriated in antiquity (Hunter, Nervegna, Fontaine). But unlike the 'author-centrism' on Aristophanes and Menander, this 'city-centrism' is not the result of chance and the vicissitudes of textual transmission. Sicilian comedy set aside, Greek comedy of the fifth and fourth century does have Athens at its centre, linguistically (by being written in the Attic dialect) as well as conceptually and thematically.

The agenda, then, for this Companion to Greek Comedy is this: what happens if we look at the Greek comic tradition as a *continuum*, spanning the fifth and fourth centuries (and beyond)? What, from a diachronic perspective, remains similar and what turns out to be different? Where are discontinuities? How about if we try to abandon, or at least try to shift (as far as the evidence permits), some of the traditional focal points – which means putting Aristophanes and Menander at the very centre – in favour of a more integrated approach which views Aristophanes and Menander, the playwrights who are by far the best documented, as part of a much broader competitive field of rival playwrights working in an organic, ever-evolving art form? And is there a way of putting into perspective the Athenocentrism of our evidence, especially by looking at Sicily and its vibrant comic theatre? Last but certainly not least, what happens if we look at Menander exclusively from the perspective of the Greek comic tradition that he was shaped by and which, in turn, he himself helped shape, as opposed to having his impact on Roman comedy always at the back of our minds somehow (which happens very regularly)?

All contributors were given this overarching agenda at the very start of the project, and they have all been pursuing it in one way or another. Their accounts, of course, differ widely, and each contributor has chosen some specific emphasis. But it is important for the reader to bear in mind this agenda which each contributor chose to respond to in his or her own way. The result is a Companion which adopts a broad and integrative approach (historical, textual, theatrical, socio-linguistic, theoretical, archaeological, iconographic), covering themes of literary, linguistic, social, political, cultural and legal history. Like every Companion, this one aims to provide informed as well as inspiring and thought-provoking discussions, written by an international team of specialists, of central aspects that are accessible to students of Greek literature (at all levels) as well as the non-specialist reader. Its twenty-three chapters are arranged in five parts, an organization which provides the user with a wide range of possible reading experiences (on which see more below). While some chapters deal with topics that have received a significant amount of scholarly attention in recent decades, others tackle areas for which there is comparatively little existing research (comedy and the law, for instance, or even comedy and religious practice). Moreover, space was, quite deliberately, made for some themes that have not been addressed systematically in a while (one example is heroism in comedy, or the question of what social historians can and cannot make of the evidence provided by comedy). It should also be mentioned at this point that some pieces adopt positions that are not necessarily considered orthodox in the field at this very moment (on fourth-century comedy before Menander, for example, or on the relationship between Greek and Roman comedy). This too is intentional: if the chapters of this Companion – individually, in clusters or as a whole – were to stimulate fruitful controversy and further research, a prime objective of this project would have been achieved.

Ways of reading this Companion

The target audience of the Companion genre is notoriously diverse, encompassing specialists in the field, Classicists at all levels with various degree of proximity to the field, non-Classicists at all levels with interest in the field, and finally that most elusive target audience of all, the 'general reader'. Like all specimens of this genre, this Companion too attempts to integrate the needs and interests of all those groups without alienating and losing any of them. While each of the parts can be read as one entity, the numerous interconnections (some of which I will be trying to point out in what follows) invite 'cross-reading' of this Companion. Last but not least, the index at the end has been designed to enable thematic readings across the whole volume.

Purpose and structure of the Introduction

The purpose of this Introduction is not only to present, in a compressed manner, the chief arguments of each chapter, but also to try to embed those chapters within this Companion as a whole (and, to a much lesser extent given the space constraints, within the study of Greek comedy in general). Most of all, the Introduction should be an appetizer of sorts, making its readers want to explore for themselves the richness and complexities of each chapter and section (which cannot possibly be conveyed by the Introduction). The approach taken is a sequential one, proceeding section by section, with frequent sign-posting of connections across sections. Authors' names are highlighted in bold upon their first (significant) mention, a technique which may also serve as an inbuilt mini-index for quick orientation within the Introduction.

The individual parts

In its first part, **SETTING THE STAGE (IN ATHENS AND BEYOND)**, this Companion contains five chapters which open up the field in a variety of dimensions: conceptually, by attempting the placement of *kômôidia* within some topography of 'genre' (Konstan); socio-dynamically, by exploring the position of the two main surviving playwrights, Aristophanes and Menander, within the wider dynamics of state-organized dramatic festivals and competitive poetics with their many rivals (Biles); chronologically, by embarking on the (difficult) attempt to construct a plausible continuous narrative of the development of the genre in the fourth century between the two strongholds of documentation, Aristophanes and Menander (Sidwell); geographically, by avoiding the limitations of Athenocentrism and expanding the field of vision to include comedy in Sicily (Bosher); and materially, by giving proper discussion to the large amount of visual evidence (especially theatre-related vase paintings) which invaluably complements and expands the surviving textual evidence (Csapo). It is within this multi-dimensional panorama thus created in the first five chapters that this volume as a whole is to be seen.

First, David **KONSTAN** explores how the concept of 'genre' helps to understand fundamental features of fifth- and fourth-century Greek comedy. This task is complicated, on a theoretical level, by the fact that 'genre' is not an unproblematic concept and best treated as a moving target than a fixed category of analysis. Also, the limited quantity and nature of evidence currently available imposes serious challenges and limitations. Bearing all of this in mind, Konstan's overall argument is that while the playwrights and their audiences had a clear sense that the performance occasioned by *kômôidia* was demarcated from that of *tragôidia*, those boundaries nevertheless remained fluid, and even lent themselves to being transgressed in what Konstan calls an 'evolutionary dance' of *kômôidia* and *tragôidia* (which has probably already begun in the fifth century). Drawing on Frye's notion of archetypes and Todorov's critical discussion of them, Konstan embarks on a nuanced exploration of genre-specific poetic practices that operated not as rules but as artistic challenges for both the creators and the consumers of *kômôidia*. Konstan gives special attention to New Comedy's focus on domestic situations and greater affinity to tragedy, with a particular focus on the generically different treatment of *erôs*.

Despite the necessarily 'Aristophanocentric' and 'Menandrocentric' bias which characterizes the study of Greek comedy, there are nonetheless openings for a broader assessment of genre-related issues beyond those two comic playwrights. The exemplary edition of the fragmentary evidence by Austin and Kassel has, over the past fifteen or so years, enabled a significant amount of fresh research on the rivals of Aristophanes and Menander. This work has considerably expanded the field of vision and deepened our understanding of Aristophanes and Menander, on the one hand, and the fragmentary playwrights, on the other. It includes monographs devoted entirely to Cratinus and Eupolis, respectively, as well as works on the practice and poetics of comedy as a competitive business. As Zachary **BILES** points out early on in his contribution on the rivals of Aristophanes and Menander, competition had to be particularly fierce (and overt) among comic poets, since tragedy, by generic convention, could not frame its competitiveness (which surely existed) within the same rhetorical frameworks that comedy had at its disposal, possibly from the earliest stages of its development onwards. Especially the so-called parabasis, a metrically and discursively distinct section delivered by the comic chorus, is comedy's showcase for articulating, via the choral persona, its competitive poetics. It is these poetics which constitute Biles' core interest. But the spirit of aggressive poetics pervades Aristophanic comedy beyond the confines of the parabasis: it extends to choice and presentation of characters (Pericles, Cleon or Socrates, for example), and to the appropriation of metre and dramatic techniques. Comic poets, however, do not only take on other comic poets. In addition, there is rivalry with comedy's glorified and beautiful sister art, tragedy, as part of its ongoing quest for generic self-assertion, self-definition and self-elevation. This, in fact, was an area of competitive poetics that Aristophanes was interested in to a high, perhaps even exceptional, degree.

Biles discusses in detail a particularly fascinating case study, the likely interaction between Aristophanes' *Knights,* performed at the Lenaea in 424, and Cratinus' *Wine Flask (Pytinê)* a bit more than a year later. There is a compelling case for assuming that Cratinus' whole play is a response to the way in which Cratinus was represented in the parabasis of the Aristophanic *Knights*. In other words, Cratinus went all out when getting right back at Aristophanes, and with consummate skill in the art of comedy-making. The success was overwhelming, and dealt a big blow to Aristophanes: Cratinus' play won first prize at the Great Dionysia in 423, a competition where Aristophanes' own *Clouds* finished 'only' third. Aristophanes' subsequent indignation is more than palpable in the revised parabasis of *Clouds*, which was written in response to this humiliating defeat. In our evidence, this instance marks a highlight both for its intensity and its creativity, and it falls within the period which saw the most engaged and colourful competitive poetics, the last decades of the fifth century. Afterwards, there is a notable downscaling in frequency, flamboyance and dynamics, a tendency that can already be observed in the two early fourth-century Aristophanic comedies *Assembly Women* and *Wealth*. By the time of Menander, the tendency, pre-figured in tragedy, of prioritizing plot integrity and realism (of sorts) would largely forestall the kind of dramatic rupture and discontinuity that overt competitive poetics needs to thrive. Victory over rivals remains much-coveted among comic playwrights, but the discourse of competition becomes largely a static add-on at the closure of a performance rather than the colourful *tour de force* it had been a century earlier.

While Biles had already been dealing a fair amount with fragmentary evidence (and reflected on the methodological implications of using it), the problems, and the fascination, of such evidence are compounded in the area discussed by Keith **SIDWELL**, namely fourth-century comedy before Menander. Problematic as this whole field may be, it is nonetheless far from being the 'desert' that Gilbert Norwood, in 1931, had made it out to be. Sidwell in fact starts by reminding us of the scope and diversity of what we *do* have after all: two early fourth-century comedies by Aristophanes (*Assembly Women* and *Wealth*), complete save for their choral songs; a substantial and diverse body of material evidence, consisting of theatre-related vase paintings, terracotta figurines and masks, reliefs and, last but not least, the archaeological remains of actual theatres (most notably Epidaurus); inscriptions, containing precious evidence concerning, for instance, the plays and playwrights who competed in dramatic festivals along with their sponsors (the *chorêgoi*); and a series of later sources, dating up to the Byzantine period: Athenaeus' *Deipnosophists*, Pollux's *Onomasticon*, Stobaeus, the *Suda* lexicon and a number of *Prolegomena on Comedy*. None of these items is unproblematic, and each source needs to be used carefully and with circumspection. But as Sidwell demonstrates, when put together, the evidence allows for better and bigger insights than one might initially think possible.

Taking his cues from two crucial passages in Aristotle (from the *Poetics* and the *Nicomachean Ethics*, respectively) Sidwell endorses a model which challenges the orthodox assumption of a single, linear development from fifth-century 'old' via (early and mid-) fourth-century 'middle' to late fourth-century 'new' comedy. Instead, Sidwell proposes, we are looking at 'two separate highways': satirical comedy, on the one hand, and plot-based comedy, on the other. The former, with its vitriolic (though increasingly disguised) invectives against individuals, is gradually being 'regulated out of existence', because it is being perceived by the social and political elite as a threat to stability and their own claims to power. In particular, Sidwell wonders whether the mythological and paratragic plays that appear to have been so popular in the period between 380 and 350 have to be understood as satirical, using myth and paratragedy as code and camouflage for invectives against known individuals. But while satirical comedy peters out, it is the other 'highway', that of plot-based comedy, which actually leads somewhere as the fourth century progresses, culminating in Menandrian comedy. One fascinating consequence of the model developed by Sidwell is that Menander is firmly situated within Greek comedy of the fourth century, since Sidwell argues that much that is characteristic of Menandrian comedy is pre-figured in comedy of the 350s and earlier.

The chapter by Kathryn **BOSHER** breaks the Athenocentric mould that has dominated the study not just of Greek comedy but of Greek drama more broadly (and many other areas of fifth- and fourth-century Greek literature). She introduces us to the intriguing and important, though fragmentary and much under-documented, world of Sicilian comedy (which was written in the Doric dialect, unlike Athenian comedy which was composed in Attic Greek). One of the distinct (and novel) features of her work is its top-down approach to the study of theatre in the West: especially the powerful Syracusan tyrants Gelon, Hieron and, in the fourth century, Dionysius I emerge as 'prime movers', and principal beneficiaries, of the mass medium theatre (note at this point that Bosher's approach to Sicilian comedy via cultural politics is complemented by the socio-linguistic analysis pursued in the later chapter by Willi on the language of comedy).

Bosher argues that by lending support to an indigenous dramatic talent like Epicharmus or recruiting a star poet like Aeschylus from Athens, the Sicilian tyrants appropriated, instrumentalized and ultimately re-shaped the local theatre to suit ideological and political agendas that are fundamentally different from those which Aristophanes, Menander and their respective rivals interacted with in Athens (which, for the most part of the fifth and fourth century, is under democratic rule). Also noteworthy is the fact that there is no evidence of indigenous Sicilian tragedy, even if strong interest in tragedy from Athens is implied by the successful attempt of the Syracusan tyrant Hieron (who ruled from 478 to 467 BCE) to draw Aeschylus to his court. Without an indigenous stage rival, Sicilian comedy, certainly during the lifetime of Epicharmus in the late sixth and early fifth centuries, appears to have been operating in a cultural economy quite different from that of the fifth- and fourth-century playwrights composing Athenian comedy, who were constantly exposed to both stimulus and pressure from Attic tragedy.

Bosher's discussion of Epicharmus in particular, in conjunction with the material evidence (theatre buildings and theatre-related vase paintings) and what can be gathered about the tyrant's cultural politics, demonstrates that there is good evidence for a continuous comic tradition in the West from the late sixth through the fifth century (and possibly longer). There is also strong reason to believe that the Western theatre, like its Athenian counterpart, had a competitive element, with the adjudication of prizes by judges. This tradition, which must have been rich and diverse, is in no way 'marginal' or 'peripheral'. On the contrary, it could be trend-setting: after all, no lesser a source than Aristotle (in chapter 5 of the *Poetics*, a passage discussed in the chapter by Sidwell on fourth-century comedy before Menander) attributes the introduction of plot-based comedy in Athens to the Western comic tradition.

Yet very significant gaps in our knowledge of the Western comic tradition remain (and are unlikely to be filled without the discovery of new textual evidence). A glaring one is the chorus. On the basis of Athenian drama one would expect the chorus to be a crucial component of Greek stage art, but whether or not Epicharmus' comedies even had a chorus continues to be disputed. Nor is the precise nature of the 'mimes' written by Sophron at the end of the fifth century currently determinable with certainty. And to what extent had the Sicilian and the Attic tradition of comedy converged by the fourth century? How many of the plays underlying the quite numerous fourth-century comedy-related vase paintings from Sicily and South Italy are Western Greek plays written in Doric rather than Athenian comedies written in Attic? Does this distinction even make sense in the fourth century, or would by that time Sicilian playwrights, for instance, compose not in their local dialect but in Attic, the dialect of the increasingly canonical fifth-century Athenian playwrights (comic and tragic) who by the fourth century at the latest had become pan-Hellenic cultural icons?

The kind of material evidence just mentioned, theatre-related vase paintings, is a central concern of the chapter on the iconography of comedy by Eric **CSAPO**. It is one of the striking characteristics of the study of Greek comedy that, for all the gaps in our knowledge, there is a substantial amount of visual evidence in a variety of media (vase paintings, terracotta masks and figurines, reliefs, mosaics) – evidence which scholars working in other areas of theatre history (Shakespearean theatre, for instance) would love to have! With standard catalogues listing over 4,500 items and with the number of known comedy-related vase paintings hitting the 600 mark (and counting), Csapo seems justified in saying that 'one could claim that Greek comedy is as well represented in the remains of ancient art as in the remains of ancient texts'. Using visual evidence is not unproblematic, in part because the shift of medium, from the ephemerally performative to the materially fixed, entails crucial shifts in agendas, conventions and contextualizations. Moreover, the difficulties that arise very much depend on the kind of question that is put to the evidence: a fourth-century South Italian vase painting, for instance, may tell us very little about how a particular play was actually staged (in South Italy or elsewhere) but nonetheless provide us with an excellent impression of, say, costuming conventions, theatrical gestures, stock characters or themes that were popular with fourth-century audiences.

In his chronologically arranged and richly illustrated select survey Csapo takes us from archaic Greece to late antiquity, impressively documenting how great the impact of Greek comic performance on visual culture continued to be, even at times when there were apparently very few or no more live performances. It becomes more than obvious that, despite the difficulties involved, this evidence cannot possibly be ignored but, like the textual evidence (which of course comes with its own sets of problems as well) has to be an integral part of any attempt to understand the nature and continuous impact of Greek comedy (note that several other chapters, especially those by Sidwell on fourth-century comedy before Menander, Ruffell on character types, Revermann on divinity and religious practice, Foley on gender and Nervegna on contexts of reception, draw extensively on the visual evidence).

COMIC THEATRE, the second major section of this Companion, examines central features of comic dramaturgy: structure and dramatic technique, characterization, theatricality, the nature and dynamics of performance, audience relationship and, last but certainly not least, comic language. Using Aristophanes' *Birds* and *Wasps* as focus plays, C. W. MARSHALL introduces the reader to standard structures and structural devices, notably the parabasis, which shaped the creation of fifth-century comedies. Other fundamental aspects of comic production like the dramatic festivals or the nature and availability of certain theatrical resources (especially actors and stage space) are also being discussed. Menander operates within a similar framework of comic production, even if the nature of comic playwriting changes, clearly under the increasing influence of (Euripidean) tragedy. Marshall also demonstrates some of the methodological difficulties that arise when trying to reconstruct comic performances from what we have to work with, namely texts which lack stage directions (ancient playwrights appear not to have written stage directions at all, even when they knew that they would not be supervising the production(s) of their own plays).

The design of character(s) is at the heart of comic theatre and crucially informs its effect. As Ian RUFFELL's discussion of 'character types' demonstrates, there is no single template of character construction and deployment that would apply to fifth- and fourth-century comedy alike, even if certain tendencies are sufficiently clear and demarcated. Thus Menander's comedies, and quite certainly most, if not all, comedies written by the late fourth century, principally revolved around character types like 'soldier', 'courtesan', 'loner', 'flatterer', 'parasite', 'slave' and 'cook'. Ruffell shows in detail how a playwright like Menander uses these 'dramatic shorthands' very much with the competence and expectations of his audience in mind, regularly in fact playing *against* those expectations in order to enrich the theatrical experience. Each character type would commonly be associated with standard traits, which would find theatrical expression in a combination of visual and verbal meaning-generating systems: narrative, action, names, costume, props and, last but certainly not least, masks. A classification of forty-four such masks is preserved in a work by Pollux (second century CE) which is usually assumed to derive from a Hellenistic source, hence applicable to the situation around the time of Menander. Ruffell therefore tabulates and discusses this fascinating evidence in some detail (eyebrows are critical!), pointing out that there may not, or not always, be a one-to-one match between this typology and actual theatrical practice. Ruffell concludes this chapter by going back to the fifth century and to the comic ancestors of the types seen in Menander. Major differences here include the prominence of (more or less self-sufficient) comic routines and *noms parlants*. Often, character shorthands in Old Comedy are motivated more locally by the associative logic of the joke rather than bigger structures like plot, sub-plot or overall 'rounded' and consistent characterization. In particular, Old Comedy indulges in shifts and complexities: the identity of a character (including the chorus) is not necessarily stable over the course of a play or one-dimensional. Multiple and layered identities in plays like *Acharnians*, *Knights* and *Peace* create poly-dimensional characters that are plausible yet hilariously impossible compositions.

This section's final chapter on comic language by Andreas **WILLI** utilizes in particularly illuminating ways the over-arching agenda of this Companion, namely the holistic view of Greek comedy as one continuum. In his symmetrically structured analysis, Willi first emphasizes continuities of comic language in the areas of dialect, register, function and mode before looking at the material the other way round and pointing to discontinuities in exactly those four areas. Discontinuity, Willi demonstrates, is more pronounced: 'There is no other genre in ancient Greek literature whose language changed so fundamentally within less than two hundred years.' These discontinuities manifest themselves, among other things, by how Athenian comedy written in the Attic dialect both adapts to and at the same time resists the levelling of dialectal difference towards a 'Common Language' (*koinê*) in the course of the fourth century; or by how the continuous shifts of linguistic register, a crucial characteristic of Greek comic theatre before New Comedy, play out in detail. One important feature of Willi's discussion is the integration of Sicilian comedy (that is, effectively, Epicharmus) into the analysis, thereby fully acknowledging the remarkable fact that Greek comedy, unique among the Greek literary genres, existed not in one but in two distinct and equally recognized dialect versions throughout the fifth century. Willi's very important chapter, which is deliberately written in a way so as to be accessible to the Greekless reader as well, connects with just about any chapter of this Companion, but particularly with Konstan (genre), Bosher (Epicharmus), Ruffell (character), and two chapters of the subsequent section, Halliwell (laughter) and Roselli (class).

The eponymous **CENTRAL THEMES** of Part III are laughter, utopianism, comic heroism, class, gender and religious practice. Laughter is placed first for a reason: put simplistically, the prime function of comedy (especially when competitively performed in the way Greek *kômôidia* was) is its potential to solicit in the audience laughter of some kind at any point in time. Or, in Stephen **HALLIWELLS**'s opening words: 'Take the *idea* (or possibility) of laughter entirely out of the equation, and comedy vanishes with it.' And there is indeed a compelling amount of evidence to suggest that this is precisely how the Greeks who reflected on the nature of comedy in antiquity saw the relationship between this art form and the 'laughable' (*geloion*).

Laughter is, of course, not a monolithic affective response but exists in multiple forms within a continuum oscillating between low or high intensity, involvement and aggression, part of which is captured in the useful, if often blurred, distinction between (playful) 'laughing with' and (aggressive) 'laughing at'. Halliwell's adoption of a double perspective – laughter vis-à-vis audience during performance and laughter as part of the social world enveloping that performance – enables him to describe and analyse the bond of 'reciprocal gratification' created by comic performance. A clear separation of Aristophanic and Menandrian comedy is mandated by the evidence. In Aristophanes laughter is an omnipresent potential 'background noise', ready to punctuate the performance at any time with relentless predictability. Halliwell's discussion of, for instance, the opening of *Frogs* shows a playwright deliberately capitalizing on the whole range of possible (and potentially divergent) responses that are available to the spectator(s), intentionally blurring the distinctions between 'highbrow' and 'lowbrow' comedy, and between playful and aggressive laughter. One of the functions of laughter here is the feeling of liberation experienced by an audience that is invited to be complicit with the 'shamelessness' of comic characters who push or even straightforwardly disrespect rules and social norms. Menander, on the other hand, makes substantial shifts in the theatrical strategies involving laughter. Here, laughter is often absent, suspended or deferred, hence unpredictable and in fact very powerful when and if it occurs. The significantly less aggressive nature of laughter in Menander makes for a comic experience that is less extreme and more sympathetically tolerant than the one provided by Aristophanes.

A central and striking feature of many Greek comedies is the utopian nature of their plots: Athenian citizens, among other outrageous feats, mount huge dung-beetles to fly to heaven and bring the goddess Peace back to earth, or found a new (and, ideally, better) city high up in the sky. In his discussion of comic utopianism, Ian **RUFFELL** sets out what is conceptually and materially at stake when the real and the non-real (or even anti-real) collide in comedy's imaginative creations of 'possible worlds'. This important topic leads to a core problem of interpreting Greek comedy (especially that of the fifth century): while it is fairly easy to see what comedy is arguing against (civil war, corruption, abuse of power by individuals, etc.), what does comedy actually stand *for*? What does it positively advocate, in affirmative and socially constructive ways? Here comedy's exploration of 'possible worlds' enables the liberating (and entertaining!) articulation, if not necessarily the endorsement, of changes and transformations that are either unthinkable or difficult to explore in other discourses: a life without hunger, women as free and autonomous agents, or people living with each other in constant peace. This puts much of Greek comedy at the forefront of innovative speculative thinking, not just in the ancient Greek world. One of Ruffell's major concerns is situating Menander within the continuum of utopian thinking in Greek comedy. While prima facie Menandrian comedy may appear 'realist' and even 'anti-utopian', Ruffell argues for a shift that makes it *differently* utopian: instead of fantastic displacement of social reality in 'possible worlds' Menander has re-conceptualized comedy's mission to a replication of social reality which is idealized to such an extent as to be utopian in its own right (minus the possibility of change).

Closely connected to Ruffell's chapter is the discussion by Ralph **ROSEN** of the character who primarily enacts and embodies those comic utopias, the 'comic hero'. Picking up the baton from Cedric Whitman's 1964 book *Aristophanes and the Comic Hero*, Rosen details the complex, often ambivalent attributes of comic protagonists: strong-willed, clever, selfish, excessive, independent (often to the point of being isolated), grotesque, articulate, abusive and resourceful (to name but some). The fact that many of those attributes are anti-social and unsympathetic in nature led Whitman to conceptualize the 'comic hero' within the Greek notion of the *ponêros* ('rascal' or 'rogue'), and to locate much of that person's heroism in the degree of, and in the justification for, being such a 'rascal' (*ponêria*). Rosen not only situates Whitman's approach within the thinking of his time, but also tries to develop further the notion of the 'comic hero', widespread as it actually is in scholarly thinking (if not always overtly so). To this purpose, Rosen emphasizes that the 'comic hero' does not exist *per se* but is always a creation of deliberate authorial composition in conjunction with generic pressure. The latter implies, most of all, that a 'comic hero' *cannot* be a perfect human being but *has* to be compromised in one way or another: it is, after all, the shortcomings, failures, incongruencies and deficiencies that make those characters funny, and relatable, in the first place. It is precisely the clash between the pretence of straightforward heroism and the reality of a more complex and ambiguous real-life figure which constitutes the *comically* heroic. Rosen is particularly interested in how comic poets, especially Aristophanes, cast themselves in the role of the 'comic hero' accomplishing extraordinary feats (like confronting that monster Cleon!), notably by means of self-representation in the parabasis. The intrinsically ambiguous and imperfect nature of the comically heroic also means that in the idealized social reality that characterizes the comedy of Menander there is no place for heroes of that ilk.

The subsequent chapter by David Kawalko **ROSELLI** (re)introduces into the discussion of Greek comedy a notion that is fundamental but rarely applied full-scale: class. There is a strong connection with Rosen's preceding chapter, because Roselli sees comic protagonists as 'microcosms of class conflict'. More generally, as an expression of relationships between social groups (which may pursue identical or opposite interests), class and its theatrical representation tell us a great deal about both comedy as one expression of ideologies and about the society which chose to fund, watch and evaluate those plays. The important issue of audience sociology (including the economics of play going) is in fact an early big theme in Roselli's chapter where it receives the detailed discussion it deserves. Roselli argues for theatre audiences that were broadly stratified in sociological terms (note that other views have been adopted on this issue, for instance in Sommerstein's contribution to this volume). In particular, Roselli takes a strongly affirmative stance on as controversial an issue as the presence or absence of women in the Athenian audience.

His prime interest, however, is the representation of class and class struggle in the plays themselves. While slavery is legitimized rather than critiqued, it is the differences between the free which become major drivers of comic projects in Aristophanic comedy, as working-class heroes radically challenge the status quo and thereby the establishment maintaining it, often with the result of at least a temporary erasure of class distinctions. There is, however, no unqualified idealization of the lower classes, on the grounds that they also endorse and facilitate the rise of unscrupulous 'demagogues'. Issues of economic inequality are further complicated when combined with issues of gender, as in Aristophanes' *Assembly Women*. Menander, unsurprisingly, emerges as socially much more reactionary and conformist, with an emphasis on endorsing and validating existing hierarchies and class distinctions (the common motif of the elite woman being restored to her proper social status after prolonged misrecognition as socially inferior is a case in point). If there is equality in Menander, it is situated not in the material but in the ethical realm, with human nature serving a levelling function in the creation of an individual's character and predisposition.

'Performing gender in Greek Old and New Comedy', the chapter by Helene **FOLEY**, sees the representation of gender in comedy as fundamentally constructivist: in a theatre tradition where only men are allowed to put on (literally) the physical markers of both femininity and, even more prominently, masculinity (large leather phallus and all!), the 'staginess' of gender and gender relations is particularly evident. That said, the grotesqueness of both the male and female comic body decreased in the course of the fourth century until, by the time of Menander, there was much closer approximation to real-life proportion, beauty and youth than before. In Old Comedy, Foley demonstrates, there can be a partial tension between a male character's civic discourse (emphasizing courage, moderation and reason, as Trygaeus does in *Peace*) and the anti-civic notions of excess and lack of restraint that are articulated by his grotesque comic body. In general, Foley argues, the men in both Old and New Comedy experience much greater leeway in the freedom and range with which they can push, expand, contradict or reverse gender-based stereotypes whereas women, across the comic tradition of the fifth and fourth century, adhere much more to traditional gender roles and stereotypes. This is very evident in New Comedy with its domesticated females whose agency tends to be confined to the matter of preserving, defending or uniting natal or marital families or children (concerns that are, however, absolutely central to the interests and ideology of New Comedy). But also in Old Comedy, even a boldly (and hilariously) transgressive heroine like Lysistrata in the end reverts to, even helps restore, the status quo of gender relations, while during the very act of heroic transgression negative stereotypes of femininity (especially excessive desire for drink and sex) are constantly being activated.

The remarkable and, at least to this extent, unparalleled fact that Greek comedy not only allows but clearly thrives on ridiculing the divine with impunity is the starting observation of Martin **REVERMANN**'s discussion of 'Divinity and religious practice'. The festival frame of licence and sanctioned ridicule is certainly one of the enabling factors here. Another is the long tradition in the Greek religious imaginary of associating the divine with the laughable (often in the form of the grotesque) that can be seen in Greek literature (as early as Homer) and in Greek ritual practice. This applies especially to ritual associated with Dionysus, who was the patron deity of theatre and whose worship may have been a central formative factor in the emergence and formation of comedy (at least in Athens). Moreover, Dionysus functioned, at least in Athens, as the principal deity of worship at the two annual dramatic festivals (the Lenaea and the Great Dionysia). That Dionysus was a very popular comic, even buffoonish character is safely attested not only from Aristophanes (especially *Frogs*) but also Eupolis (*Taxiarchoi*) and Cratinus (*Dionysalexandrus*). Revermann argues that considering the widespread ridicule of the patron deity as, in the last resort, celebratory and complimentary rather than aggressively denigrating is the only plausible exegesis, not least because the ridicule is by definition ineffectual in that it, ultimately, cannot possibly affect in any way the (unassailable) stature of the divinity as divinity.

In Menander, to be sure, the divine is the all-powerful 'background force' which is both representationally and conceptually above and exempt from even the possibility of comic ridicule, very much in the vein of what can be observed in Greek tragedy throughout. But even in fifth-century Old Comedy the picture is rather nuanced. Not only do gods in comedy lack the kind of awe and threat potential which they have in tragedy. Comedy's approach to various deities also differs. While gods like Dionysus and even Zeus seem to have occupied one end of the spectrum, Athena and Demeter appear to be interestingly protected from the antics of the genre (with *Lysistrata* and *Women at the Thesmophoria* proving to be revealing test cases). Local sensitivities, in the case of Demeter possibly inherited from comedy in Sicily (where Demeter, and not Dionysus, was closely connected with theatre), may well be at the root of this phenomenon. Revermann ends his chapter by discussing whether or not it is legitimate to speak of a distinct theology of Greek comedy.

The title of Part IV of this Companion, **POLITICS, LAW AND SOCIAL HISTORY**, reflects the diversity of the its four chapters, all of which concentrate on comedy's interactions with its political and social environment in general and select socio-political structures in particular. This includes festivals, as micro-forms of social organization, especially the two competitive dramatic festivals at Athens where Greek comedy, like tragedy and satyr play, was being performed (although there were increasingly performances outside of Athens in the whole Greek cultural continuum). Similarly,

Athenian law is seen as a socio-political structure which comedy continuously interacts with as well.

In his chapter on 'The politics of Greek comedy' Alan **SOMMERSTEIN** quickly establishes as his focus the political in the narrow sense, defined as 'matters concerned with the state'. Sommerstein's central concern is to demonstrate that and how at no point Greek comedy, a state-sponsored art form (!), was indifferent to the political in this narrow sense, even if the interest differed for individual poets and periods. Of equal importance is the corollary of this statement, namely the observation that those in power were never indifferent to comedy either. Sommerstein's focus throughout is on Attic comedy, which is Athenocentric in its political and ideological bias (Bosher's discussion of Sicilian comedy and its relationship to local autocratic rule therefore offers a fascinating complement to this chapter). For Sommerstein a major indicator of comedy's political nature is its satirical (or 'iambic') vein, the biting humour directed at individuals (which is also discussed, in more general terms, in the chapters by Sidwell and Halliwell). We catch glimpses of this in the treatment of Pericles in some fragmentary plays by Cratinus (especially his *Dionysalexandrus*), which may be part of what apparently led to restrictive legislation passed in 440/39 (repealed in 437). But it is Aristophanes' lampooning of Cleon, the leading Athenian politican of the 420s, that provides a uniquely documented impression of the dynamics that could emerge. *Acharnians* (performed 425) and especially *Knights* (performed in 424) are anti-Cleon plays and apparently triggered legal action taken by Cleon against his fellow-demesman Aristophanes. Whatever happened at court, however, did not succeed in silencing Aristophanes: *Wasps* (performed in 422, months before Cleon's death at the battle of Amphipolis) prominently adopts and hilariously develops the anti-Cleon theme once again. Striking also is the public response: *Knights*, the most vitriolic of the anti-Cleon plays, won first prize at the Lenaea in 424 – and Cleon was reelected as one of the ten Athenian generals very shortly after. How is this possible? Sommerstein puts forth the ingenious idea that the Athenian citizen collective that (re)elected Cleon as general was demographically distinct from a more, though not exclusively, elitist and upper class Athenian theatre audience (who would, in one way or another, influence the ten judges casting the actual votes at the dramatic competitions). If, however, we follow the argument developed by Roselli (pp. 242–6) that Athenian theatre audiences were diverse and broadly stratified in socio-economic terms, we are dealing with some version of compartmentalization and *doublethink*: in the theatre, an Athenian citizen might well reward acidic criticism of a politician with a first prize – while still voting for that same politician in the Assembly.

The political nature of fourth-century comedy between about 380 to the beginning of Menander's career in the 320s is harder to pin down, and it is interesting to compare Sommerstein's account of this period with the scenarios entertained by Sidwell. As far as the late fourth century is concerned, Menander, argues Sommerstein, is quite unpolitical in the narrow sense (while frequently being political in the broader sense). One indicator of this may well be that in recent years both the notion of a pro-democratic and that of a pro-Macedonian Menander have seriously been argued for by scholars. The fact that most of Menander's career took place after the fall of democracy in Athens (in 322, to be restored only in 282) is surely very significant in this context: Attic comedy and Athenian democracy had for well over a century been cross-fertilizing each other, even if that relationship appears never to have been unproblematic (thus Sommerstein labels Attic comedy from the 440s to 400 as 'right-wing', meaning that it was critical of radical democracy though not anti-democratic). There is, however, fascinating fragmentary evidence from other playwrights of the late fourth century which suggests that there were exceptions to Menander's avoidance of the narrowly political, and that comic playwrights still dared use aggressive humour against local politicians.

Dramatic festivals as micro-forms of social organization are the subject of the chapter by Edith **HALL**. As part of its busy festival calendar, the city of Athens staged two dramatic festivals, the Lenaea in January/February and the Great Dionysia in March/April, while there were also performances in the *demes* across Attica (a number of which had local theatres). 'Staged' is an appropriate expression here, since especially at the Great Dionysia the city state of Athens appropriated the occasion to put on a theatrical display of its power and what is commonly referred to as its 'civic ideology', all of which frames the actual performances of plays. It is usually difficult to pin down the precise interface and dynamics between those frames, all of which are meant to stabilize the socio-political cohesion of the city state, on the one hand, and the plays, on the other, which often appear to de-stabilize or at least problematize the forces of cohesion within social organizations like the polis or the nuclear family (this applies to both comedy and tragedy). This situation becomes even more complicated as soon as the ritual dimension of those festivals is also taken into account. Both Athenian dramatic festivals, and apparently dramatic performances in Attica as a whole, were put on in honour of one deity: Dionysus, the god of transgression and liminality (hence the god of theatre). In other words, the dramatic festivals are also ritual frames, and this too can create contradictions and disconnects as, for instance, between the worshipped Dionysus in the ritual frame and the ridiculed Dionysus on the comic stage (some of this is explored in Revermann's chapter on divinity and religious practice).

Hall, however, is primarily interested in the function of festivals *within* the dramatic fiction of the plays. Festivals and festive activities are quite frequent in Aristophanes, while there only few instances in the (little) Menander we have. In her discussion Hall opposes a Bakhtinian view which would see festivals as intrinsically subversive and would emphasize the notion of licence and carnivalesque reversal. Instead she argues that, on the contrary, festivals are integrated into the dramatic fiction to articulate and stabilize mainstream opinion and the collectively sanctioned status quo, both at the pan-Athenian and at the pan-Hellenic level. This point is substantiated in a series of case studies which take the reader through several of the preserved Aristophanic plays.

Victoria **WOHL**'s chapter re-invigorates the study of an under-discussed but central issue, the relationship between comedy and Athenian law. If we know one thing about Athenian theatre audiences, it is that many of the spectators would regularly serve as jurors in Athenian court trials. The system's need to staff its big juries (which could exceed 500 jurors, depending on the case) implied that the Athenian spectators' average familiarity with, and interest in, things legal must far have exceeded that of any other audience in theatre history (even those audiences in early-modern London or Paris with their play-going law students). This is important when, for instance, trying to reconstruct how an Athenian audience would conceptualize the issues at stake in a play like *Oedipus the King*. Law and legal discourse constitute, to deploy Wohl's phrasing, a 'vulgar tongue' spoken by the entire populace. Comedy, ever the appropriating genre, fully used, even internalized this shared language: the *agôn*, comedy's formalized frame of staging conflict and opposing views (see also Marshall's chapter) is but the overt culmination of this tendency. Also, the very fact that there is an adjudication of prizes to the competing plays at the Athenian dramatic festivals bears obvious resemblance to legal procedure: the plays' audiences are also, ultimately, their jurors.

Wohl sees the theatre and the lawcourt as functional equivalents, and as vital platforms for shaping and articulating the kind of public discourse that characterized Athenian democracy. Subjecting everything and everyone to comic ridicule is analogous to the critical examination of all claims and positions in a court of law under the rule of democracy, and a sign not of cynical indifference but of deep political commitment. The justice done by the comic freedom of speech (*parrhêsia*), like that done by a court of law, is a socially constructive and self-affirmative exercise in democracy as practised in Athens. While the relationship of comedy and the law can at least initially be problematic, even one of opposition ('antinomian'), Wohl argues that usually comedy is, ultimately, eager to overcome any such discrepancy and present itself and the law as mutually supportive. Interestingly, by the time of Menander this tendency has become very much the norm, with characters in New Comedy being so familiar and at ease with the law that they regularly appropriate it for their own purposes.

The final chapter of this section, the co-authored piece on 'Comedy and the social historian' by Susan LAPE and Alfonso MORENO, also deals with a question that is central and regularly features in undergraduate exam papers but which has rarely been posed, at least overtly and fully, in recent scholarship of the past few decades. Their detailed and nuanced chapter, the longest in this Companion, seeks to correct what the authors see as an imbalance in the value for the social historian that has been attributed to Aristophanes and Menander, respectively. For Menandrian comedy with its 'naturalism' has often been seen as a rather straightforward reflection and representation of socio-economic realities in Athens, whereas the Aristophanic plays with their big and phantastic transformative projects were considered distortions by default. And Menander's focus on the domestic (the *oikos*, or 'household') has often been considered to be different from the communal and political concerns of Aristophanic comedy with its interest in matters of the city-state (polis). Lape and Moreno, by contrast, point out that both playwrights can integrate the binary of polis and *oikos*, in the form of 'polis as *oikos*-writ-large' and '*oikos* as polis-writ-large', respectively. If this is taken into account, the continuity between Aristophanes and Menander in matters of civic ideology is, in the authors' words, 'striking'.

RECEPTION, the fifth and final part of this Companion, focuses on an area that has very much been an expanding field over the past couple of decades (reflected not least in the fact that most Companions these days include reception in one way or another). This Companion, however, is different in several respects. With its five chapters this final section is larger than similar chapters in other Companions, ensuring that reception is not perceived as a final gesture of courtesy but as a research area of such import and intrinsic interest that it merits the same amount of space as any other. Also, the scope is different in that the section traces the dynamics of reception not only in modern times but since antiquity. Lastly, the history of textual transmission, discussed in the chapter by Nigel WILSON, is considered part of reception. The result is a very diverse series of chapters with significant connections both within the section and the volume as a whole.

The chapters by Richard HUNTER and Sebastiana NERVEGNA can, and should, be read as complementary, since the two authors discuss texts and contexts of ancient reception, respectively. Hunter situates comedy in the ancient tradition of rhetorical and ethical criticism for which, he argues, comedy was 'good to think with' not just because of formal and linguistic aspects but also because of comedy's strong interest in character and human interaction. Moreover, its vibrant theatricality was something that the writers of that tradition, members of a cultural elite which put a premium on rhetorical display and public performance, would latch onto easily and with profit in cultural capital. But whereas Menander quickly established himself for this tradition as one of the exemplary stylists of Attic literature who was providing the elite with dramatic idealizations of its own human ideals, elite criticism took a much more differentiated view of Aristophanes and of Old Comedy in general. On the one hand, there is the formal appeal of an art form written in Attic Greek and preserving, in Quintilian's words, 'the purest grace of the Attic language' (10.1.65). But the subject matter of this comedy type could strike a critic like Plutarch as too inappropriate, outspoken and disrespectful to the point of being shameless (apart from often being arcane in its allusions and topicality). For others like Lucian or Dio Chrysostomus, however, it was precisely those aspects that were appealing and could serve as models of salutary and socially constructive forms of critical public discourse. But regardless of which view was adopted, the antics of fifth-century comedy in its Aristophanic guise never managed to outshine the insights and handy one-liner wisdom that could be culled from Menander and the characters he created.

This picture drawn by Hunter is suitably complemented by Nervegna's focus on contexts of reception, i.e. the social rather than, broadly speaking, literary dimension of appropriation. Theatres, dinner parties (*symposia*) and schools are the three social institutions analysed, and each appropriated differently what comedy had to offer. As a school author, Menander provided safe and conformist instruction, something which cannot exactly be said about Aristophanes who, Nervegna reminds us, was not only often obscene but also considered to be 'stained with Socrates' blood' (a stigma that was to linger for a long time). Dinner parties appeared to be easier to conduct without wine than without Menander, at least for someone like Plutarch (*Sympotic Questions* 721b). As for theatres, the exact nature and duration of comic (re)performance culture are harder to determine. But in the late first century CE it is Dio Chrysostomus (*Or.* 19.5) who explicitly contrasts tragic performances without lyrics (i.e. mainly choral passages) with full comic performances as the norm of his day.

The phenomenon, discussed by Nervegna, of Menander functioning as *the* model for comic play-writing in general further attests to his profound and far-reaching cultural impact in the ancient world. It also ties in seamlessly with the subsequent chapter which completes the triad of discussions exploring reception in antiquity, Michael **FONTAINE**'s 'The reception of Greek comedy in Rome'. If integrating Menander within the tradition of fourth- and fifth-century comedy had been a major theme throughout this whole Companion, Fontaine extends this by emphasizing the strong links, thematic and formal, between the Roman comic playwrights Plautus and Terence and the Greek comic tradition, especially that of the late fourth century (Menander, Philemon and Diphilus). Fontaine concludes that, as operatic adaptations of Greek source material, 'Roman' comedy is a species of Greek comedy or, more to the point, Hellenistic literature. His stimulating and defamiliarizing discussion of Plautus and Terence as Hellenistic authors and playwrights features a number of close readings, including the substantial passage (preserved on papyrus) of Menander's *Dis Exapatôn* (*The Double Deceiver*) which can, uniquely, be matched and compared with Plautus' appropriation at *Bacchides* 494–562. Play titles and their transformations too are important and revealing evidence. Comedy's appeal to Hellenized elite audiences in Rome is one of Fontaine's particular concerns, as is utilizing Linda Hutcheon's seminal work on the dynamics of adaptation in the twentieth century to bring out more clearly the nature of Roman comedy as operatic adaptations, as 'musicals' rather than 'drama'.

Gonda **VAN STEEN**'s chapter on the modern reception of Greek comedy brings this Companion to a fitting conclusion. As with reception in antiquity, there is an imbalance between Aristophanes and Menander – now, however, with the polarity inverted. This is mainly because Menander did not start to be a full-bodied comic playwright until he was, literally, resurrected from the sands of Egypt in the twentieth century. There could, in other words, be no modern performative and theatrical reception of Menander at all until very recently. And even after the major papyrus finds of the twentieth century, especially the publication of the Bodmer papyrus codex in 1959 (which contains the whole of the *Dyscolus* and significant parts of *Aspis* and *Samia*), Menander on stage remained confined to academic theatre, often with institutional links to Classics departments. Aristophanes, however, always was a person of interest, even if that interest fluctuated greatly. This was in spite of the fact that he was never an easy and unproblematic artist to appropriate and engage with: those stains of Socrates' blood, familiar from Nervegna's chapter, proved to be very hard to erase. Needless to say, obscenity as well as the carnivalesque features of Aristophanic comedy constituted both an appeal and an obstacle. Nicodemus Frischlin's Latin translation of five Aristophanic comedies from 1586 marks the beginning, and an early highlight, of modern reception. But it is not until the twentieth century, really, that Aristophanes and his plays in performance start to make significant and diverse impact beyond the narrow circles of the cultural and bookish elite. Aristophanic plays of particular interest are those which pursue a pacifist-utopian agenda of some sort (especially *Peace* and *Birds*) and plays which easily lend themselves to proto-feminist (mis)readings (*Lysistrata* and *Assembly Women*). Aristophanes' interest in theatricalizing social transformation, dissidence and utopian thinking made him particularly appealing to artists with political leanings towards the left. Modern Greece, which is of particular concern to Van Steen, often turns its illustrious and flamboyant son into an 'Aristero-phanes', the leftist Aristophanes (sometimes combined with an emphasis on folklorist traditions, as in Karolos Koun's *Birds* of 1959). And it comes as no surprise that the Greek 'Aristero-phanes' often caused predictable tensions with the militantly conservative forces in power. Whatever the particular instantiation, the provocative edge of Aristophanic comedy is never lost. This important fact is brought home in one of the most recent appropriations discussed by Van Steen at the conclusion of this Companion, the 'Lysistrata Project'. Created as a means of opposition to the (second) Iraq war in 2003, its world-wide reach, made possible by the (then) new media of an interconnected world, quickly established the 'Lysistrata Project' as a prime example of that new and emerging species 'global theatre'. This remarkable phenomenon compellingly illustrates not just the continuing relevance but also the undiminished vitality and inspirational power of Greek comedy.

PART I

Setting the stage (in Athens and beyond)

I

DAVID KONSTAN

Defining the genre

When Dicaeopolis, in Aristophanes' *Acharnians*, stepped forward to address the audience directly, and, casting aside his dramatic identity for the moment and speaking, as the convention of the parabasis permitted, in the voice of Aristophanes himself, declared, 'I know what I myself suffered at the hands of Cleon, because of last year's comedy' (377–8), no Greek in the audience had any doubt about what *kômôidia* referred to: it was Aristophanes' play, *The Babylonians*, that had been produced the previous year, as part of the festival of the Great Dionysia, in which Aristophanes had lambasted Cleon mercilessly, and had suggested that the allied cities were slaves of the Athenian people or *dêmos*. It appears that Cleon took legal action against Aristophanes for this satire.[1] However, the point to which I wish to draw attention is that, for contemporary Athenians, the word *kômôidia* designated a specific type of drama, intended for production in a well-defined place and context: a state-sponsored civic holiday, which included dramatic and other performances along with various religious rituals and public events. What is more, it would be staged alongside other *kômôidiai*, with which it was in competition for a prize awarded by a panel of judges. An Athenian was as sure about the performance situation of a *kômôidia* as a modern Anglican entering a church would be of the reference of the term 'hymn'.

Of course, these outer conditions did not exhaust the sense of *kômôidia*. Tragedies (*tragôidiai*) too were mounted at the Great Dionysia and the Lenaea, the other official theatrical festival in fifth-century Athens, and were judged against one another. There were also contests in the choral singing of dithyrambs. An Athenian knew perfectly well the differences among these several types of performance, on the basis of their form and content. Thus, dithyrambs did not involve actors, whereas tragedy and *kômôidia* did.

---

[1] On the *Babylonians*, see Welsh (1983); on ostensible attempts to prosecute Aristophanes, see Sommerstein (2004a). I wish to thank Anna Foka and Stavroula Kiritsi, as well as Martin Revermann, for helpful comments on an earlier version of this chapter.

The latter two were distinguished, in turn, by the nature of the masks and costumes that the actors wore, comic masks in particular tending to the grotesque. Nevertheless, these features too seem extrinsic to what one means by 'genre' today, and in fact they do not cover all that an ancient theatre-goer would have understood by *kômôidia*. And yet, to go further raises questions that are far more difficult to answer precisely.

Later in *Acharnians*, Aristophanes' earliest play to survive in its entirety, the chorus remark that Aristophanes 'has been slandered by his enemies on the grounds that he *kômôidei* our city and insults the people' (630–1): *kômôidei*, the verbal form derived from *kômôidia*, clearly means something like 'satirize' or 'ridicule', and refers to the kind of lampooning that *kômôidia* was known for. Yet this is not quite the entire story with the verb, for shortly afterwards the chorus defends Aristophanes inasmuch as he '*kômôidei* what is just [or justly: *ta dikaia*]' (655): the sense here must be that his plays deliver a just message, albeit in a comic or satirical manner. Whatever the precise sense of the term, it is clear that the Athenians associated *kômôidia* with a particular kind of literary style. This would appear to bring us closer to the modern sense of 'genre', yet it raises problems of its own. Apart from the circularity involved in inferring the nature of *kômôidia* from a word meaning 'treat in the manner of a *kômôidia*', this kind of invective or derision was not characteristic of all the kinds of drama that went under the name of *kômôidia*, for example, the type of play written by Menander. Were there, then, two distinct genres that cohabited under the name *kômôidia* – what are today (following an ancient distinction) called Old Comedy and New Comedy – or is there a good reason to see all the plays that were identified as *kômôidiai* as sharing a single form?

At the end of Plato's *Symposium*, when almost all the participants have left or fallen asleep after the night-long conversation, Socrates remains awake and is attempting to convince Aristophanes and Agathon, the tragic poet whose victory was the occasion for the party, that the abilities to compose tragedy and comedy pertain to the same individual, and that anyone who has mastered the art of tragedy can do comedy as well (223D). That Aristophanes and Agathon have to be compelled to accept this conclusion, and indeed that Socrates feels the need to argue for it at all, indicates how radically distinct tragedy and *kômôidia* were perceived to be. And in fact, among all the names of Greek comic and tragic poets that have come down to us, and there are hundreds, it appears that no one ever produced plays of both kinds.[2] It was only with the Roman adaptations by Ennius and

---

[2] See Taplin (1986). Ion of Chios (490/80–420s BCE) was famous for trying his hand at a wide variety of genres, including tragedy; that he also wrote a comedy, however, hangs

others that the same writer began to compose both comedies and tragedies. This change was no doubt facilitated by the fact that most of the drama produced in Latin was adapted from Greek models, and so it was less of a stretch for the same poet to produce versions of both kinds. In addition, for reasons that we shall come to shortly, Roman dramatists did not seek their models in the Old Comedy of Aristophanes and his contemporaries, but rather in the New Comedy of Menander and his, writing a century or so later (and within a century or less of their Roman imitators); tragedy and *kômôidia* (or *comoedia*, in Latin) continued to be recognized as distinct forms, to be sure, but a case can be made that in some respects the two arts had grown closer in the course of the fourth and third centuries BCE (see below). Even so, the Greek poets themselves never thought, or dared, to cross the divide, though the comedians could and did parody their tragic counterparts; the artists in both camps stuck to their own form, evidently in the belief that they were working in distinct and incompatible media. If we seek analogies to such exclusiveness today, we might cite the relative rarity of musicians who compose or perform both classical music and jazz (playing the clarinet in particular involves different embouchures in the two traditions).

Tzvetan Todorov, in a famous article on genre published in the *Dictionnaire encyclopédique des sciences du langage* (1972), affirmed that no genre exists in isolation: it is always defined against a constellation of neighbouring forms, and exists in a dynamic tension with them. What is more, these forms are not given *a priori*, but emerge historically; nor do such forms reach a stable or final condition, what Aristotle called their *telos*, at which point they are no longer subject to further evolution. Rather, every new composition in the genre produces an alteration in it, with the result that it is constantly subject to change and deformation, and at a certain point may lose its identity and come to constitute a new form – a process that is influenced, necessarily, by developments in the neighbouring genres in relation to which it is articulated. This is why, in 1928, the Russian formalist critic Boris Tomashevsky insisted that 'no firm logical classification of genres is possible. Their demarcation is always historical, that is to say, it is correct only for a specific moment of history.'[3] One may imagine such a movement in the transition from Old Comedy to New (perhaps by way of the shadowy Middle Comedy, identified by Plutarch and later ancient sources, on which see Sidwell, Chapter 3), whether or not one presupposes an essential generic

on a single testimony, regarded as dubious by most scholars. See Revermann (2006a) 97; Jennings and Katsaros (2007a) 3 with n. 13.

[3] Tomashevsky (1928: 1977) 55, cited in Bordwell (1989) 147.

difference between the earlier and the later forms.[4] What is more, this shift will have been coordinate with parallel developments in related genres such as tragedy, even if we are too poorly informed about them to trace any clear progress.[5] An advantage of the theoretical approach of Todorov is that it at least invites inquiry into how the evolution of comedy may have dovetailed with that of other forms; indeed, the possibility of a certain rapprochement between tragedy and comedy in the fourth century and later is a subject that would repay further investigation, making use of the remains of later tragedy, sparse as they are, and taking into account the possibility that the *Rhesus* ascribed to Euripides might, as some scholars hold, date to this later period.[6]

In his book, *Genres in Discourse*, Todorov took aim principally at the archetypal theory of Northrop Frye (1957), who saw all of literature as manifesting one of four overarching patterns: the comic, the romantic, the tragic and the ironic, which Frye associated respectively with spring, summer, autumn and winter.[7] The fundamental feature of comedy is that the protagonist is reconciled with society at the end. This can happen in various ways. For example, a powerful protagonist may, by strength of character and ingenuity, reconstruct the world according to his desire: this schema corresponds to Aristophanic comedy. Alternatively, society may change in such a way as to enable the hero or heroine to achieve the object of desire, very commonly through a marriage: this is the pattern for Menandrean or New Comedy (Frye also characterizes these two types as high mimetic and low mimetic, respectively, and he thought of the low as typically succeeding the high in historical sequence).

---

[4] Csapo (2000) 115 remarks: 'The genre transformation best represented by the remains of ancient Greek literature is that of comedy'; but he warns against seeing Aristophanes and Menander as defining Old and New Comedy, since 'the plays of Aristophanes and Menander were selected for us precisely in order to save a given theory of evolution, and one that is misleading at best' (121); contrast Revermann (2006a) 106: 'there is...good reason overall to consider Aristophanes as typical of the genre'.

[5] On Hellenistic developments in tragedy, see Griffith (2008) 69–73. What we call classical Greek tragedy may itself be seen as a collection of various kinds of drama, including romantic quasi-comedies such as Euripides' *Helen*, revenge plays such as Euripides' *Medea* and *Orestes*, and grand epic narratives like Aeschylus' *Oresteia*; for the sub-genres of tragedy, see Kitto (1966); Most (2000); Mastronarde (1999–2000) and (1999–2000a); Griffith (2008), who states that *tragôidia* and *kômôidia* were 'both quite capacious and also subject to changing definitions and conventions' (60).

[6] A detailed case for the late dating of the *Rhesus* is made by Fantuzzi (forthcoming). Liapis (2012) lxxi–lxxv also argues for a fourth-century date (or even later), and that the play deliberately imitates (now canonical) Euripidean style.

[7] In another classification, literature is organized according to three modes – the comic, the tragic and the thematic – each of which is manifested in a series of five forms: mythic, romantic, high mimetic, low mimetic and ironic.

Frye's categories are sometimes referred to as genres, despite their broad sweep and high degree of abstraction, which fail to take account of such elementary determinations of form as dramatic enactment as opposed to recitation or narration: comedy at the level at which Frye discusses it can pertain as much to novels or even lyric poetry as to the theatre. Indeed, some classifications of literature draw the lines precisely between the third-person narration characteristic of epic or the novel, the dialogic form specific to drama, and first-person lyric, and while this particular set of categories is modern (more specifically, a legacy of Romanticism),[8] Plato, in the *Republic* (392D–394D), similarly sets apart epic and drama when he divides literature into three types: straightforward narrative, which does not contain speeches; imitation or *mimêsis*, which contains only speeches delivered by a character in the work, without narrative (the example is precisely drama); and a mixture of the two forms, which one finds, for example, in Homeric epic.[9] Now, these categories, whether Plato's or the modern version, are very ample; as John Frow remarks of the modern division, 'these three forms, which are adjectival in nature rather than nominal – the epical, the dramatic, the lyrical – are larger than the individual genres, which they contain'.[10] And this is surely even more true of Frye's grand archetypes. Nevertheless, even that ample vision of the tragic and comic as archetypes, which cuts across the distinction between narrative and dialogue, or epic and drama, is already present in Aristotle's *Poetics*. Having observed that Homer and the philosophical poet Empedocles have nothing in common save metre (1447b17–18), Aristotle goes on to suggest a classification of literature and other arts, such as painting, according to the virtue of the characters represented in them: that is, whether they are better than we are, like ourselves, or worse than we are. Thus Homer, Aristotle affirms, is among those who represent people as better (1448a11–12). In this respect, the *Iliad* and *Odyssey* are akin to tragedy, whereas the *Margitês*, a burlesque epic employing the iambic metre that was also ascribed to Homer, is the model for *kômôidia* (1448b38–49a1; for *kômôidia* as representing characters who are base cf. 1449a32–3). And yet, Aristotle also recognizes that the *Odyssey* provides something of the pleasure specific to *kômôidia*, insofar as it has a double kind of reversal, in which the good end up happily and the bad in ruin

---

[8] It is found in the Preface to *Cromwell* (1827), by Victor Hugo, who adopted it from Schlegel, Schelling, and others; cf. Rajan (2000) 233–6.

[9] Cf. Dionysius of Halicarnassus *On Thucydides* 37; Aristides Quintilianus *On Music* 2.10.32–7. Aristotle makes the further observation that narrative can relate simultaneous events, and may contain parallel story lines, unlike dramatic poetry (*Poetics* 1459b22–8; cf. scholia A [Aristonicus] on *Iliad* 10.299a).

[10] Frow (2006) 60; see also at 59 on the very dubious ancient origins of this classification, which, as Frow notes, is wrongly ascribed to Aristotle.

(1453a30–6).[11] At this level of generality, in which *kômôidia* consists in a happy turn of events for the protagonists, the plays of Aristophanes and Menander are both clearly comic; however, they share this description with numerous tragedies (e.g., Aeschylus' *Oresteia*, Sophocles' *Philoctetes* and *Oedipus at Colonus*, Euripides' *Ion*, *Iphigenia among the Taurians*), as well as with works that are not necessarily dramatic at all.

We have been remarking that, once we leave aside such ostensibly extrinsic and non-literary features as the festival context, costume, and other elements of performance, which appear marginal to the issue of genre (as it is understood today), we encounter definitions of comedy or *kômôidia* that are either too narrow or too broad – or both at once. If we understand *kômôidia* as the genre that *kômôidei*, that is, which 'satirizes' or the like, then *kômôidia* is closely related to invective or iambic verse, to which indeed it was often likened;[12] but in this case the term fails to include the works of Menander and his contemporaries, which we, like the ancients, classify as a species of comedy or *kômôidia*. If, however, we look to the nature of the plot, then the presence of a happy ending does indeed cover both Old and New Comedy, but also many other works that were not labelled as *kômôidiai* (e.g., satyr plays and the ancient novels). The situation is no better if, with Aristotle, we draw the distinction between tragedy and *kômôidia* on the basis of the kind of character they typically represent – that is, virtuous or vicious, since this too results in casting the net too widely – or again, too narrowly, since Menander's characters are in general not base, and may indeed be nobler than we. At this impasse, perhaps we do best to return to the specific characteristics of Old Comedy and New, leaving aside, for the time being, the question of whether they are best described as one genre or two.

As I have said, an ancient Athenian audience, whether in the fifth century or the fourth and later, would have had no difficulty in knowing whether the performance they were watching was a *kômôidia*. Thanks to this knowledge, moreover, they would be aware, broadly speaking, of the nature of the work they were about to see and hear, though the expectations of fifth-century spectators would not be the same as those of later audiences. Indeed, this is the primary function of genre: it provides what we may call a horizon of expectation, against which one may perceive the extent to which the present work conforms to and at the same time modifies the tradition to which it belongs.[13] As Todorov has argued, 'any instance of a genre will be

[11] For the idea of 'the tragic' already in Plato, see Halliwell (2002) 109–11.

[12] See Rosen (1988).

[13] Revermann (2006a) 97 observes that spectators would recognize 'a genre grid even before a single word had been spoken'.

necessarily different' from those that preceded it; what is more, by virtue of this difference, '*every* work modifies the sum of possible works'.[14] Far from operating as a constraint, then, or as a set of rules, generic norms are a constant challenge to artists, and require in turn a high degree of critical competence in the public. What, then, was the ancient audience, assembled in the theatre, prepared to see when it was time for a *kômôidia*, whether this was after the performance of a set of tragedies (three at the Greater Dionysia, with the addition of a satyr play; perhaps just two at the Lenaea) or on a separate day devoted to the genre?[15]

In the fifth century, spectators would expect to see a play with three speaking actors (or possibly four) and a chorus, all or almost all dressed in outlandish, padded costumes, and many bearing large leather phalluses; some of them, especially in the chorus, might even be dressed as animals or other strange entities, such as clouds. These outfits, which were specific to Old Comedy (they were wholly abandoned by Menander's time, and foreign both to tragedy and satyr play), were a sign of what the audience already knew: that the play they were about to see would be ribald and fantastical, departing from the more naturalistic conventions which obtained for tragedy. The audience would not be shocked, for example, at the spectacle of an ordinary man feeding a dung beetle so that it grew as large as Pegasus, and could carry him to heaven where he might liberate the goddess of peace. But it might well have been surprised to see a play open with a woman dressed in an ordinary garment, like Lysistrata at the beginning of the play named for her. No phallus here; perhaps no excessive padding beneath her cloak. Was Aristophanes announcing, right from the start, a new kind of heroine on the comic stage, and so a new variation on the conventions of Old Comedy? Jeffrey Henderson has suggested that the representation of the heroine in *Lysistrata* was in fact a departure from the traditional form.[16] I would add only that the cue signalling such an innovation was perhaps already evident to the original public in a feature of costume which for us may pass wholly unnoticed. This is the kind of subtlety that a sophisticated manipulation of generic canons permits.

An ancient audience, whether in the fifth century or later, would also know that the characters on stage would speak in verse, and in a range of metres that, at least for spoken dialogue, was similar to that of tragedy and the satyr play. However, they would be aware as well that, in *kômôidia*, the metrical rules would be looser than in the other kinds of drama (this is

---

[14] The first quote is Todorov as cited in Gledhill (1985) 60, the second is Todorov (1973) 6.

[15] On the differences between the dramatic festivals, see Csapo and Slater (1995) 123f.

[16] Henderson (1980b) and (1987b) xxxvii–xl.

true of New Comedy as well as Old). So finely attuned were they to this difference that they could recognize allusions to, or parodies of, tragedy by the verse form alone, when the writers of *kômôidia* deliberately mimicked the metrical constraints of the more elevated genre. By contrast, the number of resolved feet in Lysistrata's opening speech, while modest for *kômôidia*, would nevertheless have been one more sign that this was not tragedy (compare, for example, the nurse's speech with which Euripides' *Medea* begins). In this respect, moreover, *kômôidia* differed from satyr plays as well, if we may judge by Euripides' *Cyclops*, which is the sole example to survive complete, and the substantial fragments of other such dramas. Beyond metre, the audience at a *kômôidia* in the time of Aristophanes would anticipate a linguistic register that was highly varied, including colloquialisms and vulgar language, extravagant multisyllabic coinages, occasional imitations of non-Attic dialects or ungrammatical and even nonsensical expressions on the part of barbarians (that is, non-Greeks), and 'high-falutin' phrases in the style of tragedy, especially useful for mocking the sister genre. Fifth-century tragedy had its own special diction, which was distinctively elevated in comparison with comedy; to take a single example, the word *demas*, meaning 'body' or 'physical form', is poetic, frequent in Homer and occurring nearly a hundred times in Euripides (fourteen in Aeschylus, eighteen in Sophocles); but there seems to be just one instance in Aristophanes, in a fragment and, what is more significant, a lyric passage (fr. 364, cited in Athenaeus 11.478).[17] Yet we find the word in the second line of Euripides' *Cyclops*, and so it was evidently at home in the satyr play, even in the iambic verse that was standard for dialogue; indeed, the diction of the satyr play is an area that has so far been largely neglected, and would repay further research.[18] With Menander, the situation is again different: he and his contemporaries for the most part avoided both the high poetic language of classical tragedy and the extravagant idiom of Aristophanes, and sought to reproduce, within the constraints of the poetic form, the speech of everyday life (the term *demas* is absent from what survives of Menander's plays).[19]

Consistent with the linguistic tone, spectators at a *kômôidia* would be prepared to see on stage characters from everyday life, and even, in the case of Old Comedy, specific well-known individuals from among their contemporaries. Tragedy had experimented briefly with historical themes (e.g., Aeschylus' *Persians*), but had abandoned this practice soon after *kômôidia*

[17] The word occurs also in Plato Comicus, fr. 173, from his *Phaon*, again in a lyric metre, though it is part of a dialogue.
[18] But see Griffith (2005b) and López Eire (2003).
[19] On the complex issue of diachronic linguistic variations in the language(s) of Greek comedy see Willi (2002a), (2003b) and Chapter 8.

became institutionalized as part of the dramatic festivals (in the 480s, probably 486), and henceforward confined itself almost exclusively to stories derived from myth. We know from Aristotle that Agathon had tried out the use of fictional or invented names for the characters in one of his tragedies, but even here we may doubt that they could be mistaken for ordinary folks, like the types who populated *kômôidiai*. If someone appeared on stage bearing the made-up name Dicaeopolis, meaning something like 'Just City' (possibly a pun on the real name Eupolis, one of Aristophanes' rivals), or Philocleon, 'Cleon-Lover', as in Aristophanes' *Wasps*, not to mention a character actually called Cleon and representing the famous demagogue himself, it was a sure sign that this was Old Comedy, just as the stock names Demeas for an older man, or Moschion for a younger, were the hallmark of New Comedy. These names were excluded from tragedy or satyr plays. It is not the case, however, that if a mythological figure called Heracles or Athena had a title role, one could infer that this was necessarily a tragedy, any more than one could conclude that a play featuring Odysseus and Polyphemus was necessarily a satyr play in the manner of Euripides' *Cyclops*; for plays of just this sort were composed by Cratinus, an older contemporary of Aristophanes who was a dedicated poet of *kômôidiai*. What is more, such travesties on mythological themes persisted into the fourth century: Plautus' *Amphitryo* gives an idea of the nature of such dramas, and may well be based on a fourth-century Greek original. The ancient critic Platonius (date unknown), in his essay *On the Distinctions among Comedies* (*Prolegomena* 1, 4.29–31 Koster), writes: 'The character of Middle Comedy was like Aristophanes' *Aeolosicon* and Cratinus' *Companions of Odysseus*', and he adds that the latter was a parody of the scene in Homer's *Odyssey* (cf. 5.51f.). While the accuracy of the details in Platonius' testimony is open to doubt, it is clear that the boundaries between the genres were more fuzzy, or at least different, than we might imagine, if we were to judge solely by the eleven surviving plays by Aristophanes (divinities and heroes do play important, if ultimately subsidiary, roles in Aristophanes' *Peace*, *Birds*, *Frogs* and *Wealth*).[20]

A feature that Old Comedy shares with tragedy and the satyr play is the chorus, which had become vestigial in *kômôidia* by the time of Menander, serving at most as a kind of musical interlude between acts.[21] It appears

[20] On Platonius, and the question of Middle Comedy generally, see Perusino (1989), Nesselrath (1990) 149–87 and Sidwell, Chapter 3.

[21] The chorus plays a much reduced role in the last two surviving comedies by Aristophanes, the *Assembly Women* and especially the *Wealth*, and this, along with other peculiar features, has led some scholars to see a shift toward Middle or New Comedy beginning with these early fourth-century plays. Contrast Zelnick-Abramovitz

that the chorus in satyr plays was regularly composed of satyrs – hybrid creatures with the lower parts of a goat, the upper being human – or sileni, like satyrs but equine below (there may have been exceptions to this rule). This convention would readily distinguish the genre from tragedy, but not necessarily from *kômôidia*.[22] Although lyric metres are characteristic of all forms of choral singing, moreover, there is a notable difference of linguistic register between *kômôidia* and tragedy, as well as divergences in metre, to which the fifth-century audience was undoubtedly attuned.[23] But the chorus was more than an additional actor on stage; it was composed of Athenian citizens (in the Lenaea, it might include metics, according to a scholion on Aristophanes *Wealth* 953), who trained hard to master the songs and dance steps, and so behind the masks there was the potential for a special kind of identification between the chorus and the audience that was lacking in the reduced cast of characters typical of New Comedy (and very likely of tragedy too in the later period). Despite the considerable differences between tragedy and *kômôidia*, fifth-century Greeks perhaps perceived a certain similarity between, say, the chorus of rural charcoal burners in Aristophanes' *Acharnians* or old men and women in his *Lysistrata* and the city elders who constituted the chorus in Aeschylus' *Agamemnon* or Sophocles' *Oedipus at Colonus*.

At the beginning of this chapter, I mentioned the parabasis, that is, the episode in Old Comedy in which the actors left the stage and the chorus or chorus leader, partly or wholly dropping their dramatic role, addressed the audience directly. Parabases (there are sometimes two) are a feature of most of Aristophanes' plays, although he gave them up toward the end of his

---

(2002), who argues, largely on the basis of its political theme, that our *Wealth* of 388 is a very slightly altered version of an earlier production, dating to 408, from which it differed only in 'structural changes and some allusions to contemporary events and persons' (44); cf. also Revermann (2006a) 98 for the essential continuity between early and late comedies of Aristophanes.

[22] Revermann (2006a) 103f. notes that *Satyroi* was the title of various comedies in both the fifth and fourth centuries, e.g. by Phrynichus and Timocles, and cites possible evidence from vase paintings, including the Getty Birds and the Cleveland Dionysus crater (on South Italian vases depicting satyr drama, see Carpenter (2005)). For (seven or eight) comedies that featured a chorus of satyrs, along with other similarities, and fundamental differences, between comedy and satyr play, see Storey (2005). The outstanding case of cross-over is Cratinus' *Dionysalexandrus*. Bakola (2005) argues that the main chorus did indeed consist of satyrs, and that what makes it a comedy rather than a satyr play is its structure; nevertheless, she cites this play as 'an unparalleled case of interaction between two dramatic genres' (57). See also Bakola (2010) and (2013) for further discussion of such interactions in Cratinus.

[23] On linguistic registers see Silk (1980) and (2000a) 160–206, on metre Parker (1997). On the problem of defining and measuring audience competence in the fifth and fourth century BCE see Revermann (2006b).

career.[24] We have no way of knowing whether they were equally common in all of Old Comedy, along with the accompanying ode and antode, epirrheme and antepirrheme, and pnigos that made up what we think of as the complete parabatic sequence. But a fifth-century audience of *kômôidia* would not be surprised to see such a rupture of dramatic illusion, or what is known today as 'the fourth wall', right in the middle of the action. This is not to say that the neighbouring genres maintained a strict barrier between the action on stage and the real world: where there was a prologue or epilogue in a tragedy, the speaker might address the audience directly, and New Comedy maintained the same convention. Indeed, a character in New Comedy might turn to the spectators even in the course of the regular action, hailing them as 'gentlemen' (*andres*) and inviting them to act as judges, as it were (e.g., in Menander's *Samia* at 269, 329, 447, 683). And yet, in Menander it is as though the audience were momentarily incorporated into the world of the play, assuming the role of bystanders or observers of the events – fulfilling, in a sense, one of the functions assigned to the chorus in fifth-century drama; in the Aristophanic parabasis, by contrast, the chorus steps out of the dramatic situation, and acknowledges the context of the theatre. Nevertheless, Menander's modest metatheatrical gesture in *Samia* may have been more of a surprise for his audience than Aristophanes' flamboyant but predictable device.

We have observed that Aristophanes employs the verb *kômôidein* in the sense of 'mock' or 'deride', and that he both mentions living contemporaries and, on occasion, gives them a role in the action (this too diminishes in his last two plays). The poets of Old Comedy, such as Aristophanes and Eupolis, took for their theme current political situations, for instance the war with the Spartans and their allies, the threat to traditional values posed by the so-called sophists, the control of popular opinion by what they viewed as upstart or unscrupulous leaders, and the corruption of the court system. This too the public took for granted, and granted in turn a special licence to *kômôidia* in respect of such liberties. There is some evidence to indicate that even in the fifth century there were efforts to limit this practice, and to treat attacks on individuals by name as libellous.[25] The extent to which the poets of Old Comedy actually advocated specific policies in their plays, as opposed to simply making fun of prominent targets, is debated, with some scholars maintaining that Aristophanes was out to raise a laugh and nothing more, while others argue that he sought to influence public opinion

---

[24] On the structure of parabasis see Marshall, Chapter 6; on its role in competitive poetics see Biles, Chapter 2.

[25] Cf. Halliwell (1991), Carey (1994). Csapo (2000) 119 notes that there 'is no evidence for ad hominem plots, which feature a real life character at the center, before the 420s'.

more substantially.[26] However that may be, by confining itself to fictional characters, and generally maintaining the theatrical illusion, New Comedy relinquished the direct topicality of the older form. This does not necessarily mean that it became apolitical, only that any social commentary had to be inferred from the overall trajectory of the story, rather than from explicit attacks on public figures. In a sense, this was true also of Old Comedy, as the controversies over Aristophanes' own political stance suggest. One consequence, however, of eliminating or reducing the parochial references characteristic of Old Comedy is that New Comedy could now appeal to a more international public. Indeed, it was not only performed in cities far from Athens, thanks to travelling companies of actors, but was often written with the expectation of being produced abroad; this is why playwrights could now compose far more *kômôidiai* than there were slots at the two Athenian festivals.[27] The universality of New Comedy also explains, at least in part, why Roman playwrights preferred to adapt this form rather than the Old Comedy of Aristophanes and his peers.

With its new focus on domestic situations, New Comedy may in fact have drawn closer to tragedy, or at least to the kind of tragedy we know from Euripides (cf. Satyrus, *Life of Euripides* = *P.Oxy.* 1176 fr. 39 col. 7). Aristophanes delighted in tweaking Euripides, and while it may be true that he shared with the great tragic poet certain traits of style and outlook – sufficient for Cratinus (fr. 342) to have coined the portmanteau word *euripidaristophanizein* (whatever the precise meaning of the term was in context) – his critique may have been designed to show to advantage his own chosen genre against its more respectable sibling.[28] Characters in New Comedy might quote verses from tragedy, as when a slave in Menander's *Aspis* (407–32) manages to cite at least four tragic poets within twenty-five lines (cf. *Men at Arbitration* 1123–6, where the slave Onesimus quotes Euripides' *Auge* by

---

[26] Out to raise a laugh: Dover (1972); Halliwell (1984); Heath (1987); politics: Ste Croix (1972); Sommerstein (1984); Henderson (1990); Carey (1994). Laughter is, of course, essential to comedy, see Halliwell (Chapter 9) who further distinguishes Old and New Comedy (or at least Aristophanes and Menander) by their approach to laughter; thus, Menander, unlike Aristophanes, 'exploits . . . laughter's conspicuous suspension or absence', and does not shy away from arousing 'emotional anguish'.

[27] Csapo (2000) 125–7 agrees that travelling companies made a difference in the nature of comedy, but points out that 'Athens remained the privileged venue for any ambitious dramatist' (127).

[28] See Heiden (1991). Revermann (2006a) 101f. notes that paratragedy goes as far back as Epicharmus, along with Cratinus, Phrynichus and Strattis, with comic titles such as *Medea*, *Philoctetes* and the like. Platter (2007) 9 maintains that parody and the crossing of genres are essential to the carnivalian tradition: 'Whenever a genre is allowed to claim for itself a superior (transcendent) status over others . . . there parody appears to contest the dominance of official speech.'

name); but such paratragic effects always serve to characterize the speaker as sententious or the like, or else are cited as nuggets of genuine wisdom; they are never parodic of tragedy itself or of specific tragic poets. It is perhaps telling that there appear to be no references to contemporary tragedians in New Comedy, as opposed to the classic figures of the fifth century: the New Comic poets evidently did not see themselves in competition with the other genre.[29]

Nevertheless, even though there might be striking similarities between the two genres on the level of plot that are not shared with Old Comedy – some of these are indicated below – we can be certain that no one watching a play of Menander ever doubted that it was a *kômôidia*, not a tragedy. Plutarch remarks (*On Eros*, as cited by Stobaeus 4.20.34) that all of Menander's plays involve passionate love or *erôs*, and from what we can judge on the basis of fragments and other sources this would seem to be broadly the case for New Comedy as a whole, although, as we have seen, mythological travesties continued to be written (this does not exclude an amorous theme, of course), and there will presumably have been no more place for romance in the Greek model for Plautus' *Prisoners of War* (*Captivi*) than there is in the Latin adaptation. By way of contrast, erotic love was rarely a central motive in tragedy. When it was, as in Euripides' *Hippolytus* and *Stheneboea*, it was women who were subject to such passion, and even here, the character Aeschylus can boast in Aristophanes' *Frogs* (1043–4) that, unlike Euripides, he never represented a woman in love. When a man was moved by *erôs*, it was normally a marginal or offstage circumstance, as in the case of Sophocles' *Women of Trachis*, where Heracles' passion for Iole sets in motion the tragedy of Dejanira.[30] Correspondingly, it is only a man's *erôs* that drives the plots of New Comedy, so far as we can tell; when women are represented as being in love, it is always a matter of a young courtesan reciprocating the affection of her urgent lover. It is impossible to say whether this distinction in the ascription of erotic passion continued to demarcate tragedy and comedy in the fourth and third centuries, or whether tragedy began to be more hospitable to erotic themes, and thus to exhibit a certain rapprochement with its sister genre.

While the plots of New Comedy are infinitely varied, they all conform to certain norms that may be said to constitute the premises of the genre. The protagonist is typically a man, very often young (this in contrast to Aristophanes' plays, which in general centre around a married, middle-aged

---

[29] See Slater (1985).

[30] It can be doubted, I think, whether the erotic affection between Achilles and Patroclus portrayed in Aeschylus' *Myrmidons* was central to the action, which revolved rather around a conflict between Achilles and Agamemnon; see Michelakis (2002) 22–57.

man or woman), who is in love with a young woman (pederasty, while alluded to in New Comedy, seems never to have constituted the core story). In the end, the two will be united, but for there to be dramatic tension, there must be some obstacle to the affair. The nature of the obstacle depends in part on the status of the woman: if she is known to be freeborn and from a citizen family, then the denouement will be a marriage, and if either the boy or the girl is still under paternal authority, then parental permission will be required (for example, the boy's father may object to union with a poor family, while the girl's father may be cranky enough to oppose any conjugal connection, as in Menander's *Dyscolus*). If the girl is not a citizen, she will most often be a courtesan, that is, a woman who makes a living through liaisons with men, or else a slave prostitute. Here, what is needed is cash, in order to pay for the services of the courtesan, if she is independent, or to purchase her from the brothel-keeper who is her master; since young men are typically indigent, the main blocking figure is likely once again to be the boy's father, who is naturally hostile to such an unprofitable relationship. These affairs do not normally end in wedlock. Sometimes, however, the young woman turns out to be a citizen after all, as revealed in the recognition scene that is characteristic of the genre. This will happen only if the young man in question is her first and only lover, for one of the rules of New Comedy is that women who have had pre-marital or extra-marital sex are not marriageable (widows with children are perfectly eligible), and there was no point in bringing a woman's citizenship to light, only to leave her in limbo, with no possibility of having a family.

The above patterns are far from exhausting the possible permutations of the New Comic plot. Married men too fall in love, in which case the obstacle may be a wife, or indeed a son who is his father's rival in the affair. Confusion of identities is another typical motif. If we take the basic engine of the plot, however, to be not the satisfaction of *erôs* per se, but the drive to reaffirm the structure of the family or *oikos*, restoring lost or kidnapped children to their proper parents, joining citizen households through legitimate wedlock (New Comedy seems to have observed the rule, first promulgated by Pericles in 451, that in Athens, at least, prohibited marriage between citizens and non-citizens), and demarcating such unions clearly from casual affairs with courtesans or other interlopers, then the parallels with a tragedy such as Euripides' *Ion* stand out clearly.[31] And if, in the *Ion*, the true father of the protagonist proves to be a god, this is no different from what happens in

---

[31] On Euripides' *Ion* and comedy, cf. Zacharia (1995); on the emphasis on preserving the *oikos* or household in New Comedy, see Le Guen (1995); Lape (2004) and Lape/Moreno, Chapter 18.

Plautus' *Amphitryo* (it is worth noting that Plautus himself refers to this play as a tragicomedy, the first known occurrence of the term). Indeed, relations between parents and children are nearly as important a theme in New Comedy as erotic attachments.

The mixing of genres, or '*Kreuzung der Gattungen*', commended itself to Hellenistic taste, and it is possible that the process was already under way in the fourth-century theatre, through intertextual relations and transfers between tragedy and New Comedy that we are no longer in a position to appreciate because of the almost complete loss of drama from this period.[32] Might there have been a shift from the high mimetic to the low mimetic mode (to use Frye's terms) in tragedy as well as in *kômôidia*? The idea must remain speculative. But before we accept the notion of a progressive convergence of the two genres, tragedy and *kômôidia*, we may take a final look at the plot structure of Old Comedy, which also, to judge from the surviving plays of Aristophanes, had its characteristic shapes. In Old Comedy, the protagonist, who was, as we have observed, typically a common citizen of middle age, conceives an extravagant plan to improve his own situation or that of society as a whole. It may be a private peace with Sparta (*Acharnians*) or a collective action to bring about an end to the Peloponnesian War (*Peace*, *Lysistrata*); outwitting creditors by sophistical arguments (*Clouds*); establishing a utopia in the sky (*Birds*), or reforming Athens by resurrecting its greatest tragic poet (*Frogs*); instituting a communist regime run by women (*Assembly Women*) or capturing the god of wealth so as to bring prosperity to all (*Wealth*). The hero or heroine overcomes all obstacles by sheer will and imagination, and in many cases defends the newly won order of things against sceptics and opportunists (it must be noted that *Knights*, *Wasps* and *Women at the Thesmophoria* do not conform to this paradigm, and even among those I have subsumed under it some do so only loosely).[33] These bold heroes have little in common with the often feckless lovers of New Comedy, who depend on clever slaves, parasites or sheer luck to overcome the obstacle to their amour. But they do bear a certain resemblance to the resourceful Odysseus in Euripides' *Cyclops*, who achieves the liberation of his comrades and the sileni by his wiliness and courage (escape from captivity may have been a common feature of satyr plays) and, rather more distantly,

---

[32] Indeed, mixture was occurring already in the fifth century, if Euripides' *Alcestis* was, as the scholia indicate (AB, argument), 'more comic' or 'more satyrical' for being the fourth play in the tetralogy, that is, in place of the satyr play. Revermann (2006a) 96f. argues that cross-overs between genres only make sense on the assumption that the Greeks recognized generic categories (the closest approximation to the word for 'genre' was *genos*).

[33] See Rosen, Chapter 11, for a discussion of the comic hero and its applicability to Aristophanic comedy.

to the character of Orestes in the Euripidean play that bears his name, who recovers from the bout of madness caused by the murder of his mother and proceeds to take on the whole city of Argos which had condemned him to death for the matricide.[34] Granted, the analogies are imprecise, at best. In any case, it is not my intention to argue for the same degree of generic interference or cross-over that may have obtained between New Comedy and later tragedy. I wish only to suggest that *kômôidia* and tragedy may have begun their evolutionary dance as early as the time of Aristophanes, each genre responding to changes in the other (or others) and continually redefining themselves against one another, as each new work modified 'the sum of possible works'.[35]

Further reading

The best introduction to the questions of genre discussed in this chapter is Csapo (2000) and the volume in which it was published (= Depew and Obbink [2000]). Genre, especially Old Comedy, is of central concern to Silk (2000a), Revermann (2006a), Bakola (2010) and Ruffell (2011). Janko (1984) is an attempt to reconstruct, by using much later sources, Aristotle's theorizing on comedy in the lost second book of the *Poetics*. An anthology of theories of comedy (mostly not ancient Greek comedy) is Lauter (1964). Hutcheon (1985) as well as Palmer (1987) and (1994) provide stimulating contemporary and (post)modern perspectives on the problem of comic form and narrative.

[34] Cf. scholia MTAB to Euripides' *Orestes* 1691 on the *komikê katalêxis*. It is worth noting that fifth-century tragedy shared with Old Comedy the formal feature of a debate between characters (known as the *agôn*), although it was less sharply defined as a structural element in tragedy.

[35] Willi (2008) argues that Sicilian comedy, as represented by the fragments of Epicharmus, is stylistically similar to that of Aristophanes, but emerged in a context in which tragedy was absent. Epicharmus did, however, lampoon Aeschylean diction, and so was conscious of the tension between his chosen genre and Attic tragedy. But this is not to suggest that we must ascribe the evolution of similar forms to a given set of relations among genres. Silk (2000a) 97 maintains that 'tragedy is not *per se* comedy's opposite; and comedy is not dependent on tragedy'. On comedy's interactions with epic poetry, which can similarly be traced back to Epicharmus, see Revermann (2013).

2

ZACHARY P. BILES

The rivals of Aristophanes and Menander

Rival poets and poeticized rivalry

It is worthwhile, in the first place, to consider why we speak of 'rivals' in thinking about Greek comedy, and whether or to what extent this designation of comic poets is appropriate. An important recent collection of articles on Aristophanes' poetic predecessors, contemporaries and successors, well demonstrates by its title, *The Rivals of Aristophanes*, the premium that is placed on the competitive backdrop of comic performance. In this case the term shows a reflex of scholarly criticism, since the volume's true objective is to identify contributions to the genre by comic poets whose plays have not been transmitted to us anywhere near as completely as the eleven surviving plays of Aristophanes. That is, rivalry *per se* figures into the discussions almost not at all, so that the difference here between Aristophanes' 'rivals' and 'other comic poets' is slight at best. By contrast, it is hard to imagine a similarly focused volume on Athenian tragedy receiving a comparable title. And yet to speak of 'tragic rivals' is no less appropriate. Among the most important evidence for assessing the history of Athenian dramatic performance are the fragmented remains of inscribed monuments of the festival competitions that were set up in the fourth century BCE and later, but depend on official records going back to the early phases of the festival's organization in the sixth and early fifth centuries.[1] Those documents are also the ultimate source of production information included in the ancient summaries of tragedies and comedies (known as hypotheses), which were composed originally by Hellenistic scholars and are included in many of the manuscripts of the plays. Both sources assure us that direct competition between poets in a formally organized competition (*agôn*) was the standard performance context for both genres, a characteristic that distinguishes Greek drama from other theatre traditions. That picture can be extended further, since festival competitions were likewise the social milieu in which many forms of Greek

---

[1] Olson (2007) 379–91; Millis and Olson (2012).

43

poetry thrived in the archaic period and earlier. From this perspective the modern emphasis on rivalry in comedy begins to look unjustified, at least to the extent of identifying anything unique about performance conditions of that genre in antiquity. On the other hand, if rivalry was not the exclusive preserve of comic poets, a number of considerations indicate that competitive resonances were peculiarly strong in comedy. Of these considerations, two are addressed here, one based on formal organizational details, the other on poetic qualities.

While the organization of tragic competitions at the City Dionysia goes back to the sixth century, comedy's inclusion in the programme can be dated more specifically to the 480s (probably 486). Even when they were performed alongside each other, the format of entries in tragedy and comedy was hardly equal: three tragic poets competed, each with three tragedies and a satyr play (a tetralogy), while three comic poets competed with one play each. That picture emerges from the production histories included in the hypotheses and is corroborated by inscriptional evidence. The hypothesis to Aristophanes' *Wealth*, however, names five comic poets at an *agôn* in 388 and hence suggests an alternative reconstruction. Moreover, this expanded comic programme can be retrojected into the fifth century on the strength of the sheer number of comedies plausibly dated to the Peloponnesian War years, a situation further attested to by the notice that Plato Comicus placed fourth in the 420s or 410s. The five comic poet programme is gaining momentum,[2] and its implication for a comparison of tragedy and comedy is this: while the tragic format established literary and performative scale as qualities of this genre, the increased field of poets participating in a comic *agôn* intensified the competitive element itself. If anything, that distinction only became more pronounced in the 440s once the Lenaea were organized; here tragedians participated on a diminished scale (two poets, each with two tragedies), while comic poets apparently competed in their usual numbers (three or five). It was a built-in feature of the comic competitions, therefore, that the audience and judges had a potentially more demanding task in discriminating between more entries, while the poets were forced to respond to those increased demands.

As a poetic form, comedy embraced its agonistic underpinnings in a way that tragedy, with its spatio-temporal distancing and more integral dramatic illusion, simply could not.[3] Although there must have been implicit rivalry, for instance, in the tragic poets' efforts to put a new spin on a shared body of subject material, there is little explicit reference to these rivalries in the tragedies themselves. And though the point should not be overemphasized,

[2] For the evidence and criticism, see Storey (2002).   [3] Taplin (1986).

it is curious that one of the few overt indications of tragic rivalry (*Electra* 518–46) shows Euripides comparing himself not to one of his contemporaries, i.e. rivals, but to Aeschylus, whom he never faced in live competition. On the other hand, presumably either Euripides' *Electra* or Sophocles' responds to the other, but the relationship, if there is one, is so covert that scholars cannot agree on the sequence and direction of influence.[4] In the tragic tradition, evidence for direct rivalry comes to us by and large from anecdotes purporting to document episodes of intense competition between tragic poets; even if these traditions are fanciful, they presumably reflect what was plausible and could be believed. But tragic poetry itself stays above the fray. Indeed, available evidence suggests that the pre-performance event called the *proagôn*, at which poets led their troupes before the theatre and delivered an address in anticipation of the performance, was reserved for tragic poets as an opportunity to tout their plays and engage their rivals.[5]

Unlike tragedy, comedy internalized the kind of competitive posturing and self-promotion that may have featured at the *proagôn*.[6] As even the most casual reader of Aristophanes' plays recognizes, mockery and ridicule of fellow comic poets are recurring features, and there is ample evidence from the comic fragments to show that carrying out such assaults on the poetic credentials of rivals became a staple of the genre during the fifth century. A good many such literary insults come as momentary diversions from the immediate dramatic situation, as when the chorus of knights suddenly mention Aristophanes' rival Cratinus, who was competing at the contest where *Knights* was performed, and bundle him together with the Paphlagonian as an object of their loathing: 'If I don't hate you [i.e. the Paphlagonian], may I be a blanket in Cratinus' house' (*Knights* 400) – this last comment in reference to that poet's alleged incontinence. Such remarks, surprising and disjointed though they often are, keep the performance keyed to the poetic contest and help characterize the plays themselves as agonistic gestures, tantamount to challenges by one poet to another.

By far the most striking and elaborate of comedy's agonistic overtures, however, is the parabasis. This choral component occurs (usually) at a play's midpoint and marks a pause in the dramatic action as the chorus addresses the audience directly on any number of topics, all of them inevitably reflecting their poet's superiority and the contrasting deficiencies of rivals. Needless to say, the characterizations of poets and poetry featuring in parabases are exaggerated and contain much bombast, but are directly inspired by the

[4] E.g., Finglass (2007) 2–4. Neither play is securely dated.
[5] Wilson (2000) 95–7; Revermann (2006a) 169–71; Biles (2011) 40–6.
[6] A scholion on *Wasps* 61 reports that Euripides (and so tragedy) figured in the plot of Aristophanes' *Proagôn*.

poetic contest itself, the stakes of which it is among the parabasis' chief functions to make relevant to the performance. Furthermore, the themes of Aristophanic parabases often reflect themes in the surrounding dramatic action, so that the parabasis implicitly presents an image of the poet as he embodies the play with which he confronts his rivals.[7] This interlacing of agonistic elements in the parabasis and surrounding plot is observable, for instance, in the way that the slight against Cratinus alongside the Paphlagonian at *Knights* 400 (above) interconnects with the chorus' clarification in the parabasis of the supposed reasons for Cratinus' incontinence and the explanatory force it has for his poetic shortcomings in comparison with Aristophanes. So too, this parabasis situates Aristophanes within a framework of poetic succession at the dramatic festivals that parallels the contest of political succession in which the Sausage-seller and the Paphlagonian find themselves. The 'drama' of Aristophanes' putative ascendancy over Cratinus and other poets in the parabasis thus interacts with themes in the dramatic plot, so that the Sausage-seller's eventual victory effectively works toward the same outcome for the poet. In short, the parabasis can transform the play itself into an agonistic act by the person who represents the creative nucleus for the entire performative endeavour.

An observable trend in Greek comedy is a downscaling in the frequency and degree of poeticized rivalry. The high water-mark for intense and open engagement between rivals is in Old Comedy of the last decades of the fifth century, i.e. Aristophanes and his rivals, and that material accordingly figures prominently in the discussion to follow. The trajectory of later changes is already apparent within Aristophanes' career, in the difference between the vibrant competitive colouring of his early plays and the more static – agonistically speaking – quality of his later plays, *Assembly Women* and *Wealth*. By the time of Menander and poets of New Comedy, overtly poeticized rivalry disappears almost entirely, as will be shown in the closing paragraphs.

Plays for (an) agonistic production

The agonistic styling of the parabasis and other related elements give comic rivalry immediacy and explicitness. Hence, unlike Euripides' activation of inter-generational competition in his reference to Aeschylus, in comedy the activation of rivalry tends to locate the performance in the here and now of a narrow period of dramatic production or even a single festival contest.

[7] Bowie (1982); Hubbard (1991); Biles (2011) 29–32.

Consider the following passage with which the chorus' impersonation of Aristophanes in the parabasis of *Clouds* ends (*Clouds* 549–59):

> It is I who punched Cleon in his belly at his height
> but was not so crude as to leap on him again once he was down.
> But these others, from the moment Hyperbolus gave them a hold,
> they keep trampling the wretch over and over, along with his mother.
> Eupolis started it when he brought out his *Marikas*,
> making a travesty of our *Knights* – the bastard! –
> and fixing a drunken hag to it, all to make room for a lewd dance;
> Phrynichus created her long ago, that one a sea-monster tried to eat.
> Then Hermippus in turn aimed his poetry at Hyperbolus,
> and now all the others press hard on Hyperbolus
> in imitation of my eel similes.

The agonistic posturing evident in Aristophanes' self-congratulatory tone and denigration of other poets is one thing; equally striking is the specificity of his remarks. Three comic poets, Eupolis, Phrynichus and Hermippus, are explicitly named, and a fourth, Plato Comicus (who produced a play titled *Hyperbolus*) is seemingly targeted as well. These comments belong to the revised *Clouds*, of uncertain date but clearly after the plays alluded to in the passage, beginning with Eupolis' *Marikas* which one ancient scholar places in 421. *Clouds* is positioned against poets of the period to which it belongs, all of them active and apparently successful in the contests by this time. By contrast, earlier in the parabasis Aristophanes' chief gripe was the defeat of the original *Clouds* in 423 by poets referred to only vaguely as 'run-of-the-mill' (*Clouds* 524). From the hypothesis to *Clouds* we know these were Cratinus and Ameipsias, who took first and second place, respectively. In the build-up towards Aristophanes' recommendation of his play to the audience at the close of the anapaests (*Clouds* 560–2), that original rivalry (obviated in one sense by Cratinus' death) is forgotten in preference to the rivals he was likely to encounter at an anticipated *agôn* of the 410s. That the revised play was never produced implies that Aristophanes' thoughts turned to the competition he might face early in his planning, which is itself sure evidence that the second *Clouds* was meant to be performed.[8]

Passages like this urge us, in emulation of the Athenian audience's experience, to resituate comedies in their original competitive moment, paying careful attention to the trends and transformations of the genre that were taking place as poets did their best to outshine their rivals. It is in these terms

---

[8] Revermann (2006a) 326–32; Biles (2011) ch. 5.

that Aristophanes has his chorus reflect on the failure of *Clouds* one year after the fact in *Wasps* (1049–50):

> But among wise spectators the poet's reputation remains intact,
> even if in driving past his rivals he crashed his idea.

As my earlier comments on the intertwining of the poet's self-promotion in the parabasis with the surrounding plot suggest, the poeticization of agonistic themes in the plays needs to be explored alongside the purely literary historical project of determining where individual poets and plays fit within a chronology of production and contest histories. On occasion the outlines of specific rivalries come to light, and we can assess particular ways in which dynamic competition shaped a play's thematic design. The most conspicuous test case is the rivalry of Aristophanes and Cratinus in the years 425–23. Passages in *Acharnians* (Lenaea 425) and *Knights* (Lenaea 424) show Aristophanes taunting his veteran adversary, with the amusing caricature of Cratinus in the latter comedy's parabasis apparently inspiring Cratinus to come up with the imagined scenario in *Wine Flask* (*Pytinê*). It was with this play that Cratinus delivered Aristophanes' defeat with the original *Clouds* in 423. The plot's premise is outlined in a partial summary of the play in an ancient commentator's remark on *Knights* 400. 'Cratinus' himself featured as the play's protagonist,[9] and the central problem was the poet's failing marriage with Comedy, the embodied genre, who wants a divorce based on complaints of her husband's inattention to her: he is ruined by drink and his poetic productivity has been severely diminished as a result. This fanciful scenario is clearly based on the *Knights* parabasis (and beyond that an earlier Cratinean model),[10] which features a Cratinus similarly ruined by drink (especially *Knights* 534f.) and (along with other poets) losing his edge in the competitions when Comedy, the genre embodied as a courtesan, suddenly casts him aside (*Knights* 516f.). Unfortunately the plot summary of *Wine Flask* does not tell us how these tensions were resolved, but several fragments allude to a pointed competitive response by Cratinus,[11] not least the notice (fr. 213) that he heaped abuse on Aristophanes in this play.

One of Cratinus' more striking modifications of the Aristophanic scenario is a change in the type of relationship he has with his genre, from courtesan-lover to wife-husband, for the latter suggests a stronger and more legitimate commitment between them, and also entails greater control on Cratinus' part over his romantic/poetic fortunes. Moreover, the play's title looks to a

---

[9] Rosen (2000) and Chapter 11.
[10] Biles (2002) 170–7; Bakola (2008) 11–15; Bakola (2010) 17.
[11] Sidwell (1995); Biles (2002) 185–7; Ruffell (2002) 157f.; Bakola (2010) 60–3.

particular kind of wine-vessel (fr. 201), one that resisted destruction and thus might survive the attack on Cratinus' drinking paraphernalia contemplated at one point as a remedy for the situation (fr. 199). The likeliest explanation is accordingly that Cratinus and Comedy were reconciled in the end, with the poet returned to a healthy state of poetic production (fr. 198), quite possibly in tandem with a reassertion of a pre-existing Cratinean poetics of inspiration through alcohol (perhaps, in greater moderation),[12] especially (though not only) if fr. 203 is correctly assigned to this play:

> You could not produce anything clever while drinking water.

That comment is attributed to Cratinus without play title in a Hellenistic epigram, where it is preceded by the claim, likewise ascribed to Cratinus: 'Wine is a fast horse for a refined poet.' If this also derives somehow from Cratinus and *Wine Flask*, it may be telling that a *fast* horse is stipulated, since the emphasis on speed is explained most economically by recourse to festival agonistics. From this vantage point, Aristophanes' summary assessment of his undoing with *Clouds* through the chariot metaphor at *Wasps* 1049f. (above) may be a pointed adaptation of a Cratinean sentiment. Apart from these indications of a lively dynamic of poetic challenge and response articulated in the successive plays of two rival poets, perhaps the most compelling point to be made about *Wine Flask* is simply that Cratinus transformed what had been a competitive challenge contained in a rival's parabasis into the plot of an entire play. *Wine Flask* stands, in other words, as the most ambitious surviving example of a comic poet's effort to reach agonistic ends by poetic means.

Navigating the corpus of fragments

With *Wine Flask* we are well informed by ancient sources about the play's date of production (423), can gauge fairly exactly its position within an ongoing rivalry between Cratinus and Aristophanes attested to in the plays themselves, and have a fair number of (comparatively) lengthy fragments and testimonia for *Wine Flask*, most important of which is the partial summary of the plot. Accessing comic agonistics in the same way for all of the 50 or so poets, 369 plays (titles are often all there is) and thousands of fragments we have from just the first roughly 100 years of the genre's history (a fraction of the original volume) is impossible. Though we can hope that ever more fragments of ancient copies of the plays will be identified in papyri, the bulk of the

---

[12] On the contribution of a 'Dionysiac poetics' to Cratinus' stage biography, see Bakola (2010) 17–20 and *passim*.

corpus of fragments is transmitted to us by later scholars and readers, whose interests in the material are often specialized and idiosyncratic; an additional degree of separation from the original plays is involved, since many of our source authors for fragments did not read the plays themselves but relied on citations by others before them.[13] Linguistic and metrical anomalies, curiosity over cultural phenomena such as food and clothing types, and references to a particular *kômôidoumenos* (i.e. a historical figure referred to in a comedy) are among the chief reasons a word, line or passage attracted their attention. Accordingly, in approaching the corpus of comic fragments one ventures onto a virtual sea of disjointed and intricate literary material where even the most modest interpretation can founder on hidden shoals. Add to this, whereas tragedy's mythical plot scenarios provide a set of landmarks to set a course by, comic plots are so fantastic and full of surprises (the distinction is humorously addressed in a long passage by one comic poet, Antiphanes fr. 189) that one is forced to navigate the material virtually without any bearings. Indeed, reconstructing plays from comic fragments is at times like trying to make out the design of a ruined sea-vessel from the wreckage and stray bits of flotsam that make it to shore. The surviving pieces of evidence may be few and the forces affecting the individual selection of components entirely random, so that there is no easy way of telling whether what one encounters has any real significance for the overall integrity.[14] Making head or tail of any individual play from fragments is more often than not simply beyond our means, let alone understanding how these plays interacted with one another in specific and meaningful ways. And yet the enterprise is not so hopeless as all this suggests, since by peering through the waters from different angles and in different light, some details start to emerge.

Of critical importance for beginning to make sense of the fragments is an assurance that the formal poetic structures of comedy, long used in analyzing Aristophanic plays, can be identified in the work of other poets.[15] Prologues, parodoi, the epirrhematic *agôn*, parabases, iambic scenes (for these terms, see Konstan, Chapter 1 and Marshall, Chapter 6) can be identified in many instances on the basis of poetic metre and subject matter. Hence, for instance, the individual identification of three chorus members as the cities Tenos, Chios and Cyzicus in frr. 245–7 of Eupolis' *Cities* probably belongs to a parodos of the sort found at *Birds* 297–304. Comparison is justified, but Eupolis' roll-call was on a much grander scale to judge from the number of lines dedicated to these three cities alone.[16] At times sharper distinctions come into play, as with Cratinus' jibe through the term

---

[13] Olson (2007) 26–32.   [14] Dover (2000) is a fine demonstration of these points.
[15] Whittaker (1935); Quaglia (1998).   [16] Storey (2003) 217f.

'euripidaristophanizer' against Aristophanes' pretensions to intellectual subtlety (fr. 342). The passage alludes to a delivery format of question and
response with the audience found in Aristophanic prologues (*Wasps* 72–86,
Peace 43–8), but the anapaestic tetrameters in combination with the polemi-
cizing content point to a parabasis. If from a parabasis, its metrical form is
that generally preferred by Aristophanes for this segment of the play. But an
abundance of fragments using other long-line metres in combination with
'parabatic' style authorial and choral claims indicate that there was greater
flexibility in this poetic form, and a poet's choice of metre may have been
one additional way he could 'brand' his poetry. Thus, in a passage of literary
invective in which Eupolis claims to have co-authored *Knights* and given it
to 'baldy' (= Aristophanes) as a gift (fr. 89), the poet cants his remarks in
so-called eupolideans.[17] Since the parabasis of the revised *Clouds* is, fairly
uniquely for Aristophanes, also in that metre and because there is thematic
contact between it and this fragment on the issue of *Knights*' originality (on
which more below), Storey's suggestion is highly appealing that the choice
of metre in these passages may itself be 'part of the intertextual exchange'.[18]
In short, the reflection of structural elements in the fragments allows us to
place a number of them within a rough blueprint of a 'standard' comedy,
which can further guide our thinking, since the individual formal structural
elements often serve specific purposes in moving a plot along. Moreover,
identifying ways in which poets deployed these formal elements differently
sets us on a course toward identifying unique aspects of a play or a peculiarity of an individual poet's style, or even signs of direct literary engagement
and response between poets.

Contributions to assessments of the fragments also come from two forms
of archaeological evidence. The inscriptions for dramatic productions mentioned in the opening paragraphs are key for reconstructing the chronology, both specific and relative, of poets' careers and their productions. That
knowledge naturally creates a framework to support conclusions about individual poets' engagement with one another or paths of influence between
them.[19] Passages like the parabasis of *Knights* which details poetic succession in the comic contests and that of *Clouds* with its assault on a series of
poetic rivals demand to be placed alongside this documentary evidence and
take on new poetic force thereafter.[20] Increasing use is also being made of
the visual evidence from vase paintings, especially South Italian vases of the
fourth century, that are often influenced by Athenian comedy. In some cases

---

[17] Parker (1988) 116f. On this rivalry, see Sidwell (1993) and (1994); Kyriakidi (2007).
[18] Storey (2003) 388.
[19] Recent discussions of this material in Rusten (2006) and Biles (2009).
[20] Biles (2001); Biles (2011) 109–21, 181–7.

the (re)performance of specific plays inspires the composition, among them one possibly inspired by *Wine Flask* with 'Cratinus' and 'Comedy' tussling over a wine jar.[21] Even where specific plays cannot be identified, however, vase paintings that can plausibly be regarded as comically inspired by such visual clues as mask-types and stage-phallus reveal much about the theatrical conventions utilized by the poets and how they supported the expression of comic ideas. Revermann, for instance, draws conclusions about a pervasive notion of 'comic ugliness' from this evidence, while Bakola finds support for Cratinus' generic cross-fertilization of comedy and satyr play in one vase's striking intermingling of comic and satyr play conventions.[22] All such inferences from these visual fragments naturally feed back into interpretations of the textual fragments.

Considerable advances have been made in recognizing the contributions of other poets to the genre by taking thematic soundings in the corpus of fragments. Perusal of the fragments quickly reveals a number of shared interests, pointing to a situation, in some ways akin to tragedy's shared mythical subject matter, where comic poets constantly recycled and reshaped a common stock of themes and tropes.[23] Many of the studies contained in *The Rivals of Aristophanes* (2000) fall into this category, charting to varying extents the treatment across the genre of themes such as food and feasting; women, foreigners and other identity groups; politics and religion; and (broadly speaking) comic vision. Not surprisingly, comic rivalry is itself one prominent theme, and the various ways poets talked about themselves and their poetry are catalogued by Sommerstein.[24] Chapters on comic themes in this volume address these approaches in fuller detail; suffice it to say here that Aristophanes' place within a vibrant genre, and not as its sole representative, becomes more conspicuous as a result of tracing how ideas familiar from his plays are handled by his predecessors, contemporaries and successors. In one instance, to which I now turn, the shaping of the genre along thematic lines by a community of poets can be placed within a specifically agonistic framework.

Plotting political attack in comedy

The passage from the *Clouds* parabasis quoted at length above (*Clouds* 549–59) provides a (patently self-serving) assessment of comedy's escalating engagement with political themes and political targets, detailing

---

[21] See Taplin (1993) 43f., Csapo, Chapter 5.
[22] Revermann (2006a) 145–59; Bakola (2010) 110–12.
[23] Heath (1990) 152.   [24] Sommerstein (1992).

as it does Aristophanes' virtual discovery of demagogue-comedy with his sustained attack on Cleon as the Paphlagonian in *Knights*, which in turn served as a model for a series of later explorations of this mode of comic plot in other poets' assaults on Hyperbolus. It is certainly true that a number of fragments of Eupolis' play *Marikas* fall rather easily into the general conception and plot scheme provided by *Knights*.[25] Thus, to mention the more significant points of comparison,[26] Marikas is a fictional name for Hyperbolus that suggests, much like the Paphlagonian for Cleon in *Knights*, a servile and foreign status;[27] those elements of character are reflected in each demagogue's streetwise education (frr. 194, 208), which ensures that there is a marked contribution of underhanded tactics to their political behaviour (fr. 193). As in *Knights*, Marikas is in a position of subservience to a master (fr. 192.118, 150), who can punish his slaves (fr. 203) and at one point calls a meeting of the assembly (fr. 192.148–50) where the demagogue presumably displays his political talents. The debt to Aristophanes' play implied by these points may even be acknowledged outright in two allusions to *Knights* at frr. 192. 135f. (Cleon mentioned in close proximity to *paphlazein*, 'to bluster', i.e. the pun involved in Aristophanes' Paphlagonian) and 201, where the chorus proclaim to the audience that they 'do not ride on horseback', an assurance that *Marikas* is not just *Knights* reheated.

It is difficult to decide what to make of the attempt in this last passage to mark intertextual disjunction (is it ironic, bantering, or otherwise?); it is, however, worth noting that Aristophanes' claims in *Clouds* about Eupolis' debt to him are thought to lie behind the parabasis' claim in Ar. fr. 58 (in eupolideans) that someone made 'three tunics out of one of my [Aristophanes?] cloaks'. That there is some truth in Aristophanes' claims seems likely from what we have of *Marikas*, although the usual caveats in reconstructing comic plays from the fragments still apply, since one cannot help noticing a tinge of circularity in the methodology for assessing similarity between the plays: applying the model of *Knights* (on Aristophanes' word!) tends to constrain the results in the absence of any independent evidence of *Marikas*' plot. What Aristophanes surely sought to dismiss, and what Eupolis presumably aimed to emphasize, were the ways he developed the demagogue-comedy paradigm differently, as signs of his independent creativity tend to suggest.[28] In short, the entire exchange over poetic 'discovery',

---

[25] One of the more extensive fragments of *Marikas* (fr. 192) belongs to an important category of evidence, a papyrus from an ancient commentary on the play organized by lemmata (thirty-five separate quotations) followed by commentary.
[26] See more fully, Storey (2003) 202–4.   [27] Cassio (1985).   [28] Storey (2003) 214.

borrowing and adaptation of a comic sub-genre is cast in overt agonistic terms.[29]

Aristophanes' remarks about the impact of his brand of demagogue-comedy take on a decidedly different character based on points of silence. As Sommerstein (2000) observes, Aristophanes' catalogue of imitators overlooks his slightly younger rival Plato, who composed a play entitled *Hyperbolus* in the early 410s, not to mention an earlier demagogue-comedy in the later 420s titled *Peisander*. On the one hand, this raises the possibility that adducing Plato in the criticism in *Clouds* required no great intellectual stretch on the audience's part, thanks to the explicit and harping mentions of Hyperbolus at *Clouds* 551 and 557f. In that case, moreover, Aristophanes' attempted suppression of his rival's place in the literary schema he presents appears the more unjustified in light of the significant contribution Plato made to this comic sub-genre, by attacking his political targets not through the (still transparent) means of an allegorical plot and fictional names as in *Knights* and *Marikas* but by actual name, to judge from the play titles themselves and several fragments (frr. 108, 182; cf. 185). What is more, the political humour may have been no less disarming in its directness, if (e.g.) fr. 105 from *Peisander* offers, through the metaphor of 'keeping women in line', a sober assessment of Athens' cold calculation of self-interest in the administration of its empire, worthy of Cleon himself.[30] The possibility that Plato advanced a counter-claim of being the first to wage war on Cleon (fr. 115) may bear on these points,[31] since it implies that Aristophanes' grand and repeated assertions on this score (see also *Wasps* 1029–37, *Peace* 751–60) did not go uncontested among his rivals. Far from marking any sort of culmination or momentous literary discovery, when set beside Plato's comedies *Knights* appears rather as one point along the way toward the fuller realization of political comedy, through a succession of efforts by various comic poets.

One of Sommerstein's subsidiary objectives is to sketch the possibility that the political climate in Athens at specific moments fostered or forestalled the development of demagogue-comedy, which implies that these developments in comic style were not simply a matter of individual genius but rather comedy's constant testing of boundaries and a good deal of opportunism. If true, Aristophanes' feud with Cleon (*Acharnians* 378–82, 502–7) in the wake of his second comedy, *Babylonians*, in 426 BCE might represent a prime

---

[29] The possibility that the early lemmata in fr. 192 belong to Eupolis' self-positioning in the play before the parabasis can be assessed in this light; cf. Storey (2003) 206f.; Bakola (2008) 20–4.

[30] Sommerstein (2000) 440.   [31] Olson (2007) 212.

example of this dynamic at work in the development of demagogue-comedy.[32] Just how openly this play dealt with political issues is difficult to assess from the fragments, and one ancient scholar's summary (Schol. *Acharnians* 378) of the play's political criticism is clearly, though not necessarily completely, dependent on the passage of *Acharnians* it aims to explain. At any rate, the latter testimonium (cf. *Acharnians* 628–32) implies that in *Babylonians* Aristophanes was more interested in ridiculing Athenian democratic institutions and political behaviour, and rather less so in attacking individuals *per se*, at least on the scale of *Knights*. *Acharnians* in 425 BCE likewise attacks Cleon indirectly by flaunting the demagogue's response to the previous play, while by turning his sights on Lamachus Aristophanes perhaps took aim at a safer target. In any event, the assault on Lamachus is neither as sustained nor central to the play, and certainly is not as acerbic as that on Cleon in *Knights*. To be sure, bringing Lamachus on stage in a more light-hearted way may have opened doors for the specific form that Plato's escalation took. Hence, Aristophanes' own plays before *Knights* lend some credence to the developmental model for explaining demagogue-comedy, and the pattern comes into clearer focus when Cratinus' style of political comedy is considered as antecedent to Aristophanes' literary-historical account in *Clouds*.

Cratinus' influence on comedy's engagement with political themes rests on several considerations: scattered political humour in fragments of his plays; his reputation for having a caustic tongue, acknowledged already by Aristophanes himself (*Knights* 526–30, *Frogs* 357); and the later characterization of his socio-political focus by ancient scholars, one of whom describes Cratinus using comedy as a 'public scourge' to expose the social and political atrocities of his fellow citizens.[33] Indeed, with Cratinus we may be at or at any rate drawing near the headwaters of trends leading to demagogue-comedy, since it is during his career that personal abuse shows up in the fragments. With Cratinus' reputation in place, one might expect Aristophanes' claims for *Knights* to ring hollowly in the theatre of the mid-420s. In fact, the evidence of at least one Cratinean play suggests otherwise. *Dionysalexandrus*, which was most likely produced in the early years of the Peloponnesian War, is the one fragmentary comedy whose plot is known to us nearly in full, thanks to a papyrus of an ancient summary (*Dionysalexandrus* test. i) of the sort prefixed to Aristophanic plays. It was a mythological burlesque in which Dionysus and his satyrs are inserted into the episode of the Judgement of Paris on Mt Ida, with the god humorously disguising

---

[32] On Aristophanes and Cleon see Storey (1995); Sommerstein (2004a) 164–6.
[33] Rosen (1988) 37–42.

himself as the shepherd, but ultimately being foiled in his attempt to claim Helen for himself when Paris arrives on the scene, keeping Helen and giving the god up to the Achaeans. Just as important as the plot summary is the appended critical notice that 'in this play Pericles is effectively ridiculed *by suggestion* (*di' emphaseôs*) for having brought the war on Athens'. What this comment, above all the italicized phrase, means and how much faith we should place in it, are matters of debate.[34] One point of support is provided, however, by Hermippus fr. 47, in which someone hails Pericles as king of the satyrs, for if this remark is rightly assumed to depend on Cratinus' play, the implication is that Dionysus was identified with Pericles (momentarily or extensively) and this identification was conspicuous enough that an audience hearing Hermippus' remark could make ready sense of the allusion. In all events, 'the war brought on Athens', according to the summary, must be the Trojan War,[35] and an attempt has been made to explain each mythological datum in the plot summary with details of Pericles' political activity.[36]

Even if those explanations are correct, the play's political message appears to have been anything but direct and represents an additional degree of separation – beyond even the Aristophanic mode of political allegorizing in *Knights* – from the explicit demagogue-comedy found in Plato. What can be gathered from several other Cratinean plays suggests that *Dionysalexandrus* was not this poet's only attempt to cultivate this sort of political comedy.[37] Cratinus' penchant for personal abuse notwithstanding, his brand of demagogue-comedy relied on an established comic form, mythological burlesque, that is barely represented in the surviving Aristophanic plays; to it Cratinus added depth, complexity and topicality by mapping political identities onto traditional characters and events.[38] Finally, significant too is the contribution to *Dionysalexandrus* of themes and plot patterns drawn from satyr drama,[39] since it broadens the range of inter-generic influences on comedy beyond Aristophanes' intense engagement with tragedy, and specifically Euripidean tragedy (acknowledged in Cratinus fr. 342), observable in such plays as *Acharnians*, *Women at the Thesmophoria* and *Frogs*. In cases like this, comedy as a genre takes on entirely new appearances based on the evidence of the fragments.

---

[34] Reassessed in detail by Bakola (2010) 198–206; cf. Revermann (1997) 198f.; Ruffell (2002) 151f.

[35] Wright (2007).

[36] Schwarze (1971); results summarized in English in Rosen (1988) 51–3; Bakola (2010) 183–8.

[37] E.g., Farioli (2000).   [38] Sifakis (2006) 27–9.

[39] Bakola (2005) and (2010) 81–117; cf. Silk (2000b) 303–6.

Genre-transformation and rivalry transformed in New Comedy

The preceding considerations demonstrate how attention to and further research on the comic fragments sheds light on Aristophanes' place within the development of comedy and makes it increasingly possible to assess these other poets in their own right. Interaction between poets ensured that comedy remained a dynamic and evolving genre, and more drastic transformations lay in store in the century after Aristophanes' death, as the genre developed toward a situational comedy of manners that abandoned the caustic and topical socio-political humour which so impressed later readers of Old Comedy (Konstan, Chapter 1). Although the poetic *agôn* remained the social occasion for these performances, a shift toward dramatically circumscribed plots, conforming to an aesthetic of heightened (if not perfect) realism, brought with it a diminution in the kinds of direct assaults on rivals and broad poeticization of agonistic themes in the plays traced in previous pages, above all with the disappearance of the parabasis.

In this respect, as with others, comedy by the time of Philemon, Menander and Diphilus became more like tragedy, so that now anecdotes contain the only direct references to specific rivalries (e.g., Aulus Gellius 17.4.1f.). One of the few allusions to antagonistic exchange, between Menander and Philemon (Philemon fr. 198), casts these poets in a scenario more redolent of their domestic plots than to heated rivalry over poetic prestige. A small handful of fragments certainly have a metapoetic ring about them, like the criticism of a dim-witted listener in Philemon fr. 131 (cf. Diphilus fr. 108):

> It's hard when a simpleton of a listener sits there;
> in his foolishness he doesn't hold himself accountable.

The agonistic resonance comes out by comparison to Cratinus' castigation (fr. 360) of the audience for failing to recognize the merits of his play until too late:

> Hail, oh magnificently useless host of laughers,
> best judges of my poetry ... after the festival is over.
> Blessed did your mother, the ruckus of the bleachers, deliver you.

But the differences are also instructive: Cratinus' is a direct address repudiating the audience, Philemon's is canted in third person discussion; Cratinus identifies the stakes of *judging* plays head-on, Philemon refers more vaguely to *listeners*; the distinctive archilochean metre of Cratinus' remarks sets them apart and suggests a parabatic overture,[40] Philemon's are metrically (and probably dramatically) indistinct iambic trimeters. In short, the attempt to wring metapoetic force out of the Philemon passage may be entirely mis-directed; at the very least it is so seamlessly integrated with the dramatic situation as to be virtually untraceable.

Still, the formulaic prayer for victory in the final lines of Menander's *Dyscolus* situates that performance in the contest. Likewise, the jeering over the old man's fallen state in the final scene of that play also emphasizes the 'victory' of the performers (959, 965), as props redolent of celebration are brought on stage (963f.) and direct appeals are issued to the audience for their kind applause (966f.).[41] With its overt agonistic gestures, the scene's poetic pedigree is unmistakable, going back to finales like those of *Achar-nians* and *Wasps* that attempt to bridge success in the dramatic enterprise with victory in the poetic *agôn*.[42] Prayers for victory similar to that at the end of *Dyscolus* appear elsewhere in Menander, while the appearance of another such prayer in a fragment of one of Menander's immediate succes-sors (Posidippus fr. 6) suggests the currency of this closural format in New Comedy.[43] Striking in that case is the more modest and stylized articulation of the agonistic posturing that was once a chief feature of the parabasis. In fact the development of such prayers may be heralded by the lively appeal to the judges in Aristophanes' *Assembly Women* (1154–62), just before the *exodos*. Moreover, the converging tendencies of comedy and tragedy are also observable, since a close parallel for these closing prayers for victory also exists in the final lines of several Euripidean tragedies.[44] The direction of generic influence is not easily unravelled, but the upshot for an apprecia-tion of rivalry in later comedy is clear enough: poeticized rivalry of the sort familiar from fifth-century poets largely disappeared as agonistic gestures became mere static add-ons to the performance under the influence of an aesthetic that demanded dramatic integrity in a plot.

And so we end where we began, with rivalry and competition in New Comedy resembling more closely the position of tragedy to Old Comedy in the fifth century. And as with tragedy, there can be no doubt that competi-tion contributed to the composition, performance and audience experience of New Comedy. But without as many overt cues provided by the poets

---

[40] Bakola (2010) 40f.   [41] Cf. *Lysistrata* 1316–21.

[42] On closural victory sequences in Old Comedy, see Wilson (2007a), with adjustments to his interpretation in Biles (2011) 86–94.

[43] Gomme and Sandbach (1973) 288.

[44] E.g., *Phoenician Women* 1764–6; these endings are generally regarded as spurious (Mastronarde (1994)), a product of post-classical book-production or perhaps reperformance in fourth-century competitions of Old Tragedy.

themselves, the enterprise of tracing the enduring effects of rivalry on the genre necessarily changes. We might still achieve those ends by considering, for instance, the extent to which Menander's deployment of stock characters shared by his contemporaries represents something peculiar or even novel, and thus amounts to his attempt to create a distinct Menandrean comedy (see Ruffell, Chapter 10). Needless to say, persuasive conclusions along these lines can be reached only if Menander's dramatic style is assessed in comparison with what can be made of his rivals.[45]

Further reading

The fragments of Greek comedy have been newly edited by Kassel and Austin in *Poetae Comici Graeci* (= *PCG*) (1983–). Storey (2011) has compiled a three-volume Loeb-edition of comic fragments (with introductions and English translations). The thematic selection of fragments and commentary in Olson (2007) provides an excellent introduction to the corpus for those with Greek, while Rusten (2011) contains a large selection of fragments in English translation; both of these works include wide-ranging presentations and discussions of the various sorts of evidence at our disposal. The evidence for the history and organization of the dramatic competitions is presented and discussed in Pickard-Cambridge (1988) and Csapo and Slater (1995). For the epigraphical evidence, see Olson (2007) 379–91 and, more fully, Millis and Olson (2012). The standard work for the chronology of Old Comedy is Geissler (1969), but here too a reassessment of the evidence by Stefan Schröder is underway. Rivalry in Old Comedy is a point of focus in Sidwell (1993), (1994), (1995); Biles (2002), (2011); Ruffell (2002); Bakola (2008). Since *PCG*, work on the fragments has intensified with monographs and commentaries on specific poets now proliferating: Storey (2003); Kyriakidi (2007); Telò (2007); Orth (2009); Pirrotta (2009); Bakola (2010). More focused studies in articles and book chapters likewise abound; old and more recent standards include Whittaker (1935), Dover (1972) 210–18 and Heath (1990), while the essays in Harvey and Wilkins (2000) as well as the other articles cited in this chapter are also good starting points.

[45] A point also stressed by Nesselrath (2011).

3

KEITH SIDWELL

Fourth-century comedy
before Menander

'Between the excitingly varied landscape of Old Comedy and the city
of Menander stretches a desert: therein the sedulous topographer may
remark two respectable eminences, and perhaps a low ridge in the
middle distance, or a few nullahs, and the wayfarer will greet with
delight one or two oases with a singing-bird or so; but the ever-present
foreground of his journey is sand, tiresome, barren, and trickling'.

(Norwood (1931) 38)

'Gilbert Norwood likened Middle Comedy in a slightly
uncomplimentary manner to a desert. Perhaps one might more
correctly see in it a sort of valley between the two peaks of Old
Comedy and the comedy of Menander'.

(Nesselrath (1990) 340)

Nesselrath's image for the period under scrutiny is much nearer the mark
in one respect than Norwood's. The earlier scholar describes only the post-
apocalypse scene, in which nothing much of interest remains, while the later
at least attempts to envisage the original topography, before the choices and
the accidents of survival took their heavy toll. From the latter viewpoint, in
fact, Norwood's depressing picture is in every respect mistaken. We have
evidence that Athenian comedy was in good shape for the whole of this
period (point 1 below). We can also name individual poets who won the
consistent approval of the Athenian public of this time and at least one whose
reputation survived well into the following century (point 2 below). We have
two complete plays and a considerable body of fragmentary material from
the comedies of this time, as well as some possible Roman reworkings from
the period, and we know several more names of poets of whom nothing
much else has survived (point 3 below). We have a body of visual evidence
which allows us the possibility of seeing what Athenians saw on stage during
these years, even if we cannot tie much (or any?) of it to individual comedies
(point 4 below). Finally, we have extensive evidence that the scholars of
antiquity studied and preserved this material until at least the end of the
second century of our era (point 5 below).

(1) The remains of several inscriptions assure us that comic competitions and the *chorêgia* with them continued uninterrupted for the whole of this period.[1] From one we know, for example, that in 389/8, the archonship of Antipater, either at the Lenaia or the Dionysia, Aristophanes won with *Wealth*, Nicochares was second with *Spartans*, Aristomenes third with *Admetus*, Nicophon fourth with *Adonis* and Alcaios fifth with *Pasiphae*.[2] This evidence also tells us that the number of entrants into the comic contest was at least five.[3] Another inscription listed (apparently in order of the winning of their first victory) the numbers of first prizes gained by individual poets (see 2 below).[4] Two inscriptions from the deme of Aixone, probably from the year 340/39, make it indisputable that local comic competitions and the local *chorêgia* were alive and well in the middle of the century (and this is confirmed also by literary evidence).[5]

(2) The remnants of the Victors Lists, though lacunose, tell us that Anaxandrides won four victories at the Dionysia and three at the Lenaia, that Antiphanes won eight victories at the Lenaia (and another five at the Dionysia), Eubulus six and Alexis between two and four (he also won at least once at the Dionysia). Menander is reported to have gained only eight victories over his whole career,[6] so this makes him certainly less successful than Antiphanes, and more or less on a par with Anaxandrides and Eubulus (about whose Dionysia victories we know nothing). In the later fourth or early third century, Demetrius of Phaleron (who governed Athens from 317 to 307 BCE) wrote a book *About Antiphanes*, and in one of the surviving *Prolegomena on Comedy* the findings of which can be traced back to the Alexandrian period, Antiphanes (possibly along with Alexis) is recorded as being one of the best comic poets of his time.[7] The taste for Menander as a great comic poet, then, is a product of later critics and cultural conditions.

(3) Aristophanes' *Assembly Women*, dating from the 390s, and his *Wealth*, produced (as we have seen) and victorious in 389/8, are our only two fully extant fourth-century plays. We have fragmentary remains of other

---

[1] *IG* II² 2322 and 2325. Mette (1977) 140–2, 167–8, 175–6, 211–18.

[2] Indirectly, since this information actually survives in hypothesis III (Wilson) to Aristophanes' *Wealth*, though its source will have been Aristotle's *Didaskaliai* (lists of festival performances), which in turn depended upon the original inscription.

[3] As it may also have been for most of the fifth century: Luppe (1972).

[4] Mette (1977) 175f.

[5] See *IG* II/III² 1202 and Athens, E.M. 13262. Mette (1977) 136. Ghiron-Bistagne (1976) 86–90.

[6] Aulus Gellius 17.4.6.

[7] *PCG* Antiphanes T5 (= Diogenes Laertius 5.81); Nesselrath (1990) 163. Koster (1975) *Prolegomenon* III, line 46.

comic dramatists whose careers spanned the fifth and fourth centuries, even if we often do not know the dates of most of their plays (see the appendix to this chapter below). Of the comic dramatists whose careers belong squarely within the fourth century before Menander (allowing for the fact that some had careers which overlapped with his), we have no complete plays. We are sometimes given the number of comedies written by individual playwrights – for example, Alexis is said to have produced 245 and Eubulus 104 – but the reliability of these numbers is difficult to check.[8] Ancient scholarship describes this period as 'Middle Comedy' (see below) and reports the over-all number of poets as 57 and the known plays as between 617 and 800.[9] But we have (not counting the dubious ones) only 621 titles and 1,272 fragments (see the appendix to this chapter below). We also know just the names (sometimes with some uncertainty) of some playwrights, sometimes along with their number of victories, sometimes with titles of some of their plays, but with no surviving fragments (see the appendix to this chapter below). Finally, Alexis appears in a list of sources for Roman comedies given by Aulus Gellius: Plautus' *Aulularia* and *Poenulus* have been plausibly suggested as derivatives of specific Alexis plays.[10]

(4) Alongside the textual material, we have an enormous stock of visual remains. We can usefully divide this into three basic categories: inscriptions and reliefs, vase paintings and theatrical memorabilia (clay masks, terracotta and bronze figurines, etc.).[11] The fragments of one relief from Athens (Csapo, Figure 5.5) help to demonstrate (along with some literary and epigraphic evidence) that the comic chorus was still dancing in the fourth century. And one early fourth-century Attic vase shows what may be a chorus of old women preparing for their performance.[12] But the vast majority of vase paintings showing comedy are from Western Greece, and, for our period, are problematic. Since Taplin (1993),[13] it has been generally accepted that many of these so-called 'phlyax vases' do refer either directly to Attic comedies or at least to a form of comedy which was very strongly influenced by Attic comedy. However, the ones we can actually tie down (such as the 'Würzburg Telephus': Csapo, Figure 5.13) appear to

[8] Alexis: *Suda* α 1138, Eubulus: *Suda* ε 3386.
[9] Numbers of poets and plays: Koster (1975) *Prolegomenon* III, lines 45–6. Numbers of plays: Athenaeus 8.336d.
[10] Aulus Gellius 2.23.1. Arnott (1996a) 29–31.
[11] The catalogues of Trendall (1967) and Webster (revised Green) (1978) are still the best place to gain first access to them. See also Bieber (1961) and Hughes (2011).
[12] For the chorus in the fourth century, see Hunter (1979); Rothwell (1995). Old woman chorus: Heidelberg B 134. Side (a) Bieber (1961), 49 fig. 208.
[13] See also Webster (1948).

relate to fifth-century plays.[14] Among the latest of these is the *c.* 350 Paestan crater from Pontecagnano painted by Assteas with the Phrynis/Pyronides scene from Eupolis' *Demes* (*c.* 410).[15] It is difficult, therefore, to be absolutely certain that we have isolated an example of Middle Comedy. It has been suggested, for example, that the *Chorêgoi* vase represents a fourth-century Athenian comedy, since paratragedy was important at this time (see below).[16] But it was also important in fifth-century comedy, and we have no text to which to tie the scene depicted. A vase from Paestum, around 350, and by the same painter (Assteas) who painted the scene from Eupolis, shows an old man in comic costume lying across his money-box, being assaulted by two thieves as his slave looks helplessly on. This might well be from a fourth-century comedy and maybe even from an Athenian one, if these plays were exported to the West. But since scenes of assault and battery, forcible restraint of an old man and theft are known from Old Comedy,[17] there is nothing to tell us that this is not an unknown Old Comedy rather than a fourth-century play, such as the *Treasure-Store* of Anaxandrides or the *Vanishing Money* of Antiphanes or Epigenes.

The figurines of actors and the masks represent a consistent series stretching from the last quarter of the fifth century right down to the period of Menander.[18] For example, there survive two Athenian sets of terracotta figures of comic actors from around 400.[19] The heavily padded costumes, with the prominent phallus for the male characters and the ugly masks, are certainly similar to the costumes shown on the later vase paintings from South Italy and it is reasonable to suspect some cross-fertilization between Athenian and Western Greek comic theatre, since such terracottas became popular throughout the Greek world.[20] The grammarian Pollux provides a list of comic masks which derives from Alexandrian scholarship,[21] and with this and the abundant physical remains of terracotta figurines, masks and representations of masks, scholars have been able to reconstruct a typology of characters for the comedy of the fourth century before Menander.[22]

---

[14] Csapo (1986); Taplin (1993) 36–40.   [15] Hughes (2003); Telò (2007) 28–33.

[16] Taplin (1993) 55–66; Shapiro (1995b).

[17] 'Robbing the miser': side (a), Berlin, Staatliche Museen F 3044, calyx crater by Assteas, *c.* 350 BCE, from St Agata. Trendall (1967) p. 50 no. 76 (70); for illustrations, see Bieber (1961) fig. 509, Hughes (1996) 102 plate 10 and (2011) 50 fig. 10. Scenes of assault and battery: e.g., Pheidippides' attack on Strepsiades in *Clouds*, Bdelycleon's imprisonment of Philocleon in *Wasps*, the slaves stealing Paphlagon's oracles in *Knights*.

[18] Green (1994) 37 and 63.

[19] Webster (1978) 45. For illustrations, see Green (1994) fig. 2.13 p. 3; Bieber (1961) 46f.

[20] See Green (1994) 63–84 for a fuller discussion of the visual evidence for this period.

[21] Pollux 4.133–54.   [22] Webster (1978) 13–26.

(5) The *Deipnosophists* by Athenaeus and Pollux's *Onomasticon* from around the end of the second century CE, the fifth-century anthology of Stobaeus and the *Suda*, a vast dictionary of the classical world composed in tenth-century Byzantium, give us the majority of the information we have about the comic poets of the fourth century, and this later scholarship is also the source of most of the fragments we possess. A number of *Prolegomena on Comedy* also survive from indeterminate dates, some of which deal with this period.[23] However, most of the material provided by these later sources can be traced back to the third century BCE and the activities of librarians from Callimachus to Aristophanes of Byzantium.[24] The fact that Roman poets utilized the comedies of Alexis for their own plays shows that some of this material was in circulation at Rome up to the end of the second century BCE, and Athenaeus' large-scale citations demonstrate that it was at least still possible to read works which included material from fourth-century comic drama, even if we cannot believe the claim of one of his characters (8.336d) to have read and excerpted more than 800 comic plays from this period.

Nature of fourth-century comedy

From the lists given in the appendix to this chapter below (under Ancient Sources [b]), it is very clear how much we have lost. Even so, we do know quite a lot about fourth-century comedy before Menander and the survival of two complete plays and a swathe of fragments (to say nothing of the visual material) certainly allows us to get some sort of picture of what the comedy of this period was like. We can tell, for example, that the type of fantastic plot favoured by Aristophanes and his rivals in the fifth century continued into the 380s, because we still have a complete text of his *Wealth*. And his *Assembly Women* (late 390s) shows that political satire was still alive and well. Lines 194–212, where Praxagora practises her radical proposal to hand over power to the women, demand that the audience still be *au fait* not only with Athenian political institutions, but also with the names and reputations of individual contemporary Athenians.

When we move into the period after *Wealth*, we can recognize a great many titles which suggest stories derived from myth or tragedy (such as Eubulus' *Medea* and *Titans*), a vogue which is all but finished by the time of Menander (who wrote no play of this type). Aristotle in the *Poetics* (1453a–36f.) mentions a comedy in which Orestes and Aegisthus end up as friends, and this may help us speculate that major reversals of the traditional stories were crucial to the plots of these plays. Still, traditional elements, such as

---

[23] Collected in Koster (1975).   [24] Nesselrath (1990) 172–87.

Heracles' gluttony, already notable in Aristophanic comedy (e.g., *Frogs*), continue to occur. Here is (probably) Heracles in Antiphanes' *Omphalê* (fr. 174.1–5):

> How could a noble man ever withdraw
> From this house, when he sees those white-skinned loaves
> Packing the kitchen in their serried ranks,
> And sees them changing shape in the tandoor?

Outside the comedies which travestied myth or parodied tragedy, invention was freer and, according to the (prologue?) speaker (perhaps Poetry or Comedy?) in Antiphanes' *Poetry*, much more difficult than for any tragedian (fr. 189.1–6; 17–22):

> The tragic genre's blessed in everything.
> First off, their audience already know
> The plots, before a single word is said.
> The poet only needs to give a hint.
> If I say 'Oedipus', they know the rest...
> For us it's different, *we* must make it up,
> New names, the past, the present, how it ends,
> The prologue. If there's anything left out
> By a Chremes or a Pheidon, he'll be booed.

The period is also marked, as the preceding fragment of Antiphanes suggests with its mention of Chremes and Pheidon, by the gradual appearance of themes and stock characters which would become more developed in Menander's work. In Alexis fr. 212.1–7 from his *Soldier* of the late 340s, for example, we see two characters in debate over possession of a baby, a theme reminiscent of Menander's *Men at Arbitration* (218–371 (Arnott)):

> A: Take this back. B What is it? A: Something I took from you.
>   I'm bringing back the child I took away before.
> B: Why? Don't you want to bring it up? A: Well, it's not mine.
> B: Nor mine. A: But it was *you*, recall, gave it to *me*.
> B: I didn't *give* it. A: What d'you mean? B: I gave it *back*.

The fragment incidentally contains a sly dig at a famous contemporary verbal quibble by the orator Demosthenes. In 343, when Philip of Macedon offered the small island of Halonnesus to Athens, the great anti-Macedonian politician is reported to have told the Athenian *dêmos* not to accept it if Philip was *giving* it, but only if he was *giving it back*.[25] This shows that even in a

---

[25] Reported by Aeschines 3.83; Arnott (1996a) 70f.

comedy now seemingly concentrating on social themes, the real world may not be far away.

Three of the major stock characters which appear at this time are the Parasite, the Hetaira and the Cook. The Cook's typical pomposity is underlined in this fragment from the *Milesians* of Alexis (fr. 153.6–19), as he instructs his hirer in the mysteries of his art. Important to note here is the use of strictly tragic iambics and riddling phraseology which scholars since antiquity have related to the dithyramb.[26] This appears to be a stylistic feature developed in and more or less confined to this period of Greek comedy, as is also the long passage in anapaestic dimeters which usually catalogues a meal (e.g., Anaxandrides fr. 42, Antiphanes fr. 130, Ephippus fr. 12).[27]

> Cook: Your cook's task merely is to make the dishes well
> And nothing else. Now if the intending diner comes
> On time, he gives a great boost to the art indeed.
> But if he misses the appointed hour to eat,
> So that the chef must warm the roasted meat again
> Or hurry to complete the roasting not yet done,
> The diner steals the proper pleasure from the art.
> Hirer: Enlist this cook at once into the sophists' guild!
> Cook: Why are you people standing there? My fire is hot,
> The watchdogs of Hephaestus thick and fast do haste
> Lightly to heav'n. For them some unseen law of force
> Has linked their birth with passing on from life at once.

As far as we can tell, the greater proportion of what remains after Aristophanes appears to conform to either the mythological/tragic burlesque or to the social comedy which would eventually triumph in Menander's day over other sub-genres. But we know of several plays which have the names of contemporary individuals (e.g., Aristophon's *Plato*, Eubulus' *Dionysius* and Timocles' *Nannion*), and since such titles were given in the fifth century to satirical comedies attacking individuals (e.g., Plato's *Cleophon* and *Hyperbolus*), we cannot discount the survival in some form of the fifth-century tradition of 'roasting' known persons by representing them as characters on the stage (like Paphlagon/Cleon in Aristophanes' *Knights*). For example, the following fragment parodies lines 39–48 of Aeschylus' *Eumenides* to set the scene in Timocles' *Autocleides Plays Orestes* (fr. 27):

> Around the wretched man sleep the old hags,
> Nannion, Plangon, Lyka, Phryne, Myrrhine,

[26] Scholion on Aristophanes *Wealth* 515; Hunter (1983) 19f., 166f.; Nesselrath (1990) 241–66.

[27] Nesselrath (1990) 267–80.

Gnathaina, Chrysis, Pythionike, Kobalis,
Lopadion, Hierocleia.

The names of the women here are probably those of real hetairai of the later
fourth century,[28] and the Autocleides referred to in the title is probably the
one mentioned by Aeschines (1.52). The title together with this description
and the way in which the work it parodies was dramatized might also be
taken as evidence that Autocleides himself appeared as Orestes in the play.
Timocles' career belongs around the mid-fourth century (he is only two
places above Menander in the Lenaia victors list), and while it may occasion
surprise to find so late an example of personal satire, it is in fact in line with
the literary evidence we have for this time. Around the middle of the fourth
century, Aeschines (1.157) refers to an attack made on an individual in a
comic chorus at a local festival. Isocrates (8.14) is still complaining about
the gossip-mongering comic poets who are washing Athenian dirty linen in
public. And Plato (Laws 935d–36b) is legislating as though satirical comedy
were still a problem.

Problem of development

The main difficulties we have, then, apart from the simple lack of texts, are
how to understand what actually happened to satirical comedy in the fourth
century and how to account for the very obvious differences even between
the last play we can examine of Aristophanes (Wealth) and the first we
possess of Menander (Samia?). Gone is the complex formal structure, discussed in more detail by Marshall (Chapter 6), of agôn, epirrhematic syzygy,
parabasis (already absent, though, from Aristophanes' fourth-century plays)
and the critical part played in the action by the chorus (though the choral
odes are also missing from Assembly Women and Wealth). In its place is
the five-act episodic plot-structure familiar from the later Western theatrical
tradition which picked it up from Menander's Roman imitators. Gone are
the fantastic elements (cities in the clouds, choruses of cities, Comedy as the
poet's wife, women holding men to ransom over political ideas, the magical
healing of Wealth etc.), and the iambic attacks on political figures. Instead,
we have full-blown domestic comedy, with plots that operate in realistic
mode, with everyday language, and virtually no reference to the details of
current political life (except for background), let alone iambic insults. It
may be the case, however, that we do not understand clearly quite how the
Athenian comedy got from its fifth-century manifestation to its Menandrian

---

[28] Eubulus wrote plays entitled Nannion and Plangon, and mentions Phryne in his Neaira
(fr. 25.2). Antiphanes wrote a Chrysis. For Lyka, see Amphis fr. 23.3.

form, because there was no direct evolution, a possibility suggested by the continued existence of satirically grounded comedies. To tackle this problem, we will need to look closely at the way in which scholars since antiquity have attempted to organize the material they had into accounts of comedy's development.

'Middle Comedy'

As mentioned earlier, in antiquity the period of comedy between Aristophanes and Menander was called 'Middle Comedy', a category clearly devised to provide a developmental link between the fifth-century genre they called 'Old Comedy', on the one side, and the later fourth century 'New Comedy', on the other. But in the early modern period, scholars also began to note that Aristotle had spoken only of 'Old' and 'New' comedies (at *Nicomachean Ethics* 1128a23–5). Consequently, the argument has raged ever since among students of Greek comedy whether to use the tripartite or the bipartite division in dealing with the genre's development, and even whether there was such a thing as 'Middle Comedy' at all.[29]

We have from ancient sources three distinct ancient usages of the term 'Middle Comedy' and each appears to derive from a different period.[30]

(1) One of the *Prolegomena on Comedy* which survives from later antiquity but certainly reflects earlier scholarship accompanies its tripartite scheme of 'Old', 'Middle' and 'New' Comedy with lists of poets for each period.[31] Nesselrath has shown conclusively that the list for 'Middle Comedy' is truncated. That it was originally much longer is proved by the designation of comic poets as 'of Middle Comedy' in sources such as Athenaeus, Pollux and the *Suda*. He suggests that the lists and the periods arose out of the pioneering cataloguing work done at the library in Alexandria from the end of the fourth century onwards, because early scholars like Callimachus and Eratosthenes were very interested in questions of chronology and had access to helpful works such as Aristotle's *Didaskaliai*. Since in this model Menander is the crucial high-point of 'New' Comedy, Nesselrath argues that the final form of this evaluative tripartite chronology (which as well as listing also *ranks* the best practitioners) was developed in the third century, some years after Menander's death, most probably by Aristophanes of Byzantium.[32] Along with this chronological and evaluative

<hr/>

[29] For an overview of this debate, see Nesselrath (1990) 1–28.
[30] Cf. Sidwell (2000) 247–50.   [31] Koster (1975) (*Prolegomenon* III, lines 42–52).
[32] Nesselrath (1990) 172–87.

approach came also an attempt to explain literary development by noting changes such as the loss of the parabasis, the restricted role of the chorus and the types of plot now favoured.

(2) A treatise on comedy known as the *Tractatus Coislinianus* (*The de Coislin Treatise*) from the title of the Paris manuscript collection in which it was found designates 'middle comedy' as a sort of 'mean' between the extremes of 'old' and 'new' comedy.[33] Janko has argued that the contents of this piece accurately reflect the lost second book of Aristotle's *Poetics* (which we know dealt with comedy), but Nesselrath has shown in detail that the treatise belongs to the later Peripatetic tradition, because of its vocabulary, its conceptual framework, and its abuse of pre-existing Aristotelian material.[34] Its tripartite treatment of comedy, then, borrows an Aristotelian idea, that of the 'mean' between two extremes, to deal with what its writer presumably saw as a mixture in the comedy of this period between the satirical attack of 'old comedy' and the complete lack of it in 'new comedy'.

(3) A completely different model is offered to us by those works in the *Prolegomena* tradition which deal with the three different periods (which they sometimes call 'first', 'second' and 'third', sometimes 'Old', 'Middle' and 'New') by linking them to restrictions on satirical attack.[35] In the first period, attack is completely open and can be employed against anyone. In the second, poets are required to make their personal attacks 'enigmatic' or 'symbolic', although with this proviso they can still satirize anyone they like. In the third phase, satirical attack is limited to slaves and foreigners: poets can no longer attack Athenian citizens. Some attempt is also made in this tradition to link the changes to *political* events (the first change to enigmatic attack to the period of the Thirty Tyrants in 404–3 BCE, the second to the hegemony of the Macedonians).[36] Allied to this scheme must be the observation in one source (Platonius) that masking conventions changed between 'old', where caricatures of the faces of the person being attacked were the norm, and the 'middle' and 'new' phases where this was no longer tolerated. This is because such attack must be regarded as no longer 'open' but as 'enigmatic' – the audience had to *guess* now who was being satirized. Note, however, that this comment assumes that the target was a character on stage (like Lamachus in *Acharnians*), not someone merely *named* in an invective attack.

---

[33] Koster (1975) 63–7 (*Prolegomenon* XV).

[34] Janko (1984); Nesselrath (1990) 102–49.

[35] Koster (1975) (*Prolegomena* I (Platonius), IV, XIaI (Tzetzes), XIc, XVIIIa (Scholia to Dionysius Thrax)).

[36] Koster (1975) (*Prolegomenon* I, lines 13–18 and 59–63).

Model (3) does not fit with either of the others, because it is not an attempt to describe the evolution of *all* comedy, just of satirical comedy. In any case, it seems clear that Menander was *not* using his comedy to attack slaves and foreigners, so that 'new comedy' on this model is not equivalent to 'New Comedy' on models (1) or (2).

Aristotle on comedy

The key differences between model (3) and the others in fact tally with two observations made by Aristotle. The first of these is at *Poetics* 1449b5–9:

> Composing plots originated in Sicily, but of the Athenian comic poets Crates was the first to abandon the iambic form and compose arguments, that is plots, of a general nature.

Here Aristotle clearly distinguishes between two different types of comedy. One is 'the iambic form', which within the context of his overall argument must refer to *satirical* comedy. The other is a comedy which has 'plots of a general nature'. According to Aristotle, Crates instituted the non-iambic comedy at Athens, under Sicilian influence, in the middle of the fifth century.[37] Modern scholarship has not paid close enough attention to Aristotle's distinction, but we will see reason below to regard it not as a peculiarity of this philosopher but as a reflection of a polis-generated view, which treated satirical comedy differently from the plot-based type.[38]

The second observation comes at *Nicomachean Ethics* 1128a23–5:

> One can see this from the 'old' and the 'new' comedies. The humour in the first was open treatment of shameful things (*aischrologia*), but in the second rather merely hinting at them (*hyponoia*). This makes a big difference as far as decorum is concerned.

Other evidence shows that 'speaking shameful things' (*aischrologia*) about individuals was considered a fundamental aspect of the personal satire of what we call 'Old Comedy'.[39] Aristotle is concerned here, then, with contrasting two different approaches to personal satire. An ancient

---

[37] Csapo (2000); Sidwell (2000); (2009) 306–8.

[38] For example, Arnott (2010) in his otherwise excellent and authoritative chapter on 'Middle Comedy' does not mention this passage and continues to treat the development of comedy as a single line (325–31). Where scholars have engaged with the model argued for here (first adumbrated in Sidwell (2000)), they have skated past the evidence itself, asserting either that the conclusions I draw have little support there (Hughes (2011) 23) or that the evidence itself is so tainted by later ancient scholars' own socio-political conditions as to be unusable (Ruffell (2011) 9).

[39] Lysias fr. 53 (Thalheim).

commentator on this passage tells us that *hyponoia* means 'satirizing enigmatically'.[40] So Aristotle is not speaking here of what model (1) calls 'Old' and 'New' comedy, but, like model (3), of an open and an enigmatic stage in the comedy of personal abuse. If this is the type of comedy he termed the 'iambic form' in the *Poetics*, then it looks very much as though he was concerned in exactly the way model (3) is with the nature and history of the satirical form. This may well be seen in one of his definitions of comedy, where he again contrasts the way comic poets compose plots with the *modus operandi* of those he calls 'writers of *iambus*' (*Poetics* 1451b5–15) – the former focusing on 'general probabilities', the latter dealing with 'the particular'. At *Poetics* 1449a32f., he also appears to have at the back of his mind another type of comedy which does present persons of full villainy and aims to hurt (the iambic form?), giving as the counter-type the comedy of plot which he prefers and hinting that its laughable mask substitutes something designed to cause pain (the caricature mask of satirical comedy?).[41]

Model (3), then, details the history of the iambic form and is at least very close to Aristotle in the way it treats its material. If it does not derive from what Aristotle said ('about iambus and comedy') in the lost *Poetics II*, it will certainly have been composed in the fourth century, when this type of comedy still existed and its nature could be seen and analysed. Models (1) and (2), on the other hand, while showing some knowledge of Aristotle's concerns, must belong later since they demonstrate no understanding of what the master meant by 'the iambic form' or by 'old' and 'new' comedies. Indeed, it seems likely enough that the reason model (1) uses the categories 'old' and 'new' is precisely because they were evidenced in Aristotle. However, since in the *Nicomachean Ethics* passage Aristotle may well have been using the terms with merely local significance (that of contrasting the unfortunate ethical effects of open satire with those of enigmatic satire), they might not represent his historical structure for the genre at all.[42] What the later commentators did, then, was to confuse models (1) and (3), assuming that they were attempting to explain the same phenomena. They may, in fact, have even truncated the 'Aristotelian model' to make it fit better with model (1), since there are signs in the evidence for model (3) of several more stages in the history of satirical comedy, including a final complete ban (Horace *Ars Poetica* 281–4).[43]

<hr/>

[40] Aspasios (*CAG* 19.1, p. 125, 31–5 (Heylbut)).

[41] See further Sidwell (2009) 317–26.

[42] But Platonius' grouping of 'Middle' and 'New' *together* as opposed to 'Old' does reflect the same sort of contrast.

[43] See nn. 36 and 45.

It may be said, with some truth, that all of these ancient conceptions of the development of comedy are merely 'models'. However, the 'Aristotelian model' can claim to be in origin at least nearly contemporary with the developments it describes and well within second-hand reach of the fifth century. Moreover, it reflects the thinking of (if it was not actually composed by) a scholar who was deeply interested in political history (witness the massive *Constitutions* project, of which only the *Athenian* survives) and the history of drama in Athens (witness the lost *Didaskaliai*). But there is also an independent argument to support the basic historicity of model (3). The ancient commentaries often appeal to the idea of restrictive legislation on comedy, especially on its ability to name names (*onomasti kômôidein*).[44] But ancient scholars also believed that 'naming names' was fundamental to 'Old Comedy', and they do not appear to have had any evidence in their *texts* of such restrictions.[45] Hence, not only did they not invent those legal restrictions, but it is likely that the state used them as model (3) proposes, to make it less obvious textually and visually just *who* were the real individuals behind the on-stage characters. It follows that it was the polis, rather than Aristotle, which first identified satirical comedy as an independent genre – and as a threat. It behoves us, therefore, provisionally at least, to regard this 'Aristotelian model' as the one which might help us better to understand how to organize the remnants of comedy from the later stages of Aristophanes' career to the beginning of that of Menander.

Towards a new account of fourth-century comedy before Menander

Let us propose a new topography. Norwood and Nesselrath have in common (along with the vast majority of students of this topic) the idea of a path which leads directly from fifth-century comedy to Menander. But Aristotle reveals the remains of two separate highways, one for satirical comedy and the other for the non-iambic comedy of plot. And the 'Aristotelian model' provides details of one – the satirical road – which ultimately leads nowhere, because it was regulated out of existence. As for the other track, it would be reasonable to assume that it is the one that leads from Crates to Menander (with, however, many thematic twists and turns), both because what we see in Menander's plays conforms to the Aristotelian definition of comedy (plot central, with characters given chance names) and because the visual

[44] E.g., the scholia on *Acharnians* 1150, *Birds* 1297a, Aelius Aristides *Orationes* iii.8 [L-B].
[45] Ammonius, Herodicus and Galen all wrote large works on the people attacked by name in Old Comedy (scholia on *Wasps* 947c, 1238a; Athenaeus 13.586a; Galen *On his Own Books* 17).

material gives us an unbroken line in mask-types from the later fifth century to Menander.

One major problem we have in tracing the satirical comedy into the fourth century is that we define it (as ancient scholars also did) by the occurrence of *named invective*. The acceptance of model (3) as independent and early obliges us rather to see the true focus of satirical comedy as its *characters*. They will have represented real individuals (whether named, like Socrates or Lamachus, or given pseudonyms, such as Paphlagon or Labes) around whom, in their caricatured forms, the plots were constructed in the way best calculated to ridicule them. Restrictions on naming, then, which may have started during the early career of Eupolis, will have referred to the association of individuals satirized as characters on stage with their own real names.[46]

The introduction of enigmatic satire, with restrictions both on giving characters their real names and caricature masking, might be seen as a compromise between the *dêmos* and the former oligarchs, since the wealthy were the usual targets of comic satire ((Xenophon) *Constitution of the Athenians* 2.18) and thus dated early in the period of the restoration of democracy (*c.* 403 BCE: see n. 36). But this and the later restriction have made the continuing iambic form all but invisible to our scrutiny. Nonetheless, the requirement not to attack openly does help to account for the loss of the parabasis, which Old comic poets had sometimes used to speak about their satirical targets. It may also help us to understand better the later careers of fifth-century satirical dramatists such as Aristophanes and Plato (who had written eponymous attacks on Peisander, Hyperbolus and Cleophon). In fact, they continued writing satirical plays, but enigmatically. Aristophanes' *Assembly Women* and *Wealth*, *Aeolosikôn* and *Kôkalos* (associated in the Alexandrian tradition with the emergence of the 'Middle Comedy') will therefore have been constructed to attack the individuals represented on stage as characters in them.[47]

Meanwhile, Plato's turn towards mythical subjects will simply have been a cover for continuing political satire, and this may be why he was singled out by the composer of the 'Aristotelian model' as an exemplar of what happened to iambic comedy under the enigma law.[48] As for the introduction of the

---

[46] Eupolis and legal restrictions: Koster (1975) *Prolegomenon* XIaI (Tzetzes), lines 87–8. The nonsensical explanation which follows, in which Eupolis is either badly mistreated or killed by Alcibiades for satirizing him, will be a later attempt to account for what was left unexplained in the 'Aristotelian model'. For the whole issue, Sidwell (2009), 222f.

[47] Sidwell (2009) 337–40.

[48] Koster (1975) (*Prolegomena* IV, line 17, XIaI, lines 97–105, XIb, line 37, XIc, line 40, XVIIIa, lines 41–2). See Rosen (1995) on Plato as 'middle comedy'.

third restriction, where only slaves and foreigners could be attacked, it is possible that it came into force in the 340s, because Isocrates and Plato were still complaining about the deleterious effects of satire until just before then. However, if so, open attacks on slaves and foreigners must also have been allowed under the first 'enigmatic' phase, because of Eubulus' *Dionysius* and Mnesippus' *Philippus*.[49] Assuming that openly naming Athenian citizens as characters was forbidden obliges us to regard Timocles' Autocleides as a non-citizen, which is plausible, even if there is no firm proof (cf. Aeschines I.52). But Aristophon's *Plato* presents a difficulty. If Plato *was* a character (there is no proof in this case), however, it may belong to the period after Plato's death (347), since Aristophon's first victory postdates Alexis', which may have been in the late 350s. We would then have to assume that putting famous *dead* Athenians on stage may not have fallen under the terms of the legislation.[50]

If this view represents the reality, then we badly need a new investigation into the continuing tradition of iambic comedy in the fourth century. This must be prepared to treat the mythological and paratragic plays of the period 380–350 BCE, identified by Nesselrath as the unique contribution of 'middle comedy', as potentially satirical.[51] Demonstration that they are will then depend upon conjectures about which Athenian *individuals* are best satirized by being represented as particular characters from myth or tragedy (as Pericles clearly was well-caricatured by Cratinus as Olympian Zeus) and what political situation is best allegorized by the choice of this subject (as the Trojan War apparently was used to parallel the Samian War in Cratinus' *Dionysalexandrus*).[52]

Plot-based comedy, on this reconstruction, was the direct beneficiary of the increasingly restrictive controls upon the iambic form, going back at least to the ban on satire enacted under Morychides (which lasted from 440–437 BCE).[53] Once the confusion of a single line of development is removed, it is relatively easy to track its development in the fourth century. The very fact that we now for the first time know of non-Athenian poets making it big in Athens and sometimes big enough to be honoured with citizenship is a good indication that these were involved in an 'international' form of comic

---

[49] *Dionysius* must be before 368, if so, since he was an Athenian citizen after that date: Hunter (1983) 116f.
[50] Euripides was perhaps a character in Eubulus' *Dionysius* fr. 26.3–4 (Hunter (1983) fr. 27, p. 120) and the move had good precedents (in Aristophanes' *Frogs* and Eupolis' *Demes*).
[51] Nesselrath (1990) 204–41, 335f.
[52] Pericles as Zeus: Cratinus fr. 73, 118, 258, 259. Trojan War = Samian War: Storey (2006).
[53] Scholion on *Acharnians* 67.

production, not tied to the specifics of the Athenian political situation.[54] And we can see from the famous fr. 189 of Antiphanes (quoted above) that the level of invention required of the comic poet here can only be that of a writer of plot-based, character-type comedy of the kind praised by Aristotle in *Poetics*. It is Anaxandrides (first victory 376 BCE) of whom we are told that 'he was the first to introduce love-affairs and the rapes of virgins' into comedy.[55] Moreover, it is clear from the fragments of Alexis (350s onwards) that the Menandrian intrigue-comedy was already being formed in the thirty years before Menander's first production (see fr. 212, quoted above). Arnott has even suggested that in Alexis' *Cauldron* we have not only the model for Plautus' *Aulularia* ('Comedy of the Pot'), but also one of the main influences upon Menander's *Dyscolus*.[56] The arrival on the scene during this 'Middle' phase of such stock characters as the Parasite, the Courtesan, the Cook and the conniving Slave is another indication that the world of Menander's comedy was already coming into existence when he began his career.[57]

On this analysis, vital questions remain to be answered. When precisely did each of the restrictions on the iambic form come in? Did any comic poet write *both* types of comedy or was a gulf fixed between the writers of the iambic form and those of the plot-based? Which plays are enigmatic iambic comedies and what were their targets? Did writers of the iambic form parody the other type of comedy? Only when we attempt to provide answers will the contours of our two highways become clearer.

Further reading

The difficulties of the area and the major questions (in my view) still left unanswered make recommending a single account problematic. For a contrasting view of comedy's development see Arnott (2010). Chapters 2 and 3 in Green (1994), especially pp. 34–8 and pp. 63–88, provide important analyses of the visual evidence for the early emergence of non-satirical, plot-based comedy. For more specific areas, see the following: Rothwell (1995) on the chorus in fourth-century comedy; Hughes (2003) and (2011) on fourth-century representations of comedy; Csapo (2000) and Sidwell (2009) app. 1 on the changes from fifth- to fourth-century comedy. For those who wish to pursue the topic at a higher level, the comprehensive account by

---

[54] Foreign poets: Alcaeus, Alexis, Amphis (?), Anaxandrides, Antiphanes, Dionysius of Sinope, Sophilus. Awarded Athenian citizenship: Alcaeus, Antiphanes.

[55] *PCG* T1 (= *Suda* α 1982).   [56] Arnott (1996a) 859–64.

[57] Nesselrath (1990) 280–330. The fragmentary evidence of Aristophanes of Byzantium's studies of Menander's influences also suggests this: Nesselrath (1990) 182f.

Nesselrath (1990) (in German) is fundamental (also note the important review, in English, of this book by Csapo (1993b)).

Appendix: Ancient Sources

(a) *Commentators on comedy*

Aristotle, *Poetics*
Athenaeus, *The Sophists at Dinner (Deipnosophistae)*
Pollux, *Onomasticon*
Prolegomena on Comedy (collected in W. J. W. Koster ed., *Scholia in Aristophanem* I. IA *Prolegomena de comoedia*, Groningen 1975)
Stobaeus
Suda

(b) *Fourth-century comic poets*

(i) Poets who span fifth and fourth centuries (with title and fragment numbers from Kassel and Austin (1983–))

Alcaeus: 8 titles and 33 fragments
Ameipsias: 7 titles (2 definitely fifth century) and 39 fragments
Archippus: 6 titles (1 fifth-century victory) and 61 fragments
Aristomenes: 5 titles and 16 fragments
Aristonymus: 2 titles and 8 fragments
Aristophanes: 5 fourth-century plays attested and at least 27 fragments (from *Kôkalos* and *Storks*; dating of fragments from the two *Aeolosikôn* plays uncertain)
Autocrates: 1 title and 3 fragments
Cephisodorus: 3 titles and 14 fragments
Crates II: 4 titles (one fragmentary)
Diocles: 6 titles and 17 fragments
Epilycus: 1 title and 9 fragments
Eunicus: 2 titles and 2 fragments
Euthycles: 2 titles
Heniochus: 8 titles and 5 fragments
Heraclides: 1 fragment
Metagenes: 5 titles and 20 fragments
Nicochares: 9 titles and 28 fragments
Nicophon: 6 titles and 30 fragments
Philonicus: no titles and no fragments

Philyllius: 10 titles and 33 fragments
Plato: 30 titles (1 definitely dated fifth century and 1 fourth century) and 291 fragments
Polyzelus: 5 titles and 13 fragments
Strattis: 18 titles and 90 fragments
Theopompus: 19 titles and 97 fragments

(ii) Fourth-century poets of whom something remains (with title and fragment numbers from Kassel and Austin (1983–))

Alexis: 146 titles and 328 fragments
Amphis: 28 titles and 49 fragments
Anaxandrides: 40 titles and 80 fragments
Anaxilas: 22 titles and 43 fragments
Antidotus: 3 titles and 1 fragment
Antiphanes: 137 titles and 327 fragments
Araros (son of Aristophanes): 6 titles and 21 fragments
Aristophon: 8 titles and 15 fragments
Axionicus: 4 titles and 11 fragments
Callicrates: 1 title and 1 fragment
Clearchus: 3 titles and 6 fragments
Cratinus Junior: 8 titles and 14 fragments
Demonicus: 1 title and 1 fragment
Dionysius of Sinope: 4 titles and 10 fragments
Dromo: 1 title and 2 fragments
Ephippus: 12 titles and 28 fragments
Epicrates: 2 titles and 10 fragments
Eriphus: 3 titles and 7 fragments
Eubulus: 58 titles and 147 fragments
Euphanes: 2 titles and 2 fragments
Heraclides: 1 fragment
Mnesimachus: 7 titles and 11 fragments
Nausicrates: 2 titles and 3 fragments
Nicostratus: 23 titles and 39 fragments
Ophelion: 4 titles and 6 fragments
Philetairus (son of Aristophanes): 13 titles and 20 fragments
Philippus (son of Aristophanes): 4 titles and 3 fragments
Philiscus: 7 titles and 3 fragments
Sophilus: 9 titles and 10 fragments
Sotades: 2 titles and 4 fragments

Straton: 1 title and 1 fragment
Theophilus: 9 titles and 12 fragments
Timocles: 28 titles and 42 fragments
Timotheus: 4 titles and 2 fragments
Xenarchus: 8 titles and 14 fragments

(iii) Fourth-century comic poets of whom only names or names and
some titles remain

Alcenor: 1 Lenaia victory
Apollinaris (possibly belongs later in the century)
Asclepiodorus (but this might be Cephisodorus): at least one Lenaia victory
Athenocles: at least one Lenaia victory
Augeas: only 3 titles known
Choregos: at least one Lenaia victory
Dionysius II
Dioxippus (date uncertain): only 5 titles known
Euboulides: 1 title known
Euthias (but he might also be an actor)
Euthycles: 2 titles known
Procleides: 1 Lenaia victory
Pyrrhen: 1 Lenaia victory

4

KATHRYN BOSHER

Epicharmus and early Sicilian comedy

Sicily and South Italy provide us with evidence for more than 300 years of ancient Greek comic theatre. Some of the earliest known comic dramas were composed in Syracuse, and both Aristotle and Plato comment on Sicilian theatre, the former on early Sicilian comic playwrights, the latter on later raucous audiences.[1] Vases with painted pictures inspired by comic performance have been found in substantial quantities in Apulia and Paestum in Southern Italy, and also in Sicily.[2] Graves on the island of Lipari, off the north coast of Sicily, untroubled by grave robbers for centuries, have yielded hundreds of ceramic figurines of comic and tragic actors.[3] The ruins of ancient Greek stone theatres dot the modern Sicilian landscape from the south-eastern corner in Syracuse to the north-western Mt Iaitas and Montagna dei Cavalli, from the western Heracleia Minoa to the north-eastern Tyndaris.[4]

Despite this wealth of archaeological and literary material, the Greek comic theatre of Sicily and South Italy is rarely studied as a unified tradition. This is in part because the evidence is fragmentary and falls under the purview of various sub-disciplines within Classics, and in part because of a scholarly focus on Athens. The fifth-century comic dramas of Epicharmus of Syracuse have often, for example, been analyzed to try to determine their relationship to Athenian comedy. Likewise, fourth-century comic playwrights Alexis of Thurii and Philemon of Syracuse travelled to Athens, and their stories are intertwined with the history of Athenian New Comedy. The comic vases found in South Italy and Sicily were at first thought to represent

---

I am very grateful to the editor and to Eric Csapo for helpful comments.

[1] Aristotle *Poetics* 1448 a 30; Plato *Laws* 659 a–c.
[2] Trendall (1967), and J. R. Green's forthcoming updated version of this work. See the beginning of Csapo (Chapter 5) for Green's new estimate of 592 extant West Greek comic vase paintings.
[3] E.g., Bernabò Brea (1981) and Bernabò Brea and Cavalier (2001).
[4] Eleven theatres appear in the archaeological record and ten more are recorded in ancient sources, or argued for by modern scholars, or both. For a discussion and extensive bibliography, see Marconi (2012). For an overview, see Rossetto and Sartorio (1994).

a subliterary comic genre native to the West, later brought into literary form by Rhinthon of Tarentum, but, on the basis of new evidence (especially the 'Würzburg Telephus' crater) Taplin and Csapo have now shown that several vases represent Athenian comedy, and in particular Aristophanes.[5] Sicilian and South Italian theatre buildings are often described as architecturally derivative of the theatre of Dionysus at Athens and, together with the comic figurines of the Hellenistic period, are interpreted as symbolic of the enormous popularity and dissemination of Greek drama from Athens. Thus, the evidence from the West is commonly used to help explain the development of Athenian theatre and the spread of Attic drama outside Athens in the fourth century and later.

In this chapter, the same evidence is put to a different purpose: to outline the history of Greek comedy in the Sicilian and, to some extent, South Italian contexts of local performance and literary traditions. Nevertheless, Athenian influence was strong and is an important aspect of the history of the comedy of the West. Unlike the ancient Sicilians themselves who claimed comedy as their own invention,[6] my aim is not to produce a history of a pure Sicilian comedy as rival to Athenian drama, but rather to try to understand the hybrid and complex traditions that grew up in this ancient New World. What was the history of comedy in the Greek West?

Settled between the eighth and sixth centuries BCE by Greek emigrants from mainland Greece, the Aegean islands and Asia Minor, western Greek cities had already grown to be enormously prosperous by the end of the sixth century BCE (see map).[7] For the next two centuries, however, power struggles among these new cities, between classes within cities, between Greeks and non-Greeks, and among ambitious and powerful individuals played havoc with city affiliations and the development of individual polis allegiances. Perhaps in response to the repeated destruction of real social and political bonds, the symbols of city unity and self-definition were proclaimed everywhere on sculpture, on massive civic and religious buildings, in

---

[5] This view was first put forward by Webster (1948). See further discussion in Csapo, Chapter 5.

[6] Aristotle, *Poetics* 1448a 28–34 (KA test. 4): 'The Dorians lay claim to both tragedy and comedy, both the Megarians, from the time when democracy had arisen among them, and those in Sicily, for the poet Epicharmus was there [not] long before Chionides and Magnes. Some of those in the Peloponnese lay claim to tragedy.' See also 1449a37–b9 (KA test. 5).

[7] A beautifully illustrated survey of Greek settlements in the West, both the first waves from old Greece and secondary foundations from Western cities themselves, can be found in Cerchiai *et al.* (2002, English version 2004). On ethnic identity in the West, see e.g., Hall (2002) 90–124.

N

ETRURIA

APULIA

Paestum

LUCANIA

Tarentum

Metapontum

Thurii

Iaitas

Tyndaris Lipari

Segesta Himera

Locri

Rhegium

Motya

Hippana

Selinus

SICILY

Catana

Heracleia Minoa

Megara Hyblaea

Agrigentum

Gela

Syracuse

Carthage

Camarina

Map: Some cities of South Italy and Sicily in the classical and early Hellenistic period.

contemporary literature and in the later ancient historical and poetical works from and about the region.[8] It is within these socio-political efforts to stabilize local identities and establish connections with the wider Hellenic world that I propose to situate the regional tradition of comic theatre in Sicily.

[8] See e.g., Marconi (2007) 29–60 and Malkin (1994).

Archaic performance traditions in Sicily

Cult traditions more or less tenuously associated with the development of theatre appear in the Western Greek record, as indeed they do in that of mainland Greece. Archaeological sources point to early and complex interactions between cult and performance. Komast iconography depicting dancers with padded stomachs and buttocks was produced in various places in the West,[9] and on the Phoenician/Carthaginian island of Motya, just off the west coast of Sicily, masks associated with eastern cult have been found. Like the masks of the cult of Artemis Orthia at Sparta, these cannot be securely placed in a direct line of influence to Greek comedy, but they do suggest local contexts for the development of performance traditions.[10] Komast vases and Spartan cult performance are both part of the Dorian tradition of laughter rituals that have some background connection to comedy, produced by two important cities in the Doric-speaking region of Greece: Corinth and Sparta. It is curious to note that the two cities for which we have the most evidence of theatre production in the West, Syracuse and Tarentum, were founded by Corinth and Sparta, respectively.

As in mainland Greece, Greek Sicilian and South Italian theatres themselves are generally situated in or near cult sites, and although most of the stone theatres date from the late classical or Hellenistic period, their physical and social connection with local cult may suggest a more long-standing and embedded cultural function for ritual performance.[11] Very early socio-political spaces resembling theatres can be found in the West as well. For example, at the end of the seventh century, in the city of Metapontum, south of Tarentum, a very large building was constructed, with seating in a complete circle around the performance space in the centre. We cannot tell if this space was used for formal theatre or not, but some kind of social and political gathering must have happened here. Most interesting for us, this singular structure was converted into a regular semicircular theatre in the

---

[9] Smith (2007) 59–60, and for a more general discussion of the connections between Komasts and theatre, see Carpenter (2007) 41–7 and Csapo and Slater (1995) 89–95. See Csapo, Chapter 5 for pictures and discussion.

[10] On masked ritual in Sparta see Athenaeus 621d; Hesychius s.v. *brydalicha*, s.v. *bryllachistai*, s.v. *Lombai*, all translated in Csapo and Slater (1995) 97.

[11] Todisco (2002) 167–92. Polacco and Anti, archaeologists of the theatre of Syracuse, argue that comedy developed out of the cult of Demeter at Syracuse, just as tragedy developed out of the cult of Dionysus at Athens (Polacco and Anti (1981; 1990)). See Kowalzig's discussion of the cult of Demeter, grain supply and the economics of importing Athenian plays to Sicily (2008). Nielsen (2002) 80 suggests that cult theatre provides the foundation for literary drama, because it contained a 'plot and individual actors besides the chorus, and performed as part of a liturgy'. Therefore, she suggests 'this kind of drama . . . constitutes a kind of missing link between chorus dancing and rituals on one hand, and literary drama on the other'.

fourth century.[12] This physical conversion of the circular area to a theatre suggests a local progression towards formal theatre.

It is likely that performances of subliterary[13] comic dramas took place in the West as in many societies, but it is hard to verify this since, without texts, the traces of performance vanish quickly. Later written sources, however, describe a number of cults in early Syracuse whose rites and festivals provided occasions for the early development of performance traditions: we have descriptions of early ritual exchanges of obscenities at a Syracusan Thesmophoria festival in honour of the goddess Demeter, and elsewhere a description of a *kômos* (a drunken procession) involving rustic song and animal costumes at a festival of Artemis Lyaia.[14] Athenaeus records that one Diomos was the first to invent the form of rustic song (perhaps similar to the ones performed at the festival of Artemis Lyaia), and that the earliest known Sicilian comic playwright, Epicharmus (fl. *c.* 480s–470s), mentioned Diomos in two of his plays.[15]

From these archaeological and anecdotal records, we see glimpses of archaic traditions of performance in the Greek West, intimately tied to cult and likely to have been regional and varied. Underlying the examples briefly set out here, we must imagine a complex network of commercial and artistic exchange between the peoples and cultures who came into contact with each other in this region, including Greeks from various cities and parts of the Mediterranean, Phoenicians/Carthaginians and Etruscans. Likewise, social and political tensions among the Greek poleis, and to some extent with native Sicilians, would perhaps have found expression in the now lost public ceremony and theatre of the emerging classical cities.

Literary performance traditions and theatre

An anonymous ancient writer on comedy, found in some manuscripts of Aristophanes, reports that the Syracusan comic poet Epicharmus 'first gathered together the scattered fragments of comedy'.[16] It is not clear exactly what this means, but it does suggest that Epicharmus relied on local comic

---

[12] Mertens and de Siena (1982); Mertens (1982). For a brief description of the theatre in English, and some beautiful photographs, see Cerchiai *et al.* (2002, English version 2004) 140f.

[13] I use the term 'subliterary' to describe performances that were not drawn from, nor were later recorded in, a text. I regret the implication of inferiority in the prefix 'sub', which I do not intend.

[14] Diodorus Siculus V 4,7; Scholion to Theocritus, Prolegomena Ba 17–Bb 14 (Wendel p. 2). The first can be found in the Loeb translation, and a translation of the second is in Csapo and Slater (1995) 98–9. On the festival to Demeter, see Kowalzig (2008).

[15] Athenaeus XIV 619a–b (KA fr. 4).   [16] Anon. De com. 9 p. 7 (KA test 6).

traditions to some extent. He writes in the Doric dialect native to Syracuse (see Willi, Chapter 8).[17] Indeed, Aristotle, Themistius, the Suda, Theocritus, Lucian and Diomedes Grammaticus also write more or less directly that Epicharmus was at the very beginnings of the development of literary comedy, a comedy that may have grown out of the performance traditions of religious cults.[18]

Epicharmus was not a lone literary figure in early Syracuse. In the century before him, the poet Stesichorus of Himera (seventh–sixth century BCE) on the north coast of Sicily and other poets associated with early stages of performance appear in the historical record, and in conjunction these names suggest that there were public performances very early on in Sicily.[19] Then, in the early classical period, Syracuse was host to many renowned poets, and this artistic atmosphere may have encouraged the evolution of cult theatre to a more formal literary level. The Syracusan tyrants of the Deinomenid family, Hieron (478–467) and his brother Gelon (485–478) before him, gathered about themselves an impressive group of poets and literary figures, including Pindar, Aeschylus, Simonides and perhaps Bacchylides. These names suggest a vibrant court culture full of exchange of ideas and literary innovation. Indeed, we can see this engagement in the fragments of Epicharmus himself: in his play *Argument and Argumentina* he makes reference to yet another Sicilian poet, Aristoxenus of Selinus, and, elsewhere, a scholiast reports that Epicharmus made fun of Aeschylus' use of a rarely used verb meaning 'to do honour to'.

Theatres and the comic dramas of Epicharmus

The tyrant Hieron did more, however, than invite and support great literary figures. He may also have built a theatre at Syracuse, though it is impossible to tell if this fifth-century theatre was on the same site as the monumental theatre visible today.[20] Although later renovations of the

---

[17] Willi (2008) 125–60.

[18] These anecdotes and more can be found in Greek in the edition (2001) of Epicharmus in vol. i of Kassel and Austin (1983–), and in Spanish translation in Rodríguez-Noriega Guillén (1996) 1–12.

[19] Stesichorus wrote poems that may have been meant for choral performance and would then have been best suited to larger outdoor performances, as Burkert suggests (1987) 52f. See Willi (2008) 51–118 on Stesichorus and the development of a West Greek colonial literature. For the story of Arion performing in Sicily, see Herodotus I, 23. Burkert (1979) makes a case for performances by Kynaithos. On the curse tablet from Gela, which references *chorêgoi*, see Jordan in Wilson (2007c) 335–50; Wilson (2007b) 351–77; and Dubois (1989) no. 134.

[20] For a recent discussion, see Marconi (2012) 175–207 who argues for a third-century BCE dating of the monumental theatre at Syracuse based on inscriptional evidence.

monumental theatre itself echo elements found at the theatre of Dionysus at Athens, some local anomalies suggest a local attempt to grapple with problems of stage design, rather than the borrowing of a ready-made Athenian model. Indeed, both Polacco and Moretti have argued that other Sicilian theatres seem to copy architectural elements of the theatre at Syracuse, in addition to, or perhaps even rather than the theatre of Dionysus at Athens.[21] This is not to suggest that the theatre of Dionysus had no architectural influence in the West, but only that Athenian ideas may have been incorporated into a nascent tradition of theatre building in Sicily.

What was performed in the early theatre of Syracuse? In addition to Aeschylus, perhaps, and other large-scale poetic performances, we have the names of three comic playwrights writing in Doric Greek: Epicharmus, Phormis and Dinolochus, together with titles of many of their plays. A very late reference to Phormis developing the backdrop for stage action suggests that these plays were staged and performed in public.[22] Dinolochus, for his part, is cited as both rival and son of Epicharmus.[23] Each of these comic writers seems to have produced many plays, enough even for competition among themselves. A collector of proverbs, Zenobius, explains Epicharmus' line 'it lies on the knees of the five judges' as follows: 'Proverbial, as it means, they are under another's control. The proverb arose because five judges used to judge the comic playwrights, as Epicharmus says.'[24] If this explanation is accepted, it may support the view that the Syracusan comic playwrights competed against each other in festivals with formal judging. We cannot be certain of the circumstances of performance, but these ancient references do indicate that there was at least a small contingent of comic writers in fifth-century Syracuse.

What role did such comedy play in the city? Was Epicharmus' work merely written versions of rough entertainment, fleeting skits with no more import to the city and citizens than an hour's distraction? Epicharmus' plays have often been thought to consist mainly of mythological burlesque, jokes about food and other coarse humour, clever word play, pithy aphorisms and the development of character types.[25] Some philosophical fragments, collected

His essay is followed by an extensive bibliography for both the monumental and rectilinear theatres at Syracuse (203–6).

[21] Moretti (1993) and Polacco (1987) argue for the influence of the theatre of Syracuse on other Sicilian theatres.

[22] Suda 609 (KA Phorm. test. 1).   [23] Ael. Nat. an VI 51 (KA test. 2).

[24] Zenobius, vulg. III 64 (KA fr. 237); see also Hesychius π 1408 (KA fr. 237).

[25] Norwood (1931) 97–113 adds the conflict of abstractions, like land and sea, to burlesque and comedy of manners. Pickard-Cambridge lays stress on Epicharmus' development of character types, but writes also that it includes 'the kind of farce and horseplay that is always an element of popular comedy of a not very advanced type'

under the heading *Pseudepicharmeia* or Pseudo-Epicharmus, are generally rejected as spurious, or are thought to have been derived from clever jokes in the plays, and to be meant, above all, for entertainment.[26]

The literary and historical circumstances of Epicharmus' productions, however, suggest that he may have taken up contemporary political subjects. The two plays of Aeschylus, thought to have been imported to Syracuse by Hieron, suggest that the Syracusans, or their tyrant, favoured subjects with immediate contemporary relevance in their theatre. One, *Persians*, is about the Persian wars of a few years before;[27] the other, *Women of Aetna*, celebrates Hieron's refounding of the city of Catana in 476.[28]

It is likely that the tyrants supported Epicharmus in the same sort of way, and for similar reasons, that they did Aeschylus and the other poets of the court.[29] If Epicharmus' plays are considered together with those of Aeschylus, it seems reasonable to search the fragments for evidence of contemporary, topical subjects. Indeed, some of Epicharmus' comedies, like the tragedies of Aeschylus, seem to be about current events. One play title, *Persians*, suggests a parody of Aeschylus' play of the same name and perhaps, therefore, its subject was also the Persian Wars. In another play, *The Islands*, a scholiast to Pindar's first Pythian records that Epicharmus described Hieron preventing the tyrant Anaxilas of Rhegium from destroying the Locrians.[30] Several of Epicharmus' plays seem to be set in Sicily; others include both local and contemporary references to contemporary coins and current religious festivals.

Epicharmus is perhaps best remembered for the first attested comic parasite. In the play *Hope or Wealth* he has left us a pathetic monologue in this character's voice:

> I'll dine with a willing host – he has only to invite me.
> I'll dine with an unwilling host – he need not even invite me!
> I am charming at the event, I turn up the
> Laughter and I praise the host.
> If anyone wants to say something against him,

(Pickard-Cambridge and Webster (1962) 281f.). Kerkhof (2001) notes the parody of myth, and also the invention of character types in his discussion of Epicharmus' influence on Attic poets.
[26] Cf. Pickard-Cambridge and Webster (1962) 247f.
[27] On the question of whether *Persians* was performed in Syracuse, cf. Herington (1967) 74–85, who has collected the primary evidence at 82f., and Griffith (1978) 106 and n. 5. See Taplin (2006) on this performance as tragedy's entry into a celebration culture.
[28] Dougherty (1993) 83–102.
[29] Svarlien (1990–1991). Cf. Bremer (1991) on the payment of tragic poets both in Athens and elsewhere.
[30] See also n. 48 below.

I berate the guy! I get very upset!
And then, when I have eaten a lot and drunk a lot,
I go away. No boy carries a lamp for me.
I creep, slipping in the darkness,
Deserted. And if I happen on the patrols
I say, by the gods, it is a good thing
Because they only want to beat me up.
And then, roughed up, I go home,
And I sleep, without bedding. And I don't feel it at all, at first,
While the unmixed wine heals me in my mind . . . [31]

This self-aware parasite is matched by the complex figure of Herakles that Epicharmus gives us. Salomone has shown us how Epicharmus presents a nuanced view of many comic characters.[32] Epicharmus' Herakles, for example, though a comic glutton, stuffing his face in low comic fashion (KA fr. 18), elsewhere perhaps seeks to excuse or explain himself to his companion, Pholus: 'But I do all these things out of necessity/ I think nobody is wretched or suffers disaster willingly' (KA fr. 66).

Andreas Willi has demonstrated how Epicharmus' plays can be read in a wider tradition of early Sicilian literature, together with Stesichorus and Empedocles, among others. He analyzes Epicharmus' subtle characterization and complex reworking of myth, and exposes a greater social and political purpose. For example, he argues persuasively that Epicharmus' *Odysseus Automolos* involves a *real* defection of Odysseus to the Trojans, the indignities he suffers at their hands and his shame at having defected so basely. Willi concludes that Epicharmus' mockery of the heroes of epic is both inherently democratic and reveals a colonial desire to rebel against traditional epics.[33]

There is not necessarily a contradiction between the democratic character of the comedy and the tyranny in which Epicharmus lived. Although great power and great wealth allowed the Deinomenid tyrants to support the arts on a grand scale, their motives seem to have been more complex than straightforward celebration of their own power as absolute rulers. Like other demagogues of the Greek world, the Sicilian tyrants seem to have tried to present themselves, not as absolute rulers, but as popular, even perhaps democratic, leaders. Their support of theatre may have been part of this exercise in self-presentation.[34]

---

[31] KA fr. 32. The Greek passage is in iambic trimeter. This is a loose translation in which I try to represent colloquial speech. For a close translation, see Olson (2007) 421.

[32] Salomone (1981).

[33] Willi (2008) 162–92; and in English in Willi (2012). See also Revermann (2013) 106–10.

[34] I take up this problem in Bosher (2006).

Epicharmus' comedies are important in the history of Greek comedy, but they are difficult to categorize because they are so fragmentary. A notorious problem in interpreting Epicharmus alongside the canonical Athenian plays is the question of whether or not Epicharmus' comedies had a chorus at all. At present, we have no lyric metre and we have no explicit reference to a chorus in the fragments. On the other hand, many of the play titles are plural (e.g., *Bacchai*, *Dionysoi*, *Persai*) and these titles may refer to the choruses in the plays. One may also adduce Pollux's note that Epicharmus used the word *chorêgos* (chorus leader, or, in the Athenian sense, producer) when he meant *didaskalos* (teacher, or director – presumably of choruses).[35] On the other hand, that there were choral performances of other genres of poetry on the island does not necessarily strengthen the argument that Epicharmus himself used a chorus in his plays.[36] The only comic Sicilian writer whose work survives from the second half of the fifth century, Sophron, wrote mimes without a chorus, although the word *choragos* appears in his mimes as well.[37] Certainly, the comedies composed by denizens of Italy in later periods, Plautus and Terence, were able to dispense completely with a chorus, and yet remain closely tied to their Greek New Comedy models, although already even in these the chorus interacted at best marginally with the plot of the drama. It is quite possible that there was a chorus in the plays of Epicharmus, but the absence of any fragment that confirms it suggests that the chorus was less important to Epicharmus than it was, for example, to his counterparts in Athens.

The generations that followed Epicharmus considered him part of the wider Greek tradition, for they identified him as one of the great dramatists and philosophers of the fifth-century Greek world. As early as Plato and Aristotle, he is listed in the canon of major Greek writers. Plato compares him with Homer, for example, and Aristotle with Crates.[38] Although this is in large part a tribute to the quality of his work, which we are less able to appreciate since so little has survived, it is also a sign that the plays were works which, like those of Aeschylus, could appeal to many other audiences in the Greek world, besides that of his own city of Syracuse.

---

[35] Poll. IX 42 (KA fr. 13).
[36] E.g., Stesichorus probably wrote choral pieces; from Gela, a curse tablet discussed in context by Wilson (2007b) demonstrates that there were choral performances; and Aeschylus' imported plays probably included choruses.
[37] Sophron fr. 147.
[38] Plato *Theaet.* 152 E (KA test. 3); Aristotle *Poet.* 5 1449b 5 (KA test. 5).

Democratic interlude

With the end of Deinomenid rule in Syracuse, when the third brother was expelled from the tyranny in 467, evidence for comic theatre in Sicily becomes sparse. During the rebellions and upheavals in Syracuse that accompanied the democracy in the second half of the fifth century, there is very little evidence of performance of plays at all. Plutarch's story about Syracusans freeing Athenian prisoners who could recite Euripides suggests an eagerness for public theatre in Syracuse in the period of the failed Sicilian expedition (415–413).[39]

On the other hand, we have many fragments from the mime writer of the second half of the fifth century, Sophron. The mimes take up topics in daily life, with an emphasis on obscene and sexual themes. They are divided into women's mimes and men's mimes, according to the gender of the main characters and the topics presented, and they are, unlike the comedies of Epicharmus, written in prose.[40] The dating of Sophron's work is made difficult by a note in the Suda, which makes him a contemporary of both Xerxes and Euripides. This impossible conflation of two periods (the early and late fifth century) may have arisen because the two writers were confused with each other: Epicharmus, who would have been a contemporary of Xerxes, and Sophron, later in the fifth century, a contemporary of Euripides.[41] Indeed, the similarities between the two dramatists' work are striking. Despite the frequent adoption of Attic or Ionic dialects by other prose writers of his day, Sophron uses a Doric dialect like Epicharmus. Likewise, both seem to either leave out or minimize the role of the chorus. They take up many of the same themes, specific references and jokes. In his edition of Sophron, Hordern suggests that Epicharmus' non-mythological dramas were important and direct influences on Sophron's work.[42]

The tradition of Doric mime writing did not stop with Sophron, but continued in the fourth century under the tyrant Dionysius I with Xenarchus, who is reported to be Sophron's son. This family relationship may well be untrue, but it suggests a connection between the work of these two mime writers. Little survives of Xenarchus' work, but the Suda compares him to Sotades, noting that Xenarchus wrote farces or 'phlyakes'.

---

[39] Plutarch *Nicias* 29; Satyrus *Life of Euripides* (P. Oxy. 1176, fr. 39, col. 19).
[40] For a full description of Sophron's mimes, see Hordern (2004) 1–34.
[41] Hordern (2004) 3f.; see Olson (2007) 4, 11f., who dates Sophron to the first half of the fifth century.
[42] Hordern (2004) 6f. See also Willi (2008) 13f. (and 119–61 for some detailed discussion of linguistic similarities).

There is, then, some evidence for a continuous comic tradition in the West through the fifth century, which can be traced through the work of these comic writers. If Sophron's mimes were only performed at small symposiastic parties of the elite (which, despite a few suggestions to the contrary,[43] is the prevailing view) is this enough to have perpetuated a popular comic tradition that can be viewed, in some sense, as continuous since the time of Epicharmus? The literary remains of this Western Greek comic tradition may be too sparse to allow us to come to a conclusion. If we consider, however, the wider political situation, and take account of the next great trove of comic remains, the comic vases from the West, a general outline comes into clearer focus.

After the heyday of Epicharmus, his colleagues Dinolochus and Phormis, and the visiting Aeschylus in the first half of the fifth century, there is little evidence for *public* performance of plays until the sudden appearance of a series of Western Greek comic (once called 'phlyax') vases at the beginning of the fourth century (for description and illustrations see Csapo, Chapter 5).[44] These vases started to be produced in South Italy and Sicily at the beginning of the fourth century and petered out by its end. For a long time, scholars thought they represented a native subliterary tradition of South Italian and Sicilian farces, and the name given them in the nineteenth century, 'phlyax', referred to an early Italian name for local subliterary farces, 'phlyakes'. In the last few decades, Csapo and Taplin have, in part on the basis of new evidence, demonstrated that some of the vases represented Athenian comedy, and in particular Aristophanes (see Csapo, Chapter 5). This was revolutionary, for it meant that Aristophanes spread far more widely and earlier than had previously been imagined, but also because it demonstrated the complex theatrical world of several Western Greek cities, especially Tarentum.[45] There have been, therefore, two competing theories to explain the vases: the first that they represent a subliterary Western Doric tradition (for which the evidence, apart from the vases themselves, is scattered and late), and the second, that they represent sophisticated Athenian imports (for which the evidence is a handful of vases, though these are convincing). What makes the vases so puzzling, however, was that there were so many of them (more than 250 still exist); that they were so widespread (all over the south of Italy and Sicily); and that, nonetheless, the type of comedy represented on them was so

---

[43] Hunter (1993) 31–44.

[44] A point noted already by Webster (1948) 19 in his ground-breaking discussion of the relationship between Western Greek comic vases (then 'phlyax' vases) and Athenian theatre.

[45] Taplin (1993 and 1987); Csapo (1986). On the possibility of the reperformance of Lysistrata in Tarentum, see Revermann (2006a) 254–60.

standardized. Is it likely that local subliterary farces would have been represented suddenly in such a standardized form over such a wide area? On the other hand, how do we explain how Aristophanes was imported suddenly and over such a large territory without leaving any significant trace in the literary or historical record? The sudden appearance of the comic vases seems less extraordinary, however, if they are considered with the fairly active theatrical tradition of comic theatre in the West that we have mapped out in much of the fifth century. Aristophanes' plays, among others, could have been absorbed into this tradition.[46]

Hieron I to Dionysius I

There is evidence of popular theatre in the early fifth century under Hieron and Gelon (that is to say, Aeschylus, Epicharmus, Dinolochus, Phormis and the building of the early theatre) and again in the early fourth century under Dionysius I (when we have a record of Xenarchus and we see the sudden proliferation of Western Greek comic vases). The conditions were similar in both periods: both tyrants seem to have supported an active literary scene at their courts. Hieron is reputed to have surrounded himself with Bacchylides, Pindar, Aeschylus, as well as Epicharmus, Phormis and Dinolochus. Likewise, Dionysius I not only surrounded himself with literary and philosophical figures, but also, infamously, tried his own hand at writing plays. It is even more telling that both tyrants seem to have used tragedy to advance their own political ends: Aeschylus wrote a new play celebrating Hieron's establishment of a 'new' city, Aetna; Dionysius, infamous in antiquity for the harshness of his rule, seems to have filled his plays not only with adages about justice and good government, but even more ironically with criticism of tyranny itself![47] Both tyrants used tragedy to whitewash their own dictatorial practices. Not only tragedy but, in both cases, comic plays seem to have been turned to propagandistic use by the tyrants. Xenarchus, writing mimes in the tradition of Sophron, is reported to have been commissioned by Dionysius to mock the Rhegians; likewise, in his play *The Islands* Epicharmus described Hieron protecting the Locrians from a harsh dictator, Anaxilas of Rhegium.[48]

---

[46] See Dearden (1988) for discussions of mixed influences on Western Greek comic vases.

[47] E.g., Snell (1971) fr. 3 and 4.

[48] This episode is recorded in a scholiast to Pindar *Pythian Two*, prompted by lines about the harshness of Phalaris who is unfavourably compared to Hieron. It seems likely that the scholiast's reference was made to Hieron here because the play also attempted to show Hieron's good character in contrast to that of wicked tyrants.

Dionysius' use of theatre seems to be similar to, if not perhaps even modelled on, that of the two Syracusan tyrants who preceded him, Gelon and Hieron. If this is the case, the question of the literary or performative character of Sophron's work is not really the deciding factor. If Sophron was simply composing his mimes for the literati during the turbulent and democratic upheavals of the latter half of the fifth century, this is sufficient for the tradition of local comic theatre to have continued where it mattered, among the powerful, who, when their day came, turned it to their own political purposes, propaganda, as well as entertainment of the general population.

Here we return to the puzzle about the Western Greek comic vases: why so many so suddenly, so widespread and so similar? As Dearden argues, these similarities among the pictures on the Western Greek comic vases, found all over the West, suggest that they represent some kind of standardized theatre. He concludes that this homogeneity 'makes it difficult to maintain the concept of impromptu drama'.[49] If we posit Dionysius as a supporter of theatre, like his predecessors Hieron and Gelon, we have a possible solution to this sudden widespread advent of depictions of popular theatre. That is, if Dionysius was actively supporting theatre, and public performance, as Hieron had done, then it seems reasonable that similar performances would have within a few years begun to be performed in various parts of South Italy and Sicily under his control, and cities outside his control may still have felt the influence of a sudden encouragement of the arts. If we look to the next grand tyrant of Syracuse, Hieron II, the same technique seems to be in evidence, for it is under his rule that many of the great theatres of Sicily were built, some with his name or that of his wife etched on a commemorative stone. Moreover, Epicharmus was still very much in the foreground in these later periods. This is apparent not only in his influence on Sophron, and some similarities in themes between his plays and the Western Greek comic vases themselves,[50] but also in the work of the tyrant Dionysius' son, who seems to have made an edition of Epicharmus' letters. Likewise, under Hieron II, a bronze statue featuring an epigram of Theocritus (well known as an imitator of Sophron), perhaps erected in the theatre of Syracuse, commemorated the brilliance of Epicharmus and his tremendous effect on the city of Syracuse as a poet and luminary.

If we imagine the tyrants as the prime movers of large-scale theatrical productions, not only later with Hellenistic buildings of grand theatres but

---

[49] Dearden (1988) 34f.
[50] Gigante (1967) 94f. and Hunter (1983) 122f. suggest certain Western Greek comic vases represent specific plays by Epicharmus.

also in their support of earlier writers like Epicharmus, then the problem of a subliterary native tradition feeding into the Western Greek comic vases no longer needs to be relied on for the argument that there was a Western, Doric tradition of theatre. The tyrants' ties with the larger Greek world, moreover, give ample opportunity for the importing of Athenian plays, as for example Aeschylus in the early part of the fifth century, and Aristophanes at the beginning of the fourth.

Although the great Hollywood expansion of Athenian theatre westward in the fifth century and later must have influenced the theatrical scene in Sicily, it seems less likely that it was the catalyst for theatre in the West than that Athenian theatre was absorbed into an active theatrical tradition which the Syracusan tyrants Gelon and especially Hieron had developed in the early fifth century, and which the tyrant Dionysius I picked up in the fourth century. Although even in the fifth century the plays of the Athenian Aeschylus were presented in Sicily, they were imported to serve the particular aims of the tyrant Hieron, and, likewise, Dionysius I may have supported both local and imported plays for reasons of propaganda. In this way, we can piece together a history of early comic theatre in the West, a theatre that accepted and was influenced by the great Athenian playwrights but was still driven by its own political and social needs. Unlike Athens, the cities of Western Greece took part in a theatre whose public and grand form was created by the tyrants, not by the democracy.

Further reading

Dearden's essays on comedy in the West include good introductions to key problems in the study of West Greek theatre, for example, Dearden (1990). Likewise, Wilson (2007b) gives an up-to-date discussion of performance in the West, and Denard (2007) describes Sicilian and South Italian traditions within the broader scope of non-literary regional performance traditions. For a wide-ranging collection of sources, and an extensive bibliography, see Todisco (2002).

The best comprehensive study in English of Epicharmus within the wider tradition of tragedy and comedy is still Pickard-Cambridge and Webster (1962), though this has now been updated in German by Kerkhof (2001), together with Willi's fascinating discussion of Epicharmus in the tradition of Western Greek writers (Willi (2008)). Olson (2007) provides a new translation and notes to key fragments of Epicharmus. On Sophron, Hordern's introduction to his translation and commentary is very useful (Hordern (2004)). For Western Greek Comic vases and figurines Green (1994) is a good place to start, and Taplin (1993) a good place to continue. On theatres, Rossetto and Sartorio (1994) give an encyclopedic overview of sites throughout the Mediterranean and a bibliography on each theatre.

For an introduction to the history of ancient Sicily, Finley's engaging and elegant study (1979) is now somewhat out of date, but the gap will soon be filled by De Angelis' survey of Sicilian history from *c.* 750 to *c.* 250, forthcoming from Oxford University Press. Carratelli's (1996) enormous and richly illustrated volume collects a wide range of essays by scholars on various questions to do with the Western Greeks. On the re-discovery by modern archaeologists of the Greek presence in Southern Italy see Ceserani (2012).

5

ERIC CSAPO

The iconography of comedy

The standard catalogues of artifacts related to Greek comedy (*MMC, MNC*) list over 4,600 items. And the rate of accumulation of new material is impressive. The catalogue of West Greek comic vase paintings, published in 1967 (*PhV*), listed 185. Richard Green, who is working on a new collection, now knows of 592. Although a picture might not always amount to a thousand words, one could claim that Greek comedy is as well represented in the remains of ancient art as in the remains of ancient texts.

Despite this, iconography has received nothing like the attention paid to the texts. Paradoxically, perhaps, the most serious obstacle to progress in the study of theatre iconography is the structure of the modern university. In the last century there was a trend, in many countries, to assimilate Classics Departments to departments of languages and literatures or history, and to relocate researchers in ancient material culture in departments of Fine Art or Archaeology. This rift makes it very difficult for students to acquire the requisite learning in both fields. But the problem runs still deeper. These material conditions have shaped much current scholarship. A recent book by Penny Small (2003) makes a positive virtue of the two solitudes by arguing that it is in the very nature of texts and artifacts to be autonomous and indifferent to one another. The book is called *The Parallel Worlds of Classical Art and Text,* the point being that parallel lines never cross. This is not a position that encourages interdisciplinary research.

Discouragement of this sort is too easy to find at present. Oliver Taplin coined the term 'iconocentric' to describe scholars (usually trained as archaeologists or art historians) who (usually while spruiking the virtues of very different and incompatible 'methodological' or 'theoretical'

I would like to thank my fellow researchers at the theatre archive at the Centre for Classical and Ancient Near Eastern Studies of Australia (Dick Green, Andrew Hartwig, Sebastiana Nervegna and Peter Wilson) for discussion of many of the artifacts that appear in this chapter. I would also like to acknowledge the assistance of an Australian Research Council Discovery Grant.

straightjackets) extenuate the utility of art for theatre history, if they do not deny it outright, and urge us to receive what appear to be theatrical scenes as 'myth' or pure 'fantasy'.[1] One has to know that there is a history behind this divorce, though perhaps not as long and bitter as some modern reconstructions would make it: one can, for example, read accounts that speak of iconography's servitude to philology in the nineteenth-century German academy, of how images were never valued except as a tool for the restoration of lost or incomplete texts, or of how Carl Robert heroically 'paved the way for the emancipation of iconographical studies from classical philology'.[2] Institutional rivalry and territoriality has generated sensitivities that have made red flags of words like 'illustration', words that never now appear in scholarship except in demonstrations that they do not exist, demonstrations that are easy enough, if, as Small insists, the term 'illustration' implies 'pictures that match (or should match) the text in the way that Sir John Tenniel's engravings fit Lewis Carroll's *Alice in Wonderland*'; it does not follow, however, that the only alternative to blatant anachronism is to speak in terms of a representation 'that has only a loose connection with the text'.[3] The relationship of ancient art and ancient comic texts is capable of more subtle positions than almost total dependence and almost total independence.

The important point, however, is that as far as dramatic artifacts are concerned any argument structured on an opposition between 'art' and 'text', painting and literature, or iconcentrism and philology is fundamentally wrongheaded. Drama is not texts and not even literature, although it can be treated that way – and in university courses today normally is. But the ancients never did, at least not until late antiquity. They knew their drama primarily (and in most cases exclusively) from performance. Dramatic performance is a visual (even if not just a visual) art and the visual arts in Greece shared in a commonwealth of motifs: painters, sculptors, coroplasts, mask-makers, costume designers, scene-decorators and even actors learned from one another, even if they adapted what they saw to the needs of their own particular medium. The purpose of this chapter is to offer a brief survey of the iconographic genres related to ancient comedy and, at the same time, to demonstrate, through a closer look at a few examples, that iconography, even though it may not illustrate like John Tenniel, can

[1] Taplin (2007) 2f., 22–6 with an excellent discussion of the controversy over tragedy-related vases.
[2] The narrative of servitude and liberation is not the only option for a history of classical archaeology: contrast, for example, Isler-Kerényi (2007) 81 (whence the quotation) with Schindler (1985) or Martin (2008) 317f.
[3] Small (2005) 104.

Figure 5.1 Fragment of Attic black-figured dinos, *c.* 575 BCE, Agora P 334

sometimes have a very close relationship with theatre, especially comic theatre, and can make important contributions to our knowledge of ancient drama, of the conditions of its performance, and of the conditions of its production.

Attic artifacts depicting choruses

From about 730 BCE dancers we call 'komasts' begin to appear on vase paintings in Corinth. The motif soon spreads to many other parts of the Greek world.[4] They are normally drunk, playful, frequently obscene and often associated with public sacrificial processions and feasts. Komasts appear on Athenian vases from the early sixth century BCE (Figure 5.1) where they are closely linked with Dionysus. Some think that Attic komasts are a mere iconographic borrowing with no reference to Attic ritual. At first, like Corinthian komasts, they wear costume with padded breasts, stomachs and buttocks that represent grotesque naked bodies and are sometimes fitted with phalloi, but the komasts soon grow stylized and in later Attic art they appear simply as naked male dancers. Though they dance the same dance in the same place, their movements are rarely co-ordinated.

Komasts cease to appear in Attic art about the middle of the sixth century BCE, but evidently not because of flagging interest in Dionysian entertainments. Peisistratus is generally credited with the creation (or possibly the

[4] Csapo and Miller (2007) 13–21, 41–117, 196–220.

Figure 5.2 Attic black-figured dinos, Ptr. of Louvre E 876, *c.* 560 BCE, Louvre E 876

revamping on a large scale) of the Athenian Dionysia, and though 570 BCE is still too early for his tyranny, it is from that date that Attic art reveals a sudden efflorescence of Dionysian imagery, with new subjects and treatments entering the repertoire, and a particular fascination with Dionysian processions, processional dances, or likely reflections of the Parade (*pompê*) that

Figure 5.3 Attic black-figured lip-cup, *c.* 550 BCE, Florence 3897

marked the beginning and the climax of the Great Dionysia.[5] The Return of Hephaestus became a popular mythic subject, but is completely assimilated to a carnival parade in which drunken and sportive satyrs, komasts, maenads and sacrifices accompany the god (Figure 5.2).[6] From this period we have our first scenes of Dionysus being escorted into town on his ship-cart. This is the time of our first and only depiction of a chorus of men carrying the giant phalloi that formed the main spectacle of the Dionysian Parade (Figure 5.3). From *c.* 570 we have our first depictions of regimented satyrs moving in step and, perhaps most significantly, the first vase paintings of imaginatively costumed men, moving and singing to what appears to be a carefully synchronized beat, usually led by a piper, and typically wearing the costumes of animals or animal-riders which suggests an interest in mimetic movement.[7] Figure 5.4 is a late example of this group of '*kômos* vases' (of which scarcely more than twenty examples survive). Dated around 510 BCE it shows a group of costumed ostrich riders moving towards a small figure wearing a satyr mask with a piper behind him. The gesture the little satyr makes as he faces the chorus shows he is the leader, or *exarchos*, and an improviser of verse to which the chorus sings a refrain (one can compare

---

[5] Carpenter (1986); Shapiro (1995a) ch. 5; Csapo and Miller (2007) 22–3, cf. 16–18; Csapo (2013).
[6] Hedreen (2004).   [7] Hedreen (2007); Green (1985a).

Figure 5.4 Attic black-figured skyphos, *c.* 510 BCE, Boston MFA 20.18

the gesture of the man at the front of the phallus pole in Figure 5.3 – it is from the interaction of the *exarchos* and the phallic chorus that Aristotle inferred the origin of comedy).[8] The series lasts only until about the time of the formal introduction of a comic competition to the Athenian Dionysia (on the usual chronology 486 BCE).

About the time that the *kômos* vases die out, artifacts depicting dramatic choruses first appear. These are never very many. Those suspected of a connection with satyr play are highly mythologized if they are meant to depict dramatic choruses at all. By contrast, tragic choruses are sometimes depicted with a degree of realism that leaves no doubt about their dramatic identity. Though much of the choral imagery that survives is found in vase painting, it is likely that the motif imitates or copies the imagery of choregic monuments.[9] The prize at the comic competitions in Athens was not given to the poets but to the choruses they trained and it was customary for the sponsor (*chorêgos*) of a dramatic chorus to commemorate a victory by dedicating a painting or relief in (or on the road to) the Sanctuary of Dionysus. A few reliefs associated with such monuments survive and, unsurprisingly, some of them show performing choruses. Given that the function of such monuments was the memorialization of a victorious choral performance, we can expect that the details of costume and dance on these monuments would have conformed at least to normal practice if not necessarily to practice on a specific occasion. We do, in fact, have the remains of two choregic monuments, both *c.* 350–340 BCE, that depicted comic choruses in

[8] Arist. *Po.* 1449a, 9–12; Csapo (2006/7). [9] Csapo (2010a).

Figure 5.5 Fragments of a choregic relief, 350–340 BCE, Agora S 2098

performance.[10] One of them, Figure 5.5, shows the remains of seven choreuts in formation, five in the first rank, whose masks are badly damaged, and two in the second rank of choreuts, whose masks survive intact because recessed behind the right shoulders of the first rank. Originally the relief probably held two full ranks of six files leaving us to imagine another two ranks behind them. Ancient scholars tell us that four ranks of six files was the normal formation of a comic chorus. Their high step is a movement that normally accompanied the regular marching metres typically used in the *parodos*, parabasis and, more rarely, in the *exodos*. Lines on the arms and legs show that the choreuts wear bodytights to the wrists and ankles. Under their chitons we see the bulk of the same buttock, breast and belly padding worn by comic actors (and the komasts before them). On neither this nor the other relief is it possible to tell if comic choreuts normally wore

[10] Agelidis (2009) 49–51.

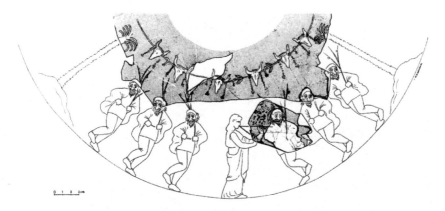

Figure 5.6 Reconstruction of a fragmentary red-figured chous, *c.* 360 BCE, Benaki 30895

the phallus (as comic actors invariably did until the time of New Comedy).[11] The dance step conceals this detail.

Figure 5.6 nicely demonstrates the way vase painters occasionally make use of choregic imagery. It is surprisingly close in subject and treatment to the two choregic reliefs. Once again we have six choreuts representing the first rank of 'marching' formation and moving with the same stylized high step if we can trust the reconstructive drawing: but note that the reconstruction is heavily influenced by the Agora reliefs (it does contain some clear errors: it should have put the choreuts' hands on their hips not tucked in belts). The choreuts appear as two half-choruses each facing the piper at centre, but the vase painter may have shaped this for symmetry. The choreuts appear to wear the usual padded *sômation* (literally = 'little body') under their chitons. Once again we cannot tell if they wear a phallus. They carry leafless branches (not the usual leafy branches of suppliants and worshippers) in a sanctuary setting indicated by the bull skulls (*boukrania*). Intriguingly, although only the piper's hands survive they are in added white, the conventional colour of female flesh. From what we know of theatre practice it is unlikely that females performed as theatre pipers and it may be that the piper in this painting (and perhaps on some choregic monuments) was fancifully assimilated to abstractions like Victory, or Comedy (both feminine nouns in Greek).[12]

Two remarkable Attic vases showing men dressed as fighting cocks may relate to the comic chorus (Figures 5.7–8). Figure 5.7 has been variously identified with the chorus of Aristophanes' *Birds* or with the actors in the *agôn* of Aristophanes' *Clouds* (an ancient scholion to verse 889 informs us

[11] Revermann (2006a) 156f. [12] See Taplin (1993) 105–10.

Figure 5.7 Attic red-figured calyx krater, *c.* 425 BCE, formerly Malibu 82.AE.83

that the Greater and the Lesser Arguments appeared in the manner of fighting cocks). But cocks cannot represent the chorus of *Birds* since the species, all carefully enumerated in the play, do not include cocks. Moreover, most experts at stylistic chronology date Figure 5.7 considerably earlier than 414 BCE (one expert dates it as early as 450 BCE). Figure 5.8, unknown until just a few years ago, shows the same costume rendered by a different artist. It has as yet no precise stylistic dating, but is helpful in other ways. As Figure 5.8 clearly shows one, but only one of the cocks (the reverse shows a piper), it does not favour the identification with the *agôn* of *Clouds* either. Two cocks seem necessary to signal a cockfight. A single figure better represents the unity of a chorus than it does a confrontation. But even if we cannot name a play, these images together make a strong case for a dramatic model. The easiest conclusion is that both were inspired by a production or productions of the same comedy. The costumes are far too close in similarity

Figure 5.8 Attic red-figured pelike, *c.* 425 BCE, Atlanta 2008.4.1

to be the result of a coincidence of painterly fantasies. Moreover, the stark theatrical realism of these images surely excludes the notion that the artist intended to draw fantastic or mythical creatures: Figure 5.7, for example, details even the string with which the leftmost cock's phallic spur is tied to the performer's left foot.

Attic artifacts depicting actors

Attic artifacts show actors (as opposed to choreuts) only after 430 BCE and almost exclusively comic actors. Comic actors appear on small vessels (especially *choes*, ritual pitchers used at the festival of the Anthesteria) and figurines. Choes generally have a wide repertoire of imagery, but a consistent preference for Dionysian and childish themes – the Anthesteria had a close

Figure 5.9 Attic red figured chous, Painter of the Perseus Dance, *c.* 420 BCE, Athens NM BΣ 518. Drawing by E. Malyon

connection with both Dionysus and childhood. There are in fact a small number of choes on which children appear wearing the costume of comic actors. These *are* painterly fantasies with only a remote connection to theatre (though a connection nonetheless). However, a chous and an oinochoe do prove that Athenian vase painters took an interest in comic theatre beyond the imitation of choregic imagery.

Figure 5.9 is a drawing reconstructing the details of a much damaged chous of about 420 BCE. Its connection with comedy has been repeatedly denied, but mostly the vase has been ignored.[13] Most work on ancient iconography in the past century has been decidedly normative, especially since the methodology craze of the later twentieth century (pretenders to a rigorous methodology rarely prize diversity) and this chous is, if anything, unusual. The situation was certainly not helped by the fact that this chous was known only through a poor photograph and a drawing by a Gilléron fils, who along with his father, has been accused in archaeological circles of fanciful and even dishonest reconstruction. After its initial publication, the actual pot was buried in a museum storeroom until 2006 when a

[13] The history of the vase is summarized by Hughes (2006b).

careful study by Alan Hughes confirmed the accuracy of Gilléron's drawing (Figure 5.9 is a slightly corrected redrawing by E. Malyon).

This remarkable painting attempts to capture, on the surface of a small vessel, the whole sweep of the theatre. It is the only ancient artifact to show a seated theatre audience and the only Attic artifact to show the low raised (wooden) stage that normally stood before the building that we refer to as the *skênê* (or 'stage building'). The form of the chairs (*klismoi*), upon which sits our audience represented by two figures, is probably an accurate reflection of the honorary front row seats (or *prohedria*) used in the late fifth-century Theatre of Dionysus: we have the fifth-century foundation blocks upon which the chairs were set, as well as chairs of the same shape imitated in marble from the later fourth-century theatre (others sat on wooden or, later, stone benches).

On the stage prances a figure with the attributes of Perseus: the sickle (*harpê*) and the magic bag (*kibisis*). He is shown in heroic nudity, but one detail (apart from being on a stage) shows him to be an actor; Hughes confirms that he has lines at his wrists and ankles indicating that he wears the bodytights, unique to ancient dramatic performers, that allowed actors to appear naked without actually being so. Remarkably, however, Perseus does not show any sign of the normal comic actor's body padding, nor the grotesque features of a comic mask. The only features that prevent Perseus appearing as a tragic actor are the undignified vigour of his step, the unkempt appearance of his hair and beard, and the large phallus that, on careful inspection, Hughes confirms to be tied in a loop (as comic figurines and actors on West Greek pottery sometimes wear it).[14]

The combination of some highly realistic detail (the tights, the looped phallus, the stage, the audience) and a lack of realism in other respects (no padding, no obvious mask) is hard to explain. It would appear as if Perseus still shares some of the ideal beauty of his heroic form known from tragedy and mythical representation. It may be that the artist feared that a more grotesque presentation of the hero, whose iconography had already been established in tragedy and serious art, would be unrecognizable.

Figure 5.10 is a scene on a crudely painted wine jug that was tossed into a well in the Athenian Agora along with several similar jugs decorated with grotesque or humorous characters.[15] This is the only extant Attic vase that can be connected with a known comedy. The jug shows two characters. The one on the left is labelled '–onysus' which can certainly be restored as 'Dionysus'. The one on the right is labelled 'Phor' which can with high probability be restored as 'Phormio'. These are the principal characters of a

---

[14] Hughes (2006b) 425. [15] Crosby (1955); *MMC* AV10–14.

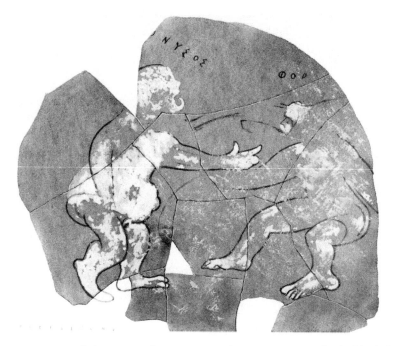

Figure 5.10 Attic polychrome oinochoe, *c.* 400 BCE, Agora P23985. Drawing by Piet de Jong

comedy by Eupolis called *Taxiarchoi*, first produced in Athens around 415 BCE.[16] An ancient summary tells us that in this play Dionysus 'learns from Phormio the ways of generals and wars'.[17] The play was remembered for the humour generated by the contrast between their characters. Dionysus was doubtless his usual comic persona: soft, lazy and effeminate. Phormio was an actual Athenian general with a reputation for tough old-fashioned discipline: in the play 'Phormio' proclaims that his nickname is 'Ares' (fr. 268.14f.). The play's fragments indicate that Dionysus received lessons in holding a shield, making camp, living in squalor, dining on raw onions and rowing. Phormio's posture on the oinochoe suggests a lesson in oarsmanship. If Dionysus is the speaker of the complaint 'hey you at the bow, will you stop splashing us?', this fragment may belong to the scene here represented (fr. 268.50f.). Enough of 'Dionysus' survives on the jug to indicate the standard comic body suit with breast, belly and buttock padding. His large head and gaping mouth possibly hint at a mask, but the painting is fast and crude and nothing very accurate was intended.

In the last decade of the fifth century BCE Athenian coroplasts begin manufacturing dramatic figurines. They were perhaps initially intended as

[16] Storey (2003) 246–60 discusses the play's date and contents.   [17] Σ Arist. *Peace* 348.

souvenirs of the Athenian Dionysia. The four that can be assigned a fifth-century date were found in Athens, but by about 375 BCE they are found all over the Mediterranean world. By 350 BCE they came to be imitated by local manufacturers in such diverse locations as Corinth, Olynthus, Akanthos, Thasos, Asia Minor, Cyprus, Cyrene, Egypt, Naples, Paestum, Locri, Tarentum, Heracleia (Policoro), Lipari, Sicily (especially Syracuse) and even Emporion (Ampurias) in Spain.[18] Manufacture throughout the Greek world continues right through the second and into the third centuries CE.[19] Apart from a few satyrs and silens with indications of costume, all of the dramatic figurines show actors (not choreuts) and for nearly a century all are comic. No tragic figurine is datable before the Hellenistic period and when tragic figurines do appear they are also exclusively actors. The manufacture and export of terracotta representations of dramatic masks tells a similar story, beginning in early fourth-century BCE Athens, widely exported and soon imitated. But here too the representations are of actors' masks, not choreuts'.

The iconography shows that actors caught hold of the popular imagination from about 430–400 BCE in Athens. Unlike the largely generic images of choral performance, scenes with actors are often highly specific.

West Greek artifacts depicting actors

About 440 BCE Metapontum and Tarentum begin to produce their own red-figured pottery. Initially it was indistinguishable in style and technique from Attic. Athenian craftsmen probably emigrated to the Dorian cities in order to set up workshops closer to a market (both Greek and indigenous non-Greek) that had already for well over a century been a major importer of Attic pottery. Apulia (Tarentum) and Lucania (Metapontum) produced pottery very close to the mainstream of Attic production until about 400 BCE. After that West Greek pottery began to develop a unique style that spread to new centres of production in Sicily, Paestum and Campania. The earliest comic vases appear soon after 400 BCE. We know of about 250 vases that depict scenes of comedy or comic performers. We will examine three vase paintings of comic scenes that I find particularly helpful for thinking about the relationship of West Greek art to theatre.

The first of these is an early product of the man who probably 'set the fashion at Taranto for decorating vases with scenes connected with the theatre'.[20] Figure 5.11 is ancient art's most ambitious experiment at capturing the

---

[18] *MMC* 39–66; Green (1994) 68–78; Green (2008) 20, 215.
[19] *MNC* 1, 68–74.   [20] Trendall (1988) 138.

Figure 5.11 Apulian red-figured calyx krater, Tarporley Painter, *c.* 400 BCE, New York, MMA 24.97.104

experience of drama on the surface of a vase. It is particularly successful in evoking the aspects of drama that made it unique as a representational art: the vast and varied spaces of the theatre, the acting, the costume, the words, and even the movements.

The first feature is not entirely unique: Figure 5.9 also attempted to capture the breadth of the theatre from the stage to the first row of spectators. In Figure 5.11, on the far right and moving left, we see the double doors of the *skênê* building, a raised stage holding an actor with the mask of an old woman, a basket with two goats, and a dead goose. Below the stage at orchestra level are two actors, both 'stage-naked' wearing the body tights, the *sômation* with enlarged breasts, belly and buttocks (note the fine detail of the buckle between belly and buttocks on the central figure) and a phallus. The central figure wears the mask of an old man and holds his hands in the air. To his left a younger man approaches holding a stick. Between them hovers a disembodied mask. On the far left, a youth watches the scene. He is not part of the comic action: he has no mask or costume, hovers on a higher plane and is mysteriously labelled *tragôidos*, which can mean tragic choreut, actor or poet. Whatever his intended identity, he functions as an audience, rising above the orchestra as if in the *theatron* and gazing at the actors.

This is the only theatrical artifact of the classical period to attempt to preserve actors' voices. Words issue from the mouths of the speakers. The old woman on the stage says 'I hand him over to you', which is the sort of formula one might use when offering a slave up for torture by a civic author-ity (the only condition under which evidence from slaves was admissible by Athenian law). The old man in the centre of the *orchêstra* on tiptoes with his hands raised says 'he has tied up my hands'. Slaves were often suspended before a beating. The young man holding the switch is presumably going to do the work. He says 'Norarettéblo' which means as much in Greek as it does in English. The words, however, mean something in ancient Circassian. They are interpreted to mean 'He stole them from over there in their yard.' Scythians were used as police in ancient Athens, and Circassian is a Scythian language.[21]

The dialogue, although we do not know its order, adds an element of time and movement.[22] So does the oddly oblique trail of letters issuing from the old man's mouth. The painter did not misjudge his space, he very deliberately permits the letters to rise up sharply and then stop dead at the level of the old man's mouth in imitation of the movement by which the old man was suspended. Trendall was disturbed at the absence of visible ropes and Beazley invented a far-fetched scenario of magical 'binding' to explain their absence.[23] What we have, rather, is a splendid example of illusionistic comic acting. The Tarporley painter chose a scene that showed the comic actor at his best, toe-dancing and pirouetting in imitation of a man being whipped while suspended. It was a virtuoso act and evidently popular. We have a similar scene at Aristophanes' *Frogs* 618–73.

Figure 5.12 shows another scene from the same comedy, although the vase painting was drawn perhaps as many as thirty years later, and by a different artist (although the McDaniel Painter was an apprentice of the Tarporley Painter). Figures 5.7–8 and 5.11–12 are the only sure instances in antiquity of a single comedy being represented by two distinct and different images. We see the same male characters in a wrestling ground (symbolised by the herm on the left with a cloak and oil bottle on its head, another oil bottle is in the old man's hand). The old man is oiling himself, indicating that they are about to fight. It really is the same comedy, we are not being fooled by the reappearance of the masks and the stick. The proof is the care with which the artist reproduces the detail of the basket containing two kids juxtaposed to a goose. The combination must be unique to this play and it is evidently included in these vase paintings as an important clue to the play's identity. We can only infer that this scene came earlier than the other (because the goose is still alive), but the Tarporley Painter and the McDaniel

[21] Mayor, Colarusso and Saunders (2012) 13.   [22] Marshall (2001).
[23] Beazley (1952) followed by Taplin (1993) 30–2 and Schmidt (1998).

Figure 5.12 Apulian red-figured bell krater, McDaniel Painter, *c.* 370 BCE, Boston MFA 69.951

Painter probably expected much more from their customers. Attic and West Greek vase paintings sometimes label characters but never give playtitles. Taplin infers (and I think he is right) that part of the fun for the consumer was puzzling out the identity of the play behind the image.[24] For this reason the comedy has come to be known as 'the Gooseplay'.

This pair of vase paintings presupposes considerable familiarity in South Italy with comic drama. This is hardly surprising, given that nearby Sicily had a comic tradition reaching back a century.[25] What is surprising is that the lines on Figure 5.11 are written in the Attic dialect, even though the Greek dialect spoken in Tarentum (and most of West Greece) was Doric. Name labels that appear on other West Greek comic vases are also normally Attic. We do not in fact need to infer that the comedy was written in Attica (though we will in a moment examine a certain case of Attic drama appearing on Apulian pottery). The necessary inference is rather that by 400 BCE Attic comedy so dominated the theatre that Attic was recognized as the appropriate dialect for comic dialogue (just as Doric was thought appropriate for choral lyrics).

[24] Taplin (1993) 27–36.   [25] See Bosher, Chapter 4.

Figure 5.13 Apulian red-figured bell krater, Schiller Painter, *c.* 370 BCE, Würzburg H5697

For want of any better evidence for illustrated dramatic texts in antiquity, some scholars have seized upon the inscription of text in Figure 5.11. In fact the inscription points very strongly in the other direction. The lines spoken by the three characters are not in verse.[26] This indicates memorywork not copywork on the part of the artist. This observation is confirmed by the appearance of a heta, a letter of the Tarentine alphabet, in the old woman's lines. Not only is the heta non-Attic, but it represents a pronunciation that is non-Attic and would have made the verse impossible to fit into any iambic trimeter.[27] These details seem to indicate that the artist is not trying to write verse, but remembering the gist of a dialogue, not getting the foreign dialect quite right, and writing the sounds down in a way that comes naturally only to a Tarentine. None of this is consistent with close contact with a text, but it is consistent with an attempt to reproduce a sequence of action seen in the theatre.

Figure 5.13 gives us as clear a correspondence between an artifact and a text as we could hope to find. Aristophanes' *Women at the Thesmophoria* is a prolonged parody of Euripides' *Telephus*. At the climax of Euripides'

---

[26] Beazley (1952) tried to force the words into a line and a half of iambic trimeter, but arbitrarily changed the quantity of some vowels to do so.

[27] The lengthening effect of an aspirated rho in the dialogue of Attic drama 'is almost invariable' (West (1987) 17). This means the old woman's words would form a short syllable followed by four longs.

Telephus the disguised Telephus is discovered to be an enemy infiltrator at the war-council where the Greeks are planning an expedition against Troy. In order to save himself, Telephus grabs Agamemnon's infant son and then jumps, like a suppliant, upon an altar, holding a knife to his hostage's throat.

In Aristophanes' play Euripides' 'in-law' is shaved, and then disguised with an effeminate head-band, fancy shoes and a dress in order to infiltrate the Thesmophoria (an exclusively women's festival characterized by fasting and abstinence) where the women of Athens plan revenge against Euripides for his misogyny. News comes that a man has infiltrated the rites and suspicion falls upon the in-law who is discovered to be male when they peek under his tunic. The in-law then grabs what appears to be the baby of one of the women and jumps upon an altar threatening it with a sword. As several women run in search of kindling to burn the in-law off the altar (and disconnect him from the divine protection altars were thought to give), the following dialogue takes place (lines 730–55):

> IN-LAW: *(to the women)* Go ahead, kindle! Burn! *(to the baby)* But you, off with this wrap right now! For your death, child, you have only your mother to blame. Hey, what's this? The girl has turned into a skin full of wine and wearing booties at that! O most flagrant women! O most bibulous of creatures, stopping at nothing to contrive an opportunity for a drink! Great boon for the bar-tender; great bane for mankind! Bane too for dishes and the loom! MIKA: *(to her servant)* Mania, throw lots of brushwood beside the altar! IN-LAW: Go ahead throw it down alongside. But you! Answer me this question! Do you claim to be the mother? MIKA: To be sure, ten months I bore her! IN-LAW: YOU bore her? MIKA: Yes, by Artemis! IN-LAW: At three pints an obol, or what? MIKA: What have you done? You've stripped my child naked, tiny as she is, you pervert! IN-LAW: Tiny! I'll say she's tiny!! How old is she? Three or four Wine Pitchers? [A reference to the annual drinking contests of the Anthesteria]. MIKA: About that, plus however many months to the Dionysia. But give her back! IN-LAW: No, by this Apollo here! WOMAN: We'll set you on fire, then! IN-LAW: Go ahead! Burn! But this baby is going to get her throat cut, this instant! WOMAN: No! I beg you! Do whatever you like to me, but spare her! IN-LAW: I see you have a very maternal nature. But her throat will be cut nonetheless! WOMAN: Oh my child! *(to her servant)* Mania, give me the sacrificial basin so that I can at least save the blood of my baby.

The details on the vase correspond exactly to the implied action: the *Telephus* parody on the altar, the wineskin with booties, the woman rushing towards the threatened wineskin with a vessel to catch the 'blood', the headband of the figure on the altar, the longish tunic which hides the actor's phallus, the beardless face and razor splotches. Even the mirror has a place in the shaving scene just before this episode. We clearly have something very close to what we might legitimately call a representation of the climactic moment in the performance of Aristophanes' *Women at the Thesmophoria*.

There are, however, also discrepancies. Austin and Olson list several omissions that show that the artist is not giving us a perfectly accurate representation of every detail that from the text we know a stage-production must have included.[28] Our scene, for example, does not show the brushwood that the text suggests was by this point already piled around the altar. An omission of this sort does not cast doubt upon the connection between this painting and a scene from Aristophanes' play. It does, however, demonstrate that vase painters are generally less interested in accurately documenting every detail of a performance than in producing an attractive, clear and recognizable image. One must first take into account the fact that artists and actors have different resources at their disposal. On stage there could be no doubt that the in-law is on an altar: the audience sees him take refuge on the altar and then the brushwood is piled up around it. The viewer of the vase painting, however, does not share the knowledge that an audience would gain from a sequence of action seen in a performance. It would be counterproductive to obscure or hide the altar by surrounding it with brushwood. Indeed, as Austin and Olson remark, the recognition of this scene as the climax of *Women at the Thesmophoria* depends on the iconic clarity with which the configuration of the altar and suppliant conform to the visual patterning of Euripides' play, the object of Aristophanes' parody. This would only be frustrated by the addition of such incidental performance details we can infer from the text, as the presence of brushwood, a servant, a statue of Apollo and the very un-beggar-like (and hence un-Telephean) effeminate shoes we know were worn by the in-law. In other words, many (on the whole minor) discrepancies between the painter's image and the actors' performance may arise, paradoxically, out of the painter's very desire to provoke recognition of the specific performance from whose details he deviates.

The details that are in the text, but not in the painting, are much less revealing than the details that are in the painting, but not in the text. On this vase, there are two types of added detail that I find interesting. The first is detail that recalls or foreshadows moments elsewhere in the narrative. Though it is true that West Greek vases in general aim to capture a single important moment within a narrative, deviations from the temporal unity of the image may actually aid in the recognition of the scene. There is, for example, no reference to a mirror at this point in the play.

---

[28] Austin and Olson (2004) lxxvi–lxxvii.

In the past I have argued that the mirror may simply suggest the feminine ambiance of the Thesmophoria.[29] But the Schiller Painter is not particularly garrulous and I suspect that the mirror has more point. It appears in an earlier scene in which the in-law is shaved and dressed in female disguise. In the hostage scene the mirror appears to allude back to the dressing scene for the sake of imparting essential background to the visual narrative: it is important that we recognize that the person who at first sight looks like a woman is only 'dressed up' as a woman. The mirror, in other words, is added as a clue to the interpretation of a scene to which it does not strictly belong. (There is no need to suppose that the mirror was left hanging on the stage at the end of the dressing scene and continued to be visible in this one.) The razor splotches on the in-law's face are also there by the painter's art and not by the mask-maker's: a mask in production might well have had such splotches, but they would not be easily visible to even the closest members of the audience. The important point is that the painter has chosen to include them here (like the mirror) and evidently does it in order to allude to the shaving scene as a further clue to facilitate recognition.

But there are also some details that are not in the text at all, not even hinted at. The bibulous woman in the *Women at the Thesmophoria* asks for a *sphageion* which is a large basin employed in sacrificial ritual to catch the blood of a sacrificial victim. Instead, we see the old woman rushing forward with a giant drinking cup or *skyphos*. The substitution is perfectly consistent with a text that systematically confuses the language of sacrifice and the language of wine-tippling, but nothing in the text would have permitted us to guess the extension of this pattern of incongruity to the shape of the vessel used to collect the 'blood' of the wineskin.[30] The detail surely reproduces the stage-action of the play in production – it is unlikely that a vase painter invented the detail in the expectation that his customers would remember that the text called for a *sphageion*.

Both the absence of details in the text and the presence of details not in the text indicate that the artist is not in fact illustrating a text. Details imported from earlier moments of the play show that he is concerned to enhance the recognizability of an action that would simply be 'given' in the case of a book illustration. Other details, however, that cannot be inferred from the text cannot plausibly derive from any source other than a stage production.

In the last twenty-five years the study of West Greek pottery has pushed ancient theatre history in unexpected directions. It provides strong evidence

---

[29] Csapo (1986) 385; cf. Balensiefen (1990) K6–K20.
[30] For parallels (esp. Ar. *Lys.* 199), see Revermann (2006a) 244–6.

that what we used to regard as 'Attic' comedy was in fact by 400 BCE known and performed in other parts of the Greek world. Indeed, since West Greek and especially Apulian pottery was exported to the non-Greek Italian hinterland, it raises important questions about the degree to which non-Greeks had also acquired familiarity with comedy in the fourth century BCE.[31] West Greek artifacts also indicate that the process of canonization that made Aristophanes, Cratinus and Eupolis the standard triad of 'classic' Old Comic authors was well underway even by the first half of the fourth century BCE. Though there are about 140 comic scenes in Attic and West Greek red-figure from comedies that we cannot recognize, it is remarkable, given the slimness of our textual remains, that three scenes from plays of Aristophanes (including Figure 5.13) and two scenes from Eupolis (including Figure 5.10) are recognizable and give evidence of reperformance as much as fifty years after their performance in Athens.[32]

Artifacts related to New Comedy

Red-figured vase painting dies out in both Athens and West Greece in the last quarter of the fourth century BCE and along with it dies any iconographic tradition that we can connect with Old (or Middle) Comedy. Almost immediately, however, a very different iconographic tradition appears. From the late fourth century BCE we have over 3,500 artifacts that show scenes, characters or masks from New Comedy; they appear in every possible artistic medium and represent a tradition that continues well into the sixth century CE.

For theatre historians the scenes of comedy are of primary interest. Many come in multiple copies. We have over 200 objects that reproduce over fifty scenes from New Comedy: many artifacts reproduce a scene in its entirety, while others reproduce (or 'extract') only one or two figures.[33] As a group they are surprisingly coherent. Whole scenes, for example, tend to focus on the interaction of three main characters (additional characters are normally reduced in size); background details are often minimal, but the masks, stage, costume and all the props that might be required for identification are usually given in exacting detail; and all can be shown on stylistic grounds to be derived from Early Hellenistic painting. In fact Green has offered some very compelling arguments for thinking that a coherent set of Early Hellenistic panel paintings, possibly commissioned to decorate a public building of the

[31] See especially Robinson (2004).
[32] For a fuller discussion of identifiable comedies, see Taplin (1993) 36–47 and Csapo (2010b).
[33] There are now several additions to be made to *MNC* 1, 85–98.

Figure 5.14 Cameo, *c.* 100 BCE, Geneva, Musée d'art et d'histoire, 1974/21133

late fourth or early third century BCE, lies at the core of the corpus of New Comic artifacts.[34]

After the third century CE many of our paintings and mosaics of comic scenes come with labels that identify the specific comedy they are meant to illustrate. This permits us to identify securely fifteen of the fifty original paintings reconstructed by Green and Seeberg. All are plays of Menander. And since the distribution of these inscribed scenes is wide and fairly random (appearing at such diverse locations as Ephesus, Khamisa, Chania, Mytilene, Kastelli Kissamou, Daphne, Zeugma and Ulpia Oescus), it is a reasonable guess that plays of Menander constitute the other 70 per cent of our New Comic scenes. This adds another important element of homogeneity to the hypothesized set of Early Hellenistic paintings. In fact, in all cases where we can check the scenes against our texts, we have either opening scenes, climactic scenes, or 'title-scenes' (i.e. scenes that give their name to the play: the arbitration scene, for example, represents Menander's *Men at Arbitration*).

Figures 5.14–16 help exemplify the long and complex history of New Comic artifacts. They are three of nine known copies of a scene from

[34] Green (1994) 111f.

Figure 5.15 Marble relief, first century CE, Naples, Museo Nazionale 6687

a comedy that Handley and Green suggest might be the title-scene from
Menander's *Drunkenness* (*Methê*).[35] Figure 5.14, a gem of about 100 BCE,
shows five figures, three larger, and two smaller, on a well-defined stage
platform. From left to right we see a pair of old men, the one on the left
physically restraining the one on the right. In the middle is a piper, shorter
than the others by a head. On the far right is a young man, who is unsteady
on his feet and supported by a slave. The young man exuberantly raises his
right hand which holds a garland. With our knowledge of New Comedy we
can easily guess that the old man being restrained is the outraged father of
the youth who enters on the right, drunk, after a night of debauchery. The
piper indicates that the youth's drunken entrance was accompanied by song,
like the singing entrance of the drunken Callidamates propped up by his girlfriend Delphium in Plautus' *Mostellaria* I iv. The same scene, although with
a richly detailed stage backdrop, appears on a relief, Figure 5.15, produced
more than a century later and found near Naples.

The other illustrations (mostly figurines) only reproduce the drunken
young man supported by his slave. Two of these extracts, however, have

[35] Green (1985b); *MNC* I, XZ 41; add Vanaria (2001).

a great deal to tell us about the comic scenes in general (especially if Green is right in arguing that the originals formed a coherent set). One of the figurines was excavated from an undisturbed grave at Halae in Boeotia with a firm context date of no later than about 280 BCE. Green argues from the wear on the mould that the production of this terracotta must have begun much earlier than the deposition of the figurine. It is in any case likely that the original scene was produced about 300 BCE.[36] The surprising but necessary conclusion is that the original painting was created within Menander's lifetime, or at latest, very soon after his death in 292 BCE. We could not ask for a closer and better witness to the visual impact of the performance of Menander's plays.

All the clues therefore suggest that we have a reliable visual record of costumes, props, and gestures from fifty scenes, one from each of fifty plays, that derive from a contemporary source. The trick is in determining which artifacts copy their archetype with accuracy. The close correspondence between Figures 5.14 and 5.15 indicates that there is a very good chance that at least some of the Early Hellenistic archetypes were copied with reasonable fidelity up to the end of the first century CE. A later version of 517 CE shows, however, just how far the later copies could digress.

Figure 5.16 is one of our latest dramatic artifacts from antiquity: it is an ivory diptych of Anastasius. In 384 CE the consuls of Rome and Constantinople were granted the exclusive privilege of commemorating their year in office by the production of diptychs. As the consul's principal duty was to organize spectacles, diptychs frequently depict public entertainments. Here we see, in the upper band, horse-racing, and, in the lower band, jugglers, acrobats, and two dramatic figures. The mask on the taller figure shows a beardless man who leans upon his much smaller servant. If not for the exuberantly raised right hand, now without a garland, we might fail to recognize our drunken youth. Now, oddly, his mask has the *onkos* (elevator hairdo) that is characteristic of tragic masks from the Hellenistic period onwards, but he does not wear the elevator boots of tragedy. Our comic pair has now simply become a symbol for classical drama, but inserted by an artist who did not recognize or understand dramatic costume conventions. The appearance of the drunken young man and his slave on this diptych is not to be taken as an indication that Anastasius included comedy in his games. The imagery on these diptychs is frequently generic and different diptychs sometimes have identical scenes. We have yet to find clear evidence of any public performance of comedy after the third century CE.

---

[36] Green (1985b) 468.

Figure 5.16 Ivory consular diptych of Anastasius, 517 CE, St Petersburg ω 263 (Byz 925/16)

Menander's *Theophoroumenê* is the most represented (but hardly the most read) play of antiquity. We now know of at least eleven copies of a single Early Hellenistic archetype.[37] Figure 5.17 is a mosaic produced by a Samian artist around 100 BCE and later transferred from an unknown location to the 'Villa of Cicero' in Pompeii. It is the oldest and most careful rendition of the complete scene although there are some 'extracts' that may be somewhat older. It shows from left to right, a small piper's assistant (unmasked and holding the pipe-case with an extra mouth piece), an actor playing the role of a female piper (in colour one can easily see the contrast between the conventionally dark male flesh of the nape and hands and the white female flesh of the mask and bodytights), then two young men singing and dancing, the first playing cymbals and the second playing a *tympanon,* both orgiastic rhythmic instruments with a particularly close association with the cult of the Great Mother (Cybele). The central door of

[37] To *MNC* 1, XZ 39–40, add Stephani (2000) 289 fig. 4; Markoulaki *et al.* (2004) 371; Çelik (2009) 45f. and see the important study by Nervegna (2010).

Figure 5.17 Mosaic by Dioskourides, 125–100 BCE, Naples, Museo Nazionale 9985

the *skênê* is visible to the right. Comparison with two much later inscribed scenes in Mytilene and Kastelli Kissamou leaves no doubt that this is from the beginning of the title-scene of Menander's *Theophoroumenê* (the 'God-possessed Girl'). A papyrus fragment appears to preserve dialogue from immediately before the illustrated scene:

> SLAVE? (reporting a conversation): . . . 'My gifts', – you hear? – the girl says, 'they took away my gifts'. He says, 'Why did you accept them, slut? How do you know this guy who gave them to you? What were you thinking? A young man [giving gifts to a girl!] And why are you walking around outside wearing a garland? Are you crazy? Then why can't you be crazy locked up inside?' KLEINIAS?: That's nonsense! She's not just putting it on, Lysias. LYSIAS: It can be put to the test. If she really is divinely possessed she'll come leaping

out here in front. (To the piper.) Pipe [a tune] of the Mother of the Gods, or rather of the Korybantes (her priests)! And you, stand here by the door of the inn! KLEINIAS?: Yes, by Zeus, excellent! Truly excellent! I like this! A perfect spot to watch from!

Although it is not easy to tell precisely what is going on, the gist is clear. A girl inside an inn behaves as if she is possessed by Cybele, the Mother of the Gods, but there is doubt whether she is genuinely possessed or simply pretending. The young men Lysias and Kleinias decide to put the matter to the test by playing music that they suppose will bring her out of the inn if she really is possessed.

The vast majority of our complete theatre scenes from this period belong to reliefs, paintings and mosaics, created not by what we might call great artists, but by skilled craftsmen who made a living decorating the interiors of private houses. These craftsmen frequently copied famous masterpieces, and among them scenes from Menander had extra appeal for those interested in 'classic' images: they were classics of art as well as of drama. The dramatic scenes in fact furnish the best evidence we have for the use by ancient craftsmen of visual models in the form of copybooks.[38] Although ancient craftsmen usually felt free to adapt their images to a general programme of interior decoration (rearranging or reversing figures in a scene, for example), there are certain kinds of deviations from a known archetype that are most easily explained as errors based on misunderstanding of visual models. We can see something of this process beginning on copies of our *Theophoroumenê* scene from Stabiae (Figure 5.18) and Pompeii (Figure 5.19) both of which were buried by the eruption of Vesuvius in 79 CE. On Figure 5.17 one can see a shadow cast by the tympanon player upon the wall of the *skênê* just in front of the cymbal player. On Figure 5.18 this shadow has become a non-descript sugarloaf-shaped lump. But on Figure 5.19, a damaged, but otherwise careful copy of the archetype, we see that this shadow has been interpreted as an altar – the base is visible in the bottom centre of the image. Possibly, as Figure 5.18 suggests, an edition of a copybook with scenes of Menander was circulating in the Bay of Naples in which the shadow looked very much like an altar and ended up being replaced by one.

The most striking deviations from archetypes appear on artifacts produced after the third century CE. Figure 5.20 is one of many panels decorating the triclinium floor of a fourth-century CE house in Mytilene. The floor shows seven panels from plays of Menander (all labelled) consistently arranged so that, of the three main characters, two look and gesture toward the right in

[38] Csapo (1997); Donderer (2005/6).

Figure 5.18 Wallpainting from Villa in Campo Varano, Stabiae, first century CE, Naples, Museo Nazionale 9034

such a way as to guide the viewer's eye from one panel to the next, moving from left to right and top to bottom like a text, until one gets to the end. For this reason the scenes on several panels have been intentionally and demonstrably manipulated, and at least two panels have undergone a complete left to right reversal. One of these is the scene labelled *Theophoroumenê*. The piper's assistant, now holding a pipe (note the case with a jutting mouthpiece) has migrated from the left to the right. This also happens in another fragmentary version at Pompeii and at Kastelli Kissamou.[39] But in this panel there is also massive corruption, so much so that many have been fooled into thinking that we have a different moment from the same scene (which, if true, might very likely resuscitate the illustrated-text theory). A careful look at Figure 5.20, however, shows that the figure farthest left retains the stance of the tympanon player (and even holds an instrument that is halfway between a tympanon and a cymbal), while the figure second from the left has the stance of the cymbal player, only reversed. Corruption is obvious, however, from the fact that the dancing young men are dressed as slaves (the hanging tails of the cloaks wrapped around their waists were evidently

[39] See Nervegna (2010).

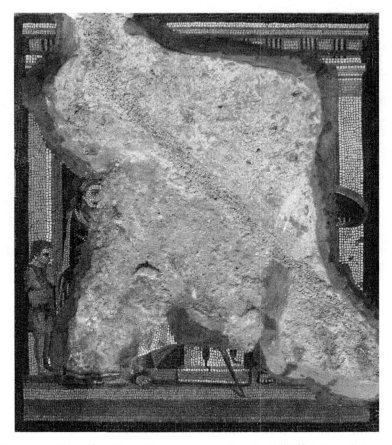

Figure 5.19 Mosaic from Pompeii, 1st century CE, Deposito dell'Ufficio Scavi di Pompeii
inv. 17735

misread as the trailing scarves that in iconography after the first century BCE
become the attributes of slaves). The leftmost character nevertheless has a
young man's mask and is labelled 'Lysias', which is certainly the name of a
free youth (and the name of one of the young men in our papyrus). 'Kleinias'
second from the right has displaced the piper.

The fact that archetypes of our Menandrian scenes were produced within
his lifetime does not in itself guarantee their reliability as evidence for performance. Nonetheless, that we are not dealing with a purely free artistic
imagination but with representations of scenes of dramatic performance is
obvious for a number of reasons. The placement of labels with play titles,
often with the name of Menander and even (at Mytilene and Daphne) act

Figure 5.20 Mosaic, Triclinium, House of Menander, Mytilene, fourth century CE

numbers is a not inconsiderable index of the artists' intention to show a comedy in performance. True, these were added to copies of the archetypes only at a late date, but these additions were not arbitrary: in the case of plays for which we have both texts and scenes, the scenes make an easy match with the openings (*Synaristôsai, Perikeiromenê*), climactic scenes (*Samia, Sikyônios*) and title-giving scenes (*Men at Arbitration, Theophoroumenê, Phasma*) known from our texts. From this it should be pretty clear that the artist(s) knew the plays and intended the images to evoke them. The artifacts display another remarkable feature that shows them to be very close, not just to the plays as known from our texts, but to the performance tradition. Careful study of the entire corpus of New Comic artifacts reveals a consistent and limited set of masks that substantially conforms to the types attested by Pollux in a catalogue that is certainly derived from sources quite unconnected with the iconographic tradition.[40]

The artifacts, in sum, retain a great deal of information about performance conditions from at least the time of Aristophanes to the time of

[40] *MNC* i, 6–51.

Menander. They are not photographs, but they nonetheless have far more than 'a loose connection' with theatre. Artists select what they think important for us to see and what they thought important was most often details that were likely to prompt recognition of a play. With few exceptions recognition was prompted by visual details, not verbal clues, and sometimes visual details that could only have been known through performance. It is only from the third century CE onwards, when the performance tradition dies out, that labels appear on the copies of Early Hellenistic scenes. By that time, we may suppose, the average viewer, without experience of a living tradition of comic performance, was in a poor position to play the guessing game. It is also in this late period we find that the greatest manipulation and corruption in copies of scenes from Menander, including such glaring errors as dressing a free youth in the costume of a slave or depicting comic actors with tragic masks. In broad outline the history of dramatic artifacts begins, grows and ends with the beginning, growth and decline of theatre (and not dramatic texts). Even in detail the contents of dramatic artifacts reflect the contents of performance and not the contents of texts. It is indeed true that the 'lives' of artifacts and texts never meet in any significant sense. But it is trivially true, because texts are irrelevant to this discussion, except as another important avenue of approach to the subject we approach through the artifacts, which is theatre performance.

Further reading

Green (1994) is highly readable and by far the most important introduction to the relationship of art and theatre in general. Chapters 1–6 and 9–10 of Csapo and Miller (2007) present current thinking about archaic vase painting that can be related to early drama or to performance genres that anticipated drama in some meaningful way. Taplin (1993) is the starting point for all modern discussions of the comic vases from the Greek West. Taplin (2007) is by far the fullest and best discussion of West Greek tragedy-related vase paintings. In the first two chapters of Csapo (2010b), I offer some reflections on the continuities and discontinuities between Attic and West Greek theatre-related vase painting. Revermann (2006a) contains the first systematic use of iconographic material for the study of stagecraft in Old Comedy.

Green (1985b) is the seminal work for understanding the background to Hellenistic and later theatre-related art. I follow Green's lead, farther than he himself is willing to go, in Csapo (1997) and in chapter 5 of Csapo (2010b).

Nervegna (2013) offers the fullest and best discussion of the iconography of Menander to date. Green and Handley (1995) and Moraw and Nölle (2002) contain beautifully illustrated and expert discussions of material evidence for drama (the latter contains a particularly notable chapter by Froning on masks and costumes).

PART II
Comic theatre

6

C.W. MARSHALL

Dramatic technique and Athenian comedy

A spectator attending a performance of a comedy at the City Dionysia or at the Lenaia came with a set of expectations about what he was going to see.[1] The expectations were conditioned by a variety of performance genres, but above all by theatre: previous comedies and tragedies helped shape these expectations and provided a framework within which a poet could experiment. This chapter will articulate some of the key elements of this set of expectations, and examine how it changed by the end of the classical period. In almost every case, however, conclusions need to be drawn from the limited selection of comedies surviving and from a handful of later discussions. This requires a 'best fit' approach, and new evidence could easily overturn established opinions, and opposing views could be found for almost any claim expressed. Though comedies had been part of the dramatic competitions since 486 at the Dionysia and *c.* 442 at the Lenaia,[2] a clear picture of the horizon of audience expectations only really begins with *Acharnians* in 425-L.[3]

The core of the ancient comic experience was the chorus, and the core of the comic chorus was the parabasis. At the Dionysia, twenty-four citizen performers would sing and dance, accompanied by a professional musician playing an *aulos* (a reeded double pipe); non-citizens could perform at the Lenaia. They would perform original and metrically complex songs, being

[1] While I believe that women were not excluded from attending theatrical performances (see e.g., Sourvinou-Inwood (2003) 177–84 and 194–6), none of what follows depends on that conclusion.

[2] Pickard-Cambridge (1988) 41–2, 71–4, 82–3. When the festival in which a play competed is known, it is indicated after the date with a D or L.

[3] The presence of classical wells and a road part of the way up the slope of the later *theatron* suggests that the size of the audience in the Theatre of Dionysus during the fifth century was much less than has been thought: Csapo (2007) and Goette (2007) suggest a capacity audience of 6000–7000, less than half that of the rebuilt Lycurgan theatre used by Menander.

lead in their movement by a *koryphaios* ('head speaker'). Songs were often strophic, composed in metrical pairs of *strophê* and *antistrophê* (turn and counterturn). The metrical equivalence likely also meant repeated melody and choreography, with the *strophê* indicating movement in one direction and the *antistrophê* repeating those movements in the reverse, though we do not know how rigidly such correspondences were maintained.[4] A group this large would dominate the visual field of the audience, and many titles of fifth-century comedies derive from the identity of the chorus. Unlike the straightforward alternation between choral and character parts which predominates in tragedy, 'Aristophanes had a number of devices at his disposal for articulating the structure of his plays, with varying degrees of clarity and emphasis, into parts which vary in length, independence, and importance.'[5] The chorus likely was reduced in size over the fourth century and came to have less to do with the main plot.[6] It nevertheless continues to be a meaningful musical presence, even though the precise nature of the songs has not survived, with the manuscripts for *Assembly Women*, *Wealth*, and Menander indicating where a song had once existed.[7]

While a spectator might expect several songs in a fifth-century comedy, the heart of a play was the parabasis.[8] The parabasis (literally a 'step aside') often presented direct audience address separate from the main plot of the play. In *Birds*, the chorus retains its avian identity, but more often it is abandoned altogether, in a narrative hiatus. The structure of the parabasis in Aristophanes seems rigid:

(1) *kommation* ('little song'), a brief introduction sung by the chorus or the *koryphaios*;

(2) the anapaests, pointed advice from the *koryphaios* in a regular stichic metre (often anapaestic tetrameter, though other metres are attested);[9]

(3) *pnigos* (the 'choker'), a climax to the anapaests delivered by the *koryphaios*, apparently recited in a single breath as a showpiece;

(4) the ode, a strophe sung by the chorus;

---

[4] This suggestive idea is developed by Wiles (1997) 87–113.   [5] Poe (1999) 194.

[6] Hunter (1979) presents a useful overview of the fourth-century chorus. Though there is no certain evidence that the chorus size was reduced in Athens, the development of the shape of the performance space required (and perhaps caused) a different conception of the use of dramatic space; the most likely solution is a smaller chorus, perhaps of seven or eight, as attested later still at Delphi (see Sifakis (1971a) 418 and 420).

[7] Hunter (1979); Rothwell (1995); Lape (2006).

[8] Sifakis (1971a); Bowie (1982); Hubbard (1991); Imperio (2004a).

[9] It is useful to distinguish stichic metres, where the metrical form repeats from one line to the next (which were spoken or perhaps chanted), from so-called lyric metres, where each line might be metrically distinct, and which were sung in accompaniment to the *aulos*.

(5) the *epirrhêma* ('words added after'), chanted by the *koryphaios* (typically sixteen or twenty lines, in trochaic tetrameter);

(6) the antode, the antistrophe to the ode, sung by the chorus;

(7) the *antepirrhêma*, metrically corresponding to the *epirrhêma* and chanted by the *koryphaios*.

Even when not all of these elements are present (*Clouds* has no *pnigos* (3); *Peace* no *epirrhêmata* (5 and 7); *Women at the Thesmophoria* no odes (4 and 6), *Frogs* nothing before the ode (1, 2, 3)), the order is constant and consequently seems directed at deeply held audience expectations. Other playwrights may not have adhered so strictly,[10] and there was evidently a dissolution of the parabasis in the fourth century (*Assembly Women* and *Wealth* have no parabasis), but this constitutes the core of Aristophanic comedy. The last four items (4–7) may be called an 'epirrhematic syzygy', and *Knights*, *Peace* and *Birds* contain a second parabasis consisting of just these elements (*Clouds* and *Wasps* possess wilder variants).[11] While the parabasis interrupts the plot, it remains part of the performance of the play, which continues without interval.

The chorus' initial entry is also clearly marked for an audience.[12] The *parodos* in Aristophanes follows a spoken (or mostly spoken; see *Women at the Thesmophoria*) introductory scene (prologue) of 200–300 lines. The normal metre for spoken dialogue is the iambic trimeter. Even here, though, variations are possible, and *Frogs* apparently provides *parodoi* for both choral identities (frogs at 209, which proves to be a false lead, and initiates at 323). These songs typically have responsive elements (i.e. strophic pairs), can involve characters, and again provide visual and musical articulation of the play's structure.[13]

A freer syzygy structure also patterns other scenes within the plays, and it seems likely that ancient audiences would perceive pairs of songs and pairs of either stichic speeches (producing an epirrhematic syzygy) or iambic exchanges (producing an iambic syzygy) as meaningful units in themselves; recognizing this is a significant achievement of modern metrical scholarship.[14] Such structures can be elaborated with the insertion of a short passage of introduction, conclusion (a *sphragis*), encouragement (a *katakaleusmos*), a *pnigos*, etc. Most Aristophanic plays offer an *agôn* ('contest'; pl. *agônes*), in which opposing parties debate a key theme of the play

---

[10] Storey (2003) 356–62.   [11] Totaro (2000).

[12] Hamilton (1991) 349. See also Zimmermann (1984).

[13] Aristotle mentions both *parodos* and parabasis when describing the structure of Old Comedy (*Poet.* 1449b 4, *EN* 4.2 1123a 23, *Rhet.* 1415a 9–22).

[14] Sifakis (1992) 123 n. 5; Poe (1999) 191.

in epirrhematic form.[15] These are not ancient terms, however, and it is the
larger structure that the audience would perceive as meaningful. It is also
unwise to be too prescriptive on matters of form, since our evidence comes
from a single playwright whose practice varies significantly over his career.
We simply cannot say what is representative for the genre as a whole. Further, some iambic scenes are not patterned in pairs, and they evidently stand
alone as dramatic units.

Some clarity can perhaps be gained from Aristophanes' *Wasps* (422-L),
which can serve as an ongoing example later in this chapter as well.[16]

a. 1–229   Iambic scene – the Prologue.
b. 230–316   Parodos. The entry song uses both strophic and non-strophic
              elements, involving both chorus and characters.
c. 317–525   Two epirrhematic syzygies. These prepare for the formal debate – a
              'proagon'.
d. 526–727   Epirrhematic syzygy. The same pattern recurs a third time, but now
              at greater length as Philocleon and Bdelycleon debate in the *agôn*.
e. 728–1008   Iambic scenes. These two spoken scenes are each preceded with a
              lyric component, and this creates the feel of a syzygy and unites the
              two scenes.
f. 1009–1121 The parabasis, which includes a detailed account of Aristophanes'
              early career.
g. 1122–1264 Iambic scene. This is another spoken scene, which prepares for the
              final movement of the play.
h. 1265–1291 The second parabasis.
i. 1292–1537 Iambic scenes. These two scenes are separated by a choral song (a
              stasimon) at 1450–73, which marks the final iambic section
              (1474–1537) as the *exodos*.

Even here, the structure is complex and the terminology generally unhelpful. Yet the general plot can be articulated through these units. Before the
chorus arrives, the audience meets Philocleon, who is addicted to jury duty
and who has been locked in his house by his son and slaves (a.). Following the choral entry, Philocleon tries to escape his captivity and Bdelycleon
agrees to a debate (c.). Following the debate (d.), preparations are made to
allow Philocleon to serve as a juror in a trial at home, and the trial takes
place (e.). Following the parabasis, Bdelycleon prepares to take an apparently rehabilitated Philocleon to a symposium (g.). Following the second
parabasis, Philocleon returns from the party with a female piper (*aulêtris*),
whereupon he dances and is generally abusive (i.). Each of these units

[15] Gelzer (1960); and see Zieliński (1885).
[16] MacDowell (1971) and Sommerstein (1983) and (2001) 264–72 offer commentaries in
English on the play.

(a, c, d, e, g, i) is roughly the same size (143–279 lines, with an average length of 218) and each is clearly marked for the audience by the dramatic structure of the play as it reveals itself in performance. The remaining elements (b, f, h) are the distinct choral units of the *parodos*, parabasis and second parabasis. Thematic links (e.g. the role of sickness and disease) help unify the overall play.[17]

The structure of Old Comedy is not straightforward, and every play is unique. Even in general outline, one can see the pressures for streamlining this traditional form. The apparent elimination of the parabasis (the beginning of which is already seen in *Frogs* 405-L) and the subsequent reduction of the chorus lead to a new standard of four act-dividing songs, which sets the pattern for five acts in Western theatre. While some have seen the roots of a five-act structure in Old Comedy, this will not have been perceptible to an audience.[18] In Menander, one recurrent plot pattern has the principal intrigue resolved by the end of act four, with the final act introducing and resolving a second problem in much shorter compass.[19] Even with a reduced chorus, music remains important to Menander, though it has left a smaller impact on the written scripts. The prominence of the *aulos*-player at the end of *Dyscolus* (316-L) is part of this larger pattern foregrounding music in comedy.[20]

The performance space for comedy was comparatively bare. The *orchêstra* was backed with a wooden stage building, or *skênê*, painted to look like a more permanent construction. Whatever its precise shape,[21] the entire performance space and the actors' movements upon it form a unified entity that can be examined.[22] There may have been a few low steps leading to the front of the *skênê*, but performers could freely travel over the entire performance area. Over the course of the fourth century, this wooden area was raised, and eventually there was a clear separation from the *orchêstra* and what was now the stage. The *skênê* roof extends the performance space vertically, and Old Comedy made use of devices for 'special effects' that had been established

---

[17] Banks (1980); Sidwell (1990).

[18] Hamilton (1991), building on others, offers a model whereby the five-act structure of New Comedy finds its antecedents in Old Comedy. This may reflect the historical development, but it diminishes the centrality of the chorus to the experience of a comedy by the audience. Sifakis (1992) offers a folktale-based narrative structure, which also downplays the central patterning function of the chorus.

[19] Hunter (1985) 40–2.   [20] See also Taplin (1993) 105–10.

[21] The shape of the *orchêstra* in the fifth century is not known: Scullion (1994) 38–41 and Wiles (1997) 23–62 argue for a circular shape, Goette (1995) 22–30 for a rectangular (or trapezoidal) shape. As the performance space changes in the fourth century, different performance dynamics emerge, and Menander's dramatic action can often be seen to be shaped by the long and narrow stage used at the time (see e.g., Arnott (2000a) 121).

[22] von Möllendorff (1995) 112–50; Revermann (2006a) 107–45.

in tragedy: the *mêchanê* and the *ekkyklêma*.[23] Aristophanes' metatheatrical jokes provide the technical vocabulary used in the theatre for these
devices: the crane operator is the *mêchanopoios* (*Peace* 174, fr. 160) and
characters are told to 'have themselves rolled out' on the platform used to
reveal interior scenes (e.g. *Acharnians* 408f.). Comedy uses these devices to
accomplish fantastic visual feats (flying a dung beetle to Olympus in *Peace*,
flying the rainbow goddess Iris in *Birds*, revealing the inside of the tragedian
Euripides' house in *Acharnians*), but it is always at least implicitly invoking tragic precedent. Significantly, the *mêchanê* seems only to be available
at the Dionysia: this supports the conclusion formed on other grounds of
assigning *Lysistrata* to 411-L and *Women at the Thesmophoria* to 411-D,
and perhaps supports the possibility that the Lenaia was not celebrated at
the Theatre of Dionysus in Athens, but elsewhere, next to the Dionysion in
Limnais.[24]

Specific controversies concerning the stage space remain insoluble with
present evidence, and opinions are sharply divided. No fifth-century comedy (or tragedy for that matter) requires more than a single, central *skênê*
door, though a raised *skênê* with three doors was in place by the Lycurgan
reconstruction and expansion of the Theatre of Dionysus in the third quarter of the fourth century.[25] This development may have coincided with the
separation of *skênê* from *orchêstra*, and the domestic plots of New Comedy,
firmly localized on a city street, make clear use of the three doorways. While
the easy use of multiple doors in later comedy is evident (even if Menander seems to prefer using only two), there would be a surprising number
of missed opportunities for comedy if these resources had been available
to Aristophanes. It is simpler to assume that, when desired, small super-
structures could be attached to the *skênê* somehow to create, for example,
windows (in *Assembly Women*) or a chimney (at *Wasps* 143–51).[26] There is
no clear evidence for painted panels or the use of set dressing (bushes for an
outdoor location in *Birds*, for example), and it seems probable that this was

---

[23] Dearden (1976) 50–85; Newiger (1989); Russo (1994) 50–8.

[24] On the *mêchanê*, see Russo (1994) 3. On the plays of 411, see Austin and Olson (2004)
xli–xliv. Slater (1986) argues for the Lenaian theatre, Scullion (1994) 52–65 against.

[25] Dale (1969) 103–18 (orig. 1957), *contra* Dover (1966a). The best fifth-century evidence
for three *skênê* doors is Eupolis fr. 48 (*Autolykos*, a play known to exist in two
versions): 'They live here [*enthad*'] in three shacks, each one having his own home'
(Storey (2003) 10, and see 93–4). If it were known that this were from a prologue
establishing the stage locale, three doors would seem guaranteed by the 410s; other
interpretations remain possible, however.

[26] Sommerstein (1998) 28–30 and 214 discusses windows, while also arguing for three
skênê doors; MacDowell (1971) 150–2 discusses the chimney.

left to the audience's imagination. *Wasps* again provides an exception, since evidently a net of some kind was visible over the *skênê* (131–2, 164, 367–8). When an altar was needed either the altar to Dionysus in the *orchêstra* (the *thymêlê*) or some temporary structure at a central location could be employed. In general, we should resist assumptions of theatrical naturalism: the outdoor, naturally lit performance space did not lend itself to the literalistic representation of every detail. While the Menandrean stage did tend towards creating a unity of place, there was no corresponding concern to match time in the dramatic world with the real time experienced by the audience: a character can run from Athens to Sparta and back in minutes, if needed (*Acharnians* 134–75).[27]

In the fifth century, plots typically revolve around a single hero, whose movements around the performance area can allow a dizzying range of locations to be represented on the bare stage.[28] The audience accepts that the character is where he says he is – 'ready to jump from one happy improvisation to the next'[29] – and the *skênê* can represent multiple locations over the course of the play, even if changes are rare following the *parodos*.[30] This flexibility of stage space is usual: *Wasps* is the only Aristophanic comedy where the *skênê* door represents the same location throughout the play, and the use of stage space, particularly the spatial tension localized on the *skênê* door, is 'recognizably congruent with tragic stagecraft'.[31] A century later, there is a much fuller sense of the stage world as independent of any character's implicit authorial fiat: 'Menander's characters live vastly more complicated lives.'[32] The New Comic stage, without the *orchêstra*, creates a long and narrow performance area that also shapes performance choices.[33] While it is meaningful to discuss the existence of dramatic illusion in the presentation of the narrative, it can be violated at any point for the sake of a joke and instantly reasserted, which creates an air of contagious ribaldry.[34]

---

[27] Lowe (1988) 40f.; Arnott (1987).　　[28] Lowe (1988) 38–40; Lanza (2000).
[29] Dale (1969) 109.
[30] Thiercy (2000). Cf. Lowe (2006) 52: 'the prologue is a place where space is still in the process of being created'.
[31] Lowe (2006) 51, and see 49–51; 'Aristophanes shares with tragedy a strong sense of the stage door as a boundary between symbolically-opposed onstage and offstage worlds' (63).
[32] Lowe (1987) 134: 'In the *Dyskolos*, up to ten offstage locations can be occupied at any time... Some of these invisible lines of continuity are simply there to serve the cumulative texture of naturalism, the illusion of a world that continues to exist outside the fragment made visible in the theatre.'
[33] Arnott (2000c).
[34] Lowe (1988) 43f.; Poe (2000) 276–80; and see Muecke (1977); Chapman (1983); Taplin (1986); Slater (1995).

All comedies were written, in the first instance, for performance in competition, and the audience was alert to the judges' decisions, with a prize being
awarded for both the play (awarded to the *chorêgos*, or 'producer') and the
lead actor (who represents the small troupe paid for by the polis).[35] Plays
were either presented all on the same day (as at the Lenaia, and typically
at the Dionysia) or spread over three days, with a comedy following each
tragic tetralogy (as may have occurred during the Peloponnesian War).[36]
Comedies were sumptuous affairs, and there are many indications that the
chorêgos was expected to provide visual opulence.[37] The state determined
a *chorêgos* for each play, who was responsible for many of the financial
commitments.[38] As part of a catalogue of such expenditures, the speaker of
Lysias 21.3 boasts that he paid 16 minas (1,600 drachmas) for the victorious
comedy of Cephisodorus (about whom very little survives) at 402-D, including the dedication costs associated with the victory. While this is less than the
amount he claims to have paid supporting productions through other liturgies, this large sum probably reflects expenses for costumes, props, extras
and the additional costs associated with training a larger chorus. When
jokes are made about the apparent poverty of costuming (as at *Frogs* 404–
13), this is less likely to reflect reduced visual richness and more likely a
self-referential joke given that this is the chorus' second costume, having
appeared as frogs a few minutes before.[39]

Whereas it seems to have been usual for tragic playwrights to direct their
own work, this is not so for comedy. Comic playwrights often staged
plays 'through' a *didaskalos* ('director'): Aristophanes used Callistratus,
Philonides and his son Araros; Eupolis used Demostratus and Eubulus used
Philippus, another son of Aristophanes.[40] Rather than conceive of this as
a process of dramatic apprenticeship, it is better to see comic playwrights
employing specialists capable of maximizing the impact of humour in performance. Philonides directed Aristophanes' *Wasps* (422-L), *Amphiaraus*
(414-L) and *Frogs* (405-L), for example, and victories would be registered
in the name of the director.[41] Following the initial performance, plays could

---

[35] Marshall and van Willigenburg (2004). Prizes for actors were established in 449 for the
Dionysia and *c.* 440 at the Lenaia (Pickard-Cambridge (1988) 93).

[36] Storey (2002).   [37] Lowe (1988) 44–6.

[38] On the division between public and private expenditures, and a rough tally of the (high)
costs of the Dionysia *c.* 415, see Wilson (2008).

[39] Marshall (1996), answering Allison (1983).

[40] Pickard-Cambridge (1988) 84–6; MacDowell (1982); Hunter (1983) 13–16.

[41] For *Wasps*, see Slater (2002) 111f.; Sommerstein (2001) 264. See also Henderson
(2007) T23. Philonides may have been victorious, apparently as director and comic
poet, at 410-D, if he is the *Phil* [at *IG* 2².2325.64. The victory monument of Socrates of
Anagyrous (*IG* I³ 969 [=*SEG* 23 (1968) 102]) celebrates the tragedian Euripides not as

be reperformed in Athens or elsewhere. Some plays were revised (or their titles reused for other dramas) and entered again in competition; *Frogs* was reperformed in 404, evidently as an encore outside of competition; and there are indications that Athenian comedy was performed in major centres in South Italy from *c.* 400 onwards.[42] These reperformances could have used altered scripts, and a gap clearly existed between the performance and what happened to survive on papyrus.[43] An Athenian vase likely from the 410s presents a clearly theatrical scene: two actors dressed as fighting cocks face each other, with an elaborately-robed *aulos*-player standing between them.[44] The actors wear apparently identical costumes with erect phalluses, though their postures differ slightly. This is certainly a representation of Old Comedy, and some have wanted to see it depicting an extant Aristophanic play. If it does depict a play we have (and of course it need not do so), it seems more likely to represent the original production of *Clouds* (423-D), in which the *agôn* seems to have been performed by two fighting cocks emerging from cages, than it does to the chorus of (a reperformed?) *Birds* (414-D), where the extant text presents a female chorus costumed individually.[45]

All performers (choristers, actors and extras) were masked. Old Comedy delighted in the human body, and emphasis is regularly placed on the grotesque: actors wore full-head masks with exaggerated expressions and usually a padded body suit that gave the impression of nudity, with distended buttocks, bellies and chest, and (for male characters) an oversized limp phallus, which could at times be used as a prop by other characters (as at *Wasps* 1341–4).[46] This corresponds closely to what one sees in many South Italian red-figure vases depicting comic scenes, at least some of which represent exported performances of Old Comedy in the fourth century.[47] Through the fourth century, the element of the grotesque in Athenian comedy diminished,

---

poet but as *didaskalos* (Wilson (2000) 130–6). Even if the director wins the prize, it does not follow that the playwright was unimportant or unknown publicly.

[42] Butrica (2001) 51–62; Sommerstein (1993); Taplin (1993).

[43] Revermann (2006a) 66–95.

[44] This vase, the so-called 'Getty Birds' has been repatriated to Italy; its former catalogue number is Malibu, J. Paul Getty Museum 82.AE.83.

[45] *Birds*: Green (1985a), (1991a) 30; Taplin (1993) 101–4. *Clouds*: Taplin (1987) and Csapo (1993a). If correct, the vase would reveal that the *agôn* originally was musical, at least in part – a fact otherwise unknown. A newly discovered Attic pelike (= Figure 8 in Csapo, Chapter 5), painted by another artist, depicts a single fighting cock using identical iconography. This persuades Csapo (2010b) 9–12 to see both vases as depicting chorus members of an unknown comedy.

[46] von Möllendorff (1995) 150–222; Foley (2000); Revermann (2006a) 145–59. Against the possibility that an erect phallus was used for the rejuvenated Philocleon late in the play, see MacCary (1979).

[47] Taplin (1993); Piqueux (2006).

so that by Menander's time there may not have been much to distinguish comic young men from tragic ones.[48] Masks primarily aided identification of characters, and in exaggerated style connoted age and sex.[49] The recurrent theme throughout classical comedy of inter-generational conflict is thereby reinforced visually. In addition, animal choruses or choruses of personifications could also be depicted (*Goats, Wild Beasts, Cities, Seasons,* and *Islands* exist among titles of fragmentary plays). Each character had a unique, iconic mask, and by manipulating a few variables the mask-maker (*skeuopoios: Knights* 232) could create caricatures of prominent Athenians who might be in the audience (as Socrates was during *Clouds,* according to Aelian *VH* 2.13).

On top of the body suit, which (with a detachable phallus) apparently served for most characters of either sex, actors would wear costumes that reflected contemporary dress. Layering costumes on top of each other allowed disguise and impersonation within the dramatic world, while always emphasizing theatrical artifice to the audience: Dionysus opens *Frogs* wearing a grotesque body suit, on top of which is an effeminate saffron gown (*krokôtos,* likely worn over a *chitôn,* which itself was likely enough to identify Dionysus), on top of which is a disguise consisting of a lionskin and (oversized?) club.[50] The audience sees all these layers, and Dionysus' mask, and is expected to possess the competence to register and integrate these discrete elements into a composite, of a comic Dionysus impersonating Heracles. Actors would play multiple roles, changing mask and costume and (likely) vocal characteristics to assume a new part. As part of leveling the playing field for competition, the number of speaking actors was fixed at three (as with tragedy) or four.[51] In addition to the chorus and actors, non-speaking performers, all in lavish costumes, filled the stage with additional bodies. Comedy revels in such materiality, and these individuals and the many stage props (which often were oversized for the large outdoor performance space) could clutter the stage with delightful distorted representations of the everyday.[52]

---

[48] Green (2006). On the relationship between mask and character in Menander, see MacCary (1969), (1970), (1971), (1972); Brown (1987); and especially Wiles (1991).
[49] Marshall (1999).   [50] Stone (1981); Muecke (1982a); Compton-Engle (2003).
[51] Marshall (1997) and (2013) argues for three; MacDowell (1995) for four. Less persuasive is the possibility of 'apprentice actors' used to speak a single line or two. The adaptation of texts following their initial performance for non-competitive contexts means that certainty will always be impossible.
[52] English (2000) and (2005) argues for a reduction of props over Aristophanes' career, but inadequately distinguishes between props, elements of costume and elements of set. See Poe (2000) 283–7, and, on the use of extras for carrying props, 272–6 and 292–5.

Each of these theatrical elements could be manipulated to become a source of humour. Consider the trial in *Wasps* 891–1008, an iambic scene that appears immediately before the delayed parabasis, and so is placed prominently in the comedy's structure.[53] Three speaking actors represent Philocleon, the jury-addicted old man, Bedelycleon, his son who is staging a domestic trial as part of his father's therapy, and an anthropomorphic dog, who will serve as a witness. Each actor plays a coded representation of Cleon, Athens' most notorious politician at the time: 'Love-Cleon', 'Loathe-Cleon' and the Dog (*Kuôn* for *Kleôn*, both from the deme of Cydathenaeum) who indicts another dog, Labes (for Laches, another politician: 895–97). However the dog was represented, any or all of these masks might be marked with Cleon's distinctive eyebrows, identifying the object of mockery without explicitly using his name. Each of the twenty-four old Athenian jurors in the chorus wears a wasp costume that somehow equates the wasps' stingers with the comic phallus. The trial conforms to audience expectations of Athenian juridical practice, humorously adapted from the civic to the domestic context. The use of space, as performers spread throughout the playing area (including the *orchêstra*) would visually reinforce the spatial relationships familiar to many in the audience from the actual courts. Props support this identification: a rooster (934), a chamber pot (corresponding to the water clock used to time courtroom speeches, and into which Philocleon mimes urination: 935–41),[54] and two large ladles, which serve as voting urns (852–5, 986–8). Reference at 820 to a makeshift version of the shrine of Lycus at the court could point to the *thymêlê*, rupturing the dramatic illusion for the momentary jest, or to some comically inappropriate household item that served as its stand-in. After initial barks (903), the Dog, surprisingly, begins to speak (907–30). Extras (*mutae personae*) present a parade of at least seven kitchen implements (936–9), depicted either as large props being carried by servants or (somehow) as unique personifications of a Bowl, Pestle, Cheesegrater, etc.[55] The defendant Labes is summoned, played by another extra, and who, since he is not one of the actors being judged and is forbidden from speaking, silently yields the floor to Bdelycleon (943–5, 949–51). Similarly, the Cheesegrater takes the stand, but Bdelycleon interprets whatever silent gestures it makes (962–6). To elicit pity from the jury, his puppies appear on stage (emerging from the *skênê*, evidently these child actors were also clothed in canine costumes), evoking both the transparent

[53] Reckford (1987) 251–62; Storey (1995) 16–19; MacDowell (1995) 165–70.
[54] See also 856–9. Reckford (1987) 259 suggests that the stage business at 995 would make this the natural water source to throw on Philocleon.
[55] MacDowell (1995) 166 n. 24.

tactics of the contemporary courtroom and the pathetic depiction of children in tragedy (975–8). When Bdelycleon casts the only vote, he is tricked into placing his pebble into the wrong ladle and consequently Labes is acquitted (986–94).

So many specifics of a scene like this are uncertain. What is known, though, is that the playwright expected at least part of his audience to be able to make sense of all the nuances, as well as to appreciate the poetry and music, the political satire and his conscious (if deliberately unconvincing) distancing gestures to avoid the appearance of personal attack. Though different spectators might privilege different elements of the variegated comic tapestry, all sources of humour combine to create the overall effect. Unlike tragedy, individual entrances and exits of characters do not articulate the advancement of the plot or the play's basic structure. The combination of slapstick, verbal humour and prop comedy clearly add to the enjoyment of the situation, even if we are not in a position today to describe with archaeological precision how they did so. In part because of the involvement with the playwright in the performance, stage directions were not written in scripts,[56] and we must work imaginatively to envisage the ancient performance, considering tempo and pacing, delivery, gestures, blocking, audience encouragement, the presence of judges and the festival atmosphere generally.

Many questions remain, and *Wasps* provides a host of difficulties that show the limits to our understanding of the play. A partial list demonstrates how much of classical comedy was bound up in performance and how many specific decisions were associated with dramatic technique. Leaving aside ordinary movements associated with blocking and vocal delivery and the many difficulties already discussed with the trial scene, we might note the following ten problems:

(1) Three characters are sleeping in the performance area as the play begins. How was this pre-set accomplished? How long had the actors been there? How does an actor mime sleeping when the eyes of the mask remain always open?

(2) At 58–9, reference is made to slaves throwing nuts to the audience as an effort to win their favour. How often did this occur? Can the insistent statement that it did not happen in this play serve as evidence to suggest that it did?

(3) At 177–97, Philocleon appears on the underside of a donkey. Was this a pantomime donkey, performed by two actors, or a static prop, pulled out perhaps on the *ekkyklêma*? The echoes of Odysseus leaving

---

[56] Revermann (2006a) 320–5.

the Cyclops' cave are reinforced regardless, but which way does the donkey face? If it is revealed with its rear end stubbornly pointed out, Philocleon's head would be suboptimally placed.[57]

(4) Who plays the boy who enters with the chorus and sings part of the *parodos* in lyric dialogue with the *koryphaios*, beginning at 248: an actor, an extra, a chorister, an actual youth? Is he alone, or were there others, and if so how many?

(5) Many of the play's opening scenes present Philocleon attempting to escape onto the stage. The separate attempts open themselves to a number of possible stagings. What does the audience see, for instance, at 379–99, when Philocleon is apparently grappling with a rope, perhaps from the *skênê* roof?[58]

(6) At 398–9, Bdelycleon orders a slave to beat his father with a sacred wreath. Is this an instance of (fictional) father-beating, an extreme part of the physical violence that is typical in comedy, or is the action somehow avoided?[59]

(7) At 456–60, Bdelycleon and Xanthias treat the chorus as they would wasps, attempting to smoke them away. How much smoke did their prop censer make in the outdoor theatre space? What does this mean for the visual reinforcement of the jurors-as-wasps conceit that runs through the play? Did the chorus respond with mimetic swarming behaviour?

(8) At 1122–68, Philocleon dresses himself for the coming symposium in a heavy wool cloak and Laconian shoes. Layering costume in this way evokes other comic scenes of disguise, but does it call attention to the artificiality of Philocleon's rehabilitation? Clothes make the man, in this case, and point to the performative nature of social institutions in real life, but are we to see Philocleon here as an actor? And does the audience perceive this whole scene (1122–264) as actually taking place indoors?[60]

(9) At 1341–86, is the *aulêtris* Dardanis played by a real woman (a non-citizen or slave hetaira, likely, in a body stocking to simulate nudity) or by a man in a padded costume? To what extent is this scene anticipated with earlier images of sexual excitement?[61]

(10) At 1500–37, who played the sons of Carcinus, and to what extent were their movements crab-like? How did this final dance relate to the previous dances foregrounded in the play?[62]

[57] Sommerstein (2001) 269; MacDowell (1988) 5f.; Bowie (1990) 33.
[58] MacDowell (1988) 5; Poe (2000) 280–2.   [59] Lowe (1988) 46f.; Poe (2000) 271.
[60] Purves (1995) 17; Poe (2000) 266f., 271.   [61] Bowie (1990).
[62] Borthwick (1968); Vaio (1971) 347–51; MacDowell (1971) 326–32; MacCary (1979).

Other plays would produce other problems, but, whatever the answer to individual questions, the ancient *didaskalos* will have made choices for each of them, and the answer would be instantly comprehensible to the original audience.

Menander demonstrates that a similar range of performance activity was possible on the New Comic stage. Long narrative prologues from human or divine characters evidently develop from Euripidean tragedy, which can also serve as an intertext patterning events.[63] Role-sharing, integration of the *aulos*-player and the chorus into the dramatic narrative, choral identity, and (possibly) metatheatrical reference to masks as seen in *Dyscolus*, for example, show affinities with Aristophanes, though to a lesser extent.[64] Comic routines apparently developed between the stock character of the *mageiros* (a sacrificial butcher and cook) and sheep (*Dyscolus* 393 and *Samia* 399) and the domestic plots could require prop babies (e.g., *Men at Arbitration* 302). Visual surprises are regular: *Perikeiromenê* contains a delayed prologue by a personified Failed Recognition (*agnoia*), which follows some short scenes in which we meet the eponymous woman whose hair has been cut short, requiring a specialized mask.

A short extant passage from Menander's *Perinthia* (*POxy* 855) points the way towards the exuberant slapstick of Roman New Comedy (even though this scene was not preserved when Terence adapted *Perinthia* for his play, *Andria*). The conventionally named slave Daos has sought sanctuary at the stage altar, where he flees his master's wrath. The setting therefore involves doorways to the house of Laches (Daos' master) and to the temple of some god. Though it would be impious to force Daos from his refuge, Laches plans to smoke him out, making him uncomfortable enough that he leaves on his own. Laches, carrying a lit torch (2–4), leads four slaves carrying firewood from his house (1f., 7–10). Daos' panic increases when Laches quotes Daos' own words from earlier in the play back at him (11–16; cf. fr. 3); this suggests that there had been an eavesdropping scene in which Laches had heard Daos boast (or that Daos has been ratted out by a fellow slave). Spoken lines make it clear that at least two of the three non-speaking slaves ignore Daos' pleas for help (4–6), and that Daos' fear-induced bowel movements reduce the appeal of staying on the altar (17f.). Laches' command to 'Light the fire!' (20) raises the stakes of the slave's predicament further. The rhythm and pacing of the delivery in this scene, as Daos discovers his schemes have been less successful than he has imagined, demonstrate some of the extremes of stage action evident in the surviving fragments of Greek New Comedy. While this scene is unusual within the surviving Menander

[63] See Porter (1999–2000).　[64] Marshall (2002).

fragments, the number of terracotta figurines depicting comic slaves sitting on an altar demonstrates the high frequency of this stock scene, with the use of fire serving as a conventional solution to a recurrent dramatic situation.

So much of the meaning that resides in performance is simply not recoverable. While words often reinforce stage action, it is the visual that dominates the interpretative frame given to the audience.[65] Conclusions about pace, delivery, the actor's voice, the quality and scope of gestures and movements, melody, and (perhaps most crucially) comic timing must derive from analogy and remain painfully elusive. Comedy was meant to be interpreted by an audience in performance and, even with the broad strokes that surviving evidence requires us to use, it is possible to perceive how much depth is provided by dramatic technique. Plays must be understood in terms of the theatre for which they were produced and, even if the picture remains frustratingly incomplete, what evidence there is must become the essential anchor for any literary interpretation.

Comedy is a genre aware of its theatricality, and, even when audience tastes no longer favoured the outrageous utopic fantasies of the fifth century, the physical awareness – the tangibility of comedy – was always foregrounded. In different ways, Athenian comedy was always metatheatrical, and found new ways of demonstrating its debts and awareness of other theatrical genres and the process of theatre itself.[66] These debts were particularly to Athens' primary artistic form in the classical period, tragedy, and in time comedy came to be perceived as tragedy's opposite, even though the similarities between the two genres are often overstated.[67] Throughout the classical period, Athenian comedy created its meaning through a dizzying combination of words, music and performance. Audiences were expected to possess a sophisticated awareness of politics, previous poetry and the realities of theatrical production, and to be able to make wild imaginative leaps with allegory, metaphor and fantastic imagery. Dramatic meaning is created and reified through the play's spatial realization, both in Athenian competition and as an exportable cultural commodity.

Further reading

In addition to the works listed in the footnotes, the following are suggested as starting points for further reading. The standard account in English of the

---

[65] Lowe (1988) 49; Poe (2000) 259, 288–92.
[66] Muecke (1977); Dobrov (2001) 87–156 and 189–211; Slater (2002); Marshall (2002).
[67] See Silk (2000a) 42–97 and Lowe (2006); Taplin (1986) argues for a clear separation between the genres, a notion challenged by Ruffell (2008), Foley (2008), and Griffith (2008).

structure of Old Comedy remains Pickard-Cambridge and Webster (1962) 194–229, which consolidates the ground-breaking work of Zieliński (1885) and Mazon (1904). Storey (2003) 348–66 provides a model for applying this to a fragmentary playwright, building on Whittaker (1935). Neither Dearden (1976) nor McLeish (1980) is completely reliable for matters of production, and the cautious and encompassing Pickard-Cambridge (1988, most of which dates to the revisions done in 1968) as well as Csapo (2010c) are the best starting points for many issues concerning theatrical production in Athens. Lowe (1988), Poe (2000) and Csapo (2010a) offer essential statements on how Old Comedy creates meaning visually. Revermann (2006a) provides important needed methodological discussions and a detailed examination of *Clouds*, *Lysistrata* and *Wealth*, and more integrative work like this is needed. Russo (1994) presents some eccentric views but always keeps performance at the forefront of his interpretations. Wiles (1991) offers an invaluable structuralist understanding of Menander's characters. Frost (1988) details character entries and exits in Menander, but does not engage with larger issues of performance. Green (1989), (1995 [1998]), and (2008) offer comprehensive bibliographies on theatre production in antiquity, and has sections on Greek comedy, which summarize the extensive material remains that depict comedy in the fifth and fourth centuries. These images (vases, mosaics, terracotta figurines, etc.) are catalogued by Trendall (1967) as well as Webster (1978) and (1995).

7

IAN RUFFELL

Character types

In a famous fragment of Antiphanes' *Poetry* (fr. 189), a character compares the resources available to tragedy and comedy in terms of inherited characters and stories. Mention Oedipus and the audience knows what will happen to him and who the other main characters are; comedy needs to invent everything – names, back-story, situation, crisis. 'If some Chremes or Pheidon leaves any one of these out, he's whistled off stage' (20f.). The main focus here is plot, but embedded in this are claims about the use of recurring characters, the audience's knowledge of those characters, their stories and associations. Comedy supposedly lacks these advantages and is forced to rely on its own devices. This is, at best, a half-truth. Middle Comedy, the period of Antiphanes, was a time when Greek comedy was increasingly rooted in typical or 'stock' characters – the use of Pheidon and Chremes as shorthand for comic characters is itself an indication.[1] The trend develops further into the strongly type-based drama of Menander and his contemporaries, where stock characters were married to a relatively circumscribed set of plots in which love and/or paternity were a central element, with the overcoming of personal and social barriers the main concern.[2] Such stock characters have been held to be either directly or indirectly, spiritually or actually, the ancestor of character types in one broad strand of popular Western comedy, through Roman comedy on into *commedia dell' arte* into (among other things) modern British pantomime and Punch and Judy shows (and other European puppet traditions). Analogies have also been drawn with domestic situation comedy on television.

---

[1] Chremes appears as early as Aristophanes' *Assembly Women*, with Chremylus in *Wealth*; Chremes is not in extant Greek New Comedy, but appears in four out of Terence's six reworkings of Greek originals (*Woman from Andros*, *The Self-Tormentor*, *Eunuch*, *Phormio*), and in all but one (*Eunuch*), the character is an old man. See also Horace, *Art of Poetry* 94. Strepsiades is son of Pheidon in *Clouds* 134. For Chremes and Pheidylus (for whom, see Philippides, *Ana* fr. 6.2) in similar generalizing terms, see Alciphron 4.2.5.

[2] On comic plots in this period, see Lowe (2000) 180–221.

The stock characters of comedy require, like the inherited stories of tragedy, a high degree of theatrical competence from the audience. The comic elements provide a different route to a similar set of theatrical advantages. The notion of a 'stock character' or 'character type' may combine up to four related elements: a restricted set of personality traits; a consistent social role (and/or profession); a restricted role within the fiction (plot function); and a name (or restricted set of names). These personal, social and fictional characteristics may be, and in the case of Greek comedy were, specifically signalled by visual cues: mask, above all, costume and props. In these terms, it is easy to overstate the rigidity of stock characters, even in New Comedy. In the crudest terms, the set of types available to the New Comic poet is much wider and less rigid than, say, that of *commedia dell'arte*.[3] The development of these comic types depended upon a hundred years of competitive pressures. Many can be traced back in some form to the fifth century, but earlier comedy had a wider set of comic and dramatic shorthands, some of which wholly or partly fell out of use or were replaced; in the fourth century, the trend was away from the more idiosyncratic characters of Old Comedy towards more generic, but grotesque, social figures and towards the more circumscribed range of plots.[4] One strand dealt with the seamy side of Athenian social life, one populated by expensive courtesans, money-grubbing spongers (flatterers and, later, parasites) and by cooks with a vastly overinflated sense of their own importance.[5] A vogue for mythological burlesque in the first half of the century was itself, when not out-and-out parody of tragedy, a collision of stock characters from one milieu (gods and heroes) with this underbelly of respectable society. Trends towards a more naturalistic presentation can already be seen in the course of the fourth century, before the final shift to the more naturalistic presentation and plots of New Comedy. The fathers and sons of New Comedy also emerge in this period, but in a broader form. An observation in an unknown play by Antiphanes gives the flavour:

[3] That is not to say that the variations achieved in the deployment of such types in *commedia* are not manifold. For useful comparisons, see Brown (1987) 186f. and Wiles (1991) 121–8.
[4] For Middle Comedy, see Arnott (1972); Webster (1970a) 37–97; Nesselrath (1990), (1993), (1995), (1997); and Sidwell, chapter 3.
[5] On courtesans, see Henry (1985); flatterers Ribbeck (1883); Arnott (1968); Brown (1992); and cooks Dohm (1964); Dobrov (2002). On food in comedy, see generally, Wilkins (2000). The development of a roster of courtesan masks and of cook masks dates to Middle Comedy: Webster and Green (1978) types V, W, X, XA, XB, XC, XD for courtesans; P and (less conclusively) PP for cooks.

No old man has yet devoured his patrimony,
nor has he wasted it stupidly either, nor freed
a prostitute, nor laid himself open to a lawsuit by breaking down a door.
In this way old age is sensible but it doesn't have a good time.

Antiphanes, unknown play fr. 236

At all periods, too, theatrical demands are married to an element of social stereotyping, more obvious in Old Comedy, but perhaps more pernicious in New. This chapter will explore the nature and development of these comic shorthands, their role in comic plot and motivation, and their relationship to comic chcaraterization more widely conceived.

Evidence and typologies

The case for seeing Middle and New Comedy in terms of strongly typed characters derives to a large extent from evidence external to the texts themselves. The grammarian Julius Pollux preserves a classification of forty-four masks for 'new comedy', probably going back to a Hellenistic source.[6] Many of these types were well attested in the fragments of Greek comedy preserved in Athenaeus and elsewhere, but before the recovery of Menander on papyrus evidence for the detailed handling of these characters derived largely from Roman comedy and its associated scholarship. The process of Roman adaptation is somewhat better, if still imperfectly, understood now and I will be leaving that out of the discussion here.[7] Further taxonomical sources have been adduced. Peripatetic ethical theory (especially the *Nicomachean Ethics* and Theophrastus' *Characters*) has been associated both with New Comedy and with Old Comedy, but although it is possible to see some Aristotelianism in Menander, it does not help to explain the character types;[8] still less does it explain Old Comedy, as I discuss further below. Some critics have

---

[6] Pollux, *Onomasticon* 4.143f. For a brief discussion of Pollux's sources and discussion of the typology, see Pickard-Cambridge (1988) 177–9, 223–31. Aristophanes of Byzantium wrote a treatise *On Masks* and is often cited as an ultimate (indirect) source (so Csapo and Slater (1995)393–402, who provide a useful translation of Pollux), but this is doubted by Pickard-Cambridge, followed by Webster *et al.* (1995) 6. Pollux also has a brief account of comic costume in a broader classification at 4.118–20, which is less helpful.

[7] Fundamental on Plautus is Fraenkel (2007). The process can be observed directly in two places: parallel fragments of Caecilius Statius' adaptation of Menander's *Necklace* preserved by Aulus Gellius (for some discussion, see Ruffell (2010), with bibliography) and the overlap of Menander's *Dis Exapatôn* with Plautus' *Bacchides*: see Handley (1968), (1997); Bain (1979); Anderson (1993) 3–29 and Fontaine, Chapter 21.

[8] The biographic tradition which made Menander a pupil of Aristotle (Diogenes Laertius 5.36) is influential here.

also sought to flesh out Pollux's comments with Hellenistic physiognomic works, but this is, at best, a shotgun marriage.[9]

As well as the growing evidence of Menander's actual practice, a rich and expanding vein of contemporary evidence has been found in the archaeological record, where representations of the stage and in particular of characters and masks become increasingly popular over the course of the fourth century and then beyond. This encompasses a wide range of materials and an increasingly wide distribution: terracotta figurines and masks; vases in different traditions; mosaics; wall painting. Since the pioneering work of Robert, attempts have been made to marry the archaeological evidence to Pollux, on the one hand, and to the textual evidence, on the other.[10] Nonetheless, the archaeological evidence is helpful in many ways. It suggests some broad trends which are compatible with the literary evidence: progressively less grotesque bodies over the course of the fourth century, particularly in younger women, in young men and finally old men. Classification of the evidence in its own terms suggests an intersection with Pollux rather than a one-to-one match, with some of his masks reflecting Middle Comedy survivals, or developing out of Middle Comedy precursors. The extent of this overlap remains disputed, not least because of the paucity of some of Pollux's descriptions, particularly of women (see Figure 7.4), and the uncertainty over some of the terms used. Some scholars see a very tight correlation between the two; a more cautiously positive estimate is that there is a solid overlap but a reasonably significant gap.[11]

What is interesting about such typologies is what they can tell us about the resources available to productions of comedy, on the one hand, and audience knowledge and expectations, on the other. For this reason, it is still helpful to start any account of New Comedy, at least, with Pollux's classification: it represents one attempt to explain why and in what respects masks were significant. In both archaeological and theatrical terms, they are quite broad types: but masks were by their nature quite ephemeral and the

---

[9] See Krien (1955); Webster (1970b) 76–86; and more recently Wiles (1991) 85–90; for scepticism Pickard-Cambridge (1988) 230; and Poe (1996) 314f., who points to selective quotation.

[10] See Robert (1911); Simon (1938); Bieber (1961). The state of play is represented by Webster and Green (1978) and Webster et al. (1995). Green (1994) is particularly helpful on quantitative and developmental issues. For the 'phlyax vase' tradition, see Webster (1948); Trendall (1967) with a typology of characters; Green (1985a); Csapo (1986); Taplin (1993); Hughes (2003).

[11] Webster et al. (1995) 6f. suggest a maximum of twelve (over twenty-five) not securely attested. By contrast, Bernabò Brea (1981) claims that forty-three of Pollux's forty-four types can be seen in the extensive numbers of theatrical figures and masks found on Lipari. Scepticism about the closeness of Pollux and the material record is expressed by Brown (1987) 184f.; Wiles (1991) 80–2; and Poe (1996) 309–11.

Type	Description
Grandad	The oldest; close-cropped hair; gentle expression in his eyebrows; thin cheeks; full beard; pale-skinned, downcast eyes, cheerful forehead
Grandad 2	Thinner, with a more intense look; pained; rather sallow; full beard; red-haired; cauliflower ears
Leading	With a roll of hair; hook-nosed; wide forehead; right eye-brow raised
Long-beard with flowing hair	long beard; roll of hair; slow expression; no brows raised
Hermonian	Receding; full beard; raised eye-brows; glaring
Wedge-bearded	Receding; pointed beard; raised eye-brows; rather grumpy
Lycomedean	Curly-haired; long beard; one eyebrow raised; indicates a busybody
Pimp	As above, but smiling and drawing together his eyebrows; receding or bald
Hermonian 2	Shaved (cheeks) and wedge beard

Figure 7.1 Pollux's typology I: old men

scope for individual tweaks (as well as special masks) quite significant.[12] Key signs that need to be decoded include: amount, style and decoration of hair; presence and nature of beard (men); fullness or thinness of cheeks; presence and nature of wrinkles or creases; shape of the lips; shape and character of the eyes and, especially, eyebrows. Raised eyebrows indicate an active and lively personality, not necessarily a positive one, and particularly in men (see Figures 7.1 and 7.2): compare the Leading Old Man (single raised eyebrow) or the more dyspeptic Hermonian or Lycomedean (raised eye-brows), the sinister pimp (eye-brows drawn together and grinning) to the more equanimous Grandad and positively slow Longbeard-and-flowing-hair. The Perfect Young Man and all species of flatterer and parasite share raised brows (no doubt signalling inventive means of crawling and sucking-up to the rich man). Pollux is here trying to capture the complex means by which a 'look' is conveyed, with perhaps excessive emphasis on the eyebrows. In any case, it should be emphasized that the configuration of the eyebrows does not offer only one kind of expression; rather, angle of the mask is important for conveying different perspectives.[13] Hair-style plays a similarly significant, but less expressive, role for women, particularly courtesans. With the

[12] On the construction of the mask, see Webster *et al.* (1995) 2–4.
[13] Wiles (1991) 95–8 on the leading slave mask, attached by him to Daos.

Class	Type	Description
Young men	Perfect	Somewhat ruddy; athletic; a few creases in his forehead; roll of hair; raised eyebrows
	Dark	Younger; low eyebrows; cultured rather than a jock
	Curly	Rather young; rather ruddy; curly hair; raised eyebrows; one crease in his forehead
	Soft	Hair like Perfect Youth; youngest; pale skin from indoors life; looks rather soft
	Rustic	Dark skin; thick lips; snub nose; roll of hair
	Flowing haired	Soldier and boaster; dark hair and skin; flowing hair
	Flowing haired 2	As above, but softer and blond-haired
Parasites	Kolax (Flatterer)	Dark (no more than from the *palaestra*); rather hook-nosed; sleek; rather malevolent look, with eyebrows raised
	Parasite	As above, but thicker ears; and more cheerful expression
	Work of art	Greying; shaved; richly dressed; a foreigner
	Sicilian	No further information

Figure 7.2 Pollux's typology II: young men

partial exception of the older women, female masks are less expressive in the forehead/eyebrow region (see Figure 7.4).

In a number of places profession (active, retired or co-habiting courtesan; pimp), social status (free; freedman; slave, see Figure 7.3) or lifestyle (flatterer or parasite), or age could be inferred from the mask. Other professions might be reasonably deduced (soldier).[14] Mask is reinforced by costume and props. For example, Festus suggests that the Maison mask was used for sailors and other types as well as cooks. Characteristics could also be suggested by the mask, e.g. interfering (*polypragmosynê*), or hinted at. Ethnicity could also be suggested: the Maison was a local (*politikos*) cook, whereas the Grasshopper (Tettix) type was from elsewhere (*ektopios*).[15] Relationships could be deduced with degrees of accuracy. For example, the slave girl with brushed hair would naturally be taken to belong to a courtesan. The role in the plot might also be inferred from appearance. The *pseudokorê* (literally

[14] Webster *et al.* (1995) 26 argue that the Grandad Slave was not necessarily a freedman; Pollux is ambiguous.
[15] Athenaeus 14.659a.

Type	Description
Grandad	Grey hair; a freedman
Leading	Red hair in a knot; raised eye-brows; forehead drawn together; stands to slaves as Leading Old Man to the free
With hair down	Receding, red hair; raised eyebrows
Curly	Red, receding hair; ruddy; cross-eyed
Maison	Balding, with red hair. Greek cook (Athenaeus); or sailor (Festus)
Grasshopper	Dark and bald, except for a few black hairs on head and cheek; cross-eyed; non-Greek cook (Athenaeus)
Flowing-haired Leading	Like Leading Slave, except for hair

Figure 7.3 Pollux's typology III: slaves

'False girl' or 'False virgin') seems to refer to girls who have been seduced or raped (e.g., Pamphile in *Men at Arbitration*).[16]

Type and character in New Comedy

In order to see this working in practice, a good starting point is Menander's handling of the broader stock types that he inherits from Middle Comedy: soldier, flatterer and courtesan.[17] With the exception of the cook, it seems that Menander largely plays against expectations – not so much to *reverse* expectations as to *enrich* characterization both of the typical characters themselves and those with whom they are interacting. The soldiers who play leading roles in Menander (Thrasonides in *The Man who was Hated*, Polemon in *Perikeiromenê (The Girl with the Cropped Hair)* and

---

[16] For this interpretation, Robert (1911) 41 nn. 2, 7; Bieber (1961) 96f.; and Green and Handley (1995) 77. Simon (1938) 101, followed by Webster (1970b) 86 and Wiles (1991) 177–80 interprets this as indicating a courtesan who turns out to be a long-lost girl able to marry legitimately (examples below). Gould and Lewis (i.e. Pickard-Cambridge (1988) 228) translate as the former, but seem to endorse the latter. Gilula (1977) (improbably) suggests that the pseudokore indicates a cross-dressed character.

[17] Other types such as the pimp are harder to see in extant Menander. See e.g., the exiguous fragments of *Symaristôsai*, the model for Plautus' *Cistellaria*, and *Kolax (Flatterer)*. Cooks in extant Menander play a largely subordinate role; see n. 5 above. Slaves have been widely discussed: see Wiles (1991), especially 165–71, 188–92; and, with cooks and courtesans, Krieter-Spiro (1997), especially 156–89, with bibliography. It is important to note that slaves are not the prime movers in extant Menander as the Cunning Slave (*servus callidus*) is in Plautus.

Class	Type	Description
Old women	Dried-up or Wolfish	Rather tall; finely wrinkled forehead; white-haired; sallow; cunning (or crooked) gaze
	Fat	Thick creases in a fat face; wears a ribbon around her hair
	Domestic, House-keeper or Sharp Crone	Snub-nosed; two teeth stick out of each gum
Young women	Talkative	Hair frames face and is brushed down; straight eye-brows; light-skinned
	Curly	As above, except for hair
	Girl	Centre parting; black straight eye-brows; slightly sallow, pale skin
	'Fallen' girl (*pseudokorê*)	Paler than the girl; hair bound around the front of her head; resembles a young married woman
	'Fallen' 2	As above, but no centre parting
	Talkative and greying	Greying, with parting; ex-courtesan
Courtesans	Concubine	As above, but with hair framing the face
	Experienced	Ruddier than the Fallen Girl; locks of hair around the ears
	Young	No jewellery; hair tied with a ribbon
	Golden	Lots of gold jewellery in her hair
	With scarf	Hair is held in a decorated scarf
	Little torch	Hair pulled into pointed knot
Slaves	Cropped	Short hair; wears only a belted chiton
	With brushed hair	Parting; rather snub-nosed; saffron, belted chiton; serves courtesans

Figure 7.4 *Pollux's typology IV: women*

Stratophanes in *The Man from Sicyon*[18] are good examples. In no case are they a straightforward bombastic boaster of the sort that would come to be known in Roman comedy as a *miles gloriosus* and which is implicit in

[18] Bias in *Kolax (Flatterer)* would be another interesting case if we had more of him. Cleostratus in *The Shield* (like the brother in *The Man who was Hated*), has a brief role but one critical to the plot – with that name and that back-story, he is likely to have been characterized as a soldier variant.

Pollux's association of the loose-haired type with an *alazôn* and soldier; but, equally, it seems clear that such qualities were exploited in the plays. Visual and other essential attributes such as the name serve as a constant reference point which bring in these associations.[19]

The most straightforward and closest to the bombastic soldier is Polemon, who at the beginning of *Perikeiromenê (The Girl with the Cropped Hair)* punishes his young mistress Glycera (Sweetheart) by cutting off her hair. He reacts in anger on being told, mistakenly, that she was having an affair with his neighbour (and in fact her long-lost brother) Moschion.[20] His anger is described as uncharacteristic (163–5) but plays off the stereotype, as the reactions by his slaves indicate (Sosias, 172–4; Doris, 185–7).[21] Polemon is, however, still infatuated and keeps sending his slave Sosias to find out how she is and what is going on (177–80, 354–60). His household, particularly Sosias, keep the military image in mind, particularly in an abortive attack on the neighbour's house at the start of Act III to retrieve Glycera.[22] In this scene, we see more of the real Polemon – not drunk and permitting Pataicus to persuade him to accept a non-violent solution. The swaggering soldier still peeps through – Pataicus asks him not to shout (489) – but Polemon is desperate to win over Pataicus, convince him that he has done right by Glycera and so win her back: he stammers, invites Pataicus in to inspect her dresses and goes into raptures over her beauty (512–25). In Act V, Polemon recants his earlier jealous, drunken behaviour (985–8). Pataicus hands over Glycera to be Polemon's wife, but warns him, 'From now on forget about being a soldier, so you don't do any thing at all rash' (1016f.) and Polemon readily agrees and begs forgiveness from Glycera (1018–20). In the end, Polemon learns about himself, but this is no straightforward transition, but rather a complex, three-dimensional character portrait, which focuses the exaggerated, bombastic traits of the soldier into jealousy and distracted passion; he is, though, fundamentally decent at heart.

Thrasonides is, on current evidence, still further removed from this baseline, if never wholly removed from it.[23] One reason is that *Misoumenos (The Man who was Hated)*, like *The Shield*, puts much more emphasis on the horrors of war and its disruptive effects on families.[24] Thrasonides has brought

[19] Names might translate as 'Son of Recklessness', 'Fighter' and 'Conspicuous Soldier', respectively.

[20] For Moschion's character, see 140–4 (prologue speech); Act II *passim*; 369–72.

[21] The text of Menander used is Sandbach (1990), with reference also to Arnott ((1979), (1996b) and (2000b)), where he differs or offers a more recent text.

[22] For martial language of the household, see also 175, 388–96.

[23] So Choricius 42 = *The Man who was Hated* fr. 1 (= test. 1 Arnott); cf. fr. 10.

[24] Daos' description (23–82) of the Lycian campaign emphasizes both profit and horror, not least in the description of the battlefield.

back from the war in Cyprus, a captive, Crateia, with whom he has been living as man-and-wife.[25] Following him back with the loot is his servant, Getas (33–6). The loot happens to contain the sword of Crateia's brother. Under the impression that Thrasonides has killed her brother, Crateia has turned on him. Thrasonides, despite his name, is more baffled than angry,[26] but like Polemon, he does have a slightly over-exuberant character, manifested in melodramatic self-pity, from his opening apostrophe of the Night (especially A4–12) to his increasing desperation as the play moves towards its climax in Act IV and V:[27]

> Crateia's father has arrived, you say?
> Now you will prove that I have been born either blest
> or the most thrice-accursed of all living creatures.
> For if he does not approve of me and does not give me
> her with full authority, Thrasonides is dead:
> and may that not happen. Let's go in; there's no longer
> any point in guessing the outcome – we have to know.
> I enter hesitantly and trembling.
> My soul foretells, Getas, some trouble.
> I am afraid. All the facts are a better thing
> than speculation, I suppose. I might be surprised.
>
> *Misoumenos* (*The Man who was Hated*)
> 259–69 = 660–70 Arnott

Use of asyndeton, use of the future indicative in the protasis of a future conditional, the grandiloquent language and hyperbolic utterances switch back and forth with tentative optimism. As Act IV moves to its conclusion, Thrasonides' efforts to convert the informal arrangements into a legitimate marriage fail. In an extensive monologue, Thrasonides develops his comic throes of tragic passion, reflecting on bearing the burden of love as a disease (356–65 = 757–66 Arnott) into an extended self-absorbed monologue, which culminates in a series of options – nobly letting her go and hoping that hate turns to pity; living a withdrawn, ascetic life in silent reproach; and finally pretending to commit suicide.[28]

Courtesans, by contrast, have both a much wider spectrum of roles inherited from Middle (and Old) Comedy, and also much clearer evidence of playing against type. In the examples above, the courtesan as long-lost girl is played three ways, with variations on character and plot function: Crateia,

---

[25] A37–40 = 37–40 Arnott.   [26] A95–7 = 95–7 Arnott, with a curse directed at Getas.
[27] Acts II and III are essentially missing.
[28] 790–809 Arnott, whose text is considerably more complete than that of Sandbach. The report of a fake suicide in Act V may be illustrated on a mosaic from the House of Menander at Mytilene (Webster *et al.* (1995) 6DM2.10 and XZ16): so Arnott.

like Philoumene in *The Man from Sicyon*, bought as a slave, Glycera being directly pimped by her guardian. A more seasoned professional is the flute-girl Habrotonon, in Polemon's entourage, who flounces off after a series of *double entendres* by Sosias in the siege of Moschion's house (232–5 = 482–5 Arnott). For the professional courtesan, the typical character appears to have been one where mercenary actions and motives were expected.[29]

The best developed courtesans that we can see in the plays in their current state are another Habrotonon, in *Men at Arbitration*, and Chrysis, the eponymous woman from Samos in *Samia*. Neither fits the stereotype, although again there are hints of it in both. Chrysis by her name suggests the 'golden' courtesan of Pollux.[30] Like Glycera, she is an object of suspicion from her partner, this time because of a parallel pregnancy – hers with her client, Demeas, and that of Plangon, raped by Demeas' son Moschion. She volunteers to look after Plangon's baby, but by a series of coincidences and mishaps Demeas comes to believe that it is Chrysis' child by Moschion (Act III) and reacts accordingly. In a rant, he (improbably) absolves the louche Moschion of responsibility and puts the blame wholly on Chrysis (330–56), characterizing her as a sexual predator preying on innocent, drunk young men, and resolves to throw her out:

> You're quite the thing. In town
> you'll see exactly who you are.
> The other girls like you, Chrysis, charge only ten
> drachmas, run to dinners and
> drink unmixed wine until they die – or
> they starve unless they do this quick and willing to please.
> You'll know this, I know, as much as
> anyone, and you'll realise what you are and how you went wrong.
>
> *Samia* 390–7

As further complications ensue, the neighbour Niceratus, who is initially sympathetic to Chrysis' plight, comes to have a similar idea (556f.) before matters are resolved. One of the major motors in terms of plot and characterization is thus the audience's use of the courtesan type to explain the expectations of the fathers and to set against the truth of the situation known to them and some of the other characters.

Habrotonon in *Men at Arbitration* is a short-term hire from a pimp rather than a long-term partnership (fr. 1; 136–8), and is part of the

---

[29] See e.g., *Kolax (Flatterer)* 128–30 = E233–5 Arnott; *Dis Exapatôn* 19–30, 91–102.

[30] Some support for the association might also be gained from her rich dress on a Mytilene mosaic (Webster *et al.* (1995) 6DM2.2 and XZ31). The name, however, was evidently not restricted to courtesans: see the nurse in *The Man who was Hated* 555 Arnott (= *POxy* 4408.268f).

characterization of Charisius, her client, and his fondness for wine and women. He is currently drowning his sorrows away from home after his wife Pamphile has given birth impossibly soon after marriage and exposed the child, unaware that the baby is in fact his. Despite starting out as incidental entertainment – with complaints about her virginal state for the time she's spent at Charisius' place (43of.) – Habrotonon becomes the prime mover in the play. She works out what must have happened and indeed was on hand in the night as a witness to the aftermath of a rape (464–92). The devious means she adopts to confirm her suspicions play on a more traditional type, as she poses as the wronged woman (493–538). Charisius' slave Onesimus points out that this is not entirely philanthropic, as she is sure to win her freedom this way – acknowledged by Habrotonon (538–66) in a (for once) candid assessment of the sex industry in Menander.[31] Habrotonon further discovers that Pamphile is in fact the child's mother (853–77) intervenes again (with Onesimus) to convince Charisius of the fact (932–78). Onesimus comes to the fore in Act V, to handle Pamphile's father, the obnoxious Smicrines; but there seems to have been a sub-plot involving Charisius' friend Chaerestratus, who has fallen for Habrotonon. In this way, she will live happily ever afterwards: 'no ordinary courtesan' (984f.), as Chaerestratus says at the beginning of the act.

Similar playing with expectations occurs with the flatterer class. Again, *Kolax (Flatterer)* sets out some of the expected relationships and has good examples of the theory and practice of sucking up to the boss.[32] Elsewhere in Menander, there are more interesting variations. Chaireas is labelled a parasite in the *Dramatis Personae* to the *Dyscolus*, although neither fawning nor financial or alimentary rewards are depicted. Rather, Chaireas presents himself as an expert in the management of love affairs (or elite marriage matches) on a friend's behalf, a stance that looks back in part to the milieu of courtesan comedy, but is out of place here. Chaireas' 'fixer' role is replicated in that of Theron in *The Man from Sicyon*, in the political sphere. The big twist is the flatterer in love, a sub-plot framing the main action. In the opening scene, the target of Theron's affections is describing his character to a female friend in uncomplimentary terms suggestive of the typical flatterer. Somehow Myrrhine learns to love Theron, and at the conclusion to the play there is a double wedding: Stratophanes to Philoumene and Theron to Myrrhine. Again with the flatterer we see elements of inherited dramatic role and subtle variation.

---

[31] Contrast 43of.

[32] A rant about flatterers by a slave (?Daos), 85–94 = C190–9 Arnott; frr. 2–4, 7–9 Arnott; see also perhaps 95–119 = D200–24 Arnott.

Returning to *Dyscolus*, we see Menander playing off two types of Young Man against inherited types, plot functions and each other. Gorgias, as elsewhere in extant Menander, is a poor rustic; he probably wears the mask of the Rustic Young Man.[33] He is looking out for his sister, who lives with the bad-tempered Cnemon; Sostratus is the sophisticated urbanite out hunting, who takes a fancy to his sister. Sostratus is somewhat over-eager but also indecisive, as he seeks to use a series of over-lapping proxies – slave Pyrrhias, flatterer Chaireas and (abortively) his father's more experienced slave Getas, who is busy. Unwilling to wait, Sostratus has to act on his own behalf (259–68).[34] On encountering Sostratus, Gorgias immediately assumes the worst, that Sostratus is one of these typical men out to take advantage of a poor, unsophisticated girl, on the basis of his general look (258), which would have included the mask, perhaps that of the raffish Second Flowing-Haired Young Man,[35] as well as his elegant cloak (257). There is a clash of personality and ethics here as well as a rural/urban and rich/poor set of oppositions.[36] Gorgias' prickliness is conveyed in stiff, even pompous language: 'Young man, would you mind stopping for a rather serious word with me' (269f.). Perhaps surprisingly, for a rustic, he also deals in grand abstractions and principles, on reputation, wealth, leisure and the changeability of fortune.[37] Sostratus, meanwhile, rejects Gorgias' charge with hurt candour and defends his good intentions, pointedly returning Gorgias' 'young man' (*meirakion*, 311). Gorgias recants his hostility and is recruited to the cause of marriage. Gorgias remains practical, suggesting Sostratus save himself the trouble of a lost cause; Sostratus is not dissuaded (322–49) and is even prepared to work the fields himself to further his case, to Gorgias' astonishment (350–92).[38] Expectations are played with, as Gorgias' practicality wins out; Sostratus' dreaming gains only a sore back. When Cnemon falls down the well, it is

[33] Webster (1970b) 79f. and Handley (1965) 35 suggest that the dark-skinned, flat-lipped, snub-nosed rustic mask indicates cowardice, stupidity and sexual licence, on the basis of [Aristotle] *Physiognomica* 811a and 812b, although cowardice is associated with 'excessively' dark skin there (Egyptians and Ethiopians are specifically mentioned).
[34] For Sostratus as the eager lover, see Zagagi (1979).
[35] Exuberant but with softer, loucher elements. So Handley (1965) 36 and on 258, following the suggestion of Webster (1949) for Moschion. Wiles (1991) 185 suggests the Curly Haired Young Man on similar grounds. The Pale Young Man is a better option for Moschion: see especially *The Man from Sicyon* 199–202 and 209f.; for sexual incontinence associated with effeminacy, see Davidson (1997) 164–6.
[36] See my other chapter in this volume, Chapter 10.
[37] 242–6, 271–88, 293–8. Handley (1965) on 269ff compares the debate between the two slave/rustics Daos and Syrus in *Men at Arbitration*, but also notes (on 271–87) Aristotle's observation that rustics are fond of generalizations (*gnômotypoi*, *Rhetoric* 1395a6).
[38] Again, for Sostratus as eager lover, see Zagagi (1979).

Gorgias who jumps down and pulls out the old curmudgeon, while Sostratus can do very little other than make cow eyes at his sister and let go of the rope (666–85). The final settlement depends on the generosity of Sostratus and his father, Callipides, but the key plot device depends upon the positive aspects of the rustic type.

In these examples, we can see the kinds of theatrical resources available in New Comedy to establish character and plot function – mask, description, actions, utterances and name. Names, like masks, can bring in a range of associations and expectations, from profession through to plot function and personal characteristics. Some, such as Cnemon, appear to be unique or rare; others, such as Gorgias, Moschion, Daos (a schemer, albeit usually unsuccessful) and Smicrines (typically a miser), are both more frequent and much more consistent.[39] Visual, verbal and dramatic cues bounce off each other for comic effect both about characters – Gorgias in discursive mode, Sostratus as labourer – and in terms of false expectations in both dramatic characters and the audience themselves. As in the cases of Gorgias and Sostratus, these interactions also serve to enrich the individual instantiation of the type: the type, inherited from the comic tradition, is a dramatic shorthand, specifically realized as an individual character.

Type, function and humour in Old Comedy

A number of the types of New Comedy clearly stem ultimately from Old Comedy, although the versions of such types in Old Comedy differ in form, both more individualized and less consistent. It might be possible to see, for example, in the older male heads of household in Aristophanes (Dicaeopolis and Trygaeus) distant ancestors of the put-upon fathers of Menander as well as the prototype for the countryman; or in the offspring at odds with their parents (Pheidippides and Bdelycleon) the distant ancestors of Menander's young men. Lamachus' appearance in *Acharnians* anticipates later soldiers. The best examples of stock types that persist, however, come from outside of Aristophanes' extant plays. The figure of the courtesan was explored repeatedly by Pherekrates.[40] In at least some instances the plots were clearly fantastic in nature and the preoccupation with drink and sex that is extended to the free women in *Lysistrata* and *Assembly Women* finds an airing in this more specialist arena. Aristophanes' own use of female entertainers and sex

---

[39] A *fixed* association has been argued by MacCary (1969), (1970), (1971), (1972) and broadly supported by Wiles (1991) 90–9; the counter-arguments of Brown (1987) suggest that this is too strong.

[40] In *Epilêsmon/Thalatta*, *Koriannô*, *Petalê* and possibly *Lêroi*. See Henderson (2000). For the origins of social comedy in this period, see Segal (1973); Handley (1985) 391–8.

workers is more limited, as in the role of trophy sex-objects in *Acharnians* 1198–231 and *Wasps* 1326–449, and as sexual distraction in *Women at the Thesmophoria* 1160–231. Reconciliation in *Lysistrata* also falls into this category.

Another social type put centre-stage was the flatterer or sponger (*kolax*). Eupolis' *Kolakes* (*Flatterers*) featured a chorus of them, and they explored their lifestyle at some length:

> As for the life that flatterers lead, we'll
> tell you: hear how we are a suave bunch
> in every way. First of all, we have a slave attendant on us
> – someone else's as a rule and he does little work.[41]
> I have these two lovely cloaks.
> I regularly change one of them for the other when I drive
> to the market. Then, when I see some man,
> a fool, but rich, I immediately make for his vicinity,
> and if the wealthy mark ever says anything, I praise it highly,
> and I am stunned with apparent enjoyment of his words.
> Then we go to dinner, each one of us to a different person's house,
> after another's barley-cake. There it's necessary for a flatterer
> to say many pleasantries immediately – or be thrown out.
> I know Acestor, the tattooed man, has suffered that fate;
> for he uttered a tasteless joke, and then the slave took him to the front door
> and handed him over to Oineus in a criminal's collar.
>
> Eupolis *Kolakes* (*Flatterers*) fr. 172

As well as his political plays such as *Poleis*, Eupolis' output featured a number of plays on the lifestyles of the rich and famous in which such characters played a role: *Autolycus* I and II and *Philoi* being the most obvious. The interest in both matters sympotic and sexual was developed further in Middle Comedy.

Perhaps the most interesting example of the handling of stock characters is that of the slave. In the fifth-century works of Aristophanes, slaves can have a stock character and a circumscribed role. Their most substantial use in earlier Aristophanes is for knockabout exposition, as in the prologues of *Wasps* and *Peace* and the second half of *Frogs*, or for door-knocking scenes (*Acharnians*, *Birds*, *Women at the Thesmophoria*) or otherwise for incidental use. Their characterization, such as it is, is limited (fearful, fond of drink; or like their masters). In Aristophanes, the suggestion is made that slaves were regularly the object of violence, although in extant Aristophanes it is the *threat* of

---

[41] The end of the line is corrupt; the translation renders Porson's emendation (see K-A's apparatus).

violence above all.[42] The opening of *Frogs* also alleges that routines with slaves carrying baggage were a hackneyed sight on the comic stage.

Xanthias in *Frogs* develops these elements into a more rounded and active character, playing with the idea of master and servant in an often ironically self-reflexive fashion. In part, he looks ahead to the fourth century. Already in Aristophanes' *Wealth* the role of Cario is much more extensive than that of his fifth-century peers. Dover suggests that the freeing of slaves for the battle of Arginusae in 406, alluded to frequently in *Frogs*, may have been a significant factor.[43] Other factors could lead to expanding the slave role: the two slaves in *Knights* extend their exposition to become the prime movers of the plot in its early stages, with one continuing to play a significant role as far as the parabasis. The allegorical nature of *Knights* may be the explanation here, with the slaves being suggestive of Demosthenes and Nicias.

Other minor characters have a relatively circumscribed set of activities and may also have been similarly cued visually. The barmaids of *Frogs* 549–78 do not have an exact parallel, but jokes about them earlier in the play (*Frogs* 114) and in *Wealth* 426 suggest that at the very least there is a social stereotype being exploited here and probably a comic type too. Other female sellers are close kin: bread-sellers in *Wasps* 1388–412 and a veritable market-full in *Lysistrata* 452–65. The sycophant occurs in three of Aristophanes' plays (*Acharnians*, *Birds*, *Wealth*) being a nuisance to the schemes of the protagonist and is given short and violent shrift on each occasion. In the first of these, he is named (Nicarchus), but not so in the latter two plays. Although a portrait mask could have been used for Nicarchus, it is unclear whether this would have been done for such a small role; likewise with oracle-mongers in *Peace* and *Birds*, although Hierokles (*Peace*) appears to have been a reasonably public figure.[44]

For the most part, Aristophanic dramatic shorthands lie in different directions: in the 'speaking names' of its characters, particularly (but not exclusively) its protagonists, and in caricatures of people from the actual world. In the former case, the name can provide a running joke within the fiction that motivates plot elements;[45] in the latter, there is a complex interplay between caricature and stock figure. Euripides, certainly, appears on stage in three of Aristophanes' dramas, with many of the same characteristics. Agathon, too, at the beginning of *Women at the Thesmophoria* draws on the earlier representation of Euripides, as Euripides himself acknowledges,

---

[42] *Peace* 741–8, with, e.g., *Wasps* 3, 1292–6, *Clouds* 56–9.
[43] See generally Dover (1993) 43–50.
[44] See IG I³ 40.66 and Eupolis, *Cities* fr. 231. For the public role of such figures, see Bowden (2003); Parker (2005) 112f., 116–18.
[45] On handling of names, see Olson (1992).

and the jokes around them operate in parallel fashion (Euripides' crippled legs in *Acharnians* and Agathon's dress and character in *Women at the Thesmophoria*), while the play with gender and sexuality seems to align Agathon with Phrynis in Eupolis' *Demes*. To be sure, individual caricature plays a part and the jokes are reworked in new directions, but there are underlying similarities and repetitions too. Pericles and Aspasia form a central pairing for the generation before Aristophanes, while Cleon and, in particular, Hyperbolus play a similar role in the 420s and early 410s.[46] In the fourth century, the development of the stock figure of the courtesan itself depended to a large extent on representations of courtesans from the actual world.[47]

A further example of the stock character at work in Old Comedy is the divine figure. In the current state of our evidence, Dionysus is the best example. We know, for example, of his central role in Eupolis' *Taxiarchoi* displaying the same soft and cowardly character which is in evidence in much of the earlier part of *Frogs*.[48] His caricature would have developed through Cratinus' *Dionysoi* (*Companions of Dionysus*) and Cratinus' *Dionysalexandrus*, Aristophanes' own *Dionysos nauagos* (*Shipwrecked Dionysus*) and Aristomenes' *Dionysos askêtês* (*Tradesman Dionysus*) to name the most obvious.[49] Other gods clearly played a role too. Herakles' appearance in *Frogs* is predicated upon an established comic caricature (cf. *Peace* 741), and there is enough evidence to support that elsewhere in the fragments. Of mythological characters, Odysseus and the Cyclops are perhaps the two best represented. The mythological characters would again go on to be developed in the mythological burlesque strand of Middle Comedy. Both out-and-out tragic parody (especially by Strattis) and mythological burlesque are well established in the repertoire by the late fifth century.

The material evidence for the period of Old Comedy is not as extensive as we might like, and for the period before Aristophanes it is impossible to draw many conclusions in relation to character types. By the end of the century, things look more promising. The best evidence, in many ways, is that from the New York group of terracottas, whose types continue through most of the fourth century but now look to derive, at least in part, from the late fifth century.[50] The personnel look like Middle Comedy: the 'yellow' series, including Herakles and a nurse, have been associated with a comic *Augê*, while the 'red' series features recognizable types (old men, slaves, courtesan).

[46] See Revermann (1997); Sommerstein (2000); Ruffell (2002).
[47] See Nesselrath (1997) 277f. for some discussion.
[48] See Storey (2003) 246–60 and Revermann, Chapter 14.
[49] The date of the last two are uncertain, but Cratinus' plays certainly predate *Frogs*.
[50] See Webster and Green (1978) 45f., AT9–23; Green (1994) 34–8. For illustrations, Bieber (1961) fig. 164. 185–91 and Pickard-Cambridge (1988) 89–95.

It has been suggested that the evidence of Aristophanes is distorting our sense of the comedy of the time and that Aristophanes was in his comic choices quite conservative.[51] This is possible: the set of figurines would be consistent with some of the humour which he mocks; but at the same time he exploits such humour himself too. Scholars in recent years have rightly pointed out the wide variety of plays in what is termed Old Comedy; but all the same, there does not seem to be a major poet of that period whose output *as a whole or even in greater part* looks quite like that in the New York group: even Pherekrates, with his courtesans, or the supposedly plot-conscious Crates.

There is, then, a variety of social types and individual characters, or a mix of the two, who function in terms of repeating traits that can be reused and reprised. In some cases, this is bound up with a recognizably similar function within the plot (slaves, sycophants, creditors, witnesses). More generalized accounts of characters in terms of plot function have also been proposed and, indeed, a functional analysis is implicit in most accounts of the formal structure of Old Comedy.[52] The story (on this model) is the Hero seeking to pursue their scheme, opposed by a Villain, aided by a (sometimes divine) Helper. Following achievement of their goals, the Hero(ine) is annoyed by Intruders who seek to deprive him/her of their enjoyment or otherwise gain a slice of the action. This works reasonably well for *Acharnians*, *Peace* and *Wealth*, but less consistently well for other plays. A better way of thinking about it is that there are characteristic *routines* and characteristic classes of character who may be particularly associated with specific routines, but not a single *Ur*-structure. Even with the comic hero, a consistent plot function is considerably complicated in plays such as *Peace*, *Wasps*, *Women at the Thesmophoria* and *Frogs*.[53] Scholars have further attempted to generalize Aristotelian types – the dissembler (*eirôn*), boaster (*alazôn*) and buffoon (*bômolochus*) – at a structural level, with little plausibility. At a smaller scale, the *bômolochus* has proved more persistent in the guise of a short-term dramatic function. In examples such as Calonice in the prologue of *Lysistrata*, buffoonish interjections are the primary role of a minor character.[54] Much more complex (and usual) are examples such

---

[51] Green (1994) 36.

[52] The most systematic functional analysis is by Sifakis (1992), adopting explicitly the models derived from folk-tale by Propp (1968). For a classic account of formal structure, see Pickard-Cambridge and Webster (1962). The variant by Cornford (1914: 1934) is particularly close to a functional model.

[53] On the comic hero, see further Rosen, Chapter 11.

[54] These derive ultimately from the *Nicomachean Ethics* and Theophrastus' *Characters*, from which (ultimately) is derived the comic typology of the *Tractatus Coislinianus* (Janko (1984), especially 216–18). For attempts to generalize some or all of these, see Ribbeck (1876); Süss (1905), (1908); Whitman (1964); McLeish (1980). For criticism,

as Dionysus in *Frogs*, who is by turns coward, buffoon and sensitive literary critic.

This points to the principal characteristic of the use of character shorthands in Old Comedy. They are driven by the logic of the joke, not as a short-cut to rounded characterization in the first instance.[55] For this reason, a stable taxonomy is unable to account for Old Comedy in the round, still less is it possible to derive a *sociology* of Attic comedy as a reflection of *actual* society.[56] This is not to say, however, that characters in Old Comedy are one-dimensional or lack complexity or indeed that there is no characterization as we might normally understand the term. Rather events and characters are motivated by a variety of factors, including the shorthands I have outlined above.

So, on the one hand, characters in Old Comedy have complex but often anti-realistic motivation. They are, further, often over-coded, serially or concurrently, with characters or character types drawn either from the actual world or from parodic and intertextual engagement with other literary, poetic or dramatic contexts. Thus in *Knights*, Paphlagon is at different times one or more of a slave/steward, a market-trader and a politician suggestive of Cleon, sitting in the front row; Dicaeopolis in *Acharnians* and Euripides in *Women at the Thesmophoria* play versions of Euripidean characters, while both Dionysus and Xanthias impersonate Heracles in *Frogs*, all with differing degrees of transparency to audience and to other characters. Dicaeopolis further speaks extensively as a comic poet or producer; such metatheatrical self-awareness can be seen more widely on the small scale.[57] Complexity (and at the extremes, outright impossibility) of character is paralleled by the flexibility of choral identity, which frequently expands to encompass a self-consciousness about their role as comic performers, most obviously but not exclusively in the parabasis. They can also speak as the poet, as well as for the poet. The most flexible choral identity is that of *Peace*, which moves between the overlapping categories of Greeks, Athenians and

and a functional interpretation, see Silk (2000a) 232f. Ussher (1977) makes the more persuasive case that Theophrastus was *inspired* by Old Comedy.

[55] See especially Dover (1972) 59–65, who describes this as 'discontinuous characterization', and Silk (1990) and (2000a) 207–55, who talks of 'imagistic' and 'discontinuous-recreative' character, respectively, rather than joke-driven character.

[56] As attempted by Ehrenberg (1962).

[57] For *Acharnians* and tragedy, see especially Foley (1988); for debates over the comic identity that Dicaeopolis embraces, see Mastromarco (1979); Halliwell (1980); MacDowell (1982); Bowie (1988); and Sidwell (1994); on Dicaeopolis' flexibility of identity, see Fisher (1993). For costume and disguise, see generally Muecke (1982a). For comic metatheatricality, see Taplin (1986); Slater (2002); and Ruffell (2008), all with further bibliography. For the allegorical elements of *Knights*, Newiger (1957) remains fundamental.

farmers, as well as embracing different modes of self-awareness.[58] So identity as well as motivation in Old Comedy, both choral and individual, is impossible, inconsistent or unstable in conventional narrative terms, to a greater or lesser extent. This instability and flexibility needs to be built into any interpretation and analysis of the genre.

On the other hand, a realist and even psychological dimension to these characters is not entirely absent either. A lot of the jokes (events and utterances) would not work without a degree of more personal motivation. For example, Philocleon and Bdelycleon in *Wasps* are, to be sure, embodiments of political positions and both Bdelycleon's initial brain-wave and Philocleon's responses play on their extreme positions. Extremism, class politics and violence are all embodied in Philocleon's outrageous behaviour throughout the play. And yet psychology plays a part; forcing Philocleon to change requires him to be broken mentally (at least temporarily). More interestingly, the characterization of Bdelycleon as snooty, pretentious and arrogant (134f.), as well as ostensibly caring for his father, and the exploration of the emotional basis of Philocleon's ideological stance (especially 546–630) all serve to play an important element in comic and narrative motivation.[59] Comic shorthands and joke-driven characterization serve to create an awful, fascinating, plausible yet impossible figure, the essence of Old Comedy.

Conclusion

It has been a truism of much classical scholarship on Greek drama that characterization on the ancient stage differed fundamentally from that on the modern stage, the latter exploring psychological realism and rounded individuals, and the former exploring ethical stance rather than character. Such a stance draws heavily on Aristotelian ideas of *êthos* and reacts against psychoanalysis. The stock characters of New Comedy are often accounted for under a similarly restrictive notion of character, but such a position over-simplifies both fictional and social processes. As more recent work on tragic characterization has emphasized, both social and fictional interactions themselves depend on shorthands for processing both character and

[58] Speaking as the poet: *Clouds* 518–16, *Wasps* 1284–91; slipping between identities, *Peace* 729–74. For *Peace*, see especially Cassio (1985). Scholars have tended towards regarding the parabasis as a ritual fossil, but for an alternative perspective see Hubbard (1991). Bierl (1999) argues that choral fluidity in general in Old Comedy is a function of ritual performance. The approach taken here is to explain the phenomenon in the round in terms of comic motivation.

[59] For empathy, particularly in relation to Philocleon, see Dover (1972) 125–7; and Silk (1987); Silk (2000a) 369–75.

situation.[60] The use of character types in New Comedy involves analogous social and fictional shorthands to explore individuals, through interaction with situations and other individuals – not, it is true, in a deeply psychological fashion, but equally not in a monochromatic or entirely exteriorized fashion either. Nor does Old Comedy exclude individual motivation and characterization, but in the interplay of repetition and innovation and the joke-based structures, they are only one element among many. The continuity in terms of comic empathy and personality, on the one hand, and social stereotypes and the social grotesque, on the other, was the basis for the development of Old Comedy into Middle, and thence to the more naturalistic form of New. Type and character are mutually interdependent, in comedy as in life.

Further reading

Pollux's classification of characters is most easily accessed in Csapo and Slater (1995). Its value in relation to New Comedy is assessed by Poe (1996). A particular issue is how closely names, types and masks go together: see MacCary (1969), (1970), (1971), (1972) and Brown (1987) for the poles of the debate. Wiles (1991) recasts the debate in a semiotic framework. Krieter-Spiro (1997) discusses some of the more obvious and specialized character types, slaves, cooks and hetairai, and has references to earlier bibliography. On slaves specifically, see Akrigg and Tordoff (2013). Characterization in Old Comedy has been approached in typical (Ribbeck (1876); Süss (1905), (1908)), social (Ehrenberg (1962)), heroic (Whitman (1964)) and functional (Cornford (1914: 1934); Sifakis (1992)) terms, and continuities have been noted with the more stock characters of later comedy (Segal (1973); Handley (1985)). Most recently, emphasis has been placed upon the fluidity and complexity of characterization in Old Comedy, for which see especially Silk (1990) and (2000a).

---

[60] See Easterling (1990) and Goldhill (1990), the former relying on Goffman's frame analysis, against earlier work by Easterling (1973), (1977) and Gould (1978).

8

ANDREAS WILLI

The language(s) of comedy

Continuities

The peripeteia in the fourth act of Menander's *Dyscolus* begins with a cry for help. In an attempt to recover a hoe and a bucket his maid Simiche had dropped in a well, the play's title figure, grumpy old Cnemon, has himself fallen into the depth. In order to rescue him Simiche first entreats the cook Sicon, who is at work nearby, but when Sicon refuses to help she turns to Gorgias, Cnemon's estranged stepson and friend of rich young Sostratus who would like to, and eventually will, marry Cnemon's lovely daughter (Men. *Dysc.* 620–38):

Σιμ. τίς ἂν βοηθήσειεν; ὦ τάλαιν᾽ ἐγώ.
τίς ἂν βοηθήσειεν;
Σικ.   Ἡράκλεις ἄναξ,
ἐάσαθ᾽ ἡμᾶς πρὸς θεῶν καὶ δαιμόνων
σπονδὰς ποῆσαι. λοιδορεῖσθε, τύπτετε·
οἰμώζετ᾽· ὦ τῆς οἰκίας τῆς ἐκτόπου.
Σιμ. ὁ δεσπότης ἐν τῶι φρέατι.
Σικ.   πῶς;
Σιμ.   ὅπως;
ἵνα τὴν δίκελλαν ἐξέλοι καὶ τὸν κάδον,
κατέβαινε, κᾆτ᾽ ὤλισθ᾽ ἄνωθεν, ὥστε καὶ
πέπτωκεν.
Σικ.   οὐ γὰρ ὁ χαλεπὸς γέρων σφόδρα
οὗτος; καλά γ᾽ ἐπόησε νὴ τὸν Οὐρανόν.
ὦ φιλτάτη γραῦ, νῦν σὸν ἔργον ἐστί.
Σιμ.   πῶς;
Σικ. ὅλμον τιν᾽ ἢ λίθον τιν᾽ ἢ τοιοῦτό τι
ἄνωθεν ἔνσεισον λαβοῦσα.
Σιμ.   φίλτατε
κατάβα.
Σικ.   Πόσειδον, ἵνα τὸ τοῦ λόγου πάθω,

Σιμ. ὦ Γοργία, ποῦ γῆς ποτ' εἶ;

Γο.   ποῦ γῆς ἐγώ;
τί ἐστι; Σιμίχη;

Σιμ.   τί γάρ; πάλιν λέγω·
ὁ δεσπότης ἐν τῶι φρέατι.

Γο.   Σώστρατε,
ἔξελθε δεῦρ'· ἡγοῦ, βάδιζ' εἴσω ταχύ.

Simiche   Who can help? Ah, poor me! Who can help?
Sicon   Good lord Heracles, by the gods and divinities let us get on with our
          libations. You swear, you hit – go to hell! What a weird place...
Simiche   The master's in the well.
Sicon   How?
Simiche   How? He was just going down to get the hoe and the bucket out, but
          then he slipped at the top, and fell in.
Sicon   Isn't that this extremely nasty old guy? Well done, by Heaven. Good
          woman, now it's your turn.
Simiche   What?
Sicon   Take a mortar or a rock or something like that, and throw it in from
          above.
Simiche   Good man, please go down!
Sicon   By Poseidon, to experience the proverbial fight with a dog in the well?
          No way!
Simiche   Oh Gorgias, where on earth are you?
Gorgias   Where I am? What's the matter, Simiche?
Simiche   What the matter is? Once again: the master's in the well!
Gorgias   Sostratus, come out; and you, show us the way, go in, quick!

Calls for help are not uncommon in Old Comedy either. One of our earliest
examples occurs in Aristophanes' *Acharnians* when Dicaeopolis turns up at
Euripides' house and wants to borrow some tragic dresses. He too is first
turned away, by Euripides' servant, but eventually he gets what he wants
(Ar. *Ach.* 393–415):

Δι. ὥρα 'στὶν ἤδη καρτερὰν ψυχὴν λαβεῖν.
    καί μοι βαδιστέ' ἐστὶν ὡς Εὐριπίδην.
    παῖ παῖ.

Οἰ.   τίς οὗτος;

Δι.   ἔνδον ἔστ' Εὐριπίδης;

Οἰ. οὐκ ἔνδον ἔνδον ἐστίν, εἰ γνώμην ἔχεις.

Δι. πῶς ἔνδον, εἶτ' οὐκ ἔνδον;

Οἰ.   ὀρθῶς, ὦ γέρον.
    ὁ νοῦς μὲν ἔξω ξυλλέγων ἐπύλλια
    κοὐκ ἔνδον, αὐτὸς δ' ἔνδον ἀναβάδην ποεῖ

τραγῳδίαν.

Δι.   ὦ τρισμακάρι᾽ Εὐριπίδη,
ὅθ᾽ ὁ δοῦλος οὑτωσὶ σοφῶς ἀπεκρίνατο.
ἐκκάλεσον αὐτόν.

Οἰ.   ἀλλ᾽ ἀδύνατον.

Δι.   ἀλλ᾽ ὅμως.
οὐ γὰρ ἂν ἀπέλθοιμ᾽. ἀλλὰ κόψω τὴν θύραν.
Εὐριπίδη, Εὐριπίδιον·
ὑπάκουσον, εἴπερ πώποτ᾽ ἀνθρώπων τινί.
Δικαιόπολις καλεῖ σε Χολλῄδης ἐγώ.

Εὐ. ἀλλ᾽ οὐ σχολή.

Δι. ἀλλ᾽ ἐκκυκλήθητ᾽.

Εὐ.   ἀλλ᾽ ἀδύνατον.

Δι.   ἀλλ᾽ ὅμως.

Εὐ. ἀλλ᾽ ἐκκυκλήσομαι. καταβαίνειν δ᾽ οὐ σχολή.

Δι. Εὐριπίδη–

Εὐ.   τί λέλακας;

Δι.   ἀναβάδην ποεῖς,
ἐξὸν καταβάδην; οὐκ ἐτὸς χωλοὺς ποεῖς.
ἀτὰρ τί τὰ ῥάκι᾽ ἐκ τραγῳδίας ἔχεις,
ἐσθῆτ᾽ ἐλεινήν; οὐκ ἐτὸς πτωχοὺς ποεῖς.
ἀλλ᾽, ἀντιβολῶ πρὸς τῶν γονάτων σ᾽, Εὐριπίδη,
δός μοι ῥάκιόν τι τοῦ παλαιοῦ δράματος.

Dicaeopolis	Now it's time to seriously take heart. I've got to go to Euripides. Hello, hello!
Servant	Who's there?
Dicaeopolis	Is Euripides at home?
Servant	Not at home at home he is, if you have insight.
Dicaeopolis	How 'at home' and also 'not at home'?
Servant	Correct, old man. His mind is out collecting phrases, so not at home, but he, he is at home, upstairs, writing a tragedy.
Dicaeopolis	Oh three times blessed Euripides, since your servant answered so wisely! Call him out.
Servant	Impossible.
Dicaeopolis	All the same. I wouldn't go away, but I'll knock the door. Euripides, dearie Euripides. Heed me, if thou hast ever heeded a man. Dicaeopolis calls you, I'm from Cholleidai!
Euripides	No time to spare.
Dicaeopolis	Then wheel yourself out!
Euripides	Impossible.
Dicaeopolis	All the same.
Euripides	I'll wheel myself out. But I haven't got time to come down.
Dicaeopolis	Euripides–

Euripides   What dost thou speak?
Dicaeopolis   You're writing upstairs, although you could do it downstairs?
              No wonder you write about cripples. But why do you wear the
              rags from tragedy, a pitiful garment? No wonder you write about
              beggars. But, Euripides, please, I entreat you on my knees, give
              me some little rag of that old play.

The differences between the two passages are glaring, thematically and formally. However, just as one might nevertheless group them together in a
single category of 'entreaty scenes', certain similarities are also undeniable
if one takes a distanced look at their linguistic set-up. Relevant continuities
here concern four areas: the texts' dialect, register, pragmatic function, and
mode of speech.[1]

Dialect

During the fifth and fourth centuries BCE Ancient Greek was dialectally very
diverse. Distinct local varieties were spoken and written in every city or
region and, at least initially, none of these dialects had a higher status than
all the others. When Greeks from different places met, everybody continued to use their own dialect, as the varieties were similar enough to ensure
mutual intelligibility. Only with the growing political and cultural importance of Athens did this situation begin to change. The Athenian dialect,
Attic Greek, gradually became an international medium of expression, first
in prose writing, later more generally. As a consequence it began to lose its
most peculiar local features and, under the influence of the competing Ionic
and Doric dialects, acquired a number of originally un-Attic characteristics.
The end product of this amalgamation process was the so-called 'common'
or 'Koine' Greek of the Hellenistic period.[2]

The phonological and morphological material used in our two sample
passages (or indeed in almost every other similar-sized passage from Old,
Middle or New Comedy) shows unambiguously that they are written in
Attic.[3] For instance, Dicaeopolis' καρτερὰν ψυχήν and Sicon's τῆς οἰκίας
would sound differently in both Ionic (καρτερὴν ψυχήν, τῆς οἰκίης) and Doric
(καρτερὰν ψυχάν, τᾶς οἰκίας). Of course certain diachronic changes can be
observed here and there, as one might expect for texts written at a distance

---

[1] In the footnotes reference will be made only to some major contributions on comic
language; Willi (2002b) provides a more comprehensive bibliographical sketch.
[2] On the history of Greek consult e.g. Meillet (1965); Palmer (1980); or Horrocks (2010).
[3] For Aristophanes see Hoffmann, Debrunner and Scherer (1969) 116–19; Hiersche
(1970) 163–9; López Eire (1986); and Willi (2003a) 232–69; for Menander a detailed
treatment is lacking, but see Körte (1931) and Hiersche (1970) 178f.

of roughly a century, but on the whole an Aristophanic text is dialectally close to a Menandrean one. Since both Aristophanes and Menander were Athenians, this may be unsurprising, but it is equally true of the fragments of, say, Menander's contemporary Philemon from (Doric-speaking) Syracuse or the slightly earlier Alexis from Thourioi in Southern Italy. Hence, just as there was a convention invariably to use an established dialect in many other literary genres of classical Greek literature (see below), so the use of Attic must have been conventionalized in comedy by the end of the fifth century at the latest. Largely this situation must have come about because the comic competitions at the Athenian Lenaia and Dionysia festivals, with their predominantly Athenian audience, constituted *the* institutional forum for the genre. However, while Old Comedy did have a close connection with polis life in Athens, it would be rash to assume that Middle or New Comedy also lived exclusively in and for this one city. It is unlikely that a Philemon or a Menander, who wrote around 100 plays each, let alone an Antiphanes, who wrote more than twice that number, did this only for the Athenian market. If the minor third-century poet Machon of Sikyon could stage his comedies at Alexandria (test. 1, from Athen. 14.664a), a similar artistic demand abroad must have existed for his greater predecessors.[4]

Register

Turning to comedy's register we will at first limit ourselves to a similarly superficial analysis. The term 'register' refers to a linguistic variety used in a specific communicative situation.[5] The register of, say, an academic discussion is different from that of a chat at the local pub: different words are used, the pronunciation may be more or less careful, sentences polished or not, etc. Very broadly one may therefore separate formal from less formal, or more colloquial, registers. Considering the entire range of Greek literary genres, comedy – both Aristophanic and Menandrean – undoubtedly gravitates towards the colloquial end. Strictly speaking, it is of course impossible to prove this, for we would need recordings of actual informal conversations in Ancient Greek to show that they were linguistically more similar to a comic dialogue than to a tragic one, an orator's speech, or a piece of historiography. However, there are a number of features in comic language which are rare in other texts and whose functional value, for instance in terms of expressiveness, appears to make them particularly suitable to colloquial or

---

[4] Compare the wide dissemination of Athenian tragedy, as discussed by Taplin (1999).
[5] On registers in Ancient Greek see Willi (2010b), with bibliography.

informal registers as we know them from modern languages.[6] To cite again a few examples from our sample passages, the phrase οὐκ ἐτός '[it's] no wonder [that] . . .' in Dicaeopolis' οὐκ ἐτὸς χωλούς/πτωχοὺς ποεῖς occurs mainly in comedy, rarely in Platonic dialogue, and never elsewhere; the frequency of the varied oaths in Sicon's utterances (Ἡράκλεις ἄναξ, νὴ τὸν Οὐρανόν, Πόσειδον) is unparalleled in other genres; and even the inconspicuous added -ί in Dicaeopolis' οὑτωσί is an emphatic particle which is commonly found attached to pronouns and adverbs in comic dialogue, less often in oratory, and hardly ever in tragedy.[7] The consistency with which phenomena like these are found throughout our comic texts, and in the mouth of otherwise dissimilar stage characters, allows us therefore to regard colloquial everyday Attic as the basic or default register of Old, Middle and New Comedy alike.

Function

A further basic similarity between the languages of Old and New Comedy relates to their pragmatic function. At the level of the stage action, most comic utterances share the functions of real-life ones: they establish contact ('Who could help?'), express feelings ('Go to hell!'), communicate facts ('The master's in the well'), aim at appropriate supportive responses ('Please go down!'), and so on. At a higher level, however, the comic text has another overarching aim: to entertain and make laugh an audience that does not take part in the verbal exchange and is therefore directly addressed only rarely, as in the parabaseis of Old or the prologues of New Comedy. The methods employed in pursuit of this higher pragmatic function are, of course, far from uniform and subject to considerable change.[8] In Old, or at least Aristophanic, comedy more weight is given to two types of humour which operate at the linguistic surface and which can be termed 'paradigmatic' and 'syntagmatic'. Paradigmatic humour exploits the associative relationships linguistic expressions have in the mind of the hearer, be it for formal or semantic reasons. Typical examples include ambiguities, punning and word-play – as when Dicaeopolis is said to be from the deme Cholleidai because Χολλῄδης

---

[6] See (after Lottich (1881); Legrand (1910) 331–40; and Dittmar (1933)) Del Corno (1975) 36–47 and Krieter-Spiro (1997) 217–33 on Menander, and López Eire (1996) on Aristophanes.

[7] On deictic -ί see Dover (1997) 63f.; Martín de Lucas (1996).

[8] See Halliwell, Chapter 9. Aristophanes' verbal humour is analysed in e.g., Kronauer (1954); Michaèl (1981); Bonanno (1987); Silk (2000a); Kloss (2001); López Eire (2002b); and Robson (2006); his metaphors and imagery in Newiger (1957); Komornicka (1964); Taillardat (1965); and Moulton (1981). Again the situation in Menander is less thoroughly explored, but note Cavallero (1994).

evokes χωλός 'lame' (thus Σ Ar. *Ach.* 406; for a semantic example see e.g., Ar. *Clouds* 1156 playing with the ambiguous meaning of τόκος 'offspring' and 'interest') – or also the invention of comic metaphors and speaking names (e.g., Κινησίας for a love-sick husband in the *Lysistrata*: cf. obscene κινέω 'to bang'). Syntagmatic humour, on the other hand, results from the incongruous juxtaposition of linguistic items. For instance, in Dicaeopolis' Εὐριπίδη, Εὐριπίδιον· ὑπάκουσον, εἴπερ πώποτ' ἀνθρώπων τινί the stylistically neutral initial vocative first clashes with the subsequent diminutive as an intimate form of address, and this again with the next phrase which is parodically borrowed from solemn prayer language.[9] Although neither of these two types of linguistic humour is entirely unknown in New Comedy, a comparison with the Menandrean sample text illustrates well that comic language generally entertains in a different, less local, manner here. No doubt there is also a clash between, say, Sicon's rough words and Simiche's humble ways, but it is less marked – or more 'motivated' – than what we find in Aristophanes. Also, it does not involve stylistic parody, nor is it violating basic communicative rules (e.g., 'Avoid ambiguity'). What incongruity there is arises from the speakers' words only inasmuch as these reflect incongruous characters. Even so, the projected audience response to the scene remains laughter and the verbal arrangement is thus still essential to the comedy's success or failure.

Mode

Finally, earlier and later comedy resemble each other as far as their principal mode of speech is concerned. In both Old and New Comedy descriptive and narrative monologues[10] as well as songs had their place, but the most prominent mode is the mimetic representation of dialogue. Obviously, mimesis has to be understood broadly in this context. A conversation like that between Dicaeopolis, Euripides' servant and Euripides himself defies any notion of naturalistic conversational behaviour, and even the Menandrean sample is unnatural in the sense that the ancient Greeks did not normally talk to each other in iambic trimeters. Yet, the fact that comedy provides at least an approximative image of natural speech production makes it invaluable to the linguistic historian. Without comedy, be it Aristophanic or Menandrean, our idea of what a real conversation in Athens must have sounded

---

[9] On diminutive vocatives in Aristophanes see Schmid (1945); on the parody of prayers and ritual language Kleinknecht (1937); Horn (1970); and Willi (2003a) 8–50.

[10] On monologues and monologue technique, especially in Menander, see e.g., Blundell (1980); Lamagna (1998); and Nünlist (2002).

like would be even vaguer – or, quite literally, more Platonic – than it is anyway.[11]

Discontinuities

Despite its focus on continuities, the preceding discussion already had to concede that the language of comedy is a universe of change as well as stability. Given the relatively abstract nature of what has been said so far, it will not come as a surprise if a closer analysis confirms what our sample passages suggest: that discontinuity prevails. There is no other genre in ancient Greek literature whose language changed so fundamentally within less than 200 years. In order to understand how and why we will again look separately at each of the four areas individuated above.

Dialect

To start with dialect, we have so far neglected the existence of Doric comedy. Its greatest representative, Epicharmus, was active in Syracuse long before Aristophanes, Eupolis or Cratinus – indeed, if we believe Aristotle (*Poet.* 1448a33-34 = Epich. test. 4), even before Chionides and Magnes, two of the early authors of Attic comedy. The extent to which Doric comedy influenced its Attic sister genre is a matter of dispute, but there is little reason not to accept Aristotle's remark (*Poet.* 1449b5–7) that one of the central features of classical Attic comedy since Crates (and probably the one feature that survived best into New Comedy) is rooted in this Western tradition: the presence of a unitary story-line in every play. In comparison with this, the second source of influence highlighted by Aristotle, improvised phallic songs (*Poet.* 1449a9–14), seems less pivotal to the subsequent evolution of the genre. All the more, the dialectal appearance of Attic comedy, which is often simply taken for granted, deserves our attention. Greek literary genres typically perpetuate the use of that dialect in which they were written during their formative period. Greek epic, for example, once it had found its canonical form in the Homeric poems, continued to be composed ever after in 'epic Ionic', even though it had also existed before Homer and in parts of the Greek world where Ionic was not normally used. Similarly, Greek tragedy, a product of Athens, retained the Attic dialect when it was transferred to Sicily through Aeschylus, by invitation of Hieron of Syracuse. Not so comedy. However revolutionary the introduction of plots *à la Sicilienne* must have been, and however much Attic comedy as we define it existed

---

[11] See e.g., Dickey (1995) on forms of address.

only after this formative shift, the new Sicilian ingredient did not in any way affect the use of the Attic dialect which must have characterized the subliterary phallic songs mentioned by Aristotle. In other words, by existing in (at least) two equally recognized dialect versions throughout the fifth century BCE, in (Doric) Syracusan as well as Attic, comedy is the odd one out among Greek literary genres; and that raises the question why.

Unfortunately, most Epicharmian fragments are short and/or badly preserved. Even so a look at the following damaged lines from his *Pyrrha and Prometheus* may help to find an answer (while also illustrating Epicharmus' Doric dialect).[12] We are apparently witnessing a conversation between Pyrrha and Deucalion who are advised by a third person (Prometheus?) to build an ark large enough for both of them as well as food and drink for a month, in order to survive the Flood; but Pyrrha seems to suspect that Prometheus only means to cheat them and steal either the ark itself when it is ready or, perhaps more likely, those of their belongings which they will not have taken inside (Epich. fr. 113.4–15):

παλίκαν τὸ μ]έγαθος; :: ἁλίκα χ᾽ ὗμ᾽ ἐγχά[δηι
κ]αὶ μηνιῆιον ἐφό[διον
] . [.] . ε λάρναχ᾽ οὕτω ποικίλ[αν
]ε ποικίλας ἀπόχρη κἀφελ[
ἀπ]οχρησεῖ· στεγάζειν δεῖ μόνο[ν
λά]ρναξ κἢν στέγαι κἢτ [
(Πυ.)]ἐστ[ὑ]ποπτεύω γα καὶ δέδοικ᾽ ἐγὼν
μὴ δ[τ]ὰ σκευάρια πάντα βᾶι φέρω[ν
ὁ Προμα[θεὺς]ἧσθαι προμαθεούμενος
κάρτα τ[   ]κόν τε χἀμαρτωλικόν
αἰ γένοιθ᾽ ὃ ισ[   ] Προμαθέος
μηδαμῶς του[   ]ν, ὦ Πύρρα, κακ[

[Deucalion?]   What size?
[Prometheus?]   Large enough to hold you two [. . .] and provisions for a
                month [. . .]
[???]   [. . .] such a colourful ark [. . .] colourful [. . .] is sufficient
                and [. . .]
[Prometheus?]   [. . .] will be sufficient: one will just have to put a roof on [. . .]
[???]   [. . .] ark and on the roof [. . .]
[Pyrrha.]   [. . .] I do suspect and fear that [. . .] Prometheus takes all the
                stuff and is off with it [. . .] foreseeing very [. . .] and deceitful
[???]   If it came about what [. . .] of Prometheus
[Deucalion?]   Do not [. . .], Pyrrha, bad [. . .]

---

[12] On Epicharmus' language see Cassio (2002); Bellocchi (2008) 262–9; and Willi (2008) 119–61; on his style also Berk (1964) 42–54.

In terms of content not much can be learned from a passage like this. Importantly, however, we see how three mythological figures converse with each other in what looks like pure Syracusan Doric, not a literary Doric as in choral lyric texts or the like. To be sure, most of what we know about Syracusan comes from the fragments of Epicharmus so that this statement might look circular. However, we do know enough about the various Doric dialects as a group to say that (a) at least there is nothing here that would seem odd for 'real' Syracusan, and (b) certain Epicharmian forms, such as προμαθεούμενος (instead of προμαθεύμενος), would be unusual in other Doric literature; that is, their belonging to a local dialect actually spoken, not just written, is most plausible. Meanwhile, in Epicharmus too we find a good number of features that point to a colloquial register, such as in the above sample the exceptional adjective ἁμαρτωλικός (with the productive suffix -ικός, for more usual ἁμαρτωλός) or the diminutive σκευάρια, which is predominantly found in comedy. *Mutatis mutandis* the situation is therefore the same as in Attic comedy, the difference really residing only in the basic dialect, not in the stylistic level of expression. But the fact that even mythical heroes (such as Prometheus) are made to speak like ordinary men suggests that it is precisely this assimilation of the stage characters' language to the language of the audience that lies at the heart of comic discourse: the issue is not so much linguistic naturalism (which would be a silly notion with regard to a mythical past) but linguistic closeness. Where other genres distanced themselves from the audience by means of their explicitly 'literary' code, fifth-century comedy did the opposite – and that entailed the use of the present audience's dialect, no matter what else any individual author's wish to preserve or highlight the genre's legacy could have suggested. That this special relationship between genre language and audience language may have been lost later on, with Attic Greek truly becoming a genre-conditioned, not audience-conditioned, dialect in Middle and New Comedy, has already been said; but since this loss happened at a time when dialectal differences were being levelled in favour of Attic-based Koine Greek anyway, the production of a fourth-century comedy in Attic outside Athens will no longer have seemed as outlandish as the production of a comedy in Syracusan Doric at the Lenaia would have been a century earlier.

Yet, by talking about a well-defined '(primary) audience dialect' we might again be simplifying things too much. Like any natural language, Attic Greek was not diachronically stable. The eventual transformation of spoken Attic into spoken Koine Greek is one difficulty. Already in antiquity there was some debate about how 'Attic' Menander's Attic still was. The purist grammarians Phrynichus (*passim*: e.g., *Ecl.* 394, 402, 408 Fischer) and Pollux (e.g., *Onom.* 3.29) condemned it, arguing that too many lexical elements typical of Koine Greek had already crept in. However, although it is indeed possible to single out certain words that were not used by the classical authors of the late fifth century, it is impossible to regard Menander's vocabulary *in toto* as fully Koineized.[13] To give but one or two examples, the word for 'ship' is still normally ναῦς, not πλοῖον, and that for 'slave' can still be παῖς, instead of παιδίον. Similarly, word formation, syntax and phonology remain distinctly Attic wherever a sensible boundary can be drawn between Attic and Koine Greek at all.[14] Words like the one for 'sea', for example, consistently appear with ττ, not σσ (i.e. Attic θάλαττα, not Koine θάλασσα), and when in Menandrean syntax the dual number virtually disappears or the subjunctive encroaches on the domain of the optative it is primarily a matter of nomenclature whether one wants to diagnose here a 'Koineized' form of Attic or simply a 'late-fourth-century' one.

But what we cannot, of course, tell is how many Athenians in Menander's theatre really still spoke such 'good' Attic: perhaps most of them, perhaps only a small minority. And a similar problem arises when we look back at the Attic of Old Comedy. In Aristophanes' last comedy, *Wealth* of 388 BCE, a number of linguistic features are noticeably 'late' when compared with how Aristophanes wrote in his earlier plays. On its own the relatively short time-gap between *Wealth* and the preceding Aristophanic plays (*Assembly Women, Frogs*) cannot account for these innovations. Hence, the change in style which manifests itself in a greater openness for less conservative forms of expression may instead relate to a change in the character of the comic genre, *Wealth* being a less polis-oriented comedy than its predecessors.[15] In other words, as long as Aristophanes was writing polis-comedies (or 'Old' as opposed to 'Middle' comedies), his dialect may have been consciously conservative, favouring traditional over innovative Attic wherever actual usage was divided. If this is true, it entails that the Attic heard on stage was not necessarily the same as the Attic spoken by a majority of the audience. Rather each comic poet could (or had to) decide afresh where to situate himself on the scale between linguistic conservatism and linguistic innovation. If we had more than fragments of Aristophanes' rivals, it would probably be possible to discern some of this synchronic genre-internal differentiation. As it is, we are at best left with some vague intuitions. Thus, the greater frequency with which the so-called 'Antiatticist' grammarian (second century CE) cites the fifth-century comedians Plato and Phrynichus in order to

[13] The contributions by Bruhn (1910); Durham (1913); and Klaus (1936) are still useful; on Menander's reception by the grammarians see Lamagna (2004).
[14] See Poultney (1963); Rosenstrauch (1967); Horrocks (2010) 52–5; López Eire (2002a).
[15] Willi (2003b).

disprove stricter purists and show that a certain word or expression did occur in 'classical' Attic, may indicate that the dialect of these two poets was less traditionalist than that of, say, Cratinus and Aristophanes.[16]

Register

The truism that different writers may have written differently is equally valid when we next reconsider the register of comedy. In everyday life some people unavoidably express themselves in more educated ways, others in more vulgar ones. So, just as there was a diachronic range of Attic Greek(s) at any point in time, there was also a range of colloquial registers to act as default registers for comedy. For whatever it is worth, Aristophanes himself attacked the coarse humour of some of his rivals (*Frogs* 12–15; cf. *Clouds* 524–5, *Wasps* 66) and such humour may well have been expressed in similarly vulgar language. But vulgar and obscene words and expressions are not absent from Aristophanes either, and some evidence for them is found already in Epicharmus. Moreover, as far as Attic comedy is concerned we must bear in mind that such material might simply reflect a generic inheritance from iambography and/or phallic song-writing. After all, although some sources observe that Cratinus and Eupolis were particularly fond of λοιδορία ('abuse'; see Cratinus test. 17, 25, Eupolis test. 2, 20, 42), the abuse of public figures (and, in connection with this, a high degree of freedom of speech) had an important social-regulatory role also in Aristophanes' plays.[17]

More important than any individual's divergence from an imaginary generic average, therefore, are the omnipresent register discontinuities *within* each comic text. Until now we have concentrated only on what has deliberately been called the 'default' register of comedy. But it is hardly an exaggeration to say that the continuous shifting of registers is the single most important defining feature of comic language before New Comedy.[18] On one level we see this when we compare different constituent parts of a classical comedy. An Aristophanic parabasis often comes across as less colloquial

---

[16] For a more detailed argument along these lines see Willi (2010a); Aristophanes' relative conservatism is highlighted in Willi (2003a) 232–69, to be held against López Eire (1991) 9–61.

[17] On the origins and function of comic abuse and *aiskhrologia* see Rosen (1988); Degani (1993); Treu (1999); Bowie (2002); Saetta Cottone (2005); and Halliwell (2008) 215–63; on obscenity in Aristophanes Henderson (1991a); on terms of abuse and negative evaluation also Müller (1913) and Dover (2002). For some less prominent material in Epicharmus and Menander see, respectively, Willi (2008) 150 and Legrand (1910) 611f.

[18] Silk (2000a) 110–17, 136–40; cf. Dover (1970).

and more stately than a passage in iambic trimeters, both in the spoken parts and in the odes which may even contain non-parodic lyrical elements (words, syntax).[19] On another – and yet more crucial – level, comic parody itself is recognizable only because it highlights, and exploits for humorous purposes, differences between linguistic varieties. Some of the most easily recognizable examples concern not registers, but foreign dialects, as when Dicaeopolis in *Acharnians* meets a Megarian and a Boeotian or when Lysistrata talks to her Spartan friend Lampito. The rendering of these foreign dialects appears to be fairly accurate and thus constitutes a precious source for our knowledge of fifth-century non-Attic Greek.[20] To be located somewhere between a foreign dialect and a register of Attic is the broken Greek of characters like the Persian ambassador in *Acharnians*, the Triballian visitor in *Birds*, or the Scythian archer in *Women at the Thesmophoria*. These passages are important because they tell us something about Athenian perceptions and representations of 'barbarians'.[21] Most common, however, is register parody properly speaking. A prime example occurs in our sample passage from *Acharnians*. Euripides' τί λέλακας, for instance, contains a high-flown verb λάσκω which, with the meaning 'to utter aloud', is peculiar to tragedy; and the servant's οὐκ ἔνδον ἔνδον ἐστίν employs a type of chiastic oxymoron that is typically associated with (sophistic/Euripidean) tragedy. But it would be wrong to infer from this scene that similar register parodies are always consistent in the sense that, for example, 'tragic' utterances could only come from 'tragic' poets and their entourage. In fact, Dicaeopolis himself is increasingly affected by the Euripidean note in the conversation, and at the end it is he who takes leave with the paratragic words καὶ γάρ εἰμ᾽ ἄγαν ὀχληρός, οὐ δοκῶν με κοιράνους στυγεῖν 'for over-molesting I am, albeit unwitting of the masters' spite' (Ar. *Ach.* 471–2).[22] Overall, such more or less unexpected departures from the default register are frequent and varied enough throughout the plays of Aristophanes to suggest a description of his language as quintessentially 'centrifugal'; and the same is probably true of Old Comedy more widely, given parodic fragments such as Archippus fr. 27 (with a treaty in officialese between Athens and the fishes); Cratinus fr. 259 (with a para-epic genealogy of Pericles' wife Aspasia born of Καταπυγοσύνη 'Lewdness'); or Eupolis fr. 16 (with a hymn to the Graces, αἶσι

---

[19] See Mastromarco (1987).
[20] See especially Colvin (1995), (1999), and (2000); cf. Kloss (2001) 34–54.
[21] Cf. Willi (2002c) 142–9 and (2003a) 198–225, after Friedrich (1918); Brixhe (1988); and Sier (1992).
[22] On Aristophanic paratragedy see Rau (1967); on parodies of other styles and registers e.g., Adami (1901); Burckhardt (1924); Bernabé (1995); Kloss (2001); and the literature cited in n. 8 above and n. 26 below.

μέλουσιν ἑψητοί 'who care for boiled fish'). In contrast with this, the language of (certainly Menandrean) New Comedy, like that of nearly all other literary genres of Ancient Greece, is 'centripetal': most utterances converge on the default register and those that do disrupt it – as does, for instance, Men. *Sicyonian* 169–70 with a sudden switch into paratragic style – frequently aim at heightened emotionality rather than comic effect.[23]

Function

While the preceding analysis thus corroborates our earlier suspicion that comedy over time loses some of its generic uniqueness, we must not conclude from this that it also loses its generic autonomy. On the contrary, because of Old Comedy's stylistic diversity, which relies on the interplay with various forms of the linguistic Other, one might rather argue that Old Comedy is a *less* autonomous genre than New Comedy. However, (Aristophanic) Old Comedy is not to the same extent 'heteronomous' as some of the mythological persiflages must have been which are hinted at by many titles of Middle Comedy (and Doric comedy before). The way in which these latter plays lived off other texts was more comprehensive, and not just because, to judge from the fragments we have, the parodic element seems to have been more thematic than linguistic there. If an Aristophanic play – even one like *Women at the Thesmophoria* or *Frogs* – were stripped of all its parody, something essential would still be left: a cultural, social and/or political message. Hence, notwithstanding the importance of the entertainment function of comic language, language in Aristophanes also has an overtly didactic purpose. Old Comedy argues and ridicules on behalf of the sovereign *dêmos* of Athens.[24] For obvious reasons it can do so only through the medium of language. Admittedly this second, didactic, function largely falls to the *signifié* side of language, which lies outside the scope of this chapter, whereas the entertainment function is more often a matter (also) of the *signifiant* and as such of greater relevance here. But the linguistic centrifugality we have diagnosed for Old Comedy also has to be seen in a 'political' light.[25] By making fun of all that is deviant from the linguistic 'norms' set by the *dêmos* and embodied in the colloquial default register, comedy endorses these norms and reinforces civic cohesion among an audience which, despite its heterogeneity, discovers that it can laugh at one and

[23] See Oliva (1968); Sandbach (1970) 126–36; Webster (1974) 56–67; Hurst (1990); see also Nesselrath (1993) on Middle Comedy.

[24] Henderson (1990), after [Xen.] *Ath. Pol.* 2.18; see also Carey (1994); Henderson (1998).

[25] See Willi (2002c).

ANDREAS WILLI

the same target: those 'alien voices' the average Athenian was socially and culturally bound to encounter in his or her city. Thus, it is no coincidence that the literary registers parodied preferentially by the poets of Old Comedy are those of tragedy and epic – two genres, that is, whose socio-cultural status was least likely to be questioned outside the institutionally carnivalesque framework provided by the comic performance.[26] Vice versa, the shift from the parody of tragedy to that of dithyramb in Middle Comedy (e.g., Ar. *Wealth* 290–315, Antiphanes fr. 55, 110, Anaxandrides fr. 6, Eubulus fr. 56) also acquires a new significance. From a purely formal point of view it may make little difference if paradithyrambic extravagant compound adjectives take the place of equally recherché paratragic nouns in –μα, but the laughter they are supposed to provoke is no longer the same. To laugh at tragic language had a communal dimension, but to laugh at the language of dithyramb was primarily a statement of cultural and aesthetic attitude (see already Ar. *Birds* 1372–1409).[27]

Mode

In this context, a further development deserving attention is the disappearance of dialect parody. We have seen that dialect parody occurs with some frequency in Aristophanes. In addition there is some, though often elusive, evidence for it in the fragments of other writers of Old Comedy (e.g., Crates fr. 1, Eupolis fr. 147, 149, Strattis fr. 29, 49). In Middle Comedy, whose thematic focus is less specifically Athenian, a similar dialectally configured 'us vs. them' dichotomy may no longer have worked well. It is true that Alexis fr. 146 also makes reference to the use of Doric instead of Attic, but what is at stake there is not a polar opposition to the audience's local identity, but a doctor's special language. Similarly, the fake doctor in Menander's *Aspis* (444–64; cf. 374–9) has to speak Doric in order to sound impressive (presumably because the most eminent medical schools were located in Doric Cos and Cnidus). Hence, starting already with a doctor's Doric utterance in Crates fr. 46 – a fragment which thus jeopardizes any clear-cut chronological boundary between Old and Middle Comedy – we can trace the development of a stock character who is associated with a foreign linguistic variety

[26] For Bakhtinian/carnivalesque readings of Old Comedy, see e.g., Carrière (1979); Goldhill (1991) 167–222; von Möllendorff (1995); and Platter (2007). Note that Aristophanes' predilection for paratragedy need not be representative of Old Comedy as a whole: see Silk (2000b); Revermann (2006a) 101–4.

[27] On dithyrambic parody in Middle Comedy see Nesselrath (1990) 241–66 and Dobrov (2002); on paradithyramb in Aristophanes Zimmermann (1997); and on the cultural implications of the phenomenon Csapo (2004).

(and who is perhaps ultimately inherited from subliterary Doric farce: see Athen. 14.621d).[28]

The mimetic mode involved with such stock characters is somewhat different from the one we observe in Dicaeopolis' conversation with Euripides and similar passages. Whereas the latter is limited to an approximative imitation of human dialogue (however communicatively derailed this dialogue may be), the former respects a vague form of naturalistic coherence and consistency. Up to a point, of course, a figure such as Aristophanes' Euripides in *Acharnians* is also a standardized tragedian whose use of tragic language is intrinsically motivated; and indeed, despite the presence of certain individualizing traits, this Euripides is perhaps linguistically more similar to the stage Agathon in *Women at the Thesmophoria* than to the Euripides appearing in *Frogs*. Overall, however, stage figures who are continuously characterized, notably by linguistic means, remain the exception rather than the rule in Aristophanes.[29] Even the dithyrambic poet of *Birds*, the tragedians Aeschylus and Euripides in *Frogs*, or the philosopher Socrates in *Clouds*, for all of whom a consistent linguistic identity could have been designed and all of whom do speak unlike ordinary Athenians at times, do not belong to this category.

Truly naturalistic mimesis, meanwhile, is something incompatible also with stock characters. Their creation is the dramatic counterpart to the recognition, by scholars like Theophrastus, of a number of character types in real life.[30] As such it is a first step towards a better understanding of individual psychology, but not more. We cannot therefore overrate the novelty of the linguistically consistent and naturalistic depiction of idiolects which we find with Menandrean figures such as the stiff Gorgias in *Dyscolus* or the youthful Habrotonon in *Men at Arbitration*.[31] It would even be reductionist to see the roots of this innovation exclusively in earlier stock-character comedy. Much rather it is a feature inherited from mime, a genre whose early interest in an adequate representation of natural language use gleams through the scanty fragments of the Syracusan writer Sophron. By way of illustration one may contrast the individualized language of Menander's cook Sicon in our initial sample with the bombastic and riddling stock-character language of a Middle Comedy cook (A) conversing with

[28] See Gigante (1969); Gil and Rodríguez Alfageme (1972); Rossi (1977).

[29] Dover (1976), after Plut. *Mor.* 853c–d; cf. Silk (1990) and (2000a) 207–55; Del Corno (1997); Beta (2004) 259–77.

[30] Broadly speaking, the differential treatment of women's speech also falls under this heading: see Bain (1984) on Menander and Sommerstein (1995/2009), Willi (2003a) 157–97 and Duhoux (2004) on Aristophanes.

[31] See Zini (1938); Sandbach (1970); Webster (1974) 99–110; Del Corno (1975) 19–33; Katsouris (1975); Arnott (1995); Krieter-Spiro (1997) 234–50.

ANDREAS WILLI

an exasperated employer (B) in Antiphanes' *The Parasite* (fr. 180; cf. e.g.,
Antiphanes fr. 55, Strato fr. 1):[32]

(A)   [...] ἄλλος ἐπὶ τούτωι μέγας
ἥξει τις ἰσοτράπεζος εὐγενής (B) τίνα
λέγεις; (A) Καρύστου θρέμμα, γηγενής, ζέων
(B) εἶτ᾽ οὐκ ἂν εἴποις; ὕπαγε. (A) κάκκαβον λέγω·
σὺ δ᾽ ἴσως ἂν εἴποις λοπάδ᾽. (B) ἐμοὶ δὲ τοὔνομα
οἴει διαφέρειν, εἴτε κάκκαβόν τινες
χαίρουσιν ὀνομάζοντες εἴτε σίττυβον;
πλὴν ὅτι λέγεις ἀγγεῖον οἶδα

A And another one will come after this, large, table-equalling, well-born–
B What are you talking about?
A A nursling of Carystus, earth-born, sizzling–
B Won't you say it? Get away!
A A casserole, I mean, but you might perhaps call it a dish.
B Do you think I care what its name is, if some call it a 'casserole' or a
   'throw-a-role'? All I know is you're talking about a vessel.

However pompous actual fourth-century cooks may have been, that they
commonly used the literary words Antiphanes' character selects is out of
the question. Moreover, although some experimenting with high-flown gastronomic poetry did take place at the time (Philoxenus, Archestratus; cf.
Pl. Com. fr. 189), there is no intrinsic connection between the role of the
cook and his linguistic register. So even if in one sense language is indeed
more strictly conditioned by character in a case like this than it would (usually) have been in Old Comedy, in another sense its far-from-naturalistic
use nevertheless remains closer to Aristophanic than to Menandrean practice. Admittedly, some of the earlier brilliance may have disappeared, the
metaphors have become less colourful, the puns (even) flatter (as in the
untranslatable κάκκαβος/σίττυβος example), the verbal inventiveness tame:
comic names retreat and witty word coinages make room for a revival of
the lexical catalogues known from some of the less charming Epicharmian
fragments (e.g., frr. 40–61).[33] But comic language has not yet been placed
in the naturalist painter's picture frame where Menander has it. It is still
a toy to be played with at will by the poet, ultimately free from any but
the most general constraints of its mimetic mode. The fundamental change

[32] See Nesselrath (1990) 257–62, 297–309; Wilkins (2000) 369–414; Dobrov (2002).
[33] But verbal accumulation also exists in Aristophanes: see Spyropoulos (1974); Silk
   (2000a) 132–6. On the loss of metaphorical colouring in New Comedy see Chiarini
   (1983); on the non-comic character of New Comedy names Brown (1987); and on
   comic word formation in Old Comedy e.g., Uckermann (1879); Peppler (1910), (1916),
   (1918), (1921); da Costa Ramalho (1952); and Handley (1953).

in taste to which Menander's comedy testifies must have come later, promoted if not triggered by the loss of Athenian independence. Thematically comedy had long abandoned politics by then. But by becoming an image of real life, its language was only now taking leave from the stereotypes inherent in group representation. The civic community which had roaringly laughed the linguistic Other off the stage no longer existed. Instead, each spectator smilingly waited to hear his or her own voice rise from the comic stage.

Further reading

Since publications on the language(s) of comedy usually deal with specific formal or functional aspects, rather than the field in its entirety, pertinent references are best accessed through the footnotes to each section. A variety of approaches is represented in collective volumes such as De Martino and Sommerstein (1995); Thiercy and Menu (1997); Ercolani (2002); and Willi (2002a). Important recent monographs include Henderson (1991a); López Eire (1996); Colvin (1999); Kloss (2001); Willi (2003a); Beta (2004); and Robson (2006), all of which focus on Aristophanes as a particularly diverse object of study.

PART III

Central themes

9

STEPHEN HALLIWELL

Laughter

εἴπω τι τῶν εἰωθότων, ὦ δέσποτα,
ἐφ᾽ οἷς ἀεὶ γελῶσιν οἱ θεώμενοι;

Shall I give them some of the usual stuff, then, master –
The things that *always* make the audience laugh?

Aristophanes *Frogs* 1f.

[W]e do not know how the words sounded, or where
precisely we ought to laugh.

Virginia Woolf, 'On not knowing Greek'

Laughter is both a fundamental parameter of comedy and a quintessential
symptom of its elusiveness. Take the *idea* (or possibility) of laughter entirely
out of the equation, and comedy vanishes with it. Yet to invoke laughter
for the purposes of explaining 'the comic' seems only to compound the
problem of how to rationalize what gives comedy (of any particular kind)
its distinctive character. In Greek, the expression τὸ γελοῖον, 'the laughable'
or 'the ridiculous', is often practically synonymous with 'comedy', *kômôidia*,
itself. Aristotle, for instance, explicitly regards the former as the essence of
the latter at the start of Chapter 5 of the *Poetics* (1449a32–7).[1] Prior to this
Aristotle had already assumed the link in question when describing Homer,
supposed author of the mock epic *Margites*, as a pioneer in comedy: 'he was
the first to delineate the form(s) of comedy by dramatising the laughable
rather than composing invective [i.e. *iambos*]' (*Poet.* 4.1448b36–49a2). All
Greeks would have agreed that comedy could not be conceptualized or
interpreted without intrinsic reference to laughter. In Plato's *Symposium*,
Aristophanes is happy to 'play the laughter-maker' (γελωτοποιεῖν, a verb
that might here even be stretched to mean 'be a poet of laughter'), since
making others laugh 'belongs to the territory of my Muse'.[2] As a treatise
from late antiquity or the Byzantine era sums it up, 'comedy begins from

---

[1] Plato's *Philebus* also links the audience psychology of comedy (48a) to the nature of 'the
laughable' (48c).
[2] Plato, *Symp.* 189a–b: what Aristophanes does *not* want is to be 'risible', καταγέλαστος,
lit. 'laughed down'; cf. my text below.

and ends with laughter'. Or, as another such treatise pithily puts it, laughter is 'the mother' of comedy.[3]

But if comedy needs the idea of laughter for its (self-)definition, how is laughter itself to be accounted for without setting up a circular appeal to what is comic, ridiculous or amusing? The problem calls for a double perspective. In the first place, allowance must be made for the active collaboration of audiences in responding to and fulfilling the strategies of humour enacted on stage. For reasons both pragmatic and psychological, a comic audience's laughter can hardly be a continuous, unvarying accompaniment. Rather, it *punctuates* a (successful) performance with appropriate rhythms of involvement and approval, thereby complementing and enhancing the work of the actors. Yet for a modern reader or critic the psychology of ancient audiences is always itself an interpretative hypothesis, not a fixed point of reference: where laughter is concerned, we should posit an interplay between stage and spectators without trying to syllogize that relationship in terms of necessary cause and effect. The second component of a desirable perspective on the nexus of comedy and laughter requires some attempt to correlate the dynamics of comic theatre with a culture's wider uses of, and attitudes to, laughter in the social world. But here it is prudent to bear in mind that comedy need not simply replicate those cultural habits: it can also manipulate, stretch and even challenge them. Furthermore, the operations of laughter are subject, like other aspects of Greek comedy, to processes of historical change, especially in regard to the evolution from Old to New Comedy. The present chapter will therefore give separate treatment to the work of Aristophanes and Menander, exploring some of the ways in which laughter can be taken as an index of the relationships between their contrasting styles of comedy and their audiences' frames of reference.

It is an important preliminary to recognize that classical Athens (in this respect partly reflecting the wider currents of Greek culture) possessed a complicated set of views about the social workings of laughter.[4] Those views evaluate occurrences (and, indeed, the *idea*) of laughter on several scales of judgement, two of which are particularly pertinent here. One of these distinguishes between acts of laughter expressive of hostility and antagonism (including *hybris*, aggressive offensiveness) and those which serve as markers of 'playful', shared pleasure: it is standard to describe the former as

[3] *Prolegomena de comoedia* XIIa, perhaps by Tzetzes: Koster (1975) 50. *Tractatus Coislinianus* IV: Koster (1975) 64.12; Janko (1984) 24f.
[4] For fuller documentation of the Athenian and Greek attitudes indicated here, see Halliwell (2008). Woolf (1992) 104 (cf. 93 for my second epigraph) recognizes that laughter is culturally conditioned, but her intuitions on the Greek side are rather hazy.

'laughing down' (καταγελᾶν) someone, i.e. exposing them to derision and shame, whereas the laughter of play involves a pretence of ridicule and arises from the pursuit of reciprocal gratification. The other evaluative scale embraces (perceived) differences between sophisticated and vulgar or witty and crude manifestations of humour. These two scales are in principle independent of one another (e.g., aggressive laughter might be judged 'sophisticated', playful laughter 'vulgar', by particular agents or observers) but they can clearly intersect.

The distinctions just mentioned are far from secure; the same laughter can all too easily be evaluated from divergent points of view or according to the expectations of different contexts. The resulting uncertainties and complications are magnified (and toyed with) in comic theatre. Playwrights and performers clearly need to create a bond of reciprocal gratification with their audiences: comic theatre itself is, in that sense, a culturally institutionalized enactment of 'play'.[5] But laughter is also depicted at work in the social world *inside* the plays, and there is always in consequence a sort of two-level structure to an audience's relationship to the possibilities of comic laughter. Those possibilities are partly a matter of dramatic display and partly embodied in the (collective) experience of the spectators themselves. How far those two levels converge or move apart is a factor in determining the ethos or spirit of particular kinds of comedy.

Aristophanes not only has an acute instinct for comedy's vital yet slippery relationship to laughter; he converts that instinct into a way of *making* comedy. The start of *Frogs* provides an explicit, teasing illustration of this process. Xanthias' opening question to Dionysus, quoted as my first epigraph, initiates an exchange whose element of metatheatrical self-reference has been extensively analysed.[6] Laughter is central to the play of ideas in the passage, but ambiguously so. In a voice which is half the actor's, half the character's, Xanthias asks permission to indulge in stage routines associated with baggage-carrying slave roles like the one he is playing. Dionysus' voice is equally layered, in his case between the identities of character and *spectator* ('when I'm watching plays', 16), the latter linked to his status as god of theatrical festivals and therefore ultimate arbiter of comic success. He responds by warning Xanthias against the sort of jokes that depend on vulgar bodily reference, including scatology (8, 11): these make the god feel physical disgust (4, 11). Over and above the evident paradox that Aristophanes' own play (half-)exploits the routines which Xanthias suggests are typical of

---

[5] In its festive institutionalization, it may also be related to, or overlap with, practices of religious ritual: on this larger question, which is particularly relevant to Old Comedy, see Halliwell (2008) 206–14, 243–63.

[6] E.g., Silk (2000a) 26–33; Slater (2002) 183–5.

inferior playwrights (13f.), the passage poses a larger comic conundrum. If an audience laughs at this opening scene (and it may start doing so even before a word is spoken, when it *sees* the antics of the semi-disguised Dionysus and his donkey-riding slave),[7] what is it laughing at – recycled comic clichés (if that is really what they were) or the ironic deprecation of them, Xanthias' vulgarity or Dionysus' 'discriminating' tastes? More pointedly, if it laughs at the suggestion of 'things that *always* make the audience laugh', is it proving itself predictably easy to please or showing its own sophistication by enjoying a game of double bluff between performers and spectators? And how could any audience be collectively sure of the difference?

Given this conundrum, which leaves the idea of laughter hovering as an uncertain test of comic effect, I want to stress that actual theatre audiences are always (mixed) realizations of *potential* audiences. In the absence of independent documentation of individual performances, this means that when framing hypotheses about audiences we are always dealing with multiple possibilities abstracted schematically from actuality. That is not, however, an impediment to interpretation. Dramatic meaning is never in any case reducible to actual audience response/reception (any more than it is reducible to conscious authorial intention). We can coherently focus on the types of response available to spectators, while accepting that the contingent particulars of individual audiences lie largely beyond reconstruction.[8] But the opening of *Frogs* complicates things further. It makes it hard to imagine any spectator being able (or needing) to isolate any one way of laughing at the scene. The comic effect itself depends on a *(con)fusion* of possibilities; critics confident of finding a specific Aristophanic 'statement' in the passage are succumbing to a mirage.[9] The scene seeks to activate laughter precisely by exposing its fluid, volatile nature. When Xanthias concludes that 'this neck of mine . . . is getting choked but isn't allowed to raise a laugh' (19f.), he is complaining about the suppression of his comic voice in the very act of exercising it.

There is a connection here, especially in Dionysus' sarcastic reference to the 'clever tricks' or 'would-be subtleties' (*sophismata*: 17) of other playwrights, with a more general feature of Aristophanes' work: the manipulation of a distinction between sophisticated (clever, original, witty) and

---

[7] Compare, as a retrospective 'clue', Heracles' barely suppressed laughter at the sight of Dionysus, *Frogs* 42–6.

[8] For one perspective on Athenian theatre audiences, see Revermann (2006b); cf. Revermann (2006a) 159–75. See also Roselli, pp. 242–6.

[9] Henderson (1991a) 188 translates Dionysus' distaste into Aristophanes' own 'contempt' for scatological comedy, presuming the playwright a reliable witness to other poets' practices and claiming, with special pleading, that Aristophanes himself exploits scatology at length in 'only a small number of scenes'.

vulgar (bodily, clichéd, coarse) modes of comedy. This distinction, which tracks the larger scale of social values mentioned above, is employed in ways that require a cooperative sense of irony on the part of spectators, who may find themselves drawn into an implicitly ambivalent relationship to (supposedly) 'highbrow' and 'lowbrow' forms of theatrical experience. If laughter counts as the *raison d'être* of his genre, Aristophanes purports to offer his audiences a superior version of it. In the prologue of *Wasps*, a slave tells the audience not to expect 'laughter filched from Megara' (57); the play will stage something 'cleverer than vulgar comedy' (66). 'Megarian' comedy was a disparaging Athenian label for traditional routines of slapstick and obscene farce: the slave is claiming, for *Wasps* itself, higher standards of comic interest (though not *so* high as to sound pretentious).[10] But among the things the slave declares off the menu is a repeat of Aristophanes' own earlier 'pounding' of Cleon (62f.). This is a sly trick, a comic half-truth: Cleon will be a repeated target of satire in *Wasps*. The result is a sort of boomerang joke when the prologue ends (133f.) by announcing the two main characters' names, Cleon-lover (Philocleon) and Cleon-loather (Bdelycleon)! As for the idea that *Wasps* will avoid trite, indecent ('Megarian') cues for laughter, this should not be taken at face value. One need only think of the scene where the drunken Philocleon asks a naked girl to grip his phallus and requests a reward for his 'prick' for having abducted her from a symposium at which she was, he states, expected to fellate the guests.[11] An attuned audience of Old Comedy would not have treated the slave's predictions in the prologue as factual information but as a means of extracting possibilities of laughter from the tension between a rhetoric of refined taste and the comic pull of gross physicality.

Something comparable can be seen at work in the (partially) revised parabasis of *Clouds*. Here the poet's first-person voice defends the 'cleverness' of the work in response to its defeat in 423 by the plays of 'vulgar men' (524), and contrasts its 'intellectual' standards with the allegedly coarse practices of Aristophanes' rivals. The playwright's persona boasts that he never resorts to hackneyed routines (e.g., ostentatious use of the comic phallus, obscene dances, the angry old man who hits others with a stick); he is constantly ingenious and original, whereas his rivals go on repeating the same kind of stuff (including imitations of Aristophanes' *own* earlier plays). This kind of agonistic bragging is itself a form of comedy. Aristophanes is not as innocent of obscenity and exchanges of blows as the parabasis

---

[10] See 'not *too* portentous' (λίαν μέγα, 56), 'not cleverer than you spectators' (65): compare the claim of theatrical 'inclusiveness' at *Assembly Women* 1155f., where the judges are split into 'the clever' (*sophoi*) and 'those who enjoy laughing' (τοῖς γελῶσι δ' ἡδέως).

[11] *Wasps* 1341–7, with further anatomical byplay with the girl at 1373–6.

suggests, while the description of *Clouds* as a modest, Electra-like maiden without a red-tipped phallus (534–9) is itself a burlesque blurring of gendered personifications. So when the playwright decries arousing 'laughter for the little boys' (539) – who did indeed form one segment of the audience of comedy[12] – he is (partly) feigning a superior 'taste', yet doing so in a manner which counts on the audience to recognize the paradoxes and confusions of laughter on which Old Comedy often trades. Is a spectator who appreciates the implicit conceit of 'Electra without a phallus' really showing more refinement than the hilarity of boys who react to byplay with an actor's enlarged phallus?

Ambiguities between 'sophisticated' and 'crude' comedy, together with the complications they introduce into the experience of laughter, are not restricted to the poetic self-images constructed in Aristophanes' parabases. They form an almost pervasive factor in his work. They arise above all from a running counterpoint between the typically uninhibited, earthy, mocking behaviour of Aristophanic protagonists (see below) and, on the other hand, the intricate components (verbal virtuosity, clashes of tonal register, dramatic twists, situational ironies) which contribute to the full poetico-theatrical fabric of each play. A key effect of this counterpoint is to make it difficult, and sometimes futile, to distinguish psychologically between laughing *with* and laughing *at* the characters or behaviour depicted on stage.

It is a hallmark of most Aristophanic protagonists to indulge in hostile derision ('laughing down', *katagelôs*, as Greek characteristically calls it) towards targets who, even if of high political, military or social status, are presented as unable to take effective reprisals for this treatment.[13] In such cases, the audience is arguably invited to align its laughter with the protagonist's ridicule, or at any rate to enjoy the latter vicariously. Obvious examples of such material are Dicaeopolis' jeering at the general Lamachus (*Ach.* 572–625, 1072–42); the Sausage-Seller's contempt for the Paphlagonian (*Knights* 271–1408 *passim*); Peisetaerus' scornful dismissal, in the post-parabatic scenes of *Birds*, of various characters who wish to enter his new city; and Lysistrata's effeminizing humiliation of the Commissioner (*Lys.* 430–613). But even this selection of instances illustrates that there is no simple psychological formula for equating this style of derision with occurrent social or political attitudes. Lamachus, for example, with his

[12] See e.g., Ar. *Peace* 50, 766, Eupolis fr. 261 (despite textual problems); Plato, *Laws* 2.658d, Theophr. *Char.* 9.4, 30.6.
[13] It is a more general fact that most explicit references to laughter in Aristophanes concern derision: see Sommerstein (2009) 107–11, though he lumps together open and concealed derision (107 with n. 5). On the varying ways in which the self-assertiveness of Aristophanic protagonists functions, see Rosen, Chapter 11, on the 'comic hero'.

comically useful name ('Mighty-Battler'), is cast as a belligerent but inept militarist; yet his repeated election as general in this period shows that while comic ridicule of him might be popular, the Athenians did not collectively wish to dispense with his military services. Even in the case of Paphlagon in *Knights*, theatrical amusement over his worsting and downfall does not guarantee any specific political judgement on the real Cleon. There is a gap between an audience's 'echo' of the protagonist's laughter in the fantasy world of an Old Comedy and the pragmatic evaluations and allegiances that are forged under the pressures of actual political circumstances. And with satirized figures who are 'types' not individuals, the asymmetrical relationship between theatrical laughter and real-world attitudes is just as clear: Athenian spectators who may have relished the discomfiture of the Inspector at *Birds* 1021–34 need not have been expressing (or endorsing) a belief that the whole of Athens' imperial bureaucracy should be dismantled.

But there are further layers of complication to be uncovered here. Aristophanic comedy displays protagonists whose outright mockery of others blatantly overrides the norms and restraints of contemporary social mores.[14] No Athenian soldier could with impunity have publicly belittled an Athenian general as Dicaeopolis does Lamachus. Still less could a group of women have physically humiliated a major magistrate of the city as Lysistrata and her friends do the Commissioner. At such moments, and in the larger scenarios to which they belong, an audience is offered an opportunity to derive pleasure from the reckless 'shamelessness' of the characters, i.e. their total disregard for the constraints of social decency in language and action. This is particularly marked with Dicaeopolis' obscene taunting of Lamachus when he flaunts his phallus and sarcastically invites the general to play with it (*Ach.* 592); with the Sausage-Seller's boast, at the climax of his defeat of Paphlagon, of having once been a male prostitute (*Knights* 1242); or – the *ne plus ultra* – with Peisetaerus' satyr-like threat to rape the goddess Iris (*Birds* 1253–6). But if (a genuine conditional) such scenes encourage an 'echo' of the protagonist's self-assertiveness in the spectators' own laughter, this need not involve 'identification' of a kind which we can straightforwardly correlate with the social profile of audiences: any hypothesis, for example, which posits elderly, war-weary farmers sharing Dicaeopolis' taunting of Lamachus in *Acharnians* will not work for *Knights*, whose protagonist is young, urban and, to begin with, politically insouciant. And what about *Lysistrata*? The

---

[14] This is not to deny that aggressively hostile laughter could occur in real life: for a fourth-century Athenian instance, with the competing interpretations of those involved, see Halliwell (2008) 33–8.

male majority/totality of spectators in 411 evidently cannot simply have 'identified' with Lysistrata or her fellow women in socio-political status.[15] Rather, the typically outlandish spirit of Aristophanic mockery promotes, through the release of laughter, a kind of audience complicity which frees spectators from their actual social roles and positions. In that sense, a male Athenian audience of *Lysistrata* might enjoy the ease with which the protagonist out-manoeuvres, out-argues, and thoroughly derides the (misogynistic) Commissioner; but it must also have been able to enjoy the play's *general* exposure of male characters to ridicule.[16] To laugh 'with' Lysistrata is not the same as to side with the situation of real women in Athenian society. It is a response to seeing the structures of that society distorted and manipulated in bizarre, even dreamlike, ways, in a plot whose trajectory passes through the tension of sexual frustration (in both female and male characters) before reaching a celebratory goal of political and sexual harmony.

'Shamelessness' is an indispensable trigger for much Aristophanic laughter. But it amounts to more than 'bad' behaviour; it centres on comic transgressions of the boundaries of restraint which had a normative purchase on social action. As both Plato and Freud agree, transgressive behaviour on stage prompts and allows the release of psychic energy (irrational pleasure for Plato, libido and aggression for Freud) in the laughter of theatre audiences.[17] In Aristophanes' case, and perhaps in Old Comedy more widely, laughter both requires and effects a sort of loosening of (male) spectators' identities, enabling them to laugh about the blurring of distinctions – between humans and gods, free and slave, leaders and masses, war and peace, male and female, even tragic and comic – that impinge on life outside the theatre. We may think of (and experience) such laughter as a perpetually *potential*, readied response to Aristophanic absurdity (i.e. to its dislocations of reality), and as incited to *erupt* by particular 'peaks' of dramatic expression, carefully shaped in performance by skilled actors. Consider, for instance, the point in *Lysistrata* where the protagonist prepares for formal mediation between Athenians and Spartans by asking naked Reconciliation

---

[15] The ongoing debate about female spectators, on which see Roselli, pp. 242–6, makes little difference here: whether or not there were women present (on which I am broadly agnostic), nobody believes they were more than a small minority.

[16] There is not a single specimen of successful masculinity in the play: geriatric half-chorus; ineffectual Cinesias; Athenian and Spartan envoys embarrassed by painful erections (1077–99) – how could an Athenian audience collectively feel that this motley crew mirrored *their* masculinity?

[17] At Plato, *Rep.* 10.606c, comic spectators echo the shamelessness on stage in their own release of inhibition; Freud (1976) 283 'admits feeling ashamed afterwards over what one was able to laugh at in the theatre'. See Freud (1976) 140–4 for aggression and libido, separately or conjointly, as sources of jokes, which are themselves for him a species of 'the comic'.

(*Diallagê*) to bring the men forward 'in a feminine, intimate manner – if anyone refuses his hand, lead him by the *prick*' (*Lys.* 1118–19). The entire context encodes, both visually and verbally, a radical incongruity and clash of registers: the diplomatic domination of men by a haughty female (with 'tragic' overtones: cf. 1124) is superimposed on a grotesque confusion of sex and geo-politics in the confrontation between the desperately priapic envoys and the symbolically sexual-cum-territorial body of Reconciliation herself.[18] Lysistrata's words at 1118f. cap all this in a moment of sudden obscenity, providing the linguistic piquancy of a 'lapse' in the tone of her public discourse to the ambassadors.[19] Laughter is itself a bodily release, capable of carrying various charges of affect or surges of emotion. Here, as often in Aristophanes, there is an (implicit) complementarity between the dramatic rupture of social norms and the audience's collusion in an escape from shame and inhibition. Beyond that psychological mechanism, it is difficult to rationalize what happens at such moments. If we laugh at the 'joke' in the last word of line 1119, we cannot easily distinguish between enjoyment of the obscene frisson itself (like the small boys of *Clouds* 539), Lysistrata's own demeanour (meant to 'shock' the men, underline her ruthlessness, betray exasperation?), and the fluid social fantasy of the whole situation, a war ended by sexual abstinence (an inversion of the most famous of all Greek myths, the seduction/abduction of Helen as the cause of the Trojan war).[20]

Aristophanic comedy, I have tried to suggest, *internalizes* (in both its habits of self-reference and its choices of material) cultural dichotomies between aggressive mockery and playful make-believe, sophistication and vulgarity, clever ideas and the 'grotesque realism' of the lower body.[21] In doing so it typically exhibits shameless agents whose antics can induce a kind of vicariously shameless laughter on the part of spectators ('laugh and consider nothing shameful', says the Unjust Argument to Pheidippides at *Clouds* 1078), while also inviting their appreciation of the intricacies and ambiguities of comedy's own processes of dramatic artifice. There is no single rule by which to make sense of the various slants that Aristophanes gives to such audience psychology. But much of what qualifies as Aristophanic laughter revolves around a willingness to relish the ironic

---

[18] See Konstan (1995) 45–60 for shrewd analysis of this scene.

[19] Note that the whole of *Lys.* 1116–19 (with gestures) 'puns' on sexual foreplay. For obscenity in Lysistrata's mouth, see 109, 124 (but in a register of conspiratorial female intimacy).

[20] *Lys.* 155f. deftly makes this thought subconsciously available to spectators.

[21] For the concept of the grotesque realism of the lower body, see Bakhtin (1968), e.g., 19–31.

implications of being gratified by displays of rampantly transgressive behaviour. When Philocleon in *Wasps* attends a socially exclusive symposium, the kind of occasion at which 'sophisticated' humour was ideally in order, he drunkenly disregards the feelings of other guests and displaces playful banter with hubristic derision; subsequently, as we have already noticed, he engages in an obscene charade with a naked slave-girl and mocks his son's attempts to control him.[22] Comedy, we might say, here frames an episode of laughter itself out of control, imagining its capacity to run amok and cause multiple offence. Yet it does so for the pleasure of its own audience, whose festive mentality may liberate them from any troubling scruples about what such actions would mean in the world of practical consequences outside the theatre.

The salient differences between Aristophanes and Menander, or between Old and New Comedy more generally, reflect a major evolution in Greek paradigms of 'the comic'. One of the dimensions of this development can be understood as a substantial shift in theatrical strategies vis-à-vis laughter. Whereas every surviving Aristophanic play gives scope for laughter from its very first line – indeed, even *before* the first line[23] – and involves a constant 'ground bass' of imminent laughter, Menander quite often exploits the very reverse of this, laughter's conspicuous suspension or absence (and the consequent unpredictability of its eventual appearance). The start of *Aspis* illustrates this phenomenon strikingly. The play opens with an *ersatz* funeral procession for Cleostratus; a symbolically battered shield replaces the soldier's missing body. The scene is heavily redolent of tragedy, above all in the function and tone of the 'messenger speech' delivered by the loyal slave Daos. Menander's original audience(s), familiar with the grammar of the genre, would have known intuitively that this sombre scenario, whose details extend to the gruesomely bloated faces of four-day-old corpses (69–72), could not continue indefinitely without comic 'correction'. There is bound, they would realize, to be a tilting back of the dramatic scales (to use a trope found in another Menandrian opening of a similarly dark, unsettling kind);[24] the plot will have to find a route away from the atmosphere of death and grief. But such expectations do not throw open the first scene of *Aspis* to laughter. Quite the reverse. They presuppose spectators able to appreciate

[22] *Wasps* 1299–1387; see n. 11 above. See various terms for laughter at 1305, 1320, 1362.
[23] Anticipatory comic stage business is retrospectively deducible from textual clues at e.g., *Ach.* 29–31, *Clouds* 11f., *Wasps* 1–14, *Birds* 1–9.
[24] *Perikeiromenê* 169, where the delayed prologue by *Agnoia* (Ignorance) reassures the audience that the distress they have already witnessed will turn out for the best; see Halliwell (2008) 404–28 for a reading of this play in terms of the suppression and release of laughter.

the deliberate suppression of laughter both on stage and in the theatre. And they carry an implicit promise of a *deferred* reward for accepting the mood of the initial situation on its own terms: the dramatic and psychological impact of comic release will be all the stronger for the removal of obstacles which originally impeded it.

The starkness of *Aspis*'s paradoxically 'anti-comic' opening has to be retrospectively reinterpreted in the light of the delayed prologue. This is delivered by the goddess Chance (*Tychê*), who gives spectators the truth about the situation, including a guarantee of Cleostratus' safe return. *Tychê* does not immediately transpose sombreness into laughter, however; she warns the audience that the circumstances will bring further upheaval for all concerned (137). But she does confirm something crucial which more acute spectators might have sensed fleetingly in the opening scene itself: that Smicrines, uncle of Cleostratus, is a nasty, anti-social character (a 'loner', *monotropos*: 121) obsessed with getting his hands on others' property (114–23, 138–46). This negative description arouses and legitimizes the prospective pleasure of seeing Smicrines exposed to derision; his vices, we are assured, will ultimately be unmasked (144f.). Critical to the process of making such unmasking apt for laughter, rather than for more uncomfortable feelings of anger or loathing, is the fact of Smicrines' self-ignorance. He betrays this to the audience in soliloquy at an early stage by his devious desire to avoid being thought avaricious (149–55), a strategy abandoned at the first excuse (394–6); and the trait is trenchantly underlined by Daos' later appeal, in conversation with him, to the Delphic principle 'know thyself' (191). Self-ignorance is identified at Plato, *Philebus* 49b–c as a key factor in making certain characters laughable. For this purpose it has to be accompanied by an inability to take retaliation, which makes it all the more significant that in *Aspis* the prologue by the goddess Chance (*Tychê*) contains a reassurance that Smicrines, despite his impulse to snatch Cleostratus' property (and sister), will ultimately prove unable to harm others (143–6).

It is basic to the tonal dynamics of *Aspis* that the release of opportunities for laughter, including the exposure of Smicrines to (moral) derision, is a gradual, non-linear process. Unlike Aristophanes, who distributes a sense of absurdity (modulated only in degrees of intensity) throughout the entire texture of his plays, Menander typically works with blocks of material which vary greatly in relation to 'the laughable'.[25] In the case of *Aspis*, he does not allow Act I to finish without creating an abrupt switch of tone from the work's initial starkness to the earthy vulgarity of low-status characters talking out of earshot of the citizens on whom they rely for work. That switch

---

[25] This is an aspect of what Zagagi (1994) 46–59 calls Menandrian 'polyphony'.

occurs with the unexpected entrance of a Cook (216), followed shortly
afterwards by a Waiter (233). Both figures had been hired for a wedding
(between Chaireas and Cleostratus' sister) which has now been cancelled
because of Cleostratus' supposed death. Both are preoccupied with loss of
earnings, which makes them assume a selfishly jaundiced view of the turn
of events. The Cook grumbles that 'as soon as I find work, somebody goes
and dies' (216); he speaks with grim humour (and dramatically ironic ignorance) of 'some corpse that's turned up from Lycia' (224f.), and he abuses
his assistant for failing to take advantage of the household's grief by stealing some oil (226–32). The Waiter in turn puns unfeelingly on how 'cut
up' he will be, like the grieving relatives, if he does not get paid (233–5);
he calls Daos a 'maniac' (ἀπόπληκτε: 239) for having dutifully brought all
his master's property home (instead of absconding with it), and he goes
on, as a Thracian slave showing contempt for a Phrygian, to call Daos
a 'nancy' (ἀνδρόγυνος: 242). In a manner highly characteristic of Menander, the mood of the scene is delicately unstable. It creates a space within
which an audience, knowing that the family's distress will soon be reversed,
can be amused rather than disgusted by the coarse cynicism of Cook and
Waiter. At the same time, however, the audience knows that the distress
is still 'real' for the family itself, not least for the loyal slave Daos. The
latter's presence on stage is therefore crucial. His anxiety to see the back
of Cook and Waiter (221, 235) is telling, and could be fleshed out subtly
by a good actor: Menander typically takes pains to differentiate between
the ethical sensitivities even of non-citizens. Daos cannot prevent the other
slaves from lowering the tone, but he can prevent the audience's laughter
from losing touch with the unresolved crisis within Cleostratus' extended
family.

Any spectator who did lose touch with that point could hardly appreciate
Act II of *Aspis*, which only permits the scales to turn decisively against
Smicrines after first dwelling on the misery his behaviour causes to others.
In a scene which complements the play's opening by showing just how far
Menander is prepared to stretch the material of comedy into the zone of
emotional anguish, Chairestratus, younger brother of Smicrines, physically
collapses when made aware of Smicrines' plan to marry Cleostratus' sister
(and thereby gain legal entitlement to her brother's property). But this quasi-
tragic moment, which may even have made use of the *ekkyklêma* or 'stage
trolley' (employed to display 'interior' scenes in tragedy),[26] turns out to be a
brilliant theatrical hinge for a reversal in the work's direction. What begins

[26] Daos' instructions to 'open the doors' at 303, and to take Chairestratus back inside at
the end of the scene (387), support this hypothesis.

as a genuine, despairing collapse (299–300) triggers in Daos the idea of *feigning* Chairestratus' death – play-acting it as a 'tragedy' (329) and thus luring Smicrines into a trap.

The audience is now placed in a position to relish the dissimulation of Chairestratus' death and the scenes of 'over-acting' which support it in Act III: first, Daos' own contribution, with its wonderfully hammed up spasms of (semi-)tragic quotation (399–428), then the 'fake doctor' scene (428–64) in which the duping of Smicrines includes a diagnosis of his *own* impending death (464). The laughter suitable to accompany these scenes marks the spectators' 'virtual' participation in the conspiracy; they are collaborators in its theatrical realization. The disarming of Smicrines' threat to the family makes laughter a sort of bond between stage and auditorium: Daos' mischief, in its self-conscious 'scripting' and play-acting, requires the spectators' mirth for its completion.[27] Yet this throws into ironic relief the way in which the audience itself had originally been unable to see through the misreports of Cleostratus' death in the play's opening scene. Menandrian laughter, unlike the 'shameless' pleasures offered by Aristophanic comedy, is in part a gauge of fluctuations in the audience's as well as the characters' relationship to events.

The principle of ineffectual self-ignorance which makes Smicrines a deserving object of ridicule can help illuminate various sections of Menander's work. But the principle is nuanced in ways which yield a spectrum of results, not a fixed effect. Smicrines in *Aspis* represents, in fact, one extreme of that spectrum. As we have seen, he causes severe distress to others; and if the statement in the prologue by the goddess Chance (*Tychê*) that after his exposure he will 'return to where he started from' (146) can be relied on (the end of the play is lost), Smicrines seems to have been treated as ultimately unredeemable. Most scholars accept that he was probably mocked and punished in some manner, as Cnemon is at the end of *Dyscolus*. But there may have been a discernible difference between the ridicule of these two loners. However uncertainly and problematically, Cnemon is forced into a kind of social reintegration: he is compelled to attend the wedding party.[28] It looks, by contrast, as though Smicrines was condemned to remain isolated in the anti-social predicament of his own making. What's more, Cnemon is given the dramatic space to attempt a kind of self-justification (*Dysc.* 708–47), in a speech which itself silences laughter and expresses condemnation of those

[27] Daos wants the fake doctor to be played by someone 'witty and a bit of a rogue', ἀστεῖον, ὑπαλαζόνα (375): it is a matter of not just deceiving Smicrines but making a delicious charade of it. For this and other details of metatheatricality in *Aspis*, see Gutzwiller (2000) 122–33.

[28] *Dysc.* 954–64.

driven by greed for 'profit' (720), while Smicrines, the bearer of that very trait, merits no such opportunity to justify himself (so far as we can tell). Cnemon, for all his irascible misanthropy, is nowhere described as suffering from outright 'wickedness' (*ponêria*), as Smicrines is (*Aspis* 116); on the contrary, in his peculiar way Cnemon is a 'hater of the wicked' (μισοπόνηρος: *Dysc.* 388). Although the gaps in *Aspis* prevent us from following through the details of this contrast, what survives is sufficient to alert us to some of the different shades of laughter which Menander directs towards the limitations and weaknesses of his characters.

Another Smicrines, father of Pamphile in *Men at Arbitration*, illustrates a further part of this spectrum. Knowing only that his daughter has been abandoned by Charisius, her husband, and that Charisius is living with a courtesan, Smicrines has prima facie justification for his indignation and concern over the potential squandering of Pamphile's dowry (126 ff.).[29] Yet Smicrines appears a focus of ridicule at more than one juncture, not least in the climactic passage in Act V where the slave Onesimus exercises irony at his expense, lectures him on the importance of character for happiness, and even calls him stupid (1078–1131). Why should the concerned father of the wronged Pamphile be made to some extent laughable? The answer involves a conjunction of his pardonable ignorance with his not-so-pardonable and overwrought temperament. Smicrines is initially in the dark about the baby whose birth causes his daughter's marital problems (and whose temporary guardianship he unwittingly adjudicates in the arbitration scene of Act II); in Act III he falls victim to the illusion that the baby is a child of Charisius and the courtesan Habrotonon (621ff.). Almost everyone else in the play also suffers from some degree of ignorance, but in Smicrines' case it is compounded by his precipitate actions, for which others criticize him.[30] Menandrian comedy, quite unlike the ethos of Aristophanes' plays, conveys a nagging sense that ignorance is a besetting factor in the human condition: much depends on how individuals adapt to its consequences. Smicrines is made less attractive by a penchant for haranguing, bullying and insulting others, not always with sufficient reason;[31] he is called 'the curmudgeonly one' (χαλεπός: 1079), an epithet applied also to Cnemon (*Dysc.* 325, 628, 747). Yet he is subtly different from Cnemon, and the pressure of his daughter's marital crisis mitigates his agitated behaviour. Even so, Smicrines is made to look to some extent ridiculous because his irascible, headstrong

[29] But there are hints that Smicrines may be *too* concerned with money: see 126–31, 749–50, 1065–7 (implying Sophrone's criticism), 1079; cf. (probably) fr. 6.

[30] Sophrone and Onesimus both count him 'precipitate', προπετής (1064, 1111).

[31] Various examples at lines 160, 228–30, 716 ff., 749 ff., 1062, 1072f., 1100, 1113, 1122.

impulses put him at the mercy of circumstances. His character, as Ones-imus sarcastically demonstrates in Act V, turns ignorance into an element of self-ignorance.

If individual Menandrian figures like those I have highlighted become tar-gets of ridicule on account of specific failings, others move fitfully in and out of the spotlight of laughter on account of a more general fallibility. In *Samia*, every single character, until the dénouement of Act IV, lacks cru-cial information about either the facts of the situation or the beliefs and motives of others. The result is a tangle of misunderstandings and cross-purposes. But Menander is careful to correlate these with emotionally plau-sible standpoints, including Moschion's mixture of shame and respect for his adoptive father, Chrysis' unselfish willingness to help conceal the identity of Moschion and Plangon's baby, and Demeas' anguish when he believes that Chrysis and Moschion have sexually deceived him. Since everyone is shown as unavoidably vulnerable to (partial) ignorance, no one is uniquely ridiculous; and during the first three acts the main promptings to laugh-ter are either incidental moments of conversational wit (such as Demeas' comments on the Black Sea, 98–100, 110–11) or the product of acciden-tal clashes of perspective such as that involving Demeas and the Cook at 357–68. In Act IV Menander creates a characteristic paradox: he almost simultaneously brings the darker emotions of the play to their culmination in Demeas' outraged sense of betrayal (478–90) *and* allows the situation to tip over into high farce, as Niceratus, infected by Demeas' misunder-standing, accuses Moschion of incest and even 'murder' (492–520) before going ludicrously berserk himself (556–82). With supreme dramatic (and metatheatrical) irony, it is motifs from tragedy, translated into comic hyper-bole, which both fuel Niceratus' rage and bring it back down to earth.[32] The tonal oscillations and juxtapositions of scenes in *Samia* leave choices for actors to make (and audiences to respond to) in the precise inflection of what can be perceived as laughable. But all the main characters are given understandable, even touching, sensitivities which constrain the scope for unqualified mirth – until, at any rate, the climactic burst of comic energy in Niceratus' melodramatic frenzy. Menander tests both his spectators and the demands of his genre by making laughter not an automatic right of comic theatre but a spasmodic, fluctuating response to the predicaments in which his men and women find themselves.

Menandrian drama operates a much tighter economy of the possibilities of laughter than its Aristophanic ancestor had done. Aristophanes creates a

---

[32] Niceratus invokes tragedy, with wild overstatement, at 495–500; Demeas wittily invokes it, at 589–98, to bring him back to his senses. For a broader perspective on generic interactions between comedy (both Old and New) and tragedy, see Konstan, Chapter 1.

diffuse impression both of absurdity (breaching norms of plausibility, ratio-nality, cause-and-effect) and of shameless, often obscene, excess (breaching norms of restraint and decency); he thereby provokes laughter as a reac-tion to a wholesale dismantling of normality. Menander, by contrast, keeps much closer to the contours of credible social psychology and behaviour, even when the events of his plots involve exceptional twists and turns. He tends to anchor opportunities for laughter – whether 'inside' the plays or on the part of the audience – in an awareness of the ways in which various character types (young and old, free and slave, male and female, but with numerous sub-types in each category) try or fail to cope with the unpre-dictabilities of life. Aristophanes allows many of his characters a general licence for uninhibited scurrility; he also builds into his audience's experi-ence a chance to surrender to such scurrility themselves by laughing 'with' his self-assertive protagonists and 'at' the tribulations of those, whether real or fictive, who fall foul of them. Menander, on the other hand, sets out to evoke laughter much less pervasively and with only occasional flickers of scurrility (mostly confined to slave roles).[33] If he sometimes still exploits the 'with'/'at' polarity, as in the respective positions of Daos and Smicrines in *Aspis*, he also appeals to a more tolerant, less aggressive laughter which recognizes that, in an expanded Greek world in which individual status is increasingly insecure, exactly who counts as ridiculous, and why, may depend on an unstable interplay between intentions, social circumstances and contingency.

Further reading

Two modern classics on the psychology of laughter are Bergson (1980), translating the French original of 1900, and Freud (1976), translating the German original of 1905. Both contain valuable insights, but they regard laughter more as a matter of psychological universals than a subject with its own cultural history. Contrast Bakhtin (1984), whose treatment of laughter as an index of larger social relations and forces has proved an influential landmark. Halliwell (2008) attempts to place ancient Greek attitudes to laughter within a web of cultural values and mentalities; chapters 4 and 5 deal with aspects of Old Comedy, chapter 8 with Menander. The essays in Desclos (2000) deal with various Greek representations of laughter; for a collection concentrating on theatre see Mureddu and Nieddu (2006). Most

---

[33] This change of ethos was a longer-term trend in Attic comedy, as shown by the pre-Menandrian distinction at Aristotle, *EN* 4.8, 1128a22–4, between 'older' comedies which relied on 'obscenity' (*aischrologia*) and 'modern' comedies which exhibit more 'innuendo' (*hyponoia*).

books on Greek comedy do not address laughter as a topic in its own right; the title essay in Sommerstein (2009), dealing with Aristophanic references to laughter, is an exception. Lowe (2008) includes a lively overview of some conceptions of comedy/humour. Robson (2006) tackles Aristophanes, especially his obscenity, from an angle influenced by modern theories of humour. Variations of dramatic tone and mood in Menander are well brought out by Zagagi (1994). Arnott (1997) surveys particular forms and techniques of Menandrian humour.

10

IAN RUFFELL

Utopianism

Among the many paradoxes of Old Comedy, perhaps the most striking is that it combines acute social commentary and political interventions with the expression and realization of wishes of the most thoroughly impossible kind, in the creation of a transformed world or an alternative society. A golden age returns or is found elsewhere or integrated into Athenian society or politics; nostalgic visions of the recent past are (re-)constituted; a good life is sought with the birds or the fishes; protagonists seek equal distribution of wealth and absence of labour; women achieve power; there is an end to war. Such comic utopianism poses in a particularly sharp fashion the problem of the individual aims and actions of comic characters, the problem of the politics of individual authors or of the genre as a whole, and the problem of humour, as Athenian *realia* collide with culturally, historically or logically impossible worlds.

Such collisions of worlds afford the opportunity to explore both social/political critique and aspirations. They are a key source of humour and rarely systematic, but by playing with, representing and developing social, political and economic ideals, the transformations of comedy play a distinct role in the speculative thinking of the period. In being prepared to contemplate and explore, however humorously, notions such as economic equality, women as political agents, or, from a modern perspective, perhaps the most laughable of all, a world at peace, Old Comedy seems in its own way to have been at the forefront of public speculation, going beyond and perhaps even leading the radical edge of Greek ideas. Over the course of its development, however, Greek comedy proceeded to move decisively against these sorts of transformative plots and worlds. In place of flagrant impossibilities, novel social or political schemes and the enactment of change that an audience can choose to believe in, Middle and New Comedy ushered in a stable, apparently realistic world in which the comedy of manners and morals takes place. And yet, as I shall argue, this comic world of Menander, in its own way, is just as utopian as the self-consciously extravagant worlds of Aristophanes and his contemporaries.

Popular ideals

Utopian thinking goes back to the beginning of Greek poetry, albeit oriented towards the past and wedded to a myth of decline. In the *Iliad*, it is a given that previous generations of men were physically superior,[1] but the idea is most fully articulated by Hesiod, with his account of the races of Men in *Works and Days* (109–201). Like other narratives of decline such as the Edenic Fall, Hesiod's sequence of decline combines the material and the moral. Spontaneous production of food and absence of labour and strife are the mark of the world of the golden race; the current race of iron is plagued both by decline in justice (*dikê*), especially in the ruling class, and in a corresponding increase in labour and misery. Hesiod's account is rooted in the privations of the subsistence economy and is largely pessimistic in character: this is utopia as absence and loss, but also as critique.

By the fifth century BC, the assumptions behind the account of mankind's fall were being questioned. Materialist and rationalist thinking competed with traditional assumptions, and that shift was reflected on the tragic stage. The comic poets also exploit Hesiod's foundational myth and its central concerns, but reverse the narrative direction so that its return or (re)discovery in some form becomes a central element in a number of comic plots, either as a goal in its own right in a sequence of plays on theme,[2] or else as a mark of comic success in quite different plots.

As in other popular uses of similar foundational myths, there is a mix of individual and/or social aspirations and a strong element of social critique.[3] The earliest play on the theme, Cratinus' *Wealth Gods*, probably of 430/29, is allegorical or semi-allegorical. The chorus of wealth gods are Hesiodic Titans who are returning after the end of a tyrant's rule, apparently exploiting the widely used Zeus/Pericles association, to restore the lost Hesiodic world of plenty. A major early scene dealt with the (unjust) distribution of wealth in the person of Pericles' associate Hagnon. The play also seems to exploit tragic re-working of Hesiod, too, via the Aeschylean *Prometheus Unbound*.[4] Whereas the tragedy appears to have offered an optimistic

[1] *Iliad* 1.260–72, 5.302–4, 12.447–9, 20.285–7.
[2] Fragments of this sequence are preserved by Athenaeus. See Baldry (1953); Ceccarelli (2000); Ruffell (2000) for discussion and bibliography. See also Wilkins (2000) 103–55 for wider discussion of agricultural fertility in the comic tradition.
[3] See especially Hill (1972) on the period of the English Revolution.
[4] West (1979).

rapprochement between tyrant and rebel, with humanity the winner, the extant fragments of the comic play appear to emphasize polarity, with the *dêmos* finally freed both politically and (it seems) economically. Other plays in the sequence which explore worlds of spontaneous abundance seem to have developed other themes implicit in the Hesiodic account and responses to it. Crates' *Wild Beasts* and Teleclides' *Companions of Amphictyon* exploited the language of Empedoclean or Pythagorean philosophy, the former apparently linked to the chorus of animals,[5] the latter invoked in an attack on the law-courts familiar from Aristophanes;[6] peace plays a role in Teleclides and Pherecrates' *Persians*.[7] The utopian world imagined in *Wealth Gods* already mixed traditional golden age elements with the trappings of culture, and the clash afforded both humour and satirical possibility. Spontaneous production (fr. 172) apparently included bread-rolls and barley cakes from Aegina (fr. 176.2–3).[8] Subsequent plays developed the incongruous possibilities. Crates' *Wild Beasts* featured a fantasy of a self-organizing banquet (furniture and food) with fish concerned about their own cooking times (fr. 16) and another on a self-organizing bathing apparatus (fr. 17). Teleclides' *Companions of Amphictyon* took a more environmental turn: a narrated landscape of spontaneous food and drink surrounding diners; rivers of wine with bread on top or of soup with lumps of meat; self-roasting fishes; roast thrushes zooming into diners' mouths. Other plays in the sequence present narratives of similar landscapes, to be found in distant locations and to be reached by more or less absurd means: Pherecrates' *Diggers* (the underworld) and *Persians*, Aristophanes' *Fryers* (underworld again), plus Metagenes' *Thurian-Persians* and Nicophon's *Sirens*.[9]

In the fully preserved works of Aristophanes, it is peace that is the principal context for hints at the golden age theme, particularly in *Acharnians* and *Peace*, where the success of both Dicaeopolis and Trygaeus is marked by the acquisition of a range of foodstuffs. Certainly, these are not acquired through spontaneous natural production, but from a return to the countryside and, in *Acharnians*, from trade with Megarians and Boeotians coming to Dicaeopolis' personal market. Nonetheless, the re-ordered worlds of these plays are both associated with the spontaneous golden age utopia. As the chorus note of Dicaeopolis in *Acharnians*, 'To *him*, all good things are coming of their own accord' (978) before launching into a rejection of war. Whatever else is going on in the world of *Acharnians*, the paradoxically

[5] Crates fr. 19.1f., cf. Empedocles fr. 141.
[6] Teleclides, fr. 2, cf. Empedocles fr. 136. Compare *Birds* (below) and *Wasps passim*.
[7] Teleclides, fr. 1.1–3, cf. *Persians* fr. 137.1f.
[8] More orthodox fertility in *inc. fab.* fr. 363.
[9] Neither of the latter pair seems to have been performed at Athens.

personal polis which Dicaeopolis has created is given golden age attributes. In *Peace*, the goddess Peace may be rescued and preside over proceedings in the form of a statue, but her involvement otherwise in the action of the play is in the form of Festival (Theoria), handed over to the city, and Harvest-Time (Opora), who is attached to Trygaeus. Civic, religious and personal dimensions of peace are all explored in this play and again suggest a version of the golden age. Wealth and justice are the core issue in *Wealth*, where the curing of Wealth's blindness means the restoration of a link between justice and wealth. The terms in which Chremylus' household is described in the new dispensation (*Wealth* 802–22) are extremely close to those of the golden age plays and spontaneous wealth underpins many of the assumptions of the play.

How much weight should be attached to such wish-fulfilment remains a bone of contention among critics. The golden age theme represents in extreme form generic tendencies towards on the one hand the happy ending and on the other an emphasis on food and (to a lesser extent) sex. Comparative evidence is mixed. Emphasis on the material, the comic and the grotesque is a characteristic of a number of popular traditions, including the mediaeval carnival culture explored by Bakhtin as a radical and disruptive background for Rabelais.[10] Worlds of exuberant, spontaneous and surreal fertility feature in a wide variety of Western contexts and cultures – the Pays de Cockaygne, Schlaraffenland, Lubberland – and with varying degrees of satire, escapism and aspiration. The American folk song, *The Big Rock Candy Mountain*, derives from this tradition and will be familiar to many Classicists through the use of the 1928 version by Harry McClintock on the soundtrack to the Coen Brothers' *O Brother, Where Art Thou?* (2000).[11] McClintock's song, with its implausible combination of cops with wooden legs and cigarette trees amid the more conventional aspirations for food and drink, encapsulates the combination of social critique and desire.

Satirical worlds

It is a mark of most fictional and political utopian writing that the projected societies are more often a means to reflect on the world of the writer or reader than to present a blueprint for a new society. So it is with most

[10] The similarities between carnival and Old Comedy at a sanctioned Dionysian festival have been discussed by a number of critics, particularly Carrière (1979) and Goldhill (1991). The relevance of the model is doubted by Henderson (1990) and Pelling (2000) 125f. A more Bakhtinian approach to the grotesque and carnivalesque is taken by Edwards (2002) and von Möllendorff (1995).

[11] See McClintock (1972).

Aristophanic utopias. One of the plays most often discussed in the context of his utopianism is *Birds*. In common with plays such as *Diggers* or *Fryers*, this play exploits a pattern of journeying to a new location and inventing or discovering there a source of happiness. While there is always an interplay between utopian world as aspiration and utopian world as reflection on the actual world, *Birds* is a supreme example of that non-place (*ou-topos*) being used for satirical and critical purposes.[12]

Peisetaerus' expedition to live with the birds is motivated by a desire to evade Athenian political activism, intrusion and interfering (*polyprag-mosynê*), which is couched almost entirely in terms of law-court activity (39–41). What he actually invents is a whole world of trouble, which engages explicitly and implicitly with Athenian activism across a much wider polit-ical spectrum. Living up to his name (Friend-Persuader), Peisetaerus sells Tereus and incidentally Euelpides (Optimist) on the idea of founding a bird city (172) and starving the gods into submission (185–97) and then sells the same idea to an initially hostile chorus of birds by persuading them of their own divine right. As this plan develops (similar development takes place in *Acharnians*, *Knights* and *Clouds*), Peisetaerus achieves one goal (living with the birds and enjoying a life of comfort) by losing the bigger picture (living the quiet life). The absurdity and flimsiness of this project are empha-sized by the coining of the name 'Cloud-Cuckoo-Land' (*Nephelokokkygia*: 818–23) and Peisetaerus later comments that the building of the wall sounds like a pack of lies (1167), but naturally it succeeds.

The extent to which any of the locations in *Birds* are a *good* place (*eu-topos*) is questionable. The initial environment is somewhat hostile (20), more reminiscent perhaps of wilderness anti-utopias, such as Pherecrates' *Wild Men* (Lenaia 421/0) or Phrynichus' *Hermit* (Dionysia 415/4, third behind Ameipsias' *Revellers* and Aristophanes' *Birds*).[13] More significant is that when the polis is founded it starts looking rather like a Greek city and particularly Athens, with Peisetaerus as the populist leader, albeit at times looking more like a *tyrannos* (so, explicitly, at 1673, 1708) than an informal leader of the people (*prostatês tou dêmou*). By the end of the play, Peisetaerus has achieved both political and cosmic supremacy, which is undoubtedly good *for him* and can be vicariously enjoyed by the audience. This is certainly far from the original aim of enjoying the quiet life (being *apragmôn*), but thereby is contrived both a fantasy of self-empowerment – a

---

[12] Plays such as Eupolis' *Golden Race* also seem to mix alternative locations and politics, although evidence is thin; for discussion, see Ruffell (2000) 490–2. Perhaps closest to *Birds* was Archippus' *Fishes*.
[13] On these, see Ceccarelli (2000); Ruffell (2000) 493–5.

number of Aristophanic leading characters feel disempowered, particularly politically – and a critical examination of Athenian politics.

This examination takes place less through the scheme of the protagonist than through the comic clash of worlds on stage and off, as events snowball. The birds' polis is named like a human city (820–5), has a patron bird (826–36), is built and defended in part like a human city (the bird wall, 837–42, 1122–74), sends heralds (843–5), has democratic institutions but also suffers from other excrescences of human politics such as (alleged) traitors and executions (1583–5), all of which were familiar from Greek politics. Quite a lot of importance has been attached by critics to the cooking of the executed conspirators and the offering of them as food. Clearly, the short joke does play on the idea of cannibalism *if this were a human city*, for a lot of its humour, and can thus be seen as commenting on the horrors of *stasis*. But as with most of the humour in the post-parabasis part of the play this scene relies on bird-human *differences* too for its effect: the dish is, after all, being used to bribe Heracles. The birds themselves are not being characterized as turning into cannibals.[14] Thematically, the presence of factionalism and summary executions within the bird polis is much more significant. The birds' action against the gods, while mythically drawing on gigantomachy and titanomachy, is more immediately drawing on circumvallation of other cities, as most recently and horrifically in the Athenian forcible reincorporation of Melos into its empire (explicitly at 186). Revolts, counter-revolts and intervention by the major powers in Greece all drew on and in turn amplified political *stasis* in Greek cities, at this time largely but not exclusively between oligarchic and popular/democratic forces. Above all, perhaps, the overweening ambition of Peisetaerus recalls the Athenians' most recent act of political hybris: the Sicilian expedition.[15]

Although *Nephelokokkygia*, then, looks like Athens, it also suffers from the interventions of Athens within the fictional world of the play, which seeks to treat the bird city as a member of its empire. Among the many arrivals seeking to exploit the situation to their own end are an Athenian inspector of weights and measures and also a sycophant, who are then rudely dispatched. A number of political experts turn up too, a town-planner, Meton, and the rather more comically derived decree-seller. This is a familiar comic attack on rival political experts, but also perhaps ties into the imperial theme in relation to the founding of Athenian cleruchies. The dithyrambic poet Kinesias turns

---

[14] Though of course birds do eat other birds. For cannibal birds, see Bowie (1993) 168–9, cf. Hubbard (1991) 181.
[15] So there are allegorical elements, but this is not to go as far as Katz (1976), who sees detailed points of contact and specific politicians and generals hidden under the characters.

up because dithyrambs are usually characterized as airy and empty (but again implying political emptiness), while the exclusion of the father-beater imparts a somewhat conventional moral dimension to *Nephelokokkygia*. *Nephelokokkygia* is then a world of paradoxes: like Athens but also suffering from Athens, human and non-human, anti-imperialist and imperialist. This paradox goes to the heart of comic utopias, being often both aspirational and satirical.

Uses of history

Both types of comic utopias that I have been discussing are quite self-consciously impossible in nature. Closer to home are idealizing projections of the recent past. Such nostalgia is always in some sense conservative, but as with more geographically or temporally distant utopias, the satirical dimension is to the fore, with aspects of the past – notably politicians, poets and education – being used to criticize the present. The tactical nature of this is well illustrated by Euripides in *Frogs*, who in the same play is used both as a stick to beat younger poets and as a target in his own right, or by Pericles who progresses from major satirical target, as still in *Acharnians*,[16] to one of four representatives of better times in Eupolis' *Demes*.

The satirical attacks do imply positives. Nonetheless, there is rarely a systematic presentation of and preference for a past world. When there is a stand-up fight between past and present, the present often puts up a good show with its own criticisms of the past (so Euripides in *Frogs*), or the past is obviously flawed. The Stronger Argument in *Clouds* is both slightly seedy and thoroughly incompetent. Insofar as there is a consistent notion of the past, it is a notion of Athenian *power*: the glory days of the Persian Wars and the early Delian League. Aeschylus' association with these good times and a better generation of leaders is central in swinging Dionysus behind his political advice in *Frogs*.[17] In *Knights*, the rejuvenation of the old, deaf Demos (People) to the time of the Persian Wars and Athenian success (1319–34) is a sleight-of-hand that achieves a happy ending that only serves to accentuate the central criticism of political practice as it has been skewered in the play. Moreover, any sense of unalloyed idealizing of the past in Old Comedy is undermined by the readiness of Aristophanes to mock simple nostalgia. In *Wasps* the age and infirmity of the old chorus of jurors is played for laughs on their entrance (230–72), while their happy reminiscences of

---

[16] 526–39. Many of the attacks by fragmentary poets are conveniently assembled by Plutarch *Pericles*, especially 3.4–7, 16.1–2 and 24.9–11.
[17] For the contrast, see 1454–9.

slack guard duty and petty theft at Byzantium (235–9) are a world away from (and undoubtedly more realistic than) the shining rejuvenated Demos of *Knights*. The even older Athenian democratic-nationalists of *Lysistrata* are even more obviously figures of fun.

The alliance against the Persians and notions of Greek unity are evoked occasionally, particularly in *Lysistrata* (1128–34; cf. *Peace* 107f., 406–13), but that aspect of the past serves to point up Greek and Athenian weakness and reinforce desire for Athenian power and hegemony rather than any genuinely panhellenic sentiments.[18] Suggestions of unity against the common enemy also serve to highlight the effects of Persian gold and the desire for Persian gold in the politics of the day.[19] Persian gold also features in *Wasps* as part of a social projection used by Bdelycleon to set against Philocleon's view of Athens as an activist's ideal. Bdelycleon's modest proposal for the Athenian tribute is a mass dinner which is modelled on a Persian institution (706–11). Dining and Persian wealth are also crossed with later versions of the golden age plots. Connotations of excess luxury were presumably at stake in Pherecrates' *Persians* and Metagenes' *Thurian-Persians*, although at least in the first of those two Persian luxury may be something to be liberated and appropriated as well as mocked.

Personal, social and economic models

The careful juggling of past and present is not disinterested: the areas of politics, poetry and education are all ones in which comedy and comedians are engaged themselves and *their* innovation is promoted by themselves, particularly in relation to their own radical suggestions and plots.[20] Particularly challenging are plays where there is encouragement to derive social or political implications from the transformed circumstances of an individual. This is, in a sense, what is happening in *Birds*. In *Acharnians*, it is far more extreme, with Dicaeopolis' decision to create a personal peace leading to a localized economy and politics, based on his household (*oikos*) and playing on his name (*dikaios* 'just', *polis* 'city'). Even more than in *Birds* this domestic/personal version of the polis co-exists and interacts, within the dramatic world, with a fictional version of the Athenian polis, while the audience in the theatre, who themselves also represent a further version of the polis, are

[18] For this self-interest, see the conclusion of *Knights*, above, and *Lysistrata* 652–5. Panhellenism is heavily over-estimated by Hugill (1936). For the relationship between hegemony and panhellenism, see Perlman (1976).
[19] See *Acharnians* 61–127, *Birds* 1027–30; Henderson (1987b) 199f.
[20] See Gomme (1938) 108f., who attaches more weight to the poetic claims than the political ones; Sommerstein (2009) 120f. and Ruffell (2002).

also heavily implicated in the proceedings. These collisions set up a series of comparisons and analogies as well as serial impossibilities (and a lot of the humour). From this perspective, the question of *Acharnians* is not whether Dicaeopolis' personal peace treaty is a just action *as an Athenian citizen in the real world*, but whether a peace treaty between Sparta and Athens would be just and beneficial to Athens *if Athens as a political entity were to behave like Dicaeopolis*. The interaction between the individualized Athens and the Athenian individuals, who want a drop of the benefits of peace without obviously pursuing a peace policy (the treaty-wine standing for both), thus provides humour, critique and a positive implication.[21]

By contrast, in the last two of Aristophanes' extant plays, the possibility of social transformation is much more directly addressed, above all in economic terms. In the *Assembly Women*, Praxagora's plan for economic and sexual communism under the helm of women is by far the most planned of any utopian scheme in Old Comedy. To the extent that the transformation in *Assembly Women* is entirely conducted in terms of public policy and on the human plane, it is also the most possible. In *Wealth*, the transformation operates beyond the human plane, with the curing of the god Wealth, but unlike, say, *Acharnians* or *Birds* the social implications are foregrounded in both the goals of the central character (95–8, 218–21, 386–8) and in the transformed world (750–62). The new economic order in *Wealth* is set up in the first instance as a moral order, the curing of the god leads to wealth now being justly rather than blindly allocated, but there are clearly political implications. Excrescences excluded from the new order include the sycophants who are victims of other utopian worlds.[22] More significantly, it is the *distribution* of wealth that is at issue in the play – the class analysis is quite explicit and breaks apart traditional and conservative associations of social and moral worth encapsulated in terms such as *agathos* and *khrêstos*, language that Aristophanes himself has on occasion used.[23] The default assumption here is that wealth under the current dispensation is ill-gotten (30f., 87–94).

The handling of wealth in both plays, not least their respective emphasis on radical redistribution and on the social implications of wealth, has led critics to see them as marking a radical departure in Aristophanes' career.

[21] For the contrast, see Foley (1988). On Dicaeopolis, this account follows Parker (1991) against those who over-emphasize his selfishness, not least Whitman (1964). To Parker's bibliography add Bowie (1993) 18–44 and Wilson (2007a) 271–8. See also Rosen, Chapter 11. McGlew (2002) 57–85, especially 76–8, emphasizes the broadly positive movement of the play.
[22] 850–958, cf. *Acharnians* 910–58 (cf. 818–29), *Birds* 1410–69.
[23] Especially in *Frogs* 718–37, although the precise referents are unclear: this may mean little more than 'not the current lot', as it is for Aeschylus at the close of the play.

This has been seen as a response to changed political and economic circumstances after the defeat of Athens in the Peloponnesian War and even, for biographical critics, as a personal crisis.[24] Other explanations, particularly in German scholarship, seek to account for this apparent departure by suggesting that the plays are ironic. Most substantively, in both plays, there is strong internal opposition to the utopian vision at the heart of the plot. In *Assembly Women*, we see one character enthusiastically adopting the new system and contributing his property to the common store, but this is pitched against another Athenian who not only will not contribute but also expects to enjoy the benefits of the new system (730–833).[25] In *Wealth*, Poverty mounts a defence of a system where economic inequality is structural and work is necessary, and is chased off stage for her pains. In both plays, on the ironic view, the impossibility of communism as a viable system is being highlighted. Further elements have been adduced: the horrors of *sexual* communism, with three old women fighting over Epigenes in *Assembly Women*; ivory ovens and other impossible transformations in *Wealth*.[26] *Assembly Women* and *Wealth* would thus both articulate the impossibility of economic and social equality *and* demonstrate the horrors of the working system.[27]

There is no dispute that there is internal opposition to the new political orders in both plays which question their logical and/or practical basis. Both pose a sharper challenge than we see in any other play except perhaps the opposed visions of *Wasps*. Yet their predictions of doom seem unfulfilled: *Assembly Women* proceeds to a communal feast; *Wealth* sees wealth being redistributed. Indeed, the complaint against the old women in *Assembly Women* is that they are *too effective* at policing the new equality. There are other filters through which to see the opposition: the characterization and appearance of Poverty only amplifies her unconcern for human suffering, while her distinctions between poverty and beggary are sophistic in every sense. The 'dissident' is in many ways closer to the sycophants of *Acharnians* or *Wealth*, seeking to sustain the old order at the expense of the new. That the loyal Athenian's handover of pots and pans is orchestrated as a Panathenaic procession (730–45) also serves to marginalize the 'dissident' from the majority of Athenian citizens who voted for the new regime. None of these points is dealing a fatal blow to the central characters' schemes. Rather, the plays are exploring questions in comic fashion

[24] See especially Sommerstein (1984), with comments by Ruffell (2006) 68–70.
[25] These have been variously identified. Sommerstein and Wilson both leave them anonymous.
[26] Heberlein (1981) 45f., with comments by Sommerstein (1984) 319, 323f.
[27] Slater (2002) 228f. notes the inconsistency.

(including implausible methods and consequences) but not in a simplistic fashion. Nor do they suggest that an audience would have left the theatre bent on revolution, but there is political food for thought here among the laughs.

The differences between these and earlier plays can also be over-stated, both in terms of the handling of wealth and the complexities of the plot. The moral and political associations of wealth (and the underlying suspicion of the rich) go back to Hesiod and is, as I have argued, at the least implicit in the golden age plays of Old Comedy. The plot of *Wealth* relies quite heavily on the assumptions of such plays and its mythological and divine dimension is familiar from Cratinus' *Wealth Gods* or Teleclides' *Companions of Amph-ictyon*. A number of earlier plays by Aristophanes also show a suspicion of power, associate wealth with political and moral corruption and mock the rich and their habits, despite more broadly sympathetic representations of the Knights in *Knights* and scorn for all populist politicians. Certainly, the late plays take the concept further, to the extent that they are the nearest that an Aristophanic play comes to questioning the Athenian democracy as a system. What we have in both is, however, a more radical version of democracy rather than its rejection: the extension of democratic principles into the economic as well as the political sphere.

Assembly Women is also developing a series of plays which feature women in charge (*gynaikokratia*), most famously in *Lysistrata*. While some critics have suggested that any scheme by women would have *necessarily* been *so* ridiculous and implausible as to undermine fundamentally any utopian scheme,[28] care is taken to sustain and explain the intervention of Praxagora, just as it is earlier with Lysistrata, in terms that are both pointed and themat-ically integrated. Indeed, while women's intervention is, in fifth- and early fourth- century terms, socially and politically *implausible*, it is logically and culturally *more* possible than many other comic plots. Even so, *implausibility* of method need not undermine the positive desires that are *also* being artic-ulated. Indeed, if anything the successful realization of goals in *Lysistrata* and *Assembly Women* has a positive feedback on the implausible method – and indeed has facilitated the space for the productive redeployment of these plays in the very different cultural context of the twentieth and twenty-first centuries.

In their explorations of wealth and redistribution, and indeed in their use of gender, the comedies of Aristophanes were clearly one of the primary means by which political and in particular speculative thinking became a wide part of public discourse in Athens. Clearly, the genre fed on and was

[28] For example, Wilson (1982) 157–61; Zimmermann (1983) 74.

in dialogue with other genres and modes of discourse. For example, Euripidean women, particularly Melanippe, contribute to Lysistrata, while some at least of the golden age plays drew on Empedoclean language and concepts. But in both cases the parodic elements play a small part on a much larger canvass. In *Assembly Women*, however, critics have long pointed to similarities between the economic and sexual communism and that of Plato in *Republic* V. There is general agreement that Plato's attempt is later, but this has not stopped critics positing that Aristophanes is drawing on or satirizing an earlier oral version or on a common ancestor, although Aristotle's account of such theories does not throw up close analogues.[29] Critics have been considerably less happy to see Aristophanes influencing Plato, although Plato's debt to other genres is in other respects clear, including comedy.[30] As in other instances, it is likely that Aristophanes is taking a set of ideas from a variety of sources and running with them – comic approaches to wealth, including sympotic elements; novel societies like those of *Birds* or *Fishes*; Dorian, particularly Cretan, style communal meals;[31] comic women's obsession with sex; political calls for redistribution going back to the time of Solon; and, perhaps, philosophical speculation – and coming up with something original. Aristophanes' version, to be sure, is far more radical (and funny) than Plato's, with the principle of equality extending across all classes as well as genders, albeit not to the extent of abolishing slavery.

The bourgeois ideal

Already in *Assembly Women* and *Wealth*, we are seeing increasing amounts of abstraction and generalization. The initial scenarios in both cases suggest a period of political and economic crisis, but the projects in both cases are far less wedded to contemporary politics than *Acharnians*, *Birds* or *Lysistrata*. In the fourth century before Menander, it is hard to see the descent of comic utopianism owing to the fragmentary state of the evidence.[32] Generalized reflections about wealth and attitudes to wealth are not uncommon in fourth-century comedy, but are shaped by the interests of excerptors and generally unhelpful in relation to plot. We are on firmer ground when we

---

[29] Closest is the equal land distribution advocated by the shadowy Phaleas of Chalcedon (Aristotle, *Politics* 1266a31–67b21).

[30] See especially Nightingale (1995); for criticism of this near-orthodoxy, see Tordoff (2007) 242–5.

[31] The arrangements in Aristophanes are closer to those of Crete than Sparta, at least on Aristotle's account (*Politics* 1272a12–21, cf. 2.1271a26–37).

[32] Antiphanes' *Anthropogonia* fr. 34 is particularly tantalizing.

arrive at Menandrian comedy, a good sixty years after Aristophanes finished competing. Menander offers a very different approach to utopianism,
both drawing on earlier comic traditions and fundamentally rejecting them.
The principal difference is that no longer is utopianism tied in any respect
to the schemes of comic characters nor is the comic world itself open to
transformation. Indeed, it is in the very fixedness of the comic world that
we can see the utopian dimension to New Comedy. Utopian ideas can
be expressed by characters, and their propositional attitudes project ideal
worlds (for them). In the permanence of the comic world, we see the rejection of such ideals. Characters who idealize worlds beyond the comic norm
are definitively excluded and marginalized.

Both elements are clear in Menander's *Dyscolus*. The eponymous grouch,
Cnemon, stands squarely in the tradition of characters who reject society
and idealize a solitary life. Such anti-civilizations go back to the Cyclopes
of the *Odyssey*, but were a minor tradition within the alternative worlds
of Old Comedy. Pherecrates' *Wild Men* and Phrynichus' *Hermit* are of this
sort. The character of Timon described in *Lysistrata* 805–20 may derive
from a similar comic context. Cnemon is an extremist who lets land lie
fallow rather than risk engaging with passers-by (136–8), has alienated his
step-son, Gorgias, and begrudges even talking to the god of the neighbouring shrine. He is violent towards people who approach him and refuses to
lend any cooking equipment. His character drives a lot of the humour in
the play, but it is also the central plot device: Cnemon will not allow his
daughter to marry, except to someone like himself (i.e. no-one, 326–38).
Issues of wealth and poverty and town versus country are also intertwined
here. The rich young townsman Sostratus takes a shine to Cnemon's daughter, but is initially assumed to be taking advantage by Cnemon's step-son,
Gorgias. Unlike Cnemon, whose poverty is a lifestyle choice, Gorgias is genuinely poor and suspicious of the rich. Overcoming these suspicions and
becoming convinced of Sostratus' genuine affection, he advises Sostratus
to make like a countryman. This leads to humour at the expense of Sostratus as he tries to work the fields on Gorgias' property in a conspicuous
fashion.

Fortunately, Cnemon falls down a well, which allows Gorgias to save
the day. Cnemon, having been hauled out by his step-son, gives a major
speech (708–47) in which he explains his chosen lifestyle but concedes that
some kind of social interaction is useful, agrees to be reconciled with his
step-son, settles half of his property on Gorgias and half on his daughter
as a dowry and allows Gorgias to arrange the girl's marriage. In an ending
that emphasizes mutual respect, Sostratus' father accepts the love-match,

but Sostratus persuades him further to settle his daughter on Gorgias – and together they persuade Gorgias to accept. Sostratus emphasizes the need for the rich man to accept the changeability and impermanence of fortune and for the poor man not to be stiff-necked and proud.

All is well that ends well, then – except that it does not end well for Cnemon. Despite Cnemon's limited concession, at least as far as his daughter and step-son are concerned, he still reserves the right to be anti-social. Indeed, he even goes so far as to claim, in a manner rather like a character from Old Comedy, that there would be benefits if everyone were like him: no courts, gaols or war, and 'each person would have enough and be content' (743–5). So Cnemon, like the internal opposition in *Assembly Women* or *Wealth* has a voice, but it is a voice that has no endorsement within the world of the play.[33] If anything, *Dyscolus* marks out the utopian schemes of Old Comedy only to reject them. The treatment of Cnemon in the final scene of the play reinforces this point. Rather than the old man being left alone to enjoy his solitude, he is punished for his ill-temper and forced to interact. The cook Sicon and slave Getas reprise the earlier scene where they came calling to ask for materials and were sent packing. This time, they do not take no for an answer. The last part of the final scene is devoted to them deliberately annoying Cnemon by banging on his door to ask for stuff and ultimately by forcing him to come to the party. Cnemon's grand isolation is, eventually, frustrated and he is forced to participate.

Cnemon's concession (746) that the social model may be more pleasurable, despite law-courts, prisons and war, is sarcastic, but it goes to the heart of the comic world of Menander. It *is* pleasurable given certain moral, social and political assumptions – the sort that seem to lead consistently to happy endings in his plays. There is a certain validation by Menandrian characters of the farmer and of work, and conversely a certain suspicion of the town if it leads to indolence, but Cnemon's fetishising of poverty and agricultural labour is undoubtedly rejected. Poverty in Menander is hardly noble and is something to be avoided (see 209–11) and sustenance of class oppositions and antagonisms is rejected, as in the case of Gorgias and Sostratus, where both sides are acting in good faith.[34] The poor farmer, observes Chaireas early in the play, is excessively fierce (129f.), a position echoed by Gorgias (295f.). It is, however, the poor man who can be moderate and reasonable and a friend in need, like Gorgias, or the rich man who behaves honourably, like Sostratus, who have the happy life and are rewarded in both wealth and

---

[33] See in more detail Konstan (1995) 93–106, who gives him slightly more play.
[34] For a fuller treatment of moral values in Menander, see Arnott (1981).

love.[35] If Cnemon's rationale is a materialist one, that everyone should have a moderate amount (*metria*: 745), for others in Menander it is necessary to *act* with moderation (*metriotês*: *The Shield* 257). That is, as Onesimus puts it in *Men at Arbitration*, 'doing nothing outrageous and nothing stupid, so as to live well' (1098f.). It is difficult to imagine a character in Old Comedy standing for it.

Dyscolus is the closest that Menander comes to flirting with the grotesque; elsewhere, Menander's realism depends upon the minimizing of such disruptive elements and the repetition of broadly middle-class families whose unity is threatened but ultimately restored. It is not that Menander's world wholly excludes extremes of either poverty or wealth (either actual or prospective) or wholly elides external crises beyond the immediate polis such as war, but both serve only to introduce crisis into the family.[36] Responses to such internal and external crises and threats consistently reinforce the avoidance of extremes of behaviour or character. In Menander's presentation of worlds where social differences are minimized, where moderation is rewarded and happy endings result in family unity and social solidarity, he is far more utopian and idealizing but far less challenging than the worlds presented in Old Comedy. This is the comedy of utopian consolidation, not utopian critique.

Conclusion

The writers of Greek comedy engage with a range of social and political issues, and one of the ways in which they do so is through the construction, discussion and manipulation of ideal worlds. These ideals can represent and articulate genuine aspirations as well as operate as a form of social and political critique, and as such can articulate a double desire for social change and explore, through the comic and anti-realist world, some of the central issues. This being comedy and not propaganda, such progress is rarely straightforward, and within these explorations comic writers can integrate opposition as well as display successful achievement of a character's goals. As we move from Aristophanes (and perhaps Old Comedy more generally) to Menander, there is a change in the deployment of utopias from a goal-oriented, transformative and flexible environment to a much more static re-articulation of an idealized world. There is also an ideological shift which may reflect external politics or biography or both. Menander can

---

[35] So Gorgias at 271–87, but reinforced by the progress of the play. See generally Rosivach (2001).

[36] For Menander and the outside world, see especially Hofmeister (1997).

share with Aristophanes the projection of oppositional worlds or worlds at odds with the fictional reality, but what Aristophanes articulates, which Menander does not or can not, is the possibility of change.

Further reading

The tradition of golden age comedies is discussed, from different perspectives, by Ceccarelli (2000) and Ruffell (2000) as well as Ruffell (2011) 386–96. On 'possible worlds' see Ruffell (2011) chapter 2. Utopianism intersects with concepts of the carnivalesque and grotesque, for which see Carrière (1979), Edwards (2002) and Halliwell (2008). It also intersects with the broader issue of the political impact of Old Comedy: see further the readings to Chapters 12 and 15. For the world of New Comedy and its politics, see Konstan (1995) and Rosivach (2001).

II

RALPH M. ROSEN

The Greek 'comic hero'

Readers and audiences have long used the term 'comic hero' with little concern that it is in any way problematic. We identify comic heroes in literature, television and film as readily as we do tragic heroes and we casually treat each of them as if they are natural categories, first established by the Greeks and considered one of their major contributions to literary criticism. Careful scholars will point out that our specific conception of tragic and comic heroes owes more to eighteenth- and nineteenth-century European aesthetics than to ancient theorizing,[1] but both terms continue to be retrojected onto the great protagonists of Greek tragedy and comedy. Tragic heroes are for the most part easier to analyze than comic ones, if only because critics can always invoke the authority of Aristotle's *Poetics*. Even though Aristotle never formulated an explicit concept of the 'tragic hero', it has never been difficult to infer one from his discussion of ideal tragic characters (ch. 13). Nowhere in what remains of the *Poetics*, however, do we find any hint of *comic* heroism, and, given his apparent literary tastes, it seems unlikely that he would find the term either appropriate or accurate for the kinds of comedy he was familiar with.[2] This chapter will be concerned with this anomaly, specifically why the idea of the 'comic hero' remains so appealing to critics of comic genres in general, and what it reveals about Greek comedy in particular that Aristotle seems to have missed.

[1] This is especially true of tragedy (Lambropoulos (2006) 7–10 and *passim*), but comedy was hardly neglected. Hegel, e.g., regarded comedy as one of the highest artistic forms; cf. Gellrich (1988) 33; Roche (1998) 135–40. For the modernity of the term 'tragic hero', see Jones (1962) 12f., who objects that it is anachronistic when referring to Greek tragedy, and Halliwell (1998) 165 n. 33, who finds the term, despite its lexical anachronism, legitimate for describing 'major individuals [in Greek tragedy] who belong to . . . a heroic tradition of myth'.
[2] Aristotle seemed to prefer the sedate, domestic New Comedy of his own day over the more outrageous, fantastic comedy of fifth-century Athens, with its fondness for highly individualistic, self-willed protagonists, but Halliwell's caution ((1998) 273–4) against inferring too much about Aristotle's tastes in comedy from the *Poetics* is sound. Still, it is likely that Aristotle would have found the notion of a 'comic hero' to be an oxymoron.

For all intents and purposes, the notion of a comic hero as applied specifically to ancient Greek comedy was 'invented' in 1964 by the American Hellenist Cedric Whitman (1916–1979).[3] That was the year he published his Martin Classical Lectures, *Aristophanes and the Comic Hero*, in which he argued vigorously – and radically for the time – for a 'wholeness of poetic vision' (9) in Aristophanes that both inspired and organized 'his baffling richness of texture'. The chief orchestrating force behind this vision, Whitman argued, is the notion of a comic hero, the strongly drawn protagonist found at the centre of nearly every extant Aristophanic plot.[4] In a very real sense, the present chapter would probably not have been written if Whitman had not made such an extended, theorized case for the importance of the comic hero in understanding Aristophanes. The reception of his study within Classics, however, was troubled from the beginning and its influence oddly oblique. After most of the initial reviews were hostile to lukewarm at best, the book was subjected to something approaching a tacit *damnatio memoriae*, infrequently cited or taken seriously by subsequent Classical scholars.[5] Yet somehow it gradually became acceptable to speak of the 'comic hero' as if the meaning of the term were self-evident and uncontroversial.[6] In retrospect, it is clear that Whitman deserves much of the credit for this development in the study of Old Comedy, even though one suspects that most scholars who have used the term casually since the 1960s have been unaware, or unappreciative, of its detailed treatment in his book. What this situation shows is that, despite the many reservations voiced at the time of its publication, something about its detailed and consistent

---

[3] On Whitman's life and career, see Briggs (1994) 702f.

[4] Whitman, in fact, would locate a full-blown comic hero in only five of the eleven Aristophanic plays, *Acharnians*, *Knights*, *Wasps*, *Peace* and *Birds*. He excludes *Women at the Thesmophoria*, *Assembly Women* and *Wealth* entirely from his list, and finds *Clouds*, *Lysistrata* and *Frogs* problematic. See Whitman (1964) 51f. As we shall see below, however, even these plays can be accommodated to a certain extent within a broader view of comic heroism. See also Konstan, Chapter 1 on the comic hero.

[5] See e.g., Austin (1965); Dover (1966b); Dunbar (1966). Dunbar's conclusion summed up the response of many early reviewers: 'For those who know their Aristophanes this book provides a frequently stimulating and sometimes enlightening experience, but it is alarming to think of its being read by non-specialists and innocent undergraduates who may be led by the august names of the publishers to assume that it is a more scholarly work than it is.' Herington (1965) is the one conspicuous exception, who praised Whitman for 'something unattempted ... from antiquity to the present day, and that is a full and systematic study of Aristophanes ... as a poet; a comic poet'. Herington had plenty of criticism as well, most of which echoed those of other reviewers – for example, that Whitman's comic hero was overly schematic, sometimes tendentious and ill-suited to many of the plays – but he had a better grasp than others of Whitman's work as a post-philological, literary analysis.

[6] See e.g., Dover (1972) 58, 93, 98, 126, despite his own (1966b) patronizing review of Whitman.

presentation of the comic hero percolated into the scholarly consciousness and made sense as a means of understanding the dynamics of Aristophanic comedy and cognate forms in other comic traditions.

Exactly how and why, and in some cases, whether, the idea of the comic hero is useful for understanding Greek comedy as a whole will be the task of this chapter. This will entail, in effect, scrutinizing Whitman's foundational model anew, in the light of how our conception of Greek comedy has evolved through the intervening decades. We will consider briefly the premises and cultural biases that informed not only Whitman's particular formulation of the comic hero, but also the scepticism he encountered from so many scholars at the time. Are we justified in regarding comic heroism as a natural category of sorts, one that we can identify in ancient texts and describe even if authors and original audiences had no critical lexicon for discussing it themselves? Or is it merely a convenient, but artificial, construct intended to bestow on comedy, without real cause, some of the 'seriousness' and efficacy associated with its generic relative, tragedy? How does the concept of the comic hero get us any closer to an appreciation of 'meaning' in Greek comic texts?

We may begin with Whitman's classic formulation of the comic hero. In the passages quoted below, I have italicized key terms and concepts to highlight the qualities supposed to characterize comic heroes (emphasis added):

> For Old Comedy is a *heroic* form. *However it may comprise political or social satire* and all the rest, *these do not define it*; they can, and do, exist in other forms. It is the *heroic* dimension, and the *nature of the comic hero*, which are decisive, and demand the *grand* style. Now whatever is heroic is *individualistic*, and tends towards *excess*, or at least *extremes*. It asserts its *self* primarily, and formulates its actions and experience in *isolation* from society as such and in relation only to the universe at large, whence its *metaphysical* implications. This unity of self-conception and *self-assertion* gives to the *heroic* spirit a kind of *purity*, but hardly what we would call consistency, for at any moment the hero may flout all expectation in deference to the *private* mysteries of his own will... Heroism is, one might say, 'inner-directed'... appearances sometimes to the contrary, no abstraction ever controls the hero in quest of wholeness. (24f.)

> There is good reason to think that the qualities of *imagination and cunning* went hand in hand with *heroic courage* as being the most admired traits among the ancient Greeks... *Craft, and persuasiveness of speech*, are means to achieving mastery, and if the comic hero is, in a way, merely the greatest and most successful of *impostors*, it is due to his imagination and his unscrupling *cleverness*, rather than to any higher gifts of courage or nobility. (28)

> [Aristophanes] repeatedly staged figures who represented ... the *salvation of the self* in all its individual waywardness, *wickedness*, and attachment to life. The result is a *grotesque*, appealing fellow, who extends one hand towards the blacker recesses of the psyche and the other towards the divine world of perfect *supremacy and freedom*. It is primarily this central and symbolic figure who raises the art of Aristophanes *above mere satire* and gives it a wider meaning.
>
> (53)

There is much in this commanding description of the comic hero that by now sounds familiar, especially his egotism, wily imagination and cleverness of speech. He is a paradoxical figure, who, on the one hand, routinely violates any number of social and legal protocols in his behaviour on stage, but, on the other, never seems to offend the audience. He is 'wicked', 'wayward', and 'grotesque', but somehow at the same time, amusing and easy to forgive. He embodies, in short, many transgressive traits that in real-life would be censured or punished by the same people who endorse and laugh at them in the context of the theatre. For Whitman, many of these qualities were captured by the Greek term *ponêria*, a notoriously multivalent word, but which we might serviceably translate here as 'roguishness' or 'rascality'.[7] Whitman locates various antecedents for Aristophanic *ponêria* in such figures as the infant Hermes in the *Homeric Hymn to Hermes*, who precociously (and comically) stole the cattle of Apollo for no other reason than to assert his own selfhood,[8] or Odysseus and Penelope in Homer's *Odyssey*, both of whom resort to trickery at various points in the poem. In Whitman's words, the aim of *ponêria* 'is simple – to come out on top; its methods are devious, and the more intricate, the more delightful' (30). As a reasonably straightforward description of many characters in Greek literature, not just comedy, this is uncontroversial enough. But Whitman finds something *heroic* about this *ponêria*, and claims that the 'true *ponêros* knows that [he is] justified by that heroic end so dear to every Greek – the joy of victory' (30). And again, in the same paragraph, he concludes that the 'protean resourcefulness and tenacity of purpose ... has its own kind of transcendence'.

---

[7] The most recent discussion of the semantics of *ponêria* is Storey (2008) 129–32, who finds Whitman's focus on roguishness tendentious: 'Although there may be places where the meaning of "morally bad" or "wicked" is tempered by sense of humor ... I think that we should take its occurrence in comedy as essentially meaning "evil" or "bad" with moral overtones' (132). It is worth noting, however, that Whitman's positive, often ironic, application of *ponêria* to comic heroism does not imply that all occurrences of the term in Old Comedy must have the same valence. For an analysis of the term in the context of fifth-century Athenian political and economic history, see Rosenbloom (2002). Also Rosen (2007) 244 n. 1.

[8] Discussion at Whitman (1964) 31–4; 'The *Homeric Hymn to Hermes* offers a kind of archetypal tale of *ponêria*' (34).

The first question we might ask is what exactly is 'heroic' or 'transcendent' about a person who embodies so many anti-social, narcissistic, even villainous qualities? Variations of this question were asked by reviewers of Whitman's book at the time, and British reviewers in particular had little sympathy for his attempt to turn the principal rogues of Old Comedy into paradigms of humanistic self-validation.[9] It is a truism that acts of literary interpretation reflect aspects of one's contemporary cultural *Zeitgeist*, and Whitman is no exception. In retrospect, his elevation of the comic hero was probably a response to a perceived blandness in American culture of the 1950s, and to the post-War boom in technology and science that seemed to threaten deep-rooted strains of individualism in American history.[10] The heroism and transcendence that Whitman found in Aristophanic heroes, therefore, was construed as a form of *justified* transgression, practically a form of civil disobedience against oppressive social structures that threatened a liberated cultivation of the self.[11] To a certain extent, one can see what he was getting at, at least when it comes to Aristophanic 'heroes': there is an egotism and unscrupulousness (what Whitman would wrap up in the term *ponêria*) about most of these figures – Dicaeopolis in *Acharnians*, Sausage-Seller in *Knights*, Trygaeus in *Peace*, for example – but their political or social agenda are throughout represented as desirable for all right-thinking people; and they are heroic because, as the pretence goes, they are largely powerless men (or present themselves as such) fighting an entrenched system of considerable power.

[9] E.g., Herington (1965) 319, wondered whether the concept of the comic hero might in itself be a 'baffling contradiction'.

[10] Whitman (1964) 42, cites approvingly, for example, a then recent German work on the grotesque (Kayser (1960)), who 'finds its essence in the dark absurdity of the world viewed coldly as a puppet show. The grotesque is the "figuration of the alienated world", where the categories of our world orientation fail'. 'Alienation', 'coldness', 'absurdity', a mechanized universe – all terms associated with the mid-twentieth century, post-War malaise that characterized so much intellectual discourse of the time. The same cultural background doubtless lay behind a parallel resurgence of interest in the 'tragic hero' during this period. B. M. W. Knox's highly influential Sather Lectures on Sophocles at Berkeley, published as *The Heroic Temper: Studies in Sophoclean Tragedy* in 1964, the same year as Whitman's book, would in time show how much more receptive scholars were to hypostasizing 'tragic heroism', while 'comic heroism' always remained a fraught concept. See also Knox (1957), where some of the seeds of his Sather lectures were sown. By 1961, Knox had become the Director of Harvard's Center for Hellenic Studies, and so formally (if not geographically, the Center is in Washington, DC) one of Whitman's colleagues, so it is easy to imagine a good deal of intellectual cross-fertilization between these two great humanistic scholars.

[11] Whitman (1964) 41: '*ponêria*... provides the liberating wings, so to speak, but it may not seem sufficient in itself, though supported by the most determined individualism, to justify the term "heroic"'.

It is also easy, however, to see why so many people bristled at Whitman's study. Even today, most scholars remain fixated on Aristophanes as a 'political' poet, if only in the minimal sense that sees his plots as ultimately directed *outwards* at the political currents of the day.[12] Contrast, then, Whitman's insistence that the plays are not really about 'the political salvation of Athens, but a far deeper kind, the salvation of the self in all its individual waywardness, wickedness, and attachment to life' (53). Whitman is aware of the paradoxes inherent in claiming heroic stature for a scoundrel, and is clearly grasping for some way to account for why it is that audiences embrace such figures so readily. The strategy he adopts, however, of allowing the comic hero his contradictions and chalking it up to the scrappy nature of the comic world (see 39) is hardly satisfying. Why exactly should we forgive the nastier aspects of the Sausage-Seller's *ponêria* in *Knights*, but jeer at the play's other *ponêros*, the Paphlagonian, the famous stand-in for the controversial politician, Cleon?[13] Whitman unwittingly raises a similar dilemma when he discusses the comic, but not quite *heroically* comic, elements in Homer's treatment of Thersites in the *Iliad*, the Greek soldier who stood up to Agamemnon at Troy but was summarily beaten down and bloodied by Odysseus in response. Whitman says of Thersites that, despite the comic touches in Homer's portrayal of him, he is 'pathetic, and closely resembles what Dicaeopolis would have been had he succumbed in the assembly to the herald's "Sit down and be quiet" ... Thersites embodies something of the state in which the comic hero finds himself before he becomes heroic, before his nascent selfhood feels the conviction to assert itself, by *ponêria*, in a Great Idea' (47). But surely Thersites' indignant outburst against the Achaean leaders was as much an attempt to assert a 'nascent selfhood' as Dicaeopolis' speech at the Athenian assembly at the opening of *Acharnians*. What, then, would distinguish Thersites' merely inchoate heroism from the 'genuine' comic heroism of a Dicaeopolis?

In fact, Whitman himself comes close to answering this question when he considers other figures in Greek literature whose status as comic, or proto-comic, heroes is problematic – characters who seem to exhibit at least some of the qualities of comic heroism, but who for some reason are not usually read as such. Whitman brings up, for example, the Cyclops as he is portrayed in Homer's *Odyssey* and Euripides' satyr play *Cyclops*,

---

[12] Whitman was well aware of the tendency also of his day to read much in Aristophanes as political and didactic, and his attempt to downplay this approach is notable for its iconoclasm, especially for the time; see his ch. 1, 'Criticism and Old Comedy', 1–20.

[13] For a discussion of this question, see Rosen (2007) 78–91; the play makes it clear that the Paphlagonian is supposed to be a 'bad' character, and the Sausage-Seller 'good', so the audience is set up for differing conceptions of *ponêria*.

and notes that the differences between the two portraits have less to do with differences in character than with the different attitudes that each author brings to their respective versions. The Cyclops will always be a monstrous, man-eating *ponêros*, but whereas Homer, from within the epic genre, makes him a brute ultimately defeated by Odysseus' own *ponêria*, in Euripides' comedic satyr play, this same character comes off as far tamer and innocuously humorous.[14] And more subtle variations of the problem can be found in Aristophanic characters themselves: Strepsiades in *Clouds*, for example, is certainly a *ponêros* – he wants to cheat his creditors, learn to argue unscrupulously, and in general live a life as much as possible devoted to the promptings of his unrepressed animal nature (*physis*) rather than to the restraints of human law and convention (*nomos*) – but in the end he is punished for his behaviour, and he comes to regret the path of *ponêria* he tried to cultivate. The ending of *Clouds* is famously controversial,[15] and it is easy to feel cheated precisely because we end up denied a 'true' comic hero, or at least a character with *ponêria* and self-assertion still intact when the dust clears. In *Knights*, constructed around an extended, rambunctious confrontation between the Sausage-Seller and the Paphlagonian (Cleon), two characters overflowing with *ponêria*, there is never any question that, as spectators or readers, we are supposed to endorse the former and repudiate the latter.[16]

Such dilemmas illustrate a point that Whitman never really clarified, but which can lead us to a more refined and useful conception of the comic hero than he was able to articulate. We may begin with a general principle: whether or not characters are to be considered comic heroes within a given work depends almost entirely on how the author presents them, not on a fixed set of personality traits that are supposed to mark them as heroic. The world is full of *ponêroi*, but sometimes a rogue is just a rogue – it takes a guiding authorial hand to elevate one above the others, and to endow that one with traits that will appeal to an audience. The dissonance, then, between this character's *ponêria* and his unexpected elevation is what

[14] See Whitman (1964) 48–9 and Rosen (2007) 117–71 for the importance of authorial perspective in calibrating an audience's sympathies towards controversial, even 'bad', characters such as Odysseus and the Cyclops.

[15] Strepsiades sets fire to Socrates' *phrontistêrion*, thereby repudiating the *ponêria* that the play started out by endorsing. Is there any hero of this play? If Strepsiades is supposed to be heroic at the end for his moral epiphany and his punishment of Socrates, his heroism has certainly been purged of both *ponêria* and a good deal of its comedy (although there is a certain measure of comic stage business in the very last scene; see Revermann (2006a) 226–35). Whitman too is uncomfortable with the end of *Clouds* (see 142f.). See also O'Regan (1992) 124–6 on the final scene.

[16] See n. 13 above.

creates comedy, and allows the author to forge an implicit relationship between the *ponêros* and the audience in a notional alliance against some common enemy. Sometimes these relationships are straightforward, as, for example, in the case of the most famous Aristophanic protagonists: the Sausage-Seller against the Paphlagonian (= Cleon) and the demagogic politics that he represents in *Knights*, or Dicaeopolis and Trygaeus working against war-mongers in *Acharnians* and *Peace*, respectively. But just as often these relationships shift within the play, or are ambiguous throughout, as we have just seen in the case of Strepsiades in *Clouds*, who ends up repenting of his attempts to repudiate 'traditional values'. And just where are the audience's sympathies supposed to lie in plays such as *Women at the Thesmophoria*, *Frogs* or *Assembly Women*? *Frogs*, for example, appears to construct Dionysus as its guiding heroic figure, but his stated desire at the opening of the play to resurrect Euripides from the underworld seems to change by the end when he chooses Aeschylus instead.[17] The contest between these two poets that forms the dramatic centrepiece of the play (*Frogs* 905–1413) is most successful as comedy precisely because it does not really affirm one poet or the other as 'superior', and Dionysus' own explicit ambivalence about choosing Aeschylus reveals a playwright clearly toying with his audience's sympathies (*Frogs* 1411–13). This is quite a different sort of comic 'heroism' from the one on display during the rowdy endings of *Knights*, *Wasps* or *Peace*, where the protagonists are allowed to celebrate, in complicity with the spectators, their decisive victory over the forces they spent the whole play fighting against.

We may draw several conclusions from such variant portrayals of comic heroism in Aristophanes. First, insofar as comic heroes really only exist as a function of how much authors can make audiences sympathize with them, they are hardly monolithic, and in fact, quite unstable. Everything will depend on how much authority an audience is granted to 'excuse' a character's outrageous behaviour – behaviour which they would never countenance in normal social interactions – and how much licence they have to take comic pleasure in it. Authors manipulate their audiences largely through plot and dramaturgy, although the process is hardly ever unambiguous, especially since there is always the lurking sense that comic figures, especially those who begin their lives in some hypothetical 'real world' as a true *ponêros*,

---

[17] For several very different approaches of Dionysus in *Frogs*, see e.g., Heiden (1991); von Möllendorff (1996–97); and Lada-Richards (1999), who see him overall as a serious figure, with heroic qualities, who evolves throughout the course of the play, over against Rosen (2004) and Halliwell (2012) 93–132, for whom Dionysus remains comically agnostic about how to choose legitimately between Aeschylus and Euripides – both of whom he loves, despite (as the play dramatizes) their respective poetic eccentricities.

might not be so appealing outside the comic world. Nearly all the antagonists pitted against each other in an Aristophanic agon, for example, display some measure of *ponêria*, even if the poet makes it clear that the audience is supposed to regard one as preferable to the other.[18] Such figures become comic precisely because *neither* of them *really* ought to be considered heroic by any conventional definition of the term, especially since non-comic (i.e. 'real') heroism usually carries with it a certain measure of didactic exemplarity, which often seems at odds with the shenanigans we associate with comic heroes. After all, true heroes – the ones that comic heroes are modelled on and parody with varying degrees of self-consciousness – do paradigmatically virtuous things which an audience is supposed to admire and emulate. But the fact that the *comic* hero is inherently compromised by his own *ponêria* makes it especially difficult for an audience to know just quite how to respond to the pretence of didacticism that always hovers over any kind of behaviour considered 'heroic'. It is no wonder, therefore, that in Aristophanes so much controversy remains over what exactly Aristophanes 'means', for example, by having Dicaeopolis succeed in his plan to secure a private truce in *Acharnians*, Strepsiades 'win' over Socrates in *Clouds*, Aeschylus beat out Euripides unexpectedly in *Frogs*, or Peisetaerus settle into his fantasy kingdom in *Birds*. None of these characters whom we, and presumably contemporary Athenian audiences, so readily consider comic heroes would last very long in the non-comic world, or be considered especially heroic there for their behaviour.

Another conclusion one might draw from our overview of comic heroism in Aristophanes is that, in fact, no two figures commonly regarded as comic heroes are very much alike. This observation may at first glance seem rather banal, but its consequences will lead us to a somewhat different conception of the comic hero than Whitman's comforting champion of humanistic individualism. As some critics pointed out, Whitman's totalizing notion of the heroic *ponêros* with the Great Idea tends to break down in the face of the huge variations across the plays in plot, characterization and manipulation of the audience's sympathies.[19] Some 'great ideas' come across as sillier – or more serious – than others, some characters' *ponêria* more palatable than others, and some resolutions of plot less ambiguous than others. It is

---

[18] This is different, of course, from saying that one *is* preferable to the other, or assuming that an author must somehow endorse anything about the figure who emerges as the comic hero.

[19] See e.g., Herington's discussion (1965) 318–20, and his comment, 319: 'The process of finding the Lowest Common Multiple in literature has, of course, its advantages (mostly pedagogic), but I am afraid that if we carry it too far we may reduce a diverse banquet to a sad, uniform, porridge.'

difficult, therefore, to come away from Aristophanic plays with anything like a consistent notion of comic heroism, and one wonders even whether 'heroism' is the right term to use in the first place. Whitman himself complicated matters by insisting that comic heroes are different from 'anti-heroes', characters who seem to behave like heroes, but whom the audience can end up despising and repudiating.[20] Comic heroes, by contrast, are supposed to be *positive* characters, whose heroism is in some sense genuine. It is when that heroism turns out to be either elusive or empty, as it so often seems to do, that one begins to question the very legitimacy of conceptualizing a comic figure as heroic.

One response to this dilemma would be simply to abandon the notion that the comic hero should be considered a generic hallmark of Greek comedy at all. But this seems premature, especially since even the most sophisticated readers of Aristophanes easily slip into the discourse of comic heroism when approaching many of the plays.[21] Clearly, there remains something deeply appealing and illuminating about the idea of a comic hero, despite all the problems of definition and conception that surround it, and it is worth asking what accounts for this hold on the critical imagination, and how it helps us refine our understanding of the poetics of Greek comedy. The position I will argue for in what follows is that audiences and readers respond not so much to the ways in which a comic hero lives up to some imagined benchmark of 'true', non-comic, heroism, but rather to the humour that arises from the hero's own presumption, indeed, *insistence*, in the work that he really *is* heroic, regardless of whether anyone outside of the fictional world would find anything heroic, in the traditional sense, in his behaviour. Another way to put this is to say that what is important about comic heroes is not *that* they are heroic, but that the author *says* they are. Once the author has secured the audience's sympathies, the comic hero is given *carte blanche* to construct a heroic posture in almost any way he chooses: the author has deemed the comic hero's cause to be good[22] and so there is little he can do wrong in this privileged state. Dicaeopolis, for example, may appear selfish in the way he refuses to share his newly acquired truce with others in the second part of *Acharnians* (729–1070), but only the most humourless critic

---

[20] Whitman (1964) 17 felt that the Aristophanic hero, in particular, embodied 'something peculiarly Greek, a quality of boundless, magnificent artifice whose exercise amounts to an act of heroic self-fulfillment'.

[21] And indeed, the term has been thoroughly assimilated into the critical discourse of literary historians outside of Classics. See e.g., Torrance (1978) generally, and 1–59 specifically on the Greek background.

[22] See n. 18 above: this is different from saying that the author agrees or disagrees with the comic hero's behaviour in any given context, or on any given topic the comic hero may be made to represent.

would claim that this behaviour detracts from his 'heroic' stature in the play. Comic heroes, in effect, cannot be 'unmade' once they are conjured into existence no matter how much they may fail to live up to any standard of true heroism, for such figures come pre-packaged, as it were, with a full measure of *captatio benevolentiae*.[23]

We are beginning to see that comic heroism has really very little to do with actual heroism at all, but is rather a rhetorical posture of self-promotion and self-aggrandizement. The comic hero, in other words, is reactive to the world around him; he disapproves of people or things, institutions, ideologies, practices, etc., and approaches them with an exaggerated sense of moral indignation. As Whitman suggested, the comic hero wants power – the victory over a perceived enemy[24] – but his success as a comic hero also requires the approval of the audience, and the author must carefully calibrate the comic hero's character to their tolerances. Indeed, the most fully formed Aristophanic comic heroes show little ambiguity in their behaviour: they barrel through their plays monomaniacally, aggressive and self-assured, but always from a self-avowed position of compromise and handicap. The audience supports them largely because Aristophanes makes sure that his comic heroes are the most powerful, sometimes even deafening, voice of justice in their respective plays.[25] It matters little, of course, whether in the cold light of day, away from the comic world, anyone would find any justice in these voices; it is, rather, the persistent *rhetoric* of legitimacy and rectitude that establishes both the heroism and the comedy of the comic hero.

We are in a position now, in fact, to make even stronger claims for the Greek comic hero: first, the perspective on the world granted him by the author, his relationship with other characters in the play, on the one hand, and with an audience, on the other, all suggest that he is a figure of satire; a figure, that is, motivated by indignation, beleaguerment, aggression, and

---

[23] See e.g., Whitman's (1964) discussion of the Cyclopeia in Homer's *Odyssey* (Book 9) at 48–50: we may stand back and censure Odysseus' behaviour in this scene (his 'unnecessary' visit to the Cyclops' island, his taunting and eventual blinding of the monster), but Homer never questions Odysseus' function as a kind of comic hero in this episode, or the Cyclops' role as the villain. For further discussion, see Rosen (2007) 117–71.

[24] This 'enemy' can, of course, be an abstraction (e.g., demagoguery, tyranny, censorship of speech) as well as a person or group.

[25] At the risk of redundancy (see nn. 18 and 22 above), it bears repeating that we must not necessarily equate any character's *claim* to justice within a plot to the author's opinions, or necessarily construe it as some kind of 'message' the play is trying to convey. On 'shouting' as a marker of antagonism between characters vying for heroic supremacy, see O'Sullivan (1992) 106–50, which focuses especially on *Knights*.

self-righteousness in the service of provoking laughter.[26] Secondly, in the case of Greek Old Comedy, especially, the comic hero is deeply implicated in, sometimes even identified with, the stances of the poet himself, as he positions himself as an indignant, courageous underdog, fighting for 'right' causes on behalf of all 'right-thinking' people in the audience. Indeed, in some of Aristophanes' plays, the structural analogies between the comic hero and the authorial *ego* are quite transparent, adding further layers of irony and destabilizing the various ways in which an audience might respond to a play. If, for example, the author presents himself as something of a scoundrel in the manner of a comic hero, how seriously are we meant to take his complaints and claims, which in Old Comedy often *pose* as serious and didactic?

The idea that the comic hero of Aristophanes and Old Comedy is a figure of satire merits some discussion here because it flies in the face of an orthodoxy that has developed since Whitman's study, and which has found its way into comic theorizing of other literature well beyond Classics. This orthodoxy takes its cue from Aristotle's discussion in *Poetics* 1448b–49a, where he was careful to distinguish between the general term for 'the laughable' (*geloion*), and the more specific term for 'invective' (*psogos*). *Psogos* was the Greek term applied to the kind of derisive, mocking, often scandalous speech associated with satirical genres. Aristotle made no secret that he found such literature indecorous and morally questionable,[27] and for this reason, as we noted earlier, it seems likely that he preferred the more genial New Comedy of his own time, where one finds only the slightest traces of *psogoi*, to Old Comedy.[28] Whitman takes from Aristotle's distinction a 'reminder that Old Comedy does not depend primarily upon satire, political or personal . . . but on something else, something broader and more inclusively absurd' (36). And he concludes with a flourish: 'Satire, pure and simple, has no heroic dimension. It reduces its targets, but not by including them in a larger vision.' A variant of this notion appeared independently in Bakhtin's famous formulation of the carnivalesque in his study of Rabelais, where he distinguished between the 'festive play' of real-world carnivals and the satirical mockery.[29] For him, the 'people's festive laughter' was different from what he called the 'satire of modern times' (one wonders whether he

---

[26] See Rosen (2007) 3–40 for a discussion of the nature and practice of satire and satirical literature, especially in classical antiquity. Also, more generally, with a focus on English literature, Griffin (1994), with further bibliography.

[27] See Cullyer (2006); Rosen (2006).

[28] See n. 2 above.

[29] Bakhtin (1984). Bakhtin's study, although originally written during the Second World War, was not published in Russian until 1965, and not translated into English until 1968, four years after the publication of Whitman's book. For bibliographical details,

meant to imply by this that there was no satire in ancient times!): 'the satirist whose laughter is negative places himself above the object of his mockery, he is opposed to it. The wholeness of the world's comic aspect is destroyed and that which appears comic becomes a private reaction' (12). Bakhtin's interest in 'the special philosophical and utopian character of festive laughter and its orientation toward the highest spheres' is not unlike the heroic, humanistic significance that Whitman ascribes to the Aristophanic hero. Both of them, in other words, regard satire as privately vindictive, anti-philosophical and negative, in contrast to a kind of comedy that is public, celebratory and in some sense positive. Neither seems to think that there can, in the end, be anything particularly heroic about satire or the satirist.[30]

Such a conclusion, however, is to misunderstand the very nature of satire, and to assume (once again) that *comic* heroism is some version of 'true' heroism. As we shall see, Aristophanes' plays show clearly not only that satirical genres operate with the pretence that they are very public, and even festive, but also that the purported aims of the satirist (whether we should believe them or not is another story) are not only constructive but even, yes, heroic. Satirists routinely *claim* for themselves exactly the kind of heroism we have come to associate with comic heroes, even as they offer as many cues that end up ironizing this heroism. The same can be said, as we have seen, of the most famous Aristophanic comic heroes – Dicaeopolis, Sausage-Seller, Trygaeus or Peisetaerus – all of whom adopt the conventional trappings and discourse of Greek heroism, but whose behaviour can also be decidedly non-heroic for comic effect. The move that now seems essential for any attempt to understand comic heroism accurately is to shift the traditional emphasis away from the 'heroism' part of the phrase, to the 'comic' part. Comic heroes are not, in fact, heroes *tout court*; they are characters *posing*

see the Foreword by translator K. Pomorska and the Prologue by M. Holquist at Bakhtin (1984) vii–xxiii. For recent work that approaches Aristophanes from the perspective of Bakhtin's carnivalesque theory, see von Möllendorff (1995) and Platter (2007) especially 1–41.

[30] Bakhtin is not specifically concerned with heroism in this section of his book, but it is clear that he would not regard the satirist, whom he finds so unappealing here, as heroic. There still persists among literary theorists a need to distinguish satire from comedy, and to conceptualize the former as in some sense a degraded form of the latter. See e.g., Torrance (1978) 5: 'The derision of satire tends toward the relentless diminution of its object to the lowest common denominator, the reduction of the human to the inhuman, of a personal enemy to a curd of ass's milk; but comedy, to succeed at all, must create a world of living people irreducible to inanimate things or mechanical processes.' Torrance elsewhere (47) describes Aristophanes' *Knights, Clouds* and *Wasps* in particular as 'swing[ing] toward the satirical pole of the comic vision – toward preoccupation with the real over the possible'. See also Halliwell, Chapter 9 on the laughter that arises in Aristophanes from 'satirical derision'.

as heroes, who are comic precisely because their claims to real heroism are always compromised by their own non-heroic behaviour. This is not to say that nothing a comic hero says or does in a work can ever be taken 'seriously', however broadly we use that adverb, but it does mean that the very things that make this character comic – his *ponêria*, irony, buffoonery, *aischrologia*, among the many other possibilities we have noted – also destabilize any of his *claims* to self-righteousness, seriousness or heroism.

Old Comedy offers various structural opportunities for the poet to position himself as a comic hero, and this, in its turn, confirms the points of contact between the comic hero and the comic poet *qua* satirist. Most notably, the section of the play known as the 'parabasis' allows the poet himself to 'step aside' from the plot to speak (more accurately 'claim' to speak) in his own voice about matters that may have little or nothing to do with the rest of the play.[31] While we only have complete examples from Aristophanes, all our evidence taken together shows that the parabasis was a typical moment in the play where the comic poet, usually channelled by the chorus leader speaking on his behalf, liked to address the audience, whether to boast of his literary accomplishments and his high-minded intentions, or complain that the audience did not appreciate him as they should.[32] The parabases of *Wasps* (422) and *Peace* (421) are excellent examples, and the fact that the parabasis of *Peace* repeats almost verbatim lines from the parabasis of *Wasps* highlights the conventional, almost formulaic, aspects of these digressions. Much of these two parabases is comically self-promotional, and at one point each chorus leader fashions the poet explicitly as a hero. The parabasis of *Wasps* opens with mock-censure of the audience for not fully appreciating the poet's talents, followed by a brief biographical history of his literary achievements. At 1029, the chorus leader then takes up the question of the poet's targets:

οὐδ', ὅτε πρῶτόν γ' ἦρξε διδάσκειν, ἀνθρώποις φήσ' ἐπιθέσθαι,
ἀλλ' Ἡρακλέους ὀργήν τιν' ἔχων τοῖσι μεγίστοις ἐπεχείρει,
θρασέως ξυστὰς εὐθὺς ἀπ' ἀρχῆς αὐτῷ τῷ καρχαρόδοντι,
οὗ δεινόταται μὲν ἀπ' ὀφθαλμῶν Κύννης ἀκτῖνες ἔλαμπον,
ἑκατὸν δὲ κύκλῳ κεφαλαὶ κολάκων οἰμωξομένων ἐλιχμῶντο
περὶ τὴν κεφαλήν, φωνὴν δ' εἶχεν χαράδρας ὄλεθρον τετοκυίας,
φώκης δ' ὀσμήν, Λαμίας δ' ὄρχεις ἀπλύτους, πρωκτὸν δὲ καμήλου.

(*Wasps* 1029–35)

---

[31] On the structure and function of the parabasis, see Sifakis (1971a) 53–70; Hubbard (1991); and Biles, Chapter 2.

[32] See further on the parabasis Marshall, Chapter 6.

And when he first began to produce, he did not, he says, attack mere men, but with a spirit like that of Heracles he tackled the greatest monsters, boldly facing up right from the start to the Jag-toothed One himself,[33] from whose eyes shone terrible rays like those of the Bitch-star, while all around his head licked serpentlike a hundred head of accursed flatterers; he had the voice of a torrent in destructive spate, the smell of a seal, the unwashed balls of a Lamia, and the arse of a camel. (Tr. Sommerstein (1983))

The parabasis of *Peace* begins with the claim that Aristophanes banished from his work the kind of low humour he mockingly imputes to his rivals (732–50), and from there takes up the question of the poet's targets in language repeated from *Wasps*:

> τοιαῦτ' ἀφελὼν κακὰ καὶ φόρτον καὶ βωμολοχεύματ' ἀγεννῆ
> ἐπόησε τέχνην μεγάλην ἡμῖν κἀπύργωσ' οἰκοδομήσας
> ἔπεσιν μεγάλοις καὶ διανοίαις καὶ σκώμμασιν οὐκ ἀγοραίοις,
> οὐκ ἰδιώτας ἀνθρωπίσκους κωμῳδῶν οὐδὲ γυναῖκας,
> ἀλλ' Ἡρακλέους ὀργήν τιν' ἔχων τοῖσι μεγίστοις ἐπεχείρει,
> διαβὰς βυρσῶν ὀσμὰς δεινὰς κἀπειλὰς βορβοροθύμους.
> καὶ πρῶτον μὲν μάχομαι πάντων αὐτῷ τῷ καρχαρόδοντι,
> οὗ δεινόταται μὲν ἀπ' ὀφθαλμῶν Κύννης ἀκτῖνες ἔλαμπον,
> ἑκατὸν δὲ κύκλῳ κεφαλαὶ κολάκων οἰμωξομένων ἐλιχμῶντο
> περὶ τὴν κεφαλήν, φωνὴν δ' εἶχεν χαράδρας ὄλεθρον τετοκυίας,
> φώκης δ' ὀσμήν, Λαμίας δ' ὄρχεις ἀπλύτους, πρωκτὸν δὲ καμήλου.
>
> (*Peace* 748–58)

Such poor stuff, such rubbish, such ignoble buffoonery, he has removed; he has created a great art for us, and built it up to towering dimensions with mighty words and ideas and with jokes that are not vulgar. Nor has he satirized the little man or woman in private life; rather, with a spirit like that of Heracles, he tackled the greatest monsters, striding through terrible smells of leather and the menaces of a muckraker's rage. And first of all these I fought with the Jag-toothed One himself, from whose eyes shone terrible rays like those of the Bitch-star, while all around his head licked serpent-like a hundred head of accursed flatterers; he had the voice of a torrent in destructive spate, the smell of a seal, the unwashed balls of a Lamia, and the arse of a camel. (Tr. Sommerstein (1990))

The poet, in other words, presents himself as 'courageous', self-sacrificing, compelled to fight on behalf of the people, yet underappreciated (hence the need for such a parabasis) by the very people his satire is supposed to be helping. He is hugely indignant at the perceived badness of his targets and

---

[33] The 'Jag-toothed One' here, and in the next passage, from *Peace*, refers to the demagogue Cleon. See Olson (1998) 221f. on *Peace* 754.

claims for himself (*Wasps* 1043) the role of 'public saviour' (ἀλεξίκακος) and 'purifier' (καθαρτής) of the city.

Other parabases echo similar sentiments. In *Knights*, for example, the chorus leader describes the poet as 'hating the same people' as the chorus and having the courage 'to say what is just' (τοὺς αὐτοὺς ἡμῖν μισεῖ τολμᾷ τε λέγειν τὰ δίκαια: 510). The parabasis of *Clouds* even has the chorus leader address the audience in the first person ('Spectators, I will speak the truth to you freely', ὦ θεώμενοι, κατερῶ πρὸς ὑμᾶς ἐλευθέρως τἀληθῆ: 518f.), blaming them directly for misunderstanding the original production of the play in 423 and failing to award him first prize (520–6). Here too he boasts of his attacks on Cleon (549), and ends by accusing fellow comic poets Eupolis and Hermippus of literary incompetence and plagiarism (553–62).

Nowhere in Aristophanes is the assimilation of the comic hero with the comic poet more complete, however, than in *Acharnians* (425 BCE). The protagonist of this play, Dicaeopolis, is continually cited as the quintessential comic hero, and certainly was one of the exemplary characters who inspired Whitman's ideas about comic *ponêria* and heroic rascality. Several times in the play Dicaeopolis is made to speak directly as if he is actually the playwright, each time complaining that Cleon had taken him to court the year before over his production of *Babylonians*.[34] At 377, for example, Dicaeopolis, speaks *in propria persona*, but as if he were Aristophanes himself:[35]

> αὐτός τ' ἐμαυτὸν ὑπὸ Κλέωνος ἅπαθον
> ἐπίσταμαι διὰ τὴν πέρυσι κωμῳδίαν.
> εἰσελκύσας γάρ μ' εἰς τὸ βουλευτήριον
> διέβαλλε καὶ ψευδῆ κατεγλώττιζέ μου
> κἀκυκλοβόρει κἄπλυνεν, ὥστ' ὀλίγου πάνυ
> ἀπωλόμην μολυνοπραγμονούμενος.
>
> (*Acharnians* 377–82)

And I know about myself, what I suffered at Cleon's hands because of last year's comedy. He dragged me into the council chamber and began slandering me, telling glib-mouthed lies about me, roaring at me like the Cycloborus, bathing me in abuse, so that I very nearly perished in a sewer of troubles. So

---

[34] On the question of Cleon's alleged lawsuit against Aristophanes for 'slandering the city in the presence of foreigners' in his production of *Bablyonians*, and on the larger question of Old Comedy and Athenian law, see Halliwell (1991) and (2008) 243–52, especially n. 81; Olson (2002) xxx, xlvi–li; Sommerstein (2004a) and (2004b); Rosen (2010) 235 n. 19.

[35] See also lines 497–505, where Dicaeopolis also seems to ventriloquize the poet himself. On the complex relationship between Dicaeopolis and 'the poet' in *Acharnians*, see Olson (2002) xlv–lxvii, with further bibliography at lxvii, n. 23.

RALPH M. ROSEN

now, first of all, before I speak, please let me dress up as piteously as I can.
(Tr. Sommerstein (1981))

The parabasis proper of *Acharnians* 626–64 similarly conflates voices: the chorus leader makes grandiose claims on behalf of the poet (e.g., the Athenian allies will flock to Athens to see Aristophanes because he is the one who 'took the risk of telling the Athenians what's just': 644), and concludes with a taunt to Cleon:

> πρὸς ταῦτα Κλέων καὶ παλαμάσθω
> καὶ πᾶν ἐπ᾽ ἐμοὶ τεκταινέσθω.
> τὸ γὰρ εὖ μετ᾽ ἐμοῦ καὶ τὸ δίκαιον
> ξύμμαχον ἔσται, κοὐ μή ποθ᾽ ἁλῶ
> περὶ τὴν πόλιν ὢν ὥσπερ ἐκεῖνος
> δειλὸς καὶ λακαταπύγων.
>
> (*Acharnians* 659–64)

So let Cleon contrive, let him devise what he will against me; for right and justice will be my allies, and never shall I be convicted of being, as he is, a cowardly and right buggerable citizen. (Tr. Sommerstein (1980))

The stances that Aristophanes assumes for himself in the parabases we have discussed are, in short, precisely the stances that are associated with the comic hero. The poet's heroism, like that found in many of his protagonists, lies in his many self-righteous claims – he has right on his side, he has courage in a world of cowards and fights relentlessly for the good of his audience. At the same time he is oppressed (he claims) by a world he constantly needs to educate and persuade. All the while these claims are presented with hyperbole, irony and, on occasion, even disingenuousness. The comic poet, in other words, can be every bit as much of a *ponêros* as the comic hero, full of grand ideas, preachiness and braggadoccio, but capable also of pettiness and vindictiveness, especially if the effect is comic.

We are unusually fortunate that the Aristophanic parabasis can reveal connections such as these between the poet's voice and the fictional characters in the plays, and the consequences are relevant even to other comic genres, where self-reflexive literary commentary of this sort is absent. It may well be that the very idea of a comic hero is an anachronistic product of the Romantic era, but it labels a character type that would be familiar to Aristophanes, and crucial to the kind of comedy he and his colleagues were trying to produce. Whether or not Aristophanes would have wanted to apply the word 'hero' to any of the characters that we have come to label as such, the fact remains that these characters mimic and parody a kind of behaviour that would have been recognizable to the Greeks as heroic, characterized, that

238

is, by courage, selflessness and a desire for personal glory. Post-Romantic critics, however, have consistently failed to understand that in a comic context, what makes such characters humorous is that all their heroic traits must be compromised in one way or another; they must be emptied of true heroism, while maintaining a *pretence* of earnestness and self-righteousness. As we have seen, this faux-heroism turns out to be exactly the stance that Aristophanes chose to adopt in his self-presentation as a comic poet. In turn, this stance affords us access to the way he himself conceptualized the comic hero fundamentally as a figure of satire – an aggressive, self-aggrandizing and self-righteous *ponêros* with a specific cause and a touch of abjection always hovering, humorously, over him.[36]

When we understand that the comic hero and the poet of Old Comedy are aligned in this way along an axis of satire, it becomes clear why the comedies of Menander and other poets of New Comedy in the fourth century BCE for all intents and purposes had no comic heroes. These were not, after all, satirical poets. There were focal characters, to be sure,[37] but they were not invested with the kind of intense self-assertion that we find in so many protagonists of Old Comedy, and the plots themselves were largely domestic and affective rather than public and topical.[38] Certainly, one can find in New Comedy occasional mockery and satire of contemporary practices or institutions, but this is neither sustained, as it is in Old Comedy, nor crystallized in a single character whose sense of purpose and self drives the entire plot.[39] Comic heroes, as it turns out, are very specific kinds of characters,

[36] We are fortunate to possess fragments from one of Aristophanes' older contemporaries, Cratinus (see Biles, Chapter 2), who produced a remarkable play, *Pytinê* (*Wine-flask*) (423 BCE, defeating Aristophanes' own *Clouds*) in which the main character seems to have been, unambiguously, the poet Cratinus himself. In the play Cratinus portrays himself as an alcoholic, whose weakness for wine has alienated him from his wife, an allegorized character named *Kômôidia* (i.e. 'Comedy'). The exact details of the plot are not entirely certain, but it it reasonably clear that Cratinus portrayed himself in this role as defiant and self-righteous, on the one hand, but pathetic and abject, on the other. Here we have a perfect example, in short, of an Athenian comic poet whose role as a comic hero becomes co-terminous with his role as a satirist. Further discussion of Cratinus' *Pytine* in Sidwell (1995); Rosen (2000); Ruffell (2002); Revermann (2006a) 308–11; and Bakola (2010) 59–64, 275–85.

[37] See further Ruffell, Chapter 7 on stock characters.

[38] While there seem to be no comic heroes in Greek New Comedy, something reminiscent of the character type surfaces later in Roman comedy. Anderson (1993) 88–106 has written of what he calls 'heroic badness' (*malitia*) of certain Plautine characters, usually slaves or courtesans. It may be an overstatement to claim, as Anderson does, that Plautus' 'Roman rogue emerges as a strikingly new creation', but he is right to distance these figures from the Aristophanic hero, who is normally 'a free man or woman with a different manner of operation and a quite different ethical stance'. On comic *malitia* see also Fantham (2008).

[39] On New Comedy see also Konstan, Chapter 1 and Halliwell, Chapter 9.

associated with very specific kinds of authors, who are themselves interested in very specific kinds of laughter. The poets of Athenian Old Comedy cultivated such characters to the extraordinary extent that they did because, as we have seen, they wanted to claim for their art a similar sort of heroism, which is to say a heroism that succeeds as comedy when it is at its least genuinely heroic.

12

DAVID KAWALKO ROSELLI

Social class

Social class can be approached in a variety of ways. Approaches inspired by Marx, Weber and Bourdieu (among others) attempt to explain social change and organization in a community of people with different cultural capital, occupations, life chances and relationships to the means of production. In light of ongoing debates about the concept of class it is important to note the influence of our own social context on the role of class as an analytic category in studies of the ancient world: the very debate about the relevance of class is part of class struggle. Cold War divisions associated the very idea of class with Stalinism and together with it rejected all forms of Marxism. Class also raises issues of self-worth and inequality, so discussion of it can be uncomfortable and acrimonious. It is thus convenient that class has increasingly been viewed as irrelevant despite (or because of) the increased consolidation of class power over the past two generations.[1] Perhaps as a result of these factors there has been little serious engagement with the concept of class in discussions of comedy.

Class expresses the relationship among competing social groups with opposed interests. While class struggle can be open (i.e. fighting in the streets), it is manifest in ideas and values and informs institutional structures. Class thus involves ideology, by which I refer to a type of representation aimed at validating and/or defending the values and social position of a particular group, while at the same time attempting to neutralize oppositional claims through denigration or incorporation.[2] Ideology embodies the interests of opposed classes, thus making for an unstable and complex set of

I would like to thank Martin Revermann and Victoria Wohl for helpful suggestions and criticism of earlier versions of this chapter.

[1] See Wright (2005) for different types of class analysis. Continued relevance of class: see e.g., Harvey (2005), (2010); Žižek (2000). As hooks (2000) vii notes, unlike race and gender, class has become an 'uncool subject'.

[2] See Gramsci (in Hoare and Smith (1971) 52–61 and *passim*); Jameson (1971) 380–85, (1981) 288–92; see further Rose (2006). The influential studies of Ehrenberg (1962) and Ste Croix (1972) are poor on issues of ideology.

representations. The effect of the potential (re)combination of social values can support the status quo or reconfigure social hierarchy. Ideology aims but is not guaranteed to reproduce dominant values.

Athens had its share of class struggle. A wealthy minority controlled the majority of land – one of the primary means of production – and officials forswore its redistribution ([Arist.] *Ath. Pol.* 56.2; cf. Dem. 24.149). Public funds were increasingly distributed through state pay and welfare, but the vast gulf separating rich from poor was contested.[3] Although all citizens shared political equality – itself subject to intense class warfare among the traditional elite and the radical *dêmos* – it existed alongside pervasive economic inequality. This separation of legal/political rights from property relations and class differences was a central paradox. The dominant public response was to appropriate aristocratic values (e.g., 'nobility of birth'), but there were complications.[4] Some members of the elite supported the policies of the 'radical' democracy, thereby demonstrating that ideology was not defined by class identity alone. Some professional workers celebrated values of industry, labour and technical skill in direct contrast to elite views of labourers as failed men unsuited for citizenship. Non-agricultural labour was in fact a significant part of the economy: despite the importance of farming, one-third of the citizen population and up to half of the total population may have worked as craftsmen or merchants.[5] Across a broad spectrum of society, elite ideology was dominant, but a set of values opposed (in varying degrees) to the idea of the 'noble *dêmos*' (i.e. fully assimilating aristocratic values) emerged without ultimately becoming hegemonic.

The audiences of Aristophanes and Menander

People came to the theatre with all kinds of ideological baggage. As a way to define more precisely comedy's engagement with class, I discuss briefly the controversial subject of audience composition. As a self-aware genre conscious of its performative context, comedy often contained references to spectators' roles and appeals to class interests. This was strategic, since the meaning and reception of drama ultimately resides in the spectators' minds.

---

[3] Ownership of land: Foxhall (2002), (2007); Osborne (1992); van Wees (2001); cf. Hanson (1995) 181–7; Morris (2000) 140–1. Class struggle in Athens: Rose (1999); Roselli (2007) 90–106.

[4] Economic inequalities: Raaflaub (1996); *dêmos'* appropriation of elite values: Donlan (1980) 113–53; Ober (1989) 259–70.

[5] Discussion of labour and manufacturing: Harris (2002a); Mattingly and Salmon (2001); shape of the ancient economy: Bresson (2000), (2007), (2008); Davies (2007); Möller (2007).

Despite the existence of ten official judges, spectators are generally recognized in Aristophanes as quasi-arbiters of dramatic competitions (e.g., *Birds* 440f., *Assembly Women* 1140–62). The overlapping of victory for the characters/chorus with victory for the performers in the competition (e.g., *Knights* 589–94), and the festive denouement with processions (*Frogs*, *Wealth*), feasts (*Assembly Women*), and weddings (*Birds*, *Peace*) were performative strategies designed to bridge the world of the play with the world of the festival. The effect was to jump-start the (anticipated) communal celebration of the performance's victory. Although there are wedding festivities in Menander, little attempt is made to enmesh the spectators in the performance. While Menander exhorts the audience to applaud and join in a prayer to Victory (e.g., *Dys.* 965–9, *Samia* 733–7), these formulaic exhortations are located exclusively at the end of plays: the victory coda functions like a curtain call. While there is much evidence for slaves, metics and foreigners as spectators, Aristophanes – unlike Menander – incorporates their presence into the performance (*Wasps* 78f.; *Peace* 45f.).[6] Aristophanes also singles out spectators in terms of their profession (*Peace* 543–55; *Plut.* 406f.), and with the majority of metics (and many slaves) working in non-agricultural jobs these solicitations equally target non-citizens. Openly soliciting the interests of spectators – a challenging job in light of their changing tastes (*Knights* 516) – was an important part of the dramatic competition. But differences between Aristophanes and Menander suggest a gradual diminution of explicit concern for the spectators' role during the performance in light of changing historical conditions and tastes. Decreased interest in directly addressing spectators in terms of social class was likely connected with Menander's attention to ethical character.

When the audience is directly addressed, comedy generally refers to *male* spectators but suggestively speaks of 'everybody else' (e.g., *Assembly Women* 1144f., *Sam.* 733f.).[7] The question of women in the audience has been subject to intense debate, but past scholarship has focused on the propriety of female attendance and evaluated dramatic performances in terms of civic or ritual functions. Since the evidence itself is somewhat inconclusive, much depends on how the question is framed. When viewed as a civic event, the theatre has no room for women; when viewed in terms of its ritual components, there is room for women.[8] However, a singular focus on a

---

[6] See Csapo and Slater (1995) 286–305; Spineto (2005) 277–92 for non-citizen spectators.

[7] *Lys.* 1043–53 may include an address to women: see Henderson (1991b) 139f.

[8] The debate starts in the Enlightenment: see Katz (1998). Drama as a civic event: Goldhill (1994); studies emphasizing ritual aspects: Henderson (1991b); Podlecki (1990); Sourvinou-Inwood (2003) 177–84. For a more 'holistic' approach see Schnurr-Redford (1995) 225–40; Spineto (2005) 292–315.

ritual or a civic frame is problematic, as theatre incorporates different aspects of society simultaneously, and women's ritual roles were understood in terms of their 'quasi-political' dimension. Crucially, there is *no evidence* for prohibitions against women attending the theatre (as there were for some athletic competitions). Class matters much here: while elite ideals may have circumscribed outdoor activities of some wealthy women, many poor women regularly worked outside the home (e.g., in the *agora*).[9] Attending performances would be another kind of public experience familiar to most poor women.

Much of the direct evidence for female spectators comes from Aristophanes and Plato – two slippery sources. While the same comic passages (e.g., *Peace* 965f., *Birds* 794f.) have been used to support both the presence and absence of women, it is perhaps best to note that Aristophanes sometimes makes an issue of women's presence/absence. His playful and casual engagement with the very idea of female spectators likely reflects an audience conscious that it had become a contested issue: Aristophanes' slippery treatment may result from the politicization of women's presence. For Plato's references to female spectators form part of a broader attack on Athens' radical democracy (e.g., *Grg.* 502d, *Resp.* 577c).[10] His criticisms of degenerate audiences consisting of women, slaves and poor citizens use the presence of women as a sign of cultural collapse caused by radical democracy and lower class ('mob') rule. It is thus most probable that women were in the audience, but their presence was affected by spatial arrangements in theatres.

The size and layout of the theatre had a major impact on audience composition. Traditional estimates for the size of the auditorium (*theatron*) in the fifth-century Theatre of Dionysus posit around 17,000 spectators, but recent studies more plausibly suggest a capacity of about 8,000.[11] This represents an even smaller percentage of a population consisting of 40,000–60,000 citizens out of a total of 250,000–400,000 people, the majority of whom were slaves, poor farmers and labourers.[12] Since a fee was charged for a seat on the benches in the *theatron*, it likely affected the number of women and the poor in the official seating area. To be sure, some of the spectators were wealthy, but fees did not keep poor citizens away.[13] There were

[9] For women's ritual roles see e.g., Goff (2004); women's labour: Brock (1994).
[10] See further Roselli (2007) 111–13.
[11] Traditional estimate: Moretti (1999–2000); revised estimate: Goette (2007).
[12] See Akrigg (2007) for demographic changes. Small number of wealthy families: Davies (1981) 9–37; Rhodes (1982); van Wees (2001).
[13] Spectators mostly wealthy: Bowie (1998); Sommerstein (1997). For a more socially stratified audience see Rehm (2002) 50; Revermann (2006b); and Roselli (2011). Wealthy women in the *theatron*: Plut. *Phoc.* 19.2–3; cf. Pl. *Leg.* 658d.

distributions of state funds to citizens for the purpose of attending dramatic festivals (i.e. *theôrika*), but the date of their introduction is contested. The current consensus favours a date around 350, but there is good evidence for ad hoc distributions starting earlier in the fifth century – perhaps even as early as the late 460s.[14] While the existence of entrance fees could be circumvented through *theôrika*, these distributions did not guarantee a sizeable presence of poor citizens in the *theatron* for every festival but crucially left open the possibility that for any particular festival *theôrika* would be approved by the *dêmos*.

The presence of non-official and free viewing spaces could, however, guarantee the presence of the poor (citizens, metics and slaves) and (most probably) women. The construction of theatres in ancient Greece on the sides of hills created a natural viewing space above the *theatron*. Thus, the topography of many theatres would easily accommodate spectators on the hillside. One such viewing area located in Athens above the benches in the *theatron* was the so-called 'view from the poplar'. Cratinus (fr. 372) mentions this location in perhaps what was a direct address to these spectators.[15] From this spot metics, slaves and women, who were not eligible for *theôrika*, and poor citizens, who used *theôrika* for other purposes, could watch for free. With a total audience of about 11,000 (including both official and unofficial locations), the poor would likely have made up at least half of it, if not more. This is reflected in elite criticism of the lower class theatre 'mob'. The idea of the poor and indiscriminate masses, to whom Aristophanes was believed to appeal (e.g., Plut. *Comp. Ar. et Men.* 853a), determining the outcome of a dramatic competition or a play's content was anathema to conservative critics (e.g., Pl. *Leg.* 700c–701b).[16]

Changes in theatre spaces and in the requirements for citizenship in the fourth century altered this picture of the theatre audience. Wooden benches were replaced by stone seating, and the *theatron* in the Theatre of Dionysus was extended right up to the Acropolis' fortification walls. The new stone theatre held around 17,000 (paying) spectators and eliminated free viewing spaces; similar expansions took place in deme theatres (e.g., Thorikos). In addition to remapping the spectators' space, political changes redefined the social class and ideology of the citizen body. While citizenship was extended to those born of two Athenian parents after 451/50, regardless of social class, the Macedonian-backed oligarchy in 322 limited citizenship to those

---

[14] For fifth-century *theôrika* see Roselli (2009); Wilson (2011) 38–43. Cf. Rhodes (1993) 514; Ruschenbusch (1979).

[15] See Scullion (1994) 55–7 for references to the 'view from the poplar'; Goette (2007) offers a useful overview of the archaeology of the theatre in Athens.

[16] See further Csapo (2000) 129–33.

possessing at least 2,000 drachmas (in 317 it was lowered to 1,000 drachmas). As a result, more than 12,000 former citizens were driven out as 'troublemakers and warmongers', and the disenfranchised Athenians who remained suffered 'hardship and disgrace' (Diod. 18.18.4–5; Plut. *Phoc.* 28.4).[17] Not only were there changes in the social structure, the rich likely got richer with an increased concentration of land in fewer hands. While theoric distributions were regularized by about 350, there is some evidence that entrance fees increased (Hyp. *Dem* 26; Philoch. *FGrHist* 328 F33); and in 322 *theôrika* were most likely abolished under the oligarchs. Attending performances may have become more difficult for the poor and perhaps women.[18]

There were broad shifts in the constitution of the audience. While restrictions on citizenship and mass emigrations of the poor physically reshaped the population, changes in popular taste, as reflected in the plays and in the archaeological record, demonstrate a waning interest in the overt politicization of comic performances and more sympathy for ethical issues.[19] These changes affected the audience's relationship with theatre in the later fourth century and suggest a reconfiguration of ideological divisions. In light of the elimination of free viewing spaces, the monetization of the audience and the diffusion of elite values, appealing to refined sensibilities became increasingly important (cf. Ar. *Eth. Nic.* 1128a25–7).[20]

Social class in comedy

Comedy is keenly attuned to social stratification, and the genre – much like tragedy and satyr drama – had a productive role in elaborating class struggle.[21] But comedy does not make an issue of all forms of exploitation. While the discourse of freedom and equality existed alongside widespread slavery, comic representations of class struggle focus more on differences among the free. However, this politicized version of social class is not static: in Aristophanes characters forthrightly address unequal economic conditions as a public/social problem, while in Menander a more circumscribed

[17] Economic and political changes: Habicht (1997); Oliver (2007). Financial requirements for citizenship were perhaps abolished in 307, but there is no direct evidence.
[18] Separate seating for some women is, however, suggested: Alexis' *Gynaikokratia* (fr. 41); Σ *Assembly Women* 21. There is no direct evidence for the abolition of *theôrika*.
[19] Discussion of archaeological evidence: Green (1994) 76–88; Webster *et al.* (1995) 53–76. See Csapo (2000) on the changes in dominant comic styles.
[20] But Hellenistic comedy did preserve 'popular' (and thus 'low') performance traditions: Hunter (2002).
[21] Discussion of class in tragedy: e.g., Griffith (1995); Rose (1992); Roselli (2007); in satyr drama: e.g., Griffith (2005a).

representation of class struggle emerges in tandem with changing social conditions.

Working class heroes

Aristophanes' heroes are typically commoners exhibiting demotic rather than elite sympathies, and often set off a chain reaction which interrogates class relations.[22] Dicaeopolis in *Acharnians* is a complex example combining concern over economic inequality with public policy. The disgruntled peasant borrows the costume of a beggar from one of Euripides' tragic heroes (Telephus) and with this as a disguise asks to speak about important public matters (notably against the war). Since the spectre of Telephus' poverty is reported to make the conditions of the poor seem bearable (Timocles fr. 6.9–11), Dicaeopolis' use of Telephus' rags may have found a sympathetic response (see *Ach.* 384). But as in the Euripidean model, Dicaeopolis' status and right to political participation is contested: the chorus and the general, Lamachus, question whether this beggar should be able to speak out (562, 593). While Dicaeopolis' lowly status compromises his social standing and thus presents one side of a debate in Athens concerning the right of the poor to participate in the governing of the city (e.g., Thuc. 8.65.3; Xen. *Hell.* 2.3.48), Dicaeopolis asserts that even a beggar is a useful citizen (595f.). This voice from below defends higher pay for lower-class rowers in the fleet (161f.) and critiques the high rates of state pay for elected office holders among the elite (e.g., Lamachus), while complaining that the hard-working poor have no access to such 'cushy' jobs (598–619). Dicaeopolis thus brings out some of the class issues associated with war, which is elsewhere portrayed as dividing the citizenry into rich and poor (e.g., *Assembly Women* 197; cf. *Knights* 912). What unites the community is exchange in the market. For the comic hero's yearning for the countryside, where there is no buying and selling but where all is produced of its own accord (33f.), takes material form in the money-based *agora* he sets up (e.g., 898f., 906, 957f.). The comic plan is realized in a 'market utopia' described in terms of the Golden Age (976), thus fulfilling the commoner's utopian desires.

The contested role of the lower classes in shaping economic and political policy reaches its apogee in comic representations of 'demagogues' or leaders of the radical *dêmos*. While there appears to be little political comedy in Menander, the *ad hominem* focus on political leaders was a defining trait

---

[22] See Henderson (1990), (1993), (1998) on the vantage point of the commoner and the promotion of the *dêmos*' sovereignty.

of Old Comedy.[23] Plays centred on individual demagogues (e.g., Cleon, Hyperbolus) stress their associations with the *agora* and its lower class 'hucksters' (e.g., *Knights* 128–45), while portraying their family origins as poor, servile and foreign. However, these leaders were Athenian citizens and were relatively wealthy. Insinuation of low birth and slave origins was strategic, as it suggests politicians were somehow no longer poor. This rise in social class could be attributed to graft and misuse of state funds (e.g., *Knights* 1218f.; *Plut.* 567f.); such charges were widely aired (e.g., *Lys.* 25–7).[24] Among the traditional elite, these charges underscored the unsuitability of demagogues to lead (cf. Thuc. 2.65). As noted above, the threat of the consolidation of class power by elected officials, most of whom were drawn from wealthy families, was a concern for Dicaeopolis.[25]

These politicians were flashpoints of ideological struggle. Their portrayal as merchants and craftsmen united them with the perceived supporters of the radical democracy; some may have affected lower class traits to appeal to the urban poor. Paphlagon, a comic version of Cleon, is thus surrounded by leather-sellers, honey-sellers and cheese-sellers (*Knights* 852f.), and as their patron he 'feeds' the people (255f.) through prosecutions of the wealthy (326). Paphlagon's/Cleon's threats (913–26) to make his opponents liable for military expenses (e.g., trierarchs) suggest a recognized form of class warfare (cf. *Peace* 639) by redistributing private wealth to the community.[26] Hyperbolus is portrayed as part of a bread-seller's family in Hermippus' *Breadsellers* (see fr. 209), and his 'low urban style' of speech in comedy aligned him with the urban poor.[27] The lower classes become politicized with such men as leaders: an elite critic of Cleon is branded by the poor as a pro-Spartan tyrant for barring poor citizens from exercising the laws of the city (*Wasps* 463–70; cf. *Lys.* 620f.). Such responses from the poor in comedy may have appeared to the conservative elite as bitter parody (see Ar. *Rh.* 1408b24), since many of them opposed the political participation of lower class citizens.[28] While elite views on demagogues surface in their comic representation as 'vulgar' and 'stupid' sellers (especially in *Knights*), the murder of Hyperbolus and Cleophon for partisan reasons by oligarchs reflects

---

[23] Politics in Menander and New Comedy: Lape (2004); Major (1997); social class of demagogues: Connor (1971); Davies (1981) 38–87; Henderson (1990).

[24] Cleon was allegedly fined for taking bribes to lower tribute payments (Σ *Ach.* 5–8), thus diverting funds from the state: see Carawan (1990).

[25] See further Henderson (1990), (1998).

[26] With their public influence such men as Cleon would have been in a position to carry out these threats; see Gabrielsen (1994) 73–8 for the appointment of trierarchs.

[27] Linguistic portrayal of Hyperbolus: Platon's *Hyperbolus* fr. 183. See Colvin (1999) 282, (2000) 290.

[28] E.g., Pl. *Leg.* 741a–42b; Ar. *Pol.* 1321a26–29; Xen. *Oec.* 4.3.

more than feelings of alienation (Thuc. 8.73.3; *Lys.* 30.10–13). Nonetheless, the re-election of Cleon as general in the weeks following the performance of *Knights* and the *dêmos'* continued reliance on like-minded leaders attest to their valued role among the 'commoners' beyond the theatre (see Ps.-Xen. *Ath. Pol.* 2.19).

In terms of ideology, comedy is not univocal and thus does not endorse a singular set of values.[29] While these leaders are to be driven out of the city (*Peace* 1319), there is some recognition of their 'usefulness' (*Knights* 977–84). In *Knights* the demise of Paphlagon/Cleon and the swift rise to political power by a poor but clever merchant, Sausage-Seller, with the aid of the aristocratic knights provide a symbolic model of a merchant-as-politician who does not steal from the *dêmos* (1214–28). The idea of proles as politicians is celebrated, but there is some apprehension in the adoption of elite values by the working classes, for without Paphlagon/Cleon the city has no state pay, no law-courts and no youths in the *agora*. There are clear costs associated with endorsing elite values (e.g., *Knights* 579f.).[30] Little wonder the poor are portrayed in comedy as alarmed at the slightest sign of trouble from the elite.

The ease with which commoners can out-manoeuvre elite politicians is potentially appealing with its social levelling of commoner and elite. Comedy's erasure of social divisions suggests a misrecognition of class distinctions that could be liberating to many while nonetheless favourable to elite hegemony, but despite the dominant role of the elite in shaping values in the polis, there are signs that some were promoting a different conception of the role of (poor) workers: literary and archeological evidence points to the emergent self-promotion of citizens and metics as craftsmen (*banausoi*).[31] While elite criticism of some politicians as 'working class' denigrated their economic policies and political style, such criticism in comedy could equally (perhaps more so in light of audience composition) be viewed as a satiric version of the complaints levelled at the radical *dêmos* (and its leaders) by the traditional elite (see *Peace* 184–8). By airing critical views of demagogues while appealing to supporters of the radical *dêmos*, comedy also engaged with changing perceptions about lower class workers and their politicization. Contested ideas about social class and politics are useful tools when

[29] *Contra* e.g., Ehrenberg (1962); Lind (1990); Schareika (1978); Ste Croix (1972). Henderson (1990), (1998) stresses the promotion of democratic values in Old Comedy but claims that the poets championed more traditional (i.e. less radical) leaders.

[30] See further Wohl (2002) 105–23; cf. Rosenbloom (2002), (2004) 332–9; Sommerstein (2000).

[31] A detailed study of this phenomenon is a *desideratum*. For some discussion see Himmelmann (1994) 23–48; Kosmopoulou (2002); Osborne (2000); Vidale (2002).

engaging in class struggle on the ideological plane – precisely where comedy intervened.

Representing class relations

'Working class' comic heroes are microcosms of class conflict, which can be expanded in terms of the contrasting conditions of rich and poor. In Aristophanes, the living conditions of the poor revolve around access to food, the price of commodities, meagre wages, decrepit lodgings, and concern over abuse by the wealthy (e.g., *Ach.* 792f.; *Wasps* 252f.; *Assembly Women* 422–6). The sweeping measures that are put forward as potential remedies elaborate the contentiousness of the economic status quo. Similar concerns over food and wages are found in Menander (e.g., *Dys.* 280–98; *Her.* 27–36), but poverty becomes a condition to be remedied by private solutions, notably marriage. The representation of class differences in Menander is further inflected by ethical concerns: according to the poor, it is best to minimize witnesses of one's poverty by staying out of sight in the countryside (*Geôrgos* 77–81; cf. Amphis fr. 17).

Various factors affect economic conditions. While the immigration of people from the countryside into the city at the beginning of the Peloponnesian War swelled the numbers of the poor (*Knights* 792f.; cf. Thuc. 2.14–17), impoverished conditions associated with farmers surface frequently in comedy. Market fluctuations caused the immiseration of some craftsmen and the enrichment of others (*Peace* 1158–264; cf. *Pl.* 823–958). Changes in the fortunes of different professionals led to jealousy (*Peace* 547), and mocking a craftsman's business losses (1212) is understood as an attack on his social standing (i.e. *hybris*: 1229, 1264). More dire was the loss of civic status through debt: men with outstanding financial obligations could be forced to work as debt-bondsmen (*Clouds* 240f.; Men. *Her.* 35f.).[32] Changes to the political regime in Athens under Macedonian rule contributed to a reconfiguring of economic values. In addition to the many (professional) toadies and parasites (i.e. lackeys of the wealthy) in Menander, working class professionals are presented as dependent on the rich for employment.[33] A Thracian waiter hired by a wealthy family (see *Sam.* 289) is bitter about lost wages and displaces his economic frustrations onto a Phrygian slave (*Aspis* 232–45). Cooks are common characters, as they play an important role in the many feasts (often at weddings) sponsored by the rich. Their attention to

[32] Debt-bondage: Harris (2002b). Economic conditions reflected in Aristophanes: Spielvögel (2001).
[33] See Krieter-Spiro (1997); Harvey (2000) 369–414. Nesselrath (1990) 280–330 discusses slaves and professionals in 'Middle' Comedy.

business (*Dys.* 665; *Sam.* 287f.) could appear as overzealousness denigrated by their wealthy employers (Men. fr. 409). Comic portrayal of cooks as poor professionals is itself topical in New Comedy (Adesp. fr. 1093.222f.).

What the poor lack and perhaps desire is represented by the wealthy and a lifestyle associated with consumption and privilege. Entire plays were based on wealthy individuals. Callias, who inherited his riches, is mocked in passing by Aristophanes (e.g., *Birds* 284f., *Assembly Women* 810f.) but is the main topic in Eupolis' *Flatterers*, where he is satirized for his spendthrift ways. In Menander the wealthy are fictional characters who wear fancy cloaks, throw big parties, give huge dowries, and strikingly have no illness – in short, their life is just a 'nap' (*Phasma* 34–43). Such characteristics as long hair, purple robes, a love of horses, warm baths, symposia, golden jewelry, exotic pets, flute-girls, courtesans, attendance at *gymnasia*, education, and flamboyant tastes in food distinguish the wealthy from the multitude in comedy.[34] These traits also served as flashpoints of ideological struggle. For example, long hair could be symbolic of elite privilege (*Knights* 579f.), while indicating anti-democratic sentiment (*Lys.* 561–4; *Wasps* 463–70, cf. 1317). This coiffure was popular among aristocratic knights – *kaloikagathoi* ('fine and good/noble men') – envisioned as allied with the clever among the spectators and the Sausage-Seller (*Knights* 225–29). Siding with the ordinary Sausage-Seller against Paphlagon/Cleon in *Knights* is bundled together with the spectators' pleasurable affiliation with the (long-haired) elite and the clever.[35] Long hair was a contested selling point in the construction of the demotic desire to be elite.

While some of the elite fashioned themselves as *kaloikagathoi*, Aristophanes uses the term both as a description of social class (e.g., *Clouds* 797) and in jest (e.g., *Knights* 733f., *Clouds* 101).[36] Despite the occasionally more balanced treatment of aristocrats, Aristophanes generally ridicules wealthy men for their wastefulness (e.g., Leogoras, Morychus), effeminacy (e.g., Cleisthenes, Alcibiades), and mistresses (e.g., Philonides), among other things.[37] Even what appears as straightforward endorsement of the elite (e.g., *Frogs* 687–737) is tempered with a sting in the tail: nobility means knowing how to drink and fuck (740). Although sources of wealth vary in comedy (e.g., trade, agriculture, banking, commodity production, inheritance), in Aristophanes theft and graft receive more attention; in Menander the

---

[34] Cf. Fisher (2000) on the class-based contradictions in representations of drinking and eating in Old Comedy. *Mousikê* is another site of ideological struggle connected with a rise in professional performers and changing economics in the theatre (e.g., the portrayal of Euripides in *Frogs*); see further Csapo (2004).

[35] See further Wohl (2002) 108–10.   [36] See Dover (1974) 41–5; Heath (1987) 29f.

[37] For comic references to these individuals see Sommerstein (1996).

wealthy are portrayed more sympathetically, particularly for their role in the community (see below). Descriptions of the wealthy embody both their exceptional social status and the contradictory desires and resentment of the poor.

Comic representations of social class differ in striking ways. The world-view of Menander's professionals is limited to their next job for the rich, but Aristophanes' merchants also reflect the emergent politicization of urban labourers ready to defend their rights and livelihood against the elite (e.g., *Women at the Thesmophoria* 445–58; *Wasps* 488–99). In Menander professionals are carefully differentiated: costumes identified them socially between elite and slave in terms of grotesque features, and linguistic portrayal distinguished working class from elite with a variety of subtle touches (Plut. *Mor.* 853c–e). In Aristophanes the levelling off of class differences among the citizenry made it easier to misrecognize the effects of class while contributing to a more egalitarian view, with poor workers testing the limits of this equality and participating in economic and political debates. The intensified legibility of social class in Menander's plays, performed in the changed political conditions of Hellenistic Greece, rendered a hierarchically stratified society more favourable to elite hegemony.[38]

Addressing economic inequality

Attempts to remedy unequal economic relations are generally divided between public and private measures with some ideas taking an explicitly utopian turn. In Aristophanes' *Wealth* the plight of the poor is resolved by mass enrichment. The plan is to restore the eyesight of the blind god, Wealth, so that he can shun the wicked and enrich the good. The play describes in detail the horrors of poverty (e.g., 535–47) and the contradictions between political rights and the unequal distribution of wealth (e.g., 28–31, 489–96). One questionable objection to the plan (made by Poverty herself) is that craftsmen and farmers would cease to work if they were wealthy (511–14, 525f.). Poverty's hair-splitting between the relative poverty of the 'poor' (*penêtes*) and 'beggars' (*ptôchoi*) may have been ideologically useful in obscuring social conditions by differentiating the two groups (548–56), but Chremylus has no truck with this.[39] This 'moderate' citizen (245) is unwilling to accept a subordinate economic position in a city where one's life chances are determined by money. The play's successful

---

[38] See Csapo (2002) 142–7 for comic characters' language and costume; cf. Krieter-Spiro (1997) on Menander's linguistic portrayal. Despite Aristophanes' social levelling, attention to 'barbarian' ethnicity is common; see Hall (2006) 225–54.

[39] Distinctions and similarities between 'beggars' and the 'poor': Rosivach 1991.

utopian scheme is connected with golden age fantasies and the eradication of class differences.[40]

In *Assembly Women* a similarly radical idea resolves economic inequality. The equal distribution of all resources – in brief, communism (590–610) – is achieved by women posing as citizen males and taking control of the city. Although there are objections to the women's utopian plans (746–1111), as in the case of *Wealth*, these are not straightforward condemnations; in fact, one character accepts that communism is now the law (759) and notes that others are compliant (805).[41] Many scholarly discussions, based on *a priori* assumptions about the poet's conservative views, have dismissed these utopian desires as impractical and viewed Aristophanes as ridiculing such schemes.[42] Surely it is important to note both support for and opposition to economic reforms built into these plays. Opposed views not only appeal to spectators/groups with competing interests; the articulation of economic equality from within a culture dominated by elite values unavoidably bears the marks of the struggle between dominant and oppositional ideologies.

State pay was another contentious issue in the debate over redistribution of public funds. Pay for service in the courts (*dikastikon*) began at a moment of intense factional strife around 460 at one or two obols and was increased to three obols by Cleon around 425. This would have constituted a subsistence wage for a small family.[43] Assembly pay was introduced after 403 at one obol and was quickly raised to three obols – again by demagogues. These forms of state pay were perceived to encourage political participation among the urban poor, and as a result they were bitterly opposed by the traditional elite (e.g., Thuc. 8.65.3; *Ath. Pol.* 29.5). Comedy in turn elaborates these competing views in its treatment of state payments. Some citizens are happy with Assembly pay, as it is equivalent to a bushel of wheat (*Assembly Women* 547f.). A more ambivalent spin connects increases in the *dikastikon* with demands by the urban poor (see *Knights* 797f.), who are described as using the courts to redistribute private wealth to the *dêmos* (*Wasps* 549–53, 626f.). More direct criticisms are also raised: those lowly 'wage earners' (*Assembly Women* 310) who collect Assembly pay should be killed (185f.),

---

[40] See DuBois (2006); Ruffell (2000); and Ruffell, Chapter 10 on ancient utopias.

[41] See further Ruffell (2006) 83–4, 93–8.

[42] For *Wealth* see e.g., Bowie (1993) 268–91; Konstan (1995) 75–90; McGlew (1997); Olson (1990); for *Assembly Women* see e.g., Foley (1982); Saïd (1979). Cf. Sommerstein (1984) for changes in the poet's outlook in the late plays. For more nuanced views see Ruffell (2006); Tordoff (2007).

[43] Increase in *dikastikon*: Σ *Wasps* 88a, 300b; cf. *Ach.* 657. *Dikastikon* as a living wage: Markle (1985). Since the courts did not meet everyday, these funds were not always available.

and urban workers now so eager to participate and collect their pay are denigrated.

Comic treatment of the democratic court system in *Wasps* is equally ambivalent. According to the conservative Bdelycleon, most of the state funds are stolen by elite politicians (*Wasps* 655–64, 691f.), hence the low level of remuneration for jurors. With service in the courts viewed as a form of slavery (682) and wage labour (712), Bdelycleon's solution is to institute a private court in his house for his father, Philocleon. State pay is replaced by private pay, as the chorus of poor jurors willingly withdraws from the public courts (726, 887f.). But this is not a simple condemnation of the democratic court system:[44] in the new private court Philocleon is easily – and obviously – deceived (992) into voting against the interests of the poor (909; cf. 917) and acquits the more conservative defendant supported by Bdelycleon. While both court systems are mocked, replacing the democratic court with a form of private, even familial, patronage appears problematic. Ambivalence in the comic representation of state pay and the courts is an attention-grabbing effect of the articulation of dominant and oppositional views. Social divisions are expressed through parody and criticism, while a case is made for redistributing state funds to the benefit of the poor (e.g., 304f., 605–18).

The use of gender to express economic inequality in *Assembly Women* raises additional issues. On account of the women's pale complexions, when disguised as male citizens they appear as shoe-makers (385), whose work inside limits their exposure to the sun. This detail dovetails with the perceived support of urban professionals (as a collective) for more radical economic measures (cf. 277f., 432). Despite the humour involved with cross-dressed women, the image of 'feminine' (male) citizens also overlaps with the representation of workers in conservative texts as worthless and unmanly (i.e. as women: Xen. *Oec.* 4.2–3); some wealthy men in fact refrained from speaking in the Assembly, since it was hijacked by urban workers (Xen. *Mem.* 3.7.6). To the conservative elite, political conditions depicted in the play may have reflected the dangers of radical democracy, but these 'women on top' humorously, and less threateningly, displace the spectre of the politicized urban *dêmos*.[45] The enaction of communism by *women* lacking political rights nevertheless tackles the paradox of political equality alongside economic inequality.

---

[44] Olson (1996); cf. Ste Croix (1972) 362; Konstan (1995) 15–28.
[45] See Konstan (1995) 56 for a different kind of displacement from class to gender in *Lysistrata*. The idea of 'women on top' was later used to articulate discontent with distributions of power in Early Modern Europe: see Davis (1975).

Gender and class also overlap in the representation of female merchants, who articulate the concerns of the urban poor and the sentiments of the radical democracy.[46] A widowed Garland-Seller complains about poor market conditions: she cannot feed her children, and as she needs to make money she cannot participate in festivals (*Women at the Thesmophoria* 445–58). In *Wasps*, after Bdelycleon's disastrous attempt to educate Philocleon in the art of proper sympotic behaviour, Philocleon attacks a female bread-seller (1388–98). The *nouveau riche*'s (1309) abusive treatment of the merchant is countered by her reliance on the rule of law to protect her: she summons him to appear before the market-controllers (*agoranomoi*) with Chaerephon as her witness (1406f.). This mixing of class with gender portrays the considerable role of women in the economy while also allowing for the expression of class antagonism by a politicized collective, albeit one represented by those possessing only a quasi-political status.

In contrast with Aristophanes, the possibility of modifying economic conditions is more circumscribed in Menander. Personal assistance is one way to redistribute resources. The contingent nature of wealth as a gift of fortune forms part of an argument for the rich to distribute their wealth (*Dys.* 799–812): it is to be used generously to help the poor, since one may need a favour from others in the future. While self-interested charity may serve to unite rich and poor or suggest a view of wealth based on equal opportunity through fate, it is difficult not to discern the patronage of the extremely wealthy.[47] Whereas greed and a disregard for family in pursuit of wealth is ridiculed (e.g., Smicrines in *Aspis*), the rich can manifest their good character by giving away some of their wealth (*Dys.* 800) – not by altering (unequal) economic conditions. Liturgies function in a similar fashion. As a kind of 'taxation' on the rich to fund public projects, liturgies bolster the elite's repute in Menander (e.g., *Samia* 13f.); in Aristophanes, however, a view from below stresses the cheapness of liturgists (e.g., *Ach.* 1150; cf. Antiphanes fr. 202). Crucially, liturgies did not directly address the conditions of the poor but did provide an arena for the production of cultural capital benefiting the elite. Discussion of the 'good' uses of wealth in Menander, even with the expectation among the poor that the wealthy 'look down' at them (e.g., *Dys.* 286), situates social class within an ethical frame that obscures a more politicized view of poverty.

In the absence of ideas (utopian or otherwise) to change the face of society to benefit the poor, relations with wealthy families appear as a partial

---

[46] See Henderson (1987a) 121f., (2000) 140–3.
[47] Cf. Lape (2004) 129–33; see also Wiles (1984); Hoffmann (1998). Casson (1976) argues that Menander represented the 'millionaires' of his day.

solution in Menander. Since many of his plays involve aspects of mistaken identity, recognition of citizen status, and ultimately marriage with the bestowal of a large dowry, the (apparently) low social status of some women and men can be corrected in the course of a play. There are indications that certain differences in social class were seen as unwelcome in a marriage (e.g., *Peir.* 710), and not all unequal unions succeed (*Plokion* fr. 297). But when plots of misrecognized social/civic status do succeed, the mistaken identity of female characters plays a central role.[48] Since natural merit and virtue (and fate!) rescue these individual women from the underclass, the narrative suggests a potentially progressive spin with a lower class character's rise from rags to riches. But many of these women are *restored* to their rightful status: they were misrecognized elite 'citizens' all along. This detail undercuts the potential subversion of dominant values, for the special value of (apparently) lower class *individuals* is separated from the taint of their (mistaken) social class. This narrative of misrecognized identity, modelled on Euripidean tragedy (e.g., *Ion*), reinforces differences in social class (e.g., *Men at Arbitration* 320–33) unlike the appropriation of Euripides' *Telephus* in Aristophanes' *Acharnians* for the purpose of contesting class distinctions.

Whereas Menander's wedding participants are generally restored to elite status, the numerous urban professionals are not. Their financial problems are resolved through more work. Marriage feasts celebrated by wealthy families were big business (see *Methê* fr. 218) and provided a consistent source of income for cooks and their attendants (e.g., *Aspis* 223f.). In this regard, the wealthy served a valuable economic role in the polis. In contrast with Aristophanes, lower class workers in Menander are less outspoken about the connections between political and social conditions (see *Dys.* 482f.). When a commoner complains that the wealthy should be concerned about the price of wheat for the sake of the poor, it is worth noting that he asks for pardon in expressing his feelings (*Phasma* 26–43). In Menander, inequalities based on social class are addressed through personal interactions with the wealthy, and results do vary.

Menander's emphasis on ethical character, while ultimately supporting elite ideology, nonetheless suggests a certain equality that elides class differences. When the wealthy Sostratus attempts to win a girl's hand in marriage by *pretending* to be a poor farmer (*Dys.* 368–92), the real peasant claims that this act reveals Sostratus' true nature: although rich he was still willing to lower himself to the level of the poor (767f.). The scene hints at a

---

[48] See Traill (2008) on women's social status. Not all brides come from wealthy families (e.g., Philoumene in *The Sicyonians*), but they generally become wealthy through marriage. See Lape (2004) for marriage as a means to reproduce democratic values.

broader, more egalitarian, conception of character defined by one's nature. But it is notably a rich man who is praised by a peasant, and external signs of class still validate the idea of wealth as something deserved (775).[49] As in the case of mistaken identity plots, references to a poor man's 'nobility' differentiate him from his social class (e.g., *Dys.* 723; cf. *Samia* 141f.). Such poor men (and women) either are revealed to be elite by birth or support elite values, and this diffusion of aristocratic ideology throughout society mystifies unequal economic relations.[50] In another case, a slave raising an exposed child of noble parentage fears that if the child is raised by working folk, he will feel disdain and after realizing his true nature undertake noble actions (*Men at Arbitration* 320–5). Ultimately, the child is rescued from slavery (see 468f.) and reunited with his 'true' social class/parents. A 'noble' character can be had by all, but only certain slaves and peasants are destined to have their 'true' class and citizen status revealed.

The plight of the majority of slaves remains an extreme model of class exploitation, which comedy was less interested in exploring. While poor citizens are imagined as free from labour in Aristophanes' utopian schemes, slaves are still needed physically to work and ideologically to support divisions between slave and free (*Plut.* 517f., *Assembly Women* 652; cf. Crates *Animals* fr. 16).[51] Slaves are also employed in the explanation and organization (particularly in Menander) of the comic plot (e.g., *Wasps*; *Aspis*). Despite their physical presence and identifiable stage business, slaves are often silent, as in the beginning of *Peace* (see 656f.); at times they are only signalled by rebukes from their masters (e.g., *Peace* 256; *Samia* 104f.). Although manumission (*Men at Arbitration* 538–48) and naturalization as citizens (*Frogs* 693f.) were possible for a tiny percentage of slaves, nearly all remained objects with no rights over themselves or their children (e.g., *Plut.* 6f.; *Men at Arbitration* 1072f.) – a fact reflected in comedy's frequent jokes about abusing and beating slaves (see *Peace* 742–7). In *Frogs* the potential challenges to the notion of slavery through the exchanging of costumes and social identities between Xanthias and his master, Dionysus, are limited by reference to the anomalous enfranchisement of slaves who fought at Arginusae (33f., cf. 190–3) and perhaps contained by the slaves' acceptance of servitude (743–55, 813). Some slaves even appear docile and trustworthy

---

[49] See Rosivach (2001); cf. Lape (2004) especially 121–9. See further Hofmeister (1997); Konstan (1995) especially 96–106; Masaracchia (1981).
[50] The disinterest in differentiating spectators by social class in Menander (see above) exhibits ideological effects similar to this interest in ethical character.
[51] Slaves in comedy: see e.g., Dover (1972) 204–8; DuBois (2003) 117–30 and *passim*; Hall (2006) 231–41; Hunt (2011); Olson (1989); Proffitt (2010); Wiles (1991) *passim*; for a rosier picture of slavery: Krieter-Spiro (1997); Sommerstein (2009) 136–54.

(e.g., Sosias and Xanthias in *Wasps*): these 'good' slaves support an idealized view of slavery from the perspective of slave-owners.

In terms of class struggle, refusal to understand commands, work slow-downs and escape (where possible) were options, but slaves' fundamental lack of position in the polis prevented them from challenging the effects of class domination in the political realm.[52] Comedy's representation of class struggle appears more concerned with the overlapping of economics and politics, where the poor become a political entity and encounter resistance in Aristophanes or where elite values foreclose oppositional ideologies in Menander. There is little recognition of the paradox of slavery, which is legitimized rather than critiqued. The varying degrees to which the dominant ideology was challenged and interrupted determined the ways in which class struggle played out before comic audiences.

Further reading

For a brief, historical overview of the concept of class see Day (2001); its moral significance is explored in Sayer (2005). The complex meanings of the concept of ideology are helpfully parsed in Eagleton (2007), but Williams (1977) remains helpful. Economic conditions in Athens (and beyond) are surveyed in a number of the essays in Scheidel *et al.* (2007) and in Bresson (2007), (2008); changes in society and culture in the fifth and fourth centuries are discussed in the essays in Osborne (2007). In terms of the theatre audience, the brief overview in Csapo and Slater (1995) remains useful, but see the comprehensive study in Roselli (2011). While there has been little serious engagement with class struggle in general, valuable orientation can be found in Konstan (1994), Rose (1992), Ste Croix (1981), and Vernant (1980). Lape (2004) and Traill (2008) provide useful discussion of the connections between social and political issues in Menander. Slavery (in comedy) has begun to receive more critical attention: see Klees (1998) and the essays in Alston, Hall and Proffitt (2010), Bradley and Cartledge (2011), as well as Akrigg and Tordoff (2013). In most respects, however, the study of Greek comedy and class remains to be written.

[52] In classical Athens we hear from one real slave working in a foundry, Lesis, who requests that a better form of slave labour be found for him: see Harris (2006) 271–9. The more than 20,000 slaves who escaped servitude during the Peloponnesian War (Thuc. 7.27.5) made no political claims, but the threat of slave revolts remained a concern: Cartledge (1985).

13

HELENE P. FOLEY

Performing gender in Greek Old and New Comedy

Greek comedy apparently grew in part out of an Attic festal tradition in which men sported costumes that could include visible padding and phalluses, but also involved disguise as animals or other figures. These festal performances may have aimed to promote fertility or banish spirits hostile to the community, so that issues relating to sexuality and fertility were part of the emerging genre of comedy from the start. Vases designed for Attic symposia (aristocratic drinking parties, where poetry could be recited and performed, including poetry in the 'iambic' tradition that could involve overt sexuality, insulting language and satire) could also represent 'comic' performances. Comedy did not become part of the theatrical festivals celebrated in honour of the god Dionysus until 486 BCE or thereabouts, so that its large public performances took shape in a context where tragedy and satyr play were already established, if continually evolving, dramatic forms. All of these factors are critical to understanding the representation of gender in both Old and New Comedy. Tragedy, comedy and satyr play could share story patterns based on Greek myths even if the language and gesture of comedy was far less restrained and its plots often focused on contemporary political and social issues. Comedy's parody of serious literature, including tragedy, probably influenced old comic plots giving central roles to women and eventuated in New Comedy's more extensive borrowing from the tragic repertory, especially the plays of Euripides, although its plots focused on domestic rather than public issues. The issues that all forms of Greek drama raised about closely related tensions and/or polarities between male and female, old and young, or slave and free appeared in non-literary works (history, philosophy or rhetoric) as well.

This chapter will assume this rich and complex background to the degree possible, but focus on how Old and New Comedy represented issues central to analyzing gender relations in the plays. Since the visual dimension of comedy was critical to its meaning for its original audience, I begin by examining the significance of comic costume and body language for

259

understanding the representation of gender roles, and move on to the ways in which the plays represent and perform 'masculinity' and 'femininity' over the entire period that spans Old Comedy (unless otherwise noted the extant works of Aristophanes) and New Comedy, where I draw exclusively on the mostly fragmentary plays of Menander. This analysis attempts to capture both transitions and continuities in the comic performance of gender over this period. The discussion of femininity is dealt with separately and secondly, because female characters became increasingly important to the comic plots and actions over time and were invented by male authors aiming to communicate with a predominantly or perhaps even, at the early stages, an exclusively male audience.[1] Old Comedy constantly drew attention to its status as performance through non-naturalistic costume, gesture and action that could emphasize bodily desires and appetites, through cross-dressing and other forms of deliberately partial disguise of its exclusively male actors, through frequent metatheatrical comments on the staging, through pointed parody of other genres, and through stressing contradictions and inconsistencies in its representation of all social roles, including gender roles. Its dramaturgy invited its audience to view gender roles as socially constructed even as it refused to repress human 'nature'/desire. New Comedy distanced itself from many of these theatrical techniques, while not entirely excluding them. Although advocating a role for desire and exploring the constraints that generate particular gender roles and social identities, it aimed in its plot structures and resolutions to make nature and culture appear to converge.[2]

Performing gender through the comic body

Comic costume in both Old and New Comedy helped to define, although in different ways, gendered conceptions of character. Greek art and literature represented idealized human bodies that comedy deliberately distorted or modified to a greater or lesser degree. The ideal nude male was tall, well muscled but slim, with a smaller than life-size penis and a face that generally expressed self-control rather than emotion. When dressed, respectable men ideally took care to keep their bodies and even one arm covered when performing in civic contexts. In the fourth century, Aeschines mocked orators like Timarchus or Demosthenes who had begun to gesticulate wildly and to

[1] See among many other discussions, the opposed views in Henderson (1991b), Goldhill (1994) and Roselli (2011).
[2] Rosivach (1998) 143 and Lape (2004). Lape quotes McCarthy (2000) 14: 'the naturalistic mode in comedy "perform[s] the function of hegemonic discourse" by making "the world around us seem to be one that is destined"'.

reveal inadequately disciplined masculine bodies or to sport overly luxurious (feminizing) clothing in the law courts (Aeschines 1 *Against Timarchus*).

The male costume of Old Comedy generally displayed an exaggeratedly long phallus that either hung down from beneath a short tunic or was visibly rolled up. The comic actor's body was padded on the rear, chest and belly and his mask was distorted, with receding hair and a large, open smiling mouth.[3] Some masks could apparently represent caricatured versions of the faces of known public figures (portrait masks). The actor's tights were wrinkled, and when he removed his clothing, the visible straps holding on the padding also called attention to the fact that he was wearing a costume. This costume invited the enactment of uncontrolled appetites or undisciplined gesture and, whether the mask had dark or white hair, conveyed age rather than youth, or a physical state not to be expected of a disciplined citizen of military age. When a male character's breasts were visible, his comic body perhaps conveyed a certain androgyny as well as age. The phallus on the costume was rarely erect; the erect phallus could express, as in Aristophanes' *Lysistrata*, men's uncontrolled desire, in this case for their wives, who are involved in a sex strike for peace. Some older men may also have displayed an erect phallus in the final scenes of plays, after the comic hero had acquired both success and a fertile female companion.

Female nudes in the visual arts were rare before the fourth century, and generally represented in symposiastic contexts or where a woman was vulnerable to violence. Literature and art suggest that height, moderate slimness, and firm and youthful breasts and limbs made an idealized female body attractive. Females in Old Comedy also wore smiling and distorted masks and although they were generally more fully cloaked, identical padding was revealed by the drape of the costume. When a female was shown nude, as at the end of *Lysistrata*, scholars think that the costume exaggerated female fertility: breasts, buttocks and belly.[4]

The majority of the central male characters in Old Comedy are mature or older men, and even young men, such as Strepsiades' son Pheidippides in *Clouds*, probably did not sport a youthful, attractive body even while claiming to be athletic.[5] Other male characters in Old Comedy, such as Cleisthenes or Agathon in *Women at the Thesmophoria*, wear costumes that

---

[3] On Old comic costume generally, see especially Stone (1981); Csapo and Slater (1995). For interpretation, see Winkler (1990) and Foley (2000). On the use of the mouth in Old Comedy, see Worman (2008). Aristotle (*Poetics* 1449a 35–7) thought comedy entailed the imitation of inferiors and the ugly (*aischron*). On comic ugliness, see Revermann (2006a) 147–59.

[4] A less likely alternative is that these parts were played by nude prostitutes or courtesans; see Zweig (1992) and Revermann (2006a) 157–9.

[5] Youthful characters may have been slightly less ugly, see Revermann (2006a) 151.

specifically throw their masculinity into question or cross-dress as 'women'. The women at the opening of *Assembly Women* try to represent men through adopting their beards, clothing, tans (women are ideally white-skinned, men sun-burnt), gestures, oaths, staffs and speaking style, but the scene's humour depends on the inability of all but one of them, the heroine Praxagora, to carry off this cross-dressing easily. Cross-dressing of this kind clearly reveals clichés about representing masculinity or femininity through body, voice and costume, to be discussed further below.

In New Comedy, the varied masks of young men and women, along with their costumes, which covered their bodies, represented youthful attractiveness. Slaves of various types continued to mimic the clothing and bodies of Old Comedy, although their phalluses and heavily padded bodies tend to become less prominent over time. Older men's and women's masks could show more humorous exaggeration and distortion to a varied degree, but their bodies were often less uncitizen-like than those of the slaves. Although New comic costumes were stereotyped and did not aim at being realistic, they did come closer to representing views about youth, age, gender or status in everyday life than did Old Comedy.[6]

In sum, Old comic costume deliberately distorted cultural ideals of masculinity and femininity or served to blur cultural boundaries between the genders. At the same time, because Old comic costume made its artificiality as costume transparent and permitted the audience to see through it to a greater or lesser degree due to metatheatrical techniques, it more easily represented gender as socially constructed than New Comedy, whose costumes represented stereotypes and called less attention to the physical body and its appetites. Neither the costumes nor the language of New Comedy invited self-consciousness about whether gender is based on nature or constructed by culture that we find at points in Old Comedy.

Performing comic masculinity

The behaviour of male characters in Old Comedy could both conform to and contradict the comic body represented by the actor, with its exaggerated display of sex organs, bellies, buttocks and mouths. On the one hand, characters can defecate in fear on stage, sport the occasional erection or masturbate (Strepsiades in *Clouds* or the slaves who open *Knights*), tease others with seductive behaviour (e.g., the scene where Myrrhine tortures her erect husband in *Lysistrata*), eagerly pursue or share an abundance of food, drink and festivity, and mouth language or use gesture not viewed

---

[6] Wiles (1991) offers a stimulating discussion of New comic costume.

as appropriate outside festal or comic contexts. Women and some gods (Heracles, whether god or hero, in particular) are shown as especially and naturally inclined to drink, food and sex, but male characters often aim to satisfy these desires even if capable of resisting them. Here comic behaviour both inverted proper male and female behaviour, which ideally aimed at self-control, or even celebrated the power of appetite in its male characters. In this respect, comic action called attention to the way in which law and convention repress human 'nature'.

At the same time, characters in Old Comedy can verbally lay claim to various sometimes fictional and sometimes civic gendered identities that can partially contradict their comic bodies and the anti-social behaviour that they displayed on stage and expand the range of normal masculinity. Trygaeus, the public-spirited hero of *Peace,* displays courage and altruism towards his fellow Greeks by mounting a giant dung beetle for a risky flight to the heavens in search of peace and the goddess of that name. The hero (initially heroes) of *Birds* may found a utopia in the heavens to get themselves out of debts and lawsuits in Athens, but they have, if to a miraculous degree, the intelligent empire-building skills for which their polis was noted. Dicaeopolis, the hero of *Acharnians,* insists on his identity as proper citizen of an Attic deme (595–7), even while he is outrageously making a separate peace with Athens' enemy Sparta, borrowing the identity of a tragic hero, Telephus, whom the Greeks in Euripides' play view as an enemy, and attempting deliberately to trick his fellow citizens, the chorus (if not his Athenian audience (441–4)).[7] Like many comic heroes, Dicaeopolis exposes and challenges his opponents with obscene and insulting language as well as a clever scheme. Indeed, as Jeffrey Henderson has pointed out, comic heroes tend to monopolize to great success the most insulting language in Old Comedy.[8] The deceptive and abusive figures of the iambic tradition in Greek poetry are generally anti-heroic, but comic heroes, despite being downtrodden citizens who devise plans because their lives have become unbearable or uncontrollable, often lay claim, like Dicaeopolis, to elite or heroic male identities, as well as civic ones. Even the most obscure clever citizen can achieve implausible success and win wine, food and women in the comedies' concluding scenes.

Old Comedy plays comparable games with the contradictory identities of comic authors as well. Cratinus in *Wine Flask* celebrates his poetic prowess even while representing himself as a drunk who mistreats his wife *Kômôidia* (Comedy). Similarly, in comic parabases, where the chorus can step out of

---

[7] For further discussion, see Foley (1988) with further bibliography.
[8] Henderson (1991b) ch. 3.

its role to speak for the poet, Aristophanes, even while mocking himself for a failure to win first prize or his early baldness, can make extravagant, heroic claims for how his often savagely satirical plays benefit his city. In Old Comedy, then, identity is a role (or set of roles) that can be put on and off at will without necessarily threatening a traditional masculinity or free citizen status that was often defined by the ability to help friends, take revenge on enemies, display virtues like courage (justice or temperance are rare in Old Comedy), or concern for the city/the panhellenic world. The fluidity of comic identity was enhanced by the heroes' mockery or transcendence of tragic (and human) limitations (including space and time) and by their manipulation, as in *Birds*, even of the gods themselves.

On the other hand, Old Comedy can through its male characters mock a kind of hypermasculinity that threatens to destroy the polis and in fact conceals a surrender to effete sexuality. Comedy can criticize democratic statesmen for threatening to usurp too much individual power and behave in tyrannical ways; comic poets, for example, often described the demo- cratic leader Pericles as a new Zeus. After Pericles, however, no one states- man in fifth-century Athens won comparable political authority, and rivalry among politicians, often characterized negatively by comedy as shame- less demagogues, was rampant. Comic characters mimic but distort this political rivalry among Athenian demagogues, as in *Knights*, where two corrupt figures, a tanner (the politician Cleon) and a sausage-seller, sling every kind of crude insult at each other and offer multiple forms of graft in order to win over and rejuvenate Demos, an elderly figure represent- ing the Athenian populace. Their apparently masculine manipulation of power is, however, deceptive. Aristophanes depicts the rhetoric of ambi- tious politicians as the product of playing the passive sexual role (natu- ral to women but not to men), especially as youths, in male homoerotic encounters.[9] Along similar lines, the philosopher (here sophist) Socrates stages a debate between Just Reasoning and Unjust Reasoning in *Clouds*. Just Reasoning celebrates the education and standards of masculinity of the past, which relied on repression of desire as well as self-discipline. Unjust Reasoning demonstrates the rhetorical skills necessary to justify a pursuit of pleasure and public power. He ends by revealing that the play's entire audience has already been 'buggered'. Logically, then, there is no reason why women in disguise cannot replace men as politicians and vote themselves into power, as in fact takes place in *Assembly Women* (discussed below), because a corrupted democracy has already 'feminized' them.

---

[9] See especially Rothwell (1990).

Old Comedy also delights in representing various other forms of deviation from implied standards of normal masculinity. A preference for non-penetrative sex (including oral sex as well as cunnilingus) is frequently mocked. Cleisthenes, a man whose cross-dressing makes him a permanent ally of women in *Women at the Thesmophoria*, is one kind of target. In the same play, the tragic poet Agathon comes outside, dressed as a woman, to test out a choral song. His ability to imitate women with such ease suggests to Euripides' male Relative that the role is all too natural to him (130–45). Euripides, who has identified the poet as someone the Relative might have penetrated from behind in the dark without realizing it (35), confesses that he was like Agathon in his youth (173f.). The process of becoming a tragic poet implicitly involves imitating the opposite sex to a degree that can compromise masculine identity and even poetic competence. The Relative thinks Agathon would need an infusion from behind in order to create a successful satyr play (157f.), a drama characterized above all by its hypermasculine chorus. On the other hand, when Euripides is forced to disguise his traditionally masculine Relative as a woman in order to infiltrate the women's Thesmophoria festival and to defend the poet against accusations of misogyny, the Relative's inability to play a female role 'authentically' is all too obvious to the audience, who is invited to laugh at his attempts to mimic women (very likely including the use of a falsetto voice to mark his change of role) and to defend Euripides by revealing female vices (a rhetorical stance that immediately invites female suspicion).[10]

Eventually, the Relative and Euripides borrow from the poet's tragedies in order to rescue him from imprisonment for infiltrating a festival where men are not permitted. The Relative's various literal-minded guards fail to be impressed by either man's attempts to 'play the woman' (including virtuous young and beautiful ones). Whether this failure suggests that art cannot successfully capture the other gender in performance remains a moot question, since the women are at first partly fooled by the disguised Relative and Euripides is able to get him off by borrowing a comic form of female role playing.[11] The poet disguises himself as a bawd and uses the attractions of a dancing girl to distract the Relative's Scythian guard. In *Frogs*, the god Dionysus' (characteristic) androgyny is by contrast revealed by his failure to exhibit masculine courage in the face of the 'terrors' of the underworld or facility at rowing, and by demonstrating mortal weakness when he stands up to whipping no better than his own slave.

---

[10] On this scene, see especially Muecke (1982b) and more generally Saïd (1987).

[11] See above all, Zeitlin (1981), revised in 1996.

On the other hand, Aristophanes' plays that are set before private domiciles, like *Wasps* or *Clouds*, and focus on domestic issues and conflicts between father and son, begin to pave the way for exploring male roles in terms that we find in New Comedy. In *Clouds*, the unsophisticated and beleaguered bumpkin hero Strepsiades decides to send his son Pheidippides, who at the play's opening is only interested in imitating the expensive upper class pursuits of his mother's family (horse racing), to Socrates' Thinkery in order to learn to argue his father out of his debts. The plan backfires as Pheidippides becomes a budding sophist who can offer persuasive arguments for beating his father. His transition to a pale, unathletic representative of Unjust Reasoning (whose argument is noted above) suggests that his masculinity has been compromised. Strepsiades, who is incapable of learning the new reasoning, ends by resorting to force, as he burns down Socrates' Thinkery;[12] but this resort to crude masculinity will not resolve his domestic problems. In this play, the son's youthful extravagance sets in motion accelerating distortions of the proper relation between father and son: the father fails to educate his son as a moral citizen, and the son loses the filial respect that Attic sons traditionally owed their fathers.

Wasps, by contrast, playfully reverses the normal (soon to be New comic) relation between the generations, by having the responsible son attempt to reform his immature father, who is addicted to jury duty, and to turn him into a socialite. The son manages to distract his father from his vice by staging a trial inside his own house, but fails to make his irrepressible father into a symposiast. This play's satirical treatment of old men's attraction to convicting their fellow citizens for pay in an increasingly litigious society does have a public dimension, which is represented by the chorus of old jury men, but the domestic setting and the focus on intergenerational tensions results in a characterization of male social roles that is far more 'realistic' and suitable to a private context than in other Old Comedies.

New Comedy is defined by its domestic settings and its interest in family tensions. The job of the male head of household in Athens was to reproduce his household and a legitimate male line. The father-son relation can vary in detail, but the new comic bourgeois patriarch tends to resist his son's expending substantial funds on hetairai or courtesans and fosters marriage to an Athenian woman (marriage between two Athenians was the only way to produce legitimate children).[13] New Comedy's sons typically fall madly in love with apparently unmarriageable women who are either expensive

---

[12] This represents the ending of the extant second, and probably unperformed version of *Clouds*.

[13] On the legal background to New Comedy, see especially Scafuro (1997) and, for gender issues, Lape (2004).

hetairai or eventually turn out to be Athenian daughters who have been separated from their families and are thus suitable for a 'love' marriage.[14] Another typical variant on this plot involves the rape of an Athenian virgin that results in pregnancy and the birth of a male child; these plays end in a marriage (sometimes between families of unequal wealth and status) with a legitimate heir.[15]

In the case of the fathers and sons who play out these roles, the plots offer no gap in principle between reality and drama. Nevertheless, New Comedy can create subtle variations on the performance of these standard male roles. The young men of New Comedy are ethically responsible to a point; they are willing to marry their rape victims, because they understand that their act has challenged the status of another Athenian family (even though they can be cavalier about the suffering of their victim (e.g. *Samia* 47–53)).[16] But being in love is a powerful affliction that undermines their performance of adult masculinity. Given to irrationality, suicidal impulses and cowardice before the older generation, young men cannot manage their affairs without assistance. Either they try to use (masculine) force, as does the soldier in *Perikeiromenê* (*The Girl whose Hair was Cut Short*) when persuasion is the only way to succeed with resisting women, or they avoid facing reality. In *Samia*, a young man named Moschion has gotten his neighbour's daughter pregnant while his father and the girl's father were away on a business trip. The girl gave birth to a son who is now being taken care of by Moschion's adopted father's mistress, Chryse, who has recently lost a child and is willing to nurse the baby in order to conceal its origin. Moschion wants to marry the girl, but is afraid to face the two fathers. His slave

[14] These Athenian women tend to reveal their citizen identity, even before they know of it, by their bearing; in *Dyscolus*, the misanthrope's daughter's isolation from the social world, and especially from other women, makes her an ideal marital prospect. Such characterization 'naturalizes' Athenian citizenship.

[15] For the basic plot variations, see especially Anderson (1984) and Rosivach (1998). On gender issues in New Comedy see, for book-length studies, Henry (1985); Zagagi (1994); Konstan (1995); Lape (2004); and Traill (2008), which has extensive recent bibliography, along with general essays by Heap (1998) and Pierce (1998). Rape plots derive from tragedy, where the rapist is a god; Euripides' *Auge*, *Ion*, *Melanippe* and *Alope* are some influential examples. As with tragedy, the New comic youth's misadventure always ends up producing a son, conveniently by an Athenian woman. On *Auge*, see Zagagi (1994) 55. Affairs with non-Athenians in New Comedy do not produce surviving children and respectable women never have more than one partner. The plots put an end to random and undirected male passion and make citizen women desirable (Lape (2004) 79, 91).

[16] On young men's attitudes to rape, see Rosivach (1998) 3, 39–41 and Sommerstein 1998, who points out that Old comic rapes or threatened rapes involve slaves, goddesses or married women. Their initial attraction to the young women is strictly physical (Rosivach (1998) 3).

Parmenon describes Moschion as an *androgynê,* or man-woman, for his cowardice (69).

This confirms a general sense that in New Comedy the young man will only achieve adult masculinity on marriage to a woman who can produce legitimate heirs. Thus the spoiled, wealthy, young hero of *Dyscolus*, who has fallen in love with and wants to marry the daughter of a misanthrope, must perform agricultural labour with her brother and acquire a tan that represents outdoor labour in order to prove himself worthy of a marriage alliance with a poor but noble family. In this respect the play democratizes ideals of citizen masculinity, since Attic families generally aimed to consolidate wealth through marriages with those of equal or greater wealth.[17] Several soldiers also belie their comic reputation as crude and violent braggarts with their attempts to win the affection of their beloveds in an increasingly sensitive fashion (see below). In a world dominated in the late fourth and early third centuries BCE by Macedonia, moral and legal maturity comes to define citizen masculinity more than the demonstration of military discipline that was equally required of earlier Athenians.[18]

New comic fathers of sons can quite frequently reveal patriarchal rigidity through their irascible tempers or are foiled through the strategies of their sons and their slaves to win the girl whom the son desires. Demeas, the adoptive father in *Samia*, for example, at first rejects the illegitimate baby that he thinks his mistress should not be raising in his house like a wife and then, when he discovers that the child is his son's, throws Chryse out on the street with the baby as a dangerous seductress; he is unwilling to believe that his previously respectful son could be at fault, but quick to condemn his mistress. Yet when he discovers the truth, he becomes self-critical and admits his faults. On his side, the son had persuaded his unmarried adoptive father to move his Samian mistress into the house in order to secure her from younger rivals,[19] even though the father was reluctant to shame the family by admitting to the love affair (or risk producing a bastard), and later courageously defends her. In this play both father and son are capable of moving somewhat beyond stereotyped masculine roles, perhaps because their own relation is socially constructed by adoption.[20]

The figure in New Comedy who inherits more of the versatile character of the Old comic hero is the New comic slave, who also resembles him in costume. Clever New comic slaves similarly create imaginative and deceptive

[17] Lape (2004) has the most extensive treatment of this issue.   [18] Lape (2004).
[19] As Lape (2004) 139 points out, Demeas is the only successful older lover in extant New Comedy.
[20] Attempts to define manliness are legion in the language of this play (e.g., 327, 344, 512, 631).

plots, if only domestic ones, to fulfil the goals of their young masters. In *Aspis*, for example, the elderly slave Daos ingeniously rescues the marital plans of the children of two brothers by foiling the greedy plans of the third to marry a wealthy niece. Slaves are, however, incapable, due to their status, of representing citizen-style masculinity. New Comedy confines Old Comedy's broader experimental role playing to those who cannot exercise social authority or transform either social roles or social reality. In New Comedy, nature and social mores converge after temporary resistance, so that the audience is not in the end invited to question traditional social roles or standards of masculinity.

Performing comic femininity

The desirability of young women in both Old and New Comedy can be enhanced by unavailability, either because their families defend the virtue of respectable citizen women or because, as in New Comedy, they are exotic and expensive. Reproducing sons for state or family is citizen women's central positive characteristic, but they also perform religious rites for the benefit of both institutions, as in the case of *Women at the Thesmophoria* or the hero Sostratus' pious beloved and mother in *Dyscolus*. Prone to being unfaithful or to over-indulgence in drink, comic women have learned from the constant restrictions and suspicion under which they live to be master-contrivers of plots that may or may not benefit their men.

Early Old Comedy (before 411 BCE) probably did not offer important speaking roles to female figures with the exception of goddesses, mytho-logical figures and abstractions.[21] Cratinus' wife *Kômôidia* in *Wine Flask*, who seems to have played a major role in criticizing and trying to reform her alcoholic poet husband, may have been an important transitional figure, since she acts as both an embodiment of the comic art and a wife. Speaking roles for women in Old Comedy are generally confined to married, citizen women. In two plays of Aristophanes, *Lysistrata* and *Assembly Women*, the heroines, who claim authority and the ability to transcend female stereotypes in part because they have learned how to imitate and speak like men, devise plans to rescue their societies from situations where men have failed to live up to proper male roles. Lysistrata's strategy, a sex strike by wives across Greece and a blockade of funds for war in the Athenian acropolis, appears to the play's men as an outrageous abuse of female roles, whereas Trygaeus' similar plan in *Peace* was merely madness. In fact, however, the wives play their roles either safely at home or in this public religious site where women

---

[21] See Henderson (1987b) and (1996).

traditionally performed religious roles to benefit the city and where no man can successfully penetrate until peace is established. Although many of her fellow Athenian wives are as eager to violate the strike as their husbands, Lysistrata retains an Athena-like self-control (the contemporary priestess of Athena Polias was named Lysimache, which also means disbander of battles/ armies, and the audience may have been meant to link the two figures).[22] Her passionate and articulate case for the women's suffering in war, not only the loss of their men but the young women's inability to perform their civic roles by marrying and reproducing children, makes Athenian women at least temporarily into serious citizens, as does the behaviour of the older women in the chorus, who cite women's initiation into adulthood through perform- ing civic religious roles and who tame the irascible and initially misogynistic chorus of old men. The play ends reassuringly with a return to traditional gender roles.[23]

In *Assembly Women*, the heroine Praxagora gets women voted into power by filling the Athenian assembly with women disguised as men and then remakes the state as a domestic/communist utopia. Athenian men have sup- posedly become so mired in self-interest and greed for state pay that they have taken on the private character of women, who were normally unable to participate in Attic politics. Their status is visualized on stage by Praxagora's feminized husband, who comes out of the house wearing her clothing (she has taken his) and calls on the goddess of childbirth to deliver him from constipation. Women, according to Praxagora, are much better suited to create an egalitarian government that attends to the interests of the whole polis. As women, they already know how to act in the interests of their households, share goods with neighbours, and reproduce traditional ways. For the price of sharing goods collectively and turning the city into a giant household, the women promise to reproduce and feed the city, while the men enjoy the women's labours. The argument works up to a point, but the women also legislate new sexual regulations, in which young people are required to sleep with older ones before they can enjoy those their own age. The play closes with three old hags competing brutally for a young man who had arrived to meet a young girlfriend and the summoning of Praxagora's husband to the communal banquet. As this play demonstrates, Old Comedy, like tragedy in a different fashion, expands on and occasionally questions gender stereotypes for women even while exploiting them. Yet, the open-ended conclusion of *Assembly Women* aside, old comic women remain

[22] Henderson (1987b) is sceptical about this identification, whereas others (Foley (1982) and Revermann (2006a) 236–43) accept it.
[23] On gender issues in *Lysistrata*, see especially Vaio (1973); Foley (1981); Loraux (1993); Taaffe (1993); Henderson (1980b), (1987b) and (1996); as well as Revermann (2006a).

more embedded in their hypothetical 'nature' and limited by their social roles than men.[24]

New Comedy, with its focus on domestic life, introduces a much wider range of female players, although many of them remain either invisible or mute despite their critical roles in the action. In this respect, as in its careful adherence to the legal restraints governing marriage and inheritance in contemporary Athens, respectable women in both New Comedy and reality remain as much as possible, religious occasions excepted, inside their homes and restrain their independent actions, sexuality and speech unless (at least in some instances) legitimate domestic interests are at stake and they are liberated to act by the absence of a male guardian.[25] Virgins, young women and hetairai by and large play more pivotal roles, above all in recognition scenes that borrow from tragedy, than wives, nurses or other female slaves, since the plots so often revolve around love and marriage.

As in tragedy, some new comic recognition scenes offer these young women a chance to break a dramatic silence that confines them to being objects of desire and to display assertively their moral character. In *Perikeiromenê* (*The Girl whose Hair was Cut Short*), the heroine Glycera, a poor Athenian girl who was exposed at birth, found and raised by an unrelated woman, and eventually forced to become a soldier's concubine, incurs the soldier Polemon's jealousy when she allows her twin brother Moschion, who was raised by a wealthy woman next door, to kiss her. Glycera has not identified herself to Moschion, who does not know he is adopted, in order to protect his future. After Polemon cuts off her hair,[26] the humiliated Glycera takes refuge with Moschion's adoptive mother, Myrrhine. Polemon, still madly in love, at first tries to get Glycera back by force, but is advised by Pataicus, who turns out to be Glycera's father, to try persuasion. Meanwhile, all the men involved think, incorrectly, that Glycera has left to get involved with Moschion, who is in fact attracted to her. In the scene that leads up to a father-daughter-son recognition, Glycera offers an unusually, for new comedy, articulate self-defence that demonstrates both a sophisticated awareness (note the use of irony) of the social realities that constrain

[24] For fragments of other Aristophanes plays bearing on women, see the appendix in Henderson (1996) 193–204. On gender issues in *Assembly Women*, see especially Foley (1982), Saïd (1979), Taaffe (1993), Henderson (1987a) and (1996).
[25] New Comedy avoids boy-girl dialogue or expressions of love between husband and wife (Traill (2008) 69). In contrast to Old Comedy, pederasty makes no appearance (Plutarch, *Moralia* 712c). See Traill (2008) 141, 185–8, 242 on female ethical modes in New Comedy, which are influenced by tragedy, where women often speak and act assertively in the absence of male guardians.
[26] The hair cut probably makes Glycera appear to be a slave (Lape (2004) 175).

women and a sense of self-worth produced by being, for the moment, her own mistress (*heautês . . . kuria*: 497) despite her vulnerable status (708–23):

> [What] could I [have accomplished], my dear man, by escaping to
>
> [Moschion's] mother? Consider whether I was trying to make him take me as a wife. Of course, he is by birth my equal? No. Was I trying to have him take me as his mistress? Wouldn't I have hurried to conceal it from his family then? Would he have chosen to put me up in his father's house? Would I choose to be a fool, make Myrrhine my enemy, and incur suspicion of misbehaviour that you won't abandon? Wouldn't I be ashamed, Pataicus? You came here persuaded of this and assuming that I am that type of person?
>
> Pataicus: By revered Zeus, no. I'd like you to prove what you are saying is true. I believe you.
>
> Glycera: Well, in any case, please go away. Let him [Polemon] do violence to another girl in the future.

Another good example of ethical courage that reveals a young war captive's free nature is Krateia in *Misoumenos* (*The Hated Man*), who rejects the love of the soldier who owns her because she wrongly believes, until after she reunites with father and brother, that he has killed her brother.[27]

Young women in New Comedy who are Athenian by birth find their lost parents and become able to marry the young men who are madly in love with them (perhaps because of their earlier painful loss of resources and identity as well as the absence of a male guardian) more often actively represent, like Glycera, an ethically distinct and admirable female character than unwed mothers who have been raped by men. Raped Athenian women can appear as mute brides, but they are only occasionally offered room to display an independent character and generally serve as pawns in the game of reproducing the patriarchal family. A major exception is Pamphile in *Men at Arbitration*, a young woman who exposed the product of a night rape by a young man who eventually turns out to have been her husband. The husband Charisius deserted her when her child was born five months after their marriage and has set up house using her dowry with a musician/hetaira, Habrotonon, with whom he is not in fact having a sexual relation. Eventually Charisius overhears Pamphile eloquently defending her marriage to him in response to her father, Smicrines, who wants to arrange a divorce from his profligate son-in-law. Both tragic and New comic women tend to be more devoted to their natal families than those of their husband or male partner, and hence Pamphile's defence of her marriage may give her an unusual and

---

[27] Once identified as legitimate daughters, these assertive women are apparently married off by their *kurios* (guardian) in silence.

independent character in this play.[28] Charisius now recognizes the suffering that both he and Pamphile have caused by bringing bastards into the world and feels a new sympathy for her. Eventually, Habrotonon, who had been playing music for a group of women on the night of the rape, remembers the then-distraught Pamphile by sight, and generously serves to reunite wife, husband and their child, who was rescued from exposure and temporarily claimed as her own by Habrotonon while she searched for its mother.

In their ability to devise plots, New comic hetairai descend more directly from the clever heroines of Old Comedy than the genre's respectable women, except that in New Comedy they can aim to restore and unify families not city states.[29] Although often exhibiting at least a partially dubious character (Habrotonon is lying, if in a good cause, and is hoping to be freed if she succeeds), they can as in this case play an important ethical role. Nevertheless, they rarely receive a just reward. At best, even a free hetaira could only hope for a slightly longer term relation with the young man who loves her before his family intervenes to arrange a marriage for him and he moves on. In *Samia*, Demeas' live-in mistress Chryse (discussed above) proves a rare exception. Like Habrotonon, she facilitates the plot by pretending that Moschion's baby was her own in order to tide him over until his father returned and could arrange his marriage. She is rescued from her expulsion and restored to Demeas' household in a wife-like role in part by her good relations with the women of the neighbouring family whose daughter Moschion raped, as well as her maternal behaviour. Such female solidarity in the face of patriarchal mistreatment and suspicion or threats to children is common in New Comedy (as well as in tragedy). Female virtue, as in this case, can also be confirmed by the loyalty of female slaves who not only serve but admire their mistresses.

Not surprisingly, then, women in Old and New Comedy are more similar and tied to traditional gender roles and stereotypes across time than men. Old Comedy's women act and speak mainly in those plays which emanate fully from their own world of the household and polis religion and are otherwise treated largely as silent objects of desire to be acquired by men. Aristophanes' Lysistrata, for example, finally reconciles the warring Greeks by dividing the enticing nude body of *Diallagê* (Reconciliation), functioning as a map of Greece, among them. When old comic heroines adopt fantastically expanded domestic and religious roles, negative stereotypes about women immediately come into play, especially if they act on their own desires, as in the concluding scene of *Assembly Women*, or when an Old Woman (*graus*) wants her gigolo back in *Wealth*. New Comedy's women are

---

[28] Traill (2008) 136–8.   [29] Traill (2008) 264f.

fully embedded in the household, often more spoken about than speaking. They act and sometimes even educate men largely in contexts where they are defending or uniting natal or marital families and children. They consent to marriage, but do not, unlike Old comic women, express desire.[30]

Comic men, by contrast, frequently engage in role playing and role-expanding or role-reversing actions. Old Comedy does not at its conclusions necessarily re-embroil its often outrageous heroes in the constraints required of Athenian citizens and fathers in reality; it lays claim to educating the polis while deconstructing masculinity. New Comedy allows temporary periods of festal release from or experimentation with masculine roles during which men can be socialized, by both women and men, to a more nuanced sense of identity before the plays restore a normality that can be tinged with the pleasures of a 'love' marriage or an escape from the economics of matches among those of equal wealth. More fundamentally, however, despite occasional lip service to female consent, it cements homosocial bonds and assures legitimate heirs for Athens.[31]

Further reading

On gender issues in Old Comedy, see Bonnamour and Delavault (1979); Foley (1982) and (2000); Loraux (1993); Taaffe (1993); Henderson (1996); Winkler (1990); Zeitlin (1981) and (1996). For book length studies on gender in New Comedy, see especially Henry (1985); Zagagi (1994); Konstan (1995); Rosivach (1998); Lape (2004); and Traill (2008).

[30] Traill (2008) 6.   [31] Lape (2004) 23.

14

MARTIN REVERMANN

Divinity and religious practice

Ridiculing the gods, with impunity

The mid-fourth-century bell crater from Apulia in South Italy which is the centre image of this volume's cover shows an intriguing scene: an old bearded man with a distinct crown (and an equally distinct dangling phallus) is climbing up a ladder to a statuesque-looking 'beauty in the window', assisted by a younger man who is wearing another piece of remarkable headgear and carrying a bird in his left hand as well as an unusual kind of staff in his right hand. To an ancient viewer (and, indeed, many modern viewers) the visual clues provided by this vase painting unmistakably point in two directions: comic performance and divinity. What strikes the viewer, certainly the modern one, as most remarkable here is *how* those gods are being presented. Appearing in full comic attire (stage-naked, exposed and grotesquely ugly), they are clearly meant to look ridiculous. Especially noteworthy is the consequence with which comedy subjects even the loftiest personnel to its antics, for both deities show the full extent of comic ugliness typical of male characters in comedy: the snub nose, protruding jaw, big buttocks and the long, dangling leather phallus.[1] Other vase evidence, including one of the rare items from Athens (= Figure 5.10 in Csapo, Chapter 5), corroborates the view that the divine was regularly and fully uglified in comedy at least of the fifth and well into the fourth century (whereas in Menander, at the end of the fourth century, such presentation of the divine would appear unthinkable).[2] This remarkable feature is unparalleled, to the best of my knowledge, in the history of world theatre, and supports the bigger claim, to be substantiated throughout this chapter, that when examining comedy's relationship with divinity and religious practice we witness a degree of licence and elasticity that is unusual by any standards that might be derived from the comparative study of world religions.

---

[1] On the notion of 'comic ugliness', see Revermann (2006a) 145–59.
[2] Walsh (2009) 105–64 discusses in detail the iconography of 'ridiculing the gods'.

In addition, the sheer fact *that* these are gods acting in the theatrical environment of comedy is notable enough in itself. While serious drama in the Western and non-Western theatre traditions regularly features or, more often, implies divine presence and implicates divine agency of some sort in its plots, the relationship of comedy with the divine in Western and non-Western theatre (*commedia dell' arte*, Japanese *kyogen*, farce) tends to be a more cautious and precarious one. This is surely to a large extent the result of concerns, not confined to Christianity, about the effects which the various forms of irreverence inherent in the theatrical spectacle might have on onlookers and performers alike. Greek comedy, by contrast, is quite different: from the very first fifth-century comedies we can put our hands on (Cratinus' *Dionysalexandrus* or Aristophanes' *Acharnians* and *Clouds*) until the plays by Menander in the late fourth century, the presence of divinity (conceptual, narrative and physical) is pronounced.

The reasons for this are surely manifold, and not confined to comedy's early links with Dionysian ritual (whatever their precise nature may have been). One point that needs to be made here is that, well before the invention of comedy as a distinct dramatic genre, divinity had been featuring in the *Iliad* and, less so, the *Odyssey* (as well as, presumably, other epic poetry) not only as laughing spectators but also as the object of humour.[3] There are, in other words, religious, cultural and literary templates for comedy to build on. In addition, on the synchronic axis the ongoing ritual embeddedness of dramatic performances, exclusively Dionysian in Attica though not necessarily so elsewhere, facilitated the dramatic integration of the divine. Last but certainly not least, there is the ubiquity of the divine in Greek traditional tale which provided rich imaginative trajectories to fuel the playwrights' creative and artistic instincts. A certain type of comedy, the 'mythological burlesque' which appears to have been particularly popular in the first half of the fourth century, latched particularly strongly onto traditional tale and the deities featured in it. But in one way or another the influence of traditional tale is palpable in a great many other comedies of the fifth and fourth centuries (while tragedy and satyr play are, of course, unthinkable without it).

Greek comedy, then, has a complex and multi-layered relationship with religious practice and belief (to reactivate a term that has sometimes been all but outlawed in the study of ancient religions but keeps resurfacing).[4] This relationship is also, in sheer quantitative terms, substantial. The home truth that Greek comedy, in all its manifestations, is an artistic engagement with

---

[3] Chapters 5 and 6 of Griffin (1980) remain foundational on this topic.
[4] See e.g., the literature quoted in Kindt (2012) 2 n. 7.

real life manifests itself not least in the fact that religious matters are featured in it very frequently indeed, with the result that the material provided by Aristophanes and the scholiasts on the Aristophanic plays constitutes a principal and absolutely indispensable source of evidence pertaining to religious life in Athens. This fact is easily established by taking a look at the source index of Robert Parker's important 2005-monograph on *Polytheism and Society at Athens*, where the entry for Aristophanes is by far the longest, taking up three full columns (the runner-ups are Plato, Plutarch and Euripides with about one and a half columns each). That said, Menander is a minor source – although it would be quite wrong to infer from this a lessened general interest in divinity at the end of the fourth century. Yet quantitative data says, of course, little about the depth, level and mode of reflection with which religious matters are thematized and problematized. It is questions of this kind which this chapter is primarily concerned with.

Ritual origins and the role of Dionysus in comedy

Comedy, like tragedy and satyr play, may well have roots in Dionysian ritual, even if certainty cannot be attained in this area. Aristotle surely implies this much when claiming, in an often-quoted and controversial passage in chapter 4 of the *Poetics*, that comedy arose 'from those who led off the phallic rites which even now remain a custom in many of our cities' (*Poetics* 1449a10–13).[5] Clearly linked with Dionysus are the drunk dancers with grotesque padded bodies that are found on the so-called 'komast vases' which originate in late eighth-century Corinth, then spread elsewhere and are found in Athens until about the middle of the sixth century BCE (see Csapo's discussion in Chapter 5, with his Figures 5.1 and 5.2). With these items it is certainly tempting to speculate on connections with comic performance of whatever kind. The same goes for the about twenty Attic artifacts which tend to be referred to rather vaguely as '*kômos* vases', dating from the middle of the sixth century until about the time when comedy becomes an institutionalized part of the Athenian Dionysia in the 480s BCE.[6] These vases, also discussed by Csapo in Chapter 5, depict men in animal costume

---

[5] On this passage see Storey (2010) 179–84 (with further discussion of other evidence potentially pertinent to the question of whether or not comedy has origins in ritual) and Csapo (2013) 40f. A phallic Dionysian procession is staged by Dicaeopolis and his family at *Acharnians* 241–79.

[6] The traditional, but not uncontroversial, date for this is 486 BCE for the Great Dionysia (and around 442 BCE for the Lenaea), see Pickard-Cambridge (1988) 82 and Olson (2007) 382–4.

(or riding animals) who move and sing in a synchronized way, often led by a piper (see Csapo's Figure 5.4). It is because of the combination of mimetic representation, synchronised movement and musical accompaniment that these vases have been considered to be 'proto-comic'.[7]

Whatever the historical connections between Dionysian ritual and the formation of comedy, visual correspondences between Dionysian ritual and comedy in performance as encountered in the fifth century are impossible to deny. Well attested for Dionysian ritual is the use of masks and especially (erect) phalloi,[8] both of which are, of course, key visual features of comic performance. Also, the co-existence, and potential cross-fertilization, of comedy and phallic choruses at the Dionysian *pompê* ('parade') on the first official day of the Athenian Dionysia has been impressively documented and explored by Csapo.[9]

But while comedy may well have had some diachronic connection with Dionysian ritual, the perhaps more pressing issue, certainly for those primarily interested in what was happening on the fifth- and fourth-century comic stage, concerns comedy's *synchronic* relationship with Dionysian ritual practice: how does comedy – once it is fully-developed and, in Athens, an institutionalized part of the city's dramatic festivals in honour of Dionysus – respond to and integrate Dionysian ritual, and what does this tell us about comedy? Complex and difficult as it is in insolation, this question is part of a long-standing larger debate about the interface between Greek drama and (Dionysian) ritual in general. Early in the twentieth century one extreme view was embraced, for Greek tragedy and comedy, by Gilbert Murray and Francis Cornford, respectively, scholars close to the 'Cambridge Ritualists' movement (a movement which in turn was formatively influenced by the work of James Frazer and Émile Durkheim). For them tragedy and comedy were complex elaborations of one underlying *Ur*-ritual of the dying and then resurrected Year Spirit (*Eniautos Daimôn*) out of whom the Greek god Dionysus (like many other deities) had evolved.[10] Thus Murray, in his 'Excursus' which was part of both the first (1912) and second (1927) edition of Jane Harrison's highly influential book *Themis*, set out to unearth 'the

---

[7] Green (2007) 101.

[8] See Csapo's Figure 5.3 in Chapter 5, with his discussion. Extensive discussions of the 'komast vases' can be found in Csapo and Miller (2007) 48–107. Note, however, that while the leather phallus used in the performance of fifth-century comedy is quite large, it is not usually erect (by contrast with the costume of satyrs in satyr play, whose (small) phalloi are always erect).

[9] Csapo (2013).

[10] On Murray see Parker (2007); on Frazer and Harrison see Csapo (2005) 30–67 and 145–61. Illuminating remarks on the 'Cambridge Ritualists' and their subsequent reception can be found in Csapo and Miller (2007) 1–3 and 24–32.

ritual forms' as 'preserved in Greek tragedy'.[11] Simultaneously, in 1914, Cornford pursued the same project for comedy in his monograph entitled *The Origin of Attic Comedy*.[12] Note that Murray and Cornford are, ultimately, interested not in synchronic but diachronic relationships (or 'origins', in their lingo) between comedy and ritual, since this approach reduces Attic tragedy and comedy to a concatenation of far more ancient 'ritual motives' which underlie the performance scripts we have and which need to be laid bare by the modern critic. For comedy, these motives are specified by Cornford as 'fight, agon, sacrifice, New Zeus (King), cooking, feast, marriage (courtesans, bride), komos'.[13] Quite predictably, Cornford's whole book focuses on the analysis, within the scheme of those 'ritual motives', of standard formal elements found in Attic comedy (*agôn*, parabasis), stock characters (for Cornford 'The Imposter', with various instantiations), 'phallic songs' (of which the parabasis is treated as a sub-species) and, critically, fertility rituals and the life-renewing celebratory endings which are tailored to fit the 'ritual motives' of the 'New God (King)' and/or 'marriage'. While essentially forgotten today, the repercusssions of this type of analysis extend far into the twentieth century (they can, for example, be felt in Northrop Frye's general theory of 'archetypes' in literature).

Those thin and, ultimately, circular readings along the parameters set by schematic, universalizing and reductionist interpretative categories provoked a strong, almost 'anti-ritualist' counter-reaction in some people working on Greek drama in general.[14] But it was always very hard, if not outright impossible, to adopt a radical anti-ritualist stance for Greek comedy in particular and argue that it had 'nothing to do with Dionysus'.[15] For one thing, in comedy (and satyr play) it is quite difficult to ignore the constant Dionysian 'background' – as expressed by the festival context, the chorus (regardless of their specific dramatic identity) and, most of all, comic costume – which underlies any 'foreground' (such as plot, music or choreography) that may very often have no explicit Dionysian connections. But perhaps even more importantly, there was of course always the

---

[11] Murray (1912: 1927).

[12] Cornford (1914: 1934). Murray too engaged with comedy eventually, but in his 1933 monograph on Aristophanes there is surprisingly little emphasis on ritual and schemes of renewal (see e.g., the brief general remarks at Murray (1933) 12f.).

[13] Cornford (1914: 1934) 221, which is the beginning of his 'Synopsis of the Extant Plays'.

[14] Most importantly so with Arthur Pickard-Cambridge, the author of the two highly influential books *Dithyramb, Tragedy and Comedy* (first published in 1927) and *The Dramatic Festivals of Athens* (first published in 1953).

[15] Used as a proverb in antiquity, the phrase 'nothing to do with Dionysus' (*ouden pros ton Dionyson*), on which see Pohlenz (1927: 1965) 474–9, indicates that the relationship between Greek drama, especially tragedy, and Dionysian ritual was subject to debate from early on. The debate may in fact be as old as Greek drama itself.

prominence of Dionysus, and of ritual frames in general, in Aristophanes' *Frogs*, the play which in scholarly circles at least was arguably the most influential and most often discussed ancient Greek comedy during the twentieth century.

Dionysus, at least according to the evidence we have, regularly appears to have had a prominent role in fifth-century comedy (in fact, a divine character in general can safely be regarded as part of the repertoire of standard figures that Greek comic playwrights continued to draw on, in different ways, from fifth-century comedy down to the plays by Menander).[16] Fragments, including visual evidence, from fifth-century comedies predating *Frogs* by Aristophanes' big rivals Cratinus (*Dionysalexandros*) and Eupolis (*Taxiarchoi*) strongly suggest that Aristophanes' representation of Dionysus as a buffoon and coward is not an exceptional artistic creation but following the norm.[17] This created, at least at the Great Dionysia, intriguing 'distorted mirror' effects in performative practice, as the priest of Dionysus (and possibly a statue of Dionysus as well) was present in the theatre.[18] In the audience the god, represented in all seriousness and grandeur by his priest, is watching (and was known to be watching) while, in the acting area, a caricature of this very god is playing the buffoon in full comic costume. Yet, as opposed to a human character like Cleon or Cleisthenes whose stature in real life was surely meant to be diminished by their comically distorted representation on stage, the god remains unaffected. Whatever ridicule may be heaped on the comic Dionysus on stage, it is without consequence in real life: the god towers above those comic antics with his grandeur, authority and power not only intact but arguably asserted and aggrandized, even celebrated. Comedy can ridicule the gods – but it cannot 'get to them'. In this vein, the ending of *Frogs* lends itself to such an affirmative, even celebratory reading of comic abuse: the play does make the point that, for all the ridicule, it takes Dionysus (and with him the art he patronizes, comedy!) to bring up Aeschylus from the underworld and renew the polis.[19] Even as a clown and buffoon, the god is mighty. While in comedy the gods may not be terrifying and awe-inspiring as their counterparts in tragedy are, they still retain and, if needed, exercise their limitless transformative power.

[16] On those stock characters see Ruffell, Chapter 7.
[17] See Storey (2003) 246–60 and Bakola (2010) 83–102, 101–208 and 252–72 on Eupolis and Cratinus, respectively.
[18] On the organization of the dramatic festivals see Csapo and Slater (1995) 103–38.
[19] For a range of interpretations of *Frogs*, ritual frames and the role of Dionysus see Lada-Richards (1999); Biles (2011) 211–56; Sells (2012); and Griffith (2013) ch. 6 and *passim*. All these readings, unsurprisingly, involve a high degree of metapoetics.

The prominent and socially integrative role of Dionysus in *Frogs* may be a deliberate archaizing strategy which sought to revitalize the art of comedy by reconnecting it with its Dionysian roots (an agenda which may also have been pursued, at the very same time, by Euripides in his late tragedy *Bacchae*). Another, equally intriguing avenue of metapoetics in *Frogs* opens itself up if one follows Bakola's plausible argument that Cratinus, until his death in the late 420s the young Aristophanes' most formidable rival, was advocating (especially in his *Wine Flask* of 423) a 'Dionysian poetics' which emphasized the inspirational and spontaneous aspects of artistic creativity, notably under the influence of wine, Dionysus' signature drink.[20] Staged roughly two decades after Cratinus' death, Aristophanes' *Frogs*, with its pervasive emphasis especially in the *agôn* on the artist's 'craftsmanship' (*technê*) and sober control, would then engage with this well-established dichotomy of 'Dionysian' versus 'technical' poetics in a way that is both integrative and funny: overtly endorsing the primacy of 'technical' poetics, while always acknowledging in the background the fundamental need of the 'Dionysian' element, not least through the role of Dionysus himself.

There can, ultimately, be no comedy without the 'Dionysian', a fundamental point which is reasserted with remarkable continuity throughout the history of Greek comedy: even Menander, whose divinities tend to be dignified, serious and abstract, preserves a trace of 'Dionysian' backgrounding in the form of the recurring comic chorus of revellers who are explicitly referred to as 'drunk' (*Aspis* 247f., *Dyscolus* 231f., *Men at Arbitration* 169f., *Perikeiromenê* 261f.).

Other deities

The divine agent as a stock character of Greek comedy could be recruited from the whole range of the Greek religious imaginary: the Olympian deities, a liminal figure like the deified hero Heracles, or personified abstractions (War, Wealth, Fortune, Ignorance, etc.). A farcical treatment seems to have been standard for some of them: as Dionysus is stereotypically a coward and a buffoon, so Heracles is a glutton or Zeus an adulterer.[21] The case of Zeus is a particularly interesting one because of the stark contrast with tragedy. Even bearing in mind the limits of our evidence, there is strong reason to believe that in Greek tragedy Zeus, although conceptually omnipresent

---

[20] Bakola (2005).
[21] Parker (2005) 149 n. 60 points to the ancient scholiast (on *Peace* 741) who mentions the cowardly Dionysus as a stock character (together with the gluttonous Heracles and the adulterer Zeus).

and regularly invoked in prayer (especially by tragic choruses), would by convention not appear on stage (by contrast with deities like Apollo, Athena, Poseidon or Aphrodite).[22] The taboo, if such existed, of on-stage representation in tragedy would give the highest and mightiest of the gods an added sense of remoteness and unreachability, forcefully underlining the power and unpredictability of the divine which resists comprehension (and in this case visual perception) by the human mind. Comedy, on the other hand, not only materializes the King of the Gods on its stage, but thoroughly humanizes and 'comedifies' him by capitalizing on weaknesses that were well known and humorously exploited in the epic tradition already. The visual evidence, including the Paestan bell crater (discussed at the beginning of this chapter) which can be seen on the front page of this volume, suggests that this strategy of ridiculing the divine could be encountered on comic stages at least until the mid-fourth century. For this time period, of course, our evidence suggests a particular popularity of 'mythological burlesques', with a correspondingly more pronounced on-stage presence of divine characters (see Sidwell, Chapter 3). But in this sub-genre of comedy, where gods were routinely displaced from mythological time into the mundanity of contemporary Athens, one may seriously wonder to what extent the audiences of such plays would still primarily conceptualize the divine characters as gods rather than ordinary humans and struggling citizens. In particular, 'mythological burlesque' seems to have used gods as hilarious and easily decodable 'chiffres' for contemporary politicians. This is reasonably well attested for Cratinus' treatment of Pericles as Zeus or Dionysus in the 430s or so, and may possibly have been quite typical of this sub-genre well into the fourth century.[23]

It is, however, clear that there were gradations of the farcical in the comic representation of divinity, and even comedy appears to have had limits. In particular, both Athena and Demeter seem to have been largely exempt from grotesque visual representation and verbal abuse. Cases in point would be the absence of abuse against those two deities in *Women at the Thesmophoria*, or in *Lysistrata* the peculiar representation of the female protagonist who in the course of the play is increasingly designed to invoke associations with the priestess of Athena Polias and Athena herself.[24] As

---

[22] Taplin (1977) 431–3.

[23] On Cratinus see Bakola (2010) 180–224, although the exact nature, duration and extent of this technique as used by Cratinus is contested. On fourth-century comedy see Sidwell, Chapter 3.

[24] Bakola (2010) 285–94 compares and contrasts the treatment of Athena in comedy with that of other deities. On Lysistrata and Athena see Revermann (2006a) 236–43.

far as the patron deity of Athens is concerned, such an inhibition is easy to explain and understand. For Demeter, the Eleusinian cult and its emphasis on reverent speech (or, indeed, silence) has been invoked as a factor.[25] One might also speculate whether comedy in Sicily, where Demeter and not Dionysus was the patron deity of theatre, and its early influence on the development of comedy in Athens are somehow a factor here.[26]

In Menander, who in this as in many other respects is quite certainly under the influence of tragedy (notably Euripides), the balance has swung entirely towards a serious and dignified representation of the divine, with a keen interest in exploiting the narrative and emotional possibilities that are inherent in using a divine character during the prologue section of a play. The crucial, and novel, aspect here is that of explicitly articulated divine power in the form of *knowledge*: the divine character is shown to be the site of truth and insight concerning all things past, present and future. Thus, the god Pan who opens the *Dyscolus* (which is set at a rural shrine dedicated to Pan and the Nymphs) is able to give an 'information prologue' the veracity of which is beyond doubt *qua* the divinity of its speaker. A more refined variation of this technique can be observed in the *Aspis* and the *Perikeiromenê*, both of which use deified abstracts, *Tychê* ('Chance') and *Agnoia* ('Ignorance') respectively, as 'prologue deities'. The refinement consists of the *delay* with which the information is conveyed to the audience. In the *Perikeiromenê* the delayed intervention by *Agnoia* is to reassure the audience that everything they have just witnessed will end well after all. Things are more complex in the *Aspis*. Here, *Tychê* reveals what really happened to Cleostratus only after the audience has just heard Daos' account of the same event which was wrong in its key aspect, the fate of Cleostratus (*Aspis* 97–148). The resulting blunt juxapostion of the human's limited perspective with the god's boundless knowledge not only creates superior audience awareness, hence dramatic irony, for the remainder of the comedy. It also creates pathos: the human audience, although in the know thanks to divine relevation, is made painfully aware of the limits of intelligibility that fundamentally shape the existence of every human being, including their own. And while it is true that the overall outcome will predictably be a joyful tale of survival and reunion as befits a comedy, a darker and more sobering subtext has been established for good. This subtext is, of course, highly reminiscent of the world of tragedy. The fact that *Tychê* discloses her identity only at the very end of her soliloquy (her name is the very last word she says: 148) may well

---

[25] Parker (2005) 150.
[26] On the role of Demeter in Sicily and South Italy see Kowalzig (2008).

be a metapoetic joke about the very technique of delay which has been put to work so powerfully in this opening scene.

Theologies of Greek comedy

Comedy's relationship with things and practices divine is monolithic in some aspects and very diverse in others. The divine may be presented as buffoonish (Dionysus, Heracles, Zeus even), temporarily replaced (Aristophanes' *Clouds*) or even overpowered for good by new gods (*Birds*). But the very existence and legitimacy of the gods is universally taken for granted, and does not in itself become the subject of reflection or even criticism (by contrast with some tragedy, especially Euripides). In both fifth- and fourth-century comedy, Greek and Athenian belief systems and ritual practices are treated conservatively as legitimate and self-evident models of social organization (like, for instance, slavery), and there is all-pervasive activation in language and performance of ritual frames: sacrifices, prayers, hymns (especially by the chorus), oaths, initiation, marriage, processions and so forth. That these ritual frames are regularly subjected to parody and distortion is the result of comedy being comedy, and not indicative of an ambiguous or even critical stance towards those frames themselves. Also, the range of ritual practices is wide and extends to a whole range of religious experiences, including initiation and mystery cult (*Clouds*, *Frogs*) as well as magic (the rejuvenation of *Dêmos* in *Knights*). At the ideological level, therefore, it seems legitimate to acknowledge a continuity and speak of one theology across fifth- and fourth-century comedy.

At the phenomenological level, however, this relationship manifests itself in very diverse ways synchronically and diachronically, to a point that it becomes meaningful to speak of different theologies (and, in consequence, different religious experiences). Definitely throughout the fifth and probably far into the fourth century, visual and verbal ridicule of the divine by means of grotesque costume and abusive language or behaviour was the norm, a practice for which the festival frame granted impunity to performers and onlookers alike. By sharp contrast, in the comic world of Menander the grotesquely ridiculous representation of the divine is, evidently under the influence of tragedy, replaced with a dignified one. These gods may still not be as imposing as Poseidon in Euripides' *Trojan Women* or Artemis in the *Hippolytus*. But they now do show at least glimpses of their power, notably so in the form of knowledge. The point of this display of power, however, is not philosophical (or 'theological') but, more narrowly, dramaturgical: divine power, as articulated in the information provided by gods in their prologue speeches, is to create dramatic irony and emotional involvement for the audience.

The ridicule of the gods in fifth- and some fourth-century Greek comedy can be so vitriolic because it cannot possibly have any effect whatsoever on their status within the society as configured outside of the theatre (a critical difference with human objects of comic ridicule). Gods are great to laugh at – precisely because this is not reality but 'only' theatre and festival. It is tacitly being taken for granted that outside of these theatrical and festival frames the gods are, quite simply, beyond reach and exempt from being affected by human actions. This unshakability of the status quo outside of the theatre is what the humour of a play like *Birds* rests on: it is plainly ridiculous that the gods should actually lose their power (in the same way that it is ridiculous that women should be actually on top, as they are in *Lysistrata* and *Assembly Women*). Also note that *Birds* does not, of course, feature the extinction of divinity as such but the overthrow of old gods by new ones (a familiar notion in the Greek religious imaginary). As a distinct class, gods continue to exist and thrive (unlike the gods in Wagner's *Götterdämmerung*). Moreover, the logic of the overthrow is emphatically absurd and intrinsically ridiculous: it is, after all, entities like birds or clouds which aspire to be the new gods.

In particular, no human, especially no comic protagonist, acquires the status of a divinity or a cult hero, at least not without a great deal of ambiguity and opaqueness. The most telling case in point is Peisetaerus in *Birds* who ends up as the ruler of the new gods – but he is a bird-man, hence fantastically displaced into an imaginative world. Nor is there an indication that any comic character is to receive hero cult, which is particularly interesting in view of the fact that in the fifth century there appears to have been growing interest in heroization, especially of athletes, the war dead, select politicians and military leaders, and poets.[27] The resurrected Aeschylus in *Frogs* may, once brought back to Athens, have been thought by the Athenian audience to be present again in their midst as a hero (hence capable of benign powers), as other heroized poets like Archilochus, Pindar or (possibly) Sophocles could be.[28] But this is, at most, a possible implication and not expressly stated or even insinuated. The ending of Eupolis' *Demes* may have had undertones of hero cult to honour the four resurrected politicians Solon, Aristeides, Miltiades and Pericles, as might be suggested by the chorus joining others in worship and offering them special wreaths

---

[27] On hero cult in the fifth century see Currie (2005) 89–200.
[28] Clay (2004) discusses not just the hero cult for Archilochus on Paros but attested hero cults for Greek poets in general.

(*eiresiônai*) at the end (fr. 131). That said, those leaders also seem to be characterized not as mere cult objects but as transformative and interventionist agents on a mission to renew Athens.[29] It is of crucial importance that all these instances are, of course, resurrections, i.e. imaginative returns of illustrious individuals and fantastic acts of wish-fulfilment that take place in blurred 'Dionysian worlds'. Also note that the 'common man'-type comic protagonist like Dicaeopolis can look forward to a good party and other immediate gratifications or, like Trygaeus in *Peace*, even to a fantastically outlandish *hieros gamos* ('holy marriage') with 'Harvest' (*Opôra*) – but not the prospect, however remote, of hero cult. Peisetaerus, to invoke *Birds* as a test case once more, is a city founder, hence eminently eligible for hero cult. But nothing of this sort is insinuated in the play. On the contrary, his hybrid status as (human) city founder and (divine) ruler of the new bird-gods – also rewarded with a *hieros gamos*, this time to 'Queen' (*Basileia*) – appears designed to underline the fantastically absurd nature of the plot. Some lines even comedy did not dare cross.

Comedy *is* a deeply-reflexive genre – but not about 'transcendental' questions like the nature of the divine and the human condition. Comedy is not eschatological: 'last things' are not its concern. What matters is the '(right) here and (right) now' (and the fun!). The focus of comedy is, ultimately, situated in the lives that people are living in the material world of the present. In this scheme of things, the supernatural is treated not as a scary and unpredictable power but as a known, omnipresent and accepted constant, and something that itself can even become the stuff of comic ridicule.

Further reading

Overall, the topic 'Greek comedy and religion' is remarkably underexplored. The best general discussion currently available is Parker (2005) 147–52 (part of his chapter on 'Religion in the Theatre'). Notable also are the linguistic analysis of 'religious registers' in Aristophanes provided by Willi (2003a) 8–50 and the discussion of god-related vase iconography in Walsh (2009) 105–64. Bowie (1993) and (2010) explore the relationship between myth and ritual in comedy. Unsurprisingly, the topic of Aristophanes' *Frogs* and the role of Dionysus has attracted particular attention, see Lada-Richards (1999); Biles (2011) chapter 6; Sells (2012); and Griffith (2013) chapter 6. On the divine in Menander see Vogt-Spira (1992) and Zagagi (1995) chapter 6. Ritual aspects are a central part of those

---

[29] On the difficulties of reconstructing Eupolis' *Demes* from the preserved fragments see Storey (2003) 111–74. On fr. 131 specifically see Revermann (2006a) 314f.

works which discuss the Athenian dramatic festivals in general: Pickard-Cambridge (1988); Csapo and Slater (1995); Wilson (2007c); Rusten *et al.* (2011) 93–131. Parker (2011) 171–223 discusses the Greek festival experience in general while the Dionysian procession specifically is the subject of Csapo (2013).

PART IV

Politics, law and social history

15

ALAN SOMMERSTEIN

The politics of Greek comedy

When used in reference to the ancient Greek world, the term 'politics' can bear at least two senses (cf. Carter (2007) 4). One of these is the ordinary modern sense of the word, namely 'matters concerned with the state' – questions about the state's activities in legislation, administration, foreign policy, and so on, and the activities of individuals, groups, factions or parties competing for power or influence in it. The other is the broader sense in which Aristotle (*Pol.* 1253a2f.) wrote that 'man is by nature a political animal', meaning simply that humans can only live a fully human life within an organized society. In this broader sense, Greek comedy obviously was 'political', as was every other kind of theatrical performance, being almost always produced as part of a festival of the polis (or of one of its sub-units, such as a deme) before an audience which consisted preponderantly of citizens of the polis and which the performers could address as if it were identical with the citizen body itself. It is, however, the narrower sense of 'politics' with which we shall be concerned in this chapter.

Almost throughout the period of its vigorous existence, Athenian comedy concerned itself with politics in this narrower sense, though the extent to which, and the spirit in which, it did so varied greatly with time and with individual dramatists' preferences. But comedy was never entirely indifferent to politics, and (very significantly) politicians were never entirely indifferent to comedy.

Most of this chapter will inevitably be concerned with Athens, from which nearly all our evidence comes. We do have a few scraps of relevant evidence about the other major comic tradition, that of Sicily. Probably in the 470s, Epicharmus (fr. 96) in a play called *Islands* said that Anaxilas, the ruler of Rhegium, 'had wanted to destroy Locri [Epizephyrii] completely and had been stopped by Hiero'. And a remark that the god of war, Ares, was a Spartan (Epicharmus fr. 165) suggests that one of his plays may have included some reference to the Persian war, a favourite subject in Hiero's

Syracuse.[1] But these are isolated items, perhaps indicating that Epicharmus once or twice either chose the subject of a comedy, or digressed from it, in a way that could be expected to please his monarch.

At Athens, comedy was probably political from its very beginnings. Indeed, it may even have owed its official beginning to political calculation. The first competition in comedy at the City Dionysia was in 487/6 (*Suda* χ 318); the Assembly decree authorizing it must have been passed in the preceding year, 488/7, almost simultaneously with the first use of 'ostracism' (Arist. *Ath. Pol.* 22.3f.) and the decree providing that the nine archons would thenceforth be chosen by lot instead of by election.[2] The latter two measures were evidently aimed against the aristocratic families, who had always dominated the elective magistracies and who were likely to (and did) provide most of the candidates for ostracism. The introduction of state-sponsored comic drama may well have had a similar aim in view, if existing unofficial comic performances already included satire of individuals; and the near-simultaneity of these developments suggests a single directing mind of populist tendencies, very likely that of Themistocles.[3] Unfortunately, no actual comic scripts from this early period appear to have been preserved.[4]

The first efflorescence of political comedy for which we have definite evidence began in the 440s with Cratinus as its leading figure and Pericles as its most important target. Here already, as throughout the next half-century, comedy tended strongly to single out for adverse attention those politicians who identified themselves, or were identified by their opponents, with the interests of the poorer citizens (see Sommerstein (1996)). Comedy, which (if the argument of the previous paragraph is correct) began its official life as an instrument of left-wing politics, had now been hijacked by the right.[5] I have suggested elsewhere that this was partly due to changes in the composition of the theatre audience after the introduction of, or an increase in, the admission fee;[6] it may be, too, that comedy, now that success in it could earn prizes and public recognition, was beginning to attract men with an extensive (and expensive) literary education.

---

[1] Pind. *Pyth.* 1.75–80; Eratosthenes in schol. Ar. *Frogs* 1028.

[2] Arist. *Ath. Pol.* 22.5 (put into effect for 487/6).   [3] Cf. Podlecki (1975) 9f.

[4] The scripts from which come the surviving fragments attributed to Chionides and Magnes were already suspected in antiquity of being spurious (Ath. 4.137e, 9.367f, 14.638d, 646e).

[5] Cf. Edwards (2002). By the 'left', for this purpose, I mean those who favoured the active use of the power of the state to reduce or eliminate privilege and inequality among citizens, and by the 'right' those who favoured its active use to maintain or extend such privilege and inequality.

[6] Sommerstein (1997) 70f.

Pericles was a target, during his lifetime, in at least five plays by Cratinus and in others by Teleclides and Hermippus. In addition to gibes about his appearance (the size and shape of his head)[7] and his allegedly voracious sexual appetite,[8] he is attacked on several political counts. He is spoken of as a potential or sometimes an actual tyrant,[9] and often identified as Zeus;[10] his partner Aspasia naturally becomes Hera,[11] but also Omphale (who held Heracles in slavery) and Deianeira (who poisoned him).[12] More than once he is mocked for being effective in talk (his great oratorical powers were admitted by all) but not in action, in regard to the completion of the Long Walls linking Athens with Peiraeus (Cratinus fr. 326) and, later, to his insistence on allowing the Peloponnesians to ravage Attica virtually unopposed (Hermippus fr. 47). In Cratinus' *Dionysalexandrus* he was apparently represented by Dionysus, who usurped the role of Paris in the Judgement story, and according to the papyrus Hypothesis he was 'very persuasively satirized by innuendo as having brought the war upon the Athenians' (*POxy* 663.44–8). It is doubtless significant that in the judgement scene Athena offers him not (as in most accounts) *success* in war, but *courage*, a gift which he of course rejects in favour of Aphrodite's (*ibid.* 15–19); the implication that he is a coward is made explicit, a few months later, by Hermippus (fr. 47).

Most of these references seem to belong to the last years of Pericles' life, perhaps because many earlier plays were lost before the Hellenistic period. At least one, however, belongs to the 440s (Cratinus fr. 326), so comic attacks on Pericles were well under way by then. This will be the background to the decree, passed in 440/39, which put some kind of restriction on comedy,[13] possibly by prohibiting mention of living persons; it has often been suggested that the decree was related to the recently launched Athenian war against Samos,[14] which Pericles' enemies blamed on the influence of Aspasia, a native of Miletus which was hostile to Samos (Plut. *Per.* 24.2, 25.1). By 437, when the decree was repealed, the Samian war was over – and Pericles' political position was somewhat weaker; two prominent friends of his, the sculptor Pheidias and the philosopher Anaxagoras, had recently been forced into

---

[7] Cratinus frr. 73, 118, 258; Hermippus fr. 69.
[8] [Eratosth.] *Cat.* 25 (Cratinus, *Nemesis*); Teleclides fr. 18; *com. adesp.* 702, 704 (implicitly compared to Heracles).
[9] Cratinus fr. 171.22–4 (?); 258; Teleclides fr. 45; *com. adesp.* 703.
[10] Cratinus fr. 118, 258; cf. Ar. *Ach.* 530f.
[11] Cratinus fr. 259; *com. adesp.* 704.   [12] *Com. adesp.* 704.
[13] Schol. Ar. *Ach.* 67; accepted as genuine by the sceptical Halliwell (1991) 57–9; see also Brockmann (2003) 58–61; Sommerstein (2004a) 156f.
[14] So e.g., Halliwell (1991) 58f.

exile by prosecutions or threats of prosecution.[15] This dip in his popularity
cannot, of course, have been due to the influence of comedy, politically
neutered as it then was, and there is no sign that its renewed attacks harmed
him seriously thereafter – the only thing that did was the terrible trauma of
the plague of 430.

In the seven years following Pericles' death in 429, Cleon became the most
prominent Athenian politician. There are eleven mentions of him in comic
fragments other than those of Aristophanes, but only three of these[16] are
(i) *known* to be by other dramatists, (ii) clearly hostile and (iii) likely to
date from the time of Cleon's ascendancy. It was not without cause that
Aristophanes claimed special credit for attacking him persistently and on a
large scale.[17]

Aristophanes and Cleon were members of the same deme (Cydathenaeum), and it has been attractively conjectured (Lind 1990) that their
feud sprang in part from personal or factional tensions within the deme.
Aristophanes made some kind of hostile reference to Cleon in his 426 play,
Babylonians (schol. *Ach.* 378), and Cleon retaliated by denouncing Aristophanes (or perhaps his producer, Callistratus, or both; see Sommerstein
(2004) 159f. n. 38) to the Council for 'slandering the City in the presence
of foreigners'. If, as is likely (Sommerstein (2004a) 153), he was using the
procedure called *eisangelia*, the Council had the choice of dismissing the
charge, imposing a fine of up to 500 drachmae, or sending the case for a
full trial,[18] when conviction might result in a swingeing fine or even a death
sentence. Aristophanes himself speaks only of being 'dragged... into the
council chamber' (*Ach.* 379), which implies that he was not sent for trial;
most likely the Council rejected the charge.[19] At any rate he was undeterred,
attacked Cleon several times in *Acharnians* in 425 (*Ach.* 6, 299–302, 377–
82, 502–3, 630–2, 659–64), and a year later, producing a play in person
for the first time, devoted the whole of *Knights* to a sustained and vicious
assault on him, when he was at the height of his power and popularity after
his victory at Pylos-Sphacteria in summer 425. Never before, so far as we
know, had an entire play been targeted in this way on a single politician.
The play won first prize – and a few weeks later Cleon was elected as one
of the ten generals.

[15] Philochorus *FGrH* 328 F 121 (Pheidias, 438/7); Plut. *Per.* 32.2–5 (Anaxagoras, 437/6?
see Mansfeld (1979), (1980)).
[16] Cratinus fr. 228; Eupolis fr. 331; Plato com. fr. 236.
[17] *Clouds* 549; *Wasps* 1029–37; *Peace* 751–60.
[18] Either by the Assembly, or by a jury-court. The details are much disputed; see for one
view Hansen (1975) 21–8, for another Rhodes (1979) 111–14.
[19] A moderate fine would hardly have been appropriate to the seriousness of the charge
(see Hansen (1980) 95).

Aristophanes must have expected that Cleon would try to retaliate again, and he apparently did. Our evidence does not make the sequence of events entirely clear; I have argued elsewhere (Sommerstein (2004a) 151, 160–4) that the likeliest reconstruction is as follows. Soon after the production of *Knights*, Cleon indicted Aristophanes for the very serious offence of *xenia* – exercising the rights of an Athenian citizen when not entitled to them. The penalty on conviction would be sale into slavery. At the preliminary hearing before the magistrate who would preside at an eventual trial, Aristophanes was cross-examined by Cleon (as was regular practice at such hearings) and did not do well or attract much public sympathy (*Wasps* 1285–9); afterwards he approached Cleon and offered a deal: Cleon would withdraw the prosecution, and Aristophanes would undertake to moderate his satire on Cleon in the future (*Wasps* 1290, cf. 1284). Cleon was apparently satisfied; probably he had only ever aimed at intimidating the dramatist. In Aristophanes' next surviving play, *Clouds* in 423, the main target was Socrates; several politicians are mentioned, but Cleon figures only in one passage.[20] Ten months later, Cleon found he had been double-crossed. The two leading characters in *Wasps* are named Philocleon, 'I-love-Cleon', and Bdelycleon, 'Cleon-makes-me-puke'; in all, Cleon's name is heard seventeen times, and the climax is his appearance, as prosecutor in a mock trial (*Wasps* 891–1002), in the guise of a loud-mouthed, lazy, thieving dog, 'the Hound (*Kuôn*) of Cydathenaeum'; and speaking through the chorus leader in the first person, Aristophanes gloats over having outwitted him (*Wasps* 1284–91). A few months later Cleon was killed at Amphipolis; Aristophanes in *Peace*, in spring 421, metaphorically dances on his grave, having more to say about the dead Cleon ('that Cerberus down below')[21] than about any living political figure.

Aristophanes never again composed a whole comedy around a single politician, but other dramatists did (see Sommerstein (2000)). After Cleon's death their main target was Hyperbolus, who figured prominently in plays by Eupolis (*Marikas*), Hermippus (*Bread-sellers*) and Plato (*Hyperbolus*), all within two or three years (421–18); and the effect of these persistent attacks may explain why, when Alcibiades and Nicias found in 417 or 416 that they might well be neck-and-neck in an impending ostracism vote and decided they had best join forces against some third party, they chose Hyperbolus as their victim, hoping rightly that many votes would be cast

---

[20] *Clouds* 581–94 (*Clouds* 549 comes from a passage added when the play was revised after Cleon's death). Three other politicians (Simon, Cleonymus and Hyperbolus) are mentioned *more* than once in the play.

[21] *Peace* 313–20; also 47–8, 269–72, 647–56, 752–60.

against him by the uncommitted.[22] Plato had already produced a *Peisander*, probably in 422 or 421;[23] later he wrote a *Cleophon*, which competed in 405 against *Frogs* in which Cleophon also figures prominently,[24] and probably also in the last years of the war Theopompus produced a play about a minor politician named Teisamenus. Early in 404, probably soon after *Frogs* had been restaged (see below), Cleophon was judicially murdered, because anti-democratic conspirators perceived him as an obstacle to their designs (Lysias 13.7–12, 30.10–14); his death, remembered by democrats after the restoration of 403, seems to have been fatal to the sub-genre of 'demagogue comedy'. Only one more was produced, Archippus' *Rhinon* in 402 or 401, and it was a relative failure.[25]

Aristophanes' *Frogs* itself was in a sense the most successful of all political comedies. Its main theme is the journey of Dionysus to the underworld to bring back a dead tragic poet to save his art from decline and, as we eventually discover, also to save Athens at a critical stage in the war. But half-way through the play, when the chorus regularly address the audience in the so-called parabasis, Aristophanes makes them give direct political advice – and feasible, not fantasy advice; we know that because it was implemented. One part of the parabasis in particular (686–705) apparently made an exceptional impact. Here, the chorus recommend that those who 'went wrong...through being tripped up by the wiles of Phrynichus' (i.e. those who joined or supported the oligarchy of the Four Hundred in 411) should be given the opportunity to make amends; it praises the people for being willing to give most of the rights of citizens to the freed slaves who had taken part in a recent naval campaign, but argues that it is unreasonable to continue denying many of these rights to free-born citizens who, and whose fathers, had fought in many such campaigns – referring to these same ex-oligarchs.

Frogs won first prize; and a few months later, after the Athenian fleet had been almost annihilated at Aegospotami and the city placed under siege, one Patrocleides introduced and carried a decree (Andoc. 1.77–9) calling (among other things) for the erasure and oblivion of all records of disfranchisement against those who had been involved in the oligarchy (with a few exceptions). And it was probably shortly after this that another decree was passed, commending Aristophanes by name, and ordering that he should be crowned with a wreath of sacred olive and that *Frogs* should be reperformed;[26] the

[22] Plut. *Nic.* 11; *Alc.* 13.4–9; *Arist.* 7.3f. See Sommerstein (1996) 332f.
[23] Sommerstein (2000) 439f.; differently Storey (2003) 342f.
[24] *Frogs* 678–85, 1504, 1532f.
[25] Archippus won only one first prize, almost certainly with *Fishes*, by far his best-known play in antiquity.
[26] Hypothesis I.39f. (Wilson) to *Frogs*; Ar. test. 1.35–9 KA. See Sommerstein (1993).

restaging probably took place at the Lenaea of 404, twelve months after the original production. Those who proposed it, though, may have had a sinister agenda: to fan hostility to Cleophon among key sections of the public (including the members of the Council, who ordered Cleophon's arrest and were then specially added to the jury that tried him). A few weeks after the Lenaea, Athens made a peace of surrender with Sparta and her allies. A few weeks after that, state power in Athens was made over to the Thirty, who became the bloodiest and most hated regime in the city's history.

Was Aristophanes himself a convinced anti-democrat? Neither his choruses, nor any sympathetic character he creates, ever express themselves in favour of the exclusion of the poorer citizens from political rights; in *Knights*, the destruction of Cleon (called Paphlagon in the play) is represented not as a defeat for the personified Demos, but as his triumphant escape from a servant who had made himself master. But then no one in democratic Athens, so far as we know, ever did express views openly hostile to democracy in any public forum, except at moments (such as the first half of 411) when it seemed likely that democracy would in fact soon be overthrown. And we certainly do find Aristophanes' choruses and sympathetic characters ridiculing the payment of citizens for performing non-military public functions like jury service, loathing the 'sycophant' or malicious prosecutor (and always representing him as targeting the rich), evaluating politicians by their social status, and resolutely opposing war against Sparta (while never opposing war against anyone else);[27] all of these views appear in the rambling diatribe of the 'Old Oligarch' ([Xen.] *Ath. Pol.* 1.6–7, 1.14, 1.16, 2.14, 2.19), and they all figured in the propaganda or practice of the oligarchs of 411 or 404.[28] At the very least, then, Aristophanes supported a raft of policies which were also supported by oligarchs, and which they seemed to believe (in most cases, probably rightly) would never be accepted in a democratically ruled Athens.

Did other comic dramatists follow a similar political line? Two points may be noted. First, as we have seen, at least five of them, over a period of twenty years, wrote one or more 'demagogue comedies' on the model of *Knights*, and almost invariably their targets were strong and combative democrats. Secondly, the few living individuals who receive *favourable* mention in Old Comedy were all opponents of the dominant radical democratic trend:[29] Archeptolemus (executed for treason after the fall of the Four Hundred:

[27] Sommerstein (2005) 197–202.
[28] Payment for public functions: Thuc. 8.67.3. Sycophancy: Xen. *Hell.* 2.3.12, Arist. *Ath. Pol.* 35.3. Peace with Sparta: Thuc. 8.70.2–71.1, Arist. *Ath. Pol.* 32.3. And the oligarchs of 411 assassinated Hyperbolus and other 'demagogues' (Thuc. 8.65.2, 8.73.3) just as those of 404 disposed of Cleophon.
[29] Sommerstein (1996) 334 gives references for the favourable mentions.

[Plut.] *X Orat.* 833d–834b); Nicias (opponent of Cleon, and, in Eupolis' *Marikas* (fr. 193), of Hyperbolus); Ulius the son of Cimon; the dramatist Sophocles (who when young was Cimon's protégé, when middle-aged was disparaged by Pericles, and when old supported the installation of the Four Hundred);[30] and Thucydides son of Melesias (Pericles' old antagonist). In short, our evidence indicates that from the 440s to the 400s comedy positioned itself pretty consistently on the political right.

Why then, with all the public exposure it enjoyed on such prestigious occasions, did comedy in general have so little actual political influence? We have noted that the treatment of Hyperbolus in comedy may well have contributed to his ostracism; but he would still not have been ostracized but for the collusion between Nicias and Alcibiades. And if the restaging of *Frogs* helped to destroy Cleophon, that happened at a time of extraordinary strain, when Athens was in imminent danger of total destruction, and after Cleophon had held a leading place in politics for some six years. Pericles and Cleon, though they had both evidently *feared* the possible influence of comedy, do not appear to have suffered significantly from it, and Cleon, as we have seen, was elected to a generalship shortly after *Knights* won first prize. How can this be explained?

The crucial point, I am sure,[31] is that while *notionally* the theatre audience was identical with the Athenian citizen body, and the dramatists regularly made their characters and choruses address it accordingly,[32] in *actuality* it was very differently composed. Recent excavations strongly suggest that the fifth-century theatre was much smaller than previously thought, with a capacity unlikely to have exceeded 7,000.[33] Many of these will have been officials of various kinds – magistrates, councillors, priests; many others will have been relatives or friends of persons involved in the productions as performers, *chorêgoi* or otherwise; many others again will have been resident aliens, or visiting foreigners (at the City Dionysia), or boys under eighteen (whom the dramatists regularly regarded as an important part of their audience),[34] none of whom had votes in the Assembly. All things

---

[30] Cimon: *Vita Sophoclis* 3; Plut. *Cim.* 8.8–9. Pericles: Ion *FGrH* 392 F 6 ap. Ath. 13.604d. Four Hundred: Arist. *Rh.* 1419a26–30.

[31] For a well-put case for a different view, see Revermann (2006a) 166–9. On audience composition see also Roselli, pp. 242–6.

[32] Just as speakers in the Athenian courts may use the second person plural to refer to the jury they are addressing, a different jury in a long-past trial, the Athenian assembly, an Athenian military or naval force, etc.

[33] See especially Csapo (2007) 97–100 and Goette (2007) (some caveats in Mitchell-Boyask 2008).

[34] *Clouds* 538f., *Peace* 50, *Assembly Women* 1146; likewise all Menander's concluding appeals (e.g., *Dys.* 967, *Sam.* 733–5).

considered, only a smallish minority of the general Athenian citizen public can have been in the theatre on any given day of the festival. And this minority would be self-selected, consisting of people who were interested enough in drama to spend a whole day watching it and to pay for the privilege (the fee of two obols[35] was not negligible for the poorer classes, particularly since the head of a family would probably have to take along all the free males in his household). Officials, and the friends of performers, would likewise be disproportionately well off and well educated (chorus members had to have been taught singing and dancing;[36] officials, though mostly appointed by lot, had to have volunteered as candidates, which few would do without basic administrative competence including fully functional literacy). In short, the theatre audience was a skewed sample, and those who sought its applause would quickly learn that the route to success bore rightwards.[37]

In Aristophanes' later plays, *Assembly Women* and *Wealth*, while attitudes to issues like war with Sparta[38] or public pay (now given also for attending the Assembly)[39] are little changed, there appears a notable sympathy for the poor: the wealth and population of Athens had now considerably diminished, and many who had once been comfortably off must have become impoverished.[40]

In what is traditionally called Middle Comedy, the period between Aristophanes' death about 385 and the début of Menander in the late 320s, the political element has diminished sharply, and our evidence for it is fairly scanty. We know that some plays did have political themes. A little-known dramatist named Heniochus wrote a play set at Olympia, where (as we learn from a surviving fragment of the prologue) all the Greek cities had come to make sacrifices of thanksgiving for becoming free from tributes (*phoroi*), but had then been corrupted through lodging too long with a landlady named *Aboulia* ('Folly' or perhaps 'Irresolution'), and now are being stirred up to frequent drunken violence by two other women, 'Democracy' and

---

35 For the evidence for this, see Pickard-Cambridge (1988) 265–8; add probably *Frogs* 141.

36 *Frogs* 727–9 treats education in 'wrestling-schools and choruses and culture (*mousikê*)' as a single package and associates it with the 'well-born and virtuous'.

37 This is not to claim that the theatrical public in Aristophanes' time was 'an elite audience' (a position ascribed to Sommerstein (1997) by Revermann (2006a) 169). The classes designated by the 'Old Oligarch' as the *dêmos* were well represented in audience and choruses alike ([Xen.] *Ath. Pol.* 1.13, 2.18); all that is being argued here is that they were much less well represented in the theatre than they were in the assembly.

38 *Assembly Women* 202f.

39 *Assembly Women* 186–8, 282–4, 289–310, 376–93, 547–8; *Wealth* 171, 329f.

40 Cf. Sommerstein (1984) and, on the economic difficulties experienced by many Athenians in the 390s, Mossé (1973) 12–17 and Strauss (1986) 42–69; they were well remembered half a century later (Dem. 57.30–45).

'Aristocracy'.[41] It would appear that the cities formed the chorus of the play (as in a famous play of Eupolis)[42] and that the three women named, or at least the latter two, were individual characters. We cannot date the play precisely, but it probably belongs to the period of confused warfare and politics between the end of Spartan hegemony (371) and the arrival of Philip of Macedon as a force in Greek affairs (353).

Apart from this, though, there is very little political material in what remains of plays from the period 385–350. The individual who appears most often in our evidence is Callistratus, a prominent figure in the 370s and 360s. In an ingenious fragment of Eubulus (fr. 106) someone poses a riddle:

(A) It babbles, but has no tongue; it's female, but has the same name as a male; it controls its own wind; it's hairy, but sometimes smooth; it speaks unintelligibly to the intelligent and trots out *nomos* [which can mean either 'tune' or 'law'] after *nomos*; it is one and many, and if you pierce it, it doesn't bleed. What is it? Can't you guess?

(B) Callistratus!

(A) No, wrong – it's an arsehole!

Theopompus (fr. 31) speaks of Callistratus securing foreign alliances by bribery. He was also accused of squaring political opponents at home in the same way,[43] and Anaxandrides (fr. 41) speaks of one of them, Melanopus, anointing Callistratus' feet with expensive Egyptian perfume. From the same play, *Protesilaus*, comes a long fragment (Anaxandrides fr. 42) describing the sumptuous wedding of the Athenian general Iphicrates to a Thracian princess – though this is merely a prelude to an account of the even greater gastronomic delights which the speaker's own master can provide. Elsewhere we hear of a series of attacks on the long-lived politician Aristophon, *inter alia*, for bribery, rapacity and perjury (*com. adesp.* 836). But these are slim pickings for a long period; and of an outstanding general like Timotheus, or a prominent politician like Eubulus of Probalinthus, we hear nothing at all.

It thus comes as a surprise to find, making his appearance in the 340s, a dramatist like Timocles. His forty-two fragments contain more references to individual politicians than Anaxandrides, Antiphanes and Eubulus together have in a corpus thirteen times the size.[44] A single fragment (4) mentions five

---

[41] Heniochus fr. 5; see Olson (2007) 126–8.

[42] And also, it seems, in another fourth-century play, by Anaxandrides, in which a Greek refuses to make an alliance with Egypt (sc. against Persia) because he finds Egyptian religion abhorrent (Anaxandrides fr. 40).

[43] Plut. *Dem.* 13.3 (referring to Melanopus).

[44] For a detailed study of the political content of Timocles' comedies in comparison with those of other Middle comic dramatists, see Constantinides (1969) 54–61.

leading figures, including Demosthenes and Hypereides, who allegedly took money from Alexander's ex-treasurer Harpalus in 324; in other fragments we hear of Demosthenes' bellicosity and of Hypereides' venality (Timocles frr. 12, 17), and Timocles may even have brought Demosthenes on stage as a character (cf. Timocles fr. 41). It is possible that he went relatively easy on politicians who favoured good relations with Macedon; the five men named in fr. 4 were all strong anti-Macedonians, and at least four had been among those whose extradition Alexander demanded in 335.[45] In other respects too Timocles often recalls Aristophanes: his title *The Lover of Jury Service (Philodikastes)* recalls the theme of *Wasps*, he has Dionysus as a hero, a range of exotic choruses (satyrs, heroes, Egyptians), and a play called *Orestautocleides* in which, in a parody of Aeschylus' *Eumenides*, Autocleides in the role of Orestes is surrounded, not by a dozen sleeping Furies, but by a dozen ageing courtesans (Timocles fr. 27).

But Timocles remains isolated. His contemporary, Alexis, in over 300 fragments mentions just four political figures: one (nine times) for his love of expensive food,[46] one (three times) for his extreme thinness,[47] one (twice) for his legislative harassment of fishmongers,[48] and one (just possibly) for his political activity.[49] One comedy, by Mnesimachus, was named *Philip*, and it probably was about the Macedonian king, since the fragments (Mnesimachus frr. 7, 8) mention warfare and 'eating up' cities in Thessaly and Achaea (Phthiotis); otherwise there is not one comic fragment about Philip (though two mention his boastful general Adaeus),[50] nor about Alexander during his lifetime.

A decisive event in the history of comedy, as of much else, was the end of Athenian independence, and (for the time being) of Athenian democracy, in 322. This was also almost the death-knell of any possibility of a free political comedy at Athens. Henceforth, except during occasional democratic interludes, the only living political figures referred to unfavourably in comedy (that we know of) were those who were neither in Athens, nor in control of Athens. It is significant that of the dynasts who warred for portions of Alexander's empire, the one mentioned most often in comedy

[45] Plut. *Dem.* 23.4. That Timocles' choice of targets is not *entirely* one-sided (cf. Timocles frr. 14, 19, on Aristomedes, mentioned in Dem. 10.70–3 as an appeaser of Philip) proves nothing; Aristophanes' was not either.

[46] Callimedon 'the Crayfish' (Alexis frr. 57, 102, 117, 118, 149, 173, 198, 218, 249), also mentioned five times by other dramatists.

[47] Philippides (Alexis frr. 1, 93, 148), also mentioned four times by other dramatists; cf. Hypereides, *Against Philippides*.

[48] Aristonicus (Alexis frr. 130, 131).

[49] Aristogeiton (Alexis fr. 211); cf. Dem. 25, 26, Din. 2.

[50] Under the nickname 'Philip's cockerel' (Antiphanes fr. 296, Heraclides fr. 1).

was the remotest, Seleucus, ruler of Mesopotamia and points east (and later of Syria); and even so, all the references to him are politically innocuous.[51]

Menander's career began in the late 320s. His plays are frequently 'political' in the broader sense; *Dyscolus*, for example, has often been seen as promoting social solidarity between different classes of the community.[52] But political comment in a stricter sense appears only, so far as we know, in *The Sicyonian(s)*. Act IV of this play begins with an ill-tempered dialogue between two old men of Eleusis, one rich and the other poor;[53] the former was probably named Smicrines, the latter's name is unknown.[54] One of them, possibly both, have just come from a meeting of the Eleusis deme assembly. Smicrines pooh-poohs the other's readiness to believe anyone who makes an emotional appeal: you can't expect a public meeting to judge what is true and false – a small committee will do that much better. 'By great Zeus,' says the other man, 'you're a wicked oligarch . . . You lot will be the death of me . . . I hate you and all your supercilious kind. I may be riff-raff, but [completion of sentence lost].' The two men part with mutual curses, and Smicrines shouts at the other's departing back 'Very sensible of you to run away; I'd have shut your mouth tighter than a metic's!'[55] Before the end of the act Smicrines will discover that the maker of the emotional appeal, Stratophanes, is his own long-lost son (*Sic.* 280–311); in other words, his initial judgement was completely wrong, and that of the assembly right. We certainly would not wish to infer from this that Menander was a strong democrat; he had, after all, been a friend of Demetrius of Phalerum, sole ruler of Athens from 317 to 307 (Diog. Laert. 5.79). But had he been a strong oligarch, he would hardly have written this scene in this way – nor indeed the next one (*Sic.* 176–271), which contains a full report of the assembly meeting, modelled on that of the Argive assembly in Euripides' *Orestes* (866–952). In Euripides the assembly allowed itself to be manipulated by self-interested and dishonest individuals, and voted unjustly for the death of Orestes and Electra. Here it perceives the truth (whatever Smicrines may have said) and makes the right decision. We are made to hear not only the

[51] Alexis fr. 207; Antiphanes fr. 185; Demetrius II com. fr. 1; Philemon fr. 49.
[52] See e.g., Konstan (1995) 102–5, and (with different emphases) Rosivach (2001) and Lape (2004) 110–36. The politics of Menander, in this broader sense, are admirably discussed by Hofmeister (1997).
[53] Men. *Sic.* 150–68; see Gomme and Sandbach (1973) 646–50; Belardinelli (1994) 145–57; Arnott (2000b) 240–7.
[54] He may or may not be a character who appears elsewhere in the play; see references cited in previous note.
[55] Literally 'tray's', referring to the trays of offerings carried by metics in the Panathenaic procession; see Arnott (2000b) 245 n. 4.

speeches but also the shouts from the floor (ten or eleven of them, all indicating that the ordinary folk have their hearts in the right place).[56] Whatever Menander himself may have really thought,[57] we can reasonably infer that at this time the theatrical public wanted to be told that the voice of the people was the voice of truth and justice, and that the authorities of the day were not averse to this message; which probably places the play in one of the two periods of democratic government that Athens knew in Menander's adult lifetime,[58] either in 318–317[59] or between 307/6 and ca. 300.

During most of the latter period the dominant politician in Athens was one Stratocles, whom some thought to have behaved with undue obsequiousness towards the Macedonian dynast Demetrius Poliorcetes; in particular, he manipulated the state calendar in order to enable Demetrius to go through all the stages of initiation in the Eleusinian Mysteries during a short visit to Athens.[60] These and other breaches of religious tradition were held by Stratocles' enemies to have been the cause of various subsequent signs of divine displeasure, and the comic dramatist Philippides (fr. 25), probably in 301, made a character say:

> The man who cut down the year to a single month – the man who treated the Acropolis as a hotel, and brought prostitutes into the house of the Virgin[61] – the man on whose account the frost scorched the vines[62] – the man whose impiety caused the Panathenaic robe to be torn in half[63] – the man who turned the honours of the gods into honours for a human! It is these things that subvert democracy, not comedy [or not a comedy].

The last sentence implies that a comic dramatist (quite likely Philippides himself) had been accused (quite likely by Stratocles) of having used the theatre in an attempt to subvert the democratic constitution; almost a rerun

---

[56] Men. *Sic.* 197, 202f., 223, 239, 245, 257, 264, 265f., 269.

[57] Lape (2004) sees him as consistently promoting a democratic ideology, Major (1997) as consistently promoting a pro-Macedonian one (whatever that means in an age when Macedonian dynasts were constantly fighting one another and competing for influence over the Greek city-states); but both admit that on the surface his plays are notably apolitical, by comparison not only with Old Comedy but with some of his contemporaries.

[58] On the history and politics of Athens in this period, see Habicht (1997) 36–97.

[59] So Belardinelli (1994) 69–71.

[60] Plut. *Demetr.* 26.1–4; Philochorus *FGrH* 328 F 70; Diod. Sic. 20.110.1.

[61] That is to say, he was responsible for authorizing Demetrius to lodge in the Parthenon, where he entertained some of his mistresses (Plut. *Demetr.* 23.5–24.1).

[62] Plut. *Demetr.* 12.5.

[63] In 302; the robe bore images of Demetrius and his father Antigonus along with those of Zeus and Athena (Plut. *Demetr.* 10.5, 12.3). Philippides himself procured from King Lysimachus some appropriate accessories for the new robe dedicated at the next Great Panathenaea in 298 (*IG* ii² 657.14–16).

of the long-past conflict between Cleon and Aristophanes.[64] There probably was not a formal charge, let alone a conviction, since a decree twenty years later praised Philippides for never having done anything hostile to democracy in word or act (*IG* ii² 657.48–50). Philippides may even have brought Stratocles on stage; a character in one of his plays referred to Stratocles' allegedly unhappy marriage, and did so in the second person.[65] If Philippides made his major attack on Stratocles in 301, he may have had to leave Athens almost immediately for his own safety; he was at the court of Demetrius' great rival, Lysimachus, by the time of Lysimachus' victory at Ipsus later that same year.[66]

Philippides' main impact on public affairs, however, was made outside the theatre: over a long period he secured from Lysimachus a series of favours and benefactions for Athens, for which, in a later period of restored democracy (in 282), he was awarded a golden crown, a bronze statue of himself (to be erected *in the theatre*), public maintenance in the Prytaneum, and privileged seating at all public spectacles.[67] Across a century, this younger contemporary of Menander can join hands with Aristophanes. Both lived under democracy and under oligarchy or autocracy; both were accused of political subversion in their capacity as comic dramatists; and both were later publicly honoured, in that same capacity, for their services to the Athenian people.

Further reading

The literature on this subject is vast, especially with regard to Aristophanes. Modern discussion begins with Gomme (1938), who challenged the traditional view (which went all the way back to ancient scholarship) that Aristophanes was a politically committed and partisan dramatist; his approach was deepened and developed by Forrest (1963); Dover (1972); Heath (1987); and especially Halliwell (1991), (1993), (1997), while studies defending and evidencing a position closer to the traditional one have included Ste Croix (1972); Cartledge (1990); Henderson (1990), (1993), (1998); MacDowell (1995); Sommerstein (1996), (2004a), (2005); and with particular reference to the Athenian citizen assembly, Rhodes (2004). Carey (1994) takes a nuanced position. Heath (1997) provides an extremely valuable analysis of the close similarities between the methods and topics of vituperation

[64] Cf. O'Sullivan (2009) 64–78.
[65] Philippides fr. 26: 'she turns away, but you just manage to kiss her head'.
[66] *IG* ii² 657.16–29. Menander, on the other hand, seems to have remained in Athens, and remained active as a dramatist, under all regimes.
[67] *IG* ii² 657 (services, lines 9–38; honours, lines 58–70).

in Old Comedy and in forensic oratory. See more recently Olson (2010) and Ruffell (2011). On the earlier development of Athenian comedy, see Edwards (2002); on Cratinus, Bakola (2010) chapter 4; on Eupolis, Storey (2003) especially 334–48. On Middle Comedy, see Nesselrath (1997), especially 272–7, though he probably overstates his case for 'a sustained interest... in Athenian and general Greek political developments' by dramatists other than Timocles; on Philippides, see O'Sullivan (2009). Major (1997) and Lape (2004) attempt, in sharply contrasting ways, to find a political standpoint in Menander. To the complex history of Athens in his times, the early chapters of Habicht (1997) are an essential guide, though it is handily summed up in one paragraph by Lowe (2008) 70.

16

EDITH HALL

Comedy and Athenian festival culture

The idea of the festival is inseparable from Greek comedy. Festivals often lurk in the background of Menander's plots, since they provided the occasions when youths accidentally impregnate maidens: it was at the festival of the Tauropolia that Charisios had made Pamphile pregnant in *Men at Arbitration*, it was at the Adonia that Plangon in *Samia* conceived her baby, and it was in the procession during the festival of Dionysus that the hero of Menander's *Synaristôsai* first became infatuated with a girl (fr. 337 K-A).[1] Menander's most substantial surviving text, *Dyscolus*, has at its heart a private celebration of the god Pan at a cave believed to be inhabited by nymphs in the rural deme of Phyle; the celebration includes all the standard features of larger, public festivals – a sacrificial meal, followed by drinking and dancing that goes on into the night.[2] Another of Menander's plays, *Sicyonians*, apparently ended with an all-night festival at Eleusis, presumably in honour of Demeter and Persephone.[3] But the festivals in these plays are occasions for important developments in personal and domestic relationships, especially the idealized inter-familial bonds through marriage and reproduction which it is Menandrean comedy's generic imperative to create and celebrate. In *Dyscolus*, the festival of Pan is not even one accorded an official place in the city calendar, since Sostratus' mother is only inspired to organize the sacrifice after being visited by Pan in a dream.

The festival theme performs rather different functions in the earlier comedies of Aristophanes, performed when the sovereign power at Athens was still held by the men who constituted the *dêmos*. The idea of the festival is in Aristophanic comedy intimately tied to the idea of the democratic city-state, which administered and substantially financed the festival programme. It has become rather fashionable since the 1980s to see

---

[1] Arnott (1998) 40. The Adonia was also the scene of a rape that resulted in a pregnancy in *Phasma*: see Webster (1973) 197f.
[2] On the comic processional revel (*kōmos*) in Menander, see Lape (2006).
[3] Quincey (1966) 119.

festival licence, especially somatic and sexual explicitness, as performing a critical and subversive role in Aristophanes through challenging Athenian citizens' 'conventional' prejudices and preconceptions. This line of argument often derives from the notions of the carnival and the carnivalesque which the Russian critic Mikhail Bakhtin developed in his work on Rabelais. But it will become apparent in my argument here that Bakhtin's perception of the inherent subversiveness of festival licence and humour does not chime with my own view of Aristophanic comedy's relationship with festival. I believe he uses festival to shape *mainstream* opinion, by positioning his comedy as the authoritative mouthpiece of the community's central, traditional, collective value system, rather than to subvert authority from a viewpoint characterized as oppositional, radical or marginal.[4]

The Athenians of Aristophanes' time spent a substantial proportion of their days celebrating festivals.[5] One non-Athenian author said that they operated under constant pressure of time because 'they have to hold more festivals than any other Greek city, and when these are going on it is even more difficult than usual for any of the city's affairs to be transacted' (pseudo-Xenophon, *Ath. Pol.* 3.2). The festival calendar was kept by the senior magistrate ('*archôn*'), and administering it could be difficult, since it did not always correspond either with lunar exigencies or the schedule, organized by the Council, for the meetings of legislative bodies.[6] Indeed, the chorus of Aristophanes' *Clouds* say that the gods have been blaming the Moon because the Athenians are always making mistakes in their calculations of the right days for litigation and those for performing sacrifices (615–26). Athenian festivals were also diverse: they ranged from small-scale events run on a local basis in the demes, to massive ceremonies, lasting days, at which guests were present from all over the Greek-speaking world. The archon's calendar also had to take account of the festivals held in other cult centres beyond Attica which Athenians regularly attended, such as the Olympic or Isthmian games.

One crucial function of the festivals attended by Aristophanes' audiences, therefore, was to create a sense of temporal order by routine suspension of 'normal' everyday life, and to mark the experience of the seasons and the flow of time.[7] In comedy, the parodies of plays performed at other

---

[4] For a slightly different approach to the issue of Bakhtin's overstatement of the political subversiveness of some types of festival comedy, see Eco (1984).

[5] For the changes in the financial and administrative organization of the Dionysia itself that took place between Aristophanes and Menander, see Wilson (2008). On the Greek festival experience (in Athens and elsewhere) see Parker (2011) ch. 6.

[6] See Dunn (1999).   [7] Leach (1961) 134.

Dionysiac festivals across time in previous years, such as the parodies of
Euripides' *Andromeda* and *Helen* in *Women at the Thesmophoria*, partially served to remind the audience of the rhythm of the manifestations
of their shared identity and memories as a group. But the feature which
made any major festival day different from all other days, at least for
lower-income Athenians, was that when they were conducting a festival
(*heortê*) they were not working: 'every day is a festival for those who
don't work' (Theoc. *Id.* 15.26). For the very poor, a festival might bring
a welcome opportunity to eat: Carion in *Wealth* recalls the custom of feeding the poor with bread and soup at the festival of Theseus (627). The
interruption to working activities and the availability of food, drink and
sexual opportunity during the 'suspended' time occupied by festivals are
both reflected in the consistent interest Old Comedy displays in golden
ages and utopias, worlds where material needs are met without human
labour.[8]

In addition to shaping the communal sense of temporal order, festivals
also offered a shared sense of control over space. A component of most
festivals was the processional journey to the place of celebration, with its
own bends, inclines, bridges, landmarks and traditional places where the
participants paused at shrines to perform a hymn or sacrifice. Everyone who
attended the Great Dionysia, for example, would have recently refreshed in
their minds the route taken by the opening procession, which brought the
icon of Dionysus from the Academy (an olive grove outside the city) via the
city walls and several shrines to the sanctuary of Dionysus.

A psychologically important route through the city was that taken by
the opening procession of the Panathenaea in high summer; the participants gathered at the Dipylon gate in the north of the city and moved
down the Panathenaic way via the agora (the site of much of the city's
secular business) to the sacred centre on the Acropolis and thence to the
Parthenon. In *Assembly Women*, an important scene relies on the audience's shared knowledge of the Panathenaic procession. After the women
have inaugurated the new regime, Chremes responds to Praxagora's edict
ordering everyone to take their private possessions to the agora and donate
them to the state (711–14).[9] He lines up the contents of his larder as if they
were members of the polis assembling on the first day of the Panathenaea to
progress to the agora (730–45). He begins with his sieve, which is to take

[8] This motif had certainly become popular in contemporary Old Comedy, for example in
Eupolis' *Chrusoun Genos* and Teleclides' *Amphictyones*.
[9] The man is not named in the manuscript, but should almost certainly be identified with
Chremes, the friend of Blepyrus who reports what happened at the momentous meeting
of the Assembly when the women took power.

the place of the Basket-bearer (*kanêphoros*), the young woman who led the procession:[10]

> You, beautiful flour-sieve, chief amongst my possessions,
> Move beautifully as you come outside here to me,
> So that you can be the Basket-bearer, all clogged with flour,
> Since you have devoured so many sacks of it.

She is to be followed by a blackened cooking pot (representing the Chair-bearer), a jug (the Pitcher-bearer), and other 'participants' including honey-combs, branches which may suggest the older men who took part in the procession, a tripod, oil-flasks and the 'crowd' who brought up the rear, represented by smaller items of culinary equipment. The Panathenaea marked the Athenians' New Year, and Chremes' domestic Panathenaic procession marks another fresh start, since it 'inaugurates the new age'.[11] The plan for the new age was conceived, says Praxagora, at the Skira festival (17f., 59), a women-only celebration of Demeter and Kore, connected with sowing of seed, held in the previous month. But in the world of the play the new era is not just a matter of the calendar – of the cycle of seasons, marked by sequential festivals – but of female power and communism, characterized by the joint ownership of possessions which now ludicrously march in festival procession.

This brilliant scene demonstrates how a poet of Old Comedy could create bonds between his spectators by exploiting their shared experience of festivals while simultaneously developing an absurdist flight of comic fantasy. In this he bathetically substitutes grubby culinary implements for processional leaders, traditionally distinguished by their beauty. This scene perfectly exemplifies the synergy between the Athenians' festival culture and their style of comedy, but festivals feature in other genres as well. The Homeric hymns and the victory odes of the Theban Pindar and the Cean Bacchylides reflect festival culture. Greek tragedy can be structurally informed by a particular festival (Euripides' *Electra* with the Argive festival of Hera, for example),[12] describe festivals, and provide aetiologies for others (Eur. *IT* 1138–51, *Hippolytus* 1425–30). The dialogue on the ideal civic community recorded in Plato's *Republic* takes place during a night when the Thracian goddess Bendis was first celebrated at Athens; the party portrayed in his *Symposium* takes place at the end of the Lenaea, and it is during the Panathenaea that several conversations recorded in other dialogues are supposed to have taken place (*Ion, Parmenides, Timaeus, Critias*). But there

[10] Menander was also interested in the figure of the basket-bearing young woman in the procession, since one of his lost plays was entitled *Kanêphoros*.
[11] Bowie (1993) 262. [12] Zeitlin (2003).

is no doubt that the ancient Greek literary genre which talks most and most explicitly about festivals is comedy.

During the twentieth century, the idea of 'festival' became important in a range of disciplines. For the philosopher Hans-Georg Gadamer, 'festival' is fundamental to our approach to all art: when someone *immerses* herself in an artwork, s/he is interwoven into an event, detached from regular time, and thus a participant in a more excellent reality. But s/he is also, in an important sense, assenting to perceive that reality actively, in a sustained and involved manner, through her/his eyes (and/or ears) – or, as the ancient Greeks would have said, assenting to *theôrein* it.[13] The idea of *participation* in a festival was such a strongly defined concept for Aristophanes' audience that he could create a personification of it: in his *Peace* of 421, *Theôria* conceived as a beautiful young woman, is one of the two benefits which the recovery of Peace can bestow on the Greek world – the opportunity to participate in festivals without obstruction (the other is a personification of the successful ripening of agricultural produce). Gadamer's idea of art as festival is important because he is entirely rejecting the Romantics' notion of art as something in which people were not seen as actively 'participating' at all. Instead, the Romantics had seen art as acting *upon* them by taking them into the private world of their imagination, thus removing the need to exert themselves intellectually or be practically involved in the process.

Gadamer's notion of art as festive, active *participation* illuminates the ubiquity of the idea of festival within the art-form of Aristophanic comedy. The plays were all first performed in drama competitions held at festivals, specifically at Athenian festivals of Dionysus, either the Lenaea, held in approximately the equivalent of January, and the Great Dionysia (March/April). The participants in the Lenaea were Athenian citizens and resident non-Athenians (metics); those at the Dionysia were drawn from many other Greek states allied with or subject to the Athenian empire. *Wasps*, for example, was performed at the Lenaea in 422 BCE. In a fundamental sense, then, both performers and spectators of comedy were co-celebrants in a festival of the god, and their primary group identity on these occasions was dependent neither on ethnicity nor status, but as fellow participants in the festival.

This is also true, of course, of the group identity of the spectators of tragedy, the content of which is less preoccupied with festivals. Here, one great difference lies in the temporal orientation of the genre. While tragedy is set in the past, usually the remote past far beyond living memory, comedy's temporality occurs simultaneously with (and usually as an imaginary

[13] Gadamer (1986).

extension of) the Athenian reality in which the drama competition is taking place. That reality consisted of several thousand worshippers of Dionysus gathered in a shape based on a circle, viewing each other in a self-conscious way as fellow festival participants. The group that gathered at the Dionysia, with its international dimension, also resembled the group that gathered at other interstate festivals such as the Olympia in the Peloponnese or the Athenian Panathenaea. The group that gathered at the Lenaea, meanwhile, shared many features with the groups that gathered not only at other Athenian festivals such as the Anthesteria or the Boedromia, but also those who participated in the civic institutions of the Assembly and the courts of law.

The parallelism between the Athenian communities endlessly recreated in both political and festival communities is clear in a speech made by one statesman when the body of citizens was divided. In 403 BCE the city was enduring the reign of terror of the so-called Thirty Tyrants at the end of the Peloponnesian War. The exiled democrats won a victory, after which their spokesman Cleocritus addressed the defeated aristocrats in a speech which shows how the shared experience of festivals lay at the heart of the Athenians' sense of group identity (Xenophon, *Hellenica* 2.4.20):

> Fellow citizens, why are you keeping us out of Athens? Why do you seek our deaths? For we have never done you any harm. We have taken part alongside you in the most hallowed rituals and sacrifices, and in the finest festivals. We have been your co-dancers in choruses and co-students, as well as your co-soldiers.

In Aristophanic comedy, which is consistently pro-peace, but which seeks to please as large a proportion of the audience as possible, it is scarcely surprising that so much prominence is given to Cleocritus' first category of shared experience – participation 'in the most hallowed rituals and sacrifices, and in the finest festivals' – rather than to joint military training.

Sociologists and anthropologists today understand festivals as functioning in social communities in a way that derives from the model proposed by Émile Durkheim in *The Elementary Forms of Religious Life* (1912). Durkheim argued that ordinary, everyday life, governed by the need to work and perform domestic chores in order to fulfil fundamental physical needs, weakens individual people's commitment to shared community beliefs and social bonds. It develops a sense of secular individualism that is 'centrifugal' – it pulls each person away from the society's communal centre and toward his or her separate and self-interested place on its periphery.[14] Societies are

---

[14] Etzioni (2000).

threatened by these centrifugal and individualistic pressures. The threat creates a need for activities which look towards the centre of the community rather than away from it, and reinforce commitments to mutual values, beliefs and practices. Rituals, including festivals, offer a mechanism for the symbolic recreation of society, in which its members define what is mutually sacred to them, and share highly charged experiences which form the bonds between participants to which Cleocritus, the democratic spokesman, famously appealed.

The tension between the centripetal and centrifugal impulses in societies is staged in the same episode of *Assembly Women* as Chremes' Panathenaic marshalling of his chattels in the public cause. Another citizen enters and declares that it would be the height of folly to contribute his possessions, the fruit of his sweat and thrift, to the public store (746–9). After an extended discussion, the second man secretly decides to work out some clever scheme by which he can keep his own things and yet take a share of the common feast (872–7). In Aristophanes' first surviving comedy, *Acharnians*, the entire plot is structured around the same Durkheimian tension between Athenian citizens' centrifugal, self-interested individual drives and the centripetal pressure reinforcing their shared interests and beliefs. But in the festival-obsessed world of comedy, Aristophanes can choose to symbolize the contrast between Durkheim's competing group and individual interests through the contrast between neither non-festival and festival, nor secular and sacred, but between *two types of festival* of Dionysus. The hero Dicaeopolis is a citizen from a country deme, aghast at the continuing Peloponnesian War and especially angry with the politicians responsible for the endless hostilities. He decides to make a personal thirty-year peace treaty with the Spartan enemy, in order to return to his home in the countryside, where he celebrates the local festival of Dionysus, the 'Rural Dionysia' (201f.). This is known to have been celebrated in upwards of fourteen demes in approximately December. It was a popular event, connected with arable and vegetative fertility; it featured a procession with a ritual phallus that culminated in a sacrifice to Dionysus. By Plato's time, some Rural Dionysia also included dramatic performances (*Republic* 5.475d).

After uttering the formulaic command for silence with opened sacrificial rituals, Dicaeopolis orchestrates his own household in a celebration of the local village festival (236–84). A young woman leads the procession, carrying the basket of ceremonial objects. The male slave Xanthias follows, bearing the phallus, and Dicaeopolis comes third, singing the phallic hymn. Yet the festival is arrested before it can culminate in sacrifice. The chorus, who hail from another deme (and one famous for its bellicose temperament), the men of Acharnai, seem to have been reading their Durkheim when they complain explicitly that Dicaeopolis is neglecting his responsibilities as a fellow Athenian in favour of his own individual household. They address him as 'a traitor to your fatherland: you alone amongst us all have concluded a truce, and you dare to look us in the face!' (289–91). Dicaeopolis' reintegration into the Athenian community does not come until Lamachus' slave arrives to attempt to buy an eel and some thrushes from Dicaeopolis for his master, who is about to celebrate the 'Feast of the Cups', or *Choes*, the second day of the Anthesteria (959–62). There commences a sequence corresponding to the rituals at this Athenian festival, in which small children were prominent. A herald tells the people to listen for the trumpet signal, before downing a full jug of wine. Dicaeopolis instructs the women and children to cook hares and prepare flower garlands; thrushes, eels and honey-smeared tripe are roasted (1000–7, 1040–2). The festival enters a new level of civic inclusiveness as the formerly bellicose general Lamachus arrives and another herald announces that the Priest of Dionysus has summoned Dicaeopolis: 'everything is ready' – couches, tables, cushions, garlands, perfumes, tasty treats, courtesans and pretty dancing women (1087–93). Dicaeopolis enters with two courtesans and claims that he has won the drinking competition; to close the festival and the play he leads courtesans and chorus in an energetic revel or *kômos* (1198–2002), the institution which originally gave its name to the genre of comedy (Arist. *Poet.* 3). Dicaeopolis has become a bridegroom figure, about to mate with one of the courtesans: this symbolic wedding is suggestive of the official 'sacred marriage' (*hieros gamos*) that took place between the god Dionysus and the wife of the King Archon at the Anthesteria ([Dem.] 59.73–8).[15]

Acharnians, therefore, stages a conflict between a group whose primary, warlike identity and allegiance are determined by their deme – the men of Acharnai, who worship the personification of war, Polemos (979).[16] They are initially at loggerheads with Dicaeopolis, whose identity and outlook as a peace-seeking farmer is symbolized by his membership of the rural deme of Cholleidai. Yet the contrast between these two deme-based identities is in Aristophanes' hands sharpened, with the extremity and polarization characteristic of the comic imagination, into a Durkheimian contrast between the centrifugal and centripetal impulses which make festivals necessary in any robust community. Dicaeopolis' mission is to find an identity that will include all participants in the play *and* in the wider festival beyond it. It is in Dicaeopolis' delight at the staged Anthesteria that an

---

15 See Habash (1995). Similar things can be said of the marriage of Trygaeus and Opora at the end of *Peace* (Hall (2006) 342f.) and that of Peisthetairos and Basileia at the end of *Birds* (Pozzi (1985–86) 128).

16 There was, indeed, a cult of the war-god Ares at Acharnae.

Athens-wide identity (which will maximize Aristophanes' chances of pleasing the largest possible proportion of his Athens-wide audience) is eventually discovered.

The example of *Acharnians* reveals both the benefits and limits to the usefulness of Durkheim's 'classical' model of festival when applied to Aristophanic comedy. The 'frame' festival at which *Acharnians* was performed, the Lenaea, worked to consolidate the values of the whole Athenian city-state, just like the Anthesteria with which the internal world of the comedy ends. But there were many other festivals, both large and small, celebrated by sub-groups of residents of Attica whose mutual identity was determined by other criteria – deme or class or profession or gender – micro-communities whose mutual self-interest must often have conflicted with that of the macro-community of Attica. Group identity is a fluid phenomenon. Every male citizen of Athens belonged to a particular deme, a tribe and a phratry, the last of which involved rituals of initiation and registration of membership which took place at the Apatouria festival.[17] He was also classified as belonging to one of four income brackets, a classification which affected both the civic bodies on which he served and the military services he performed: the chorus of Aristophanes' *Knights*, for example, belong to the second highest income bracket, and served as cavalrymen. Which of his group identities was temporarily prominent was a matter of immediate context. There were certainly some minor festivals celebrated by groups within Athens which shored up their 'micro-identities', such as the Prometheia (celebrated by smiths), and a festival of Poseidon Hippios, believed to have appealed primarily to the wealthier families which produced the cavalry. It was the task of Aristophanes as comic playwright in the drama festivals, held at the more inclusive festivals of Dionysus, to weld the disparate groups of Athenians into a group united not only by their temporary identity as co-celebrants of the god, but by their applause for the playwright's comic creation.

The most inclusive of all festivals was the Eleusinian Mysteries. The Mysteries were an extremely well-attended annual rite of Demeter held in the autumn at Eleusis, a deme fourteen miles north-west of Athens. The festival took eight days, and involved movements between Demeter's Eleusinian temple (the Telesterion) and a related shrine near the Athenian agora. The central procession wound all the way from the city to Eleusis, priests and

[17] Evidence for festivals relating to the *ephêbeia*, the process through which young male citizens became initiated into the status of Athenian citizen-soldier, is almost non-existent in the fifth and early fourth century. For this reason I am not here discussing interpretations of *Knights*, *Wasps* and *Clouds* which relate their plots and motifs to ephebic initiation, for which see further Bowie (1993) 45–58, 78–96, 102–12.

magistrates leading the initiates ('*mustai*') on their pilgrimage. At the climax of the rites, the *mustai* entered the Telesterion and experienced the Mysteries.[18] Initiation, which held out the promise of a blessed afterlife, was open to all who could speak Greek, free and slave alike. Cleocritus, the democratic spokesman whom we met above, appealing in 403 BCE to his co-Athenians on the ground of their shared experience of festivals, was already well known as the sweet-voiced herald who made announcements in the course of the Eleusinian Mysteries (Xenophon, *Hellenica* 2.4.20). These included the *Prorrhêsis*, the proclamation of the restrictions on those allowed to attend; this is parodied in Aristophanes' *Frogs* which premiered just two years earlier (354f.). Indeed, *Frogs* is fundamentally informed by the structure and content of the Eleusinian Mysteries, as several scholars have demonstrated in detail.[19] The play opens with a visit to Heracles, the mythical prototype of the Eleusinian initiate, who had braved the Underworld, found salvation, and subsequently enjoyed immortality. The whole play consists of a perilous journey (the standard image for the process of initiation) to an underworld inhabited by joyful, deathless celebrants of Iacchus as well as of Demeter and Persephone, and we know that Iacchus, an 'avatar' of Dionysus,[20] featured prominently in the Eleusinian procession's ritual cries. The dramatic action concludes, like the experience of the Mysteries, with a blaze of torches and communion with the dead, as Aeschylus is escorted back to Athens by the chorus of *mustai*.

More important than any of the humour and fantastic theatre which Aristophanes derives from his comic take on the Eleusinian festival is the political use to which he puts its remarkable social inclusivity.[21] Aristophanes is here calling for an Athens which enthusiastically embraces a wider citizenry than hitherto. On the one hand, he advocates the recall of Alcibiades and the reinstatement of some prominent citizens who had fallen foul of the democracy, but he also approves the recent emancipation and almost certainly naturalization as citizens of a significant number of slaves. They had been freed in recognition of their contribution as rowers in the battle of Arginusae the previous year.[22] The sheer scale of the chaos and crisis in Athens in 406, along with the acute shortage of manpower, had made even the desperate expedient of the mass enfranchisement of slaves acceptable.

---

[18] For bibliography on the Mysteries see Evans (2002).

[19] Lada-Richards (1999); Bowie (1993) 228–53. The Eleusinian Mysteries also play a role in *Clouds*: see Marianetti (1993).

[20] Bowie (1993) 230.

[21] This is not to say that there was not internal differentiation as expressed by stages of initiation within the mysteries, nor a strong sense of exclusion directed at the uninitiated. See Clinton (2003).

[22] See Hall (2006) 200.

Indeed, there is little reason to suppose that the new citizens enfranchised by Arginusae were not actually yet present in the audience at the premiere of *Frogs*: several of the lines in the dialogues involving Xanthias and in the parabasis seem designed to cultivate their applause (33f., 190–2, 693–9). Arginusae is also almost certainly the reason lying behind the creation of the clever and resilient Xanthias in Aristophanes' *Frogs*, whose role, as a slave, is unprecedented amongst previous Aristophanic comedies. The communal identity which Aristophanes is aiming at creating in *Frogs* was one which had much in common with the welcoming, inclusive formula decreeing eligibility criteria for attendance at the Eleusinian Mysteries. Aristophanes chose the festival to integrate into his comic plot with unusual care that year, and won his reward: *Frogs* was not only victorious at the Dionysia, but seems to have been revived soon thereafter.

In order to win at the drama competitions, therefore, a comedy needed to create a dominant worldview through its laughter which felt commensurate with the group identity and outlook of the audience of comedy. Allusion to joint experience of festivals was a tried and tested method of achieving this aim, at least amongst the men who attended the Athenian drama competitions. Although there has been much discussion of whether women in the fifth century could watch the tragedies, it is in my view highly unlikely that women watched the premieres of comedy.[23] Moreover, the judges were male, and the libidinal self at stake in comedy is emphatically masculine. This makes the festivals discussed in the gender role reversal plays particularly interesting. As we have seen, *Assembly Women* claimed that the women's plot to take over the running of the city was hatched at their Skira festival. Both *Lysistrata* and *Women at the Thesmophoria* were performed in 411 BCE, although we do not know which was the Lenaea play and which the Dionysia performance. In political terms, this makes a good deal of difference to the meaning at least of *Lysistrata*: the heartfelt plea for peace would have had a very different agenda (and possibly far more acerbic one) if intended for an exclusively Athenian audience at the Lenaea (where I am inclined to think it was performed) rather than a panhellenic one at the Dionysia. Yet both plays utilize the idea of female festivals to invite audiences to relate to one another in terms neither of civic nor imperial allegiance, but of biological sex and culturally defined gender. Anthropologists since the 1960s have often emphasized the festival phenomenon of role reversal in defining, through inversion, hierarchical social structures, and the patriarchal ancient Athenians seem to have found hilarious the double inversion

---

[23] On audience composition, see also Roselli, Chapter 12.

whereby male actors pretended to be women who were temporarily taking over masculine social roles.[24]

Lysistrata's opening words remind the audience that Athenian women enjoy licentious festivals of deities associated with crazed or sexualized ritual behaviour (1–3). The play also refers to more respectable festivals in which Athenian females were prominent, such as the Brauronian festival of Artemis (638f.); the Panathenaea lies behind Lysistrata's expertise in weaving, demonstrated in the extended metaphor by which she conceives administering the state as a process of textile production (667–86). Weaving was a central duty of the goddess's high priestess. She trained the teenaged high-born girls who lived on the acropolis for the nine months leading up to the Panathenaea. These two girls, the *arrêphoroi*, supervised eleven others in weaving the new robe for the goddess's statue. The chorus of *Lysistrata* remember fulfilling the role of *arrêphoros* at the festival in their younger days (638–41). But another, far more mysterious festival, attended by women alone, also lurks behind Aristophanes' plot in *Lysistrata* – the Adonia. One ancient scholar even thought that *Adôniazousai* (*Women Celebrating the Adonia*) might have been an alternative title for this comedy.

The festival of Adonis was not an official, state-sanctioned occasion, but was celebrated by groups of women who seem to have gathered spontaneously. It was viewed as an oriental import, and seems to have been conceived as occurring on the margins of civic culture during the classical period at Athens. The rituals which took place, although performed exclusively by women, were noisy enough to make an impression on Aristophanes' male audience. In *Lysistrata* the magistrate assumes that the takeover of the Acropolis by the women is connected with their Adonis cult: on his arrival, he asks (387–90):

> Has there been another outburst of the women's debauchery,
> The drumming and the nonstop cries of 'Sabazios!'
> And that moaning on the rooftops for Adonis
> Which I once heard when I was in the Assembly?

He specifies the occasion when the drunken carousing and 'lewd songs' (398) for Adonis could be heard during the debate over the Sicilian expedition. These rites were related to the myth in which Aphrodite's youthful favourite

---

[24] See the essays in Babcock (1978). When it comes to symbolic inversion of the roles of free and slave at festivals, there is far less evidence for Athens than e.g., the Roman Saturnalia, but Bowie (1993) 71 has suggested that such a practice is connected with the situation at the outset of *Knights*, where a slave is in control of the house of his master, *Dêmos*.

Adonis was killed in his youth by a boar. Adonis was ritually represented by
seeds which women planted in flowerpots, until the shoots appeared, when
they were carried up to the roofs of houses to wither in the sun. At the death
of the Adonis plants, hideous ritual lamentation ensued for the loss of the
handsome young sexual partner. Some scholars have pointed out that such a
ritual lament finds a parallel in the displacement of Aphrodite by the absence
of men during the war, the deaths of so many prospective bridegrooms in
the Sicilian disaster, and in the sex-strike initiated by Lysistrata. One recent
reading argues that the women perform a kind of Adonis festival on the
Acropolis, thus bringing a women-only, 'private' festival into the heart of
the public domain.[25] But in Durkheimian terms, insofar as Lysistrata is
'universalizing' the emotions undergone by women at the Adonia – grief
for lost erotic excitement and for the vanished beauty of dead youths –
she is indeed orchestrating a 'centripetal' emotional experience that will
create a joint worldview for all the war-traumatized polis. In 411, so soon
after the disaster in Sicily, many spectators will have been feeling acutely the
loss of young men they had loved.

The other play of 411, *Women at the Thesmophoria*, constitutes the
most extended look at a single festival in Aristophanes' surviving *oeuvre*.[26]
Although celebrated in secret by women, the Thesmophoria differed from
the Adonia in that it was state-sanctioned and state-financed. It was widely
celebrated across the Greek world, and thus would have been familiar to
any member of the panhellenic audience at the Dionysia (if it was performed at that festival rather than the Lenaea). The plot reflects the formal
trespassing, enacted at the festival, of women into male space and public
institutions. Indeed, by staging a female 'Assembly' and a 'trial' of Euripides
for his misogynist portraits of women, Aristophanes is pushing the gender role reversal that seems in reality to have structured the Thesmophoria
to its comic limits. In non-political terms, as well, the comedy draws on
attested features of the festival: the ritualized verbal obscenity is expressed
in a high proportion of obscene jokes;[27] the Kinsman is prepared as a sacrificial pig, the traditional Thesmophoria animal (221–2, 237, 239); and
the handling of sexual objects is transformed into suggestive play with the
Kinsman's ithyphallus (643–8).[28] His final release may reflect the custom
(attested in an admittedly a very late source, Hermogenes *Staseis* 29), for
prisoners to be released at the Thesmophoria. But at the end of the play,
the grudge held by the women of Athens against the men who create and

[25] Reitzammer (2008).
[26] The title of a lost play by Aristophanes, *Women Pitching Tents*, certainly implies a
festival context.
[27] See de Wit-Tak (1968). [28] See Bowie (1993) 212, 215.

consume the stereotypical picture of them in Euripidean tragedy suddenly evanesces. The men and women of Athens find a common enemy in the barbarian state-slave who is mercilessly baited. Just as the women who celebrated the Thesmophoria all over the Greek world returned to their private houses at the end of the festival, abruptly restoring the patriarchal public order, so the fictional Thesmophoria-celebrants tell everyone to go home (1228f.).

The extended parodic enactment of tragic theatre in this play, as well as the imagined location at a major state festival in a city-centre sanctuary, mean that the relationship borne by its internal content to its external 'frame' of the drama competition is closer than in most of Aristophanes' plays. The only comedy in which the relationship is more intimate is *Peace*, which featured amongst its cast, as we have already noted, a personification of the opportunity to participate in festivals, *Theôria*. The hero of *Peace*, Trygaeus, is a vine-growing peasant from Athmonon (190f.), an extra-mural deme far north-east of the city centre. Trygaeus is the most panhellenic of all Aristophanes' heroes, leading a chorus consisting of members of numerous Greek states in the retrieval of Peace. He enacts in the realm of comic fiction the present in which his audience found themselves.[29]

The previous summer had seen the Athenians defeated in the terrible battle of Amphipolis. But Cleon and Brasidas, the generals on both sides, had died as a result of this confrontation, leaving the way at last open for peace negotiations between Athens and Sparta (Thuc. 5.16.1). By the time of the Dionysia, the terms of a treaty had been agreed. Two aspects of this diplomatic procedure are central to *Peace*. First, the treaty was ratified, according to Thucydides, 'immediately after the City Dionysia' (5.20.1), which probably means that the Athenian Assembly met on the very day after the end of the festival to elect the delegation which would go to Sparta, where the truce was ratified a few days later (Thuc. 5.18f.). *Peace* was therefore performed just days before peace was inaugurated in reality, and in front of an audience from numerous Greek cities profoundly interested in the collective ceasefire. Secondly, the first clause of the treaty was itself concerned with festivals:

> With regard to the sanctuaries held in common, everyone who so wishes shall be able, according to the customs of his country, to sacrifice in them and visit them and consult oracles in them and attend the festivals in them (*theôrein*) in safety (Thuc. 5.18.1).

---

[29] I argue this in greater detail in Hall (2006) ch. 11.

The mute character *Theôria*, whom Trygaeus bestows upon the Athenians, is thus simultaneously a reference to the vastly increased right to enjoy attending festivals to be assured by the imminent treaty, and a self-conscious comment on the occasion at which the play is performed – one of the play's exceptional number of cases of 'audience participation'.

In *Peace*, the theatrical self-consciousness ('metatheatre') is emphatically related to the here and now of the theatre of Dionysus, and what Trygaeus is doing in this context.[30] Trygaeus is aware to an unusual degree of the mechanics of the theatre, admonishing the crane operator to be careful (174). When he bestows *Theôria* on the officials sitting in the front row (881–908), he breaks the physical boundary between actors and audience. There is a consistently high level of reference to the audience by the actors (50–61, 64–78, probably 263 and 286, 292–300). Characters speculate about what members of the audience are thinking (43–8, 543f., 545–51). Spectators are integrated into the action when they are pelted with grain at the sacrifice (962–5), and when the hero invites them to share the offal with him and his slave (1114–16).

On one occasion there occurs a total confusion, unique in Old Comedy, of what literary scholars used to call the 'art-life' boundary, and theatre specialists, since Diderot's *Treatise on Dramatic Poetry* (1758), have called the 'fourth wall' separating the enacted world of drama from the real world inhabited by the spectators. This remarkable Aristophanic rupture of the 'fourth wall' is the chorus' invitation to the audience at 815–18 'to thrust aside wars and dance with me your friend . . . and celebrate the festival (*heortên*) along with me'. It is impossible to be sure whether the chorus mean the festival within the play (celebrating the reinstatement of Peace), or the City Dionysia extraneous to the play (the prelude to the ratification of peace). They must mean both.

The importance of ensuring that nothing derailed the imminent treaty explains why the homology *Peace* creates between comic plot and festival context is so extreme. Trygaeus' far from frivolous mission is to create in his fantastic world a group identity that can with superficial light-heartedness accommodate not only all Athenians but all Greeks present at the Great Dionysia. This group sensibility relies on the implication that all opponents of the treaty are not only party poopers, but intent on pursuing their own self-interested (and in Durkheim's terms, centrifugal) agendas. Ultimately, the prominence of festivals in Aristophanic comedy is to be explained less in terms of the idea of licence than in terms of the medium's instrumentality in moulding opinion on both pan-Athenian and panhellenic levels.

[30] Slater (2002) ch. 6, especially 130f.

Further reading

The evidence relating to the dramatic festivals in Athens is discussed in Pickard-Cambridge (1988); Csapo and Slater (1995); Wilson (2007c); Rusten *et al.* (2011) 93–131; and (specifically on the Dionysian procession) Csapo (2013). Athenian festival culture in general is the subject of Part II of Parker (2005). Parker (2011) focuses on the experience provided by festivals from the viewpoint of the student of ancient Greek religion.

17

VICTORIA WOHL

Comedy and Athenian law

In his investigation of the political culture of the young American democracy, Alexis de Tocqueville observed that in the United States all issues ultimately end up in court. As a result, he remarks, 'all parties are obliged to borrow the ideas, and even the language, usual in judicial proceedings in their daily controversies'. Introduced by the lawyers who fill public offices and extended to the whole populace by the jury, 'the language of the law thus becomes, in some measure, a vulgar tongue'.[1]

In classical Athens, as in de Tocqueville's America, law constituted a 'vulgar tongue' spoken by the entire populace. The terminology, logic and rhetoric that characterized the *dikastêria* (lawcourts) permeated fifth- and fourth-century Athenian society, making a conspicuous appearance on the comic stage. The comic tongue – itself 'vulgar' in both senses of the word – was well adapted to fluent articulation of the lingua franca of the law: comedy borrowed freely from other contemporary discourses and absorbed them into its own worldview.[2] The communication between the lawcourts and the comic stage ran in both directions: each adopted language and themes from the other. Structurally, too, comedy and the law were similar and symbiotic, both in their internal structure and in their place within the structure of Athenian democracy. The comic *agôn* (contest) constituted a trial in which the theatrical audience was the jury. In this sense, comedy functioned as a kind of counter-jurisdiction, where issues of justice and social order could be debated and resolved, all with a wink and a giggle. But the humour in these comic 'cases' is not supplementary or superfluous: indeed, laughing at the joke – both the joke on stage and its real-world referent – is the very essence of 'comic justice'.

I would like to thank Ariel Vernon for research assistance and Martin Revermann and Alan Sommerstein for their extremely helpful comments.
[1] de Tocqueville (1862: 2003) 223.
[2] See in general Willi (2003a) and on comedy's use of legal language in particular Willi (2003a) 72–9.

That Attic comedy and law shared a common 'tongue' makes sense given that they shared the same audience, the Athenian *dêmos*. For de Tocqueville the class of lawyers, with their specialized legal knowledge and high social rank, injected an aristocratic influence into American democracy that tempered the sovereignty of the people embodied in the popular jury.[3] But Athens had no professional lawyers. It was the litigant's job to determine which laws were relevant to his case and how best to present them. Litigants could buy speeches from professional speech-writers (*logographoi*) but they delivered these themselves in court as if they were their own words. In fact, legal expertise was considered suspect, and if the litigant had any he generally hid it behind a mask of inexperience.[4] Nor was there a class of judges trained to interpret the law. Every court case was decided directly by the convict-or-acquit vote of the jury, with no instruction from experts or time for formal deliberation. Indeed, there could hardly have been deliberation given the size of juries: 201, 401, 501, or even more, depending on the sort of case. The *dikastai* – the word is alternately translated as 'judges' and 'jurors' – were average Athenian citizens, chosen daily by lot from a jury pool itself chosen annually by lot. Jurors were expected to have no more detailed knowledge of the law than they had picked up in their daily lives.[5] But given Athens' notorious litigiousness that could be quite a bit: the potential jury pool in any given year was 6,000 citizens, roughly 10–20 per cent of the total citizen body. Whether as litigants, witnesses, or jurors, Athenian citizens were in direct and constant contact with the law.[6]

This populace of experienced, though untrained, jurors was the notional audience of Attic comedy, which takes for granted broad familiarity with the language and procedures of the courts.[7] Aristophanes' *Birds*, for instance,

---

[3] de Tocqueville (1862: 2003) 217–23, 224f.

[4] On the amateurism of Athenian law and the bias against experts see especially Ober (1989) 174–7; Todd (1996); Christ (1998) 203–24.

[5] For the details of the jury system, see MacDowell (1978) 33–40; Todd (1993) 82–91. There is a clear synopsis of the Athenian legal system as a whole in Lanni (2006) 31–40.

[6] Harris (1994) 135 calculates that the average Athenian citizen would have served as a juror once every five years and heard up to twenty cases during his term. Strepsiades in Aristophanes' *Clouds* cannot pick out Athens on a map because it does not show the dikasts sitting (208). On the idea and reality of Athenian litigiousness, see Christ (1998). I focus here exclusively on Athenian comedy and law. Whether Sicilian comedy ever engaged with legal procedures in the same way as Athenian comedy is impossible to tell. None of the preserved titles of plays by Epicharmus suggests that it did, and of the few remaining fragments only one, fr. 146, contains legal terms (*dika*, *katadika*). This fragment seems to imagine a scenario similar to that at the end of *Wasps*, with drunkenness leading to lawsuits.

[7] The composition of the actual audience is a matter of debate. The general assumption that comedy's audience was broadly stratified by class and gender (see Revermann

although not directly about the legal system, is full of juridical humour. Peisetairos and Euelpides have left Athens looking for a peaceful place to live: the objectionable busyness of Athenian life is epitomized by the fact that 'Athenians spend their whole lives singing in the courts' (40f.). These two self-proclaimed 'anti-jurors' (*apêliasta*: 110) set out to build a new city among the birds, but their new community is soon infested by the same problems that plagued the old. Among other nuisances, they are visited by a 'decree-salesman' (*psêphismatopôlês*: 1038) selling 'new laws'. Peisetairos tries to drive him off but he is nabbed as a witness by the inspector who summons Peisetairos on a charge of assault (*hubris*) and seconds the charge by citing relevant decrees (1046–55). No sooner do the heroes get rid of these two litigious intruders than others appear: a son who has heard that there is no law amongst the birds (as there was in Athens) against beating one's father (1337–71); a sycophant (a vexatious litigant, who brought cases for profit) who believes that obtaining wings will allow him to ply his trade more efficiently (1410–69). The play suggests that litigiousness is an ineradicable part of the Athenian character. Its humour rests on general familiarity with legal personalities (sycophants, inspectors), legal procedure (the protocol for issuing summons, for instance), and the provisions of the statutes themselves: in another scene, Peisetairos quotes the law of inheritance verbatim to the hero/god Heracles in order to convince him that, as a bastard, he cannot inherit his father Zeus's estate and is thus better off joining their new city (1641–75).[8]

If comedy appealed to its audience as experienced jurors, Athenian litigants also appealed to their jurors as experienced theatregoers.[9] Aristophanes mentions litigants who use humour to win over their jurors (*Wasps* 566f.) and the logographer Lysias provides some conspicuous examples of the strategy. Lysias 1 *On the Murder of Eratosthenes* is the defence speech of one Euphiletus for the murder of Eratosthenes. He claims that he caught Eratosthenes in bed with his wife (homicide under those circumstances was justifiable under Athenian law); but Eratosthenes' relatives argue Euphiletus lured Eratosthenes into his house as a pretext for killing him. Euphiletus'

(2006a) 166–9) has been challenged by Sommerstein (1997), who proposes that, given the cost and effort of attending the theatre, the audience would have been more affluent, educated and politically conservative than the general citizen body. See further Roselli, Chapter 12. For my purposes here the notional identity of theatrical audience, jury and *dêmos* is more important than the real differences between the three bodies.

[8] Passages like this make Aristophanes a primary source for fifth-century legal practice and thought: see Todd (1993) 40–2; Christ (1998) 16, 53–6, 61–3, 145–7.

[9] On the audience of Athenian trials, see Bers (1985); Hall (1995) 43f.; Lanni (1997). Hall (1995) stresses the performative nature of ancient trials and reads the court case as a drama, with its own stagecraft, cast of characters and *peripeteia*.

defence rests on an argument from character (*êthos*). He paints himself as a guileless and doting husband, slow to notice the tell-tale signs of his wife's affair: a squeaking door-hinge, her made-up face. His account, as John Porter (1997) has argued, is informed by a 'comic adultery scenario'. Euphiletus' gullibility, the sexual reversal where the wife playfully locks her husband in the women's quarters while she meets her lover, the dramatic image of the couple caught *in flagrante* – all these elements have their parallels in the plots of Old and New Comedy.[10] Indeed, the parallels are so close that Porter concludes the speech was composed not for an actual trial but as a rhetorical exercise.[11] But if, as Porter suggests, Lysias' audience was familiar with the comic plot of the adulterous wife and inclined to sympathize with its bumbling but good-natured cuckold, then Lysias' defence narrative would be not just a plausible forensic strategy but an effective one.[12]

Speeches like Lysias 1 suggest a bi-directional symbiosis between the law-courts and the forensic stage, as each adopted the other's 'vulgar tongue' to address and persuade its audience. That symbiosis was particularly intimate in Attic New Comedy of the later fourth century. Adele Scafuro has shown how characters in the plays of New Comedy (the extant plays of Menander and others preserved primarily in Roman adaptations) exhibit a 'forensic disposition': they call upon the law easily, know it well, and use it adeptly to pursue their comic schemes.[13] The central scene of

---

[10] Porter (1997) 426–33: he adduces especially Ar. *Women at the Thesmophoria* 476–89 and Men. *Samia* 219–34, 238–48. Even the names of the protagonists in this forensic drama seem borrowed from the comic stage: Eratosthenes means 'strong in passion'; Euphiletus, 'well loved' (Porter (1997) 437).

[11] Porter (1997) 433–41. Contra, see Gagarin (2003).

[12] Another noteworthy example of this strategy is Lysias 24 *On the Invalid*. The speaker is suing for the continuation of his disability pension, against the claim of his opponent that his income disqualifies him from the dole. The speaker aims to show that his opponent is not serious in his charges 'but is just playing around (*paizôn*), not wishing to persuade you that what he says, but wishing to make a joke of me (*kômôidein*), as if he were saying something clever' (18). He argues this point by making a joke of himself. Throughout the speech, the impoverished invalid parodies the rhetoric and persona of elite litigants in the same way that the everyman protagonists of Old Comedy parodied the heroes of tragedy. Thus, as Phillip Harding ((1994) 203) says, the whole speech 'is a parody of the *dikanikos logos* [forensic speech], or rather it stands in the same relationship to serious rhetoric as the comic perversion of tragedy (paratragedy) does to its original – language of the high style put into the mouth of a comic character in an inappropriate situation'. Lysias 1 and 24 present the litigant himself in a comic light. This strategy carried the obvious risk that the jurors would laugh at, not with the litigant, and it was thus used sparingly. More common was the deployment of comedy against an opponent, a strategy used extensively in, e.g., Aeschines 1 *Against Timarchus*. On comedy in Greek rhetoric see further Harding (1994); Hall (1995) 56f.

[13] Scafuro (1997) 25. On law in Menander see also Omitowoju (2002) 145–7; Lape (2004) 15–17, 71f.

arbitration in Menander's *Epitrepontes* (*Men at Arbitration*) provides one vivid example. There the charcoal-burner Syros and shepherd Daos are fighting over ownership of some trinkets found with an abandoned infant and refer their dispute for arbitration to Smicrines who is, unbeknownst to any of them, the infant's grandfather. In presenting their cases, these two lowly characters make sophisticated use of both legal diction (e.g., 226–8) and forensic argumentation (including Daos' hypothetical argument at 283–6 and Syros' claim to sue on behalf of the baby at 304–7). Focusing on scenes like this, Scafuro argues that 'the courts provided a meta-grammar of protocols for settlement'.[14] Here too the lines of influence run in both directions, for Scafuro suggests that in acting out familiar forensic scenarios the characters of New Comedy dramatize the 'staginess' of Athenian law, with its creation of plausible personae, recruitment of witnesses, and formalized presentation of the issues.[15] The forensic plots of the comic stage were close kin to the dramas enacted daily on the 'forensic stage'.

This continuum between courts and theatre can be seen, for example, in Menander's *Samia*. Moschion has impregnated Plangon, the girl next door. Fearing her father, they pretend the baby belongs to Chrysis, the mistress of Moschion's adoptive father, Demeas. When Demeas learns Moschion is the baby's father he believes he has been cuckolded by his own son. The play stages a comic trial of Moschion for *moikheia* (adultery, rape or seduction) with both the courtesan Chrysis and the free girl Plangon. Not only is *Samia* replete with juridical tropes and diction (e.g., 325–45, 506–14, 571–84), but its plot is structured by Moschion's 'crimes' and his defence, presented before an audience addressed as jurors (*andres*: 269, 329). The eventual discovery of the child's true parentage acquits the youth. The laws of marriage and legitimacy are reaffirmed, as Moschion's (supposed) crime in the case of Chrysis is revealed as a misunderstanding and his (actual) crime in the case of Plangon rectified by marriage. The play ends with a wedding (complete with legal marriage formula, 725–9) that reconciles father and son, resolves conflict between neighbours, secures the legitimate reproduction of the household, and reunites lovers (both Moschion and Plangon and Demeas and Chrysis). Its romantic imbroglios staged in a forensic idiom, the comedy's happy ending offers a resolution at once judicial and dramatic.[16]

The relationship between law and comedy that appears as mutually supportive in the later fourth century may have been more antagonistic in the fifth. The end of the fifth century, with its rapid succession of

[14] Scafuro (1997) 9, and on the arbitration scene of *Epitrepontes*, 154–61.
[15] Scafuro (1997) 66f.
[16] Scafuro (1997) 101–3, 260–5; Omitowoju (2002) 197–203; Lape (2004) 137–70.

calamitous events – Athens' defeat in the Peloponnesian War, the tyrannical reign of the Thirty oligarchs, a brief but devastating civil war – changed the nature of both Athenian democracy and comedy. The popular sovereignty that defined the democracy of the fifth century gave way to a more stable but also less vibrant and immediate rule of law in the fourth, as the laws were newly codified and given precedence over the decrees of the Council and Assembly.[17] While the democracy became more institutionalized, the focus of comedy shifted from the public sphere to the private: the intensely political plays of Aristophanes gave way to the largely domestic dramas of Menander.[18] This double transformation in comedy and democracy may also have transformed the relation between them. Robert Wallace has argued that whereas fifth-century Old Comedy frequently lambasts the jury system, sometimes going so far that it came up against censorship laws designed to protect the polis, in the more 'regulated, restrained, and domesticated' Athens of the fourth century 'comic drama no longer stood in opposition to Athens' government or legal system, but reinforced their order. Laws often provide the framework for dramatic action, now in the private rather than public sphere'.[19] For him, the tight symbiosis between law and comedy in the fourth century marks a historical discontinuity from the more tense and oppositional relationship between the two discourses in the fifth century.

Many scholars have understood fifth-century Old Comedy as an antinomian discourse that stood in opposition to the norms of Athenian political and social life. The plays of Old Comedy are sometimes taken to exemplify the licence of the carnival, as described by Bakhtin, to constitute 'a second world and a second life outside officialdom' in which the structures of 'official' polis life were temporarily suspended and inverted.[20] The extant plays of Aristophanes provide some evidence for this antinomian reading of comedy. Many of the plays either begin (e.g., *Birds, Lysistrata*) or end (e.g., *Clouds, Wasps, Assembly Women*) with a fantasy of escape from society's customs, norms and laws (*nomoi*) and many more comic plots are driven by resistance to those *nomoi*. In the topsy-turvy world of *Birds*, for instance, the chorus leader in the parabasis invites the audience to come 'live pleasantly' in Cloud-Cuckoo-Land, for 'everything proscribed by law as shameful (*aiskhra*) where you live is fine (*kala*) among us birds' (755f.). He lists the

---

[17] Ostwald (1986) especially 497–524.
[18] See Lape and Moreno, Chapter 18. This schematization necessarily over-simplifies what was in fact a complex transformation in both Athenian politics and Athenian comedy; see especially Sidwell, Chapter 3 and Sommerstein, Chapter 15.
[19] Wallace (2005) 358.
[20] Bakhtin (1984) 6. See especially Carrière (1979) 29–32; Reckford (1987) 441–98; von Möllendorff (1995) 73–109. Edwards (2002) 29–32 offers a critical survey of these works; cf. Henderson (1990) 272–5, 285–7; Goldhill (1991) 176–88.

inversions: among the birds it is permissible and even admirable (*kalon*) for a son to fight his father (757–9); runaway slaves and persons of dubious (or spurious) ancestry are perfectly acceptable members of society (760–8); adultery, one of the most serious crimes in classical Athens and subject to severe legal sanction, is not only licit but facilitated by the wings that allow an adulterer to visit his lover while her husband is sitting in the theatre enjoying the play (793–6).[21]

Birds ends with a celebration of this new antinomian polis, but more typically in Aristophanic comedy the temporary escape from *nomoi* ultimately serves to reaffirm their importance and necessity. In *Clouds*, Strepsiades sets out to acquire oratorical skill so that he can 'twist lawsuits' (*strepsodikêsai*) and give his creditors the slip (434; cf. 1151–3). He sends his son Pheidippides to Socrates' 'Thinkery' to learn 'how to argue against everything just' (*panta ta dikai' antilegein*: 888) and is delighted when Pheidippides exhibits his new rhetorical skills by picking apart (in typical forensic fashion) the intent of Solon's law concerning summons for debt and proving that the law's spirit, if not its letter, works in his father's favour (1171–1212).[22] The old man is less pleased, however, when Pheidippides uses his newfound skills to argue that it is just for a son to beat his father (1405): to Strepsiades' complaint that such behaviour goes against *nomos* (1420), his son argues that *nomoi* were made by men and can be changed by them; that among animals it is natural for sons to beat fathers; that it is no less right for sons to beat fathers than fathers sons (1410–46). Strepsiades comes to rue the freedom from the law that he had earlier sought (1303–20), and the play ends with a strong reaffirmation of the sanctity of and need for *nomoi*, as Strepsiades and the chorus join to burn down the school where Pheidippides learned his antinomian rhetoric. Strepsiades chooses this course of action, moreover, in preference to 'stitching together a case' against Socrates (1481–5). The irony of lawless violence deployed to punish lawless violence merely emphasizes the point that when the law, corrupted by sophistic rhetoric, becomes unavailable as a means of resolving conflict, the only alternative is violence.

This common pattern of temporary inversion and ultimate reaffirmation of the legal status quo has led many scholars to question the relevance of Bakhtin's model of carnival to Old Comedy. As Anthony Edwards

---

[21] Konstan (1995) 29–44 analyses *Birds*' contradictory relation to *nomoi*. See also Carey (2000) 67f. and 76f.

[22] Johnstone (1999) 24–33 discusses this mode of reading the law in Athenian forensic oratory.

notes, the 'oppositional and antiauthoritarian character' of Bakhtin's carnival hardly seems to apply to Athenian comedy, which was 'precisely an official, state-sponsored genre, presented at a public festival supported by public revenues'.[23] Just how antinomian could Old Comedy be, given its performance context? Edwards argues that it was, in fact, anti-authoritarian, but that the authority it opposed was not that of elite officialdom (as in Bakhtin) but of the *dêmos*. He points to the general conservatism of Old Comedy's politics and suggests that the genre appropriated the originally demotic laughter of the carnival as a weapon against the *dêmos* itself.[24] When comedy, the vehicle of popular laughter, becomes an institutionalized arm of Athens' popular sovereignty, the people itself becomes the target of its oppositional humour. While Edwards' theory of Old Comedy's double-inversion preserves its antinomian status, other scholars have viewed the comic theatre not as an escape from the law but instead as a counter-jurisdiction working in tandem with the courts, a place where non-normative (if not outright illegal) behaviour was policed and subjected to the rough justice of public humiliation.[25] Jeffrey Henderson, in his important article 'The *Dêmos* and Comic Competition', stresses the structural homology between the courts, Assembly and theatre. In each, an individual performer (whether political orator, litigant or poet) competed before a mass audience, whose approval granted victory of his policies in the Assembly, his suit in court, or his play in the dramatic competition.[26] This shared performative dynamic, as well as a shared civic ideology, made comedy and the courts distinct but parallel institutional venues for addressing the same social and political issues. From this perspective, comic licence is seen not as saturnalian and oppositional, but as an extension of democratic *parrhêsia*, the right and duty

---

[23] Edwards (2002) 29. See also the discussion of Bakhtin in Goldhill (1991) 177–88 and his astute conclusion: 'The shifting levels of fictional representation – a hallmark of comedy – cannot be reduced to mere "comic inversion". In the interplay of comic fictions, "transgression" is not necessarily the polar opposite of "norm". Comedy in and as performance tests – *negotiates* as well as *celebrates* – the possibilities of transgression' (188).

[24] Edwards (2002) 38–41. On the conservatism of Aristophanic politics see Ste Croix (1972) 355–76 and Sommerstein, Chapter 15.

[25] Henderson (1990) 295 puts well the policing function of comedy: its ridicule 'uses complaints about disruptive but otherwise unpunishable behavior . . . as a form of social control . . . Festive ridicule, in punishing misbehavior not, or not yet, in the community's power to punish by force (as in court), thus lies somewhere between doing something about misbehavior and doing nothing about it.'

[26] Henderson (1990); cf. Ober and Strauss (1990). These scholars focus on the political, not the juridical, but the line between the two was porous in Athens: see Yunis (1988). See also Hall (1995) on the isomorphism of theatrical and forensic performance.

VICTORIA WOHL

of every Athenian citizen to speak up in public about the issues facing the polis.[27]

This *parrhêsia* operates within the comic plot: when Dicaeopolis (whose name means 'Just Polis') signs his own private peace treaty with the Spartans in Aristophanes' *Acharnians*, this citizen's frank expression of his individual opinion is imagined as a means to the end of a peaceful and just polis.[28] *Parrhêsia* also operates at the level of plays as a whole. Aristophanes' merciless ridicule of Cleon in *Knights* is a famous example: Aristophanes represents this criticism not just as an exercise of his rights as a citizen but as his duty as a self-proclaimed educator of his fellow-citizens (*Ach.* 628–64; *Wasps* 1029–50, 1284–91; *Peace* 747–60). In this case comedy functions like the juridical procedures of *dokimasia* (confirmation hearing) or *euthunê* (audit): it holds prominent individuals up for public scrutiny, exaggerating their personal flaws and the failings of their policies for comic effect and asking the democratic audience to judge the merits of its critique.[29] Indeed, these theatrical hearings could have real judicial consequences. In 426 Cleon sued Aristophanes for slandering the city (*Ach.* 377–82).[30] More gravely, Aristophanes' distorted caricature of Socrates in *Clouds* may have contributed to the philosopher's prosecution and, ultimately, his death sentence (Pl. *Ap.* 18b4–d2, 19b3–c5).

As a public scrutiny of Athens' leading figures, Old Comedy was a vital arena for the exercise of *dêmokratia*, the authority (*kratos*) of the *dêmos*: in the theatre, just as in the courts and the Assembly (*ekklêsia*), the *dêmos* sat in judgment and passed verdict on the competitive appeals of (generally elite) speakers seeking to persuade them.[31] Ps.-Aristotle's *Constitution of the Athenians* lists Solon's institution of the *dikastêria* as one of the most 'populist' (*dêmotikôtata*) features of his democratic reforms and the one

---

[27] Isoc. 8.14. For recent discussions of *parrhêsia*, see the essays in Sluiter and Rosen (2004).

[28] The extent to which Dicaeopolis acts in the common interest and his personal victory is a collective victory has been questioned, most recently by Wilson (2007a) 271–78.

[29] Henderson (1990) 307. The fact that Cleon was re-elected as strategos the year after *Knights* was awarded first prize does not invalidate this understanding of comedy's political function, but does warn us not to press the parallels too far. See Henderson (1990) 298.

[30] On Cleon's suit against Aristophanes and the legal limits on comic ridicule see schol. ad *Ach.* 378; Halliwell (1991); Wallace (1994); Henderson (1998); Sommerstein (2004b); Wallace (2005) 362–8, and on the conflict between Aristophanes and Cleon more broadly, McGlew (2002) 86–111 and Sommerstein, Chapter 15.

[31] Plato (*Gorgias* 502d) considers drama a type of *dêmêgoria* (political speech) that aims to persuade the *dêmos*. Henderson (1990) 276–307; Ober and Strauss (1990) examine the dynamic between elite competitors and mass audience in relation to the theatre; on this dynamic more generally see Ober (1989).

330

that most 'strengthened the masses', the reason being that 'the *dêmos*, having sovereign power over the verdict, also has sovereign power over the state' (*Ath. Pol.* 9.1). The 'Old Oligarch', applying his usual socio-economic lens, sees a similar power relation at work in the comic theatre: he claims the *dêmos* didn't allow comic poets to lampoon itself but only prominent individuals, who were generally rich and powerful (2.18). The *dêmos*' role as critical audience/jury seemed to ancient political thinkers a vehicle of its political sovereignty. Whether exercised through laughter in the theatre of Dionysus or through its vote in the courts, the power of the *dêmos* in its role as audience/jury enacted foundational democratic convictions: a belief in the right and duty of the *dêmos* to scrutinize its leaders and their policies; a confidence in the average citizen, with no training beyond his own native intelligence and political savoir-faire, to reach a correct verdict; a faith that the *dêmos*' judgments will make the polis *eunomos*, orderly, lawful and just.

Aristophanes' *Wasps* exemplifies with particular clarity comedy's function as a counter-jurisdiction to the courts and takes up explicitly the contribution of the jury system to the *dêmos*' sovereignty. As the play opens the main character, Philocleon, is afflicted with a strange disease (*noson*: 71): 'he is jury-crazy (*philêliastês*) like no one else and is in love with judging' (*erâi . . . tou dikazein*: 88–9). His particular passion is handing down convictions, to anyone and everyone. His son, Bdelycleon, hopes to cure him of this mania, by first locking him in the house, then (when that doesn't work) proving that jury duty is bad for him, and finally arranging for him to try a case at home and tricking him into an acquittal. Having finally forced his father to submit, Bdelycleon promises him a comfortable retirement: he takes him to a symposium (an elite drinking party), outfitting him in fancy clothes and teaching him the requisite manners. But the old dog cannot be taught new tricks: he insults the guests at the symposium, makes a fool and a nuisance of himself, and in the final scene returns from the party, drunk and disorderly, leaving a trail of pending lawsuits in his wake.

Wasps is permeated by the law at every level: language, imagery, plot, character, space, gesture. When Bdelycleon has his father try a case at home, he turns not only the household but the very stage into a *dikastêrion*; the structural parallels between theatrical audience and jury are literalized as the audience watch Philocleon try the case of the dog Labes for stealing a hunk of cheese (760–1009).[32] The scene parodies in exacting detail the procedure of an Athenian trial – complete with kitchen utensils as witnesses – and

---

[32] This parody of the courts is simultaneously a political parody, in which Labes stands in for the general Laches and the prosecuting dog from Kudathenaion (895) for Cleon. On the political dispute between the two see MacDowell (1971) 163f. on *Wasps* 240; Olson

the kinds of arguments made by litigants in real cases, from the recitation of past services to the community (950–9) to the appeals for pity from the defendant's pups (976–8). This overtly forensic scene also highlights the juridical structure of the play as a whole: the *agôn* between father and son is staged as a trial judged by the chorus (and audience) according to the dictum 'do not judge until you've heard both sides' (725f., cf. 919f.), an allusion to the dikastic oath sworn by Athenian jurors. As the two characters deliver their speeches, the poetic structure of the play melds with its legal theme. As James McGlew remarks, 'legal metaphors become literal, as Aristophanes transforms his stage into a court, interweaving the Athenian citizen's identity as juror into the play's dramatic core'.[33] What is on trial in this play is precisely the law. The play exposes to comic ridicule the foibles and failings of the popular court system. It takes aim at the decrepit, impoverished jurors whose 'waspish' ill-temper makes them always eager to convict (223–7, 403–7, 423–5, 453–5), who pre-judge cases based on prejudice and personal whim – never considerations of justice – and want 'to do some damage' with their vote (320–2, 340). It also attacks the powerful litigants who kowtow to these jurors and beg them for mercy (558–75), the sycophants who fix cases for profit (691–4), and the high and mighty (*kalo te kagathoi*) who turn their crimes into jokes and so avoid prosecution (1256–63). Above all, it assails the politics of the jury system. Philocleon argues that there is no one 'happier or more blessed than a juror, or who lives with more awesome luxury' (550f.). Supplicated by the powerful, entertained by the famous, coddled by grateful politicians (especially Cleon, who 'holds us in his arms and swats the flies away', 597), the jurors enjoy a 'mighty power' (*megalên arkhên*: 620) no lesser than Zeus's. Bdelycleon counters that jurors are in fact the slaves of those they think they rule (518f.). They delight in their jury pay, but it is only the smallest fraction of the revenue that comes in from the Empire, an Empire won through their own past naval service; most of that income is swallowed by bribe-taking politicians who pay the jurors a pittance in exchange for their faithful support in the courts (655–723). Far from a 'mighty power', jury duty is in fact a 'mighty servitude' (*megalê douleia*: 682). This *agôn* puts on trial the notion that the

(1996) 138–42. The names of the two lead characters ('Lovecleon' and 'Loathecleon') indicate the inextricability of law and politics in the play.

33 McGlew (2004) 13. The conflation of poetic and rhetorical *agôn* is particularly self-conscious in Aristophanes' *Frogs*, where the subject on trial is drama itself and the judge Dionysus, god of theatre. But the language and argumentation there is drawn more from political than forensic contest. Phrynichus' *Muses*, which competed against *Frogs* in 405, may have staged a similar aesthetic *agôn* in a more explicitly juridical idiom, to judge by the mention of the voting pebble and urn in fr. 33 K-A. On this lost play, see Harvey (2000) 100–8.

popular courts enacted the *dêmos'* sovereignty. The verdict is equivocal: the chorus declare Bdelycleon the winner but Philocleon refuses to be persuaded (725–63). But by juxtaposing the ideal of the *dêmos'* jurisprudential hegemony and the political realities (at least as Bdelycleon sees them) that limited that democratic power, the play seems to urge the *dêmos*, as Henderson puts it, 'to look through the lies, compromises, self-interest, and general arrogance of their leaders and to remember who was ultimately in charge'.[34]

Flawed as it may be, the jury system is shown to be indispensable to Athenian society. *Wasps* follows the same pattern of critique and reaffirmation of *nomoi* that we saw above in *Clouds*. Bdelycleon finally convinces his father to give up jury duty and join the symposium, but his anti-social behaviour in his new guise as hubristic aristocrat shows the need for the legal system he so adored in his old persona as punitive juror (1332–42). As he insults the other guests, abducts the flute-girl and assaults innocent bystanders, he finds himself the object of the sort of legal actions he used to convict. In the play's exaggerated antithesis, one is either juror or criminal, and when Philocleon throws away his voting urns (1339), he throws away *nomos* altogether. The resulting vision – comic licence in the form of social anarchy and rampant lawlessness – suggests that the jury system, whatever the failings or false-consciousness of the jurors, is essential to a just and orderly polis.

Wasps demonstrates that the city needs its laws. At the same time, it shows that the city – and the law – needs comedy. The play's dynamic of critique and reaffirmation suggests that the jury system be embraced only after it has been subjected to the scrutiny provided by the play itself, its flaws exposed to public view and therefore (potentially, if not actually) rectified. Justice comes, at the end of the play, not through the punishment of Philocleon's lawless sympotic behaviour nor through the 'cure' of his forensic disease, but through a vindication of his passion for the courts: the substance of his son's complaints has been acknowledged by the laughter it generated but his repudiation of the legal system is ultimately rejected. 'Comic justice' thus works together with civic justice and its institutions, reaffirming them in a form improved by comic critique.

To say this is to suggest that comic justice operates by inculcating in its audience a specific prosecutorial disposition, a readiness to laugh at – and through this laughter to put on trial – the laws, customs and institutions

---

[34] Henderson (1990) 312. He is speaking of the political project of Aristophanic comedy in general. The politics of *Wasps* are well analysed by Konstan (1995) 15–28; Olson (1996); McGlew (2004). Carey (2000) 79–83 argues that critiques of the legal system in *Wasps* and other Aristophanic comedies accurately reflect contemporary anxieties about the law.

most vital to the polis. On the one hand, this critical disposition characterizes Athenian democracy in general, with its ideology of *parrhêsia* and institutional mechanisms of public accountability. On the other hand, it is specific to Old Comedy, which both demands this sensibility of its audience and develops it by exposing virtually everything to mockery. *Wasps* invites its audience to laugh at every position, including mutually exclusive positions: both Philocleon and Bdelycleon, both the decrepit jurors and the hubristic elite, both the courts and their critics. Through its equal-opportunity mockery the play asks its audience to exercise a generalized scepticism, what Carole Clover terms 'an active paranoid imagination'.[35]

In other words, it asks its audience to adopt precisely the same indiscriminately prosecutorial attitude that it ridicules in its own chorus and elderly protagonist. Like Philocleon before his transformation, the old jurors of the chorus are suspicious, sharp-spirited, quick to anger (223–7, 404–7, 422–5, 455). This 'waspish' character is not just the ill-temper of grumpy old men (106–8); instead, as Danielle Allen has argued, it is the *orgê* (passion, anger) that, properly controlled, characterized engaged citizenship in democratic Athens.[36] If this sensibility makes these jurors over-eager to 'sting' with their convictions and thus leads to miscarriages of justice, the only solution to that injustice is more of the same sensibility: the audience must approach the jurors' prosecutorial zeal in their verdicts with their own prosecutorial zeal in the form of their laughter. They must become as waspish as the chorus, whether they are judging court cases, political debates or the comic *agôn* between Philocleon and his son. In Athens' courts the jurors swore as part of their dikastic oath 'I will listen to both the plaintiff and the defendant equally.'[37] Old Comedy's version of that oath would have the audience swear to laugh at both (or all) sides equally. Even the playwright himself is not immune, for we are reminded in the parabasis of *Wasps* (1015–50) that the play is part of a theatrical *agôn* and Aristophanes himself resembles the litigants he ridicules for entertaining the jurors with jokes and spectacles in

[35] Clover (1998) 108. The disposition inculcated by Old Comedy is akin to the cognitive state she argues is produced in modern America by the adversarial trial, a state she sees characterized by close ('paranoid') attention to points of fact and hermeneutic agility in evaluating truth claims based on them. The 'voluntary prosecutor' is another example of this sensibility in Athens: the law allowing individuals to bring charges against anyone they believed to be harming the state encouraged all citizens to think like potential prosecutors.

[36] Allen (2000) 50–9, 128–33, (2003) 83–4; cf. Konstan (1995) 19; McGlew (2004) 22. As Martin Revermann points out to me, such semi-theriomorphic choruses are extremely rare in Attic comedy; the wasp/man chorus thus functions as an embodied metaphor.

[37] Dem. 24.151. For the reconstruction of the oath's text see, most recently, Mirhady (2007) 49–51.

the hope of winning their vote.[38] This equal mockery of all positions is not a lack of political commitment on comedy's part, as is sometimes assumed, but in fact its greatest contribution to Athens' political culture, for in this way it cultivates the critical disposition, the 'active paranoid imagination', through which the *dêmos* both exercised and guarded its sovereign power in the Assembly and the lawcourts. This same disposition, I am suggesting, constituted comic justice, for when the audience was willing to laugh at everything equally, casting aside its biases and preconceptions to approach every issue with equitable scepticism and even-handed mockery, then justice was done in the Theatre of Dionysus.

Further reading

Clear and detailed overviews of the Athenian legal system are offered by MacDowell (1978) and Todd (1993). Accessible state-of-the-art essays on various aspects of Greek law, including its relation to contemporary drama, can be found in Gargarin and Cohen (2005). Pitched more for the expert but still of interest to the general reader are the essays in Cartledge, Millett and Todd (1990). Recent years have seen the publication of a number of interpretations of Athenian law as a discourse: one might begin with Carey (1998); Johnstone (1999); Lanni (2006); Wohl (2010). But the more specific topics of comedy in law and law in comedy remain under-examined: for the former, see Harding (1994); Porter (1997); for the latter, Scafuro (1997); Carey (2000); Lape (2004).

[38] The chorus count it an injustice (*adikeisthai*: 1017) that the audience failed to vote Aristophanes first prize the previous year (for *Clouds*), especially when he has done them so much good and at such risk to himself – all typical forensic tropes.

18

SUSAN LAPE AND ALFONSO MORENO

Comedy and the social historian

The comedies of Aristophanes and Menander present numerous aspects of life in democratic and early Hellenistic Athens; yet, although we find meditations on politics, wars, economic transactions, love and marriage, comic representations obviously do not passively or straightforwardly mirror historical realities. Rather, as a form of public drama, Old and New Comedy each developed its own conventions of comic-world making. Moreover, as the conventions of Old and New Comedy differ, so too do their plots or characteristic forms of content. Whereas Aristophanes' comedy is often concerned with the nature of democratic and imperial politics, Menander's comedy usually revolves around the Athenian household and its composition. Accordingly, these differences in convention and content have an impact on the way and extent to which their comedies can be used as a source for social history. That said, while there are some obvious differences in the historical narratives we can reconstruct from Aristophanes and Menander, there are also some key continuities. We know that central areas of Athenian culture remained stable through the fifth and fourth centuries, as did poets' desire to dramatize them.

As is well known, Aristophanes' comedy more explicitly engages with Athenian contemporary affairs than does Menander's comedy. Aristophanes portrays the concerns of citizens in an imperial democracy, whereas Menander depicts the familial and romantic dramas of ordinary Athenians; to be sure, the protagonists in Menander's comedies are usually citizens, but the political dimension of this identification is much less marked than in Aristophanes. Characters in Aristophanes' comedies comment directly on politicians, the worth of their policies, war, the use and abuse of the courts and the Assembly, economic and class tensions, as well as on the role of philosophers and women in the polis. By contrast, references to political institutions, politicians and even the wars that plagued early Hellenistic Athens, have been largely supplanted in Menander's comedy by a concern for the household, its composition and reproduction. Whereas

Aristophanic comedy abounds with references to known extra-dramatic realities, Menander's comedies create a self-contained repetitive fantasy where citizens worry only about their romantic lives or those of their family members.

Although Aristophanes would seem to offer much more for historians than Menander – at least on the level of narrative content – it is Menander's comedy that has long been culled as a source for social history. Aristophanes has often not been trusted as a reliable historical source because his 'purpose' was to mock, shock and entertain his audiences, rather than to inform or provide an accurate mirror of contemporary realities. In other words, the conventions of Old Comedy have been seen as veiling the historical realities that so obviously inform Aristophanic narratives. By contrast, the very fact that Menander presents his dramas of civic reproduction in the narrative mode of literary naturalism has led historians to assume that his comic representations more accurately capture something of the historical reality. Most egregiously, some critics and historians have concluded that Menander's comedy testifies to the decline of the polis and the political and the concomitant rise of private life and the individual. At the risk of over-simplification, it appears that Aristophanes' comedy has been rejected as a historical source because of the evidently extravagant generic conventions of Old Comedy, whereas Menander's comedy has been embraced as a source for a kind of social and political history on the basis of its seemingly guile-less generic conventions: its naturalism, its sustained effort to maintain the dramatic illusion, as well as the fiction that the world it presents is ordinary, natural and inevitable. In what follows, we seek to redress this imbalance by arguing that Aristophanes and Menander each offer a great deal to the social historian. But as the conventions of Old Comedy and New Comedy differ, so too do the challenges they pose to historians seeking to excavate the historical realities informing the comic plots.

Methodological problems

We begin by placing comedy in the context of other sources, and assessing their respective advantages and problems. For the fifth century BCE the picture is complicated by the extreme (even if often unacknowledged) peculiarity of the surviving evidence. First, among contemporary sources, the two principal narratives by Herodotus and Thucydides cover the beginning and end of the century, respectively, but leave the central period of almost fifty years (479–432 BCE) a yawning gap, without more illumination than a brief, chronologically imprecise, and probably tendentious excursus (the so-called '*Pentecontaetia*') introduced by Thucydides to support his idea of the inevitability of the Peloponnesian War.[1] Secondly, public inscriptions, whose frequency from the late 460s onwards leads some historians to speak of an 'epigraphic habit', can illuminate the economic and legal history of the Athenian Empire in particular, but present notorious difficulties in dating and contextualizing.[2] Thirdly, we have archaeological (including iconographic) evidence of enormous potential, but almost always unrealized, value, because it is hardly able *by itself* to fill the gaps in our understanding of economic and social *realia*. Alongside this contemporary evidence is a large body of non-contemporary material (particularly historical and biographical) that may be more or less well informed by lost contemporary sources, but which is inevitably understood through, and presented alongside with, the perspectives and presuppositions of later periods.

The situation for the fourth century BCE is not very different. Again, the principal surviving narrative, Xenophon's *Hellenica*, provides only partial chronological coverage (and, since it is usually considered to be more a *memoir* than a work of research, of historical quality usually considered inferior to that of Herodotus and Thucydides). Again, the use of inscriptional and archaeological evidence demands contextualization. And again, the use of later material risks anachronism. There are only two notable differences. The first is the survival, beginning from the late fifth century, of a considerably corpus of speeches delivered in the Athenian assembly and courts, and (closely related to these speeches) of politically conservative pamphlets composed and circulated by various authors (from the so-called 'Old Oligarch', to Isocrates, to Xenophon). The second is the now-fragmentary tradition of local historical writing, an antiquarian and also fundamentally political genre that, in the case of its Athenian version (the so-called *Atthis*), underlies the pseudo-Aristotelian *Constitution of the Athenians*. For our understanding of comedy, and ancient drama generally, the survival of philosophical texts (particularly Aristotle's *Poetics*, but also his *Rhetoric* and *Nicomachean Ethics*) is also invaluable.

Among these various sources comedy (whether Old, Middle or New) sits uneasily. Unlike tragedy, the Athenian comic genre was one which was explicitly grounded in a base of historical reality. But comedy also works by deliberately distorting reality in ways that, in the absence of other evidence, are often impossible to detect without starting from the comic evidence itself. Similar traps of circularity or *a priori* argument are encountered with epigraphic and archaeological data. Secondly, especially if one should try

[1] On the historiography of the *Pentecontaetia*, see especially Badian (1993) chs. 2 and 4.
[2] See Papazarkadas (2009) 67–88.

338

to identify the poet's personal attitudes and biases, there is the extremely fragmentary nature of the evidence to consider. Although it has of late become unfashionable to say so explicitly, orthodox opinion still considers Aristophanes a 'Cimonian conservative' (roughly an aristocratic imperialist).[3] The opposite view of Aristophanes as a liberal pacifist, though still alive in popular reception, is by contrast in disfavour.[4] No doubt Aristophanes did have political views, but given that only eleven comedies, about a fourth of his total output, survive, can we ever be sure what he believed?[5] Likewise, by Aristophanes' fifth-century competitors, Cratinus and Eupolis (together with him the canonical trio of Old Comedy), as later by Menander, not to mention even more obscure and fragmentary figures, we lack even a single complete play. The chronological scope of the evidence is also restricted. By Aristophanes we have five plays from the 420s, four more from the final decade of the Peloponnesian War (414–404), and two from its non-immediate aftermath (c. 393 and 388). Thus, even where it is possible to identify the historical base of comedy, its use raises the problem: can one generalize from a 'snapshot'?

There are essentially two responses to these difficult methodological problems. The first (and so far dominant) response is sceptical, limiting the use of comedy to an ancillary level, usually as a kind of check, in the (itself restricted) realm of political history. Such handling of Aristophanes has a long tradition: Müller-Strübing's self-avowedly polemical volume (1873), critical of the deficient use of Aristophanes by Boeckh, Grote and Curtius (among others), is representative, concentrating on the relatively minor problems of the Euboean expedition of 424/3 BCE (in *Wasps* 715–21 and its *scholion*), the five talents 'vomited' by Cleon (in *Acharnians* 6), and the nature of several Athenian magistracies (the generals and the so-called *Staatsschatzmeister*).[6] Comic topicality can easily be 'mined' in order to provide, for example, a likely date for the important Standards Decree (*ML* 45 = *IG* I³ 1453) (as Wilamowitz famously did in 1880, before he knew about the actual version, on the basis of *Birds* 1040f.), although, as we are about to see, it is no surprise that the risky method of dating from letter-forms was long preferred over Aristophanes' reference, and used to date the decree more than thirty years before 414 BCE.[7] Mining or checking is the same

[3] See Meiggs (1972) 391–5; Ste Croix (1972) 355–71 (with the phrase) and Lewis (1997) 183; Murray (1933) viii ('a Tory journalist'). Robson (2009) 180, though very cautious, is representative.

[4] This view is particularly associated with Murray (1933); see Hopper (2002).

[5] Gomme (1938); Forrest (1963); and Heath (1987) represent, on more fundamental grounds, the sceptical view.

[6] Müller-Strübing (1873).

[7] Tod (1946) 165; Meiggs and Lewis (1988) 114–17; Meiggs (1972) 167–73.

method used, for example, when Aristophanes is pitted as an alternative to Thucydides on the outbreak of the Peloponnesian War, particularly the nature of the Megarian decree(s) and the extent of Pericles' culpability (the mined texts in this case being *Acharnians* 515–39 and *Peace* 605–18).[8] The orthodox position on this question (following Ste Croix, who of all modern historians gives the most vigorous and explicit methodological statement on the historical use of comedy) remains sceptical, affirming the secondary importance of Aristophanic evidence: 'the only safe course is to *look at the other evidence first*'.[9] (Though why a student of the Peloponnesian War should first look to Thucydides rather than to Aristophanes is unclear: from 424 to 404 BCE, while the former was an exile in Thrace, the latter was a direct witness and participant in Athenian political life!) The extreme of this sceptical approach to comedy, the assumption that comic exaggeration and generic role playing was so pervasive that nothing the poet says should be taken seriously, begins with Gomme and Forrest, and finds its fullest expression in Heath.[10] Ironically, Menander suffers from the opposite problem: his comedies have long been selectively mined for what they purportedly reveal about Athenian social and legal realities, overlooking their comic context (as we discuss further below).

In any case, from Boeckh onwards, the sceptical approach has meant that comedy has not played as dominant and explicit a role in economic and social historiography as one might expect.[11] Quite the opposite. It is emblematic that despite Ste Croix's profound interest in, and encyclopaedic grasp of, socio-economic evidence, comic sources (and here one especially contrasts Ehrenberg's claim that 'we have no other source which springs so directly from the people as comedy') are practically absent from his later, Marxist masterpiece on the ancient class struggle.[12] Likewise, comedy found either peripheral or no use in the long-dominant orthodoxy of M. I. Finley and his 'Cambridge School' of economic history, although this tradition gave priority to the dominance of social forces over the economy, as posited by Max Weber and Karl Polanyi.[13] Not even the post-Finley 'new orthodoxy' (in this and other cases simply following the old methodology) seems willing to challenge this, and comedy features only sparsely in the long social and economic sections of the *Cambridge Ancient History*, as in the recent

---

[8] See particularly Ste Croix (1972).

[9] Ste Croix (1972) 232 (original emphasis), giving his first of five principles of interpretation (the rest stemming from it).

[10] Gomme (1938); Forrest (1963); Heath (1987).   [11] Boeckh (1817).

[12] Ehrenberg (1962) 9; Ste Croix (1981), with the index.

[13] Finley (1973); Osborne (1985), (1987); see Morris (1994) 352f.

and more specialized *Cambridge Economic History of the Greco-Roman World*.[14]

The second response (though by far the less popular) takes heart from the testimony that, when the Sicilian tyrant Dionysius asked to learn about the Athenian *politeia* (a term which in the fourth century meant the institutions and way of life, in short, the character of the *polis*), Plato sent him the plays of Aristophanes.[15] Beginning with Burckhardt, this is an attempt to engage comedy fully as a source for economic and social history. However, the methodology employed is problematic, with Burckhardt, for example, saying the following:

> As a source for cultural history comedy is indispensable, and the digressions (*parabaseis*), where the poet speaks directly, are of particular documentary importance; Aristophanes may be totally slanderous where he is dealing with certain individuals, but, where he depicts general conduct, can *only* have said what everyone knew and felt to be recognizable.[16]

The problem raised by this passage is that it is by no means clear that Aristophanes usually (or indeed ever) *does* speak directly in his parabases (excepting perhaps, as is usually thought, in the parabasis of *Frogs* 686 705), in Burckhardt's meaning.[17] And even if he does speak directly, scholars have asked, is he ever serious?[18] That question is probably not just fundamentally flawed, but just brings us back to the earlier (and irresolvable) question of the poet's political agenda.[19] In any case, Burckhardt makes no attempt to sustain this approach to Aristophanes. The 'general conduct' that he identifies in comedy is a general 'crisis of Greek life', the immorality and wickedness of the late fifth century, for in Burckhardt's view 'it is strikingly obvious that Greek life fell into decay during the Peloponnesian War'.[20] The sceptical replies to this are simple: that the 'crisis' was only perceptible to a 'Cimonian conservative' genuinely expressing his views – or (from those who deny that the poet's views were ever genuinely voiced) that it was

---

[14] See Cohen (1992); Lewis *et al.* (1992) ch. 8e–h, (1994) ch. 10; Scheidel *et al.* (2007), all with their indices.

[15] T 1.42–5 (Kassel-Austin); see Ehrenberg (1962) 42.

[16] Burckhardt (1898–1902) = (1998) 277.

[17] For a clear exposition of the problems see Robson (2009) 172–8.

[18] Compare Heath (1987) 19f. with Henderson (1990) 312f. On the seriousness of *Frogs*, see also McGlew (2002) 166.

[19] See Pelling (2000) 158–60; Silk (2000a) 308–10. The poet's political agenda must above all not be confused with the conventions of democratic comedy: see Edwards (2002).

[20] Burckhardt (1898–1902) = (1998) 274.

the traditional role of the comic poet to vilify and tar, to play the anti-establishment figure with his audience. In short, Burckhardt's crisis would be a mirage, his reading of Aristophanes too literal.

Conscious of following in Burckhardt's footsteps, Ehrenberg undertook the project of writing a detailed 'sociology of Old Attic Comedy' in his famous *The People of Aristophanes*, an attempt which has never been repeated.[21] For Ehrenberg it was the assumed background, the subconscious atmosphere, without which the consciously elaborated comic plot would be meaningless, that made comedy an invaluable mirror of reality.[22] Deftly side-stepping the question (which, as we have seen, Burckhardt hardly answered) of whether the poet ever spoke in his own voice, or was ever serious, Ehrenberg adopted Burckhardt's method of indirect attestation ('when a source answers our questions without intending to do so') in his reading of Old Comedy.[23]

The approach is morphological, the evidence treated simultaneously as *comédie de situation* and *comédie de moeurs*, but after providing *a tour de force* description of Athenian economy and society (including farmers, upper classes, traders and craftsmen, citizens and foreigners, slaves, the family and neighbours, money and property, religion and education, and war and peace) in the age of Aristophanes, Ehrenberg leaves us with a picture of decline not very unlike Burckhardt's. Forced by the war to evacuate the countryside of Attica and seek shelter behind the walls of Athens, to import their basic supplies from overseas, and to depend on their treasury for pay and sustenance, the Athenians were displaced from a predominantly traditional, agricultural lifestyle into an urban existence where old social bonds were broken and money became the chief medium of interaction. This reading makes the corruption of the demagogues, portrayed as war-profiteers, and the venality of the citizenry, debased and blinded by paltry distributions of *misthos*, the leitmotif of *Acharnians*, *Knights* and *Wasps*. The perversity of regarding education itself as a commodity, attributed to a whole generation obsessed with sophistic thought, is the generational crisis claimed to be at the heart of *Clouds*. Meanwhile, the terrible horrors of the war – Murray had pointed in particular to the Melian massacre – increased Aristophanes' resort to utopian or escapist plots, starting with *Birds*, and continuing with *Lysistrata*, and so on to *Wealth*.[24] Ehrenberg concludes:

> The spirit of comedy, its very nature, depended originally, even in its criticism, on the spirit of the whole people and the democratic State. Later the tendencies

---

[21] Ehrenberg (1962) 8 n. 1.   [22] Ehrenberg (1962) 8f.
[23] Ehrenberg (1962) 8.   [24] Murray (1933) 57–72.

we have characterized, above all the quietist ideal defined again and again in the middle of a terrible war, show the path which comedy took, a path which led finally to a somewhat dull and wholly unpolitical atmosphere. The two latest extant plays of Aristophanes, and especially the *Ploutos* [*Wealth*], with their narrow and materialistic dreams based on 'wishful thinking', are witnesses to a period of weakening and transition. The fantastic and Utopian exaggeration of reality in Old Comedy has vanished, while the artistic subtlety and the deeper psychology of New Comedy have not yet been achieved. So the historians of literature divined or discovered the existence of Middle Comedy which, seen from a general point of view, includes the period when poetry had left the sphere of politics... Consciously or not, they [the comic poets] adapted themselves to a new *bourgeois* audience and its standards of decency, materialism and private interests.[25]

The overall transition was principally one, to use Weber's terms, from *homo politicus* to *homo oeconomicus*: 'everybody realized to an increasing extent the importance of money, and the economic side of life gradually overpowered the political side'.[26] In this sense, Aristophanes not only documented but, 'entirely a child of his own age', was also an unconscious participant in, the 'self-destruction of the Polis': 'the poet, who fought passionately against the deterioration of the democracy brought about by demagogic leaders, was himself a demagogue'.[27]

The conclusion is sweepingly dramatic – doubtless too much so – but also worth restating even if just to highlight its continuity in more recent scholarship. Humphreys' argument that the Peloponnesian War turned Athens into a city of petty traders, and that wartime displacement from the land of Attica extended an '"economic" attitude to all questions where money was concerned', is based on the same interpretation of Aristophanes (particularly *Acharnians*, *Knights* and *Wasps*).[28] But her argument was an important modification to Ehrenberg's, who had assumed an identity between *homo politicus* and what he called the Athenian nobility: for Ehrenberg the rise of *homo oeconomicus* was quite literally the takeover of the state by a new class, the *petite bourgeoisie*.[29] Instead, Humphreys argued, the economic

---

[25] Ehrenberg (1962) 366f. On this general transition, though not on its date, Ehrenberg agrees with Rostovtzeff. See Rostovtzeff (1941) vol. 2, 1115: 'Athens in the late fourth century BC was a city of *bourgeois*, if we may trust the picture of it presented by contemporary authors such as Menander and other dramatists of the New Comedy and Theophrastus in his *Characters*; so also were other cities as we see them in the mimes of Herondas, Theocritus, and elsewhere.'

[26] Ehrenberg (1962) 362, 369 ('the victory of the economic outlook and the preponderance of "Economic man"').

[27] Ehrenberg (1962) 365; cf. 358f.; (1960) 101; cf. 97; see also Olson (2002) li.

[28] Humphreys (1978) 71, 171–4, 233.

[29] The view, inherited from Hasebroek (1928), underpins the analysis of Kurke (1999).

transformation of Athens was one that must have affected mass and elite together, altering their collective values.[30]

The Ehrenberg (or modified-Ehrenberg) line remains the standard reading of Aristophanes' development. The precarious situation in which the new Athenian *homo oeconomicus* would have found himself during the closing years of the Peloponnesian War, facing an empty treasury, a ruined army and collapsing trade, emerges in recent readings of *Assembly Women* and particularly *Wealth* (which has been called 'the first sustained text in economic theory').[31] Strauss sees the focus of the first play as macro-economic, that of the second as micro-economic: in these plays 'the Athens that Aristophanes describes... is needy, greedy, class-ridden, money-crazy and confused'.[32]

Reassessing Aristophanes

At the beginning of this process of supposed decline, six years after the first invasion of Attica, stands Aristophanes' earliest surviving play, *Acharnians*. For Ehrenberg, in 425 BCE the great socio-economic transformation was still in its early stages: the average Athenian was still overwhelmingly a *homo politicus*, and Aristophanes is thought to be attacking a disturbing, but relatively new social trend.[33] The passage where Dicaeopolis complains that the Peloponnesian War has introduced him to the necessity of dealing with the Buy Man (whereas previously he had lived in happy self-sufficiency in his rural deme) continues to be taken seriously as evidence of the earlier norm, namely the general isolation of the Greek countryside from market forces:

> For a country resident to have to buy was, by this token, an unusual experience and profoundly disturbing. In the Athens of the years of war with Sparta the importance of the market was abnormally magnified.[34]

But such a reading misunderstands the essential comic premise of the play, in which Dicaeopolis (for whom Aristophanes must have carefully chosen Cholleidai, one of the smallest and most remote Attic demes, as a home) arrives in Athens and makes a lightning journey from clueless rustic to

[30] Humphreys (1978) 171–4, 233.
[31] David (1984); Spielvogel (2001); McGlew (2002) 171–211; Ruffell (2006); the quote is from Lowe (2008) 51.
[32] Strauss (1986) 166. The economic and social situation after the Peloponnesian War has been described very differently but equally plausibly by Akrigg (2007) as one where depopulation led to a relative improvement in the living conditions of the survivors on the analogy of the European peasantry after the Black Death.
[33] Ehrenberg (1962) 88.   [34] Osborne (1987) 180.

Euripideanizing urbanite and consummate trader, fantastically buying for himself a private peace with Sparta.[35] '*Acharnians* demands an audience that, far from being unacquainted with buying and selling in a market, regards these as parts of everyday life.'[36] We must not forget in this connection that Aristophanes is responsible for much of what we know about the commodities sold in the Athenian agora.[37] Most importantly, even his earliest play presupposes an audience which is *already* accustomed to thinking economically. The audience must even appreciate the dramatic clash between political morality and the economic ethos of the ambiguous hero, who ends the play in the dubious and comically brilliant victory of a hedonistic – but aggressively self-centred and anti-social – isolation.[38]

Indeed, the tendency among current scholarship on the Athenian Empire at its height is to underline its economic nature.[39] By the start of the Peloponnesian War, Athens was already permeated by an economic mentality, which Aristophanes would have witnessed in its maturity, not its origins. The theory of the evolution of Aristophanic *homo politicus* into Menandrian *homo oeconomicus*, of the decline of Old Comedy (and Athens itself) into self-destructive *apragmosynê* – in short, all the traditional assumptions about the origins and nature of New Comedy – should be regarded with a strong dose of historical scepticism.

Far more fruitful from the point of view of social history is to observe the similarities in both method and substance, not just between Old and New Comedy, but with other forms of Athenian public performance. Dover has outlined interesting argumentative overlaps between comedy and fourth-century oratory in particular, and it is worth recalling here that Aristotle saw (*Rhet.* 1356a13) *êthos*, or moral character, as the strongest of all argumentative proofs of forensic rhetoric. Dover's analysis illuminates, among other things, the role of the poet as 'an angry, minatory moralizer'.[40] It is not at all the case, for example, that Aristophanes' attacks on professional orators, Euripides or Socrates, constitute a genuinely anti-intellectual position, as much as it is a traditional role persistently shared with democratic oratory, paradoxically displaying values 'which we should associate with a pre-democratic' (and here one might be tempted to interject *pre-capitalist*) 'wealthy class'.[41] Dover's outcome is diametrically opposed to Ehrenberg's: 'the fact that we can so often compare the standpoint, values, and techniques of Old Comedy (from *Acharnians* in 425 to *Wealth* in 388) with those of oratory even as late as 325 brings home to us the slow pace at

[35] See Olson (1991) 203.   [36] Moreno (2007) 74.   [37] See Wycherley (1957) 185–206.
[38] See Olson (2002) xliii–xliv; Olson (1991).
[39] See Kallet (2009); Kroll (2009); Moreno (2009).
[40] Dover (1974) 18–33; see also Dover (1972) 96f., 110–19.   [41] Dover (1974) 30.

which Athenian society evolved and the essential continuity between the theatrical audiences of Aristophanes and the juries and assemblies addressed by Demosthenes'.[42] A fuller literary record would show, Dover suggests, that the ridicule of politically prominent individuals (even if not as sustained as in Aristophanes) continued to be part of Athenian comedy until surprisingly late, perhaps the end of the fourth-century or later.[43] All this prompts the question of whether the perceived clear differences between Old and New Comedy are above all ones of dramatic technique, rather than of spirit.

Linguistic study is, as Dover also shows, valuable in the historical use of comedy.[44] This approach has been recently taken and expanded with particular brilliance by Willi, who explores the various registers – the languages – employed by Aristophanes, and throws open the rich socio-linguistic content of the plays.[45] Aristophanes self-consciously experimented with language, including philosophical, literary, economic, scientific and sexual terms. Here again, the moral dimension is important. To take an example from the economic register (unused by Dover), the term *kapêleia* or its cognates, normally having the technical meaning of 'retail trade' in fourth-century oratory (and accepted as such in modern *lexica*), appears in Aristophanes more than twice as often as in any other Greek author, and almost one-third of the times it appears in all of Greek literature, but does so with a moral focus, to mean a merchant who was a 'cheater' or a 'knave'.[46] The predominant use of this word in Aristophanes is in connection with war-profiteering and the pilfering of the economic resources of the *dêmos* by demagogues like Cleon. *Kapêleia* in Aristophanes is thereby set up against its moral opposite: the 'sharing politician', who in plays like *Knights* and *Wasps* operates principally by inviting the *dêmos* and the city as a whole to feast (quite literally) on the profits of empire.[47] The dramatic problem posed by this use of economic terminology is similar to that raised earlier by *Acharnians*: to what extent are economic activity, buying and selling, and individual profit socially harmful? This serious question, whether consciously posed to the original audience, or simply part of a shared and unconscious background, demanded first-hand experience not only of a market, but even more importantly of an imperial, economy.

One could doubtless push this economic interpretation of Aristophanes too hard. In particular, although the primitivist reading of the ancient economy proposed by Finley is increasingly in disfavour, its substantivist

---

[42] Dover (1974) 30.   [43] Dover (1972) 223f.
[44] Dover (1972) 77; see also e.g., Henderson (1991a).
[45] Willi (2002a), (2002b), (2003a), (2003b) and Chapter 8.
[46] Moreno (2007) 227–42.   [47] Moreno (2007) 235.

foundations (the dominance of social forces over economic, as mentioned above) are as solid as ever, and urge the reframing of our interpretation in political terms.[48] So perhaps it is more accurate to state that Old Comedy, as a source of social and economic history, is best read as an Athenian commentary on the experience of empire, in particular its resources, and the considerable social challenges this posed.

The great political question provoked at Athens by its imperial resources seems to have been not so much one of exploitation, as one of distribution. Everyone, even oligarchic critics of the regime, could agree that the Athenian thalassocracy was admirably efficient at profiting from its power, and receiving the goods of the entire world into its harbour. But who could benefit from the distribution of plots (*klêroi*) on land conquered overseas, as the Athenian democracy had begun to do since its inception in 507 BCE?[49] Who could join the rosters of Athenian jurors and other recipients of state pay (*misthos*)?[50] Who, in short, belonged to an 'Athenian master race', the imperial *polis* – and who, among the myriads of other Greeks interacting with the *dêmos* everywhere in the Aegean, did not?[51] The Citizenship Decree, the restriction of Athenian citizenship after 451/0 BCE to those individuals who were born of Athenian father and mother, is probably to be understood as a response to these questions, most likely in a context where the relevant resources could be seen as limited and therefore precious, as well as to be subjected henceforth to an intensivist form of management.[52]

In the context of an imperial city growing rich from trade, tribute and land annexations, it is unsurprising that one dominant form of social and political criticism appearing in Aristophanes, and (as far as we can tell) in other poets of Old Comedy, took the form of attacks on self-enriching politicians. Paphlagon/Cleon in Aristophanes' *Knights* can make his master Demos expand and contract through distributions of food:[53]

Paphlagon: Please hold off, so I can provide you with barley grain and a daily livelihood.
Dêmos: I can't stand hearing about barley grain! You and Thuphanes have cheated me once too often.
Paphlagon: All right, I'll supply barley meal already processed.

[48] Finley (1973); Morris (1994); Morley (2007) 13f. [49] Moreno (2009) 216.
[50] Hansen (1999) 38. [51] Badian (1993) 19.
[52] Badian (1993) 19, linking the decree to the practical limitations imposed on Athenian imperialism by its failures in the late 450s; see also Hornblower (2002) 36; for the need to restrict resources as motivating the concern with pure Athenian ancestry, see Lape (2010a) ch. 5.
[53] *Knights* 719f.

Sausage-seller: And I'll supply barley cakes ready-made, and the hot meal too; all you have to do is eat.

Dêmos: Then you two get on your marks and go to it, because to the one who treats me best I intend to award the reins of the Pnyx.[54]

In *Wasps*, those who receive jury pay are deceived into thinking their political patrons generous, when instead they are lining their pockets:

BDELYCLEON: Consider this: you could be rich, and everyone else too, but somehow or other these populists have got you boxed in. You, master of a multitude of cities from the Black Sea to Sardinia, enjoy absolutely no reward, except for this jury pay, and they drip that into you like droplets of oil from a tuft of wool, always a little at a time, just enough to keep you alive. Because they want to keep you poor, and I'll tell you the reason: so you'll recognize the trainer and whenever he whistles at you to attack one of his enemies, you'll leap on that man like a savage. If they wanted to provide a living for the people, it would be easy. A thousand cities there are now that pay us tribute. If someone ordered each one to support twenty men, then twenty thousand loyal proles would be rolling in hare meat, every kind of garland, beestings and eggnog, living it up as befits their country and their trophy at Marathon. As it is, you traipse around for your employer like olive pickers.[55]

Reality was, of course, far more complex than Aristophanes presents it. In the context of a war where the Athenian political elite was itself increasingly burdened with the demands of war-tax (*eisphora*), the rich could level similar accusations of corruption, a situation that seems very likely to have been explored by the twin choruses of rich and poor Athenians (the latter supporting the demagogue Hyperbolus) featured in Eupolis' *Marikas*.[56]

The context of a closed population, where Athenian parentage was all-important, because citizenship was exclusive and financially desirable, perhaps makes understandable yet another dominant *topos* of Old Comedy: the focus on the household (*oikos*) as a kind of microcosm of the city (*polis*) in relation to the social, economic and sexual dangers that it faced. Generational conflict, almost literal warfare between fathers and sons, abounds in Aristophanes, sometimes overlapping directly with the issue of distribution of state resources, as in *Wasps*, and generally underpinned (most graphically in *Clouds*) by the pernicious effects that contemporary rhetorical, philosophical or literary fashions were allegedly having on the Athenian youth. Set against a civic ideology where reproduction and female modesty traditionally appeared side by side (see Pericles' Funeral Speech, Thuc 2.44f.), and in

[54] *Knights* 1100–9 (Loeb trans.).   [55] *Wasps* 698–702 (Loeb trans.).
[56] Storey (2003) 203f.

a war-time context where Athens had been emptied of much of its adult male citizenry (all either dead or campaigning abroad), the rampant female sexuality and drunkenness portrayed in *Lysistrata*, *Women at the Thesmophoria* and *Assembly Women* should be understood as the comic exploration of another prominent anxiety of empire. Alongside these women in comedy, and contributing as much to the decline of Athens as the corruption brought about by demagogues and sophists, is a new generation of citizens who are very doubtfully Athenian, 'slave-born' or 'mis-minted' usurpers of democratic prerogatives.

Finally, the context of a closed population reduced by tremendous losses from plague and war, yet forced to stretch these numbers in order to defend an empire in a context of total war, explains (far better than the irascible personalities attributed to men like Cleon by some contemporaries) the particular intensity of violence and oppression displayed by Athens from the 420s until the end of the war.[57] The chorus of Aristophanes' *Babylonians* (426) assimilated Athens' allies to a gang of slaves forced to work a mill, while that of Eupolis' *Cities* (*c.* 422) seems to have made a running joke of the exploitation of the allies by likening them to slaves, women or animals.[58] Both plays fit the trend in Old Comedy, where slaves are frequently and brutally punished.[59] It is only in New Comedy that their treatment is softened (usually, with exceptions), and slaves become typecast as rogues. Xanthias in *Frogs* seems to present a crucial step in this interesting transition, taking as much violence from his master Dionysus as he gives in return.[60] He belonged to a period in Athenian history where the boundaries of citizen birth, previously unassailable, were now being crossed by slaves, freed for rowing in the Athenian cause in the dying days of the empire.

Menander

Whereas Aristophanes rails against fraudulent citizens, men whose irregular birth inevitably translates into corrupt fiscal and political policies, Menander's comedy is conspicuously lacking in such abuse. There are two reasons for this. First, the conventions of Menander's comedy effectively rule out the possibility that a citizen or potential citizen might have mixed origins: violations of the state-sanctioned rules of reproduction never occur, and in fact, are literally inconceivable in Menander's comic universe. Most of the plays employ a marriage plot pattern, telling the story of how a young citizen in

---

[57] See Hansen (1988).   [58] See Storey (2003) 218–20.
[59] See Dover (1972) 206, 213.   [60] See Roselli, Chapter 12.

love manages to marry his beloved in accordance with the laws of Athenian marriage and citizenship. Even in cases in which the comic hero seems to fall for a foreigner or slave woman, by the end of the play her true identity as a freeborn female citizen is discovered. In this way, the status of any illegitimate or bastard children that the hero has fathered is regularized, meaning that the child will have the bilateral Athenian parentage needed for eventual membership in the Athenian citizen body. Plays are all about creating the conditions for civic reproduction from the ground up, ensuring that young Athenian men and women marry for the purpose of producing legitimate offspring. Accordingly, this single-minded nativist orientation is the second reason why Menander's comedy offers little scope for the racial slurs and ancestry abuse so common in Aristophanes' comedy. There is, of course, an additional reason for the apparent absence of such insults. Whereas Aristophanes assails the birth and ancestry of men involved in Athenian politics and public life as a way of derailing their politics and policies, Menander's comedy eschews explicit politics in favour of the *oikos* or household. This is what, of course, Menander's comedy offers the social historian: a dramatically mediated case study in the *oikos* and its dynamics. This is not to say that romantic comedy lacks a political dimension or backdrop. After all, the marital and reproductive arrangements celebrated in comedy are precisely those defined as legitimate by the Athenian state. To an Athenian audience it would have been obvious that the democratic polis stands behind the romantic and family practices depicted in Menander's comedy.[61] There is one extant (but fragmentary) play that weaves democratic political practice into the romantic plot.[62] In the *Sikyônioi*, a democratically partisan deme assembly hastily convenes to determine the fate of a young woman who declares herself to be a lost or displaced female citizen. At the assembly, as reported by a messenger, two men vie for the heroine, Stratophanes, a mercenary whose democratic speech-practices dovetail with the discovery of his true identity as an Athenian citizen, and Moschion, the son of an oligarchic father who seeks the heroine for something less than a legitimate marriage. Not surprisingly, the assembly is sympathetic to the plight of Stratophanes, the more democratic speaker. Although we do not know the play's performance date, critics have argued that it must have been staged during a

[61] Lape (2004); Lowe (2008) 71f.
[62] We simply do not know how common this kind of political dynamic may have been in Menander because less than 10 per cent of his dramatic output has been recovered to date. It is clear, though, that explicit political commentary did crop up occasionally in New Comedy, see Philippides fr. 25, Timocles fr. 34, Alexis fr. 99 as well as Arnott (1996a); Burstein (1980); and Lape (2004) 58f., 62–4; Sommerstein, Chapter 15.

period in which Athens' democracy was restored.[63] This implies, of course, that the relative lack of explicit political content in New Comedy may have something to do with its wider political environment.

Unlike Aristophanes' comedy, which was written and performed in democratic and imperial Athens, Menander's career spans (roughly) 321–293 BCE, a period in which Athenian autonomy – in matters domestic and foreign – was sharply curtailed by various successor kingdoms. In fact, the Athenian polis experienced no less than seven regime changes during Menander's career. The Athenians were forced to endure Macedonian-mandated oligarchies between 322 and 319, 317 and 307, and again in 301 and 294.[64] During the periods of oligarchic rule, the traditional democratic criteria for citizenship, free birth from two native parents, was subordinated to a wealth requirement that disfranchised many who had been citizens under the democracy. Moreover, even when the democracy was formally restored in 307, its autonomy was limited by Athens' dependence on Demetrius Poliorcetes and his father, Hellenistic rulers vying for control of Alexander's empire in Greece.

Although Menander's comedy occasionally mentions political figures and even democratic institutions, as we have seen in the *Sikyônioi*, it never depicts or refers to the presence of oligarchic governments or Macedonian troops in Athens. For instance, there is no sign of Macedonian troops in the *Dyscolus*, which was performed during Demetrius of Phaleron's oligarchy and set in a remote deme known to have housed a garrison of Macedonian troops.[65] The comedy does, however, offer a strong critique of poverty as a barrier to marriage. Since marriage had long been employed as an institution of citizenship, the argument against using economic status as a criterion for marriage offers a negative commentary on the oligarchic privileging of wealth as the *sine qua non* of citizenship. Accordingly, the devaluation of economic considerations in the making of marriages (and citizens) that we find in many of Menander's plays articulates an implicit anti-oligarchic slant. In addition, it should also be mentioned that comedy generally privileges the polis and its culture over and against the new successor kingdoms. We see this especially when a mercenary in the employ of one or the other of the Hellenistic rulers appears as the romantic lead or the rival. Plays featuring a mercenary as the rival emphasize that mercenaries – emissaries of the Hellenistic kingdoms – lose out in the romantic contest to young

---

[63] See Garzya (1969); Guida (1974); and Webster (1973) 291.
[64] See Billows (1995); Ferguson (1911); Gehrke (1976); Habicht (1997); and Tracy (1995).
[65] See Wiles (1984); Lape (2004).

citizens.[66] Judging from Menander's extant plays, it appears that it is only by giving up his professional military service and reforming his character that a 'mercenary' can get the girl.[67] With such plot patterns, comedy recasts the contemporary conflict between polis and kingdom as a romantic conflict, thereby framing the contest in a way that allows for the triumph of the polis and its perspective.

This political backdrop allows us to see that the focus on everyday life in comedy probably does not provide us with evidence for a wholesale shift in cultural values, a new turn to private life, as it were. Nevertheless, New Comedy offers a wealth of information for the social historian, as scholars have long recognized. Menander's comedy has been studied as a source for law, women's history, gender, sex work, the family, economic realities and moral values in fourth-century and early Hellenistic Athens.[68] At the same time, the comic plots and conventions have also been employed to examine the history of gender and civic ideologies in Athens. While we obviously cannot cover all of this material here, we discuss some of the social realities depicted in comedy and the complexities involved in evaluating them as a source for social history.[69] We conclude with a discussion of slavery and comedy, since this area has (so far) been relatively under-exploited in the scholarship.

Comic conventions, ideology and social realities

Comedy's sexual and reproductive conventions often speak more to ideology (both the ideology of the genre and that of Athenian culture) than to social practices. For instance, comedy has been seen as providing a kind of cultural commentary on the gender system in that freeborn females in Menander's comedy never willingly engage in premarital sex. This emphasis

---

[66] For examine, in Menander's *Kolax*, the mercenary soldier is flattered in a way that likens him to Demetrius Poliorcetes (fr. 4 Sandbach). See also Elderkin (1934) on the Hellenistic backdrop to Plautus' *Curculio*.

[67] See Lape (2004) 171–201.

[68] Arnott (1981); Cox (1998); Fantham (1975); Goldberg (2007); Henry (1985); Hunter (1994); Konstan (1995); MacDowell (1982); Mossé (1989); Ogden (1996); Patterson (1998); Préaux (1957); Webster (1974); and Zagagi (1994). Krieter-Spiro (1997) and Traill (2008) examine the social dynamics within the plays. For Menander's fidelity to Athenian law, see Brown (1993) 412–20; Fantham (1975) 44f.; Fredershausen (1912) 208; Gomme and Sandbach (1973); Lape (2004); Ogden (1996) 174–80; Omitowoju (2002); Paoli (1962); Préaux (1960) 232; and Scafuro (1997). For the Hellenistic elements of Menander's comedy, see Henrichs (1993) and Patterson (1998); for the civic ideology of the fourth-century democracy in Menander's plays, see Lape (2004) and Lowe (2008) 71.

[69] See also Foley, Chapter 13 and Wohl, Chapter 17.

on female chastity is, of course, quite a departure from Aristophanic representations of sexually eager female citizens, both the married and unmarried. What accounts for this change in representational focus is less a shift in cultural attitudes and ideology than a shift in perspective. Whereas Aristophanes' depictions of hypersexual female citizens serve to justify the ideology of female sexual control articulated in Athenian law and society, Menander's chaste female citizens embody the other side of the equation, a world in which female sexual control appears as a natural and self-sustaining reality.

The mandate to preserve the sexual respectability of comic heroines accounts for another comic convention: when unmarried known female citizens are involved in sexual activity in comedy, it always comes about because of the force if not outright violence of young Athenian males. By showing that young male citizens might commit violent sexual assaults on female citizens without suffering any legal consequences, comedy provides important information for the ideology and regulation of sexual offences in Athenian law and culture. The conventions of the comic rape plot suggest that the perpetrator's intention to harm, or lack thereof, and the results of his conduct for another male citizen were more important in the construction of legal harm than the issue of his female victim's lack of consent.[70]

In some cases, it is more difficult to assess whether comic conventions surrounding Athenian marriage practices owe something to social realities as well as to ideological orthodoxies. Although comedy is scrupulously faithful to the laws of Athenian marriage, there are some discrepancies between how comic characters make marriages and what social historians suggest was the norm in Athenian society. The overarching purpose of marriage in Athens was reproductive: men married to secure children, heirs, and hence future citizens. There were, of course, additional reasons behind the particular marriages Athenians formed: kinship, friendship and economic or financial considerations are all mentioned in the lawsuits.[71] However, the common motive for marriage in Menander's comedy, *erôs*, romantic passion, is never mentioned in the lawsuits. With all due caution, scholars have suggested that Menander's comedy or New Comedy generally attests to a link between *erôs* and marriage, and perhaps to the emergence of new ideas about romantic marriage.[72] Although there is evidence that *erôs* was

---

[70] For the rape plot pattern, see Doblhofer (1994) 57–63; Fantham (1975) 44–74; Konstan (1995) 141–52; Omitowoju (2002); Pierce (1997) 163–84; Rosivach (1998) 113–150; Scafuro (1997) 238–78; and Sommerstein (1998) 100–14; see also Cole (1984).

[71] See Isager (1980/1).

[72] See Brown (1993); Rudd (1981); Walcot (1987). For erôs as a theme in Menander, see also Blanchard (2007) 71–8.

expected to develop within the context of an Athenian marriage, there is no evidence – aside from comedy – that *erôs* served as a key motive for forming a marriage.

Although there is some debate about the age of women at first marriage in Athens, social historians agree that Athenian men were around thirty at the time of first marriage, while women were perhaps as young as fourteen and/or as old as sixteen or eighteen.[73] In comedy, however, we find a very different picture, with the hero and heroine being roughly the same age. A character in Menander's *Aspis* specifically states that the best marriages are those in which the partners are the same age (263–7). In Terence's *Eunuch* (based on a Menandrian original), the young man who marries is explicitly identified as an Athenian ephebe, hence somewhere in the vicinity of 18 and 20. In addition, plays premised on a premarital rape often stress the youth of the offender-husband as a way of freeing him from the opprobrium that might otherwise follow from his action. The discrepancy between comedy and other cultural sources for the age of men at first marriage raises obvious questions: did men begin to marry earlier in Hellenistic Athens? Was comedy anticipating or advocating such a change in practice? It is certainly possible that the changed conditions of life in the Hellenistic polis prompted young men to marry at an earlier age, for some of the activities that men were traditionally involved in prior to marriage – serving as a citizen-soldier, participating in politics – were reduced in scope. Although such circumstances may have encouraged an earlier marriage age for men, we have no evidence for it aside from comic representations, which may owe more to conventions internal to comedy than external social practices.

There is a third area in which comic marriage practices depart from earlier fourth-century norms. In Athenian culture, marriage-practices generally worked to preserve existing patterns of socio-economic inequality, with the wealthy marrying the wealthy, and the less wealthy marrying the less wealthy. It was expected that a man would marry a woman with a dowry roughly in proportion to the size of his own patrimony.[74] Although a dowry was not formally required for a marriage, it protected women from mistreatment and abrupt divorce, and served as key evidence that a given union was in fact a legitimate marriage.[75] Wealthy men simply did not marry women with little or no dowry, at least according to speakers in the Attic lawsuits

---

[73] For the debate concerning the age of Athenian girls at first marriage see Golden (1990); Keuls (1985) 104; Ingalls (2001).

[74] See Foxhall (1989) 34. See also Cox (1998).

[75] Cox (1998); Foxhall (1989); Hunter (1994) 15–18; Ingalls (2002); Patterson (1991); Schaps (1979) 74f.

(Is. 3.29, 11.40). Given these conventions, it comes as something of a surprise that comedy frequently depicts wealthy men marrying the daughters of less wealthy citizens, and even being willing to forgo the dowry entirely. For instance, in *Dyscolus*, the wealthy Sostratus immediately offers to marry the heroine without having the family provide a dowry (303–9). There are reasons for suspecting that such devaluations of economic matrimonial motivations reflects a convention internal to comedy rather than a shift in Athenian practice. This is because economically mismatched marriages often come about as the result of a premarital rape and resulting pregnancy. The need to normalize the status of the child and its mother provides a reason for the marriage that overrides the wealth and class considerations that might otherwise weigh against it.

In addition to the peculiar strategies comedy employs to generate interclass marriages, there is also reason to suspect that comedy's willingness to laud such unions has to do with the larger political environment. As mentioned above, many of Menander's comedies were written and performed in oligarchic Athens when wealth was an important criterion for both citizenship and citizen marriage. In this context, the claim that wealth does not or should not matter in choosing a marriage partner carries tacit anti-oligarchic significance. This significance appears to have been especially prominent in *Dyscolus* in the confrontation between Sostratus and his father Kallippides over whether Sostratus' new-found friend Gorgias should be allowed to marry into the family.[76] The fabulously wealthy Kallippides insists that he does not want another beggar in the family (794–6).[77] By this time in the play, however, it is clear that Gorgias is not a beggar. By exaggerating his poverty and making it the sole factor in determining whether he should be allowed to marry into a wealthy family, the play draws special attention to the significance of wealth as a criterion for civic membership.

Plotting women, bastards and reproductive affronts

Despite comedy's fidelity to Athenian marriage laws, its depiction of matrimonial motivations and strategies is anything but a straightforward mirror of social practice. As we have seen, we must evaluate the comic representations in light of a number of factors, including conventions internal to comedy, other cultural evidence, and the wider ideological and political context in which comedy was performed. That said, comic depictions that

[76] See Lape (2004) on the issue of poverty in the play, see also Wiles (1984); Rosivach (1999).
[77] For the exaggeration of Gorgias' poverty, see Gomme and Sandbach (1973) 181.

appear to be shaped by dramatic conventions rather than social realities can nevertheless provide important information about social attitudes and even behaviour.

For instance, one Menandrian conceit that is obviously not an accurate gauge of the social reality is the rule that citizens never produce genuine or permanent bastards in their non-marital sexual encounters. While this reproductive convention highlights comedy's ideological commitments, we may get a glimpse of social realities in the way comic characters behave when they mistakenly believe that an illegitimate child has been born. The plots of *Samia* and *Men at Arbitration* both rely on bastardy scenarios whereby a wealthy Athenian citizen appears to have fathered a child with a woman whose background rules her out as a candidate for citizen wife. In *Samia*, Demeas has gotten his live-in lover, Chrysis, a former courtesan from Samos, pregnant. In *Men at Arbitration*, the courtesan Habrotonon conducts a paternity investigation by pretending to be the mother of a citizen's bastard child. In both cases, these women assume that they will be able to convince a wealthy Athenian man to raise rather than expose or refuse the child.

Whether or not courtesans or former courtesans were in the habit of convincing citizens to raise their illegitimate children, Athenian citizens seem to have suspected that they were. In one case, the speaker in an Attic lawsuit claims that an elderly Athenian citizen (Euctemon) was persuaded by a former prostitute to fraudulently legitimize her own sons (i.e. he was supposedly not even the father of the children he spuriously claimed) (6.19–23). Similarly, in his prosecution of Neaera, Apollodorus reports that Phrastor, a citizen, was persuaded by a courtesan (and her courtesan mother) to recognize a bastard as his legitimate son (Dem. 59.50–9).[78] Accordingly, the scenarios envisaged by Chrysis in *Samia* and Habrotonon in *Men at Arbitration* are consistent with the kinds of things the Athenians imagined really did go on. The Attic lawsuits demonstrate that the Athenians believed that some men, perhaps particularly the wealthy, raised and even legitimated their bastard children rather than having them exposed or otherwise excluding them from the household.[79] However, in both the comic and forensic sources, the assumption is that a woman, generally a courtesan, stands behind the ideological infraction.

While we see a strong gender and class bias in that prostitutes and courtesans were routinely blamed for real or imagined offences against the

[78] See Glazebrook (2005a); Hamel (2003) 158; Kapparis (1999) 36–43; Patterson (1994) 207; Carey (1992) 112.
[79] Humphreys (1993) 6.

356

overlapping norms of familial and civic membership, the bias cuts two ways in that it also indicates that wealthy men were routinely suspected of raising and legitimating bastard offspring. In this context, we might question whether the sex of an illegitimate child had any bearing in this situation. The supposed bastard children in Menander's *Samia* and *Men at Arbitration* are both male. It is possible that this supported the courtesans' confidence that they would be able to convince the fathers to raise the children. Although social historians have argued that female children were more at risk for exposure than male children, this argument pertains to a family's *legitimate* children.[80] In the case of bastards, several scholars have argued females would have had a better chance of escaping exposure than males since it was easier to circumvent the polis' legitimation procedures in the case of females.[81]

All in all, comedy does not provide clear evidence that the sex of a citizen's illegitimate child affected its chances for survival. Rather, what comedy does depict is a gender-based difference in the strategy a parent might employ to ensure the rearing of illegitimate offspring. In many of the comedies, an unwed female citizen gives birth (or has given birth) to a child. Although these women are unable to raise the child themselves, in contrast to Athenian men who find themselves in this situation, they nevertheless make provisions for the child's survival.[82] Most commonly, women give their illegitimate children to other women, friends and neighbours, to raise. The mother (a victim of rape) who employed this strategy in Menander's *Phasma* (*Apparition*) contrived an ingenious ruse to preserve her maternal role, despite the impossible circumstances. She dug a hole in the wall between her house and the neighbour's house where her daughter lived and disguised it as a shrine. In his summary of the play, Donatus tells us that the mother was able to have frequent contact with her daughter by worshipping at the supposed altar.[83]

Similarly, in Menander's *Hiereia* (*Priestess*), a priestess gives her bastard son to a female friend to rear (again a neighbour). This woman, who had two

---

[80] The evidence of comedy, however, suggests a connection between poverty and infant exposure, see Menander *Perik.* 802–12, and Terence *Heauton Timoroumenos*, and Ogden (1996) 205.

[81] Rhodes (1978) 91 and Ogden (1996) 165 suggest that female bastards were more easily passed off as legitimate due to the less rigorous procedures for monitoring female identity.

[82] In *Men at Arbitration*, however, the newly-wed Pamphile exposes a bastard son and in Plautus' *Cistellaria* (based on the *Synaristôsai*) an unwed mother gives her baby to a slave to expose. For the exposure and inevitable rescue of infants in comedy, see Murray (1943).

[83] Arnott (2000b) *Phasma* test. VI.

legitimate children of her own, seems to have passed off the priestess's child as a legitimate son.[84] *Hiereia* and *Phasma* show that although comedy's unwed mothers are unable to bring up their illegitimate children on their own, they nevertheless have an important resource in their female friendships. These plays also suggest that the fact that a child was the product of rape did not diminish a mother's interest in its survival.

Nevertheless, it is not always the case that comedy's unwed mothers have an available friend to foster their children. In *Hêrôs*, Myrrhine gives her illegitimate twins to Tibeios, a shepherd and one-time slave, to raise. Although we cannot be certain of the details given the very fragmentary nature of the play, it is clear that Myrrhine valued her children's survival more than their status *per se*. This attitude, i.e. survival at any cost, appears to have been associated with women in particular. In Terence's *Heauton Timoroumenos*, based on a Menandrian original, an Athenian man, Chremes, instructed his wife Sostrata to expose their legitimate child in the event it was female. In contrast to the cases we have been considering, the child's sex rather than its status is the motive for infant exposure in this play. But instead of obeying her husband, Sostrata gave the child to an old woman from Corinth to rear (626–30). When, years later, the husband discovers her deception, he rails against his wife's stupidity by pointing out that the child might have been sold as a slave, a fate evidently worse than death in his eyes (640). He surmizes that her thinking must have been something like 'nothing is too bad provided that she live' (641).

While all of these plays involving pseudo-bastards who are eventually recognized as legitimate have elaborate and fantastic plots, they nevertheless give us some information about women's behaviour and/or male expectations thereof. First, it seemed reasonable to portray women, even powerless unwed mothers, as going to elaborate lengths to ensure the survival of their illegitimate (or legitimate) offspring. This is not that surprising: since kinship comprised a greater portion of a woman's identity than a man's, women might be expected to show a keen interest in their children, legitimate and illegitimate. Still, there is a slight paradox here, a discrepancy between the end of civic reproduction and the means by which it is achieved. Although comic plots unerringly uphold the state's rules stipulating who could bear legitimate children with whom, in the process of doing so they depict women who value the survival of their children more than the pieties of legitimacy endorsed by genre and state.

---

[84] The details of this play's plot are mainly known from a partially preserved summary, see K.-A.'s edition of *Hiereia*, for the text.

Slaves and others in the marriage plot

The citizens who star in Menander's marriage plots are assisted by an array of supporting characters, male and female domestic slaves, prostitutes, courtesans, cooks and other 'service personnel'.[85] In fact, slaves play important roles in all of the extant comedies, whether they assist the hero in his romantic quest, act as surrogate family members, orchestrate the plot as an internal playwright, or serve as an easy target for low-brow humour. Given the centrality of slavery in Menandrian plots, it is surprising that the plays and fragments have been relatively understudied by historians, at least to date. As is the case with the representation of marriage practices, comedy provides an ideologically mediated portrait of Athenian slave culture; that is to say, it offers a one-sided history in that we only ever view slavery from the vantage of the master class. Still, it offers some valuable information.

In contrast to the rather distant relationships between masters and slaves depicted in Aristophanes, Menander portrays close and often affectionate relationships between citizens and their domestic slaves.[86] In part, this is a function of standard plot patterns whereby a domestic slave provides crucial assistance to the young citizen in his romantic quest, often to the exasperation of his father, the technical master of the household. Although this motif may not portray an existing social reality, i.e. slaves probably did not intrigue against their masters to facilitate their sons' romantic intrigues, it does capture something of the social reality in that slaves played important roles in rearing, attending and often educating the children of their masters. Likewise, comedy's portrayal of strong emotional bonds between certain types of slaves (the *paidagôgos* and nurse) and their charges seems to have a basis in social reality.[87] When slaves are treated as or act like family members, it is assumed that they have internalized the family's interest as their own. In the case of male slaves, this mean that they must help safeguard the chastity of the female family members, as in the *Misoumenos*, where a slave seeks to apprehend an old man he believes is seducing his master's mistress (617–22). A slave who failed in this task could be reprimanded. In *Dyscolus*, Gorgias berates his slave for neglecting his duty when he spied a would-be seducer speaking with Gorgias' sister: 'As it is, you stood aside, as if none of your business! Daos, you can't escape from blood ties with a sister, I don't think. We're still responsible.' (238–41). There is,

---

[85] For this term, see Krieter-Spiro (1997).   [86] See Hunter (1994) 83.
[87] See Golden (1990) 148; for Menander's *paidagôgoi*, see Krieter-Spiro (1997) for a nurse in Menander treating her ward as a daughter, see *Dyscolus* 883 with Handley (1965) 287. See also Diog. Laert. 5.11–74.

of course, some bad faith in a rebuke like this inasmuch as a slave who violated the person of a free citizen ran the risk of severe punishment, even death.

Despite the fact that the comedies depict close relationships between domestic slaves and their masters, the violence that hangs over the life and body of the slave in Aristophanic comedy remains ever present in Menander. Masters threaten old female nurses with beatings, head injuries, drowning and dousing (*Dys.* 195–6, 591, *Epitr.* 1062, 1073). Similarly, they threaten male domestic slaves with whipping, beating, burning and tattooing (*Sam.* 306f., 321–3, 440f.). Whipping, though, is by far the most commonly threat-ened punishment for slaves, which is why the slave can be 'reviled as a *mastigias* or whipping post'.[88] Although Demeas' behaviour in *Samia* – he promises to whip and tattoo his slave – appears just a touch excessive by Menandrian conventions, it can be explained by circumstances unique to the drama. Although Demeas overhears his son's former nurse calling Moschion the father of the infant he believed was his own, he is unable to torture the nurse, a regular technique for extracting the truth from slaves. In contrast to the nurses in *Dyscolus* and *Men at Arbitration*, the nurse in the *Samia* is no longer vulnerable to physical abuse because Demeas' has previously manumitted her, though she still lives in his house (237f.).

Although we find a freedwoman in the *Samia*, such appearances are rare; references to either manumission or freedmen are not very common in the extant plays and fragments. In *Perikeiromenê*, a mercenary promises to manumit a female slave for helping him reconcile with his beloved (982). It is possible that the process of manumission or the plight of freedmen was thematized in two lost plays (*Anatithemenê* 33 K-A and *Didumai* 116 K-A) because Harpocration, a second century CE grammarian, cites these works as evidence for the fees or taxes levied on manumitted slaves. The fact that slaves had to pay manumission fees and eventually the metic tax is probably one reason why we do not see domestic slaves actively lobbying for freedom in comedy. Still, some types of slaves do appear keenly inter-ested in winning their freedom both in Menander's comedy and in the Attic lawsuits.

In *Men at Arbitration*, Habrotonon, an enslaved harp girl and courtesan admits to a suspicious male slave (Onesimus) that she wishes to gain her free-dom by impersonating the mother of a citizen's child (540f., 548, see also 557–60).[89] That is, she hopes that the child's father will free her because he cannot bear that the mother of his child should be a slave. Although Ones-imus seems to desire freedom as well, Habrotonon has a more compelling

---

[88] Hunter (1994) 168; DuBois (2003) 104.　　[89] See also Furley (2009) 28f.

reason to seek it as well as the means to pay for it. Unlike Onesimus, she is not a domestic slave in the employ of a citizen family. Rather, her owner is a pimp who hires her out to customers who can afford his price. Women clearly did not want to remain in such circumstances any longer than necessary. The Attic lawsuits suggests that enslaved courtesans and prostitutes worked to buy their freedom or to convince their customers to do so on their behalf.[90] In addition to contrasting the situation of an enslaved female courtesan with a male domestic slave, *Men at Arbitration* also portrays slaves who work apart from their masters and live in what appear to be 'informal marriages'. Although slaves in Athens had no legal right to marry and in fact had no legally recognized family relationships at all, some masters allowed their slaves to live in separate domiciles in de facto marriages – the situation *Men at Arbitration* portrays.[91] What is interesting about this particular example is that it portrays slaves as something other than the appendages of their masters: one of the slaves' wives ardently seeks children, just as the citizens who star in the marriage plot.

The issue of manumission and its consequences was clearly central to the plot of *Hêrôs*, a fragmentary play which has been of particular interest to scholars interested in the history of Athenian slavery laws.[92] Roughly eighteen years before the play's opening, Laches, an Athenian citizen, had raped and impregnated a young Athenian woman, Myrrhine. She subsequently bore twins, a boy and a girl, but rather than exposing them, she gave them to Tibeios, a shepherd who happens to be Laches' freedman.[93] By a fortuitous coincidence, she then married Laches, her rapist (though neither of them recognized the other). Although the fragments do not tell us when Laches freed Tibeios, we do know that Tibeios was forced to borrow money from Laches in order to feed his family during a famine. Since Tibeios died before repaying the debt, his assumed children, the twins Gorgias and Plangon, have undertaken to repay Laches. When the play begins, the twins are living on Laches' property and working off their debt, with Gorgias working as a shepherd and Plangon spinning wool and weaving with Myrrhine, the mistress of the house who also happens to be her long-lost mother.

Just prior to the play's opening, Plangon has been raped and impregnated by Pheidias, a citizen neighbour, who, whatever his intentions might have

---

[90] See Dem. 59 on Neaera and Isaeus 6 on Alce.
[91] See Todd (1993) 186 and Krieter-Spiro (1997) 41 on comic slaves who live apart from their masters.
[92] See Ste Croix (1981) 163; Harris (2002b); Millett (1991) 78; Gomme and Sandbach (1973) 390; Todd (1993) 181.
[93] For freedpersons in comedy, see Krieter-Spiro (1997) 35f.

been, could not have married her due to her presumed status deficiency. In the meantime, Daos, a slave in Laches' household, has fallen in love with Plangon and is willing to pretend to be the father of her child. He reports that he has already gained Laches' consent to cohabit with Plangon, in other words, to set up an informal marriage of the sort we saw in *Men at Arbitration*. He is simply waiting for Laches to consult the girl's brother about the match. In the approximately fifty extant lines of the play's opening scene, Daos tells a fellow slave about his love for Plangon:

> My heart aches when I see her,
> I was raised with her, she's virtuous,
> and a suitable match for me.   (18f.)

After mocking Daos for indulging in romance – neither slaves nor impoverished citizens in comedy usually have time for love – Getas asks whether the girl in question is a slave (20). But Plangon's status is precisely the problem, as Daos' clearly realizes:

> Yes – nearly . . . in a way.
> You see, there was a shepherd living here
> In Ptelea, he'd been a slave when young,
> Tibeios, who'd got these twin children – that's
> What he himself said – Plangon, she's the girl I worship.
>
> (21–4)

Daos' dodgy description of Plangon as a slave 'in a way' (*tina tropon*) is one reason that scholars have argued that the institution of debt bondage stands behind the dramatic scenario in *Hêrôs*.[94] Although the twins (Plangon and her brother) are working in Laches' household to discharge their late father's debt, there is no indication as to whether their work is voluntary or compulsory.[95] Moreover, even if they are enslaved (temporarily), this does not tell us whether freeborn Athenian citizens were similarly vulnerable to debt bondage because the twins are presumed to be the children of a freedman.[96] What the play's scenario does intimate is that the line between freedom and slavery was porous for those at the bottom of the social ladder, i.e. for impoverished freedmen and their offspring.[97]

As the supposed children of a freedman, Gorgias and Plangon would be free persons, provided that they were born after their father's manumission.

[94] Ste Croix (1981) 163 argues the play attests the resurfacing of debt bondage in Athens under Macedonian rule. Harris (2002b) maintains that the play provides evidence that debt bondage had never been abolished in Athens.
[95] Gomme and Sandbach (1973) 390.
[96] See Millett (1991) 78; Gomme and Sandbach (1973) 390; Todd (1993) 181.
[97] On this issue, see Zelnick-Abramovitz (2005).

We might imagine his status as a freedman made Laches' look like a good candidate to parent the children in Myrrhine's eyes since she would not have been consigning them to a life of slavery. But she could not have anticipated that a famine would lead Tibeios to borrow heavily from his former master or that he would die prematurely, abandoning the twins to an uncertain fate. In Athenian culture, it was expected that children would discharge the debts of their father; in fact, Athenian citizens whose fathers were in debt to the state lost their political rights as citizens until they paid off the debt. It is possible that as the children of a freedman, the twins were similarly deprived of their freedom until repaying the debt; we simply do not have evidence for the precise legal background. Still, these circumstances do endanger Plangon with the possibility of a more lasting status reduction.

Hêrôs is exceptional for its emphasis on Plangon's potential for downward social mobility. While it is true that many of Menander's plays hinge on restoring the status and identity of a lost female citizen, there is never a question that these women might become sexually involved with slaves, even when they are temporarily enslaved themselves. In *Hêrôs*, by contrast, Plangon is nearly given to a slave to live in an informal union. Had Daos succeeded in 'marrying' her, she would not have been given her freedom when the debt to Laches was repaid. We must consider what allows *Hêrôs* to depict a situation that was otherwise taboo in Menander's comedy. On one level, the precariousness of the twins' circumstances has everything to do with Tibeios' status as a freedman. We might think that they could have established their freedom (after discharging the debt) by showing that their father had been a freedman. Since manumitted slaves were required to register their former master as a guardian (*prostatês*), the twins might have appealed to this record, if in fact Tibeios would have been able to pay fees required to create a public record of the manumission.[98] This raises the additional question of what status Tibeios would have had after his manumission. Some scholars have argued that freedmen automatically became metics and accordingly had to pay the monthly flat tax to which metics were subject.[99] It is certain, however, that Tibeios, a shepherd, would not have been able to pay this tax, especially once the famine struck. If he had been paying the metic tax but then stopped, he could have been sold back into slavery.[100] Perhaps, though, the issue of Tibeios and the metic tax is a moot point because he occupies a legally recognized status between slave and metic, which Zelnick-Abramovitz has argued existed for freedmen.[101]

[98] See Whitehead (1977) 16f.; Zelnick-Abramovitz (2005) 201.
[99] Whitehead (1977) 16f. with references cited.   [100] See Todd (1993) 198.
[101] Zelnick-Abramovitz (2005) 310.

Unfortunately, the play is less concerned to delineate the legal statuses that stand behind the plot than to show the ambiguities that might surround social status in practice. It is often remarked that the Athenians were idiosyncratic in that they used performances of citizenship to identify citizens rather than records.[102] That is, citizenship was enacted and verified by the citizen's known participation in exclusive civic rituals rather than by the inclusion of his name on a list. The Athenians seem to have reserved using public lists to identify certain categories of non-citizens, such as metics and the disfranchised.[103] For instance, when seeking to establish that his mother was a citizen rather than a slave or foreigner, Euxitheus in Demosthenes 57 emphasizes that her name is not on any of the lists associated with aliens (57.34, 55). Slaves and freedmen, however, were not included on these lists. It is possible that the need or desire to distinguish freed persons from slaves stands behind the publication of manumission lists in the later part of the fourth century. But what about the slaves? Why didn't the Athenians keep track of what they considered to be valuable possessions? It is likely because they thought they knew a slave when they saw one – not because of his or her physical appearance *per se*, but rather by their occupation and associations.[104] This was hardly a foolproof system since it appears that citizens who worked in occupations associated with slaves could and did have their civic credentials impeached.[105]

Accordingly, by labouring in occupations associated with slaves, the twins create the appearance that they are in fact slaves, irrespective of their presumed father's status. Similarly, their relationships with slaves engenders a kind of guilt by association. At any rate, Daos assumes that Plangon is a fitting wife for him because they have been raised together (19).[106] Significantly, Laches agreed to the match, even though he obviously knew her father was a freedman rather than a slave. By depicting Plangon as a hair's breadth away from the kind of downward status mobility comedy elsewhere refuses to imagine, *Hêrôs* also challenges the idea that there was a natural dividing line between citizens and slaves. That is to say, it suggests

---

[102] See Betrand (2007); Scafuro (1994); Todd (1994).

[103] See Boegehold (1990); Thomas (1994).

[104] Pseudo-Xenophon reports it was impossible to distinguish citizens and slaves on the basis of physical appearance because they dressed in the same attire, *Ath.* 1.10.

[105] For instance, in Demosthenes 57 (*Against Euboulides*), a citizenship case, Euxitheus complains that his opponents adduced the fact that his mother worked as wet-nurse (an occupation associated with slaves) and a ribbon-seller in the agora as evidence of her lack of citizenship. For women's work and social status see Brock (1994); Cohen (2001).

[106] Gomme and Sandbach (1973) 388.

that the division between citizens and slaves was based on contingencies of occupation and association, rather than on birth and innate nature. That said, the audience was likely spared from thinking too much about these unsettling possibilities by the dramatic scenario and its conventions. There is something absurd about having a freedman with the conspicuously Phyrgian slave name 'Tibeios' passing off two children named Gorgias and Plangon (always the names of citizens in comedy), as his own.[107] Similarly, Gorgias and Plangon would have worn masks associated with their true status and roles, securing the line between citizens and slaves even as it seemed to be blurred in the plot.[108]

The scenario in *Hêrôs* raises the larger question of the relationship between Menander's comedy and the ideology of slavery in Athens. On one level, comedy inevitably supports the institution of slavery in Athenian culture. By portraying a world in which every citizen is a master who can beat, bind and torture their slaves at their own discretion, comedy contributes to the naturalization of slavery as an institution. At the same time, however, the comedies often undermine the rationale employed to justify the system. This ideology is most succinctly expressed in the doctrine of natural slavery Aristotle offers in the *Politics*. In this work, Aristotle argues that persons who cannot reason for themselves because of their lack of the deliberative faculty can be considered slaves by nature.[109] He goes on to claim that barbarians or non-Greeks have the requisite mental deficiency, thereby offering a theory that supports the existing Athenian practice of enslaving non-Greek 'barbarians'.[110] In some cases, comedy recruits the Greek-barbarian hierarchy to depict slaves as inferior, in keeping with Aristotelian theory.[111] Perhaps we might expect this given Menander's often-cited association with Aristotelians and their school of philosophy.[112] More often than not, however, representations of slaves challenge ideas about the natural inferiority of the overlapping categories of barbarians and slaves.

Although we never see the Phrygian Tibeios in *Hêrôs*, the facts that he was freed, established as a shepherd, and chosen as a foster father for the

[107] Gomme and Sandbach (1973) 389.
[108] On the names, see Gomme and Sandbach (1973) 389; for the masks, see Wiles (1991).
[109] For the theory of natural slavery, before and after Aristotle, see Garnsey (1996) 13–16. For an attempt to distance Aristotle from this theory, see Frank (2005).
[110] For the non-Greek origins of slaves in Athens, see Diller (1937) 142–3; Manville (1990) 133; Morris (1998); Robertson (2008); Rosivach (1999).
[111] See *Georgos* 56f. For Greek-barbarian polarity in New Comedy, see also Long (1986) 151–6.
[112] See Gutzwiller (2000); Lord (1977); Sommerstein, Chapter 15; Tierney (1936); Wiles (1991).

twins all work against the perception that he was considered innately inferior. One might object that in *Men at Arbitration*, a slave seeking to obtain a
foundling's recognition tokens bases his argument on the idea that citizens/
freepersons were naturally superior (321–38). In this case, however, the
slave's argument is self-serving, deliberately tailored to flatter the old citizen arbitrating his case. In the *Aspis* the exchange between Daos, a Phrygian
slave and former *paidagôgos* to his master, and the Thracian waiter certainly
relies on the kind of ethnic humour that kept the Greek-barbarian hierarchy
alive. The waiter is incredulous that Daos has returned with his master's
loot when he might have safely absconded with it (239–41). Seeking an
explanation, he asks, 'where do you come from?' When Daos responds that
he is from Phrygia, the waiter identifies his ethnic identity as the source of
cowardice.[113] At the same time, he boasts of the manliness associated with
own Thracian ancestry: 'The Getae, by Apollo, a manly tribe; that's why
the mills are full of us' (244f.). The joke, of course, is that manliness here
amounts to stupidity since being put in the mill was one of the worst pun-
ishments for a slave. But the ethnic/slave humour in this scene calls attention
to dismantling of the stereotypes on which that humour rests in the prior
scene between Daos and Smicrines, a greedy old (over forty) citizen. When
Smicrines tries to enlist Daos in his scheme to marry a wealthy heiress, Daos
cites the Greek cultural adage 'know thyself' to justify his refusal (191).
When Smicrines persists, Daos ironically falls back on conventional ethnic
stereotypes:

> I am a Phrygian. Much that seems good to you seems awful to me –
> And the converse. Why pay attention to me? Your thinking is,
> Of course, far superior to mine.   (206–9)

What makes this statement ironic is not simply the fact a slave is appealing
to the ideology employed to justify his enslavement to sideline the misdeeds
of an Athenian master.[114] It is also the circumstances of the play itself that
depict Daos as the ethically and intellectually superior character and an
Athenian citizen as the indisputable villain. Because of this depiction (and
others like it), scholars have detected a strong current of social criticism in
Menander's comedy.[115] Whatever Menander's intentions may have been,
though, the undoing of the ideology of natural (barbarian) slavery we find

---

[113] For the name Daos as an indicator of Phrygian ethnic origin, see Krieter-Spiro (1997)
55.
[114] For related examples of Menandrian slaves employing popular philosophy to chide
their masters, see Furley (2009) 248, with additional references cited.
[115] See Sherk (1970) on the *Aspis*.

in the *Aspis* and elsewhere may respond in some way to circumstances in the
Hellenistic period. Alexander's conquests and their aftermath led to forms
of new social and demographic mobility for Greek and non-Greek speakers
alike. In addition to the unprecedented contact between different peoples,
there was also an increase in the practice of enslaving Greeks who had been
captured in war.[116] In such circumstances, it may have been difficult to
maintain the fiction that slavery could be justified on the basis of the slave's
innate intellectual deficiencies. On the other hand, Menander's depictions of
slavery as both an inevitable part of social life and one that could not really
be justified may capture a pre-existing cultural contradiction. Long before
Menander, Greek intellectuals pointed out that slavery was not natural
(Arist. *Pol.* 1253b21–3), a realization that appears to have affected slave-
holding practices not at all.

Conclusion

Against the traditional view, we have stressed the need to be careful not to
draw a false dichotomy between Aristophanes' political or polis-centred
comedies and Menander's social or *oikos*-based comedies. Menander's
comedies are in fact saturated with matters of civic ideology, as recent critics
have shown.[117] The continuity between Old and New comedy in this respect
is striking. For one of the hallmark features of Athenian thought centres on
the deep connection between *oikos* and polis, a connection Aristophanes
exploits for humorous effect by occasionally constructing the polis as an
oikos-writ-large, or an *oikos* as the polis-writ-small. If Aristophanes' polis-
oriented comedy contains a good deal of the *oikos*, so too polis is never
completely absent in Menander's *oikos* comedies. After all, the marriage
and reproductive arrangements so often celebrated in comedy are precisely
those defined as legitimate by the Athenian state. For this reason, we cannot
strongly demarcate the field of social history depicted in Menander's comedy from the terrain of the political or the polis at large. Rather, we must
constantly bear in mind what would have been obvious to an Athenian
audience, namely that the democratic polis stands behind the romantic and
family practices depicted in Menander's comedy.

If we choose to privilege an essential stability in terms of thematic repertoire between Old and New Comedy, we must do so with an open eye to a

[116] The practice of enslaving Greeks captured in war begins with Alexander's father, see
Rosivach (1999).
[117] Lowe (2008); Lape (2004).

series of important historical changes that affected that repertoire's dramatic representation. Whereas the democracy of Athens in the time of Aristophanes (except for brief periods in 411 and 404/3) was free, in the time of Menander it was either suspended or constrained by Macedonian influence for significant periods of time. This difference is likely to have impacted on the degree to which the poet could openly address delicate political matters.[118] Whereas Aristophanic Athens was an imperial city accustomed to the systematic extraction of wealth from neighbouring areas, Menandrian Athens was a city increasingly dependent on the benefactions of wealthy elites, including foreign kings.[119] One might summarize this as a change from the mentality of tribute (*phoros*) to one of self-sufficiency (*autarkeia*), identifiable not only in comedy but also in contemporary rhetoric and philosophy. An era of idealized autarky provides a context for reading the *Oikonomikos* of Xenophon no less than the *oikos*-based comedies of Menander. Along with the restriction on the redistributive powers of a democratic state that is no longer imperial naturally comes an increasing focus on the civic qualities of a wealthy elite, who are expected to aid the city without taking power from the *dêmos*. Here, too, the Menandrian *oikos* as a polis-writ-small is understandable. Half a century after the collapse of empire even the predatory ideal widely glorified in the fifth century seems discredited: the comic presentation of Smicrines in *Aspis* is not unlike Demosthenes' oratorical depiction of Androtion and his associates in *Against Timocrates*, their taking of booty associated with profoundly undemocratic and anti-social characteristics (*philargyria, ponêria, aiskhrokerdeia*).

Similarly, just as we might understand Aristophanic gender hierarchies, which push toward polygyny, as a strategy to address an imperial, seductive and exploitative city as *oikos*-writ-large, we might take the celebration of monogamy that informs Menandrian gender relations as more appropriate for our post-imperial, autarkically idealized polis. The same applies to comic slavery. Bearing in mind the essential point that slave numbers fluctuated in correlation to Athenian economic prosperity,[120] slavery's enduring topicality leaves no doubt that while Athens was essentially a slave-owning society, the interaction between free and slave was constant in the household, the Attic countryside, and the market. Athens therefore never had, significantly even at the height of empire, an economy that could be said to be slave-based.

---

[118] Aristophanes' *Lysistrata* and *Women at the Thesmophoria*, both usually dated to the Lenaia and Dionysia of 411, are probably directly comparable in this respect to Menander.

[119] For discussion of the complexities of Hellenistic euergetism, see Billows (1995); Ma (1999).

[120] See Sargent (1925).

Athens was therefore never, significantly even at the height of empire, a slave economy. Still, despite the softening of gender hierarchy and the increased interaction between masters and slaves in Menander's comedy, the social realities it presents remain all too familiar from the world of Old Comedy. *Plus ça change, plus c'est la même chose.*

PART V

Reception

19

RICHARD HUNTER

Attic comedy in the rhetorical and moralising traditions

For later writers Attic comedy was very 'good to think with'. Not only was it a poetic form where striking change over time could be traced and variously explained, but it could also be used to explore issues of continuing and always contemporary significance, such as the limits of free speech, the role of public criticism, and the relationship between individual and society, a theme as prominent in Aristophanes' *Acharnians* as in Menander's *Dyscolus*. This chapter offers three brief, but I hope exemplary, soundings into these later traditions. All concern how comedy and its history were understood and used in the public and private relations of the educated classes of the Hellenistic and Roman worlds. The depiction of character and the relationship between dramatic representations and real or idealized life, the extent to which New Comedy was constructed as reinforcing the humane ideals of an educated elite, and the actual effect of Old Comedy satire upon those who were satirized are themes which were far from having merely historical interest for men who were very conscious of the varying roles each of them played every day; 'life' itself was staged in public, and the dangers of unconvincing performance were very real.

'O Menander and life...'

One of the most familiar (and most misused) ancient judgements about Menander is transmitted to us by the fifth century CE rhetorician and philosopher Syrianus, in his commentary on the treatise *On Issues* (Περὶ τῶν στάσεων) of Hermogenes of Tarsus, one of the greatest rhetoricians of the imperial period (late second/early third century).[1] Hermogenes begins his discussion by listing the different ways in which people may be designated and how those designations provide a basis for rhetorical argument

---

[1] The best collections of ancient views on comedy are the *Prolegomena* in Koster (1975) and the *testimonia* for individual poets in PCG; Quadlbauer (1960) remains a useful, if superficial, survey.

from them; the fourth category is τὰ ἠθικά ('terms denoting character'), 'such as farmers, gluttons and such like' (29.18–19 Rabe). Syrianus' comment on this is as follows:

> Fourthly, terms denoting character such as farmers, gluttons and such like. The avaricious (φιλάργυροι), the difficult (δύσκολοι). He calls terms denoting character all those which offer the speaker material for confirmation or attack from character alone: thus farmers are generally solitary and hard-working and prefer the anti-social life, and the avaricious are penny-pinching and have their eye constantly only on profit, and the gluttonous are ready to do anything at all for pleasure. Menander (T 83) imitated life best of all and all his plots are filled with such characters; for this reason the grammarian Aristophanes (T 7 Slater) hit the mark exactly with the well-known verse he composed about him:

> > ὦ Μένανδρε καὶ βίε,
> > πότερος ῥ ὑμῶν πότερον ἀπεμιμήσατο;

> 'O Menander and life, which of you imitated the other?'
> (Syrianus *Commentary on Hermogenes* 22.24–23.11 Rabe)

Aristophanes of Byzantium (late second-early first century BCE) versified and varied a contemporary theory which saw comedy as an 'imitation of life',[2] and pressed home the point by making the trimeter about imitation almost as rhythmically 'unpoetic' as possible (with three resolutions in the first two metra). What is, however, too often forgotten about this testimonium is that, whatever Aristophanes meant by his praise, Syrianus sees Menander's supreme imitation of life as rooted in the representation of 'characters', and they are characters who conform, according to Syrianus, to familiar, generalizable patterns; if they are not quite 'stock characters', they are certainly representatives of 'types'. Syrianus' pattern of argument is in fact the heir of both dramatic and rhetorical traditions, which fed off, and nourished, each other from at least the fourth century BCE on.

Aristotle bequeathed to the ancient rhetorical tradition a pattern of generalizing about the 'character traits' of men of different ages and fortunes (*Rhetoric* 2.1388b–91b); orators and declaimers found such patterns very useful, for the more closely one's account of someone's behaviour fitted the expected pattern, the more convincing the account. Moreover, thoughts of 'character' immediately evoked the idea of comedy and *vice versa*. That comedy was the dramatic genre of 'character' (*êthos*), as tragedy was that of *pathos*, became a commonplace of criticism (cf., e.g., Quintilian 6.2.20); the corresponding distinction in epic was between the 'characterful' *Odyssey*

---

[2] Cf. Cicero quoted by *Prolegomena* XXVI 1–3 Koster; Pfeiffer (1968) 190–2. On Aristophanes' praise of Menander see also Halliwell (2002) 286f.

and the 'pathetic' *Iliad* (Aristotle *Poetics* 1459b14, 'Longinus' *On the Sublime* 9.15 etc.).[3] Menander himself was heir to this way of thinking and, in turn, encouraged it. The titles of very many plays of both Middle and New Comedy suggest comedies about 'characters', and at least for New Comedy we may guess that it was the probably universal pattern of comic prologues, most notably divine prologues, which encouraged a view of comic characters as 'types'; prologues give direction to a play and to the way in which an audience views it. In Menander's *Aspis* the prologizing god Tyche describes Smicrines as follows:

> He surpasses absolutely everyone in villainy. He recognizes no one as friend or relation, and doesn't give a damn whether anything is disgraceful, but he wants to have everything; that's all he cares about. He lives alone, with one old serving-woman.   (Menander *Aspis* 116–21)

Here precisely is Syrianus' 'avaricious man' (cf. *Aspis* 123, 149) with his single focus in life (*Aspis* 120 ~ Syrianus 23.4 Rabe). So too, Pan's prologue in the *Dyscolus* introduces us to Cnemon, one of those 'who can farm the rocks at Phyle' (*Dyscolus* 3f.), where life is 'toilsome (ἐπίπονος, cf. Syrianus 23.2 Rabe) and tough' (*Dyscolus* 21); Cnemon is both 'quarrelsome' (δύσκολος) and a farmer who is 'solitary and hard-working and prefer[s] the anti-social life'.[4]

It is the Euripides of Aristophanes who first intimates a 'cast list' for plays in terms of social status and family relationship:

> From the very first verses I would leave no one idle, but the wife and the slave spoke like everyone else, and so did the master and the young maiden and the old woman.   (Aristophanes *Frogs* 948–50)

The comic Euripides' point is that his plays allowed everyone, not just 'heroic males', to speak, for this was 'democratic' (*Frogs* 952), but – particularly as we look back from the perspective of subsequent developments – his assertion goes closely together with his immediately following claim that he introduced into tragedy 'everyday matters (οἰκεῖα πράγματα), the kind of things we are familiar with and which are parts of our lives' (*Frogs* 959),[5] the βιο-λογούμενα which 'Longinus' (9.15) was subsequently to find in the *Odyssey*.

---

[3] Cf. further Russell (1964) 99. 'Longinus' is probably referring principally, not to the 'events' on Ithaca, but to the cast of characters which, when viewed in a particular light, have a distinctly 'comic' feel: the rustic (Eumaeus), the young son (Telemachus), the wife (Penelope), the master (Odysseus), even the old woman (Eurycleia), and of course what binds them together is a 'recognition'.

[4] Alciphron's *Letters of Farmers* is one of the best pieces of evidence for the influence of comedy on such rhetorical literature in this regard.

[5] I have discussed various aspects of this comic claim in Hunter (2009) 18–25.

Such 'everyday matters' are not things 'which happened' but which 'might have happened', they are 'imitative of life' (rather than being 'life itself'), and as such they both foreshadow the historical development of comedy and the later scholarly account which saw in comedy 'fictions of events drawn from life' (πλάσματα βιωτικῶν πραγμάτων: *Prolegomena* XVIIIb 1.9–10, 2.10 Koster). As for the Euripidean cast of characters itself, this looks forward to how later comedy was to be described and evoked, particularly, though not exclusively (cf. Satyrus cited below), in Roman literature:[6] 'the wife' looks forward to the *matronae* (cf. Terence *Eunuchus* 37); 'the slave' to perhaps the hallmark character of comedy (cf., e.g., Terence *Eunuchus* 36 and 39, *Heauton Timoroumenos* 37, Ovid *Amores* 1.15.17); 'the master' to the *senes* and *duri patres* (cf., e.g., Terence *Eunuchus* 39, *Heauton Timoroumenos* 37, Ovid *Amores* 1.15.17); and although 'virgins' are not common speaking characters in comedy (cf. Menander *Dyscolus* 189–213), they were central of course to the way in which comic plots were imagined (cf., e.g., Manilius *Astronomica* 5.472 *raptasque in amore puellas*).[7]

It is, of course, no surprise to find the (comic) Euripides as an influential figure in the shaping of traditions about comedy, for the link between Euripides and New Comedy is a commonplace of both ancient and modern discussion, one given particular notoriety by Nietzsche in *The Birth of Tragedy*. In the dialogic *Life of Euripides* by Satyrus (late third/early second century BCE) a speaker traces a clear line of descent from Euripides to comedy:

> [? quarrels between husband] and wife, and father and son, and slave and master, or as far as concerns crucial events (*peripeteiai*), the rape of virgins, suppositious children, recognitions by means of rings and necklaces; these are the very stuff of more recent Comedy (τὴν νεωτέραν κωμωιδίαν), and it was Euripides who brought them to fullness, though they began with Homer[8]
> (Satyrus, *Life of Euripides* fr. 39 col. VII Schorn = Euripides T 137 Kannicht)

---

[6] It may be argued that Roman representations of Menander assimilate him somewhat to the nature of Roman comedy and thus, from a modern perspective, rather misrepresent (cf., e.g. Fantham (1984) 302f.), but that 'misrepresentation' is itself very instructive. Apuleius' description of the comedy of Philemon (*Florida* 16 = Philemon T 7) is a very good example of how the virtues of New Comedy were conceived within a very standard pattern.

[7] At *Frogs* 957f. the comic Euripides claims to have taught the Athenians, inter alia, 'loving (ἐρᾶν), scheming, to suspect trouble'; most editors (for good reasons) consider ἐρᾶν corrupt, but it is at least worth noting the apparent parallel at Terence *Eunuchus* 39f. describing the 'typical' plots of comedy: *falli per seruom senem / amare odisse suspicari*.

[8] I follow most editors, though not Schorn, in assuming a lacuna after the reference to Homer.

This theory of the genesis of important elements of later comedy very likely goes back to the heyday of Alexandrian scholarship,[9] but as we have seen we may trace its origins further back than that, and indeed to comedy itself. Later criticism too came very close to tracing this genetic argument to comedy itself. In one of the best-known ancient assessments of Menander, Quintilian notes that Menander himself acknowledged his admiration for Euripides and imitated him:

> As he often testifies, Menander admired Euripides greatly and imitated him, though in a different genre. In my judgement at least, a careful reading of Menander would suffice to produce all the virtues I am recommending: he fashioned so complete an image of life, there is in him such fullness of invention and fluency of expression, so completely is he adapted to every circumstance, character and emotion.　　(Quintilian 10.1.69 = Menander T 101)

Menander's 'testimony' (*testatur*) to his admiration for Euripides is presumably a reference to places in the comedies where characters explicitly quote from Euripides (cf., e.g., *Aspis* 424–8),[10] but what is important in the present context is that here too we find the very close link between the 'imitation of life' and the presentation of 'characters'. Moreover, Quintilian's concern is literature which will be of benefit to the orator and here too he is able to draw on a very long critical tradition about Euripides and Menander. What was in the *Frogs* the endless 'chattering' of Euripidean tragedy became for subsequent ages, particularly for the educated elite, an enviable rhetorical skill from which the aspiring orator could learn much;[11] one of Satyrus' speakers noted that 'in his speeches Euripides regularly spoke in accordance with the rules of rhetoric' (fr.1 Schorn = T 184 Kannicht) and, as Quintilian notes (10.1.70), Menander not infrequently included judicial debates or speeches in his plays. Of the scenes which Quintilian cites, the one which is best known to us, the arbitration scene from *Men at Arbitration*, in fact evokes a Euripidean model within a play which everywhere reveals a very sophisticated and knowing sense of theatrical history and theatrical convention.[12] Here too ancient dramatic criticism is seen to be the heir of the 'criticism' internal to drama itself.

There was another way too in which Euripides and Menander could be drawn together. In his recommendation of the two dramatists to those who

---

[9] Cf., e.g., Nesselrath (1993). For 'recognitions' as the *telos* of comedy cf. *Prolegomena* XVIIIb 2.8–9, 3.9 Koster.
[10] Cf. Satyrus, *Life of Euripides* loc. cit. (= Philemon fr. 153) where verses in praise of Euripides, spoken (presumably) by a character in one of Philemon's plays, are introduced as 'Philemon too bears witness (μαρτυρεῖ) to this.'
[11] Cf. Hunter (2009) 39–48 on Dio 52.　　[12] Cf., e.g., Hunter (1985) 134–6.

wished to train themselves in political oratory, Dio Chrysostom (18.6–7 = Menander T 102) adduces now familiar praise of Menander's powers of character portrayal, but he also anticipates criticism from the σοφώτεροι that he has preferred Menander to 'Old Comedy' and Euripides to 'the old tragedians'. It might surprise us to see the history of tragedy and comedy placed on this structurally equal footing, as though the close critical linkage between Euripides and Menander had worked back into the past to fashion an 'Old Tragedy' and a 'New Tragedy' on the pattern of 'Old Comedy' and 'New Comedy', but both poets could indeed be seen to stand at the end of a long development and to be the high point of that development; after both of them, on this model, the respective genres declined. That they seemed so close in other ways would merely confirm the structural parallel.

Dio defends his choice of 'the new' over 'the old' by an analogy: 'doctors do not prescribe the richest (πολυτελεστάτας) dietary regimes to those in need of treatment, but the ones which are beneficial'. The adjective refers not simply to price, for these are diets which are 'rich', with the implication of 'elaborate', 'varied', 'luxurious', and hence – by a familiar principle of ancient (and modern) dietetics – unhealthy.[13] A play of Menander is structurally and rhythmically much 'simpler' than a play of Aristophanes; the most obvious difference of course lies in the predominance in Menander of the iambic trimeter and the absence of the chorus – it is this which makes Menander a 'plain diet'. So too, the language of Menander is uniform in a way in which the extraordinary linguistic range of an Aristophanes is not. Dio is not really attacking Old Comedy, but is merely concerned with what will be the most beneficial reading for the budding *pepaideumenos*. The differences, however, between the 'forcefulness' (δεινότης) of Old Comedy and the realism and grace of Menander to which Dio points could, of course, be expressed much more negatively, and this is precisely what we do find in a number of places in Plutarch, most notably in the extant epitome of the *Comparison of Aristophanes and Menander* and in the *Sympotic Questions*; for Plutarch, Aristophanic comedy poses a threat to the political and social values of the educated elite which he (Plutarch) represents.[14] What for Dio is the 'rich diet' of Aristophanes is for Plutarch the disturbing 'unevenness' (ἀνωμαλία) of Old Comedy; the point is made particularly explicit with regard to language:

Aristophanes' diction contains the tragic, the comic, the pretentious, the prosaic, unclarity, ambiguity, grandeur and elevation, idle chatter and sickening

[13] The point is rather misunderstood by Garzya (1959) 245f.
[14] Cf. Hunter (2009) 78–89; the existence of that discussion precludes detailed treatment of the *Comparison* here.

nonsense. Despite all these differences and unevennesses, his style does not even assign what is appropriate and fitting to each kind.

(Plutarch *Comparison of Aristophanes and Menander* 853c–d)

Menander's language, by contrast, is 'mingled' into a perfect unity (853d–e).[15]

Comedy for an elite

Plutarch's concern in *Sympotic Questions* 7.8 is with entertainment suitable for symposia, though there is of course a wider critical agenda in play as well (as the *Comparison* makes very clear).[16] The lack of decency and order (*kosmos*) which Plutarch sees everywhere in Old Comedy offers particular dangers for men enjoying their wine, and it is the elite symposium which has, for Plutarch, replaced the theatre as the proper arena for the enjoyment of 'literature'. Such social occasions always contain within themselves the danger that they will degenerate into drunken brawling (or worse). The danger is very clear in Plutarch's description of Old Comedy:

> There is in the so-called parabases a quite untempered (ἄκρατος) and intense seriousness and outspokenness, and in its tolerance of jokes and buffoonery it is appallingly surfeited (κατάκορος) and openly shameless and stuffed full (γέμουσα) of phrases which lack decency (κόσμος) and of outrageous (ἀκολάστων) words. (Plutarch *Sympotic Questions* 711f–12a[17])

For Plutarch the parabases present a particular danger because there the non-elite citizen body is directly addressed and invited to laugh at 'the great and the good'.[18] Moreover, Plutarch's language precisely evokes the 'unmixed' wine and excess which would indeed lead to brawling and which is a symbol of the very antithesis of the elite symposium; the point is reinforced by an echo of a passage of Plato's *Phaedrus* in which Socrates retails the disgust of the *erômenos* at the way his lover talks about him:

[15] At 712d of *Sympotic Questions* 7.8 Plutarch refers to the 'enjoyable and smooth' style (τὸ τερπνὸν καὶ γλαφυρόν) of Menander's plays, and a comparison of what he has to say about Menandrean style both there and in the *Comparison* with Dionysius of Halicarnassus' account of the γλαφυρὰ σύνθεσις (*De comp. verb.* 23) is instructive; the latter too is characterized by words which blend and fit together so that no part stands out from any other.

[16] *Sympotic Questions* 7.8 has been much discussed, cf., e.g., Gilula (1987); Aguilar (1997); Imperio (2004b), and my account inevitably overlaps to some extent with earlier accounts.

[17] Very similar language is used at *Sympotic Questions* 712e of 'mimes called *paignia*, which should not be seen even by the slave boys who fetch our shoes'; the parallel is very telling for Plutarch's attitudes.

[18] Cf. 'Platonius' I 39–41 Koster, who explicitly associates the parabases with radical democracy.

the lover's reproaches are intolerable when he [the lover] is sober, but when he gets drunk (εἰς μέθην ἰόντος) and speaks with excessive and unrestrained freedom (παρρησίαι κατακορεῖ καὶ ἀναπεπταμένηι χρωμένου) they bring disgrace as well as being intolerable. (Plato *Phaedrus* 240e4–7)

The echo evokes an image not only of disgusting drunkenness, which ruins the fellowship of a symposium,[19] but also of paederasty in its least attractive form, and the absence of paederasty from Menander (in contrast, we must suppose, to Old Comedy) is to be noted by Plutarch in the immediately following section of the 'question' (712c).

According to a well-known set of linguistic and iconographic images, the symposium was a 'sea voyage', with the symposiasts as sailors.[20] Plutarch alludes to the idea as he turns from the excesses of Old Comedy to Menander's appropriateness for the symposium:

What objection could anyone make to New Comedy [as sympotic entertainment]? It is so blended (ἐγκέκραται) into symposia, that we could steer (διακυβερνῆσαι) the drinking-party more easily without wine than without Menander.
(Plutarch *Sympotic Questions* 712b)

Drinkers, like sailors, need to reach the calmness of harbour without the potentially destructive storms which Old Comedy threatens to stir up; a symposium, like a sea-voyage, can turn out well or ill. Menander's comedy brings its characters and its audience back safely to familiar calm waters; the thrust of this comedy is restorative, not radical.[21] The pattern of this movement is (again) picked up from the plays themselves. In the *Aspis*, the prologizing Tyche describes the state of the characters at the beginning of the play as 'wandering in a state of ignorance' (99); it is precisely from such a 'wandering' state, like sailors adrift on the sea, that the goddess will intervene to save them and restore them to knowledge and a state of social acceptability. In Old Comedy as we know it, however, it is as often radical change, not restoration, which is established by the end of the play, or at least restoration may operate on a large and communal scale (*Acharnians*, *Frogs*, perhaps *Knights*).

Often, of course, in Menander restoration takes the form of the familiar calmness of marriage. Plutarch calls attention to marriage as a common

---

[19] Somewhere behind these images may lie the proposal in Aristotle's *Politics* 'that younger men should not be in the audience for iambic verses or comedy until they have reached an age to share in common meals and serious drinking (μέθη) and they will be protected by their education (*paideia*) from the harmful effects of such things' (7.1336b20–3).

[20] Slater (1976) remains the fundamental starting point.

[21] Cf. the remarks of Knox (1979) 266f. on comedy and the inheritance from Euripides' *Ion*.

ending for the plays, in which social norms are restored: 'rapes of virgins regularly end in marriage' (712c). He also establishes 'marriage' as the proper end for the audience, and one which the plays themselves promote:

> Love affairs in Menander are appropriate for men who have drunk and will shortly be going off to sleep with their wives; for there is no paederasty in these plays and rapes of virgins regularly end in marriage.
>
> (Plutarch *Sympotic Questions* 712c)

The plays thus confirm the institution of marriage and the mutual fidelity of man and wife; the point is made by an obvious allusion to the end of Xenophon's *Symposium* in which the arousing and (relatively) sexually explicit pantomime of Dionysus and Ariadne makes 'the symposiasts who were not married swear that they would marry, and those who were married mount their horses and ride off to enjoy their wives' (Xenophon *Symposium* 9.7). Xenophon here may also seem to be promoting marital love – the pantomime after all showed Dionysus and Ariadne on their 'wedding night' – but the allusion points a contrast between a mime which arouses the symposiasts physically and a play of Menander, which contains no scenes remotely like the kissing and embracing of Dionysus and Ariadne, and which privileges marriage as a social institution for the procreation of legitimate citizens (cf. *Dyscolus* 842f., *Misoumenos* 444f., *Samia* 726f.), not as an opportunity for pleasurable sex.[22]

Another reason why Plutarch considers Aristophanes unsuitable as entertainment at symposia is the arcane nature of much of his subject matter:

> Moreover, just as at official dinners a wine-steward stands beside each guest, so it would be necessary for each guest to have a grammarian to explain each allusion – who is Laispodias in Eupolis (fr. 107) and Kinesias in Plato (fr. 200) and Lampon in Cratinus (fr. 62) and everyone mocked in comedy (τῶν κωμῳδουμένων ἕκαστος), so that our symposium would become a schoolroom or the jokes would be senseless and without meaning.
>
> (Plutarch *Sympotic Questions* 712a)

Plutarch conjures up the world, not just of the schoolroom,[23] but also of the scholarly and scholiastic industry which had flourished since Alexandrian times, but – at least as far as Old Comedy is concerned – enjoyed a particular flowering in Plutarch's time and subsequently; of the examples he cites, our

---

[22] For other aspects of this passage cf. Brown (1990) with earlier bibliography.

[23] The fourth-century CE rhetorician Libanius tells us that, when a young man, he was stunned by lightning one day as '[he] was standing beside my seated teacher (γραμματιστής) and reading the *Acharnians* of Aristophanes' (*Or.* 1.9). Plutarch reverses the hierarchy of teacher and pupil.

knowledge of Laispodias does indeed derive primarily from an Aristophanic scholium, and Plutarch's allusion to the scholarly activity of drawing up explanatory lists of 'those mocked in comedy' finds its echo in Athenaeus 8.344e, our source for Cratinus fr. 62, which clearly draws upon such lists.[24] The educated elite naturally loved to display their learning and *paideia* at symposia, but the kind of 'professional', curiously – in their view – banal, detailed[25] learning necessary to explain an arcane name in Old Comedy is not what they prided themselves upon; here is one measure of the difference between the symposia which Plutarch envisages and the discussions which Athenaeus dramatizes. Such scholarship was much less needed, and much less practised, in the case of Menander and New Comedy in general, in which allusions to real contemporary figures are very rare,[26] and in which the 'pleasant and prosaic' style (712b) was readily accessible to all and needed no constant glossing. To what extent this openness of Menandrian comedy, the fact that it did not need the attentive protection of scholars, contributed to the disappearance of texts we can only surmise.

What Menander did offer was plays based around ethical issues, and the enjoyment of Menander was therefore truly connected to the study of philosophy and the cultivation of 'human sympathy' (τὸ φιλάνθρωπον), which was what really mattered to men like Plutarch:[27]

> Valuable and simple (ἀφελεῖς) maxims[28] penetrate the mind and, with wine acting like fire, they soften even the hardest characters and work them into more reasonable shape (πρὸς τὸ ἐπιεικέστερον).
>
> (Plutarch *Sympotic Questions* 712c)

---

[24] For such lists cf. Steinhausen (1910). Aristophanes is not included in Plutarch's examples, although he is almost an inevitable fixture on lists of the chief poets of Old Comedy. Perhaps he is excluded as being the best known and most familiar of the Old Comedy poets: as Plutarch wishes to stress the obscurity of Old Comedy, he chooses poets who really do belong to scholars. The vast majority of fragments of Cratinus do indeed come from scholia, lexica and Athenaeus.

[25] The distaste in the repetition ἑκάστωι τὸ καθ᾽ ἕκαστον ἐξηγεῖσθαι at 712a is almost audible. One thinks of Aristotle's distinction between generalizing poetry, on the one hand, and history, on the other, which deals in the details (τὰ καθ᾽ ἕκαστον) of individual historical figures ('what Alcibiades [or Laispodias or Kinesias or Lampon, we might add] did or suffered'); it is the former which is 'more philosophical and more serious' (*Poetics* 1451b4–11). So too, Old Comedy, like 'iambic', may be characterized by 'real' names for its characters, whereas later comedy uses typical, generic names (*Poetics* 1451b11–15, Antiphanes fr. 189).

[26] Cf. Hunter (1985) 13 with n. 31.   [27] Cf. also *Comparison* 854b–c.

[28] Here too Euripides and Menander stood together in the critical tradition, cf. Quintilian 10.1.68 on Euripides *sententiis densus*, though Plutarch's point is rather different from Quintilian's. On Menander's *gnômai* see also Aelius Theon, *Progymnasmata* 91.13–25 (citing fr. 255) and 92.15–22 (citing fr. 129).

Such maxims require no 'commentary'; they penetrate us imperceptibly (ὑπορρέουσαι), unlike Old Comedy with its insistent obscurities which call attention to themselves and demand interpretation. In his account of 'simplicity' (ἀφέλεια), Hermogenes notes that 'simple thoughts' are thoughts 'which are common to all men and occur to everyone, or seem to, and contain nothing deep or intricate' (322.6–8 Rabe), and although Hermogenes has in mind the speech of such as rustics, women and children (for which he says one could find myriad examples in Menander, 323.23–324.2 Rabe), his discussion can shed light on what Plutarch wants to highlight in Menander.

If the humour of Aristophanes was, in Plutarch's view, vulgar and crude, his grace and wit (χάριτες) are in fact a prominent motif of the ancient critical tradition; an epigram, very improbably ascribed to Plato, records that the Graces established a shrine to themselves in his soul (Ar. T 130).[29] One element of this 'grace' was a quality of his language and that of Old Comedy generally; Quintilian (10.1.65) asserts that Old Comedy was almost alone in retaining the 'pure grace of the Attic language' (*sinceram illam sermonis Attici gratiam*). The two elements are mutually reinforcing because 'Attica' itself was renowned, particularly by the Romans, as the home of graceful wit.[30] Praise of the 'Attic' quality of a writer carries of course a particular charge in the period of the Second Sophistic, both because of the general stress in education at all levels upon 'the Attic classics', and because of the purifying 'Atticist' linguistic movement. Rather later, Eunapius virtually describes the fourth-century orator Libanius of Antioch as a reincarnation of Aristophanes:

> His writings are full of wit (χάρις) and comic ribaldry (κωμικὴ βωμολοχία) and elegance (κομψότης) runs over the whole . . . [He has] what the people of Attica call a sharp nose (μυκτήρ) and urbane wit (ἀστεϊσμός); he cultivated this as the peak of culture (παιδεία), drawing entirely for his style upon the ancient comedy. (Eunapius *Lives of the Philosophers* 496 = XVI.2 Giangrande)

Quintilian's praise of the language of Old Comedy is also very close to a report of the *Praeparatio sophistica* of the Atticist lexicographer Phrynichus (late second century CE); the Byzantine patriarch Photius (Ar. T 69)[31] reports that Phrynichus included Aristophanes among those writers who were 'models and rules of the genuine and pure and Attic language' (εἰλικρινοῦς καὶ καθαροῦ καὶ Ἀττικοῦ λόγου). For Menander's language, on the other hand, Phrynichus had nothing but contempt (Menander T 119), and here

---

[29] Cf. Ussher (1977) 74f.   [30] Cf. Otto (1890) 44.   [31] Cf. also T 88–9.

again we may wonder whether Atticist scruples counted against the survival of the greatest figure of New Comedy.

Old Comedy transformed

If the frankness and 'vulgarity' of Old Comedy could, when necessary, be dismissed as unworthy of the attention of an educated man, allusions to the works of Aristophanes and his fellow poets abound in the Greek prose texts of the Roman empire; the 'idea' of Old Comedy was in fact a potent and attractive one. Lucian, for example, repeatedly drew inspiration for his satire from Old Comedy, and moralists found appeal to the critical nature of Old Comedy a helpfully authorizing analogy for their own activity. Thus, for example, in criticizing the frivolity and addiction to low entertainment of the people of Alexandria, Dio Chrysostom urges them to imitate the Athenians 'who allowed their poets to reprove not just individuals, but the city as a whole, if they behaved in any way inappropriately' (32.6); so too, in the rather similar *First Tarsian Oration* (cf. below), Dio (33.44) claims that some of his audience will say that he is insulting (ὑβρίζειν) their city, just as in the parabasis of the *Acharnians* Aristophanes claims that Cleon falsely accused him of 'mocking (κωμωιδεῖν) our city and insulting (καθυβρίζειν) the people' (*Acharnians* 631). On the contrary, Dio's speeches will make men 'stronger and more sensible and better able to administer their cities' (32.7); here indeed is the claim of the Aristophanic parabasis (cf., e.g., *Acharnians* 650) and the only thing that Aeschylus and Euripides can agree on in the *Frogs*:

> *Aeschylus.* Tell me, for what should a poet be admired?
> *Euripides.* For cleverness and the advice he gives, because we make men in
>   their cities better.
>
> (Aristophanes *Frogs* 1008–10)

Dio makes a rather more complex use of the model of Old Comedy in *Oration* 33 in which he takes to task the people of Tarsus for the mysterious, and presumably immoral, practice of 'snorting' (ῥέγχειν).[32] The speech is characterized throughout by a witty and allusive tone which sets it squarely within more than one tradition of satirical writing, but Old Comedy is never far away. Dio begins by contrasting himself with the ordinary, run-of-the mill speakers who deceive the audience with empty and commonplace encomium of the city, its surrounding countryside and people (cf. also chapter 23);

---

[32] On this speech see especially Bost Pouderon (2006); brief accounts in Desideri (1978) 122–9; Jones (1978) 73–5; and Swain (1996) 214–16; cf. also Bonner (1942).

the strategy is itself commonplace, but we may recall again the parabasis of *Acharnians* in which the chorus claim that the poet has worked much benefit in stopping the citizens from being deceived and taking pleasure in empty flattery, such as when ambassadors from the allied cities proclaim Athens 'violet-crowned' or 'shining' (both standard poetic epithets) (*Acharnians* 633–42). In chapter 9, Dio then introduces the standard paradigm of Athenian willingness to put up with the criticism of Old Comedy, though this criticism is now significantly called 'abuse' (λοιδορία); this paradigm is, moreover, no longer straightforwardly positive, as it is contrasted with the Athenian unwillingness to put up with the criticisms of Socrates, though the philosopher was carrying out 'the god's instruction' and also not performing any vulgar dance such as the *kordax*. The criticism of Old Comedy is now presented as anything but an unmixed blessing:

> The comic poets viewed the *dêmos* with suspicion and feared it, so they flattered it like a master (δεσπότης), only biting gently and with a smile; it was like wetnurses who smear honey around the edge of the cup when their young charges have to drink something unpleasant.[33] So it was that the comic poets did as much harm as good, for they filled the city with arrogant pride and jests and vulgar knockabout (βωμολοχία). (Dio Chrysostom 33.10)

Old Comedy did have a serious purpose, but it was so hedged around with comic byplay to make the *dêmos* laugh that the effect was at best mixed. Dio's view of Old Comedy here overturns its own claims by drawing material from it. The picture of the poets 'flattering' the *dêmos* clearly looks to Aristophanes' *Knights*, the whole of which might be described as a contest in flattery of Demos. Like Dio's audiences (or so Dio claims), the Aristophanic Demos 'enjoys being flattered' and 'all men fear [him] like a tyrant' (*Knights* 1111–20).[34]

Dio has a second alternative to Old Comedy, alongside Socrates, to brandish as his model in this speech. This is Archilochus, all of whose poetry is (according to Dio) devoted to attacking men's faults and who was very greatly honoured by Apollo. Archilochus thus becomes the spiritual ancestor of the 'Cynic preacher' such as Dio, not least in the fact that he censured

---

[33] The closeness to Lucretius 1.936–8 is, of course, noteworthy, but of particular interest in the present context is Horace *Satires* 1.1.23–6, where Horace seems, as in *Satires* 1.4, to reject the charge of *bômolochia*, and to compare one satirical technique ('telling the truth with a laugh') to teachers who reward children with cakes so that they will learn the alphabet. Given Horace's later claims in 1.4 for the genetic relationship of Old Comedy and Roman satire, the closeness to Dio 33.10 deserves more attention than it has received.

[34] Cf. also *Wasps* 620–30.

himself; such a man will offer no 'flattery or deceit' (chapter 14). By implication, both Archilochus and the Cynic (lit. 'dog-like') Dio carry a real 'bite'
(cf. 16, 44), not the 'gentle biting' of Old Comedy (10, above).[35] Dio's
preaching is thus one descendant of Archilochus' abusive poetry, as in some
ancient theory was Old Comedy also. Aristotle sees in Old Comedy the
inheritance of iambic (*Poetics* 1449a4, 1449b8), and later theory made the
abuse (λοιδορία) of Cratinus, in particular, heir to the Parian poet (*Proleg.*
II 1–2 Koster = Cratinus T 17).[36] This may simply be a result of the fact
that Cratinus wrote an Ἀρχίλοχοι ('Archilochus and his colleagues'), but it is
quite likely that that play did indeed create some kind of analogy between
Cratinus' comedy and Archilochus' abusive poetry, and it was that analogy
which in part lies behind the later critical tradition. As is very clear from,
for example, Horace's treatment of the links between comedy and Roman
satire in *Satires* 1.4,[37] the constructions of ancient literary history were flexible tools to be adapted to the rhetorical demands of different situations;
no one will challenge the 'historicity' of Dio's account. Dio is, moreover, in
part disingenuous: laughter, such as greeted Old Comedy, is one response
which he seeks, and satirical denunciation may, in antiquity no less than
now, 'flatter' the object of the attack and actually strengthen the hold of
the practices denounced. It may indeed be that Dio's attack upon Tarsian
'snorting' is more aligned with the 'innuendo' (ὑπόνοια) which Aristotle saw
as a feature of 'new comedies' and of the 'educated man' (*pepaideumenos*),
which Dio certainly claims to be, than with the 'blunt abuse' (αἰσχρολογία)
of 'old comedies' and, we might add, of Archilochus as he was traditionally
represented (*Nicomachean Ethics* 4.1128a20–4).[38]

Further reading

The proper history of the reception of comedy in antiquity has yet to be
written. On the contexts of Menander reception in antiquity see Nervegna
(2013). Chapter 3 of Hunter (2009) considers some of the approaches to
comedy and its history taken by later writers; in addition to the works cited
in the notes to this chapter see Nervegna, Chapter 20 and the opening pages
of Van Steen, Chapter 23.

---

[35] Callimachus fr. 380 Pf. paints a probably negative picture of Archilochus' angry bite.
[36] Cf. Perusino (1989) 64–6 and Bakola (2010) 4f., 17f. and 70–9.
[37] Cf. Hunter (2009) 99–106.
[38] Cf. 33.32, 'If I am unable clearly to explain what this fault is, you should try to work it
out (ὑπονοεῖν)'; contrast the proclaimed clarity (34.5) of the *Second Tarsian Oration*,
perhaps in deliberate contrast with the manner of the *First*.

20

SEBASTIANA NERVEGNA

Contexts of reception in antiquity

Performed in theatres and dining rooms, penned on papyri, illustrated on artefacts, cited and variously echoed by Greek and Roman authors alike, Greek comedy – and especially New Comedy – enjoyed a blissful, long-lasting afterlife in antiquity. If this is not always clear for us to see, that is simply because our sources are scattered, almost hidden, in a wide range of scholarly works, from keen philological commentaries to collections of inscriptions, thick catalogues of theatre-related monuments, and a steady stream of papyri. Rich yet often difficult to read, our sources for the ancient popularity of Greek plays can all be 'institutionally framed', that is, approached through the social institutions that produced and used them. Once properly identified and placed within the right context, they can be set within the larger picture, where they often point to trends and dynamics and, inevitably, expose problems and gaps. The ancient contexts of reception of Greek comedy and drama in general are three: public theatres, dinner parties (the Greek *symposia* and the Roman *convivia*) and schools. Different as they are or may appear, these venues all shared an interest in classical and Hellenistic Greek plays and contributed to their survival, articulating it into different strands. In this chapter, I can only provide a very brief sketch of how and why public audiences, diners, students, and teachers appropriated Greek comedy and kept it alive. Needless to say, these are all difficult questions: the ancient afterlife of Greek comedy, just like that of other literary genres, shuns the grand narrative to take up the feeble tone of fragmentary accounts.

By way of introduction, two points should be borne in mind. First, the tendency to reduce one specific kind of comedy to one author only. Ancient scholars often refer to the 'best three' of both Old Comedy (Aristophanes, Cratinus and Eupolis) and New Comedy (Menander, Diphilus and

I wish to thank Anthony Alexander, Michael Fontaine, J. Richard Green and Martin Revermann for their suggestions. I am indebted to the Kudos Foundation of Australia and the University of Sydney for their generous financial support.

Philemon).[1] In practice, however, both triads were further narrowed down to one single dramatist per genre, Aristophanes and Menander. Their plays feature most commonly on papyri and in literary quotations especially in the Roman period, with illustrations of Menander's drama virtually monopolizing our visual record for Greek New Comedy. To a large extent, the afterlife of the whole genre coincides with that of Aristophanes and Menander, and, in pointed contrast with the modern reception of both playwrights (see Van Steen, Chapter 23), ancient sources are overwhelmingly tilted towards Menander. To speak with images, Menander looks good gazing at a mask, holding a book roll as well as relaxing on a couch (see Figures 20.1–20.3).

Secondly, it is difficult to identify what kind of comedy our sources refer to when individual playwrights are not named. Following ancient scholars, we traditionally speak of 'Old Comedy' and 'New Comedy', with 'Middle Comedy' sandwiched in between, thus articulating the history of Greek comedy into clear-cut, nicely divided stages. Although misleading, since New Comedy-style plays were also written and performed in the heyday of Old Comedy and because Old Comedy, with its political verve, was still blooming after Aristophanes' death, this is a functional and commonly shared distinction.[2] Ancient sources, however, do not rely on the convenient triad Old-Middle-New, or at least not consistently. Aristotle, for instance, uses 'old comedy' (*palaia kômôidia*) to refer to our Old Comedy (*NE* 1128a22). But when 'old' plays were performed at festivals along with newly composed drama, as often happened, the 'old comedy' (*palaia kômôidia*) recorded on our inscriptions includes, at least occasionally, the name of Menander and his fellow-dramatists, i.e. our New Comedy. Latin translations of these terms raise further confusion. Writing in the Late Republic, Cicero refers to Aristophanes as 'the wittiest poet of old comedy (*veteris comoediae*)'; yet, when a few years later the Emperor Augustus 'relished [Greek] old comedy (*comoedia veteri*) and often put it on at public shows', we feel uncomfortable with

---

[1] The *locus classicus* for the canonization of Old Comedy is Hor. *Sat.* 1.4.1–2 (see also Quint. *Inst.* 10.1.65–6, Vell. Pat. 1.16.3); for New Comedy, see Vell. Pat. 1.16.3, Rufinus *GrL* 6, p. 564.7 and Diomedes *GrL* 1, 488.23. Note, however, that Aristotle (*Poet.* 1448a27) already acknowledged Aristophanes as a master of this genre and that the New Comedy trio first appears on the inscription recording competitions of 'old' plays in Athens around the mid-third century (*Hesperia* 7, 1938, 116–18; SEG XXVI 208), an important reminder of the role of actors' activities in canonizing poets and genres. All dates are BCE unless otherwise stated.

[2] The identification of three periods in Greek comedy is usually attributed to Hellenistic scholars: Nesselrath (1990) 172–87, for instance, favours Aristophanes of Byzantion. For Old and New Comedy as two co-existing styles in the classical and Hellenistic periods, see Csapo (2000).

Figure 20.1 Relief of a seated poet (Menander) with masks of New Comedy, first century–early first century CE. Princeton University Art Museum (y1951–1), Museum purchase, Caroline G. Mather Fund. Photo: Bruce M. White

the thought that the moralizing Augustus found Aristophanes' plays more congenial than Menander's.[3] Fluidity of terms, linguistic inconsistency and shifting usage: they all remind us, frustratingly, of the difference between common practice and the world of scholars and antiquarians.

From performance to reperformance

Unlike the Romans of the early Empire, for instance, who could cultivate and display their literary talent by writing plays and reading them to a select audience, classical dramatists wrote only for theatrical performance. Already in the fifth century, we also hear of reperformances. As a token of respect for Aeschylus, his tragedies were revived on the public stage soon after his death, around 456; so well received was the parabasis of

[3] Cic. *Laws* 2.37, Suet. *Aug.* 89.1 with Revermann (2006a) 86.

Figure 20.2 Wall painting reproducing Menander from the House of Menander in Pompeii (I.x.4), dated to the first century CE. Reproduced with permission of the Ministero per i Beni e le Attività Culturali

Aristophanes' *Frogs* that the play was 'even reperformed', probably at the Lenaea in 404.[4] A popular decree lies behind these early revivals at the main dramatic festivals in Athens: they were an exceptional honour sparingly

[4] *Life of Aeschylus* 12, Ar. *Ach.* 9–12 (see also Quint. *Inst.* 10.1.66, Phil. *Life of Apollonios* 6.11); Ar. *Frogs* hyp. 1c Dover (quotation) with Sommerstein (1993) 461–6; Revermann (2006a) 73. An earlier comic revival, Teleclides' *Sterroi*, is dated to 430: *IG* XIV 1098a (*IGUR* 215).

Figure 20.3 Mosaic pavement: Menander, Glycera, Spirit of Comedy (*Kômôidia*), late third century CE. Princeton University Art Museum (y1940–435). Gift of the Committee for the Excavation of Antioch to Princeton University. Photo: Bruce M. White

granted by the Athenian assembly, as rare in these contexts as they would become common later on, in Athens and beyond. In the fourth century, at least some of Aristophanes' plays such as *Women at the Thesmophoria*, *Acharnians* and *Frogs*, travelled to the West to entertain South Italian audiences and to be painted on their artefacts.[5] As far as we can tell, South Italian vases with scenes from Old Comedy, erroneously called 'phlyax vases', were produced mostly in Taras (Tarentum), a Spartan colony notoriously crazy about theatre.[6] Scholars have wondered about both the knowledge the local audience had of Athenian institutions and prominent figures – the flesh and blood of Aristophanic drama – and the practicalities involved in performing these plays. Choruses in particular must have been both hard

[5] The *Women at the Thesmophoria* are reproduced on an Apulian bell krater dated to about 370 (Würzburg H5697), and the *Acharnians* on a total of three Apulian relief gutti now scattered around the world: see Green (1994) 66. The Apulian bell krater thought to reproduce *Frogs* (formerly Berlin, Staatliche Museen F 3046; dated to 375–350) survives only in reproductions. Note also a Paestan bell krater dated to *c.* 350 (Salerno, Museo Provinciale Pc 1812) reproducing Eupolis' *Demes*. On these artefacts, see Csapo (2010b) 52–67 with earlier literature.

[6] Green (1991b). On theatrical activity in Taras, see also Todisco (2002) 163–6 and Revermann (2006a) 70, 257–9 who makes a case for Taras as the reperformance venue for our *Lysistrata*.

for foreign audiences to grasp and problematic for travelling performers to stage.[7] Even so, one should not underestimate the degree of theatrical culture in South Italy, with theatrically active centres like Metapontum, Thurii and Syracuse. In the second quarter of the fourth century, potters in Taras used theatrical scenes to decorate red-figured *askoi*, wine vessels specifically produced for the indigenous market of central and northern Apulia. These vases show the degree of knowledge or at least exposure to Greek comedy not only in Greek colonies but also in non-Greek settlements in South Italy.[8]

None of these problems comes up when situating Menander's plays outside Athens. With its love stories that could take place anywhere in the Greek world, its stock characters, domestic situations and, last but not least, its easy Greek, Menander's comedy can be easily transplanted across time and place. But at this stage, as the significant increase in the number of both theatres and comedies in the fourth century indicates, one can better speak of comedies for a growing (mostly) Attic market, rather than exported from Athens to other venues.[9] In his some thirty-year-long dramatic career, Menander produced over 100 plays, at least some of which quickly entered actors' repertoires: about thirty years after Menander's death, they were already restaged in Athens under the category of 'old comedy' (*palaia kômôidia*).[10] One surmises that New Comedy, if not always Menander in the Roman period, is also to be understood when we come across 'old comedy' (generally within a competition of 'old' plays) in other festival records from the Greek East dated well into the second century CE.[11] Festival-related inscriptions are not as detailed as one would wish, but Plutarch, a prolific Greek author who lived in the late first and early second century CE, fills this gap by explicitly mentioning public revivals of Menander. He probably watched them staged by Kuintos Markios Straton, a contemporary comic actor crowned in the most prestigious festivals and renowned for his expertise in Menander's drama.[12] An earlier performer who made Menander his *forte* also crops up in the *Palatine Anthology*, where Crinagoras, an epigrammatist and politician from Mytilene active in the Late Republic and

---

[7] Taplin (1993) ch. 9; see also Taplin (1999) 38, discussing early revivals of tragedy outside Athens. On Sicilian choruses in general, see Wilson (2007b).

[8] Robinson (2004), who also considers other kinds of vases with theatrical motifs meant for the indigenous market.

[9] Csapo (2004) especially 67; see also Taplin (1993) 94.

[10] *Hesperia* 7, 1938, 116–18 (SEG XXVI 208; 254, *Phasma*). See also *IG* II² 2323.129–30, 206–7 (c. 193 and 167; *Misogynes* and *Phasma*).

[11] For a review of our evidence for revivals and their format, see Nervegna (2007) and (2013) ch. 2.

[12] Plut. *Mor.* 854A-B; *IG* II² 12664 with Plut. *Mor.* 673C.

Early Empire, records the inscription on the tomb of an actor, 'you excelled in the many dramas that Menander wrote with one of the Muses or one of the Graces'.[13]

Although both inscriptions and literary sources conjure up the picture of a lively theatrical tradition with performance of new plays hand in hand with revivals of 'old' ones, the exact format of these revivals is harder to gauge. This is partly because the epigraphic and literary records are not as specific as one would wish and partly because they are both scanty and scattered. Although Menander did not compose choral songs for his comedies, his scripts envisage and make room for interludes by a chorus often described as 'drunken young men'. Occasionally given a specific identity (they are Pan-worshippers in *Dyscolus* and perhaps huntsmen in *Hêrôs*), they delivered songs on set themes which were included in their first performance and apparently retained in later stagings.[14] At the Amphictyonic Soteria held in Delphi around the mid-third century, dramatic performances of (probably) old plays included a comic chorus of seven members in three instances and eight in one case.[15] Of great interest is a remark by the Greek rhetor Dio Chrysostom (*Or.* 19.5) in a speech dated to the late first century CE: the drama staged in his day, he writes, is mostly 'old' (*archaia*) and, while tragedies have lost their lyrics to be reduced to their iambic parts, 'all is kept of comedy'. This suggests full-length comic revivals, still punctuated by choral interludes: the late expression 'silent like a chorus of Menander' was probably foreign to theatrical practice.[16]

Variously adapted and adjusted for Republican audiences, in the hands of the authors of *palliatae*, the Roman comedies of Greek subject matter, 'old' Greek comedies became 'new' – a point Terence obsessively stresses.[17] Not that comedies of Roman subject matter, the *togatae*, were not influenced by Greek models: to craft his *togatae*, Afranius at least freely helped himself to Menander's drama.[18] Even when public dramatic performances in the Roman West thinned out, men of letters kept composing comedies fashioned after the Greek masterpieces, and especially Menander's. Pliny the Younger,

---

[13] *Anthologia Palatina* 9.513, on which see Gow and Page (1968) 259.

[14] *Dyscolus* 230f., *Hêrôs* fr. 1 with Arnott (1996b) 39. For tipsy young men as chorus members, see *Aspis* 247f., *Men at Arbitration* 169f., *Perikeiromenê* 261f.

[15] Nachtergael (1977) 299–328 with *Actes* 2–11; Le Guen (2007) 106.

[16] On this expression, see Burkert (2000).

[17] Ter. *Andria* 12, *Heauton Timoroumenos* 7, *Hecyra* 2, *Phormio* 9.

[18] Plautus securely used Menandrean models for *Kolax*, *Bacchides* (*Dis Exapatôn*), *Cistellaria* (*Synaristôsai*) and *Stichus* (*First Adelphoe*), as did Terence for *Adelphoe* (based on *Second Adelphoe*), *Andria*, *Heauton Timoroumenos* and *Eunuchus*. See Fontaine, Chapter 21. For Menander's influence on Afranius, see Macr. *Sat.* 6.1.4, Cic. *Fin.* 1.7, Hor. *Ep.* 2.1.57.

a senator and a writer of the High Empire, claims that he had recently heard Vergilius Romanus deliver to a small audience a superb comedy modelled after Old Comedy (*ad exemplar veteris comoediae*). Vergilius had already authored comedies in imitation of Menander and his fellow-playwrights, comedies which could proudly stand next to those of Plautus and Terence, yet this was his first experiment with Old Comedy.[19] In the late first or early second century CE, the politician Marcus Pomponius Bassulus both adapted some of Menander's plays and composed original ones, making a point of recording on his tombstone his literary activity, pursued not to spend his leisurely hours 'like a sheep' (*CIL* IX 1164). Apuleius also entertained himself with drama, producing, among other things, a (Plautine) version of an excerpt titled *Anechomenos* and drawn 'from Menander'.[20] Even more interesting is the case of the fourth-century CE grammarian Apollinarios of Laodicea, in Syria. In his attempt to fight back the Emperor Julian's attack against the Christians, now banned from public schools and Greek studies, Apollinarios turned himself into a novel (and even better) Homer to produce his own epos on the Hebrews. Bent on replacing the basic school works of Greek poetry with adaptations of Christian content, he also added to his poem imitations of Euripides' tragedy, Pindar's lyric and Menander's comedy (Sozomenon, *Historia Ecclesiastica* 5.18.4).

The point here is that Menander set the model for writing comedies, regardless of the use made of them. In spite of his early revivals, Aristophanes lost appeal with later theatre-goers and dramatists. It is possible that his drama was publicly staged under the philhellenic and archaizing Hadrian, who was the former master of an Athenian actor of Old Comedy (*archaia*) named Aristomenos and dubbed 'Attic Partridge', a nickname which smacks of Aristophanic language. A similar case could be made for the reign of Commodus since the festival record from Aphrodisias, in Caria, includes *archaia kômôidia*.[21] At least occasionally, later playwrights and authors in general drew inspiration from Aristophanes,[22] but Menander's and Menander-like plays were what public audiences almost invariably watched on the stage and what later 'dramatists' most consistently imitated. Against this background, it is not surprising that ancient scholars could refer to Menander

---

[19] Pliny *Ep.* 6.21. See also Synesius of Cyrene, *Dio* 18, 278, 10.
[20] *Anth. Lat.* 712 R; Men. F 431 K.-A. See May (2006) 63–71.
[21] Ath. 3.115b (see also SHA *Hadr.*19.6), *MAMA* VIII 420; Roueché (1993) 173–4, no. 53. See Jones (1993) 46f.
[22] In addition to Vergilius Romanus, see also the Hellenistic playwright Machon, who made 'Attic thyme' bloom along the Nile (*AP* 7.708, with Gow and Page (1965) 258). Bowie (2007) reviews Aristophanes' influence on Greek authors of the second and third century CE.

simply as 'the comic poet' and that a Pompeian inscription may even make him the inventor of comedy.[23]

From public theatres to dinner parties

In the competitive theatre business of the Classical period, making one's name and keeping it up was a tough job. Dramatists, *khorêgoi*, actors and choruses all rivalled for the approval of the judges and for the favour of theatre-goers whom the chorus of Aristophanes' *Knights* describes as fickle and quick to make and break a poet. Their example is Magnes, who was beloved in his youth only to be booed off the stage in his old age, the same turn of fortunes Cratinus is now facing. And to think that Cratinus used to be such a hit that, 'at a *symposion* there was no other singing than "Doro with fig-sandal" and "Artists of handy hymns"'![24] Comic distortion and exaggeration aside (Cratinus' *Satyrs* was competing against Aristophanes' *Knights*), the *symposion* is here the ground where a playwright's reception is measured. From classical and Hellenistic Athens to fourth-century Syracuse and Macedonia, guests mix wine with dramatic speeches and songs, invariably with a preference for tragedy.[25] They keep doing so under the Empire too, though now very rarely.[26] The second-century CE scholar Gellius tells us that, during their *rendezvous*, he and his friends 'often read' Roman comedies, at least occasionally setting them side by side with their Greek originals by Menander and other New Comedy poets. This is the context of their famous comparison between select excerpts from Caecilius' *Necklace* and its Menandrean model, a comparison made, as usual, to the detriment of the Roman author.[27] Gellius may well exaggerate about his scholarly meetings and, given his suspicious phrasing, may even be simply using them as an artistic device rather than an actual account, but it is still significant that the only Roman 'diners' we explicitly hear of as entertaining each other with drama are very different from their earlier counterparts. Now the scholars who populate the *Attic Nights*, they do not recite from memory but read drama. This is not to say, however, that all ancient diners were as literary minded as Gellius and his friends: dinner parties could also offer room for innovation and experiments and they are perhaps the

---

[23] *CIL* IV Suppl. III 1.7350 with Linderski (2007) especially 51–2.

[24] Ar. *Knights* 529–30. The lines cited are Cratinus, *Eumenides* PCG F 70.

[25] Athens: Ar. *Clouds* 1364–72; Plut. *Lys.* 15.3; Ephippus, *Homoioi* or *Obeliaphoroi* PCG F 16, 1–3; Theoph. *Char.* 27.2; 15.10. Fourth-century Syracuse: Timaeus *FGrH* 566 F 32; fourth-century Macedonia: Aeschin. *In Tim.* 168, Nikoboule *FGrH* 127 F 2.

[26] The latest (and wholly fictional) reference to this practice is Julian, *Symposion* 310b: Silenus sings Aristophanes' *Knights* to mock the Emperor Claudius.

[27] Gell. *NA* 2.23 with Holford-Strevens (2003) 67, 198–201.

venue of musical and variously altered versions of both Aristophanes' and Menander's lines delivered by the guests.[28]

Guests entertaining each other with drama dwindle under the Empire, but another, more interesting practice comes to the forefront, private dramatic performances. In this as in many other things, Alexander the Great left his stamp: the entertainment programme at the mass-marriage he organized in his palace in 324 included both tragedy and comedy staged by Greek actors.[29] When it comes to trends and fashions, the step from Hellenistic royal palaces to the houses of the wealthy Romans under the Republic and the Empire is, indeed, a short one. The Romans, however, conveniently owned their performers, as we read on the inscriptions from the *columbaria*, the dove-like structures where Roman plutocrats buried their household staff. These records occasionally include comic actors: we find them, for instance, in the households of Augustus' family members, his wife Livia and his nieces the Elder and Younger Marcella, and of close associates of the Emperor like the Statilii.[30] Next to working as private teachers, comic actors also generated revenues for their masters by training other actors and performing both publicly and privately.[31] Their versatility made them as expensive to buy as valuable to have: they were a hot commodity which also spoke well of their master's cultural standing. In the elegant world of Pliny the Younger, comic actors are among the entertainers an educated Roman would typically expect at a proper *soirée*. Pliny himself makes comedy a staple feature of his home entertainment, regardless of the company, of the season and even of the villa where he is sojourning.[32]

Unlike Pliny (and other sources), Plutarch uniquely specifies what kind of comedy he enjoys over dinner: Menander's. This is a conscious choice Plutarch and his friends helpfully justify with a thorough review of the various dinner shows available, from drama to mime and musical performances

---

[28] Two texts could be linked with sympotic performances: P.Oxy. 3705, which has half a line from Menander's *Perikeiromenê* with four different settings (though this text could also belong to a school context) and an unpublished *ostrakon* from Upper Egypt which apparently preserves some words from the hoopoe's song in Aristophanes' *Birds* accompanied by musical notation. See Hall (2007a) 8.

[29] Ath. 12.538b–539a (citing Chares of Mytilene), Ael. *VH* 8.7. See in general Csapo (2010b) ch. 6.

[30] *CIL* 6.3926, 4436, 6252, 6253 (see Leppin (1992) 215, 264, 260–1, 308). On *columbaria* in general, see Hasegawa (2005) chs. 2 and 3.

[31] Plut. *Cat. Mai.* 21.7 (skilled slaves as trainers), SHA *Hadr.* 19.6 (Hadrian's own performers also entered public competitions). See also *Dig.* 38.1.25, 27: Roman law allowed masters who had performers as freedmen to hire out their services and to use them as they liked. On private performers as a source of income, see Sick (1999) especially 337–42. On comic actors as teachers, see below.

[32] Pliny *Ep.* 1.15.2–3, 9.17.3, 9.36.4, 9.40.2.

(*Mor.* 711B–713F). While stylistic features, topicality and indecent humour do not make Old Comedy jive with wine, New Comedy, that is Menander, ranks even higher than the drinks. Enacted by 'men performing Menander' or by a '*kômôidos* got at a high price', Menander's plays are both perfect and integral to dinner parties for many a reason: suitable and edifying plots, pleasant style, useful maxims, and a blend of serious and funny.[33] More of their qualities emerge from Plutarch's judgement of other dinner shows which are instead to be avoided, the Pyladic dance and a type of mime called *hypothesis*. Among other things, the former 'requires a large cast' and the latter is both too long and 'difficult to stage' (711E, 712E). Note also Plutarch's reference to Aristophanes' too fiery and outspoken parabaseis as yet another strike against Old Comedy: he is envisaging full-scale revivals.[34] By default, one concludes, Menander's short dramatic actions, coupled with minimal staging requirements and a small cast, are extra advantages for their convivial use: with Menander, moral edification is married with practical concerns. Put on a stage by a troupe of actors (the same as those involved in public shows) and at least occasionally held within a competitive frame, private dramatic performances were an elaborate and costly form of dinner entertainment.[35] The big difference which marked off these performances from the public ones, one suspects, lies not in their format but in the nature of their audience, now hand-picked by the very wealthy hosts who could afford to own or rent actors and who either had a private theatre or could turn their dining room or garden into one.

This is a point worth emphasizing. Offering drama over dinner is a feature of the Roman banquet as 'a procession and a *theatron* [where] the drama of wealth is brought on', not a widespread practice as current scholarship often makes it on the basis of the extant Menander portraits and illustrations of his plays excavated in ancient houses.[36] With only one surviving portrait, Aristophanes was virtually unknown to ancient viewers and the same is also largely

---

[33] Plut. *Mor.* 673B, 531B, 712B–D. The use of *kômôidos* to refer to the entire troupe is common in theatre-related documents: see Nervegna (2007) 29 with earlier literature. For comic troupes performing in private settings, see also Petr. *Sat.* 53.13 and Gaius, *Institutiones* 3.212 (slave *comoedi* are conceived as a troupe).

[34] Plut. *Mor.* 711F–712A. See also Jones (1993) 192f. A chorus also crops up in the performance of Euripides' *Bacchae* at a betrothal party in Parthia (Plut. *Crass.* 33.2–4): though suspicious at best, this anecdote is still good evidence for what could be thought possible, at least for kings.

[35] On private theatres, see Sear (2006) 46f. Private stages: Sall. *Hist.* 2.59.1–4, Sen. *Q. Nat.* 7.32.3; private dramatic competitions: Epict. 3.4.11. As Dunbabin (1996) and (2003) especially 169–74 argue, the need for more room for entertainment (and service) also affected the lay-out of Roman dining rooms, leading to the introduction of the outward-looking sigma couch in the late second century CE.

[36] Plut. *Mor.* 528B, on which see D'Arms (1999) especially 301–3.

true of his plays, which dropped out of artists' repertoires after *c.* 330.[37] By contrast, our visual record for Menander is overwhelming. Fashioned after early-Hellenistic archetypes, Menander's portraits and illustrations of his comedies quickly found their way into Roman houses scattered throughout the Empire to be included in the decorative programme of their social areas. Not only is Menander the Greek author most widely reproduced in ancient art, but his plays also held a firm spot in dramatic iconography through-out antiquity.[38] House-owners who could entertain and impress their guests with drama were the upper-crust only (the Emperors and their associates), and those who could and wanted to deliver drama to each other were the very *crème* of ancient connoisseurs. But many could, of course, follow artis-tic trends and ape the elite's means and learning. The houses in the Vesuvian area, for instance, yielded a rich number of dramatic scenes displayed in spaces such as halls and reception rooms, yet grander areas to host perfor-mances are at best hard to find. Given their size, their dining rooms allowed 'only limited space for entertainers: a little music, recitation, a couple of dancers, but nothing really fancy'.[39]

From theatres to schools

Nothing exemplifies Menander's leading role as a school author better than his recurrent association with Homer, the founding father of Greek literature and the bedrock of ancient training.[40] Our records show that Menander owed such an authoritative position to two features of his plays, maxims and characterization, a point often combined with Menander's lifelikeness.

Surgically lifted and often variously adjusted from his comedies or simply circulating under Menander's name, *Menander's Maxims* as they eventually came to be known, entered ancient as well as medieval classrooms.[41] Copied on papyri, *ostraka* and wax tablets, they offered young students penman-ship and memorization material as much as food for thought: their themes

[37] Unlike Menander and a number of other poets (see Fittschen (1995)), Aristophanes was apparently not honoured with a statue in the Theatre of Dionysus in Athens. All we have is one headless herm from Hadrian's villa inscribed with Aristophanes' name (*IG* XIV 1140) and three heads thought to represent him. See Richter (1984) 94f. For illustrations of his plays, see above.
[38] Menander's portraits: Fittschen (1991); Bassett (2008); Nervegna (2013) 122–36. Illustrations of Menander's plays: Green and Seeberg (1995) 1.85–98; Csapo (1999); Nervegna (2010) and (2013).
[39] Dunbabin (1996) 70.
[40] Select references: *IG* XIV 1183, Stat. *Silv.* 2.1.113–19, Aus. *Ep.* 21.45–7, Ferrandus, *Life of Fulgentius* 1 PL 65, 119B.
[41] Editions of *Menander's Maxims*: Jäkel (1964); Pernigotti (2008). See also Liapis (2002) and (2006).

(wealth, women and education, for instance) inculcated values and shaped children's ethical world.[42] Later on, these one-liners with a literary pedigree acquired a new life as elegant citations meant to legitimize the compositions that few, privileged students would write under the grammarian and the rhetor – one of the many examples of economy in the use of cultural models. At this stage, however, students' exposure to Menander also included longer excerpts, mostly speeches, which Greek and Roman authors alike celebrated as models of style. They were to be used for two specific exercises, both ideally supervised by a rhetor: the 'speech in character', one of the so-called 'preliminary exercises' which build up to longer compositions; and declamations, the pinnacle of ancient training and the pastime of ancient intellectuals.[43]

The Greek saying 'a man speaks as he lives' (e.g., Quint. *Inst.* 11.1.30), a mainstay of ancient rhetoric, also found Menander's characterization by use of language quite appealing. Linguistically speaking, Aristophanes thinks in bipolar terms, Athenians and non-Athenians, be they from Sparta or Persia, and he denies his characters the individualizing speech patterns and socially differentiating expressions which are typical of Menander's.[44] Consider Gorgias in his confrontation with another young man, Sostratus, in *Dyscolus*.[45] He starts with a maxim on the instability of human fortunes, passed off as his own with an emphatic 'I' at end of the line, to go on to contrast the fate of the haughty rich, which is subject to collapse, and that of the earnest poor, which is subject to improvement. By the end of his speech, however, good fortune has become a durable possession which Sostratus, Gorgias recommends, should seem to deserve (and behave accordingly). Bookish and stiff with maxims, antithesis and old-fashioned expressions, Gorgias' little piece is also sprinkled with faulty logic. If we did not have the play but only this excerpt, its speaker could still be identified for what Gorgias actually is, a man hidden away in the country with little practice in speech-making.

---

[42] Cribiore (1996) lists over twenty school documents recording maxims by or attributed to Menander and ranging from the first to the seventh century CE. Menander is first associated with maxims on a second- or third-century CE papyrus also penned by a student, *PGiss* 348 (Pap. III Jäkel), on which see Brashear (1985). On maxims, their themes and their role in early education, see Morgan (1998) 125–44.

[43] On Menander as a model for 'speeches in character': Theon, *Progymnasmata* 2, 68, 21–4 Sp.; as a model for declamations: Quint. *Inst.* 10.1.71. For excerpts from plays by Menander or attributed to him on school-related papyri, see e.g., *PIFAO* 89 + *PKöln* 282, *POxy* 409 + 2655, *PLouvre* 7172. Stobaeus' anthology, probably dated to the fifth century CE, preserves many maxims and passages from Menander.

[44] Plut. *Mor.* 853C–E with Hunter (2000) 270–2 and (2009) 84–9. On linguistic characterization in Greek comedy, see Willi (2002b) 29–31; (2003a) 68f. and 226f., and Chapter 8.

[45] *Dyscolus* 271–87 with Sandbach (1970) 116–19.

Since ancient rhetorical training, unlike its modern counterpart, never lost sight of its oral dimension, Greek comic poetry fostered both students' writing and delivery skills. A comic actor is the first teacher of Quintilian's would-be orator (*Inst.* 1.11.1–14): next to correcting faulty pronunciation and teaching voice production, he has the tasks of harmonizing gesture and speech, correcting facial expressions as well as providing a model of delivery. But first and foremost, Quintilian stresses along with a host of ancient rhetors, speakers are to be trained to avoid staginess and differentiate themselves as much as possible from actors, who in the Roman world were mostly slaves.[46] Greek rhetors, on the other hand, tend to be less restrained in their recommendations. Consider the *scholion* to Dionysius Thrax' *Art of Grammar* attributed to Melampodos or Diomedes: 'One must [read] comic plays as in life, imitating young or old women, fearful or angry men, and all that suits the characters brought onto the stage in Menander, Aristophanes or other comic poets.'[47] Impersonating hysterical heroines like Andromache, Hecuba and Niobe was part of the Greek curriculum in the second as in the fourth century CE: there is little concern here for dangerous emotions entering pupils' souls or womanish mimicry affecting their masculinity.[48] If you were one of Libanius' students in late-antique Antioch and you were a skilled actor, you would have been picked to act out plays in front of the whole class.[49] This all points to school performances: the same teachers who fragmented Greek plays into select excerpts, from maxims to longer passages, possibly also kept them alive as performance texts.[50]

When ancient writers recommend future orators to forge their speech on Menander, consistently harping on his maxims, style and lifelikeness, they are not formulating original opinions, but rehearsing and rationalizing a well-established practice. From the Hellenistic period to the rise of Christianity as an educational force, school practices and the pedagogical discourse in general remained, to a large extent, chained to their Hellenistic structures and methods.[51] As part of the literary canon, neither Menander nor Aristophanes could be disposed of, but the use made of them differed. Consider

[46] Quint. *Inst.* 1.11.2f., 11.3.57, 181–4; see also *e.g.*, *Rhet. Her.* 3.24, 26; Cic. *De Or.* 1.251, 3.220. See Fantham (2002) 370–3; Richlin (1997) 99–105.
[47] Schol. Dion. Thr. *GrGr* I 3 p. 16, 21–5.
[48] E.g., [Hermogenes] *Progymnasmata* 9.32 (21, 14 R), Aphthonius, *Progymnasmata* 11, 45–6 Sp. See also Connolly (2001a) on the theatricality of Greek sophists' performances.
[49] Lib. *Ep.* 190.2 Norman with Cribiore (2008) 165. School performances are likely to be the contexts of the so-called 'actors' papyri' preserving dramatic texts, see Nervegna (2013) 111.
[50] This is not to say that whole plays (and texts in general) did not circulate among students. The *Bodmer Codex* of Menander, for instance, belongs to a school context: see Fournet (1992); Cribiore (2001) 200f.
[51] Marrou (1956) xiii.

papyri in schoolhands, which preserve much Menander but no Aristophanes at all. Aristophanes, who gained ground in the Byzantine period as Menander's comedies fell out of favour, entered school training at an advanced level,[52] when students had already a fluent handwriting – something which should alert us to the possibility that some of our Aristophanes-papyri could be school products. Making a large use of Menander and a limited one of Aristophanes responded to sensible practical concerns. A more accessible Greek and an easier subject matter, the same reasons why a 'typical' theatre-goer or a diner like Plutarch enjoyed New rather than Old Comedy, promptly suggest themselves. This is not to say that ancient authors did not recognize Aristophanes' merits: Cicero and Gellius celebrate his wit; pure Attic speech, charm and elegance have Quintilian rank Old Comedy as the best model for orators, right after Homer.[53] Positive comments also focused on Old Comedy's healthy political function, with its exposé of vice and faults.[54]

But Old Comedy has also a dangerous aspect, which is best exemplified by the single episode that looms most largely in the ancient (and modern too: see Van Steen, Chapter 23) reception of Aristophanes, his responsibility in Socrates' conviction. Turned into an accomplice in the plot against Socrates and allegedly paid to write the *Clouds*, Aristophanes earned much blame for Socrates' death, a catastrophic event which, in the opinion of a late author, triggered the decline of Athens and eventually of the whole of Greece.[55] If not overtly dangerous, Old Comedy is unrefined and vulgar, the work of a drunken man.[56] Low buffoonery, indecent and inappropriate words, and misuse of *parrhêsia* (freedom of speech) are, Plutarch writes, all good reasons to make both the larger and the sophisticated public turn away, and to place Aristophanes' drama next to mimes.[57] Plutarch's comments belong to a tradition which is as old as Plato and Aristotle and which casts Old Comedy as vulgar and unrefined only to bespeak uneasiness with personal abuse and slander.[58] Aristophanes' drama and its outspokenness are a direct product of Athenian democracy: so well do they represent it that Plato allegedly sent

---

[52] Cribiore (2001) 201 with earlier literature.
[53] Cic. *Laws* 2.37; Gell. *NA* 1.15.19, 13.25.7; Quint. *Inst.* 10.1.65.
[54] E.g., Cic. *Rep.* 4.11f. (who also adds that the Twelve Tables included the death penalty for public slander); Quint. *Inst.* 10.1.65.
[55] Eun. *VS* 6.2.4; see also e.g., Σ *Clouds* 627, Ael. *VH* 2.13, Max. Tyr. 3.3. [Plut.] *Mor.* 10C praises Socrates' exemplary self-control in the face of Aristophanes' ridicule of him. Pl. *Apol.* 19c is the earliest mention of Aristophanes' responsibility for Socrates' bad reputation with the jurors.
[56] Ath. 10, 429A, Σ *Knights* 92; see also Ael. Arist. *Or.* 29, especially 27f.
[57] Plut. *Mor.* 853A–854D, 712A, 712E, 71C–D. See Hunter (2000) 270 and (2009) 84.
[58] Pl. *Laws* 816d, 935e; Arist. *Pol.* 1336b.

a copy of Aristophanes to the tyrant Dionysius of Syracuse who wanted to learn about the Athenian constitution.[59] A source of anxiety already in classical Athens, *parrhêsia* is hard to fit into political and cultural contexts with little room or tolerance for it. As Connolly (2001b) argues, during the Empire the conservative tendency of ancient education put a strain on ancient teachers now struggling to match the ethical system in schools with that outside of schools. Selecting, revising and manipulating did the trick.

Reception history as social history

Once viewed through the lens of social institutions, the reception of Greek comedy opens a window on dramatic and social history alike: the different response that social institutions granted to earlier texts sheds light both on the survival of plays and on the real or projected nature of these institutions. With their family-focused plots and their moralistic stance, Menander's comedies were beautifully suited to inform the speech and articulate the thoughts of subjects to a central rule, both inside and outside theatres. As Plautus has his ill-starred fisherman answer to an old man's lecture, comic actors get applause for teaching people good things with their wise sayings even if, once at home, nobody cares for their rules of wisdom (*Rope* 1249–52). Horace (*AP* 319–22) adds that at times plays built on well-drawn characters and peppered with moral passages are well received even if they lack charm, weight and skill. It speaks well of Plutarch, Gellius and all their friends that they enjoy Menander's drama in their spare time: the learned and sophisticated elite of the High Empire makes room for self-improvement even when relaxing on a couch. Aristophanes is too hard, too 'dirty', speaks of inappropriate things and cannot use words properly. He reeks of wine and his hands are even stained with Socrates' blood. Whether performed on public or private stages, delivered in schools, copied or excerpted by students and teachers, in all of their various uses, the comedies of graceful Menander made good citizens and refined gentlemen.

Further reading

The starting point for readers interested in the ancient afterlife of Aristophanes and Menander are the *testimomia* collected in Kassel and Austin (1983–) vols. iii 2 and vi 2. Nervegna (2013) gathers and discusses our sources for the ancient afterlife of Menander in public theatres, dinner parties and schools. The iconographic evidence is collected and discussed

---

[59] *Life of Aristophanes* 40–5.

by Taplin (1993) (Old Comedy) and Green and Seeberg (1995) (New Comedy). Many sources on the afterlife of classical and Hellenistic Greek drama can also be found in Csapo and Slater (1995). Nervegna (2007) discusses public revivals of classical and Hellenistic Greek drama in antiquity with a particular focus on their format. Jones (1991) is the pioneering work on the use of Greek drama at dinner parties; see also Csapo (1999), (2010b) and Nervegna (2010) who deal with both literary and iconographic sources. Important studies on specific periods are Fantham (1984) on the afterlife of Menander in early-imperial Rome; Bowie (2007) on the use of Aristophanes' drama by Greek authors of the second and third century CE; and May (2006) especially chapter 2 on the reception of both Greek and Roman comedy in the second century CE. Green (1994) chapters 5 and 6 discuss Greek drama in the Hellenistic and Roman periods, with particular attention to the material record. The works on ancient education by Morgan (1998) and Cribiore (2001) shed much-needed light on the school use of drama by collecting and discussing both papyri in schoolhands and literary sources. For more recent works on various aspects of the reception of Greek drama, Green's review (2008) 109–18 is very helpful.

21

MICHAEL FONTAINE

The reception of Greek comedy in Rome

Old and New Comedy in Rome

Although many of the Greek texts and commentaries on them were still available as late as the second century CE, Attic Old Comedy made no discernible impact at all on the Latin-speaking population of Rome at any time, in either the creative arts or intellectual life. No frescoes, mosaics, vases, sculptures or other specimens of the plastic arts indicate any familiarity at all among the Latin populace with the genre. Among them Old Comedy was never performed, and if it was ever read, which is unlikely, it aroused almost no interest or enthusiasm among any of Rome's writers during the classical period, from the earliest poets of the third century BCE down through the end of pagan antiquity. While the inspiration for the aggression of Roman satire was sometimes sought in Old Comedy's freedom to parody men active in political affairs, the relation was merely analogical, not derivative, and it is not at all clear that Eupolis, Cratinus and Aristophanes were ever more than merely names taken at second or third hand to the few Roman authors that mention them. Even Cicero, the one author who would have been likely to do so, almost certainly never read anything of Old Comedy; verses that he seems to quote in a letter to his brother Quintus from Aristophanes' *Acharnians* (659–61), which would prove otherwise, are in fact only the lines of Euripides that Aristophanes had parodied. With the exception of an 'old comedy' purportedly written by one Vergilius Romanus in the early second century CE, references in Latin to *vetus* or *antiqua comoedia*, 'old comedy', refer almost invariably either to revived performances of the New Comedy of Menander and his peers, or to the sophisticated Latin adaptations of these comedies that we conventionally call *fabulae palliatae*, 'plays in a Greek cloak', or, more commonly, 'Roman comedy'.[1]

---

[1] Roman knowledge of Old Comedy: Quadlbauer (1960) 52–70. Old Comedy in the second century CE: Rusten *et al.* (2011). Satire and Old Comedy: Horace: *Satires* 1.4.1–8; *AP* 282ff.; Persius 1.123–5; Cicero *De republica* 4.11; contra, Cucchiarelli

Unlike Old Comedy, enthusiasm for these adaptations of New Comedy in Rome of the middle to late third and second centuries BCE was tremendous. Twenty-six of them survive, of which twenty are by Plautus (T. Maccius Plautus, *fl. c.* 210–184 BCE), and six by Terence (P. Terentius Afer, *fl.* 166–160 BCE), along with one very fragmentary play of Plautus and several hundred short and scattered fragments preserved by grammarians of Plautus and a dozen or so other comedians active in those years.

By the time Plautus began mounting theatrical performances in Rome in the late third century BCE, Latin comedy had been an established genre for a generation. By the 140s new productions were declining, and by the end of the second century BCE comedy as a vital genre was extinct; henceforth it survived only in revived performances of older scripts, occasional dabblings by amateurs and obscure poetasters probably intended for recitals, and as school texts to be read by such aristocratic Roman youths as Cicero or Julius Caesar.[2] In its heyday (*c.* 210–160 BCE), however, these Roman comedies were performed in temporarily erected theatres at up to four regular public festivals in Rome, each held annually and lasting more than one day, as well as at a number of occasional festivals, including public funerals for leading citizens of the state.

All in all, then, we have much more of these Roman adaptations than we have of Greek New Comedy itself – and yet many think we can hardly glimpse Greek comedy itself through these adaptations. Why? What was this genre of 'Roman comedy'?

How 'Greek' is Roman comedy? Roman comedy as operatic adaptation

First, a preliminary word is in order. In 1974 John Wright convincingly demonstrated that Plautus and the fragmentary Roman comedians all cultivated a 'stylistic unity', that is, the adaptations by the fragmentary comedians all probably looked at least superficially similar to those of Plautus. Wright also showed, however, that Terence, whose six comedies survive, was in many ways an exceptional poet who eschewed this stylistic unity. Accordingly, in speaking of the style of Roman comedy, 'Plautus' often refers by shorthand to 'the collective Roman Comedians except for Terence'.[3] What does this stylistic unity mean in practice?

(2001) attempts to show that Horace *Satires* 1.5 is indebted to Aristophanes' *Frogs*. Cicero and Aristophanes: Quadlbauer (1960) 55f.; Wright (1931) 80–3. Cicero's letter: *ad Quint.* 8.8.2 (= 158.2 Shackleton Bailey). Vergilius Romanus: Pliny *Epist.* 6.21.
[2] Lowe (2008) 83–7, 92–5, 130f.; Menander test. 69 (= CIL IX 1164, epitaph of Pomponius Bassulus). Caesar and Cicero: Courtney (1993) 153.
[3] See Wright (1974) 127–51, 183 and passim.

Roman comedy preserves the Greek setting of its source texts. Plays are set in Athens or, more rarely, other real locales in the Hellenized world (Cyrene, Epidaurus, etc.). While this Hellenic milieu remained the same, however, 'Roman' comedy differed from Greek New Comedy in two important structural respects that tend to be overshadowed by more salient differences. That is because students coming to Roman comedy for the first time are invariably impressed by the genre's most obvious feature – namely, that it is written in Latin rather than Greek. While this change of language is certainly its most obvious feature, it is also, I submit, probably the *least* important difference between Greek and 'Roman' comedy, and certainly a distraction from the really important differences. As we will see below, it also encourages us to approach the interpretation of Roman comedy from some misconceived premises.

One of the structural differences made by Roman comedy was the elimination of act-breaks and choral *entr'actes* in favour of continuous action. While Greek comedy was written as a series of five acts predominately in mimetic, spoken iambic trimeters, with musical interludes performed by a chorus between acts, the Roman comedians eliminated the chorus entirely in favour of continuous performance from start to finish. (In this respect comedy differs starkly from 'Roman' tragedy, which did *not* eliminate the chorus.) The other change is more original and more startling. Roman comedies transformed more than half of the simple spoken iambic verses of their models into longer verses that were chanted or sung to musical accompaniment performed on reed pipes (*tibiae*). This musicalized verse (*canticum*) includes both the fairly regularized trochaic *septenarii* – the metre resembles that of *Ode to Joy* – as well as far more sophisticated lyrical songs in constantly changing metres (in Latin, *cantica mixtis modis*), corresponding to what we would call arias and duets. The Roman poets, in other words, first massively increased the proportion of these musical verses relative to that of spoken verse (*deverbia*), and then *integrated* this song into the continuous mimesis, presenting these songs in scenes alternating at unpredictable intervals with the spoken iambic *senarii*.[4] Though it self-avowedly took much of its material for plot and character from a Greek play, then, many a Roman comedy was essentially a musical, not a 'drama' as we conceive of it, and in performance the two plays would have created a very different impression. Although it is frequently seen as a secondary consideration, this important fact cannot be stressed enough, because it dictates how the comedians

---

[4] Musical and spoken verse: Moore (2012), building on Moore (2008) and Moore (1998). Percentages: Moore (2008) 4f.; Duckworth (1952: 1994) 362f. and 369f.

themselves approached their work as a creative genre, and how we should approach their work, too.

For if we approach Roman comedy with the understanding that it is first and foremost an *adaptation* of spoken drama into operatic, musical form, rather than merely a translation from one language to another, and that it is furthermore an *operatic* adaptation, this premise does much to throw light on the changes that Plautus, Caecilius and their peers made to their models, and it helps to explain why. A convenient starting point for reorienting discussion of some other important premises along these lines is the recent republication of a famous book on Plautus.

Eduard Fraenkel and beyond

In 2007 Oxford University Press published an English translation of Eduard Fraenkel's 1922 book *Plautinisches im Plautus*, 'The Plautine in Plautus'. Eighty-five years had passed since its original publication, forty-seven since the Italian-language second edition titled *Elementi Plautini in Plauto*, 'Plautine Elements in Plautus', the title that the English translators took as their own. Why has a nearly century-old book been translated now?

This book by Eduard Fraenkel (1888–1970) is often called the starting point for Plautine research. In it Fraenkel sought to 'take up once again the old question "How does Plautus go about translating?" and to expand it into a general enquiry about the Latin poet's own creative work'.[5] Fraenkel, that is, wanted to identify 'the Plautine (element)' by discovering precisely which parts of his plays Plautus had significantly changed from his source texts, and to probe these changes for signs of Plautus' self-expression. This was something of a novelty. In Germany of the late nineteenth and early twentieth centuries, pervasive philhellenism had been leading such scholars as Friedrich Leo (1851–1914) and Wilamowitz (1848–1931) to Plautus and Terence largely in hopes of recovering the genius of Menander and his peers from what they saw as the barnacles of Roman farce; as in the plastic arts, the Greek element was primary, the Roman at best an inferior copy. For Latinists working in this milieu, then, Fraenkel's book promised a sort of liberation to explore Plautus and the Latin comedians – whom later Romans themselves had considered artists worthy of study and citation – as independent poets and creators.

By studying individual points of Plautus' style and, to the limited extent that he could, comparative Greek material, Fraenkel isolated and spoke of

---

[5] Fraenkel (2007) 3.

Plautine expansion, amplification and condensation of speeches and individual elements in the Greek models – of personification, of metaphors treated literally, of hyperbolic comparisons, of transformation and identification motifs, of mythological material, of military imagery applied to slaves, of riddles, and above all of '*Skurrilitäten*', a name Fraenkel gave to the puns, silly banter and corny or absurdist jokes that often make readers of Plautus smile.[6] Building his case cumulatively, Fraenkel tried to establish a basis for the notable change in ethos, or characterization, between Greek and Roman New Comedy, and to throw some light on the literary interests of Plautus' Roman audience.

Impressive as it seems, Fraenkel's method is open to a charge of circularity. It is quite likely, for instance, that in identifying stylistically and qualitatively buffoonish elements as 'the Plautine' Fraenkel was merely pointing to many of the very same stylistic criteria on which M. Terentius Varro (116–27 BCE), the republican scholar, relied in drawing up the authoritative list of twenty-one canonical plays of Plautus that survive today. That is, Fraenkel has probably taken us back to Varro, but only coincidentally to Plautus.[7]

Still, after the original 1922 publication of *Plautinisches im Plautus*, the recovery of Menander's *Dis Exapatôn* papyrus (see below) impressively confirmed many of Fraenkel's deductions, and, after a few initial challenges, the book enjoyed a celebrated readership. Before long, however, the success of Fraenkel's book begot a strange afterlife. Many scholars began to treat Fraenkel's conclusions collectively as gospel truth; no longer did they speak of 'adaptation' but of complete, untrammelled originality. Combined with some long-standing misapprehensions about Plautus' text, genre expectations began to change: for many, the Greek illusion was no illusion at all; the characters in Plautine comedy were not Greeks but really Romans in disguise; the play was not really set in Athens or some other Greek locale but in Rome itself, or in some in-between fantasy space, with half-Greek,

---

[6] Fraenkel apparently appropriated this term from Leo, his teacher; cf. Leo (1912) 157 and (1913) 127, 146, 215, 248, and 259.

[7] This is the inference to be made from Varro's convergent criteria of *filum atque facetia sermonis* (Gellius, N.A. 3.3.3), *iocorum venustas* and *iocorum copia* (Macrobius Sat. 2.1.10–11, with Deufert (2002) 104 n. 278), especially because in Macrobius the emphasis is on buffoonish jokes (cf. *scurra*, 2.1.12). On the 'Varronian' canon (in fact a misnomer, as Varro himself thought forty plays authentic) see Ritschl (1845) 126–54; for Ritschl's calculation 40 – 21 = 19, see Suerbaum (2002) 222 §127 T. Maccius Plautus T 66 and T 70. Ritschl thinks Varro's other nineteen were probably *Addictus, Artemo, Astraba, Boeotia, Cacistio, Commorientes, Condalium, Faeneratrix, Fretum, Frivolaria, Fugitivi, Gemini lenones, Hortulus, Nervolaria, Parasitus medicus, Parasitus piger, Satyrio, Sitellitergus* and *Trigemini*.

half-Roman characters. Beginning from these premises, then, the content of Plautus' plays soon became – whether as satire, cultural commentary, or racist caricature – a source of Roman social history.[8]

But we are getting ahead of ourselves; before proceeding further in the abstract, let us examine some sample texts in detail to see how Roman comedians went about adapting their sources.

Some texts

In comparing Roman comedy with its source texts, our selection is limited by that worst of criteria – chance survival. Still, though very few, these comparisons sometimes reveal that Roman reworkings of Greek comedy could be quite close. For example, a fragment of the *Demetrius* (fr. 5 Ribbeck[3]) of the comedian Turpilius[9] (iambic senarii):

> antehac si flabat aquilo aut auster, inopia
> tum erat piscati

> In the past, if the north or south wind would blow,
> then there was a lack of fish

preserves the sense, metre and even word order of Alexis' *Demetrios* fr. 47.1–3 (iambic trimeters):

> πρότερον μὲν εἰ πνεύσειε βορρᾶς ἢ νότος
> ἐν τῇ θαλάττῃ λαμπρός, ἰχθῦς οὐκ ἐνῆν
> οὐδενὶ φαγεῖν

> In the past, if the north or south wind would blow
> strongly on the sea, there'd be no fish in it
> for anyone to eat.

Likewise, in *Bacchides* 816–17 Plautus' maxim (iambic senarii):

> quem di diligunt
> adulescens moritur
> dies young

> He whom the gods love

faithfully replicates, again including metre, Menander's *Dis Expatôn* (fr. 4 Arnott, iambic trimeter):

> ὃν οἱ θεοὶ φιλοῦσιν, ἀποθνῄσκει νέος

> He whom the gods love dies young.

---

[8] See briefly Fraenkel (2007) xi–xvi.
[9] On Turpilius, see Wright (1974) 153–81 and Suerbaum (2002) 258f.

And in Plautus' *Carchedonius* [vulgate *Poenulus*[10]] v. 1318, *te cinaedum esse arbitror* 'I think you're a faggot' probably renders βάκηλος εἶ 'you're a queer' of Alexis' *Karchedonios* (fr. 105).

Several longer samples of Roman adaptation are also available for study, and a side-by-side comparison of them is revealing.[11]

(1) In Plautus' *Synaristosae* [*Cistellaria*], Selenium explains to the *lena*, or madam, how her rapist had wound his way into her favour (89–93; trochaic septenarii):

> Per Dionysia
> mater pompam me spectatum duxit. dum redeo domum,   90
> conspicillo consecutust clanculum me usque ad fores.
> inde in amicitiam insinuavit cum matre et mecum simul
> blanditiis, muneribus, donis.

> During the festival of Dionysus
> mother took me to see the procession. On the way home   90
> he spied me and stole along after me all the way to our door.
> Then he wound his way into mother's heart – and mine, too –
> with the nice things he said, and did for us, and gave us. (tr. Nixon)

Compare the girl (κόρη) Plangon's words in Menander's *Synaristosai* (fr. 337, iambic trimeters):

> Διονυσίων <˘˘> ἦν   1
> πομπή
> ὁ δ' ἐπηκολούθησεν μέχρι τοῦ πρὸς τὴν θύραν·
> ἔπειτα φοιτῶν καὶ κολακεύων <ἐμέ τε καὶ>
> τὴν μητέρ' ἔγνω μ'   5

> At the Dionysia there was a   1
> procession [. . .]
> He followed me right up to the door,
> and then by always stopping by and flattering <both me and>
> my mother, he knew me.   5

Apart from the differences between Greek and Latin idiom, Selenium's response is practically a word-for-word rendering of Plangon's speech in Menander: verbal correspondences, including loan words, transliterations and cognates (*pompam* ~ πομπή; *Dionysia* ~ Διονυσίων; *matre* ~ μητέρ'[α]) and ordinary lexical equivalents (*consecutust . . . me usque ad fores*

---

[10] On this and Plautus' other titles, see below.

[11] For Terence's adaptation practices, which are not examined here, see Barsby (2002a).

~ μ᾽ ἠκολούθησεν μέχρι τοῦ πρὸς τὴν θύραν; *blanditiis, muneribus, donis* ~ κολακεύων) are obvious.

Yet Plautus completely omits Menander's euphemism for the rape, 'He knew me', while the alliterative triplet *conspicillo consecutust clanculum* (91), which corresponds to nothing in Menander's text, indicates Plautus' predilection for verbal amplification and expressiveness (here, perhaps imparting a sinister or foreboding note to the words). Moreover, Plautus has recast Menander's spoken iambic trimeters as musically accompanied trochaic septenarii, in effect elevating or abstracting an ordinary conversation into an overtly artificial form of speech.

(2) A hundred-line stretch of Menander's *Dis Exapatôn, The Double Deceiver*, known from papyrus rather than quotation, parallels Plautus' *Bacchides* 494–562.[12] In the following extract, the father of a young man who is going to dissolution, named Moschus (Pistoclerus in Plautus' play), exhorts a second young man, named Sostratus in Menander's play and Mnesilochus in Plautus, to intervene and save his son. A *paedagogus*, named Lydos ('The Lydian') in each play, asks permission of his master, the old man, to help in the intervention. Though he is rebuffed, he makes his concern for his younger master's behaviour clear (Menander, *Dis Exapatôn* 11–17, iambic trimeters):

ΜΟΣΧΟΥ ΠΑΤΗΡ	ΛΥΔΟΣ	ΣΟΣΤΡΑΤΟΣ
Μ.Π.	σ]ὺ δ᾽ ἐκεῖνον ἐκκάλε[ι	11
	]ν, νουθέτει δ᾽ ἐπαν[τίον	12
αὐτόν τε σῶσον, οἰκίαν θ᾽ ὅλην φίλων.		13
Λυδέ, προάγωμεν. ΛΥ. εἰ δὲ κἀμὲ καταλίποις...		14
Μ.Π. προάγωμεν. ἱκανὸς οὗτος. ΛΥ. αὐτῳ, Σώστρα[τε,		15
χρῆσαι πικρῶς· ἔλαυν᾽ ἐκεῖνον τὸ[ν] ἀκρα[τῆ·		16
ἅπαντας αἰσχύνει γὰρ ἡμᾶς τοὺ[ς] φίλους.–		17

MOSCHUS' FATHER	LYDUS	SOSTRATUS
M.F. (*to Sostratus*)] You should call him out		11
]and rebuke him face to face,		12
And save him, and his whole household of loved ones.		13
Lydus, let's go. LY. But if you left me, too ...		14
M.F. Let's go. He's enough. LY. Sostratus,		15
Treat him harshly, assail that libertine:		16
He's disgracing all of us, who're his friends.		17

[12] *POxy.* 4407, officially published in 1997 by Eric Handley in *The Oxyrhynchus Papyri* 64: 14–42; besides Arnott's edition (= Arnott (1979) 152–66), a Greek text and English translation are also found in Barsby (1991) 191–5.

Compare Plautus *Bacchides* 494–9 (ed. Questa 2008, trochaic septenarii):

PHILOXENUS	MNESILOCHUS	LYDUS	
PH. Mnesiloche, hoc tecum oro ut illius animum atque ingenium regas;			494
serva tibi sodalem | et mi filium. MN. factum volo.			495
PH. in te ego hoc onus omne impono. Lyde, sequere hac me. LY. sequor.			499
melius multo, me quoque una si cum | hoc reliqueris.			496
PH. adfatim est. LY. Mnesiloche, cura, ei, concastiga hominem probe,			497
qui dedecorat te, me amicosque alios flagitiis suis.–			498

PH. Mnesilochus, I beg you, try to get control of his heart and mind.   494
Save a friend for yourself, and a son for me. MN. I want that to happen.   495
PH. I'm putting the whole onus on you. Lydus, follow me. LY. Very well.   499
It'll be much better if you leave me together with him, too.   496
PH. He's enough. LY. Mnesilochus, go, take charge, castigate him well: 497
He's disgracing you, me, and his other friends with his scandalous   498
behaviours.

Despite allowances for the natural idiom of each language, verbal correspondences are again easily picked out on the individual level (σῶσον ~ *serva*; ἱκανὸς ~ *adfatim*; ἔλαυν[ε] ~ *concast-iga* [from *agere*], and so on), though with some interesting differences of tone and rhetoric. Menander's Λυδέ, προάγωμεν, for instance, is inclusively polite, while Plautus' *Lyde, sequere hac me* is authoritative, and Plautus explicitly fills out Menander's aposiopesis εἰ δὲ κἀμὲ καταλίποις (14) with an apodosis (*melius multo, me quoque...si...reliqueris*: 496); on balance, Plautus' Philoxenus makes a greater use of rhetorical flourishes than his counterpart in Menander. Other differences in speaking of family relations and social cohesion are also notable: οἰκίαν θ' ὅλην φίλων refers obliquely to everyone within a household; *et mi filium*, used in an antithesis not found in Menander, is starkly personal. And Plautus has again expanded and recast Menander's spoken verses as song.

(3) Finally, a famous chapter of Aulus Gellius (*NA* 2.23.1–22) compares three extracts of Caecilius Statius' comedy *Plocium*, *The Necklace*, with its model, Menander's *Plokion*.[13] Gellius observes in comparing the first extracts that Caecilius did not attempt to reproduce some of Menander's lines (§11) but rather added *nescioqua mimica*, 'some stuff you'd find in a mime', and in the second, printed below, that Caecilius spoiled Menander

---

[13] Caecilius frr. 136–55 and 163–6 Warmington = Menander frr. 296 (C16 Olson 2007), 297 (C17 Olson 2007) and 298; Gellius' essay, which reveals that Caecilius has made substantial changes to Menander's text, as a whole repays careful study. On Caecilius, who by some accounts was Rome's greatest comedian, see Wright (1974) 87–126 and Suerbaum (2002) 229–31.

by giving the character a buffoonish quality (§13). Here is Menander fr. 297 (= C17 Olson 2007), a dialogue between Laches, speaking about his wife, and his neighbour, another man of similar age (iambic trimeters):

ΛΑ. ἔχω δ᾽ ἐπίκληρον Λάμιαν· οὐκ εἴρηκά σοι
τουτὶ γάρ; Α. οὐχί. ΛΑ. κυρίαν τῆς οἰκίας
καὶ τῶν ἀγρῶν καὶ †πάντων ἀντ᾽ ἐκείνης†
ἔχομεν. Α. Ἄπολλον, ὡς χαλεπόν. ΛΑ. χαλεπώτατον.
ἅπασι δ᾽ ἀργαλέα ᾽στίν, οὐκ ἐμοὶ μόνῳ,   5
υἱῷ πολὺ μᾶλλον, θυγατρί. Α. πρᾶγμ᾽ ἄμαχον λέγεις.
ΛΑ. εὖ οἶδα.

LA. I'm married to a Lamia with a dowry. Haven't I told you
that? A. No. LA. She rules our house,
And our fields, and <everything that>
we've got. A. By Apollo, that's tough! LA. Extremely tough.
She's unpleasant to everybody – not just me,   5
Even more to our son, our daughter. A. Sounds impossible.
LA. Mmm, I know.

Caecilius (Warmington fr. 151–5, preferable to Ribbeck³ 158–62) renders this as follows (A = 'Laches'; iambic senarii):

B. Sed tua morosane uxor quaeso est? A. Va! Rogas?
B. Qui tandem? A. Taedet mentionis quae mihi
ubi domum adveni, adsedi, extemplo savium
dat ieiuna anima. B. Nil peccat de savio:
ut devomas vult quod foris potaveris.   5

B. Oh – is your wife really difficult? A. Pfff! *Is* she?
B. Why do you say that? A. I don't like to talk about it;
The very moment that I get home and settle in,
She gives me a lowcarb-breath kiss. B. That kiss isn't such a bad idea:
she wants you to vomit up what you were drinking while you were out.   5

Without Gellius' guidance, it would be hard to tell that these passages correspond. Caecilius abandons Menander's perfectly pointed allusion to Lamia, a beautiful child-eating succubus; gone is his allusion to the woman being an *uxor dotata*, the well-dowered wife who makes her husband's life comfortable but unbearable. Gone, too, is one of the grievances that follow from this: her lording ownership of the family property over her husband, ruling the roost. Caecilius instead emphasizes the wife's ill temper (*morosa*), and clownishly reorients this grievance around her bad breath, cast in the form of a riddle-joke, which the husband, who has been out carousing to escape her control, finds offensive. Like Plautus, then, Caecilius condenses, rearranges and alters characterization, and augments vigour; unlike Menander's, his two men sound like a couple of mildly misogynistic good old boys. In Gellius' opinion (§22), Caecilius for Menander is bronze for gold.

For better or worse, the terms that Gellius sets forth in his essay, viz. of the *comparison* of Roman comedies with their Greek models, and particularly in terms of aesthetics, fidelity and naturalism vs. farce, have become the bread and butter of Roman comedy scholarship ever since. These criteria are the essence of what is called 'fidelity criticism'.

Operatic adaptation and fidelity criticism

Because it is so obvious an enterprise, fidelity criticism is the low-hanging fruit of adaptation studies. More surprisingly, recent theorization of adaptation across many literatures (broadly conceived) reveals that traditional criticisms of Roman comedy, especially Plautus, are all but inherent in the genre. As Linda Hutcheon writes, adaptations are *routinely* thought to deform, pervert or be culturally inferior to a source text.[14]

One can, of course, maintain these views if one wishes, but such judgements may not be entirely just when it comes to Roman comedy. For if we recognize that Roman comedy is primarily an *adapted* literature – from spoken or mimetic to musical drama – and only secondarily a *translated* literature – from Greek to Latin drama – then we can and should adjust our expectations accordingly. Indeed it appears that this is what the earliest Roman critics themselves did. In drawing up his canon of the ten best *poetae comici*, meaning authors of the *palliata*, Volcacius Sedigitus says nary a word about 'fidelity' to Greek models; and, like Sedigitus, Varro compares only Roman comedians to one another, not to Greek comedians. This suggests that a reorientation of our approach may be conducive to new insights.[15]

If, for example, Fraenkel had approached Plautine comedy primarily as a musicalization of drama and only secondarily as a translation – recall his word 'translated' above (*übersetzt* in the German and *traduce* in the Italian versions, respectively) – he probably would have reached many of the very

[14] Hutcheon (2006) 2f.
[15] Sedigitus' canon: Gellius *N.A.* 15.24 = Courtney (1993) 93f.; Varro: *Menippeans* fr. 399 Astbury, Courtney (1993) 96. Although early fidelity criticism is implicit in the young Julius Caesar's school composition (cf. n. 2 above) – Caesar deems Terence a *dimidiatus Menander*, 'half-pint Menander' – this opinion, like Gellius', is that of the dilettante rather than the scholar. It is formed in an academic, not theatrical, context and should never have left it.

same conclusions about Plautus' activity that he did. Here is Hutcheon on musicalized adaptation in all literatures ((2006) 30):

> To appeal to a global market or even a very particular one, a television series or a stage musical may have to alter the cultural, regional, or historical specifics of the text being adapted. A bitingly satiric novel of social pretense and pressure may be transformed into a benign comedy of manners in which the focus of attention is on the triumph of the individual.

Except for the intensifier 'bitingly', the words 'a...satiric novel of social pretense and pressure' sound much like the familiar praise of Menandrian comedy, while 'the triumph of the individual' strongly recalls Fraenkel's eighth chapter, which is generally accorded as one of his best, on 'The Predominance of the Slave's Role'.[16] Obvious examples are Plautus' *Bacchides*, *Mostellaria* and *Pseudolus*.

Hutcheon also establishes that adaptations into *operatic* form always entail a distortion of characterization and psychology, even to the point of cartoonization ((2006) 38, quoting a modern opera critic):

> It is opera, however, that has been singled out as particularly guilty on both the loss of quality and quantity counts, given its extremes of compression; again, it takes much longer to sing than to say a line of text, much less read one. Operatic recycling 'denatures' a novel, we are told, 'reducing it to a cartoon spray-painted in Day-Glo colors and outlined with a Magic Marker'.

Apart from Gellius' remark above that Caecilius added *nescioqua mimica* to what Menander *praeclare et apposite et facete scripsit*, the reader will recognize this as the most familiar criticism of Plautus in twentieth-century scholarship – not least in Fraenkel's work. One recent scholar writes (emphasis added):

> Fraenkel explains [that]... the elaboration of the [Plautine] slave as hero panders to the need of the unsophisticated Roman audience for *greater colour, less subtle distinctions* than the Greek audience of Menander.[17]

As Hutcheon is showing us, however, this change is all but bound up with the *form* of the change. In theorizing adaptations across literatures, Hutcheon also states, again regarding specifically musical adaptations ((2006) 3):

> They use the same tools that storytellers have always used: they actualize or concretize ideas; they make simplifying selections, but also amplify or extrapolate; they make analogies; they critique or show respect, and so on. Like

---

[16] Fraenkel (2007) 159–72.
[17] Leigh (2004) 25, referring to what is now Fraenkel (2007) 171f.; examples could be greatly multiplied.

parodies, adaptations have an overt and defining relationship to prior texts, usually revealingly called 'sources'. Unlike parodies, however, adaptations usually openly announce this relationship.

Here in a nutshell are the rest of Fraenkel's conclusions about Plautus' originality – but presented as obvious generic premises, to be taken for granted.

I do not mean to suggest that Fraenkel was at all wrong; on the contrary, he was right. But he came very much the long way around. It was obvious all along that Plautus and his peers had eliminated the Greek act-breaks and musicalized what had been spoken material, while many of the plays themselves openly announce their relationship to a Greek model in their prologues. If Fraenkel had, as I suggest we do here, instead approached Roman comedy as inherently *adapted* stuff, he might have considered Plautine comedy more closely in the light of the Hellenistic literature and performance that was contemporary with them. This leads us to reconsider some familiar and interrelated premises about Roman comedy in general and about Plautus in particular.

Some premises

Plautus as technītes *of Dionysus and Hellenistic author*

The origins of Roman comedy are to be sought not in Rome itself, as they frequently are in modern scholarship, but emphatically in the Hellenistic world. According to Livy, Horace and Valerius Maximus, Rome already possessed a native tradition of rustic theatrical shows, perhaps pantomimes, before Greek comedy arrived in Rome. If this dubious account is true, imported Roman adaptations of Greek comedies will have found a ready-made home within this cultural milieu, but these rustic shows cannot have been their origin or impulse.[18]

The most significant, though often underappreciated, link between Greece and Rome during the half century separating Menander's death in 292 BCE from the first recorded performance of an adapted Greek play in Rome in 240 BCE is that of the 'Artisans of Dionysus' (*hoi peri ton Dionyson technītai*). These corporations of itinerant actors traversed the Mediterranean Greek world in a regular circuit, staging performances of original and revived classics of Greek tragedy and New Comedy. They are first known to have performed in Rome toward the end of Plautus' career, in the 180s BCE.[19] And,

---

[18] Livy 7.2.3–12; Horace *Epist.* 2.1.139–63; Valerius Maximus 2.4.4.

[19] Livy 39.22.2 *artifices ex Graecia* and 39.22.10 *artifices*. Since the prologue to Plautus' *Menaechmi* mentions *ludi*, 'a festival (including theatrical shows)', at Greek-speaking

as Bruno Gentili has impressively shown, they had already been selecting, combining and musicalizing classics of earlier Greek drama for performance in these venues in novel ways.[20]

In his biography of Plautus written a century and a half later, Varro related that the Italian-born Plautus had begun a career in which he made money *in operis artificum scaenicorum*, evidently working outside of Rome. *In operis*, 'in the service of' or 'among the gangs of' is a vague expression – it might mean an actor, producer, writer, stagehand, or several other things – and it is probable that Varro chose it because he did not know himself in what capacity Plautus had worked. But there should be no ambiguity about *artificum scaenicorum*, since elsewhere Gellius, who quotes this bit from Varro's biography (*N.A.* 3.3.14), himself tells us (*N.A.* 20.4.2) that it is the Latin translation of *hoi peri ton Dionyson technītai*. Varro claimed, in other words, that Plautus had begun his career working for, with or among these itinerant troupes of Greek-speaking *technītai*. The claim is eminently plausible and, if true, would explain where Plautus became so thoroughly familiar with Greek drama.

Those who want to see Plautus as primarily a *Roman* author rather than a dramatist working in contemporary Hellenistic traditions frequently discount Varro's claim or strain its interpretation beyond its natural implications. They instead point to elements in Plautine comedy that hark back to a native Italian tradition of comedy known as 'Atellan farce'. Since this is the predominant view today, it is important to stress in response that it is a modern construct not shared by ancient Romans themselves. Horace states explicitly that, except in the case of his hungry parasites, where some influence from the Atellana is discernible, Plautus was fairly faithful to the characterization found in his Greek models. And elsewhere Horace reveals that some enthusiastic Romans in his time thought of Plautus as a second Epicharmus.[21] These critics, in other words, saw Plautus as a writer in the *Greek* tradition. While, then, Plautus' (evidently false) name Maccius probably does signal some artistic allegiance to Atellan farce – 'Maccus' is the name of the stock clown in these farces – it would be an illegitimate inference to rewrite Varro's biography on the basis of the name to

---

Tarentum in southern Italy as something both popular and familiar (29–30), obscure references to *artifices* in Plautus' prologues (*Amphitryo* 70 and *Carchedonius* 36–9 – on these titles see below) may refer to these Greek *technītai*, too.

[20] Gentili (1979) 15–62; disputed (and updated) by Nervegna (2007). *technītai*: Jones (1993); Le Guen (2001); Lightfoot (2002); at a later date, Petzl and Schwertheim (2006) with Slater (2008) (the latter offers an English translation).

[21] Horace on Plautine fidelity: *Epist.* 2.1.170–3; Fontaine (2010) 221–3; Plautus as the Roman Epicharmus: Horace *Epist.* 2.1.58, Fontaine (2010) 57 n. 41–58.

assert that Plautus began his career as an actor in the native Italian Atellan farce.[22]

Moreover, while the travelling *technītai* were musicalizing New Comedy for performance, other currents and literary aesthetics were brewing in Hellenistic literary circles. Such Hellenistic 'metaphrasts' as Aratus (*c.* 315–240 BCE), Nicander (second century BCE), and (in his Latin *Hedyphagetica*) Ennius (239–*c.* 169 BCE), Plautus' contemporary and peer comedian, were busy experimenting with adapting literary form. These poets were setting intractably prosaic, scientific content into verses in which subject matter is subordinated to elegant style, verbal tricks, ironic detachment and *jeux d'esprit*. As Roman comedy is itself a metrically refined version of more prosaic Greek trimeters, it may be helpful in the future to consider the genre and its aesthetics in much the same light.

The Plautine Canon

By emphasizing the importance of the *technītai*'s activities and of Hellenistic aesthetics over the merely formal fact that Roman comedy is a species of Latin poetry, we are in a position to clear up some other misconceived premises of the genre. There is, for instance, considerable evidence that most Plautine titles were, like Terence's, Greek rather than Latin, and that many of the Latin titles familiar to us are later accretions of grammarians, revival producers or simple misunderstandings of the text. This inference follows in part from the internal evidence of the plays, which often announce their own title in Greek form; it also follows from Cicero's casual translation (*Tusc.* 3.65) of Terence's *Heauton Timoroumenus* 'The Self-Tormentor' as *Ipse se poeniens*, a translation that flatly contradicts the play's own announcement in v. 5 of its Greek title. We must assume the same has happened with many of Plautus' titles. And since these Latin titles have been wrongly taken as a declaration of Plautus' peculiar 'Romanism' or even 'anti-Hellenism', that is, of his artistic independence from the models, we take this opportunity to distill recent scholarship and redefine the titles of the twenty-one 'Varronian' plays in the Plautine canon in Table 21.1. Untranslated titles in Table 21.1 represent proper names of leading characters, with the plural titles *Captivi*, *Bacchides* (*Bacchises*) and *Menaechmi* (*Menaechmuses*) indicating comedies of error; unlike the 'speaking' names *Gorgylio*, 'Mr Fast-and-Furious

[22] This is the suggestion of Leo (1912) 85, followed by Duckworth (1953: 1994) 50 and many others.

Table 21.1 *Plautus' Varronian plays*

Plautus' title	Transliteration	Meaning	Vulgate title and/or meaning
1. *Alazon*	Ἀλαζών	*The Braggart*	*Miles Gloriosus, The Braggart Soldier*
2. *Amphitryo*	Ἀμφιτρύων		*Amphitruo*
3. *Asinaria*		*The Jackass Affair*	
4. *Aulularia*		*The Crock Affair*	
5. *Bacchides*	Βακχίδες		
6. *Captivi*		*Prisoners of War*	
7. *Carchedonius*	Καρχηδόνιος	*The Carthaginian*	*Poenulus, The Little Punic*
8. *Clerumenoe*	Κληρούμενοι	*Those Drawing Lots*	*Casina*
9. *Emporus*	Ἔμπορος	*The Merchant*	*Mercator, The Merchant*
10. *Epidicus*	Ἐπίδικος		
11. *Gorgylio*	Γοργυλίων		*Curculio*
12. *Menaechmi*	Μέναιχμοι		
13. *Persa*	Πέρμα (?)	*The Persian*	
14. *Phasma* (?)	Φάσμα	*The Ghost*	*Mo(n)stellaria, The Ghost Affair*
15. *Pseudylus*	Ψευδύλος		*Pseudolus*
16. *Rudens*		*The Rope*	
17. *Stichus*	Στίχος		
18. *Synaristosae* (?)	Συναριστῶσαι	*Ladies at Lunch*	*Cistellaria, The Casket Affair*
19. *Trinummus*	Τρίνουμμος (?)	*Über-coin*	*The Threepenny Day*
20. *Truculentus*		*The Grouch*	
21. *Vidularia*		*The Knapsack Affair*	

Man', and *Pseudylus*, 'Mr Deceiver', the names Amphitryo, Menaechmus, Bacchis, Epidicus and Stichus, respectively, have mythological, historical or generic connotations irrelevant to their etymologies. Titles not transliterated in Greek are purely Latin; question marks indicate titles ambiguously Latin or Greek or uncertainty over Plautus' own title. None of these titles, however, necessarily is or translates the title of Plautus' model; proper names used as titles are especially suspect: *Bacchides* adapts Menander's *Dis Exapatôn* (*The Double Swindler*), and *Stichus* his first *Adelphoi* (*Brothers*), but *Truculentus* is not Menander's *Dyscolus* (*The Grouch*); likewise Terence's

Phormio (a proper name) adapts Apollodorus' *Epidicazomenê* (*The Girl Claimed at Law*).[23]

Although modern scholarship on Plautus invariably refers to the plays by the vulgate titles listed in Table 21.1, they should henceforth be abandoned as representing no more than a mixture of textual corruptions, misunderstandings and later accretions. And seen in this light, Plautus looks much more like a playwright in the Hellenistic tradition than primarily a Latin author. At the same time, the sharpened focus we gain from the revised list allows us now to consider the question: what was the purpose of Roman comedy?

The purpose of Plautine comedy: criteria of self-expression and audience

Why did Romans like these comedies, and what can we infer about the Roman appropriation of this Greek art form? Until recently scholars believed that Roman comedy was a popular entertainment produced for huge, unruly masses whose attention the comedians had to struggle to attract and hold amid other festival amusements – tightrope walkers, gladiators, and so on. Most answers to these questions were accordingly formulated from this premise. In 1998, however, new archaeological and demographic evidence overthrew that assumption, suggesting that audiences were in fact quite small. Measuring the steps of the Palatine temple of the Magna Mater, upon which spectators sat for the performance of Plautus' *Pseudylus* in April 191 BCE, Sander Goldberg calculated that about only 1,600 persons could have been present: this was a high school gymnasium, in other words, not a Colosseum – and this at a time when Rome's population may have included fully 350,000 persons. Various other considerations (reserved seats for senators, untranslated Greek words, statements in prologues such as *Menaechmi* 7–9 about preferred aesthetics in Rome, and so on) suggest that audiences of Roman comedy were aristocratic, knowledgeable, philhellenic, and, of course, de facto theatre-loving. Scholars are now reassessing their assumptions about the genre – in particular, what exactly 'Roman comedy' was, for whom it was written, and where it came from.[24] The question of

[23] On the titles *Emporus, Phasma, Stichus*, and *Synaristosae*, see Wright (1974) 92–6; on *Amphitryo, Gorgylio, Pseudylus, Trinummus*, Apollodorus' *Epidicazomene*, and Plautus' non-canonical *Baccharia* and *Satyrio*, see Fontaine (2010) *passim*. As explained in Fontaine (2010), Plautus' Greek words are best transliterated by classical norms; the practice is anachronistic, but it improves intelligibility. See also in general Gentili (1979) 32.

[24] Audience: Goldberg (1998), the fundamental study; Fontaine (2010) 183–7, with references. Festivals: Marshall (2006) 16–21. Theatre conditions in Rome: Marshall (2006); Brown (2002).

why Roman artists were interested in Greek comedy in the first place must now be completely rethought. Several positions can be staked out among recent work, but all depend first of all on what we consider to be criteria of artistic originality and how we approach the interpretation of Roman comedy.

In adapted literature, two related principles alone can be expected to throw light on individual authors' creative preferences and, by corollary, what the audience liked. One is *how* the adaptation alters its source text, in both quantity and quality, while the other and broader principle is the *selection* of what to adapt in the first place.

Across multiple Roman comedies common themes can be discerned. Confidence tricks, education, relations of sex or power among individuals, and so on, tend to predominate. It is likely that these themes already dominated in the Greek theatre or in the performances of the *technītai*. But if these were primarily the dominant themes in the larger pool of Greek comedy, can they reflect the Roman comedians' interests overall?

Although we know the names of sixty-four playwrights of New Comedy, the models for Roman comedy come predominantly from Menander, Philemon, and Diphilus, the three canonical poets of Greek New Comedy. If Roman comedy is seen as operatic adaptation, there are inherently strong economic reasons for these financially low-risk choices. Indeed, in a highly rhetorical passage, Horace suspects that this profit motive alone explained Plautus' primary artistic concerns.[25]

Yet a few striking exceptions give us pause. Like Aeschylus' *Persians*, Plautus' *Carchedonius* (*The Carthaginian*) (almost certainly from Alexis' *Karchêdonios*) presents in a surprisingly sympathetic light a protagonist who bears ethno-national ties to a recently defeated political enemy. And Plautus' *Captivi* (*Prisoners of War*) (Greek source unknown), explores themes of captivity that seem more immediately relevant to Rome amid her period of military conflict and expansion in the late third and early second centuries BCE than to the militarily neutered Athens of the late fourth century BCE.

Some have therefore suggested that Plautus selected his plays with an eye toward addressing the social or political concerns dominant in contemporary Rome. If so, why? Satire is one possibility. Another recent suggestion presupposes that Plautus (and his audience) treated Roman comedy not just as a mirror of Hellenistic or human life in general but more specifically as a mirror of *Roman* life, and that with his comedy Plautus was sensitively probing social or political tensions and concerns prevalent in contemporary

[25] *Ars Poetica* 175f.; cf. Hutcheon (2006) 5. Lowe (2008) 99f. lists Plautus' known and suspected Greek originals.

Rome; hence, for instance, Plautus selects for production the *Gorgylio*, a play which features the theft of a ring, in order to direct his audience's thoughts back to an incident in which Hannibal, the Carthaginian general, had stolen a ring; and Plautus' *servi callidi*, 'crafty slaves', are tricky because Hannibal had a reputation for trickery.[26]

I have disagreed with this line of approach elsewhere.[27] One reason is that interpretations based on politico-historical allegory are like conspiracy theories: with a few connections and a little ingenuity, they are easily devised, hard to disclaim and, despite an author's best protestations, impossible to disprove.[28] Warner Brothers studio learned this lesson recently when, to their consternation and frantic denials, the Hollywood film *300* (itself an adaptation of a 1998 graphic novel) was widely interpreted as a neoconservative allegory urging a Western attack on contemporary Iran.[29]

The other reason I fault this line of approach lies in the nature of Roman comedy. As this chapter has sought to establish, Roman comedy was largely a single phenomenon that continued literary-performative trends that were current in the contemporary Hellenistic world. Like their Hellenistic counterparts, the Roman poets were updating classic texts in new forms and with a fair amount of genre crossing for their audiences. Since Roman comedy belongs on a continuum from Greece to Rome – indeed, 'Roman' comedy is merely a species of Greek comedy, or, better, Hellenistic literature – the best, and perhaps only, evidence of Roman social history that it affords us is a clear insight into the enthusiastic adaptation of Hellenic culture among elites in Rome. Perhaps this is enough.

Further reading

I expand on many of the issues discussed here in Fontaine (2010). In addition, for those interested in the close connections between Greek and Roman

---

[26] Leigh (2004) 34.

[27] See Fontaine (2004) for some of the problems; Leigh (2004) 4–6, 12–23 for others.

[28] An example: the opening scene of Plautus' *Alazon* showcases a toadying parasite and a braggart soldier. With fulsome servility, the toady records and recounts the valorous military exploits (*virtutes*) of his warrior-patron, exploits which, he claims, he witnessed on the soldier's Eastern campaigns. This scene could be interpreted as a brilliant censure of Ennius, Plautus' peer comedian, whom M. Fulvius Nobilior as consul in 189 BCE brought along as a *poeta* on his military campaign to Aetolia (Cicero, *Tusc.* 1.3 = Suerbaum (2002) 381 §162 M. Porcius Cato T 3). A perfect allegory – except that scholars have decided that a *different* allusion, in verses 210–12, to the ongoing imprisonment of Plautus' peer comedian Naevius securely dates Plautus' play to 205 BCE, some sixteen years earlier. What happens without such controls? And what if our controls are wrong?

[29] See Cieply (2007).

comedy and for the musicalization of pieces from classical Greek drama in Hellenistic times, Gentili (1979) is essential reading (his thesis has, however, been recently challenged by Nervegna (2007); on music in Roman comedy in general, see Moore (2012)). Although Gentili (1979) should be read alongside it, Fraenkel (2007) remains the starting point for most research on Plautus and the fragmentary comedians; even where one disagrees with his conclusions, Fraenkel is always illuminating, and his discussion (225–31) of Leo's term 'Hellenistic *Singspiel*' (musical comedy), though critical, is nevertheless a helpful English-language introduction to the term. The historicist approach to Roman comedy is most prominently represented by Leigh (2004). Lowe (2008) 81–132 offers an excellent up-to-date survey of Plautus, Terence, and the other fragmentary comedians, and is warmly recommended, especially for bibliographical help and recommendations for the best editions of classical texts. Suerbaum (2002) 170–259 provides extensive bibliographies and many of the relevant testimonia for the fragmentary comedians, while the analysis of Wright (1974) on their stylistic unity remains fundamental reading. I give my views on some aspects of Terence's methods of adaptation in one essay (= Fontaine (2014)), and further explore Plautine and Terentian adaptation in two essays in Fontaine and Scafuro (2014). For the reception of Greek comedy by Greek authors of the Roman empire, see Hunter, Chapter 19 and Nervegna, Chapter 20.

22

NIGEL WILSON

The transmission of comic texts

Until the second half of the fifteenth century, all the literatures of the Western world were passed down from one generation to the next in copies transcribed by hand. Throughout this period, which lasted for two millennia or more, there were frequently times when writing material was in short supply and the number of people capable of acting as scribes severely limited. Another factor restricting production was that copies were normally produced singly, the only exception to this general rule being that in the Greco-Roman world the publishing business probably operated by having a manager dictate to a group of slaves, thereby ensuring production of multiple copies.

Given these economic conditions and the prolific output of many authors, it was inevitable that the stock of available texts was continually being whittled down, and it is clear that even the Alexandrian scholars of the third and second centuries BCE were unable, despite considerable effort, to put together a complete collection of dramatic and other texts composed in the preceding centuries. But at least they had built up extensive holdings, which suffered enormous losses in later antiquity and after. It is known that there were at least 256 writers of comedy in Greek, whose output totalled more than 2,300 plays.[1] Of these we now possess eleven by Aristophanes, one by Menander that is complete but for a few lines, and substantial parts of several others by Menander. This is much less than 1 per cent of the total production in this genre (and the percentage for tragedy is probably not much more favourable).

Comedy secured formal recognition as an element in the festivals of Dionysus in or around 486 BCE, and from that point onwards authors, especially those who won prizes, will have had a greater incentive to retain master copies of their texts. But it is very doubtful whether there was any trade in books at that date and there is not even anecdotal evidence about the

---

[1] Zimmermann (1998) 9.

circulation of texts. By the last quarter of the fifth century, however, the situation had changed to the extent that there is a reference to an area in the market-place in Athens where apparently books were on sale; this is the usual interpretation of Eupolis, fragment 327 K.-A.; the text could also mean 'where papyrus is for sale', which would be consistent with, rather than proof of, a trade in books. In addition Plato makes Socrates say (*Apology* 26D) that the philosopher Anaxagoras' book can be bought for a drachma, while there are indications that individuals could own private libraries; it is difficult to imagine that Aristophanes could parody tragedy so extensively without possessing a number of texts himself. A less well-known but important scrap of evidence comes from the orator Isocrates, who reports (*Aegineticus* 5) that the seer Polemaenetus had a collection of books on divination. It can be inferred that the date when this collection was formed was probably about the end of the fifth century. But collections of this kind formed by professionals to meet their specific needs are no proof that texts such as comedies were circulating already among lovers of literature; we are left guessing when educated people began to acquire their copies, and we need to bear in mind that public libraries did not yet exist.

Suppose an Athenian with literary interests, or someone from elsewhere drawn to Athens by its cultural prestige, attended a dramatic festival, saw a play by Aristophanes or one of his rivals and decided that he would like to read it or some others from earlier years, what would he have had to do? It is very uncertain whether a visit to the market would have supplied his need; would the theatre manager have been able to help? The variously titled officials who looked after the building are not stated to have had responsibility for the texts,[2] and it appears that the theatre did not act as a deposit library until the latter part of the following century, when the orator Lycurgus made a proposal that official copies of tragedy be kept (pseudo-Plutarch, *Vitae decem oratorum* 841F).[3] I would not exclude the possibility that some kind of informal but of necessity incomplete collection had begun to be formed in the preceding decades, but there is no evidence. So it might well be that the enthusiastic reader would have needed to gain access to the author, if he was still living, and otherwise to his family or heirs, in the hope of acquiring texts.

In the Hellenistic period and early Roman empire there was a gradual rise in the standard of living. Apart from the great libraries set up by the

---

[2] Pickard-Cambridge (1988) 266.

[3] Pickard-Cambridge (1988) 100. In this context Lycurgus is also stated to have revived a competition for comedy on the third day of the Anthesteria festival, a competition which apparently had fallen into abeyance. This information, however, is not unproblematic, see Wilson (2000) 32.

rulers of Alexandria and Pergamon there were other smaller collections, often associated with a gymnasium, and in due course some city councils established libraries. Though we are not very well informed about all aspects of cultural life in Greek cities, the habits of the reading public can be inferred to some extent from the papyri recovered from towns in various parts of Egypt, where the ruling and intellectual elite were Greek in speech and culture. A glimpse of a circle of learned readers in Oxyrhynchus in the Fayum is provided by a letter penned in the late second century (*POxy* 2192), in which the writer indicates that he needs certain texts and has a good idea of where to find them. They include the now lost work by one Hypsicrates on characters ridiculed in comedy (this must have dealt with Old Comedy rather than Middle or New). We cannot be sure how often such episodes of sophisticated literary activity occurred or in how many locations outside the principal centres of culture. But what we can say with confidence is that a certain number of texts were widely known and circulated because they had a place in the syllabus for secondary education. Inclusion in the curriculum could lead to the production of scholarly commentary or other monographs such as that of Hypsicrates; the historical allusions in Aristophanes created quite an industry among Alexandrian and later scholars, and a very small percentage of such material, many times re-edited, has come down to us in the margins of some of the medieval manuscripts. In contrast to Aristophanes the style and content of plays by the later writers were less often the object of scholarly interest; it is known that more than one scholar investigated the similarities of Menander's plots to those of plays by his rivals and concluded, perhaps unfairly, that he was guilty of plagiarism, but otherwise all that survives is a small portion of a collection of brief summaries of the plots (*POxy* 1235). As these summaries appear to have concluded with a comment on the merits of the play in question, we should probably infer that they were designed to help the reader decide which plays to choose from Menander's vast output.

It is worth noting in passing that his popularity with the wealthier members of the educated public is proved by the discovery of mosaics in a number of villas in various parts of the Roman world. A pair from the 'Villa of Cicero' at Pompei, one of which has an inscription declaring that it shows a scene from act II of the *Theophoroumenê*, are signed by the artist Dioscorides. One found at Ulpia Oescus in Bulgaria gives the title *Achaioi*, and recently a find at Zeugma on the Euphrates revealed a scene from the *Synaristôsai*. But the most famous of such monuments, of uncertain date but usually thought to be of the third century, is the set of eleven mosaics in a villa at Mytilene, each one inscribed with the name of a different play, and all but one with an indication of which act is depicted. The eleven titles include just two of which substantial portions survive, *Samia* and *Epitrepontes* (*Men at Arbitration*).[4]

Initially, it was Menander who was chosen to represent comedy in the literary syllabus. Aristophanes appears to have replaced him in late antiquity.[5] Although the reasons for this change are not entirely clear, the nostalgic admiration of Athenian achievements in the fifth century BCE, which was very powerful from the second century onwards when Greece was suffering severe economic decline, must have played its part; there were no doubt other factors, one of which will be mentioned below. Acquaintance with Menander gradually became the preserve of a small number of highly educated readers; there are occasional references to a few plays in the writings of Choricius, a professor of rhetoric in Gaza in the sixth century, and the last hint of direct knowledge is found in the first half of the following century in the letters of the Byzantine author Theophylactus Simocatta.

Aristophanes had written around forty plays, Menander just over 100 (our sources give slightly varying figures), and several other authors were prolific. To keep all titles in circulation would tax the resources of a modern publisher. In pre-modern conditions publishers and librarians were in no position to do much to stem the steady rate of reduction in the range of texts available. Although not everyone will have been unaware of the risk of texts being lost for good, there is only one report of a serious attempt to deal with the problem. In 356 the emperor Constantius II decided to establish a library in Constantinople, the eastern capital of the empire, and in a surviving panegyric by the orator Themistius (4.59b–61b) he is credited with understanding the urgency of maintaining full collections of texts, and not just the central authors, but those who appealed to a smaller circle of readers and whose works, being rare, needed to be protected from neglect. The imperial initiative may have had some effect for a time, but Constantinople, in common with other cities, was often damaged by fire, and the library is thought to have been destroyed by one such disaster in 475. Many provincial cities also had libraries, some of them set up as charitable foundations, such as the library of Celsus at Ephesus, which had an endowment of 23,000 denarii (*Inschriften von Ephesos* 7.2.5113), or the one established by Pliny the Younger at Como at a cost of 1,000,000 sesterces and with an endowment of 100,000 (*ILS* 2927), but these institutions were not equal to the task of ensuring a full stock of texts in perpetuity. The small selection of literary texts that has come down to us is largely the result of the gradual emergence of a consensus about the choice of texts to be included in the curriculum of

---

[4] MNC 2, 186 and 468–71; Abadie-Reynard and Darmon (2003) 95–9.
[5] Marrou (1956) 243 does not suggest that Aristophanes had a significant position earlier.

secondary schools. It might appear at first sight that this is too pessimistic an assessment of the situation in late antiquity, because the *Anthology* of John Stobaeus, probably compiled in the fifth century, includes excerpts from a great many plays by Menander and a fair number from other writers such as Philemon. But the impression created by the remarkably wide range of authors cited is probably misleading; some of the quotations match those in other anthologies and it is a plausible inference that they go back to a common source of an earlier date.[6]

Since the end of the nineteenth century the papyri found in Egypt have enhanced our knowledge of many genres of ancient literature. Though they have produced relatively little to interest the student of Old and Middle Comedy – perhaps the most significant exception consists of some rather enigmatic fragments of Eupolis' *Dêmoi* (three leaves of *P. Cairensis* 43227) – our knowledge of Menander has been completely transformed, essentially by three substantial discoveries. A large part of a book excavated at Aphroditopolis and now known as the Cairo codex (the rest of *P. Cairensis* 43227) proved to contain hundreds of lines from *Men at Arbitration* and significant portions of three other plays.[7] A still greater find attracted wide attention in 1959, when the *Dyscolus*, a text complete but for a few lines, was published from the Bodmer papyrus (*P. Bodmer* 4). This extraordinary volume proved to contain also large portions of *Aspis* and *Samia* (published as *P. Bodmer* 26 and 25). The third major find was part of *Sicyonios* (*P. Sorbonne* 72, 2272, 2273). Smaller contributions to our knowledge have come from two palimpsests: leaves of parchment from Greek texts that had been discarded were reused, as was fairly common practice, in both cases for texts in Syriac. A fragment found at St Catherine's monastery on Sinai (now St Petersburg MS. gr. 388) yielded fifty lines of *Men at Arbitration*, and more recently a palimpsest in the Vatican turned out to contain some verses from *Dyscolus* and *Titthê* (MS. Vat. syr. 623).

At the beginning of the Byzantine period, which for the present purpose may be reckoned from the reign of Justinian (527–565), Menander had all but disappeared. His name was known simply because it had been misleadingly attached to a collection of 877 one-line aphorisms entitled *gnômai monostichoi*; very few of them belong to him. In theory a Byzantine intellectual could also have known the passages of varying length quoted in Stobaeus' *Anthology*, but copies of that bulky collection seem to have been

[6] Diels (1875).
[7] Riyad and Selim (1978) provide a facsimile. Though the texts of the two authors were found together, it seems likely that the Eupolis fragments came from a different codex, quite possibly written by the same copyist. Körte (1912) 278 noted that the script is more careful and formal.

rather rare. With Aristophanes it was another matter. His place in the educational curriculum was safe. It may seem paradoxical that his plays and those of the tragedians enjoyed high standing in a culture which no longer had any theatres and so gave no opportunity for performances of classical drama. But Byzantine society was in some ways very conservative, not least in matters of education. Ever since the second century one of the main aims of the system had been to produce an elite capable of speaking and writing Attic Greek as it had been written by the great Athenian authors hundreds of years ago. Authors who were considered the purest exponents of Attic dialect became set texts. Menander ought to have qualified alongside Aristophanes, but for some reason was not thought to be so suitable; many authorities admired his language, but the important grammarian Phrynichus, writing in the late second century, disagreed strongly (*Ecloge* 394F), and his opinion may have been enough to tip the balance.

We know nothing of the stages by which Aristophanes' surviving plays were selected. The eleven that we can now read will not all have figured in the average syllabus of a school, but probably represent the range from which an influential teacher of late antiquity suggested that his colleagues make their choice. Judging by the contents of the extant medieval copies and by the range of citations or allusions in Byzantine writers it would seem that pupils typically read *Wealth*, *Clouds* and *Frogs*, which modern scholars refer to as the triad, and in some schools a fourth play, *Knights*, was added. Early Byzantine copies do not survive complete; there are a few scraps from sixth-century texts on papyrus or parchment (it should be noted that by this time books were no longer scrolls but in the codex form that we are accustomed to, and that parchment was much used as an alternative to papyrus because it was more durable, even if expensive and sometimes in short supply). In the following centuries, a period commonly described as a Dark Age lasting until the end of the eighth century, we lose track of the history of texts, and when signs of renewed intellectual activity appear the evidence is too scanty to furnish a full and clear picture. It can, however, be shown that John of Sardis, writing a commentary on a handbook of rhetoric by Aphthonios in the early ninth century, drew on a text of Aristophanes equipped with the marginal commentary known as scholia.[8] A few decades later the patriarch Photius in his *Bibliotheca*, a survey of more than 300 works of classical and patristic literature, unfortunately disregards poetry almost entirely; but he does reveal by an unmistakable allusion in one of his letters that he had read at least the *Wealth*, which appears to have been the first play that the

[8] Alpers (2009) 73–86.

Byzantine schoolchild encountered.[9] This is the play which normally comes first in the medieval and later manuscripts; it was probably chosen not so much on grounds of literary merit but because it is relatively easy from a linguistic point of view, and this was a consideration to be taken seriously, since the spoken language was beginning to diverge markedly from classical Attic Greek.

There are about 170 manuscript copies of one or more plays dating from the years up to 1600, by which time the printed book dominated the market for Greek texts, but only about 35 can be dated earlier than *c.* 1400, and of these very few indeed were produced before the Byzantine empire suffered the catastrophic sack of the capital city by the Fourth Crusade in 1204. The earliest and most important, despite numerous minor scribal errors, is the Ravenna manuscript (Biblioteca Classense MS. 429), written in the middle of the tenth century; of the medieval copies it is the only one to contain all eleven plays. No other witness survives from that century apart from a tiny fragment of *Birds* (Florence, Biblioteca Laurenziana MS. 60.9). From the late eleventh century we have the Venice manuscript (Biblioteca Marciana MS. gr. 474), which contains seven plays and is highly regarded by editors for the quality of the text it offers. Only two other manuscripts can be dated with certainty or probability before 1204, and they are of no great value to the editor. After the Byzantines had regained control of their capital in 1261 there was a gradual revival of scholarly interest in the Classics, in which a key role was played by Demetrius Triclinius, who appears to have directed a school in the empire's second city, Thessalonike, *c.* 1310–1320. Unlike most of his colleagues he took an informed interest in the metres of Greek dramatic texts and exploited his knowledge to correct some of the errors that had crept into the texts because of the inaccuracy of copyists. The results of his labours are visible in a number of the late manuscripts, in particular a fifteenth-century copy in Oxford (Bodleian Library, MS. Holkham gr. 88), which offers the text of eight plays. This is unusual, because by this date most copies were prepared for use in schools which limited the curriculum to the three triad plays, with the occasional addition of the *Knights*. Quite a number of copies offer only one or two plays, a fact from which one is tempted to infer that the syllabus was being reduced.

When Italians began to study Greek in the fifteenth century, they relied heavily on Byzantine refugees as teachers, and the refugees imported the school syllabus that they had grown up with. But in an age which lacked good course-books and dictionaries Aristophanes was far from being an easy author for the student, and there is not much evidence that Italians

[9] Wilson (2007) 112.

took a special interest in the plays or were able to emend corrupt passages. One of the refugees, however, Andronicus Callistus, who taught for a while in Bologna and Florence but ended his days obscurely in London, has been identified as the scribe of a manuscript (Paris, B.N. MS. grec 2715) that contains a fair number of minor improvements which should probably be credited to him.

A major step forward was the issue of the first printed edition, prepared by the talented Cretan refugee Marcus Musurus for the Aldine Press in 1498. It was not a complete edition, because he was unable to obtain a manuscript of the *Lysistrata* or *Women at the Thesmophoria* which were first printed by the Juntine Press in Florence in 1515. Nor was Musurus' edition based on the best manuscripts; one might have expected him to profit from the excellent manuscript in the Marciana collection mentioned above, but it was not available for consultation despite the wish expressed by the donor cardinal Bessarion as far back as 1468, and he relied on a copy that is now in Modena (Biblioteca Estense, MS. gr. 127 = a.U.5.10) and various manuscripts that included more than one copy of the recension prepared by Demetrius Triclinius. Most of the latter have been lost, but a small part of the printer's copy has been identified (Sélestat, Bibliothèque Humaniste, MS. 347 = K 1105e); it gives the text of *Wealth*.[10]

Printing ensured that texts would now be safe, but it was not the solution to every problem. Mistakes made by successive generations of scribes had not all been eliminated and texts circulating in the Renaissance were still disfigured by many errors, which made some passages barely intelligible. For some time the best manuscripts were either not identified or not accessible, and an enormous expenditure of scholarly effort was still needed to remedy the situation. We do now have editions that provide readable, but not definitive, texts. What are the prospects for the future? As far as the existing corpus is concerned, the progress achieved in the last century or so means that the law of diminishing returns will apply to textual criticism. But we have not reached the end of the road. Palimpsests and papyri offer us the prospect of new finds. The latter could prove to be a rich source when it becomes possible to examine the cases of Egyptian mummies. These were made from cartonnage consisting of multiple layers of papyrus, often derived from discarded books. Experiments on fragments of such cases have shown that the layers, which are stuck together, can easily be separated by immersion in a solution of an enzyme obtained from a slaughterhouse. What is now needed is a technology that is not invasive but maps the ink in each

---

[10] Wilson (2007) 4–13. The sources used by Musurus for his edition are analysed by Sicherl (1997) 114–54.

layer individually. Attempts are already being made to develop the technology, and if they are successful there is a very real possibility of spectacular discoveries.

Further reading

For the history of transmission of classical texts in general see Reynolds and Wilson (2013). Wilson (2007) details the transmission of Aristophanes and discusses problems from the perspective of the most recent editor of the text. The Aristophanic transmission is also discussed by Sommerstein (2010b). For the text of Menander and its restoration, see Gomme and Sandbach (1973) 39–57; Blume (2010) and Handley (2011); for comic fragments see Nesselrath (2010). A profound and at the same time lively introduction to the papyri from Egypt (especially the non-literary ones) and their world is Parsons (2007).

23

GONDA VAN STEEN

Snapshots of Aristophanes and Menander

From spontaneous reception to belated reception study

Reception of Plutarch's reception

The reception of Aristophanes and Menander may well be one of the oldest cases of 'spontaneous' reception.[1] Imagine the Athenian who has just watched one of the comedies and who regales his neighbours and friends by replaying some of the jokes or scenes for them: 'Stop me if you've heard this one already...'. The reception of Aristophanes and Menander may well be one of the oldest cases of 'studied' or 'directed' reception, too. It was most likely Plutarch himself who subjected both playwrights to an (unfair) comparison, and who fiercely condemned Aristophanes in favour of

I am very grateful to Philip Walsh, who researched the history of Aristophanes in the Anglo-American world, for sharing a copy of his 2008 dissertation with me and for reading an earlier version of this chapter. My gratitude also goes to Romain Piana, who kindly sent me a microfiche version of his dissertation, which covers two critical centuries of the playwright's reception in France (from 1760 through 1962). I also gratefully acknowledge three important databases from which I was able to draw: first, the Classical Receptions in Late Twentieth Century Poetry and Drama in English Database, The Open University, www2.open.ac.uk/ClassicalStudies/GreekPlays; secondly, the database of the Archive of Performances of Greek and Roman Drama, University of Oxford, www.apgrd.ox.ac.uk; and lastly, the European Network of Research and Documentation of Performances of Ancient Greek Drama based at the University of Athens, http://ancient-drama.net. All translations from foreign languages are my own, unless otherwise noted.

[1] I use the now established term 'reception' despite the difficulties that have been associated with this term and its relations to performance history, performance criticism, and the study of the classical tradition. I concur that the critical terminology of reception studies needs reviewing and/or revisiting when theatre texts are concerned. Reception theory has made deplorably little impact on the historical study of the visual art forms and expressions that accompanied the classical and postclassical plays (with the exception of vase paintings). Studies of early modern through contemporary productions of Aristophanes and Menander have yet to engage in depth with the reception aspects of the costuming, stage and set design, dance, music etc. I regret that in this chapter, too, I can only scratch the surface of this tremendously interesting area of reception that allows us to reach far beyond the study of the ancient text and its 'afterlife'.

433

Menander (*Moralia* 853a–854d).[2] Plutarch set the stage for many centuries of history and criticism in the same vein.[3] Aristophanes' reputed knock-about comedy or his *bômolochia* (or *aischrologia*), his mixing of styles, and the perceived public role of his ridicule in Socrates' conviction and death suffered under the weight of the comparison with his younger counterpart. However, Aristophanes suffered under the burden of the comparison with the grand and 'consistent' style of tragedy as well. In seventeenth-century France, for instance, Greek tragedy was honoured more than Greek comedy primarily for its influence on neoclassical drama – in particular on the plays of Racine, Corneille, and their followers. Early modern through nineteenth-century Western thinkers related to Socrates; their defence of the *philosophe avant la lettre*, or the patron of the Enlightenment, came at the expense of Aristophanes, in a reductionist treatment of his *Clouds* but also of the person of the dramatist himself.[4] Voltaire, for instance, compared himself to Socrates, or was frequently compared to him, and his bias against Aristophanes took the undertow of a personal attack. Such an approach resonated with the agendas of early modern ethical, political and aesthetic criticism. But this thinking also led the West to rediscover Aristophanes: critics from various countries joined in the widespread debate about *Clouds*, the essence and 'rules' of the playwright's comedic licence, as well as the purity of his Attic Greek and his lyrics versus the bawdiness of his verbal and visual expression of sexual or scatological matters.

An early modern interest in Aristophanes' *Clouds* strengthened a prior fascination with *Wealth*, and thus with the humanist inquiry into the playwright's potential as a moralist. Matthew Steggle aptly sets the time frame in which we need to (re)conceptualize the reception of his work – and life:

> [I]t is no longer possible to adhere to the traditional model of the reception of Aristophanes, according to which Greek Old Comedy is almost unknown until a nineteenth-century 'rediscovery' of Aristophanes.[5]

---

[2] Richard Hunter, who studies the rhetorical and political dimensions of Plutarch's *Comparison of Aristophanes and Menander*, believes that the fragmentary précis (or epitome) of a *Comparison* was likely derived from a lost essay written by Plutarch himself, see Hunter (2000) 267, (2009) 78–89 and Chapter 19. See also Lamberton (2001) 191, 192 and 207. On the role of tragedy in Plutarch's influential comparative model see recently Hall (2007b) 252f.

[3] For more information on the reception of Aristophanes from antiquity to (roughly) 1800, see Hall (2007a) and Walsh (2008) 14–24. See further Braden (2010) and Telò (2010). See also the prior chapters on 'Reception', Chapters 19–22.

[4] See further Macgregor Morris (2007) 209–21; Piana (2005) ch. 1 and *passim*; Van Steen (2000) ch. 1.

[5] Steggle (2007) 52. François Pauw discusses most of the ingredients that make up 'Old Comedy' and that, according to him, hampered Aristophanes' early modern reception

The 'missing centuries', from the Renaissance through the early nineteenth century, of the reception of both Aristophanes and Menander proved Plutarch wrong, and recent decades have further favoured the former over the latter. These centuries will be the first focus of this chapter but a few caveats are in order. The reception histories of both playwrights were never closely intertwined, not even in the rigid framework of comparison that Plutarch's lingering terms might force upon us. It would be misconceived to think of their work and legacy as mirror-images of each other. It is important, therefore, to restore each author's autonomy and uniqueness, and to reiterate that the popularity of either one hardly ever came 'at the expense' of the other.

As much as Aristophanes was a source of controversy, he was also a source of productive tension from early modern times through the early twenty-first century. His corpus inspired modern literary criticism of comedy or the theory of the comic, and it lent itself to a rethinking of the reception study of the genre of Old Comedy. The same cannot be said of the tradition of Menander, whose direct (as opposed to Roman-mediated) reception suffered from having to rely on fragmentary texts with many variants. My aim in this chapter, then, is to outline some of the trends, movements and landmark versions that characterize those 'lost' centuries in which Aristophanes' reception is hardest to trace, and to devote less attention to twentieth-century developments, the study of which is greatly facilitated by the availability of online databases. Even for those 'lost' centuries, I will necessarily have to confine myself to 'vignettes' of reception and will refer to recent studies that paint a fuller picture, especially of the playwright's reception in Britain, France, Germany and the United States.[6] A brief chapter on the reception of Aristophanes cannot attempt to be exhaustive. This study does not purport to be a comprehensive summary of the history of the poet's reception, nor does it present a critical review of scholarship on the topic. My objective is rather to outline some of the primary associations of Aristophanes in Western culture of the sixteenth through the early twentieth century, to provide a background to other scholars' discussions of the playwright's reception from the 1950s to 1960s through the present day (which nobody can discuss from a global perspective without leaving blatant, and culturally insensitive, lacunae).

(1996). Paul Botley, on the other hand, convincingly demonstrates that Aristophanes' *Wealth* figured prominently in the Renaissance curriculum of teaching and studying Greek, see Botley (2010) 88–91.

[6] See Walsh (2008) and (2009); Piana (2005); Holtermann (2004); and S.C. Day (2001), respectively. Day provides an extensive list of performances of Aristophanes' comedies in the United States in Appendix A (2001) 198–214.

GONDA VAN STEEN

Aristophanes of the lost centuries

The Cretan scholar Marcus Musurus, compiler of the first printed edition of the Aristophanic corpus (*editio princeps*, 1498) for the Venetian publisher Aldus Manutius, excluded both *Lysistrata* and *Women at the Thesmophoria*, which were not published until 1515.[7] He and many of his contemporaries probably took offence at Aristophanes' loose-lipped female figures, who were, even if only on the page, 'stains' on the sought-after classical decorum. Musurus' influential edition remained one of the standard texts for nearly three centuries. The sixteenth through mid-seventeenth-century humanists in Italy, Germany, France, England, Spain and Switzerland produced the first translations into Latin, such as the important 1538 Latin translation of, notably, *all* of Aristophanes' comedies by Andreas Divus, an Istrian humanist.[8] Greek-Latin editions appeared by the mid-sixteenth century, followed by imitations and occasional performances (most of them in ancient Greek) of primarily *Wealth* and *Clouds*. Vasiliki Giannopoulou concludes that 'the 1546 Cambridge performance of *Peace* seems to have been something of an exception'.[9] Nicodemus Frischlin, professor at the University of Tübingen, issued an early defence of Aristophanes in his 1586 Greek-Latin edition of five of Aristophanes' comedies (*Wealth, Knights, Clouds, Frogs* and *Acharnians*). Frischlin addressed the criticisms of Plutarch directly, but was more influential in the German, Dutch and English academic world than in France.[10] Typically, Aristophanes was appropriated first by the academic elite, and he only gradually became accessible to the broader public.[11]

The early humanists cast Aristophanes as an apt moralist or an ethical and didactic guide, and they valued the allegorical figures of *Wealth* such as Poverty, the title character's antipode. *Wealth* is relatively free of obscenities and personal attacks, and its language is less lyrical and more

[7] Wilson (2007) 12. For a detailed discussion of the earliest humanist editions of Aristophanes, see Wilson (2007) 10–14.

[8] Hall (2007a) 9; Wilson (2007) 13.

[9] Giannopoulou (2007) 310. Giannopoulou (2007) compiled an extensive list of translations of Aristophanes published in various languages from the Renaissance until 1920, and she includes some significant printed editions and adaptations. Her research, which was commissioned by the Archive of Performances of Greek and Roman Drama, incorporates older sources. Her findings are confirmed by Walsh, who appended an expanded chronological list of published *English* translations and adaptations of Aristophanes' plays, 1651–1902. Walsh (2008) 40–9, and appendix A, 198–207. See also the list in Walton (2006), appendix.

[10] Walsh (2008) 8f., 24–33; Hadley (2014).

[11] See further Steggle (2007), who discusses Aristophanes' reception in the context of the Renaissance and early modern theatre of Shakespeare, Johnson and their contemporaries. In Britain through the eighteenth century, Aristophanes was subjected to a variety of popular treatments, on which see Walsh (2008) 39–65.

readily intelligible. Also, the play held first place in the Byzantine triad of Aristophanes (consisting of *Wealth*, *Clouds* and *Frogs*). '[S]igns of interest' in *Frogs* and *Birds* began to show in England, France and Italy in the seventeenth century, whereas 'the "peace", "Cleon" and "demagogue" plays *Acharnians*, *Knights*, *Wasps* and *Peace*' made their first lasting impact in the late eighteenth century: translators and imitators of the latter plays creatively responded to the French Revolution, a historical moment for both supporters and detractors to relate to the classics to enhance social and political negotiations.[12] François-Benoît Hoffman wrote an intriguing revolutionary adaptation of Aristophanes' *Lysistrata*, which was staged a mere four times in 1801–1802: the moral censors banned it, sensitive as they were to the shifting political and military fate of the Revolution.[13] Other Western contemporaries equated the French revolutionary leaders with the classical demagogues such as Cleon, and they used Aristophanic references to foreground the 'excesses' of democracy. The revolutionary turmoil in Europe and in colonial America revitalized the playwright's reception in Britain, in particular, where the political content of his comedies and especially their relationship to democracy became the basis for a cutting critique of the democratic state system.[14]

Britain saw a landmark of an early Aristophanic adaptation in a burlesque play by the prolific Victorian playwright, James Robinson Planché: *The Birds of Aristophanes: A Dramatic Experiment in One Act* was staged at the Theatre Royal, Haymarket, London, in 1846.[15] Meanwhile, influential translators such as the poet John Hookham Frere gave the playwright increased visibility: his minimally adapted translations of *Frogs*, *Acharnians*, *Knights* and *Birds* offered up viable scripts for performance.[16] An 1883 premiere of *Birds* (in ancient Greek) at Cambridge claimed to revive Attic comedy in the first complete play production, but it underestimated several earlier stagings (also at secondary schools such as Dulwich College, London, where *Frogs* was presented in 1876).[17] Starting in the 1850s, Benjamin Bickley Rogers issued a series of translations that were prudishly Victorian – and that served the Loeb series for several decades.[18] It took the

---

[12] Giannopoulou (2007) 310 (quotations). [13] See further Orfanos (2007).

[14] See further Walsh (2008) ch. 2 and (2009); for the German states, see Holtermann (2004) 74–6, 317.

[15] Fletcher (1979–1981); Walsh (2008) 112, 136–8; see also Hall and Macintosh (2005) 345–7.

[16] Walsh (2008) 139 n. 91.

[17] Easterling (1999) 28, 31f., 37, 47; Stray (1998) 157, 159; Walsh (2008) 136 n. 84, 138f., 175 n. 74; Wrigley (2007), with emphasis on the Oxford productions of Aristophanes.

[18] See further Walsh (2008) ch. 3 and 161f.

publication of Aubrey Beardsley's pen and ink illustrations of *Lysistrata* (1896) to expose Britain to Aristophanes' sexual humour. Beardsley's carefully crafted but very revealing drawings accompanied a prose translation of the play by Samuel Smith. These illustrations, which embarrassed even Beardsley himself later in life, helped to 'mark a transition from Romantic and Victorian Hellenism to the modern era'.[19]

In the early 1900s, Gilbert Murray's translations popularized a pacifist Aristophanes and again galvanized the playwright's Anglo-American reception.[20] Students and amateurs active in British university drama clubs as well as Classics departments produced a fair number of early twentieth-century revivals of Aristophanes, and less elitist forms of that tradition continue to this day. The Cambridge Greek plays included *Wasps* (1897, 1909), *Birds* (1903, 1924, 1971, 1995), *Peace* (1927), *Frogs* (1936, 1947), *Clouds* (1962) and *Lysistrata* (1986).[21] For many years professional British theatre dared to invest only in *Lysistrata* and *Birds*. Terence Gray, for instance, produced *Lysistrata* in an interesting 1931 double bill with Sophocles' *Antigone*. As director of the Cambridge Festival Theatre he also staged two versions of *Birds* (1928, 1933). Norman Marshall's Gate Theatre successfully presented an unexpurgated *Lysistrata* in 1935.[22]

The French neoclassical prejudice against Aristophanes barely waned during the seventeenth and eighteenth centuries. This European divide led D. K. Sandford, professor of Greek at Glasgow University, to conclude that the playwright was a casualty of 'those egregious judges of antiquity – the French'.[23] Many French critics reduced Aristophanes to a text for reading, a source from which to mine Attic Greek. Revolutionary detractors went on to call Socrates the victim of the poet's democratic frenzy. According to Chantal Grell, 'Aristophane fit l'objet d'une réprobation quasi générale' ('Aristophanes was the object of near-universal reprobation').[24] Martin Holtermann, too, singled out the seventeenth-century French advocates of classicism as some of the playwright's most virulent enemies. He declares, with a whiff of national pride: 'It was up to intellectuals in a German context

---

[19] Walsh (2008) 149 (quotation); (2008) 12, 118, 147–50, 173–87. Walsh also includes copies of Beardsley's drawings (2008) 208–15. Most of the illustrations are available online as well.

[20] See further Stray (2007), even though Murray's work on Aristophanes does not figure prominently in this volume.

[21] Walton (1987) 352f.; Easterling (1999); Stray (1998) 157–61.

[22] Walton (1987) 342, 344.   [23] Sandford is quoted by Walsh (2008) 32.

[24] For the broader background to the reception of the classics in late seventeenth- and eighteenth-century France, see Grell (1995), especially 102 (n. 187, quotation), 316, 1105.

to develop a new taste for his comedies and to detect their political aspects.'[25] But the German states, too, took a slow start on actual stage performance of Aristophanes. It was ancient *tragedy* that Goethe and Schiller brought to the forefront of German theatre, heralding Weimar classicism. Apart from Goethe's amateur production of *Birds* (1780), Attic comedy performance was overlooked in Germany until 1908, although more or less liberal translations were available. In 1908 Max Reinhardt, the celebrated Austrian director active in Germany, put on a bawdy *Lysistrata* in Berlin.[26] Despite its immense success, it was not followed by any other significant pre-1950s attempt to reinterpret the Aristophanic repertoire for the stage, let alone to establish a tradition of comic revivals.

As in Britain, elite academic circles conceived of the earliest stage revivals of Aristophanes in North America, but the playwright soon reached broader audiences. In 1886, male students from the University of Pennsylvania staged a performance of *Acharnians* (in ancient Greek) at the Academy of Music in Philadelphia. Concerns about the play's obscenity resulted in documented acts of self-censorship.[27] This early production outstripped in importance a few American academic stagings of *Birds*, such as the one presented (in the original language) in 1903, at the inauguration of the Hearst Greek Theatre at the University of California, Berkeley.[28]

The year 1930 saw the first American *Lysistrata*, a turning point in the United States' popular acceptance of classical drama. The production of Norman Bel Geddes in Gilbert Seldes' adaptation had been inspired by the touring 1923 *Lysistrata* of the Moscow Art Theatre.[29] Notwithstanding some negative reviews, the show resisted censorship pressure and ran for more than 250 performances in several urban venues (Philadelphia, New York, Chicago, Los Angeles, etc.). In 1936, the Federal Theatre Project, the artistic offspring of Franklin Delano Roosevelt's Works Progress Administration (WPA), sponsored the creation of an African American *Lysistrata* adapted by Theodore Browne. But its premiere at the University of Washington in Seattle was closed by the WPA for being too risqué. Susan Day suggests that the ban resulted from the show's attempt to subvert white hegemony: it

---

[25] Holtermann (2004) 317. Holtermann provides a useful overview of editions, commentaries, translations and performances of Aristophanes in a lengthy appendix (2004) 279–316. For an older study of the poet's scholarly reception in Germany, see Werner (1975).

[26] See further Kotzamani (1997) ch. 2.

[27] See further S. C. Day (2001) ch. 1; Pearcy (2003).   [28] S. C. Day (2001) 145–59.

[29] On this Soviet *Lysistrata*, which toured New York and Chicago in 1925–1926, see also below. See further Kotzamani (1997), who discusses Seldes' adaptation in her ch. 4; Day (2001) ch. 2; Walsh (2008) 192f.

undermined racism with 'sophisticated, self-assured, multilevel humor' and 'laughter *about* bigotry'.[30] The war years witnessed further efforts to revive *Lysistrata*. The comedies that are typically less popular with modern audiences than *Lysistrata* and *Birds* were first staged in the United States, as in most Western European countries, after 1950.

Modern Greece as touchstone

The fifteenth through the mid-nineteenth centuries may be the centuries during which performances of Aristophanes remained a rarity, but the playwright figured prominently in the theoretical discourse about the nature of comedy.[31] Franciscus Robortellus, for instance, a mid-sixteenth-century theorist, adapted Aristotle's analysis of tragedy to comedy and delivered an influential synthesis of the Renaissance 'rules of comedy'.[32] He also upheld, however, Plutarch's verdicts on Aristophanes' lack of decorum and on his 'raillery' of 'that best of men, the most venerable Socrates'.[33] From Robortellus to Adamantios Koraes, a Greek expatriate to France and founding father of modern Greece, Socrates is *the* victim of the unchecked public ridicule that both firmly associated with the work and life of Aristophanes. The major controversies in this extended debate pivoted on the competing claims of philology, Enlightenment rationalism, moral and aesthetic criteria, and theatre practitioners' status as legitimate interpreters of the plays. These issues continued to steer the discourse on Aristophanes through the late nineteenth century, as is manifested by the inherited and expanded discussions that accompanied the playwright's belated reception in the modern nation of Greece itself: the newborn state of (nominally) 1821 had missed out on the experience of the Renaissance because of the four-centuries-long Ottoman occupation, but it adopted the poet's contemporary European reception, complete with its nodes of controversy.[34]

By 1868, *Wealth* had become the play of choice also of modern Greek translators and performers interested in reviving Aristophanes in his 'homeland'. It was the work that secured the leap from a text-based to a performance-oriented reception of the playwright. *Wealth* became the vehicle of the politico-satirical (and distinctly socialist) wit of Michael

[30] Day (2001) ch. 3, 99 (first quotation), 137 (second quotation).
[31] My choices here *qua* references reflect my aim to use the reception of Aristophanes in modern Greece as a touchstone to the playwright's reception in other locales.
[32] Herrick (1964) 79.
[33] Translated from the original Latin by Marvin Herrick (1964) 230 (both quotations).
[34] The discussion in chs. 1 and 2 of Van Steen (2000) precludes detailed treatment of the topic here.

Chourmouzes and Sophokles Karydes who, with the help of a professional theatre company, gained a first breakthrough for Aristophanes on the modern Greek stage. Their popular production, which fed a permanent taste for contemporized political satire, competed with an antiquarian staging of *Clouds*. *Clouds*, too, was produced in 1868, but qualms about 're-staging' the execution of the 'father of rationalism' in Greece itself had delayed the Athenian debut of the long-contested comedy. The long-lived French bias, mediated by Koraes, affected the modern Greek reception of Aristophanes in palpable ways. Expatriate and local Greek intellectuals were keen to promote Socrates as a 'moral ancestor' and to sideline the comic pundit.[35] However, the sought-after pedigree from the Golden Age came with Aristophanes, the 'poisoned gift from antiquity', in tow.[36]

The 1868 *Wealth* represents the kind of bold adaptation that typified, both in Greece and elsewhere in Western Europe, the risks that the urban satirical press and stage were willing to take, with Aristophanes lending the classical cover or pretext. These adaptations helped to ease Old Comedy into the legitimate sphere of contemporary amateur revivals of Greek tragedy. Aristophanes-the-satirist developed into an outspoken mouthpiece, often against oppressive censorship. He initiated a wave of free versions and imitations that swept the early twentieth-century urban stages (and comic genres), and that revolutionized the public treatment of his 'immoral' women's plays. The taboo on modern Greek stage productions of *Clouds* was only broken by the unstoppable wave of biting satire launched at the turn to the twentieth century by Georgios Soures, a political pundit, translator, and director of *Clouds*.[37] Soures and Polyvios Demetrakopoulos, another prolific Demotic translator, then upped the ante and introduced risqué versions of the women's plays in the anti-feminist vein.[38] Through the 1930s, Aristophanes remained the alibi-author behind popular (often transvestite) adaptations of *Lysistrata*, in particular. Such a para-economy of bold adaptations shook up the authoritarian and nationalist patterns that, up until the 1900s, had grounded the field of modern Greek cultural production. Key in this development was the very popular 1892 French adaptation of

[35] Kalospyros (2007) 277f.   [36] Van Steen (2000) 16 and ch. 1.

[37] Van Steen (2000) 91–102 and *passim*. On the significance of Soures' theatre, see recently Bakonikola (2007).

[38] See Van Steen (2002) on the hazardous road to respectability in modern Greek theatre that Aristophanes' women's plays took while, for years, they excluded female spectators. Especially the socialist and anti-feminist strands in the poet's reception in Greece allow for interesting comparisons with the late nineteenth-century German exploitation of his plays for contemporary political and moral interpretations of nationalism, socialism, communism and female emancipation. The former are discussed by Van Steen (2000) chs. 2 and 3, the latter by Holtermann (2004) ch. 6.

Lysistrata by Maurice Donnay, a poet, playwright, and co-founder of the Chat Noir cabaret. Since its 1892 premiere at the Grand-Théâtre, Donnay's comedy had seen substantial reworking, repetition and imitation in Paris and elsewhere in Europe.[39] Donnay radically altered the original plot, structure and themes, and he introduced ancient courtesans (hetairai), whom he cast as the odalisques of an Oriental harem. Conceding to the fascination of the *boulevard* with extra-marital love and sexual intrigue, he transformed Aristophanes' *Lysistrata* into a comedy of sexual manners that showed little concern for a current socio-political critique. The Aristophanic cachet thus helped to revolutionize and 'europeanize' the urban entertainment business with sensual or 'hedonist' spectacle *à la grecque*, which dislodged the last barriers between classical and modern, elite and mainstream, 'high art' and popular culture. A British *Lysistrata* production of 1912–1913, on the other hand, started to champion women's suffrage and female political aptitude in general. The adaptation by Laurence Housman had opened at the Little Theatre in London in 1910 and was directed by Gertrude Kingston, who also played the title role.[40] More recent theatre practitioners, too, have drawn *Lysistrata* into the discourse on feminism, to deconstruct gender stereotyping.

Revival tragedy in Greece has revealed long-lasting ties to the more conservative literary and cultural tradition. The intelligentsia promoted classical tragedy as a vehicle of German-style *Bildung*, according to the cultural role of theatre as *Bildungstheater* or, in Greece's case, classicizing, 'restored' or restorative theatre. The elite expected revival tragedy to act as a nationalist or nativist bulwark against modernist aesthetics and to serve Greece's mission of nation-building. After the barrage of the notorious *Lysistrata* productions of Greece through the 1930s, it took the avant-gardist approach of legendary theatre director Karolos Koun to transform classical drama into an instrument of modernism, with Aristophanes' comedies in the lead. Directors such as Alexes Solomos, Spyros Euangelatos and countless others debunked decades of stultifying conventions and helped to define the reception of the playwright in Greece of the second half of the twentieth century.[41] Most contemporary directors, however, have worked in dialogue or competition with, or in counter-distinction from, Koun. The outcomes of their work have revealed the greatest diversity and variation of what proves

[39] Kotzamani (1997) ch. 1; Piana (2005) ch 6, B; Van Steen (2000) 110–12. See also recently Beta (2010) 246–48; Maurogene (2007) 118–26.
[40] Hall and Macintosh (2005) 530 and n. 16. Notably, in 1911, Wilhelm Süss published *Aristophanes und die Nachwelt*.
[41] See also Solomos (1961).

to be a Protean modern Greek Aristophanes. Philip Walsh, however, issues an incisive and timely warning:

> [e]xplicitly celebrating the polyphony or multidimensionality of Old Comedy is itself a phenomenon of the past one hundred years or so; before then, dogmatic readings overwhelmingly prevailed. Negotiating contradictions was not the business of Plutarch or the French neoclassical critics . . . It is prevalent in the twenty-first century to identify and emphasize the conflicting impulses within the plays and to argue that definitive resolution is impossible, but previous generations took a very different approach. If anything, Aristophanic comedy forced them . . . to take sides on matters of politics, morality, history, and aesthetics.[42]

The modern Greek reception of Menander, on the other hand, has been rather thin, but it provides an excellent illustration of the classicizing drive behind revival drama. This reception started with a characteristic example of what has pejoratively been called the 'museum treatment' or the approach of 'faithfulness' to the archaeological as well as to the philological legacy of the past. Thus, in 1908, the Athenian Philological Society 'Parnassus' staged a premiere of Menander's *Men at Arbitration*. The production was meant to celebrate the recent discovery of papyrus fragments that had yielded substantial new finds. The performance had to put image to the text, and it was received against the backdrop of lectures and newspaper articles on the subject of the papyrus finds. After the first few years of philological excitement, however, modern Greek interest in the Menander of the stage abated. The Greek theatre historian Giannes Sideres commented: 'Thus Menander made his first appearance in our theater and was promptly forgotten. He would, however, return with honor and with successes.'[43] But Sideres did not elaborate on what that subsequent modern Greek reception held. Stavroula Kyritsi, in her forthcoming dissertation, answers the lingering questions, but she also confirms that Menander was only infrequently performed before the last quarter of the twentieth century. Even after, his plays were often staged in academic settings.[44]

New Comedy and Menander toned down the complexity of Old Comedy. Richard Hunter concurs: 'That New Comedy is structurally and tonally both simpler and more uniform than Old Comedy requires no lengthy demonstration.'[45] These characteristics of New Comedy, which Plutarch preferred to the unpredictable changes of style and tone of Aristophanes, may explain why the reception of Menander found few new incentives through the (modern) ages. Menander's tradition has not enjoyed the

---

[42] Walsh (2008) 6.   [43] Sideres (1976) 231.
[44] See also Grammatas (2009).   [45] Hunter (2000) 271.

sequence of reinvigorating dramaturgical discoveries that modern generations have made as they re-read Aristophanes. This does not exclude, however, a future era in which the perceived lack of complexity of New Comedy
may appeal to many more contemporary readers, performers and audiences,
who might find respite from their overly demanding predicament in the simple, almost foreseeable plots.

How to slice it?

The above capsule description of the modern Greek tradition in revival comedy touches on a larger problem: how to slice the huge topic of twentieth-
century developments in the reception of Aristophanes in Greece, or any
place else, without invoking another instance of local exceptionalism? In
this chapter, therefore, I can only hope to point to trends as markers of
where to look and, if at all possible or desirable, as tools to 'quantify'
the reception of Aristophanes. Recording regular productions and repeat
performances is relatively easy for those who expect to find the poet's comedies among the steady features of the grand outdoor festivals, such as the
ones at Athens and Epidaurus (both founded in the mid-1950s). But even
those physical sites that seem geared for a heightened degree of reception
can be deceptive: the classical drama festival at Syracuse in Sicily (founded
1921), for instance, featured a 1927 production of *Clouds*, but its next
Aristophanic comedy, a modern version of *Frogs*, was not performed until
1976.

Scholars have covered the reception history of Aristophanes mainly by
geographical region or country, which might appear as an odd organizing
principle to break down a centuries-long and versatile tradition. Reception study also tends to be genre-based: from translations to adaptations
to performances – a pattern that is too often presumed to be a natural progression. Article titles such as 'Lysistrata on the Arabic Stage' and
'Aristophanes between Israelis and Palestinians' disclose recent examples
of the playwright's reception with regional focus.[46] Typical divisions qua
space, with Aristophanes negotiating local conflicts and borders, are often
extended by the limits of time periods and by the possibilities as well
as the restrictions of venues and/or modes: scholarship and the edited
and/or translated text, the stage, opera, musical entertainment, experimental

---

[46] See Kotzamani (2006b) and Yaari (2008), respectively, who stress the pacifist message
of *Lysistrata*. The latter analyses a 2002 performance in Jerusalem of a play, *The War
Over Home*, that integrated three anti-war comedies of Aristophanes and that
advocated for human rights.

theatre, ballet and dance, comics, the cinema, the Internet, and all else.[47] Each of these categories enriches, but also detracts from, a more holistic perspective on the development and the reception of the multi-faceted genre of Old through New Comedy. Other scholars have examined the legacy of particular ingredients of Aristophanes' work, such as the nature of his humour, his political side (conservative or progressive politics?), the ritual and metatheatrical aspects to his art, or his blend of literary, aesthetic and socio-political criticism.[48] The concerted modern quest for a socio-political critique in Aristophanes' comedies emerged in tandem with the search for a type of proto-feminism in the women's plays (see above).[49] Recently, the Lysistrata Project, the brainchild of two North American actresses, Kathryn Blume and Sharron Bower, crossed geographical boundaries to spotlight Aristophanes' most popular comedy against the backdrop of the imminent outbreak of the Iraqi war: on or around 3 March 2003, more than 1,000 organized readings of the play took place across the globe. The Project is indicative of the ongoing movement to stage Aristophanes' work as truly contemporary and activist theatre. As Marina Kotzamani has noted, the Internet, which was an essential tool to the Lysistrata Project, has allowed twenty-first-century generations to become world citizens through theatre.[50]

Holtermann's detailed monograph examines the *political* modes in which intellectuals of the German Enlightenment interpreted, imitated and adapted Aristophanes from the late eighteenth through the early twentieth century (from *c.* 1770 to *c.* 1914). These historical foundations established Aristophanes as a political playwright in contemporary Germany. Peter Hacks built on these foundations with his utopian and neo-Brechtian adaptation of Aristophanes' *Peace*, directed by Benno Besson at the Deutsches Theater in East Berlin in 1962. The production became one of the most popular shows in German-speaking countries.[51] In the case of Africa, the geographical *cum* political approach encompasses an entire continent, as in the section 'Aristophanes in Africa' in the important 2002 book of Kevin Wetmore, Jr.[52]

---

[47] See recently Gamel (2007) on Stephen Sondheim's 1974 musical *Frogs*, in which Shakespeare and Bernard Shaw are substituted for Aeschylus and Euripides. The adaptation by Burt Shevelove was first conceived in 1941 for performance in the pool at Yale University. Issues of translation and adaptation have been the lifelong concern of Michael Walton, who devoted chs. 8 and 9 of his 2006 volume, *Found in Translation*, to the challenges of translating Aristophanes. See also Walton (2007).

[48] The literature on each one of these aspects is large. For a recent reading, however, of Aristophanic humour and obscenity, see Robson (2006) and (2008). See also Revermann (2006a) and Silk (2000a).

[49] See e.g., Angel (2002).   [50] Kotzamani (2006a) 106.

[51] See Seidensticker (2007).   [52] Wetmore (2002) 50–2.

Wetmore observes: 'it seems fairly safe to conclude that Greek comedy is not nearly as popular in Africa as Greek tragedy, in any African nation'.[53] He sees the (far more accessible) native traditions of the African continent fulfil functions similar to those of Aristophanes' work.[54] In the 1970s, South Africa, the most prominent locale of reception, saw several stagings, among them a 1971 Afrikaans adaptation of *Birds* and a 1974 version of *Lysistrata*.[55] Lastly, one is always tempted to concentrate on the well-known productions that define a local politicized tradition, such as Koun's *Birds*, and to let possibly equivalent productions escape notice, such as an interwar staging of *Birds*, directed by Aleksander Wegierko at the Polish Theatre in Warsaw.[56]

When Koun was a student in Paris, he likely saw the famous 1928 satirical revue, *Birds*, of Charles Dullin, the modernist French director, actor, teacher and proponent of (a sophisticated approach to) folk theatre. With Dullin, Koun shared the conviction that the theatre had to broaden the social basis of its audience, and that Aristophanic comedy was an ideal vehicle to reach that end.[57] Dullin envisaged a *théâtre du peuple*, or a 'theatre of the people'. At his Théâtre de l'Atelier (founded in 1922), he searched for and experimented with popular and physical forms of performance.[58] Dullin himself was likely inspired by the 1923 *Lysistrata* created by the Musical Studio of the Moscow Art Theatre, a Soviet production that cast the experience of the October Revolution as 'People's Theatre'.[59] For his Russian *Lysistrata*, director Nemirovich-Danchenko had adopted the debate form and role of the modern revolutionary rally or mass meeting: two choruses acted to oppose the women's revolution to the old men's reactionism; they embodied the envisioned model of the new Soviet theatre.[60] The production became a resounding success and left a profound impact also in the United States (see above).[61]

Koun's 1959 opening performance of *Birds* became a *succès de scandale*: its anti-clerical tenor was exacerbated by the firebrand translation of Vasiles Rotas, who attacked the Greek conservatives and their ties to US

---

[53] Wetmore (2002) 50.   [54] Wetmore (2002) 51.

[55] See further Betine van Zyl Smit (2007), who also discusses censorship scandals in South Africa.

[56] For a (minimal) reference to the latter production, see Zawistowski (1937) 378 (his figure 3), 384.

[57] On the relationship between Koun's work and that of Dullin, see also Kotzamani (2007) 180f., 185, 187; (1997) 411.

[58] See further Piana (2005) ch. 7.

[59] On the Marxist underpinnings of the utopian model of the 'People's Theatre', which quickly became canonical, see also Hall (2007a) 20.

[60] Kotzamani (2005) 79, 105f.   [61] See further Kotzamani (1997) ch. 3.

imperialism. Over the years, appreciation for Koun's Art Theatre (*Theatro Technes*) grew to the extent that his *Birds* now stands as perhaps the single most influential production of Aristophanes – a classic in its own right. The shocking premiere made the long-standing confrontation between the academic, and typically nationalist, approach and the modernist treatment of Aristophanic performance come to a head, resulting in a debate about art's autonomy in the face of a paternalistic and authoritarian government. Aristophanes was, of course, not new to censorship, whether of a religious-moral or political strain. Many were the instances, too, in which aesthetic choices and questions had become issues with political ramifications. Koun's *Birds* captured the socio-political limbo of frail optimism of Cold War Greece. Kotzamani concludes her insightful analysis of the show on a more pessimistic note, stressing the powerlessness of the ordinary birds (for the Greek people) when faced with the tyrannical tendencies that overtake the protagonist Peisetaerus: 'The production's mournful ending conveys a pessimistic message about the capacity of a new progressive state to hold against the adversity of threatening powers.'[62] The 1959 premiere met with severe political retaliation initiated by Konstantinos Tsatsos and Konstantinos Karamanlis. The outright ban drove Koun also to uphold Aristophanes as a model for a risky blend of ideological avant-garde and folk theatre aesthetics, which he then applied to his productions of innovative native and foreign plays of mainly the 1960s and 1970s. For decades, Koun's *Birds* was emblematic of village and folk traditions (including the rural festival and the Karaghiozes shadow theatre); now, half a century later, it is an icon of nostalgia for a Greece of simpler times.[63]

Greek cartoonist Niarchos predicted that Koun's anti-clerical and anti-government production of *Birds* would determine Aristophanes' modern Greek reception (Figure 23.1). Niarchos' cartoon, reprinted on the front cover of a 1999 special issue of the satirical journal *To Pontiki* (*The Mouse*), incorporates a billboard or poster that announces *Birds* as a work by the 'duo Aristophanes and Tsatsos'. Tsatsos walks up to 'co-author' Aristophanes to affirm that he, too, now owns rights to the play. Ancient and modern reception merge in an incongruous ownership of work and image.

With Koun's *Birds* of leftist hue, Aristophanes entered into, and captured, the symbolic economy of Greek popular dissidence and resilience, which helped to define the ideology of the Left throughout the twentieth century (while the rift between Left and Right widened), and which continues to exert a populist appeal on Greek society. 'Aristophanes the leftist'

---

[62] Kotzamani (2007) 189.
[63] For a detailed analysis of the scandal, its political context, and the immediate outcry, and also for more cartoons, see Van Steen (2007) and (2000) ch. 4.

Figure 23.1 Front cover of a 1999 special issue of *To Pontiki*.

or *Aristero-phanes*, 'the one who reveals himself as leftist', in the words of journalist Voula Damianakou, effectively pre-empted any subsequent reactionary appropriation of his plays.[64] Of course, popular transgression and

---

[64] Damianakou is quoted by Van Steen (2000) 131, 185.

folksy disobedience are more interesting to study than conservative movements, and they find inexhaustible wellsprings among the multi-faceted people. However, the late twentieth-century Aristophanes who has been mostly dissident, often remains entrapped in processes of stagnation and effacement of genuine socio-political criticism. While Menander was passed over, Aristophanes' comedy became an ideal, and self-perpetuating, platform for revisionism. Far more often than not, Aristophanes' plays have championed the underprivileged and/or minorities, whether those were the poor, the silenced, women, non-whites or gays. The historical dramatist likely did not have the same agendas, but his humour was spirited and versatile enough to allow for new and different levels of signification. In the right hands, Aristophanes' plays stay fresh. While the study of the ancient poet will remain the bailiwick of the classicist, credit is due to the circles of actors, directors, translators, cartoonists, illustrators and all those who have championed the important innovations, but who also need to ponder the value of provocative 'newness', or rapid modernization for modernization's sake.

Further reading

Book-length and dissertation-length studies of the reception of Aristophanes and Menander appear to be a (belated) early twenty-first-century phenomenon, which bodes well for the methodic study of the reception of Old through New Comedy in future decades. Beyond the few pages of Hardwick (2003) 64–7, such recent works include: Day (2001); Hall and Wrigley (2007); Holtermann (2004); Kotzamani (various recent publications on the – perhaps universally – most popular play, *Lysistrata*); Maurogene (2007); Piana (2005); Van Steen (2000) and (2002); Walsh (2008); and Hadley (2014) on Frischlin's seminal 1586 translation of Aristophanes. Hall and Wrigley's volume explores the relationship between performance history (histories) and select texts of Aristophanes, their translations and adaptations. Its many contributions shed ample light on the reception of Aristophanes' 'distant quest' plays (Hall (2007a) 3). Lowe (2008) has provided an extensive and up-to-date bibliography on the subject of Greek and Roman comedy at large. I also wish to acknowledge the very important research that young Greek scholars have conducted on Aristophanes and Menander, and that has gone unnoticed in English-language academia for far too long. Kaite Diamantakou-Agathou (2007a) and (2007b), for example, has analysed the topic of *Wealth* as a recurring vehicle of Aristophanes' revival. See also the special issue of a leading Greek newspaper, *He Kathemerine*, entitled *Aristophanes: Diachronic and Current* (13 June 2004).

For recent studies on reception (theory), theatre and classics, see the volume of essays, *Classics and the Uses of Reception*, edited by Charles Martindale and Richard Thomas (2006), or the first volume in the Classical Receptions Series published by Blackwell (series editor: Maria Wyke). See also Hall (2004), Kallendorf (2007), and Hardwick and Stray (2008). For a summary review of recent work in reception studies of Greek drama, see Revermann (2008). Older but still useful are the essays collected in *Living Greek Theatre* by J. Michael Walton, for discussions of revived ancient drama in Greece, Western Europe, England and North America (1987). See also Flashar's (recently expanded) comprehensive study, again with emphasis on ancient tragedy (2009, originally published in 1991).

BIBLIOGRAPHY

Abadie-Reynard, C. and J. P. Darmon (2003) 'La maison et la mosaïque des Synaristosai de Zeugma', *Journal of Roman Archaeology*, Suppl. 51: 79–99

Adami, F. (1901) 'De poetis scaenicis Graecis hymnorum sacrorum imitatoribus', *Jahrbücher für classische Philologie*, Suppl. 26: 213–62

Agelidis, S. (2009) *Choregische Weihgeschenke in Griechenland*. Bonn

Aguilar, R. M. (1997) 'Plutarco y la comedia ateniense' in Schrader, Ramón and Vela (1997): 3–28

Akrigg, B. (2007) 'The nature and implications of Athens' changed social structure and economy' in Osborne (2007): 27–43

Akrigg, B. and R. Tordoff, eds. (2013) *Slaves and Slavery in Ancient Greek Comic Drama*. Cambridge

Allen, D. (2000) *The World of Prometheus: The Politics of Punishing in Democratic Athens*. Princeton, NJ

(2003) 'Angry bees, wasps, and jurors: the symbolic politics of *orgê* in Athens' in Braund and Most (2003): 76–98

Allison, R. H. (1983) 'Amphibian ambiguities: Aristophanes and his frogs', *Greece and Rome* 30: 8–20

Alpers, K. (2009) *Untersuchungen zu Johannes Sardianos und seinem Kommentar zu den Progymnasmata des Aphthonios* (Abhandlungen der Braunschweigischen Wissenschaftlichen Gesellschaft LXII). Braunschweig

Alston, R., E. Hall and L. Proffitt, eds. (2010) *Reading Ancient Slavery*. Cambridge

Anderson, W. S. (1984) 'Love plots in Menander and his Roman adapters', *Ramus* 13: 124–34

(1993) *Barbarian Play: The Comedies of Plautus*. Toronto

Angel, M. (2002) 'A classical Greek influences an American feminist: Susan Glaspell's debt to Aristophanes', *Syracuse Law Review* 52: 81–103

Arnott, W. G. (1968) 'Studies in comedy I: Alexis and the parasite's name'. *Greek, Roman and Byzantine Studies* 9: 161–8

(1972) 'From Aristophanes to Menander', *Greece and Rome* 19: 65–90

(1981) 'Moral values in Menander', *Philologus* 125: 215–27

(1987) 'The time-scale of Menander's *Epitrepontes*', *Zeitschrift für Papyrologie und Epigraphik* 70: 19–31

(1995) 'Menander's manipulation of language for the individualisation of character' in De Martino and Sommerstein (1995) 2.147–64

(1996a) *Alexis: The Fragments. A Commentary.* Cambridge

(1997) 'Humour in Menander' in Jäkel and Timonen (1997) 65–79

(1998) 'Notes on Menander's *Phasma*', *Zeitschrift für Papyrologie und Epigraphik* 123: 35–48

(2000a) 'Stage business in Menander's *Samia*' in Gödde and Heinze (2000) 113–24

(2000b) *Menander: Volume III.* Cambridge, MA

(2000c) 'Menander's use of dramatic space', *Pallas* 54: 81–8

(2010) 'Middle Comedy' in Dobrov (2010) 279–331

Arnott, W. G., ed. and trans. (1979) *Menander.* Vol. I. Cambridge, MA

(1996b) *Menander.* Vol. II. Cambridge, MA

Austin, C. (1965) Review of Whitman (1964) in *Gnomon* 37: 618–20

Austin, C. and D. Olson (2004) *Aristophanes Thesmophoriazusae.* Oxford

Babcock, B., ed. (1978), *The Reversible World: Symbolic Inversion in Art and Society.* Ithaca, NY

Badian, E. (1993) *From Plataea to Potidaea: Studies in the History and Historiography of the Pentecontaetia.* Baltimore, MD

Bain, D. (1979) '*PLAVTVS VORTIT BARBARE*. Plautus, *Bacchides* 526–61 and Menander, *Dis exapaton* 102–12' in D. West and A. J. Woodman, eds. (1979) *Creative Imitation in Latin Literature.* Cambridge, 17–34

(1984) 'Female speech in Menander', *Antichthon* 18: 24–42

Bakhtin, M. M. (1984) *Rabelais and His World*, trans. Hélène Iswolsky. Bloomington, IN

Bakker, E. J., ed. (2010) *A Companion to the Ancient Greek Language.* Oxford

Bakola, E. (2005) 'Old Comedy disguised as satyr play: a new reading of Cratinus' *Dionysalexandros* (P.Oxy. 663)', *Zeitschrift für Papyrologie und Epigraphik* 154: 46–58

(2008) 'The drunk, the reformer and the teacher: agonistic poetics and the construction of persona in the comic poets of the fifth century', *Proceedings of the Cambridge Philological Society* 54:1–29

(2010) *Cratinus and the Art of Comedy.* Oxford

(2013) 'Crime and punishment: Cratinus, Aeschylus' *Oresteia*, and the metaphysics and politics of wealth' in Bakola, Prauscello and Telò (2013) 226–55

Bakola, E., L. Prauscello and M. Telò, eds. (2013) *Greek Comedy and the Discourse of Genres.* Cambridge

Bakonikola, C. (2007) 'The theater of Soures and its roots' (in Greek) in Vapheiade and Papandreou (2007) 209–16

Baldry, H. C. (1953) 'The idler's paradise in Attic comedy', *Greece and Rome* 23: 49–60

Balensiefen, L. (1990) *Die Bedeutung des Spiegelbildes als ikonographisches Motif inder antiken Kunst.* Tübingen

Banks, T. R. (1980) 'The ephemeral, the perennial, and the structure of Aristophanes' *Wasps*', *Classical Bulletin* 56: 81–4

Barsby, J. (1991) *Plautus: Bacchides*, 3rd edn. Warminster

(2002a) 'Terence and his Greek models' in Questa and Raffaelli (2002) 249–75

Barsby, J., ed. (2002b) *Greek and Roman Drama: Translation and Performance.* Stuttgart (= *Drama* 12)

Bassett, S. (2008) 'The late antique image of Menander', *Greek, Roman and Byzantine Studies* 48: 201–25

Bastin-Hammou, M. (2007) 'Aristophanes' *Peace* on the twentieth-century French stage: from political statement to artistic failure' in Hall and Wrigley (2007) 247–54

Beazley, J. D. (1952) 'The New York "Phlyax-Vase"', *American Journal of Archaeology* 56: 193–5

Beare, W. (1964) *The Roman Stage*, 3rd edn. London

Bekker-Nielsen, T. and L. Hannestad, eds. (2001) *War as a Cultural and Social Force: Essays on Warfare in Antiquity*. Copenhagen

Belardinelli, A. M. (1994) *Menandro: Sicioni*. Bari

Bellocchi, M. (2008) 'Epicarmo e la commedia attica antica' in Cassio (2008) 260–91

Bergmann, B. and C. Kondoleon, eds. (1999) *The Art of Ancient Spectacle*. London

Bergson, H. (1980) *Laughter*, Eng. trans. C. Brereton and F. Rothwell in Sypher (1980) 61–190

Berk, L. (1964) *Epicharmus*. Groningen

Bernabé, A. (1995) 'Una cosmogonía cómica: Aristófanes, *Aves* 685ss.' in López Férez (1995) 195–211

Bernabò Brea, L. (1981) *Menandro e il teatro greco nelle terracotta liparesi*. Genoa

Bernabò Brea, L. and M. Cavalier, eds. (2001) *Maschere e personaggi del teatro Greco nelle terracotta liparesi*. Rome

Bers, V. (1985) 'Dikastic thorubos' in Cartledge and Harvey (1985) 1–15

Bertrand, J.-M. (2007) 'À propos de l'identification des personnes dans la cité athénienne classique' in Jean-Christophe Couvenhes and Silvia Milanezi, eds., *Individus, Groupes et Politique à Athènes de Solon à Mithridate*. Tours, 201–14

Beta, S. (2004) *Il linguaggio nelle commedie di Aristofane: Parola positiva e parola negativa nella commedia antica*. Rome

  (2010) 'The metamorphosis of a Greek comedy and its protagonist: some musical versions of Aristophanes' *Lysistrata*' in Brown and Ograjenšek (2010) 240–57

Betts, J., J. Hooker and J. R. Green, eds. (1988) *Studies in Honour of T. B. L. Webster*. 2 vols., Bristol

Bieber, M. (1961) *The History of the Greek and Roman Theater*, 2nd edn. Princeton, NJ

Bierl, A. (1999) *Der Chor in der alten Komödie: Ritual und Performativität*. Munich

Biles, Z. P. (2001) 'Aristophanes' victory dance: old poets in the parabasis of *Knights*', *Zeitschrift für Papyrologie und Epigraphik* 136: 195–200

  (2002) 'Intertextual biography in the rivalry of Cratinus and Aristophanes', *American Journal of Philology* 123: 169–204

  (2009) 'The date of Phrynichos' Lenaian victory in *IG* II² 2325: a reply to Rusten (2006)

  (2011) *Aristophanes and the Poetics of Competition*. Cambridge

Billiani, F., ed. (2007) *Modes of Censorship and Translation: National Contexts and Diverse Media*. Manchester

Billows, R. A. (1995) *Kings and Colonists: Aspects of Macedonian Imperialism*. Leiden

Blanchard, A. (1983) *Essai sur la Composition des Comédies de Ménandre*. Paris
  (2007) *La comédie de Ménandre: politique, éthique, esthétique*. Paris

Blok, J. (2005) 'Becoming citizens: some notes on the semantics of "citizen" in Archaic Greece and Classical Athens', *Klio* 87: 7–40

Blume, H.-D. (2010) 'Menander: the text and its restoration' in Petrides and Papaioannou (2010) 14–30

Blundell, J. (1980) *Menander and the Monologue*. Göttingen

Boeckh, A. (1817) *Die Staatshaushaltung der Athener*, Berlin = Cornwall Lewis, G., trans. (1828) *The Public Economy of Athens, in Four Books; to Which is Added, A Dissertation on the Silver-Mines of Laurion*, London

Boedeker, D. and K. Raaflaub, eds. (1998) *Democracy, Empire, and the Arts in Fifth-Century Athens*. Cambridge, MA

Boegehold, A. (1990) 'Andocides and the decree of Patrokleides', *Historia* 39: 149–62

Boldrini, S. *et al.*, eds. (1987) *Filologia e forme letterarie: Studi offerti a Francesco della Corte*. 5 vols., Urbino

Bonnamour, J. and H. Delavault, eds. (1979) *Aristophane, les femmes et la cité*. Fontenay-aux-Roses

Bonanno, M. G. (1987) 'Metafore redivive e nomi parlanti (sui modi del Witz in Aristofane)' in Boldrini *et al.* (1987) 1.213–28

Bonner, C. (1942) 'A Tarsian peculiarity (Dio Prus. Or. 33) with an unnoticed fragment of Porphyry', *Harvard Theological Review* 35: 1–11

Bordwell, D. (1989) *Making Meaning: Inference and Rhetoric in the Interpretation of Cinema*. Cambridge, MA

Borthwick, E. K. (1968) 'The dances of Philocleon and the sons of Carcinus in Aristophanes' *Wasps*', *Classical Quarterly* 18: 44–51

Bosher, K. (2006) *Theater on the Periphery: A Social and Political History of Theater in Early Greek Sicily*. Ph.D. thesis, University of Michigan

Bosher, K., ed. (2012) *Theater Outside Athens: Drama in Greek South Italy and Sicily*. Cambridge

Bost Pouderon, C. (2006) *Dion Chrysostome. Trois discours aux villes (Orr. 33–35)*. Salerno

Botley, P. (2010) *Learning Greek in Western Europe, 1396–1529: Grammars, Lexica, and Classroom Texts*. Philadelphia, PA: American Philosophical Society

Bowden, H. (2003) 'Oracles for sale' in P. Derow and R. Parker, eds. (2003) *Herodotus and his World*. Oxford, 256–74

Bowie, A. M. (1982) 'The parabasis in Aristophanes: prolegomena, *Acharnians*', *Classical Quarterly* 32: 27–40

  (1993) *Aristophanes: Myth, Ritual and Comedy*. Cambridge

  (2010) 'Myth and ritual in comedy' in Dobrov (2010) 143–76

Bowie, E. L. (1988) 'Who is Dicaeopolis?', *Journal of Hellenic Studies* 108: 183–5

  (1990) '*Marginalia Obsceniora*: some problems in Aristophanes' *Wasps*' in Craik (1990) 31–8

  (1998) 'Le portrait de Socrate dans le *Nuées* d'Aristophane' in Trédé and Hoffmann (1998) 53–66

  (2002) 'Ionian *iambos* and Attic *komoidia*: father and daughter, or just cousins?' in Willi (2002a) 33–50

  (2007) 'The ups and downs of Aristophanic travel' in Hall and Wrigley (2007) 32–51

Bowlby, R., ed. (1992) *Virginia Woolf: A Woman's Essays*. Harmondsworth

Braden, G. (2010) 'Aristophanes' in Grafton, Most and Settis (2010) 69–70

Bradley, K. and P. Cartledge, eds. (2011) *The Cambridge World History of Slavery*, vol. 1, *The Ancient Mediterranean World*. Cambridge

Branham, R. B. (2002) *Bakhtin and the Classics*. Evanston, IL

Brashear, W. (1985) 'Gnomology', *Yale Classical Studies* 28: 9–12

Braund, S. and G. W. Most, eds. (2003) *Ancient Anger: Perspectives from Homer to Galen*. Cambridge

Bremer, J. M. (1991) 'Poets and their patrons' in Harder and Hofman (1991) 39–60

Bremer, J. M. and E. W. Handley, eds. (1993) *Aristophane: Sept exposés suivis de discussions* (Entretiens Hardt, 38). Geneva

Bresson, A. (2000) *La cité marchande*. Bourdeaux

    (2007) *L'économie de la Grèce des cités (fin VIe-Ier siècle a. C.). I. Les structures et la production*. Paris

    (2008) *L'économie de la Grèce des cités (fin VIe-Ier siècle a. C.). II. Les espaces de l'échange*. Paris

Briggs, W. W. (1994) *Biographical Dictionary of North American Classicists*. Westport, CT

Brixhe, C. (1988) 'La langue de l'étranger non grec chez Aristophane' in Lonis (1988) 113–38

Brock, R. (1994) 'The labour of women in Classical Athens', *Classical Quarterly* 44: 336–46

Brockmann, C. (2003) *Aristophanes und die Freiheit der Komödie: Untersuchungen zu den frühen Stücken unter besonderer Berücksichtigung der Acharner*. Munich

Brown, M., ed. (2000) *The Cambridge History of Literary Criticism*. Vol. 5: *Romanticism*. Cambridge

Brown, P. G. (1987) 'Masks, names and characters in New Comedy', *Hermes* 115: 181–202

    (1990) 'Plots and prostitutes in Greek New Comedy', *Papers of the Leeds Latin Seminar* 6: 241–66

    (1992) 'Menander, fragments 745 and 746 K-T, Menander's "Kolax", and parasites and flatterers in Greek comedy', *Zeitschrift für Papyrologie und Epigraphik* 92: 91–107

    (1993) 'Love and marriage in Greek New Comedy', *Classical Quarterly* 43: 184–205

    (2002) 'Actors and actor-managers at Rome in the time of Plautus and Terence' in Easterling and Hall (2002) 225–37

    (2008) 'Scenes at the door in Aristophanic comedy' in Revermann and Wilson (2008) 349–72

Brown, P. and S. Ograjenšek, eds. (2010) *Ancient Drama in Music for the Modern Stage*. Oxford

Bruhn, C. (1910) *Über den Wortschatz des Menander*. Jena

Bultrighini, U., ed. (2005) *Democrazia e antidemocrazia nel mondo Greco*. Alessandria

Burckhardt, A. (1924) *Spuren der athenischen Volksrede in der alten Komödie*. Basel

Burckhardt, J. (1898–1902) *Griechische Kulturgeschichte*, Berlin = S. Stern, trans., O. Murray, ed. (1998) *The Greeks and Greek Civilization*. London

Burkert, W. (1979) 'Kynaithos, Polycrates and the Homeric Hymn to Apollo' in G. W. Bowersock and M. C. J. Putnam, eds., *Arktouros: Hellenic Studies Presented to B. M. W. Knox*. Berlin and New York, 52–62; and reprinted in C. Riedweg, ed., *Kleine Schriften vol. 1: Homerica*. Göttingen, 189–97

(1987) 'The making of Homer in the 6th century BC: rhapsodes versus Stesichorus' in M. True *et al.*, eds., *Papers on the Amasis Painter and His World*. Malibu. 51–62; reprinted in C. Riedweg, ed., *Kleine Schriften vol. 1: Homerica*. Göttingen. 189–97

(2000) '"Stumm wie ein Menander-Chor": ein zusätzliches Testimonium', *Zeitschrift für Papyrologie und Epigraphik* 131: 23–4

Burstein, S. (1980) 'Menander and politics: the fragments of the Halieis' in S. M. Burstein and L. A. Okin, eds., *Panhellenica: Essays in Ancient History and Historiography in Honor of Truesdell S. Brown*, Lawrence, 69–76

Butler, J., E. Laclau and S. Žižek, eds., (2000) *Contingency, Hegemony, Universality: Contemporary Dialogues on the Left*. London

Butrica, J. (2001) 'The lost *Thesmophoriazusae* of Aristophanes', *Phoenix* 55: 44–76

Cairns, D. L., and R. A. Knox, eds. (2004) *Law, Rhetoric, and Comedy in Classical Athens: Essays in Honour of Douglas M. MacDowell*. Swansea

Carawan, E. M. (1990) 'The five talents Cleon coughed up (Schol. Ar. *Ach*. 6)', *Classical Quarterly* 40: 137–47

Carey, C. (1992) *Apollodoros against Neaira: (Demosthenes) 59*. Warminster

(1994) 'Comic ridicule and democracy' in Osborne and Hornblower (1994) 69–83

(1998) '*Nomos* in Attic Rhetoric and Oratory', *Journal of Hellenic Studies* 116: 33–46

(2000) 'Comic law', *Annali dell'Università di Ferrara* 1: 65–86

Carpenter, T. H. (1986) *Dionysian Imagery in Archaic Greek Art: its Development in Black-Figure Vase Painting*. Oxford

(2005) 'Images of satyr plays in South Italy' in Harrison (2005) 219–36

(2007) 'Introduction to komasts and predramatic ritual' in Csapo and Miller (2007) 41–7

Carratelli, P. (1996) *The Western Greeks*. London

Carrière, J. C. (1979) *Le carnaval et la politique: une introduction à la comédie grecque suivie d'un choix de fragments*. Paris

Carter, D. M. (2007) *The Politics of Greek Tragedy*. Exeter

Carter, D. M. ed. (2011) *Why Athens? A Reappraisal of Tragic Politics*. Oxford

Cartledge, P. (1985) 'Rebels and *sambos* in ancient Greece: a comparative view' in Cartledge and Harvey (1985) 16–46

(1990) *Aristophanes and his Theatre of the Absurd*. Bristol

Cartledge, P., E. Cohen and L. Foxhall, eds. (2002) *Money, Labour, and Land: Approaches to the Economy of Ancient Greece*. Cambridge

Cartledge, P. and F. D. Harvey, eds. (1985) *CRUX: Essays in Greek History Presented to G. E. M. de Ste. Croix on his 75th Birthday*. London

Cartledge, P., P. Millett and S. Todd, eds. (1990) *Nomos: Essays in Athenian Law, Politics, and Society*. Cambridge

Cassio, A. C. (1985) 'Old Persian *marika-*, Eupolis' *Marikas*, and Aristophanes' *Knights*', *Classical Quarterly* 35: 38–42

(2002) 'The language of Doric Comedy' in Willi (2002a) 51–83

Cassio, A. C., ed. (2008) *Storia delle lingue letterarie greche*. Milan

Casson, L. (1976) 'The Athenian upper class and New Comedy', *Transactions of the American Philological Association* 106: 26–59

Cavallero, P. A. (1994) 'El humorismo en Menandro', *Dioniso* 64: 83–103

Ceccarelli, P. (2000) 'Life among the savages and escape from the city' in Harvey and Wilkins (2000) 453–71

Çelik, Ö. (2009) 'Yukari Harbiye Mozaik Kurtarma Kazısı (Perikeiromene, Philadelphoi, Syaristosai [*sic*], Theophorosmene [*sic*])' in F. Bayram and A. Özme, eds., *17. Müze Çalişmaları ve Kurtarma Kazıları Sempozyumu*. Ankara, 41–52

Cerchiai, L. *et al.*, eds. (2002, English version 2004) *The Greek Cities of Magna Graecia and Sicily*. Los Angeles, CA

Ceserani, G. (2012) *Italy's Lost Greece: Magna Graecia and the Making of Modern Archaeology*. Oxford

Chapman, G. A. H. (1983) 'Some notes on dramatic illusion in Aristophanes', *American Journal of Philology* 104: 1–23

Chiarini, G. (1983) '*Metafora* e *metonimia*: per l'elaborazione di un modello interpretativo del teatro classico', *Res Publica Litterarum (University of Kansas)* 6: 113–22

Christ, M. (1998) *The Litigious Athenian*. Baltimore, MD

Cieply, M. (2007) 'That film's real message? It could be "buy a ticket"', *New York Times*, 5 March 2007, E7

Clay, D. (2004) *Archilochos Heros: The Cult of Poets in the Greek Polis*. Washington, DC

Clinton, K. (2003) 'The sanctuary of Demeter and Kore at Eleusis' in N. Marinatos and R. Hägg, eds. (2003) *Greek Sanctuaries: New Approaches*. London and New York, 110–24

Clover, C. (1998) 'Law and the order of popular culture' in Sarat and Kearns (1998) 97–119

Cohen, B., ed. (2000) *Not the Classical Ideal: Athens and the Construction of the Other in Greek Art*. Leiden, Boston and Cologne

Cohen, D. (2001) 'Women in public: gender, citizenship, and social status in classical Athens' in M. Gagarin and R. Wallace, eds., *Symposion* 2001. Vienna, 33–46

Cohen, E. (1992) *Athenian Economy and Society: A Banking Perspective*. Princeton, NJ

Cole, S. G. (1984) 'Greek sanctions against sexual assault', *Classical Philology* 79: 97–113

Colvin, S. (1995) 'Aristophanes: dialect and textual criticism', *Mnemosyne* 48: 34–47
    (1999) *Dialect in Aristophanes and the Politics of Language in Ancient Greek Literature*. Oxford
    (2000) 'The language of non-Athenians in Old Comedy' in Harvey and Wilkins (2000) 285–98

Compton-Engle, G. (2003) 'Control of costume in three plays of Aristophanes', *American Journal of Philology* 124: 507–35

Connolly, J. (2001a) 'Reclaiming the theatrical in the Second Sophistic', *Helios* 28: 75–96

(2001b) 'Problems of the past in imperial Greek education' in Too (2001) 339–73

Connor, W. R. (1971) *The New Politicians of Fifth-Century Athens*. Princeton, NJ

(1994) 'The problem of Athenian civic identity' in A. Boegehold and A. Scafuro, eds., *Athenian Identity and Civic Ideology*. Baltimore and London, 34–44

Constantinides, E. (1969) 'Timocles' *Ikarioi Satyroi*: a reconsideration', *Transactions of the American Philological Association* 100: 49–61

Cook, P., ed. (1985) *The Cinema Book: A Complete Guide to Understanding the Movies*. London

Cornford, F. (1914: 1934) *The Origin of Attic Comedy*. London (2nd edn Cambridge 1934)

Courtney, E., ed. (1993) *The Fragmentary Latin Poets*. Oxford

Cox, C. A. (1998) *Household Interests: Property, Marriage Strategies, and Family Dynamics in Ancient Athens*. Princeton, NJ

Craik, E., ed. (1990) *'Owls to Athens': Essays on Classical Subjects for Sir Kenneth Dover*. Oxford

Cribiore, R. (1996) *Writing, Teachers and Students in Graeco-Roman Egypt*. Atlanta, GA

(2001) *Gymnastics of the Mind*. Princeton, NJ

(2008) *The School of Libanius in Late Antique Antioch*. Princeton, NJ

Cropp, M., K. Lee and D. Sansone, eds. (1999–2000) *Euripides and Tragic Theatre in the Late Fifth Century* (= *Illinois Classical Studies*)

Crosby, M. (1955) 'Five comic scenes from Athens', *Hesperia* 24: 76–84

Csapo, E. (1986) 'A note on the Würzburg bell-crater H 5697 (Telephus Travestitus)', *Phoenix* 40: 379–92

(1993a) 'Deep ambivalence: notes on a Greek cockfight', *Phoenix* 47: 1–28 and 115–24

(1993b) Review of Nesselrath (1990), *Phoenix* 47: 354–7

(1997) 'Mise-en-scène théâtrale, scène de théâtre artisanale: les mosaïques de Ménandre à Mytilène, leur contexte social et leur tradition iconographique' in B. Le Guen, ed., *De la scène aux gradins* (*Pallas* 47, 1997) 165–82

(1999) 'Performance and iconographic tradition in the illustrations of Menander', *Syllecta Classica* 10: 154–88

(2000) 'From Aristophanes to Menander? Genre transformations in Greek comedy' in Depew and Obbink (2000) 115–34

(2001) 'The first artistic representations of theatre: dramatic illusion and dramatic performance in Attic and South Italian art' in Katz, Golini and Pietropaolo (2001) 17–38

(2002) 'Kallippides on the floor-sweepings: the limits of realism in classical acting and performance styles' in Easterling and Hall (2002) 127–47

(2004) 'The politics of the New Music' in Murray and Wilson (2004) 207–48

(2005) *Theories of Mythology*. Malden, MA and Oxford

(2006/7) 'The iconography of the *Exarchos*', *Mediterranean Archaeology* 19/20: 55–65

(2007) 'The men who built the theatres: *theatropolai*, *theatronai*, and *arkhitektones*' in Wilson (2007c) 87–115

(2010a) 'The context of choregic dedications' in Taplin and Wyles (2010) 79–130

(2010b) *Actors and Icons of the Ancient Theater*. Malden, MA and Oxford

(2010c) 'The production and performance of comedy in antiquity' in Dobrov (2010) 103–42

(2013) 'Comedy and the *Pompe*: Dionysian genre-crossing' in Bakola, Prauscello and Telò (2013) 40–80

Csapo, E. and W. J. Slater (1995) *The Context of Ancient Drama*. Ann Arbor, MI

Csapo E. and M. Miller, eds. (2007) *The Origins of Theater in Ancient Greece and Beyond: From Ritual to Drama*. Cambridge

Cucchiarelli, A. (2001) *La satira e il poeta: Orazio tra Epodi e Sermones*. Pisa

Cullyer, H. (2006) 'Agroikia and pleasure in Aristotle' in Rosen and Sluiter (2006) 181–217

Currie, B. (2005) *Pindar and the Cult of Heroes*. Oxford.

D'Arms, J. H. (1999) 'Performing culture: Roman spectacle and the banquets of the powerful' in Bergmann and Kondoleon (1999) 301–19

Da Costa Ramalho, A. (1952) Ἁπλᾶ ὀνόματα no estilo de Aristófanes. Coimbra

Dale, A. M. (1969) *Collected Papers*. Cambridge David, E. (1984) *Aristophanes and Athenian Society of the Early Fourth Century BC*. Leiden

Davidson, J. (1997) *Courtesans and Fishcakes: the Consuming Passions of Classical Athens*. London and New York

Davidson, J., F. Muecke and P. Wilson, eds. (2006) *Greek Drama III: Essays in Honour of Kevin Lee*. London (= *Bulletin of the Institute of Classical Studies* Supp. 87)

Davies, J. K. (1981) *Wealth and the Power of Wealth in Classical Athens*. New York (2007) 'Classical Greece: production' in Scheidel *et al.* (2007) 333–61

Davis, N. Z. (1975) *Society and Culture in Early Modern France*. Stanford, CA

Dawe, R. D., J. Diggle and P. Easterling, eds. (1978) *Dionysiaca: Nine Studies in Greek Poetry, Presented to D. L. Page*. Cambridge, 105–39

Day, G. (2001) *Class*. London and New York

Day, S. C. (2001) 'Aristophanes' plays in the United States: a production history in the context of sociopolitical revelations', Ph.D. thesis, Tufts University

De Angelis, F. (forthcoming) *A Social and Economic History of Archaic and Classical Greek Sicily*. Oxford

De Jong, I., H. Dik and A. Rijksbaron, eds. (2005) *Sophocles and the Greek Language*. Leiden

Dearden, C. W. (1976) *The Stage of Aristophanes*. London
    (1988) 'Phlyax comedy in Magna Graecia: a reassessment' in Betts, Hooker and Green (1988) 33–41
    (1990) 'Epicharmus, Phlyax and Sicilian comedy' in J. P. Descoeudres, ed., *Eumousia*, Sydney, 155–61

De Martino, F. and A. Sommerstein, eds. (1995) *Lo spettacolo delle voci*. Bari

Degani, E. (1993) 'Aristofane e la tradizione dell'invettiva personale in Grecia' in Bremer and Handley (1993) 1–36

Del Corno, D. (1975) 'Alcuni aspetti del linguaggio di Menandro', *Studi Classici e Orientali* 24: 13–48
    (1997) 'La caratterizzazione dei personaggi di Aristofane attraverso i fatti di lingua e di stile' in Thiercy and Menu (1997) 243–52

Denard, H. (2007) 'Lost theatre and performance traditions in Greece and Italy' in McDonald and Walton (2007) 139–60

Depew, M. and D. Obbink, eds. (2000) *Matrices of Genre: Authors, Canons, and Society*. Cambridge

Desclos, M.-L., ed. (2000) *Le rire des Grecs. Anthropologie du rire en Grèce ancienne*. Grenobles

Desideri, P. (1978) *Dione di Prusa*, Messina and Florence

Deufert, M. (2002) *Textgeschichte und Rezeption der plautinischen Komödien im Altertum*. Berlin

Diamantakou-Agathou, K. (2007a) *In the Hinterland of Ancient Comedy: Introduction to the Semiology of Space and Time in the Theater of Aristophanes* (in Greek). Athens

(2007b) '*Wealth* as a vehicle to the survival and revival of Aristophanes' (in Greek) in Vivilakes (2007) 423–32

Dickey, E. (1995) 'Forms of address and conversational language in Aristophanes and Menander', *Mnemosyne* 48: 257–71

Dickinson, T. H., ed. (1937) *The Theater in a Changing Europe*. New York

Diels, H. (1875), 'Eine Quelle des Stobäus', *Rheinisches Museum* 30: 172–81

Diller, A. (1937) *Race Mixture among the Greeks before Alexander*. Urbana, IL

Dillon, J. and S. E. Wilmer, eds. (2005) *Rebel Women: Staging Ancient Greek Drama Today*. London

Dittmar, W. (1933) *Sprachliche Untersuchungen zu Aristophanes und Menander*. Weida in Thüringen

Doblhofer, G. (1994) *Vergewaltigung in der Antike*. Stuttgart and Leipzig

Dobrov, G. (2001) *Figures of Play: Greek Drama and Metafictional Poetics*. Oxford

(2002) 'Μάγειρος ποιητής: language and character in Antiphanes' in Willi (2002a) 169–90

Dobrov, G., ed. (1995) *Beyond Aristophanes: Transition and Diversity in Greek Comedy*. Atlanta, GA

ed. (1997) *The City as Comedy: Society and Representation in Athenian Drama*. Chapel Hill, NC

ed. (2010) *Brill's Companion to the Study of Greek Comedy*. Leiden

Dohm, H. (1964) *Mageiros. Die Rolle des Kochs in der griechisch-römischen Komödie*. Munich

Dominik, W. J., ed. (1997) *Roman Eloquence: Rhetoric in Society and Literature*. London

Donderer, M. (2005/6), 'Antike Musterbücher und (k)ein Ende. Ein neuer Papyrus und die Aussage der Mosaiken', *Musiva et Sectilia* 2/3: 81–113

Donlan, W. (1980) *The Aristocratic Ideal in Ancient Greece*. Lawrence

Dougherty, C. (1991) 'Linguistic colonialism in Aeschylus' *Aetnaeae*', *Greek, Roman and Byzantine Studies*: 119–32

(1993) *The Poetics of Colonization*. Oxford

Dover, K. J. (1966a) 'The skene in Aristophanes', *Proceedings of the Cambridge Philological Society* 192: 2–17

(1966b) Review of Whitman (1964) in *Classical Review* n.s. 16.2: 159–61

(1970) 'Lo stile di Aristofane', *Quaderni Urbinati di Cultura Classica* 9: 7–23 (English trans. in Dover (1987) 224–36)

(1972) *Aristophanic Comedy*. Berkeley, CA

(1974) *Greek Popular Morality in the Time of Plato and Aristotle*. Berkeley and Los Angeles, CA

(1976) 'Linguaggio e caratteri Aristofanei', *Rivista di Cultura Classical e Medioe-vale* 18: 357–71 (English trans. in Dover (1987) 237–48)

(1987) *Greek and the Greeks: Collected Papers I.* Oxford and New York

(1993) *Aristophanes: Frogs.* Oxford

(1997) *The Evolution of Greek Prose Style.* Oxford

(2000) 'Foreward: Frogments' in Harvey and Wilkins (2000) xvii–ix

(2002) 'Some evaluative terms in Aristophanes' in Willi (2002a) 85–97

Dubois, L. (1989) *Inscriptions grecques dialectales de Sicile.* Paris and Rome

DuBois, P. (2003) *Slaves and Other Objects.* Chicago, IL

(2006) 'History of the impossible: ancient utopia', *Classical Philology* 101: 1–14

Duckworth, G. E. (1952: 1994) *The Nature of Roman Comedy.* Princeton, NJ

Ducrot, O. and T. Todorov (1972) *Dictionnaire encyclopédique des sciences du langage.* Paris

Duhoux, Y. (2004) 'Langage de femmes et d'hommes en grec ancien: l'exemple de *Lysistrata*' in Penney (2004) 131–45

Dunbabin, K. (1996) 'Convivial spaces: dining and entertainment in the Roman villa', *Journal of Roman Archaeology* 9: 66–80

(2003) *The Roman Banquet. Images of Conviviality.* Cambridge

Dunbar, N. (1966) Review of Whitman (1964), *Journal of Hellenic Studies* 86: 182–83

Dunn, F. (1999) 'The council's solar calendar', *American Journal of Philology* 120: 369–80

Durham, D. B. (1913). *The Vocabulary of Menander.* Princeton, NJ

Eagleton, T. (2007) *Ideology: An Introduction.* New edition. London and New York

Easterling, P. (1973) 'Presentation of character in Aeschylus', *Greece and Rome* 20: 3–19

(1977) 'Character in Sophocles', *Greece and Rome* 24: 121–9

(1990) 'Constructing character in Greek tragedy' in Pelling (1990) 83–99

(1999) 'The early years of the Cambridge Greek Play: 1882–1912' in Stray (1999) 27–47

Easterling, P. and E. Hall, eds. (2002) *Greek and Roman Actors. Aspects of an Ancient Profession.* Cambridge

Easterling, P. and B. Knox, eds. (1985) *The Cambridge History of Classical Literature, Volume I: Greek Literature*, Cambridge Eco, U. (1984), 'The Frames of Comic Freedom' in Sebeok (1984) 1–9

Edwards, A. T. (2002) 'Historicizing the popular grotesque: Bakhtin's *Rabelais and His World* and Attic Old Comedy' in Branham (2002) 27–55 (revised and updated version of an article first published in Scodel (1993) 89–117)

Ehrenberg, V. (1960) *The Greek State.* Oxford

(1962) *The People of Aristophanes: A Sociology of Old Attic Comedy*, 3rd edn. New York

Elderkin, G. W. (1934) 'The Curculio of Plautus', *American Journal of Archaeology* 39: 29–36

English, M. C. (2000) 'The diminishing role of stage properties in Aristophanic Comedy', *Helios* 27: 149–62

(2005) 'The evolution of Aristophanic stagecraft', *Leeds International Classical Studies* 4: 1–16

Ercolani, A., ed. (2002) *Spoudaiogeloion: Form und Funktion der Verspottung in der aristophanischen Komödie*. Stuttgart and Weimar

Etzioni, A. (2000) 'Toward a theory of public ritual', *Sociological Theory* 18: 44–59

Evans, N. (2002) 'Sanctuaries, sacrifices, and the Eleusinian Mysteries', *Numen* 49: 227–54

Falkner, T., N. Felson and D. Konstan, eds. (1999) *Contextualizing Classics: Ideology, Performance, Dialogue: Essays in Honor of John I. Peradotto*. Lanham, MD

Fantham, E. (1975) 'Sex, status, and survival in Hellenistic Athens: a study of women in New Comedy', *Phoenix* 29: 44–74

  (1984) 'Roman experience of Menander in the late republic and early empire', *Transactions of the American Philological Association* 114: 299–309

  (2002) 'Orator and/et actor' in Easterling and Hall (2002) 362–76

  (2008) 'With malice aforethought: the ethics of *malitia* on stage and at law' in Sluiter and Rosen (2008) 319–34

Fantuzzi, M., ed. (forthcoming) *The* Rhesus *Ascribed to Euripides*

Farioli, M. (2000) 'Mito e satira politica nei 'Chironi' di Cratino', *Rivista di Filologia e di Istruzione Classica* 128: 406–31

Ferguson, W. S. (1911) *Hellenistic Athens*. London

Finglass, P. J. (2007) *Sophocles: Electra*. Cambridge

Finley, M. I. (1973) *The Ancient Economy*. London

  (1979) *Ancient Sicily*. London

Fisher, N. (1993) 'Multiple personalities and Dionysiac festivals: Dikaiopolis in Aristophanes' *Acharnians*'. *Greece and Rome* 40: 31–47

  (2000) 'Symposiasts, fish-eaters, and flatterers: social mobility and moral concerns in Old Comedy' in Harvey and Wilkins (2000) 355–96

Fittschen, K. (1991) 'Zur Rekonstruktion griechischer Dichterstatuen. 1.Teil: Die Statue des Menander', *Athenische Mitteilungen* 106: 243–79

  (1995) 'Eine Stadt für Schaulustige und Müßiggänger: Athen im 3. und 2. Jh. v. Chr.' in Wörrle and Zanker (1995) 55–77

Flashar, H. (2009) *Inszenierung der Antike: Das griechische Drama auf der Bühne*, 2nd edn. Munich

Fletcher, K. (1979–1981) 'Aristophanes on the Victorian stage: J. R. Planché's adaptation of The Birds', *Theatre Studies* 26–27: 89–98

Foley, H., ed. (1981) *Reflections of Women in Antiquity*. New York and London

  (1982) 'The 'female intruder' reconsidered: women in Aristophanes' *Lysistrata* and *Ecclesiazusae*', *Classical Philology* 77: 1–21

  (1988) 'Tragedy and politics in Aristophanes' *Acharnians*', *Journal of Hellenic Studies* 108: 33–47

  (2000) 'The comic body in Greek art and drama' in Cohen (2000) 275–311

  (2008) 'Generic boundaries in late fifth-century Athens' in Revermann and Wilson (2008) 15–36

Fontaine, M. (2004) Review of Leigh (2004). *BMCR* 2004.11.30

  (2010) *Funny Words in Plautine Comedy*. Oxford and New York

  (2014) 'Dynamics of appropriation in Roman Comedy: Menander's *Kolax* in three Roman receptions (Naevius, Plautus, and Terence's *Eunuchus*)' in D. Olson, ed., *Ancient Comedy and Reception*, Berlin and Boston, 180–202

Fontaine, M. and A. Scaturo, eds. (2014) *The Oxford Handbook of Greek and Roman Comedy*, Oxford and New York

Forrest, W. G. (1963) 'Aristophanes' *Acharnians*', *Phoenix* 17: 1–12

Fournet, J.-L. (1992) 'Une éthopée de Caïn dans le Codex des Visions de la Fondation Bodmer', *Zeitschrift für Papyrologie und Epigraphik* 92: 253–66

Foxhall, L. (1989) 'Household, gender, property in classical Athens', *Classical Quarterly* 39: 22–44

    (1992) 'The control of the Attic landscape' in Wells (1992) 155–9

    (2002) 'Access to resources in Classical Greece: the egalitarianism of the polis in practice' in Cartledge *et al.* (2002) 209–20

    (2007) *Olive Cultivation in Ancient Greece: Seeking the Ancient Economy*. Oxford

Foxhall, L. and A. D. E. Lewis, eds. (1996) *Greek Law in its Political Setting: Justifications Not Justice*. Oxford

Foxhall, L. and J. Salmon, eds. (1998). *Thinking Men: Masculinity and its Self-Representation in the Classical Tradition*. London and New York

Fraenkel, E. (2007) *Plautine Elements in Plautus*, trans. T. Drevikovsky and F. Muecke. Oxford and New York

Frank, J. (2005). *A Democracy of Distinction: Aristotle and the Work of Politic*. Chicago, IL

Fredershausen, O. (1912) 'Weitere Studien über das Recht bei Plautus und Terenz', *Hermes* 47: 199–249

Freud, S. (1976) *Jokes and their Relation to the Unconscious*, Eng. trans. J. Strachey, rev. A. Richards. Harmondsworth

Friedrich, J. (1918) 'Das Attische im Munde von Ausländern bei Aristophanes', *Philologus* 75: 274–303

Frost, K. B. (1988) *Exits and Entrances in Menander*. Oxford

Frow, J. (2006) *Genre*. New York

Frye, N. (1957) *Anatomy of Criticism: Four Essays*. Princeton, NJ

Furley, W. D. (2009) *Menander, Men at Arbitration*. London

Gabrielsen, V. (1994) *Financing the Athenian Fleet*. Baltimore, MD

Gadamer, H.-G. (1986) *The Relevance of the Beautiful*. London

Gagarin, M. (2003) 'Telling stories in Athenian law', *Transactions of the American Philological Association* 133: 197–207

Gagarin, M. and D. Cohen, eds. (2005) *The Cambridge Companion to Ancient Greek Law*. Cambridge

Gallo, I., ed., (2004) *La biblioteca di Plutarco*. Naples

Gamel, M.-K. (2007) 'Sondheim floats *Frogs*' in Hall and Wrigley (2007) 209–30

Garnsey P. (1996) *Ideas of Slavery from Aristotle to Augustine*. Cambridge

García Novo, E. and I. Rodríguez Alfgeme, eds. (1998) *Dramaturgia y puesta en escena en el teatro griego*. Madrid

Garzya, A. (1959) 'Menandro nel giudizio di tre retori del primo impero', *Rivista di Filologia Classica* 37: 237–52

    (1969) 'Il *Sicionio* di Menandro e La Realta' Politica Del Tempo', *Dioniso* 43: 481–4

Gehrke, H. J. (1976) *Phokion. Studien zur Erfassung seiner historischen Gestalt*. Munich

Geissler, P. (1969) *Chronologie der altattischen Komödie*, 2nd edn. Berlin

Gellrich, M. (1988) *Tragedy and Theory: The Problem of Conflict since Aristotle*. Princeton, NJ

Gelzer, T. (1960) *Der epirrhematische Agon bei Aristophanes*. Munich (= *Zetemata* 23)

(1971) *Aristophanes der Komiker*. Stuttgart (identical with the entry on Aristophanes in the supplement volume XII of *Paulys Realencyclopädie*)

Gentili, B. (1979) *Theatrical Performances in the Ancient World*. Amsterdam

Ghiron-Bistagne, P. (1976) *Recherches sur les acteurs dans la Grèce antique*. Paris

Giannopoulou, V. (2007) 'Aristophanes in translation before 1920' in Hall and Wrigley (2007) 309–42

Gigante, M. (1967) *Rintone e il teatro in Magna Grecia*. Naples

(1969) 'Il ritorno del medico straniero', *La Parola del Passato* 24: 302–7

Gil, L. and I. Rodríguez Alfageme (1972) 'La figura del médico en la Comedia ática', *Cuadernos de Filología Clásica* 3: 35–91

Gilula, D. (1977) 'The mask of the pseudokore', *Greek, Roman and Byzantine Studies* 18: 247–50

(1987) 'Menander's comedies best with dessert and wine (Plut. *Mor.* 712e)', *Athenaeum* 55: 511–16

Glazebrook, A. (2005a) 'Prostituting female kin (Plut. *Sol.* 23.1–2)', *Dike* 8: 33–52

(2005b) 'The making of a prostitute: Apollodoros's portrait of Neaira', *Arethusa* 38: 161–88

(2006) 'The bad girls of Athens: the image and function of hetairai in judicial oratory' in C. A. Farone and L. McClure, eds., *Prostitutes and Courtesans in the Ancient World*, Madison, 113–48

Gledhill, C. (1985) 'Genre' in Cook (1985) 58–112

Gödde, S. and T. Heinze, eds. (2000) *Skenika: Beiträge zum antiken Theater und seiner Rezeption. Festschrift zum 65. Geburtstag von Horst-Dieter Blume*. Darmstadt

Goette, H. R. (1995) 'Griechischer Theaterbau der Klassik – Forschungsstand und Fragestellungen' in Pöhlmann (1995) 9–48

(2007) 'An Archaeological Appendix' in Wilson (2007c) 116–21

Goff, B. (2004) *Citizen Bacchae: Women's Ritual Practice in Ancient Greece*. Berkeley, CA

Goldberg, S. (1998) 'Plautus on the Palatine', *Journal of Roman Studies* 88: 1–20

(2007) 'Comedy and society from Menander to Terence' in McDonald and Walton (2007) 124–38

Golden, M. (1990) *Children and Childhood in Classical Athens*. Baltimore, MD and London

Goldhill, S. (1990) 'Character and action, representation and reading: Greek tragedy and its critics' in Pelling (1990) 100–27

(1991) *The Poet's Voice: Essays on Poetics and Greek Literature*. Cambridge

(1994) 'Representing democracy: women at the Great Dionysia' in Osborne and Hornblower (1994) 357–70

Goldhill, S. and R. Osborne, eds. (1999) *Performance Culture and Athenian Democracy*. Cambridge

Gomme, A. W. (1938) 'Aristophanes and politics', *Classical Review* 52: 97–109. Reprinted in Gomme (1962) 70–91

(1962) *More Essays in Greek History and Literature*. Oxford

Gomme, A. W. and F. H. Sandbach (1973) *Menander: A Commentary*. Oxford

Gould, J. (1978) 'Dramatic character and "human intelligibility"', *Proceedings of the Cambridge Philological Society* 24: 43–67

Gow, A. and D. Page (1965) *The Greek Anthology: Hellenistic Epigrams*. 2 vols., Cambridge

(1968) *The Greek Anthology: The Garland of Philip and Some Contemporary Epigrams*. 2 vols., Cambridge

Grafton, A., G. W. Most and S. Settis, eds. (2010) *The Classical Tradition*. Cambridge, MA and London

Grammatas, Th. (2009) 'Ménandre sur scène. L'expérience neo-hellénique', *Cuadernos de Filologia Clasica* 19: 141–9

Green, J. R. (1980) 'Additions to *Monuments Illustrating Old and Middle Comedy*', *Bulletin of the Institute of Classical Studies* 27: 123–31

(1985a) 'A representation of the *Birds* of Aristophanes', *Greek Vases in the J. Paul Getty Museum* 2: 95–118

(1985b) 'Drunk again: a study in the iconography of the comic theater', *American Journal of Archaeology* 89: 465–72

(1989) 'Theatre production: 1971–1986', *Lustrum* 31: 7–95 and 273–8

(1991a) 'On seeing and depicting the theatre in Classical Athens', *Greek, Roman and Byzantine Studies* 32: 15–52

(1991b) 'Notes on phylax vases', *Numismatice e Antichità Classiche* 20: 40–56

(1994) *Theatre in Ancient Greek Society*. London

(1995 [1998]) 'Theatre production: 1987–1995', *Lustrum* 37: 7–202 and 309–18

(2006) 'The persistent phallos: regional variability in the performance style of comedy' in Davidson *et al.* (2006) 141–62

(2007) 'Let's hear it for the fat man: padded dancers and the prehistory of drama' in Csapo and Miller (2007: 96–107

(2008) 'Theatre production: 1996–2006', *Lustrum* 50: 7–391

(2010) 'The material evidence' in Dobrov (2010) 71–102

Green, J. R. and E. Handley (1995) *Images of the Greek Theatre*. London

Green, J. R. and A. Seeberg (1995) *Monuments Illustrating New Comedy*, 3rd edn. London

Gregory, J. (2005) *A Companion to Greek Tragedy*. Malden, MA and Oxford

Grell, C. (1995) *Le Dix-huitième siècle et l'antiquité en France 1680–1789*. 2 vols., Oxford

Griffin, D. (1994) *Satire: A Critical Re-Introduction*. Lexington, KY

Griffin, J. (1980) *Homer on Life and Death*. Oxford

Griffith, M. (1978) 'Aeschylus, Sicily and Prometheus' in Dawe, Diggle and Easterling (1978) 105–39

(1995) 'Brilliant dynasts: power and politics in the *Oresteia*', *Classical Antiquity* 14: 62–129

(2005a) 'Satyrs, citizens, and self-presentation' in Harrison (2005) 161–99

(2005b) 'Sophocles' satyr plays and the language of romance' in De Jong, Dik and Rijksbaron (2005) 51–72

(2008) 'Greek middlebrow drama (something to do with Aphrodite?)' in Revermann and Wilson (2008) 59–87

(2013) *Aristophanes' Frogs (Oxford Approaches to Classical Literature)*. Oxford

Griffiths, A., ed. (1995) *Stage Directions: Essays in Ancient Drama in Honour of E.W. Handley*. BICS Suppl. 66. London

Guida, A. (1974) 'Note sul *Sicionio* di Menandro', *Studi Italiani di Filologia Classica* 46: 211–34

Gutzwiller, K. (2000) 'The tragic mask of Menander: metatheatricality in Menander', *Classical Antiquity* 19: 102–37

Habash, M. (1995) 'Two complementary festivals in Aristophanes' Acharnians', *American Journal of Philology* 116: 559–77

Habicht, C. (1997) *Athens from Alexander to Antony*. Cambridge, MA and London

Hadley, P. (2014) 'Athens in Rome, Rome in Germany: Nicodemus Frischlin's 1586 Translations of Aristophanes', Ph.D. thesis, University of Toronto

Hall, E. (1996) *Aeschylus' Persians: Edited with Translation, Introduction and Commentary*. Warminster

　(1995) 'Lawcourt dramas: the power of performance in Greek forensic oratory', *Bulletin of the Institute of Classical Studies* 40: 39–58, reprinted with updates in Hall (2006) 353–92

　(2004) 'Towards a theory of performance reception', *Arion* 12: 51–89

　(2006) *The Theatrical Cast of Athens: Interactions between Ancient Greek Drama and Society*. Oxford

　(2007a) 'Introduction: Aristophanic laughter across the centuries' in Hall and Wrigley (2007) 1–29

　(2007b) 'Tragedy personified' in Kraus, Goldhill, Foley and Elsner (2007) 221–56

Hall, E. and F. Macintosh, eds. (2005) *Greek Tragedy and the British Theatre 1660–1914*. Oxford

Hall, E. and A. Wrigley, eds. (2007) *Aristophanes in Performance 421 BC–AD 2007: Peace, Birds, and Frogs*. London

Hall, J. (2002) *Hellenicity: Between Ethnicity and Culture*. Chicago, IL

Halliwell, S. (1980) 'Aristophanes' apprenticeship', *Classical Quarterly* 30: 33–45

　(1984) 'Aristophanic satire', *Yearbook of English Studies* 14: 6–20

　(1991) 'Comic satire and freedom of speech in Classical Athens', *Journal of Hellenic Studies* 111: 48–70

　(1993) 'Comedy and publicity in the society of the polis' in Sommerstein *et al.* (1993) 321–40

　(1997) *Aristophanes: Birds, Lysistrata, Assembly-Women, Wealth*. Oxford

　(1998) *Aristotle's Poetics*, 2nd edn. Chicago, IL

　(2002) *The Aesthetics of Mimesis: Ancient Texts and Modern Problems*. Princeton, NJ

　(2008) *Greek Laughter: A Study of Cultural Psychology from Homer to Early Christianity*. Cambridge

　(2012) *Between Ecstasy and Truth: Interpretations of Greek Poetics from Homer to Longinus*. Oxford

Hamel, D. (2003) *Trying Neaira: The True Story of a Courtesan's Scandalous Life in Ancient Greece*. New Haven, CT

Hamilton, R. (1991) 'Comic acts', *Classical Quarterly* 41: 346–55

Handley, E. W. (1953) '-*sis* nouns in Aristophanes', *Eranos* 51: 129–42

　(1965) *The Dyskolos of Menander*. Cambridge

　(1968) *Menander and Plautus: A Study in Comparison. An inaugural lecture delivered at University College, London 5 February 1968*. London

(1985) 'Comedy' in Easterling and Knox (1985) 355–98

(1997) 'Menander. *Dis Exapaton*' in Handley and Wartenberg (1997) 17–42

(2011) 'The Rediscovery of Menander' in Obbink and Rutherford (2011) 138–59

Handley, E. W. and A. Hurst, eds. (1990) *Relire Ménandre*. Geneva

Handley, E. W. and U. Wartenberg, eds. (1997) *The Oxyrhynchus Papyri*, vol. 64. London

Hansen, M. (1975) *Eisangelia: The Sovereignty of the People's Court in Athens in the Fourth Century BC and the Impeachment of Generals and Politicians*. Odense

(1980) '*Eisangelia* at Athens: a reply', *Journal of Hellenic Studies* 100: 89–95

(1988) 'Athenian population losses, 431–403 BC, and the number of Athenian citizens in 431' in M. Hansen, *Three Studies in Athenian Demography*, Copenhagen, 7–13

(1999) *The Athenian Democracy in the Age of Demosthenes*, 2nd edn. Oxford

Hanson, V. (1995) *The Other Greeks: The Family Farm and the Agrarian Roots of Western Civilization*. Berkeley, CA and London

Harder, A. and H. Hofman, eds. (1991) *Fragmenta Dramatica*. Göttingen

Harding, P. (1994) 'Comedy and rhetoric' in Worthington (1994) 196–221

Hardwick, L. (2003) *Reception Studies*. Oxford

Hardwick, L. and C. Stray, eds. (2008) *A Companion to Classical Receptions*. Oxford

Harris, E. (1994) 'Law and oratory' in Worthington (1994) 130–50

(2002a) 'Workshop, marketplace, and household: the nature of technical specialization in Classical Athens and its influence on economy and society' in Cartledge *et al.* (2002) 67–99

(2002b) 'Did Solon abolish debt-bondage?', *Classical Quarterly* 52: 415–30

(2006) *Democracy and the Rule of Law in Classical Athens*. Cambridge

Harrison, G. W. M., ed. (2005) *Satyr Drama: Tragedy at Play*. Swansea

Harrison, G. W. M. and V. Liapis, eds. (2013) *Performance in Greek and Roman Theatre*. Leiden

Harvey, D. (2000) 'Phrynichos and his Muses' in Harvey and Wilkins (2000) 91–134

(2004) *Paris, Capital of Modernity*. New York and London

(2005) *A Brief History of Neoliberalism*. Oxford

Harvey, D. (2010) *The Enigma of Capital and the Crises of Capitalism*. London

Harvey, D. and J. Wilkins, eds. (2000) *The Rivals of Aristophanes: Studies in Athenian Old Comedy*. London

Hasebroek, J. (1928) *Staat und Handel im alten Griechland*, Tübingen (trans. (1933) *Trade and Politics in Ancient Greece*, London)

Hasegawa, K. (2005) *The Familia Urbana during the Early Empire: A Study of Columbaria Inscriptions*. Oxford

Heap, A. (1998) 'Understanding the men in Menander' in Foxhall and Salmon (1998) 115–29

Heath, M. (1987) *Political Comedy in Aristophanes*. Göttingen (= *Hypomnemata* 87)

(1990) 'Aristophanes and some of his rivals', *Greece and Rome* 37: 143–58

(1997) 'Aristophanes and the discourse of politics' in Dobrov (1997) 230–49

Heberlein, F. (1981) 'Zur Ironie in 'Plutos' des Aristophanes', *Würzburger Jahrbücher für die Altertumswissenschaft* 7: 27–49

Hedreen, G. (2004) 'The return of Hephaistos, Dionysiac processional ritual, and the creation of a visual narrative', *Journal of Hellenic Studies* 124: 38–64

(2007) 'Myths of ritual in Athenian vase-paintings of Silens' in Csapo and Miller (2007) 150–95

Heiden, B. (1991) 'Tragedy and comedy in the *Frogs* of Aristophanes', *Ramus* 20: 95–111

Henderson, J. (1980b) '*Lysistrata*: the play and its themes' in Henderson (1980a) 153–218

(1987a) 'Older women in Attic Comedy' in *Transactions of the American Philological Association* 117: 105–29

(1987b) *Aristophanes' Lysistrata.* Oxford

(1990) 'The *demos* and the comic competition' in Winkler and Zeitlin (1990) 271–313

(1991a) *The Maculate Muse: Obscene Language in Attic Comedy*, 2nd edn. New York and Oxford

(1991b) 'Women and the Athenian dramatic festivals', *Transactions of the American Philological Association* 121: 133–48

(1993) 'Comic hero versus political elite' in Sommerstein *et al.* (1993) 307–19

(1996) *Three Plays by Aristophanes: Staging Women.* London

(1998) 'Attic Old Comedy, frank speech, and democracy' in Boedeker and Raaflaub (1998) 255–73

(2000) 'Pherekrates and the women of Old Comedy' in Harvey and Wilkins (2000) 135–50

(2007) *Aristophanes: Fragments.* Cambridge, MA

Henderson, J., ed. (1980a) *Aristophanes: Essays in Interpretation.* New York (= *Yale Classical Studies* 26)

Henrichs, A. (1993) 'Response' in A. W. Bulloch, E. S. Gruen, A. A. Long and A. Stewart, eds., *Images and Ideologies: Self-Definition in the Hellenistic World*, Berkeley, CA, 171–95

Henry, M. M. (1985) *Menander's Courtesans and the Greek Comic Tradition.* Frankfurt am Main, Bern and New York

Herington, C. J. (1965) Review of C. H. Whitman, *Aristophanes and the Comic Hero, Phoenix* 19: 314–23

(1967) 'Aeschylus in Sicily', *Journal of Hellenic Studies* 87: 74–85

Herrick, M. T. (1964) *Comic Theory in the Sixteenth Century.* Urbana, IL

Hiersche, R. (1970) *Grundzüge der griechischen Sprachgeschichte bis zur klassischen Zeit.* Wiesbaden

Hill, C. (1972) *The World Turned Upside Down: Radical Ideas during the English Revolution.* London

Himmelmann, N. (1994) *Realistische Themen in der griechischen Kunst der archaischen und klassischen Zeit.* Berlin and New York

Hoare, Q. and G. N. Smith, eds. (1971) *Selections from the Prison Notebooks of Antonio Gramsci.* New York

Hoffmann, G. (1998) 'La richesse et les riches dans les comédies de Ménandre', *Pallas* 48: 135–44

Hoffmann, O., A. Debrunner and A. Scherer (1969) *Geschichte der griechischen Sprache I: Bis zum Ausgang der klassischen Zeit*, 4th edn. Berlin

Hofmeister, T. P. (1997) 'Hai pasai poleis: polis and oikoumene in Menander' in Dobrov (1997) 289–342

Holford-Strevens, L. (2003) *Aulus Gellius: An Antonine Scholar and His Achievements.* Oxford

Holtermann, M. (2004) *Der deutsche Aristophanes: die Rezeption eines politischen Dichters im 19. Jahrhundert.* Göttingen

hooks, b. (2000) *Where We Stand: Class Matters.* New York

Hopper, C. (2002) 'Spiced-up girls', *Guardian*, 14 September 2002, 37

Hordern, J. H. (2004) *Sophron's Mimes: Text, Translation, Commentary.* Oxford

Horn, W. (1970) *Gebet und Gebetsparodie in den Komödien des Aristophanes.* Nuremberg

Hornblower, S. (2002) *The Greek World, 479–323 BC*, 3rd edn. London

Horrocks, G. (2010) *Greek: A History of the Language and its Speakers*, 2nd edn. Malden, MA and Oxford

Hubbard, T. K. (1991) *The Mask of Comedy: Aristophanes and the Intertextual Parabasis.* Ithaca, NY

Hughes, A. (1996) 'Comic stages in Magna Graecia: the evidence of the vases', *Theatre Research International* 21: 95–107

   (2003) 'Comedy in Paestan vase painting', *Oxford Journal of Archaeology* 22: 281–301

   (2006a) 'The costumes of Old and Middle comedy', *Bulletin of the Institute of Classical Studies* 49: 39–68

   (2006b) 'The "Perseus Dance" vase revisited', *Oxford Journal of Archaeology* 25: 413–33

   (2011) *Performing Greek Comedy.* Cambridge

Hugill, W. M. (1936) *Panhellenism in Aristophanes.* Chicago, IL

Hugoniot, C., F. Hurlet and S. Milanezi, eds. (2004) *Le statut de l'acteur dans l'antiquité grecque et romaine.* Tours

Humphreys, S. C. (1978) *Anthropology and the Greeks.* London

   (1993) *The Family, Women, and Death.* Ann Arbor, MI

Hunt, S. (2011) 'Slaves in Greek literary culture', in Bradley and Cartledge (2011) 22–47

Hunter, R. L. (1979) 'The comic chorus in the fourth century', *Zeitschrift für Papyrologie und Epigraphk* 36: 23–38

   (1983) *Eubulus: The Fragments.* Cambridge

   (1985) *The New Comedy of Greece and Rome.* Cambridge

   (1993) 'The presentation of Herodas' Mimiamboi', *Antichthon* 27: 31–44

   (2000) 'The politics of Plutarch's *Comparison of Aristophanes and Menander*' in Goedde and Heinze (2000) 267–76

   (2002) '"Acting Down": the ideology of Hellenistic performance' in Easterling and Hall (2002) 189–206

   (2009) *Critical Moments in Classical Literature: Studies in the Ancient View of Literature and its Uses.* Cambridge

Hunter, V. (1994) *Policing Athens: Social Control in the Attic Lawsuits, 420–320 BC.* Princeton, NJ

Hurst, A. (1990) 'Ménandre et la tragédie' in Handley and Hurst (1990) 93–122

Hutcheon, L. (1985) *A Theory of Parody: The Teachings of Twentieth-Century Art Forms.* New York

(2006) *A Theory of Adaptation*. London and New York

Imperio, O. (2004a) *Parabasi di Aristofane: Acarnesi, Cavalieri, Vespe, Uccelli*. Bari

(2004b) 'I comici a simposio. Le *Quaestiones convivales* e la *Aristophanis et Menandri Comparatio* di Plutarco' in Gallo (2004) 185–96

Ingalls, W. (2001) 'Paida nean malista: when did Athenian girls really marry?' *Mouseion* 1: 17–29

(2002) 'Demography and dowries: perspectives on female infanticide in classical Greece', *Phoenix* 56: 246–54

Isager, S. (1980/1) 'The marriage pattern in classical Athens: men and women in Isaios', *Classica et Mediaevalia* 33: 81–96

Isler-Kerényi, C. (2007) 'Komasts, mythic imaginary, and ritual' in Csapo and Miller (2007) 77–95

Jackman, T. (2006) 'Ducetius and 5th-century Sicilian tyranny' in S. Lewis, ed. (2006) *Ancient Tyranny*. Edinburgh, 33–48

Jäkel, S. (1964) *Menandri Sententiae*. Lipsia

Jäkel, S. and A. Timonen, eds. (1995) *Laughter Down the Centuries*, vol. 2. Turku (1997) *Laughter Down the Centuries*, vol. 3. Turku

Jameson, F. (1971) *Marxism and Form*. Princeton, NJ

(1981) *The Political Unconscious*. Ithaca, NY

Janko, R. (1984) *Aristotle on Comedy: Towards a Reconstruction of Poetics II*. London

Jennings, V. and A. Katsaros (2007a) 'Introduction' in Jennings and Katsaros (2007) 1–16

Jennings, V. and A. Katsaros, eds. (2007) *The World of Ion of Chios*. Leiden (*Mnemosyne* Suppl. no. 288)

Johnstone, S. (1999) *Disputes and Democracy: The Consequences of Litigation in Ancient Athens*. Austin, TX

Jones, C. P. (1978) *The Roman World of Dio Chrysostom*. Cambridge, MA

(1991) 'Dinner theatre' in Slater (1991) 185–98

(1993) 'Greek drama in the Roman Empire' in Scodel (1993) 39–52

Jones, J. (1962) *On Aristotle and Greek Tragedy*. London

Jordan, D. (2007) 'An opisthographic lead tablet from Sicily with a financial document and a curse concerning choregoi' in Wilson (2007c) 335–50

Just, R. (1989) *Women in Athenian Law and Life*. London

KA = Kassel and Austin (1983–)

Kallendorf, C. W., ed. (2007) *A Companion to the Classical Tradition*. Malden, MA and Oxford

Kallet, L. (2009) 'Democracy, empire and epigraphy in the twentieth century' in Ma, Papazarkadas, Parker (2009) 43–66

Kalospyros, N. A. E. (2007) 'Adamance Coray (Koraës): the literary image of Socrates in the Greek Enlightenment and New Hellenism' in Trapp (2007) 277–98

Kapparis. K. (1999) *Apollodorus, 'Against Neaira' [D. 59]*. Berlin and New York

Kassel, R., and C. Austin (1983–) *Poetae Comici Graeci*, vols. i, ii, iii 2, iv, v, vi 2, vii, viii. Berlin and New York

He Kathemerine, 13 June 2004: special issue *Aristophanes: Diachronic and Current* (in Greek)

Katsouris, A. G. (1975) *Linguistic and Stylistic Charcterization: Tragedy and Menander*. Ioannina

Katz, B. (1976) 'The *Birds* of Aristophanes and politics', *Athenaeum* 54: 353–81

Katz, G., V. Golini and D. Pietropaolo, eds. (2001) *Theatre and the Visual Arts*. New York, Ottawa and Toronto

Katz, M. A. (1998) 'Did women of ancient Athens attend the theater in the eighteenth century?', *Classical Philology* 93: 105–24

Kayser, W. (1960) *Das Groteske in Malerei und Dichtung*. Munich

Kerkhof, R. (2001) *Dorische Posse, Epicharm und attische Komödie*. Leipzig

Keuls, E. C. (1985) *The Reign of the Phallus: Sexual Politics in Ancient Athens*. New York

Kindt, J. (2012) *Rethinking Greek Religion*. Cambridge

Kitto, H. D. F. (1966) *Greek Tragedy: A Literary Study*. London

Klaus, K. (1936) *Die Adjektiva bei Menander*. Leipzig

Klees, H. (1998) *Sklavenleben im Klassisghen Griechenland*. Stuttgart

Kleinknecht, H. (1937) *Die Gebetsparodie in der Antike*. Stuttgart and Berlin

Kloss, G. (2001) *Erscheinungsformen komischen Sprechens bei Aristophanes*. Berlin and New York

Knox, B. M. W. (1957) *Oedipus at Thebes*. New Haven, CT
  (1964) *The Heroic Temper: Studies in Sophoclean Tragedy*. Berkeley, CA
  (1979) *Word and Action. Essays on the Ancient Theater*. Baltimore, MD and London

Komornicka, A. M. (1964) *Métaphores, personnifications et comparaisons dans l'oeuvre d'Aristophane*. Wrocław

Konstan, D. (1994) 'The classics and class conflict', *Arethusa* 27: 47–70
  (1995) *Greek Comedy and Ideology*. New York

Körte, A. (1912) 'Fragmente einer Handschrift der *Demen* des Eupolis', *Hermes* 47: 276–313
  (1931) 'Menandros' Kunst: Sprache', *RE* XV/1: 751–3

Kosmopoulou, A. (2002) '"Working women": female professionals on classical Attic gravestones', *Annual of the British School at Athens* 96: 281–319

Koster, W. J. W. (1975) *Scholia in Aristophanem Pars I, Fasc. 1A: Prolegomena de Comoedia*. Groningen

Kotzamani, M. A. (1997) '*Lysistrata*, playgirl of the Western world: Aristophanes on the Early Modern Stage', Ph.D. thesis, City University of New York
  (2005) 'Lysistrata joins the Soviet Revolution: Aristophanes as engaged theatre' in Dillon and Wilmer (2005) 78–111
  (2006a) 'Artist citizens in the age of the Web: the Lysistrata Project (2003–present)', *Theater* 36: 103–10
  (2006b) 'Lysistrata on the Arabic stage', *PAJ: A Journal of Performance and Art* 28: 13–41
  (2007) 'Karolos Koun, Karaghiozis and *The Birds*: Aristophanes as Popular Theatre' in Robb (2007) 179–94

Kowalzig, B. (2008) 'Nothing to do with Demeter? Something to do with Sicily! Theatre and society in the early fifth-century West' in Revermann and Wilson (2008) 128–57

Kozak, L. and J. Rich, eds. (2006) *Playing Around Aristophanes: Essays in Celebration of the Completion of the Edition of the Comedies of Aristophanes by Alan Sommerstein*. Oxford

Kraus, C., S. Goldhill, H. P. Foley and J. Elsner, eds. (2007) *Visualizing the Tragic: Drama, Myth, and Ritual in Greek Art and Literature. Essays in Honour of Froma Zeitlin*. Oxford

Krien, G. (1955) 'Der Ausdruck der antiken Theatermasken nach Angabe im Polluxkatalog und in der pseudo-aristotelischen Physiognomik', *Jahreshefte des Österreichischen Archäologischen Instituts* 42: 84–117

Krieter-Spiro, M. (1997) *Sklaven, Köche und Hetären: Das Dienstpersonal bei Menander. Stellung, Rolle, Komik und Sprache*. Stuttgart

Kroll, J. H. (2009) 'What about coinage?' in Ma, Papazarkadas and Parker (2009) 195–209

Kronauer, U. (1954) *Der formale Witz in den Komödien des Aristophanes*. Oberwinterthur

Kurke, L. (1999) *Coins, Bodies, Games, and Gold*. Princeton, NJ

Kyriakidi, N. (2007) *Aristophanes und Eupolis: zur Geschichte einer dichterischen Rivalität*. Berlin

Lada-Richards, I. (1999) *Initiating Dionysus: Ritual and Theatre in Aristophanes' Frogs*. Oxford

Lamagna, M. (1998) 'Dialogo riportato in Menandro' in García Novo and Rodríguez Alfageme (1998) 289–302
  (2004) 'Il lessico di Menandro nella disputa sull'atticismo' in López Férez (2004) 195–208

Lamberton, R. (2001) *Plutarch*. New Haven, CT and London

Lambropoulos, V. (2006) *The Tragic Idea*. London

Lanni, A. (1997) 'Spectator sport or serious politics? *Hoi perihestêkotes* and the Athenian lawcourts', *Journal of Hellenic Studies* 117: 183–9
  (2006) *Law and Justice in the Courts of Classical Athens*. Cambridge

Lanza, M. (2000) 'Entrelacement des espaces chez Aristophane (l'exemple des *Acharniens*)', *Pallas* 54: 133–9

Lape, S. (2004) *Reproducing Athens: Menander's Comedy, Democratic Culture, and the Hellenistic City*. Princeton, NJ
  (2006) 'The poetics of the *kômos*-chorus in Menander's comedy', *American Journal of Philology* 127: 89–109
  (2010a) *Race and Citizen Identity in the Classical Athenian Democracy*. Cambridge
  (2010b) 'Gender in Menander's Comedy' in Petrides and Papaioannou (2010) 51–78

Lauter, P., ed. (1964) *Theories of Comedy*. New York

Leach, E. (1961) *Rethinking Anthropology*. London

Le Guen, B. (1995) 'Théâtre et cités à l'époque Hellénistique', *Revue des Études Grecques* 108: 59–90
  (2001) *Les associations de technites dionysiaques à l' époque hellénistique*. 2 vols., Nancy
  (2007) 'Le palmarès de l'acteur-athlète: retour sur *Syll.3* 1080 (Tégée)', *Zeitschrift für Papyrologie und Epigraphik* 160: 97–107

Legrand, P.-E. (1910) *Daos: Tableau de la comédie grecque pendant la période dite nouvelle (Κωμῳδία Νέα)*. Lyons and Paris

Leigh, M. (2004) *Comedy and the Rise of Rome*. Oxford

Leo, F. (1912) *Plautinische Forschungen zur Kritik und Geschichte der Komödie*, 2nd edn. Berlin

    (1913) *Geschichte der römischen Literatur I*. Berlin

Leppin, H. (1992) *Histrionen*. Bonn

Lewis, D. M. (1997) 'Aristophanes and politics' in *Selected Papers* (P. J. Rhodes ed.), Cambridge, 173–86

Lewis, D. M., J. Boardman, J. K. Davies and M. Ostwald, eds. (1992) *The Cambridge Ancient History*, 2nd edn, vol. V. Cambridge

Lewis, D. M., J. Boardman, S. Hornblower and M. Ostwald, eds. (1994) *The Cambridge Ancient History*, 2nd edn, vol. VI. Cambridge

Liapis, V. (2002) *Menandrou Gnomai monostichoi. Eisagôgê, metaphrasê, scholia.* Athens

    (2006) 'How to make a *monostichos*: strategies of variation in the *Sententiae Menandri*', *Harvard Studies in Classical Philology* 103: 261–98

    (2012) *A Commentary on the Rhesus Attributed to Euripides*. Oxford

Lightfoot, J. L. (2002) 'Nothing to do with the technītai of Dionysus?' in Easterling and Hall (2002) 209–24

Lind, H. (1990) *Der Gerber Kleon in den Rittern des Aristophanes. Studien zur Demagogenkomödie*. Frankfurt am Main

Linderski, J. (2007) 'The Menander inscription from Pompeii and the expression *primus scripsit*', *Zeitschrift für Papyrologie und Epigraphik* 159: 45–55

Long, T. (1986) *Barbarians in Greek Comedy*. Carbondale and Edwardsville, IL

Lonis, R., ed. (1988) *L'étranger dans le monde grec*. Nancy

López Eire, A. (1986) 'La lengua de la comedia aristofánica', *Emerita* 54: 237–74

    (1991) *Ático, koiné y aticismo: Estudios sobre Aristófanes y Libanio*. Murcia

    (1996) *La lengua coloquial de la Comedia aristofánica*. Murcia

    (2002a) 'La lengua de Hiperides y Menandro', *Habis* 33: 73–94

    (2002b) 'Recursos lingüísticos de la burla en la comedia aristofánica', in Ercolani (2002) 45–70

    (2003) 'Tragedy and satyr-drama: linguistic criteria' in Sommerstein (2003) 387–412

López Férez, J. A., ed. (1995) *De Homero a Libanio (Estudios actuales sobre textos griegos II)*. Madrid

    ed. (2004) *La lengua científica griega: orígenes, desarrollo e influencia en las lenguas modernas europeas*. Madrid

Loraux, N. (1993) 'The comic acropolis: Aristophanes, Lysistrata' in N. Loraux (1993) *Children of Athens: Athenian Ideas about Citizenship and the Division Between the Sexes*. Princeton, NJ, 143–83

Lord, C. (1977) 'Aristotle, Menander, and the *Adelphoe* of Terence', *Transactions of the American Philological Association* 107: 183–202

Lottich, O. (1881) *De sermone vulgari Atticorum maxime ex Aristophanis fabulis cognoscendo*. Diss. Halle

Lowe, N. (1987) 'Tragic space and comic timing in Menander's *Dyskolos*', *Bulletin of the Institute for Classical Studies* 34: 126–38

(1988) 'Greek stagecraft and Aristophanes' in Redmond (1988) 33–52

(1993) 'Aristophanes' Books', *Annals of Scholarship* 10: 63–83

(2000) *The Classical Plot and the Invention of Western Narrative*. Cambridge

(2006) 'Aristophanic spacecraft' in Kozak and Rich (2006) 48–64

(2008) *Comedy*. Cambridge

Luppe, W. (1972) 'Die Zahl der Konkurrenten an den komischen Agonen zur Zeit despeloponnesischen Kriegs', *Philologus* 116: 53–75

Ma, J. (1999) *Antiochus III and the Cities of Western Asia Minor*. Oxford

Ma, J., N. Papazarkadas and R. Parker, eds. (2009) *Interpreting the Athenian Empire*. London

MacCary, W. T. (1969) 'Menander's slaves: their names, roles and masks', *Transactions of the American Philological Association* 100: 277–94

(1970) 'Menander's characters: their names, roles and masks', *Transactions of the American Philological Association* 101: 277–90

(1971) 'Menander's old men', *Transactions of the American Philological Association* 102: 303–25

(1972) 'Menander's soldiers: their names, roles and masks', *American Journal of Philology* 93: 279–98

(1979) 'Philokleon *ithyphallos*: dance, costume and character in the *Wasps*', *Transactions of the American Philological Association* 109: 137–47

MacDowell, D. M. (1971) *Aristophanes: Wasps*. Oxford

(1978) *The Law in Classical Athens*. Ithaca, NY

(1982) 'Aristophanes and Kallistratos', *Classical Quarterly* 32: 21–6

(1988) 'Clowning and slapstick in Aristophanes' in Redmond (1988) 1–14

(1994) 'The number of speaking actors in Old Comedy', *Classical Quarterly* 44: 325–35

(1995) *Aristophanes and Athens: An Introduction to the Plays*. Oxford

Macgregor Morris, I. (2007) 'The refutation of democracy? Socrates in the Enlightenment' in Trapp (2007) 209–27

Major, W. (1997) 'Menander in a Macedonian world', *Greek, Roman and Byzantine Studies* 38: 41–74

Malkin, I. (1994) *Myth and Territory in the Spartan Mediterranean*. Cambridge

Mansfeld, J. (1979) 'The chronology of Anaxagoras' Athenian period and the date of his trial, I', *Mnemosyne* 32: 39–69

(1980) 'The chronology of Anaxagoras' Athenian period and the date of his trial, II', *Mnemosyne* 33: 17–95

Manville, P. B. (1990) *The Origins of Citizenship in Ancient Athens*. Princeton, NJ

Marconi, C. (2007) *Temple Decoration and Cultural Identity in the Archaic Greek World*. Cambridge

(2012) 'Between performance and identity: the social context of stone theaters in late Classical and Hellenistic Sicily' in Bosher (2012) 175–207

Marianetti, M. (1993) 'Socratic mystery-parody and the issue of *asebeia* in Aristophanes' Clouds', *Symbolae Osloenses* 68: 5–31

Markle, M. M. (1985) 'Jury pay and assembly pay at Athens' in Cartledge and Harvey (1985) 265–97

Markoulaki, S., I. Christoudoulakos and C. Frangonikolaki (2004) 'Hê archaia Kisamos kai hê poleodomikê organôsê' in A. Ausilio, ed. (2004) *Creta romana e protobizantina: atti del congresso internazionale, Iraklion 23–30 settembre 2000*. Athens. vol. 2, 355–80

Marrou, H. L. (1956) *A History of Education in Antiquity*. Trans. G. Lamb. London

Marshall, C. W. (1996) 'Amphibian ambiguities answered', *Echos du Monde Classique/Classical Views* 15: 251–65

   (1997) 'Comic technique and the fourth actor', *Classical Quarterly* 47: 77–84

   (1999) 'Some fifth-century masking conventions', *Greece and Rome* 46: 188–202

   (2001) 'A gander at the Goose Play', *Theatre Journal* 55: 51–71

   (2002) 'Chorus, metatheatre, and *Dyskolos* 427–441', *Scholia* 11: 3–17

   (2006) 'Three actors in Old Comedy, again' in Harrison and Liapis (2013) 257–78

   (2013) *The Stagecraft and Performance of Roman Comedy*. Cambridge

Marshall, C. W. and G. Kovacs, eds. (2012) *No Laughing Matter. Studies in Athenian Comedy*. London

Marshall, C. W. and S. van Willigenburg (2004) 'Judging Athenian dramatic competitions', *Journal of Hellenic Studies* 124: 90–107

Martin, R. P. (2008) 'Words alone are certain good(s): philology and Greek material culture', *Transactions of the American Philological Assocation* 138: 313–49

Martín de Lucas, I. (1996) 'Los demonstrativos con -ι epidíctica en Aristófanes', *Emerita* 64: 157–71

Martindale, C. and R. F. Thomas, eds. (2006) *Classics and the Uses of Reception*. Malden, MA and Oxford

Masaracchia, A. (1981) 'La tematica amorosa in Menandro' in *Letterature Comparate: Problemi e Metodo. Studi in Onore di Ettore Paratore*. Bologna, 213–38

Mastromarco, G. (1979) 'L'esordio 'segreto' di Aristofane', *Quaderni di Storia* 5: 153–92

   (1987) 'La parabasi aristofanea tra realtà e poesia', *Dioniso* 57: 75–93

Mastronarde, D. (1994) *Euripides: Phoenissae*. Cambridge

   (1999–2000) 'Euripidean tragedy and genre: the terminology and its problems' in Cropp, Lee and Sansone (1999–2000) 23–39

   (1999–2000a) 'Introduction' in Cropp, Lee and Sansone (1999–2000) 17–22

Mattingly, D. J. and J. Salmon, eds. (2001) *Economies beyond Agriculture in the Ancient World*. London and New York

Maurogene, M. (2007) *Aristophanes on the Modern Greek Stage* (in Greek), Ph.D. thesis, University of Crete

May, R. (2006) *Apuleius and Drama. The Ass on Stage*. Oxford

Mayor, A., J. Colarusso and D. Saunders (2012) *Making Sense of 'Nonsense' Inscriptions: Non-Greek Words Associated with Amazons and Scythians on Ancient Greek Vases: Version 1.0*, Princeton/Stanford Working Papers in Classics 1–42

Mazon, P. (1904) *Essai sur la composition des comédies d'Aristophane*. Paris

McCarthy, K. (2000) *Slaves, Masters, and the Art of Authority in Plautine Comedy*. Princeton, NJ

McClintock, H. (1972) *Haywire Mac*. New York: Folkways Records. Recorded and with notes and interviews by Sam Eskin

McClure, L. (2003) *Courtesans at Table: Gender and Greek Literary Culture in Athenaeus*. New York

McDonald, M. and J. M. Walton, eds. (2007) *The Cambridge Companion to Greek and Roman Theatre*. Cambridge

McGlew, J. (1997) 'After irony: Aristophanes' *Wealth* and its modern interpreters', *American Journal of Philology* 118: 135–53

    (2002) *Citizens on Stage: Comedy and Political Culture in the Athenian Democracy*. Ann Arbor, MI

    (2004) '"Speak on my behalf": persuasion and purification in Aristophanes' Wasps', *Arethusa* 37: 11–36

McKeown, N. (2011) 'Resistance among chattel slaves in the Classical Greek World' in Bradley and Cartledge (2011) 153–76

McLeish, K. (1980) *The Theatre of Aristophanes*. New York

Meiggs, R. (1972) *The Athenian Empire*. Oxford

Meiggs, R. and D. M. Lewis, eds. (1988) *A Selection of Greek Historical Inscriptions to the End of the Fifth Century BC*, revised edn. Oxford

Meillet, A. (1965) *Aperçu d'une histoire de la langue grecque*, 8th edn. Paris

Mertens, D. (1982) 'Das Theater-Ekklesiasterion auf der Agora von Metapont', *Architectura* 12: 93–124

Mertens, D. and A. de Siena (1982) 'Metaponto: Il teatro-ekklesiasterion', *Bolletino d'Arte del Ministero della Pubblica Istruzione*, VI: 16: 1–60

Mette, H-J. (1977) *Urkunden dramatischer Aufführungen in Griechenland*. Berlin

Michaèl, C. A. (1981) Ὁ κωμικὸς λόγος τοῦ Ἀριστοφάνους. Athens

Michelakis, P. (2002) *Achilles in Greek Tragedy*. Cambridge

Millett, P. (1991) *Lending and Borrowing in Ancient Athens*. Cambridge

Millino, G. (2000) 'Epicarmo e i Pigmei', *Anemos* 1: 113–50

Millis, B. and D. Olson (2012) *Inscriptional Records for the Dramatic Festivals in Athens: IGII2 2318–2325 and Related Texts*. Leiden and Boston

Mirhady, D. (2007) 'The dicasts' oath and the question of fact' in A. Sommerstein and J. Fletcher, eds., *Horkos: The Oath in Greek Society*. Bristol, 48–59

Mitchell-Boyask, R. (2008) Review of Wilson (2007c), *Bryn Mawr Classical Review* 2008.05.24

MMC = Webster (1978)

MNC = Webster (1995)

Möller, A. (2007) 'Classical Greece: distribution' in Scheidel *et al.* (2007) 362–84

Moore, T. J. (1998) 'Music and structure in Roman comedy,' *American Journal of Philology* 119: 245–73

    (2008) 'When did the *tibicen* play? Meter and musical accompaniment in Roman Comedy', *Transactions of the American Philological Association* 138: 3–46

    (2012) *Music in Roman Comedy*. Cambridge

Moraw, S. and E. Nölle, eds. (2002) *Die Geburt des Theaters in der griechischen Antike*. Mainz

Moreno, A. (2007) *Feeding the Democracy: The Athenian Grain Supply in the Fifth and Fourth Centuries BC*. Oxford

    (2009) '"The Attic neighbour": the cleruchy in the Athenian Empire' in Ma, Papazarkadas and Parker (2009) 211–21

Moretti, J.-C. (1993) 'Les débuts de l'architecture théâtrale en Sicile et en Italie méridionale (5th–3rd s.)', *Topoi* 3: 72–100

(1999–2000) 'The theater of the sanctuary of Dionysus Eleutheros in late fifth-century Athens', *Illinois Classical Studies* 24–25: 377–98

Morgan, T. (1998) *Literate Education in the Hellenistic and Roman Worlds*. Cambridge

Morley, N. (2007) *Trade in Classical Antiquity*. Cambridge

Morris, I. (1994) 'The Athenian economy twenty years after *The Ancient Economy*', *Classical Philology* 89: 351–66

(1998) 'Remaining invisible: the archaeology of the excluded in classical Athens' in S. R. Joshel and S. Murnaghan, eds., *Women and Slaves in Greco-Roman Culture: Differential Equations*. London, 193–220

(2000) *Archaeology as Cultural History: Words and Things in Iron Age Greece*. Oxford

Mossé, C. (1973) *Athens in Decline 404–86 BC* (English trans. J. Stewart). London

(1989) 'Quelques remarques sur la famille à Athènes à la fin du IVème Siècle: Le témoignage du théâtre de Ménandre' in F. J. Fernández Nieto, ed., *Symposion 1982: Vorträge zur griechischen und hellenistischen Rechtsgeschichte*, Cologne, 129–34

Most, G.W. (2000) 'Generating genres: the idea of the tragic' in Depew and Obbink (2000) 15–36

Moulton, C. (1981) *Aristophanic Poetry*. Göttingen

Muecke, F. (1977) 'Playing with the play: theatrical self-consciousness in Aristophanes' *Antichthon* 11: 52–67

(1982a) 'I know you – by your rags: costume and disguise in fifth-century drama', *Antichthon* 16: 17–34

(1982b) 'Portrait of the artist as a young woman', *Classical Quarterly* 32: 41–55

Müller, A. (1913) 'Die Schimpfwörter in der griechischen Komödie', *Philologus* 72: 321–37

Müller, C. W., K. Sier and J. Werner, eds. (1992) *Zum Umgang mit fremden Sprachen in der griechisch-römischen Antike*. Stuttgart

Müller-Strübing, H. (1873) *Aristophanes und die Historische Kritik. Polemische Studien zur Geschichte von Athen in fünften Jahrhundert vor Ch. G.* Leipzig

Murray, G. (1912: 1927), 'Excursus on the ritual forms preserved in Greek Tragedy' in: J. Harrison (1927) *Themis: A Study of the Social Origins of Greek Religion*, 2nd edn. Cambridge (1st edition published in 1912), 341–63

(1933) *Aristophanes: A Study*. Oxford

(1943) 'Ritual elements in the New Comedy', *Classical Quarterly* 37: 46–54

Murray, P. and P. Wilson, eds. (2004) *The Culture of 'Mousikē' in the Classical Athenian City*. Oxford

Mureddu, P. and G. F. Nieddu, eds. (2006) *Comicità e riso tra Aristofane e Menandro*. Amsterdam

Nachtergael, L. (1977) *Les Galates en Grèce et les Sôtéria de Delphes*. Mémoires de la classe des lettres de l'Academie Royale Belgique 73. Brussels

Nervegna, S. (2007) 'Staging scenes or plays? Theatrical revivals of 'old' Greek drama in antiquity', *Zeitschrift für Papyrologie und Epigraphik* 162: 14–42

(2010) 'Menander's *Theophorumene* between Greece and Rome', *American Journal of Philology* 131: 23–68

(2013) *Menander in Antiquity: The Contexts of Reception*. Cambridge

Nesselrath, H.-G. (1990) *Die attische mittlere Komödie: Ihre Stellung in der antiken Literaturkritik und Literaturgeschichte*. Berlin

    (1993) 'Parody and later Greek comedy', *Harvard Studies in Classical Philology* 95: 181–95

    (1995) 'Myth, parody, and comic plots' in Dobrov (1995) 1–27 (1997) 'The polis of Athens in Middle Comedy' in Dobrov (1997) 271–88

    (2010) 'Comic fragments: transmission and textual criticism' in Dobrov (2010) 423–53

    (2011) 'Menander and his rivals: new light from the comic adespota?' in Obbink and Rutherford (2011) 119–37

Newiger, H.-J. (1957) *Metapher und Allegorie: Studien zu Aristophanes*. Munich

    (1989) 'Ekkyklema e mechane nella messa in scena del dramma greco', *Dioniso* 59: 173–185

Newiger, H.-J., ed. (1975) *Aristophanes und die alte Komödie*. Darmstadt

Nielsen, I. (2002) *Cultic Theatres and Ritual Drama: A Study in Regional Development and Religious Interchange between East and West in Antiquity*. Aarhus

Nightingale, A. W. (1995) *Genres in Dialogue: Plato and the Construction of Philosophy*. Cambridge

Norwood, G. (1931) *Greek Comedy*. Boston, NJ

Nünlist, R. (2002) 'Speech within speech in Menander' in Willi (2002a) 219–59

Obbink, D. and R. Rutherford, eds. (2011) *Culture in Pieces: Essays on Ancient Texts in Honour of Peter Parsons*. Oxford

Ober, J. (1989) *Mass and Elite in Democratic Athens: Rhetoric, Ideology, and the Power of the People*. Princeton, NJ

Ober, J. and C. Hedrick, eds. (1996) *Demokratia: A Conversation on Democracies*. Princeton, NJ

Ober, J. and B. Strauss (1990) 'Drama, political rhetoric, and the discourse of Athenian democracy' in Winkler and Zeitlin (1990) 237–70

Ogden, D. (1996) *Greek Bastardy in the Classical and Hellenistic Periods*. Oxford

Oliva, C. (1968) 'La parodia e la critica letteraria nella commedia post-aristofanea', *Dioniso* 42: 25–92

Oliver, G. (2007) *War, Food and Politics in Early Hellenistic Athens*. Oxford

Olson, D. (1989) 'Cario and the new world of Aristophanes' Plutus', *Transactions of the American Philological Association* 119: 193–9

    (1990) 'Economics and ideology in Aristophanes' *Wealth*', *Harvard Studies in Classical Philology* 93: 223–42

    (1991) 'Dicaeopolis' political motivations in Aristophanes' *Acharnians*', *Journal of Hellenic Studies* 111: 200–3

    (1992) 'Names and naming in Old Comedy', *Classical Quarterly* 42: 304–19

    (1996) 'Politics and poetry in Aristophanes' *Wasps*', *Transactions of the American Philological Association* 126: 129–50

    (1998) *Aristophanes: Peace*. Oxford

    (2002) *Aristophanes: Acharnians*. Oxford

    (2007) *Broken Laughter: Selected Fragments of Greek Comedy*. Oxford

    (2010) 'Comedy, politics, and society' in Dobrov (2010) 35–69

Omitowoju, R. (2002) *Rape and the Politics of Consent in Classical Athens*. Cambridge

O'Regan, D. (1992) *Rhetoric, Comedy and the Violence of Language in Aristophanes' Clouds*. Oxford

Orfanos, Ch. (2007) 'Revolutionary Aristophanes?' in Hall and Wrigley (2007) 106–16

Orth, C. (2009) *Strattis: die Fragmente*. Berlin

Osborne, R. (1985) *Demos: The Discovery of Classical Attica*. Cambridge
  (1987) *Classical Landscape with Figures: the Ancient Greek City and its Countryside*. London
  (1992) '"Is it a farm?" The definition of agricultural sites and settlements in ancient Greece' in Wells (1992) 21–7
  (2000) 'An other view: an essay in political history' in Cohen (2000) 21–42

Osborne, R. ed. (2007) *Debating the Athenian Cultural Revolution: Art, Literature, Philosophy, and Politics 430–380 BC*. Cambridge

Osborne, R. and S. Hornblower, eds. (1994) *Ritual, Finance, Politics: Athenian Democratic Accounts Presented to David Lewis*. Oxford

O'Sullivan, L. (2009) 'History from comic hypotheses: Stratocles, Lachares, and *P.Oxy.* 1235', *Greek, Roman and Byzantine Studies* 49: 53–79

O'Sullivan, N. (1992) *Alcidamas, Aristophanes and the Beginnings of Greek Stylistic Theory*. Stuttgart

Ostwald, M. (1986) *From Popular Sovereignty to the Sovereignty of Law: Law, Society, and Politics in Fifth-Century Athens*. Berkeley, CA

O'Toole, L. M. and A. Shukman, eds. (1977) *Formalist Theory* (= vol. 5 of *Russian Poetics in Translation*). Oxford

Otto, A. (1890) *Die Sprichwörter und sprichwörtlichen Redensarten der Römer*. Leipzig

Palmer, J. (1987) *The Logic of the Absurd*. London
  (1994) *Taking Humour Seriously*. London and New York

Palmer, L. R. (1980) *The Greek Language*. London

Paoli, U. E. (1962) *Comici Latini e Diritto Attico*. Milan
  (1976) *Altri Studi di Diritto Greco e Romano*. Milan

Papazarkadas, N. (2009) 'Epigraphy and the Athenian Empire: re-shuffling the chronological cards' in Ma, Papazarkadas and Parker (2009) 67–88

Parker, L. P. E. (1988) 'Eupolis the unruly', *Proceedings of the Cambridge Philological Society* 34: 115–22
  (1991) 'Eupolis or Dicaeopolis?', *Journal of Hellenic Studies* 111: 203–8
  (1997) *The Songs of Aristophanes*. Oxford

Parker, R. (2005) *Polytheism and Society at Athens*. Oxford
  (2007) 'Gilbert Murray and Greek religion' in Stray (2007) 81–102
  (2011) *On Greek Religion*. Ithaca, NY

Parsons, P. (2007) *City of the Sharp-Nosed Fish: The Lives of the Greeks in Roman Egypt*. London

Patterson, C. (1998) *The Family in Greek History*. Cambridge
  (1991) 'Marriage and married women in Athenian law' in S. Pomeroy, ed., *Women's History and Ancient History*, Chapel Hill, NC, 48–72
  (1994) 'The case against Neaira and the public ideology of the Athenian family' in A. Scafuro and A. L. Boegehold, eds., *Athenian Identity and Civic Ideology*, Baltimore, MD and London, 199–216

Pauw, F. (1996) 'Aristophanes' Nachleben and other Post-Renaissance disasters', *Akroterion* 41: 161–86

PCG = Kassel and Austin (1983–)

Pearcy, L. T. (2003) 'Aristophanes in Philadelphia: the *Acharnians* of 1886', *Classical World* 96: 299–313

Pelling, C. B. R. (2000) *Literary Texts and the Greek Historian*. London

Pelling, C. B. R., ed. (1990) *Characterization and Individuality in Greek Literature*. Oxford

(1997) *Greek Tragedy and the Historian*. Oxford

Penney, J. H. W., ed. (2004) *Indo-European Perspectives: Studies in Honour of Anna Morpurgo Davies*. Oxford

Peppler, C. W. (1910) 'The termination -ικός, as used by Aristophanes for comic effect', *American Journal of Philology* 31: 428–44

(1916) 'The suffix -μα in Aristophanes', *American Journal of Philology* 37: 459–65

(1918), (1921) 'Comic terminations in Aristophanes', *American Journal of Philology* 39: 173–83; 42: 152–61

Perlman, S. (1976) 'Panhellenism, the polis and imperialism', *Historia* 25: 1–30

Pernigotti, C. (2008) *Menandri Sententiae*. Florence

Perusino, F. (1989) *Platonio: la commedia greca*. Urbino

Petrides, A. and S. Papioannou, eds. (2010) *New Perspectives on Postclassical Comedy*. Newcastle

Petzl, G. and E. Schwertheim (2006) *Hadrian und die dionysischen Künstler: drei in Alexandria Troas neugefundene Briefe des Kaisers an die Künstler-Vereinigung*. Bonn

Pfeiffer, R. (1968) *History of Classical Scholarship from the Beginnings to the End of the Hellenistic Age*. Oxford

PhV = Trendall (1967)

Piana, R. (2005) 'La Réception d'Aristophane en France de Palissot à Vitez 1760–1962', Ph.D. thesis, Paris, Vincennes and Saint-Denis

Pickard-Cambridge, A. W. (1988) *The Dramatic Festivals of Athens*, 2nd edn, revised by J. Gould and D. M. Lewis, reissued with supplement and corrections. Oxford

Pickard-Cambridge, A. W. and T. B. L. Webster (1962) *Dithyramb, Tragedy and Comedy*. Oxford

Pierce, K. F. (1997) 'The portrayal of rape in New Comedy' in S. Deacy and K. Pierce, eds., *Rape in Antiquity*, London, 163–84

(1998) 'Ideals of masculinity in New Comedy' in Foxhall and Salmon (1998) 137–47

Piqueux, A. (2006) 'Le corps comique sur les vases «phlyaques» et dans la comédie attique', *Pallas* 71: 27–55

Pirrotta, S. (2009) *Plato comicus: die fragmentarischen Komödien*. Berlin

Platter, C. (2007) *Aristophanes and the Carnival of Genres*. Baltimore, MD

Podlecki, A. J. (1975) *The Life of Themistocles: A Critical Survey of the Literary and Archaeological Evidence*. Montreal

(1990) 'Could women attend the theater in ancient Athens?', *Ancient World* 21: 45–63

Poe, J. P. (1996) 'The supposed conventional meanings of dramatic masks: a re-examination of Pollux 4. 133–54', *Philologus* 140: 306–28

(1999) 'Entrances, exits, and the structure of Aristophanic comedy', *Hermes* 127: 189–207

(2000) 'Multiplicity, discontinuity, and visual meaning in Aristophanic comedy', *Rheinisches Museum* 143: 256–95

Pohlenz, M. (1927: 1965), 'Das Satyrspiel und Pratinas von Phleius' in H. Dörrie, ed. (1965) *Max Pohlenz: Kleine Schriften*. Vol. 2, Hildesheim, 473–96

Pöhlmann, E., ed. (1995) *Studien zur Bühnendichtung und zum Theaterbau der Antike*. Frankfurt

Polacco, L. (1987) 'L'evoluzione del teatro Greco comico nel IV a.C.' *Dioniso* 57: 267–79

Polacco, L. and C. Anti (1981; 1990) *Il teatro antico di Siracusa,* part I and part II. Rimini

To Pontiki, 19 August 1999: special issue on Aristophanes' *Birds* (in Greek)

Porter, J. (1997) 'Adultery by the book: Lysias I (*On the murder of Eratosthenes*) and comic *diegesis*', *Echos du Monde Classique* 40: 421–53

(1999–2000) 'Euripides and Menander: Epitrepontes, Act IV', *Illinois Classical Studies* 24–25: 157–73

Poultney, J. W. (1963) 'Studies in the syntax of Attic comedy', *American Journal of Philology* 84: 359–76

Pozzi, D. (1985–1986) 'The pastoral ideal in "The Birds" of Aristophanes', *Classical Journal* 81: 119–29

Préaux, C. (1957) 'Ménandre et la société athénienne', *Chronique d'Égypte* 32: 84–100

(1960) 'Les fonctions du droit dans la comedie nouvelle', *Chronique d'Égypte* 25: 222–39

Proffitt, L. (2010) 'Family, slavery and subversion in Menander's Epitrepontes' in Alston, Hall and Proffitt (2010) 152–74

Propp, V. I. (1968) *Morphology of the Folktale*. Austin, TX

Purves, A. (1995) 'Empowerment for the Athenian citizen: Philocleon as actor and spectator in Aristophanes' Wasps' in Zimmermann (1995) 5–22

Quadlbauer, F. (1960) 'Die Dichter der griechischen Komödie im literarischen Urteil der Antike', *Wiener Studien* 73: 40–82

Quaglia, R. (1998) 'Elementi strutturali nelle commedie di Cratino', *Acme: Annali della Facoltà di lettere e filosofia dell' Università degli statale di Milano* 51: 23–71

Questa, C. and R. Raffaelli, eds. (2002) *Due seminari plautini: La tradizione del testo, i modelli*. Urbino

Questa, C., ed. (2008) *Titus Maccius Plautus: Bacchides*. Sarsina and Urbino

Quincey, J. (1966) 'The end of Menander's "Sicyonian"', *Phoenix* 20: 116–19

Raaflaub, K. (1996) 'Equalities and inequalities in Athenian Democracy' in Ober and Hedrick (1996) 139–74

Rajan, T. (2000) 'Theories of genre' in Brown (2000) 226–49

Rau, P. (1967) *Paratragodia: Untersuchung einer komischen Form des Aristophanes*. Munich

Reckford, K. J. (1987) *Aristophanes' Old-and-New Comedy. Volume I: Six Essays in Perspective*. Chapel Hill, NC

Redmond, J., ed. (1988) *Farce*. Cambridge (= *Themes in Drama* 10)

Rehm, R. (2002) *The Play of Space: Spatial Transformations in Greek Tragedy.* Princeton, NJ

Reitzammer, L. (2008) 'Aristophanes' *Adōniazousai*', *Classical Antiquity* 27: 282–333

Revermann, M. (1997) 'Cratinus' *Dionysalexandros* and the head of Pericles', *Journal of Hellenic Studies* 117: 197–200

   (2006a) *Comic Business: Theatricality, Dramatic Technique, and Performance Contexts of Aristophanic Comedy.* Oxford

   (2006b) 'The competence of theatre audiences in fifth- and fourth-century Athens', *Journal of Hellenic Studies* 126: 99–124

   (2008) 'Reception studies of Greek drama', *Journal of Hellenic Studies* 128: 175–8

   (2013) 'Paraepic comedy: point(s) and practices' in Bakola, Prauscello and Telò (2013) 101–28

Revermann, M. and P. Wilson, eds. (2008) *Performance, Iconography, Reception: Studies in Honour of Oliver Taplin.* Oxford

Reynolds, L. and N. Wilson (2013) *Scribes and Scholars: A Guide to the Transmission of Greek and Latin Literature*, 4th edn. Oxford

Rhodes, P. J. (1978) 'Bastards as Athenian citizens', *Classical Quarterly* 28: 89–92

   (1979) '*Eisangelia* in Athens', *Journal of Hellenic Studies* 99: 103–14

   (1982) 'Problems in Athenian *eisphora* and liturgies', *American Journal of Ancient History* 7: 1–15

   (1993) *A Commentary on the Aristotelian Athenaion Politeia*, 2nd edn. Oxford

   (2004) 'Aristophanes and the Athenian assembly' in Cairns and Knox (2004) 223–37

Ribbeck, O. (1876) 'Über den Begriff des *eirôn*', *Rheinisches Museum* 31: 381–400

   (1883) *Kolax: eine ethologische Studie.* Leipzig

   (1897–1898) *Scaenicae Romanorum Poesis Fragmenta*, 3rd edn, 2 vols. Leipzig

Richlin, A., ed. (1992) *Pornography and Representation in Greece and Rome.* Oxford

   (1997) 'Gender and rhetoric: producing manhood in the schools' in Dominik (1997) 90–110

Richter, G. M. (1984) *The Portraits of the Greeks.* Abridged and revised by R. R. R. Smith. Oxford

Ritschl, F. (1845) *Parerga zu Plautus und Terenz.* Leipzig

Riyad, H. and A. Selim (eds.) (1978), *The Cairo Codex of Menander (P. Cair. J. 43227)*, London 1978

Robb, D., ed. (2007) *Clowns, Fools and Picaros: Popular Forms in Theatre, Fiction and Film.* Amsterdam and New York

Robert, C. (1911) *Die Masken der Neuren Attischen Komodie.* Halle

Robertson, B. (2008) 'The Slave-names of IG i³ 1032 and the ideology of slavery at Athens' in C. Cooper, ed. (2008), *Epigraphy and the Greek Historian*, 79–118

Robinson, E. G. D. (2004) 'Reception of comic theatre amongst the indigenous South Italians', *Mediterranean Archaeology* 17: 193–212

Robson, J. (2006) *Humour, Obscenity and Aristophanes.* Tübingen

   (2008) 'Lost in translation? The problem of (Aristophanic) humour' in Hardwick and Stray (2008) 168–82

   (2009) *Aristophanes: An Introduction.* London

Roche M. W. (1998). *Tragedy and Comedy: A Systematic Study and a Critique of Hegel*. Albany, NY: State University of New York Press

Rodríguez-Noriega Guillén, L. (1996) *Epicarmo de Siracusa. Testimonios y Fragmentos Edicióncrítica bilingüe*. Oviedo

Rose, P. W. (1992) *Sons of the Gods, Children of the Earth: Ideology and Literary Form in Ancient Greece*. Ithaca, NY

(1999) 'Theorizing Athenian imperialism and the Athenian State' in Falkner *et al.* (1999) 19–40

(2006) 'Divorcing ideology from Marxism and Marxism from ideology: some problems', *Arethusa* 39: 101–36

Roselli, D. K. (2007) 'Gender, class, and ideology: the social function of human sacrifice in Euripides' *Children of Heracles*', *Classical Antiquity* 26: 81–169

(2009) '*Theorika* in fifth-century Athens', *Greek, Roman and Byzantine Studies* 49: 5–30

(2011) *Theater of the People: Spectators and Society in Ancient Athens*. Austin, TX

Rosen, R. (1988) *Old Comedy and the Iambographic Tradition*. Atlanta, GA

(1995) 'Plato comicus and the evolution of Greek comedy' in Dobrov (1995) 119–37

(2000) 'Cratinus' *Pytine* and the construction of the comic self' in Harvey and Wilkins (2000) 23–39

(2004) 'Aristophanes' *Frogs* and the *Contest of Homer and Hesiod*', *Transactions of the American Philological Association* 134: 295–322

(2006) 'Comic aischrology and the urbanization of agroikia' in Rosen and Sluiter (2006) 218–38

(2007) *Making Mockery: The Poetics of Ancient Satire*. Oxford

(2010) 'Aristophanes' in Dobrov (2010) 227–78

Rosen, R. and I. Sluiter, eds., (2006) *City Countryside and the Spatial Organization of Value in Classical Antiquity*. Leiden

Rosenbloom, D. (2002) 'From *poneros* to *pharmakos*: theater, social drama, and revolution in Athens, 428–404 B.C.E.', *Classical Antiquity* 21: 283–346

(2004) '*Poneroi* vs. *chrestoi*: the ostracism of Hyperbolus and the struggle for hegemony in Athens after the death of Perikles, Part II', *Transactions of the American Philological Association* 134: 323–58

Rosenstrauch, H. (1967) *Studia nad językiem Menandra*. Wrocław

Rosivach, V. J. (1991) 'Some Athenian presuppositions about the poor', *Greece and Rome* 38: 189–98

(1998) *When a Young Man Falls in Love: The Sexual Exploitation of Women in New Comedy*. New York and London

(1999) 'Enslaving barbaroi and the Athenian ideology of slavery', *Historia* 48: 129–57

(2000) 'The audiences of New Comedy', *Greece and Rome* 47: 169–71

(2001) 'Class matters in the *Dyskolos* of Menander', *Classical Quarterly* 51: 127–34

Rossetto, P. and G. Sartorio, eds. (1994) *Teatri Greci e Romani: alle origini del linguaggio rappresentato*. 2 vols., Rome

Rossi, L. E. (1977) 'Un nuovo papiro epicarmeo e il tipo del medico in commedia', *Atene e Roma* n.s. 22: 81–4

Rostovtzeff, M. (1941) *Social and Economic History of the Hellenistic World*. 3 vols., Oxford

Rothwell, K. (1990) *Politics and Persuasion in Aristophanes' Ecclesiazusae*. Mnemosyne Supplement 111. Leiden

(1995) 'The continuity of the chorus in fourth-century Attic comedy' in Dobrov (1995) 99–118

Roueché, C. (1993) *Performers and Partisans at Aphrodisias*. London

Rudd, N. (1981) 'Romantic love in classical times?', *Ramus* 10: 140–58

Ruffell, I. (2000) 'The world turned upside down: utopia and utopianism in the fragments of Old Comedy' in Harvey and Wilkins (2000) 473–506

(2002) 'A total write-off: Aristophanes, Cratinus, and the rhetoric of comic competition', *Classical Quarterly* 52: 138–63

(2006) 'A little ironic don't you think? Utopian criticism and the problem of Aristophanes' last plays' in Kozak and Rich (2006) 65–104

(2008) 'Audience and emotion in the reception of Greek drama' in Revermann and Wilson (2008) 37–58

(2010) 'Translating Greece to Rome: humour and the re-invention of popular culture' in D. Chiaro, ed. (2010) *Translation, Humour and Literature*. London and New York, 91–118

(2011) *Politics and Anti-Realism in Athenian Old Comedy*. Oxford

Ruschenbusch, E. (1979) 'Die Einführung des Theorikon', *Zeitschrift für Papyrologie und Epigraphik* 36: 303–8

Russell, D. A. (1964) *'Longinus': On the Sublime*. Oxford

Russo, C. F. (1994) *Aristophanes: An Author for the Stage*. London

Rusten, J. S. (2006) 'The four "new Lenaean victors" of 428–5 B.C. (and the date of the first Lenaean comedy) reconsidered', *Zeitschrift für Papyrologie und Epigraphik* 157: 22–6

Rusten, J., J. Henderson, D. Konstan, R. Rosen and N. Slater, eds. and trans. (2011) *The Birth of Comedy: Athenian Comedy in Texts, Documents, and Images*, 486–282. Baltimore, MD

Saetta Cottone, R. (2005) *Aristofane e la poetica dell'ingiuria*. Rome

Saïd, S. (1979) 'L'Assemblé des Femmes: les femmes, l'économie et la politique' in Bonnamour and Delavault (1979) 33–69

(1987) 'Travestis et travestissements dans les comédies d'Aristophane', *Cahiers du Groupe Interdisciplinaire du Théâtre Antique (GITA)* 3: 217–48

Salomone, S. (1981) 'L'altra faccia di Epicarmo', *Sandalion* 4: 59–69

Sandbach, F. H. (1970) 'Menander's manipulation of language for dramatic purposes' in Turner (1970) 111–43

(1990) *Menandri reliquiae selectee*, revised edn. Oxford

Sarat, A. and T. R. Kearns, eds. (1998) *Law in the Domains of Culture*. Ann Arbor, MI

Sargent, R. L. (1925) *The Size of the Slave Population at Athens During the Fifth and Fourth Centuries Before Christ*. Urbana, IL

Sayer, A. (2005) *The Moral Significance of Class*. Cambridge

Scafuro, A. (1994) 'Witnessing and false witnessing: proving citizenship and kin identity in fourth century Athens' in A. Scafuro and A. L. Boegehold, eds., *Athenian Identity and Civic Ideology*, Baltimore, MD and London, 156–98

(1997) *The Forensic Stage: Settling Disputes in Graeco-Roman New Comedy*. Cambridge

Schaps, D. M. (1979) *Economic Rights of Women in Ancient Greece*. Edinburgh

Schareika, H. (1978) *Der Realismus der aristophanischen Komödie*. Frankfurt

Scheidel, W., I. Morris and R. Saller, eds. (2007) *The Cambridge Economic History of the Greco-Roman World*. Cambridge

Schindler, W. (1985) 'Die Archäologie im Rahmen von Wilamowitz' Konzeption der Altertumswissenschaft' in W. M. Calder, H. Flashar and T. Lindken, eds. (1985) *Wilamowitz nach 50 Jahren*, Darmstadt, 241–62

Schmid, F. (1945) *Die Deminutiva auf -ιον im Vokativ bei Aristophanes*. Zurich

Schmidt, M. (1998) 'Komische Teufel und andere Gesellen auf der griechischen Komödienbühne', *Antike Kunst* 41: 17–32

Schnurr-Redford, C. (1995) *Frauen im klassischen Athen: Sozialer Raum und reale Bewegungsfreiheit*. Munich

Schrader, C., V. Ramón and J. Vela, eds., (1997) *Plutarco y la historia*. Zaragoza

Schwarze, J. (1971) *Die Beurteilung des Perikles durch die attische Komödie und ihre historische und historiographische Bedeutung*. Munich

Scodel, R., ed. (1993) *Theater and Society in the Classical World*. Ann Arbor, MI

Scullion, S. (1994) *Three Studies in Athenian Dramaturgy*. Stuttgart

Sear, F. (2006) *Roman Theatres: An Architectural Study*. Oxford

Sebeok, A., ed. (1984) *Carnival!* Berlin and New York

Segal, E. (1973) 'The *physis* of comedy', *Harvard Studies in Classical Philology* 77: 129–36

Segal, E. ed. (1996) *Oxford Readings in Aristophanes*. Oxford

Seidensticker, B. (2007) '"Aristophanes is back!" Peter Hacks's Adaptation of Peace' in Hall and Wrigley (2007) 194–208

Sells, D. (2012) 'Eleusis and the public status of comedy in Aristophanes' Frogs' in Marshall and Kovacs (2012) 83–99

Shapiro, H. A. (1995a) *Art and Cult under the Tyrants in Athens*, 2nd edn. Mainz
(1995b) 'Attic comedy and the "Comic Angels" krater in New York', *Journal of Hellenic Studies* 115: 173–5

Sharrock, A. and H. Morales, eds. (2000) *Intratextuality*. Oxford

Sherk, R. K. (1970) 'Daos and Spinther in Menander's *Aspis*', *American Journal of Philology* 91: 341–3

Sicherl, M. (1997) *Griechische Erstausgaben des Aldus Manutius*. Paderborn

Sick, D. H. (1999) 'Ummidia Quadratilla: cagey businesswoman or lazy pantomime watcher?', *Classical Antiquity* 18: 330–48

Sideres, G. (1976) *The Ancient Theater on the Modern Greek Stage, 1817–1932* (in Greek). Athens

Sidwell, K. (1990) 'Was Philocleon cured? The *nosos* theme in Aristophanes' Wasps', *Classica et Mediaevalia* 41: 9–31
(1993) 'Authorial collaboration? Aristophanes' *Knights* and Eupolis', *Greek, Roman and Byzantine Studies* 34: 365–89
(1994) 'Aristophanes' *Acharnians* and Eupolis', *Classica et Mediaevalia* 45: 71–115

(1995) 'Poetic rivalry and the caricature of comic poets: Cratinus' Pytine and Aristophanes' Wasps' in Griffiths (1995) 56–80

(2000) 'From Old to Middle to New? Aristotle's Poetics and the history of Athenian comedy' in Harvey and Wilkins (2000) 247–58

(2009) *Aristophanes the Democrat: The Politics of Satirical Comedy during the Peloponnesian War*. Cambridge

Sier, K. (1992) 'Die Rolle des Skythen in den Thesmophoriazusen des Aristophanes' in Müller, Sier and Werner (1992) 63–83

Sifakis, G. M. (1971a) *Parabasis and Animal Choruses*. London

(1971b) 'Aristotle, *E.N.*, IV, 2, 1123 a 19–24, and the comic chorus in the fourth century', *American Journal of Philology* 92: 410–32

(1992) 'The structure of Aristophanic comedy', *Journal of Hellenic Studies* 112: 123–42

(2006) 'From mythological parody to political satire: some stages in the evolution of Old Comedy', *Classica et Mediaevalia* 57: 19–48

Silk, M. (1980) 'Aristophanes as a lyric poet' in Henderson (1980a) 99–151

(1987) 'Pathos in Aristophanes', *Bulletin of the Institute of Classical Studies* 34: 78–111

(1990) 'The people of Aristophanes' in Pelling (1990) 150–73

(2000a) *Aristophanes and the Definition of Comedy*. Oxford

(2000b) 'Aristophanes versus the rest: comic poetry in Old Comedy' in Harvey and Wilkins (2000) 299–315

Simon, A. K. H. (1938) *Comicae Tabellae*. Emsdetten

Slater, N.W. (1985) 'Play and playwright references in Middle and New Comedy', *Liverpool Classical Monthly* 10: 103–5

(1986) 'The Lenaean theatre', *Zeitschrift für Papyrologie und Epigraphik* 66: 255–64

(1995) 'The fabrication of comic illusion' in Dobrov (1995) 29–45

(1996) 'Literacy and Old Comedy' in Worthington (1996) 99–112

(2002) *Spectator Politics: Metatheatre and Performance in Aristophanes*. Philadelphia, PA

Slater, W. J. (1976) 'Symposium at sea', *Harvard Studies in Classical Philology* 80: 161–70

(2008) 'Hadrian's letters to the athletes and Dionysiac Artists concerning arrangements for the "circuit" of games' (Review of Petzl and Schwertheim (2006)), *Journal of Roman Archaeology* 21: 610–20

Slater, W. J. ed. (1991) *Dining in a Classical Context*. Ann Arbor, MI

Sluiter, I. and R. Rosen, eds. (2004) *Free Speech in Classical Antiquity*. Leiden

(2008) *KAKOS: Badness and Anti-Value in Classical Antiquity*. Leiden

Small, J. P. (2003) *The Parallel Worlds of Classical Art and Text*. Cambridge

(2005) 'Pictures of tragedy?' in Gregory (2005) 103–18

Smith, T. J. (2007) 'The corpus of komast vases: from identity to exegesis' in Csapo and Miller (2007) 48–76

Snell, B. (1971) *Tragicorum Graecorum fragmenta*. Vol. I, Göttingen

Solomos, A. (1961: 1974) *The Living Aristophanes*. Originally published as *Ho zontanos Aristophanes* (in Greek). Athens. Trans. A. Solomos and M. Felheim. Ann Arbor, 1974

Sommerstein, A. H. (1981) *Aristophanes: Acharnians*. Warminster
  (1982) *Aristophanes: Clouds*. Warminster
  (1983, corr. 1996) *Wasps*. Warminster (= *The Comedies of Aristophanes* 4)
  (1984) 'Aristophanes and the demon Poverty', *Classical Quarterly* 34: 314–33.
    Reprinted with minor revisions in Segal (1996) 252–81
  (1990) *Aristophanes: Peace*, 2nd edn. Warminster
  (1992) 'Old comedians on Old Comedy', *Drama* 1: 14–33
  (1993) 'Kleophon and the restaging of Frogs' in Sommerstein *et al.* (1993) 461–76
  (1995/2009) 'The language of Athenian women' in De Martino and Sommerstein
    (1995) 2.61–85. Reprinted, with addenda, in Sommerstein (2009) 15–42
  (1996) 'How to avoid being a *komodoumenos*', *Classical Quarterly* 46: 327–56
  (1997) 'The theater audience, the demos, and the Suppliants of Aeschylus' in
    Pelling (1997) 63–79. Reprinted with updates in Sommerstein (2010a) 118–42
  (1998) *Ecclesiazusae*. Warminster (= *The Comedies of Aristophanes* 10)
  (1998) 'Rape and young manhood in Athenian comedy' in Foxhall and Salmon
    (1998) 100–14
  (2000) 'Platon, Eupolis and the "demagogue-comedy"' in Harvey and Wilkins
    (2000) 437–51
  (2001) *Wealth*. Warminster (= *The Comedies of Aristophanes* 11)
  (2004a) 'Harassing the satirist: the alleged attempts to prosecute Aristophanes' in
    Sluiter and Rosen (2004) 145–74
  (2004b) 'Comedy and the unspeakable' in Cairns and Knox (2004) 205–22
  (2005) 'An alternative democracy and an alternative to democracy in Aristophanic
    comedy' in Bultrighini (2005) 195–207 (discussion, 229–33). Reprinted with
    updates in Sommerstein (2009) 204–22
  (2009) *Talking about Laughter and Other Studies in Greek Comedy*. Oxford
  (2010a) *The Tangled Ways of Zeus and Other Studies in and around Greek
    Tragedy*. Oxford
  (2010b) 'The history of the text of Aristophanes' in Dobrov (2010) 399–422
Sommerstein, A. H. ed. (2003) *Shards from Kolonos: Studies in Sophoclean Frag-
  ments*. Bari
Sommerstein, A. H., S. Halliwell, J. Henderson and B. Zimmermann (eds.) (1993)
  *Tragedy, Comedy and the Polis: Papers from the Greek Drama Conference,
  Nottingham, 18–20 July 1990*. Bari
Sourvinou-Inwood, C. (2003) *Tragedy and Athenian Religion*. Lanham, MD
Sparkes, B. A. (1975) 'Illustrating Aristophanes', *Journal of Hellenic Studies* 95:
  122–35
Spielvogel, J. (2001) *Wirtschaft und Geld bei Aristophanes. Untersuchungen zu den
  ökonomischen Bedingungen in Athen im Übergang vom 5. zum 4. Jh. v. Chr.*
  Frankfurt am Main
Spineto, N. (2005) *Dionysos a teatro. Il contesto festivo del dramma Greco*. Rome
Spyropoulos, E. S. (1974) *L'accumulation verbale chez Aristophane: Recherches sur
  le style d'Aristophane*. Thessaloniki
Ste Croix, G. E. M. de (1972) *The Origins of the Peloponnesian War*. Ithaca, NY
  (1981) *The Class Struggle in the Ancient Greek World*. Ithaca, NY
Steggle, M. (2007) 'Aristophanes in Early Modern England' in Hall and Wrigley
  (2007) 52–65

Steinhausen, J. (1910) *Kômôidoumenoi*, Dissertation Bonn

Stephani, G. (2000) 'Mosaici Sconosciuti dall'Area Vesuviana' in F. Guidobaldi and A. Paribeni, eds., *Atti del VI Colloquio dell'Associazione Italiana per lo Studio e la Conservazione del Mosaico*. Ravenna, 279–90

Stone, L. M. (1981) *Costume in Aristophanic Comedy*. New York

Storey, I. C. (1995) '*Wasps* 1284–91 and the portrait of Kleon in *Wasps*', *Scholia* 4: 3–23

(2002) 'Cutting comedies' in Barsby (2002b) 146–67

(2003) *Eupolis: Poet of Old Comedy*. Oxford

(2005) 'But comedy has satyrs too' in Harrison (2005) 201–18

(2006), 'On first looking into Kratinus' Dionysalexandros' in Kozak and Rich (2006) 105–25

(2008) '"Bad" language in Aristophanes' in Sluiter and Rosen (2008) 119–41

(2010) 'Origins and fifth-century comedy' in Dobrov (2010) 179–225

(2011) *Fragments of Old Comedy*. 3 vols., Cambridge, MA

Strauss, B. S. (1986) *Athens after the Peloponnesian War: Class, Faction and Policy 404–386 BC*. London

Stray, C. (1998) *Classics Transformed: Schools, Universities, and Society in England, 1830–1960*. Oxford

Stray, C., ed. (1999) *Classics in 19th and 20th Century Cambridge: Curriculum, Culture and Community*. Cambridge

Stray, C., ed. (2007) *Gilbert Murray Reassessed: Hellenism, Theatre, and International Politics*. Oxford

Suerbaum, W., ed. (2002) *Handbuch der lateinischen Literatur der Antike. Erster Band: Die archaische Literatur*. Munich

Süss, W. (1905) *De Personarum Antiquae Comoediae Usu et Origine*. Bonn

(1908) 'Zur Komposition der altattischen Komödie', *Rheinisches Museum* 63: 12–38

(1911) *Aristophanes und die Nachwelt*. Leipzig

Svarlien, D. A. (1990–1991) 'Epicharmus and Pindar at Hieron's court', *Kokalos* 36–37: 103–110

Swain, S. (1996) *Hellenism and Empire*. Oxford

Sypher, W., ed. (1980) *Comedy*. Baltimore, MD

Taaffe, L. K. (1993) *Aristophanes and Women*. London and New York

Taillardat, J. (1965) *Les images d'Aristophane: Études de langue et de style*, 2nd edn. Paris

Taplin, O. (1977) *The Stagecraft of Aeschylus: The Dramatic Use of Exits and Entrances in Greek Tragedy*. Oxford

(1986) 'Fifth-century tragedy and comedy: a *synkrisis*', *Journal of Hellenic Studies* 106: 63–74

(1987) 'Phallology, phlyakes, iconography and Aristophanes', *Proceedings of the Cambridge Philological Society* 33: 92–104

(1993) *Comic Angels and Other Approaches to Greek Drama through Vase-Paintings*. Oxford

(1999) 'Spreading the word through performance' in Goldhill and Osborne (1999) 33–57

(2006) 'Aeschylus' *Persai*: the entry of tragedy into the celebration culture of the 470s?' in A. F. Garvie, D. Cairns and V. Liapis, eds. (2006), *Dionysalexandros:*

BIBLIOGRAPHY

Essays on Eschylus and his Fellow Tragedians in Honour of Alexander F. Garvie. Swansea, 1–10

(2007) *Pots and Plays: Interactions between Tragedy and Greek Vase-Painting of the Fourth Century BC.* Los Angeles, CA

Taplin, O. and R. Wyles, eds. (2010) *The Pronomos Vase and its Context.* Oxford

Telò, M. (2007) *Eupolidis Demi.* Florence

(2010) 'Menander' in Grafton, Most and Settis (2010) 582

Thiercy, P. (2000) 'L'unité de lieu chez Aristophane', *Pallas* 54: 15–23

Thiercy, P. and M. Menu, eds. (1997) *Aristophane: La langue, la scène, la cité.* Bari

Thomas, R. (1994) 'Literacy and the city-state in archaic and classical Greece' in A. Bowman nd G. Woolf, eds., *Literacy and Power in the Ancient* World, Cambridge, 33–66

Tierney, M. (1936) 'Aristotle and Menander', *Proceedings of the Royal Irish Academy* 43: 241–4

Tocqueville, A. de (1862: 2003) *Democracy in America*, B. Frohnen ed., H. Reeve trans., Washington, DC

Tod, M. N., ed. (1946) *A Selection of Greek Historical Inscriptions to the End of the Fifth Century BC*, 2nd edn. Oxford

Todd, S. (1993) *The Shape of Athenian Law.* Oxford

(1994) 'Status and contract in fourth-century Athens' in G. Thür, ed., *Symposion 1993*, Cologne, 125–40

(1996) 'Lysias against Nikomachos: the fate of the expert in Athenian law' in Foxhall and Lewis (1996) 101–31

Todisco, L. (2002) *Teatro e Spettacolo in Magna Grecia e Sicilia.* Milan

Todorov, T. (1972) 'Genre' in Ducrot and Todorov (1972) 193–201

(1973) *The Fantastic: A Structural Approach to a Literary Genre.* Trans. R. Howard. Ithaca, NY

(1990) *Genres in Discourse.* Trans. C. Porter. Cambridge

Tomashevsky, B.V. (1928: 1977) 'Literary genres' in O'Toole and Shukman (1977) 52–93

Too, Y. L., ed. (2001) *Education in Greek and Roman Antiquity.* Leiden

Tordoff, R. (2007) 'Aristophanes' *Assembly Women* and Plato, *Republic* book 5' in Osborne (2007) 242–63

Torrance, R. M. (1978) *The Comic Hero.* Cambridge, MA

Totaro, P. (2000) *Le seconde parabasi di Aristofane*, 2nd (corrected) edn. Stuttgart

Tracy, S. V. (1995) *Athenian Democracy in Transition: Attic Letter Cutters of 340–290 B.C.* Berkeley, CA

Traill, A. (2008) *Women and the Comic Plot in Menander.* Cambridge

Trapp, M., ed. (2007) *Socrates from Antiquity to the Enlightenment.* Aldershot

Trédé, M. and P. Hoffmann, eds. (1998) *Le rire des anciens.* Paris

Trendall, A. D. (1967) *Phlyax Vases*, 2nd edn. London (= *Bulletin of the Institute of Classical Studies* Suppl. 19)

(1988) 'Masks on Apulian red-figured vases' in Betts, Hooker and Green (1988) 137–54

Treu, M. (1999) *Undici cori comici: Aggressività, derisione e tecniche drammatiche in Aristofane.* Genoa

Turner, E. G., ed. (1970) *Ménandre: Sept exposés suivis de discussions* (Entretiens Hardt 16). Geneva

489

Uckermann, W. (1879) *De Aristophanis Comici vocabulorum formatione*. Marburg

Ussher, R. G. (1977) 'Old Comedy and "character": some comments', *Greece and Rome* 24: 71–9

Vaio, J. (1971) 'Aristophanes' *Wasps*: the relevance of the final scenes', *Greek, Roman and Byzantine Studies* 12: 335–51

(1973) 'The manipulation of theme and action in Aristophanes' *Lysistrata*', *Greek, Roman and Byzantine Studies* 14: 369–80

Van Steen, G. A. H. (2000) *Venom in Verse: Aristophanes in Modern Greece*. Princeton, NJ

(2002) 'Trying (on) gender: modern Greek productions of Aristophanes' *Thesmophoriazusae*', *American Journal of Philology* 123: 407–27

(2007) 'From scandal to success story: Aristophanes' *Birds* as staged by Karolos Koun' in Hall and Wrigley (2007) 155–78

Van Wees, H. (2001) 'The myth of the middle-class army: military and social status in ancient Athens' in Bekker-Nielsen and Hannestad (2001) 45–71

(2004) *Greek Warfare: Myths and Realities*. London

Van Zyl Smit, B. (2007) 'Freeing Aristophanes in South Africa: from high culture to contemporary satire' in Hall and Wrigley (2007) 232–46

Vanaria, M. G. (2001) 'Il gruppo fittile dello scavo XXXIId' in L. Bernabò Brea, M. Cavalier and F. Villard, *Meligunìs-Lipára XI.2. Gli scavi nella necropoli greca e romana di Lipari nell'area del terreno vescovile*. Palermo: 759–61

Vapheiade, E. and N. Papandreou, eds. (2007) *Questions on the History of Modern Greek Theater: Studies Dedicated to Demetres Spathes* (in Greek). Herakleio, Crete

Vernant, J.-P. (1980) 'The class struggle' in *Myth and Society in Ancient Greece*. Trans. J. Lloyd. New York, 11–27

Vidale, M. (2002) *L'Idea di un Lavoro Lieve: Il Lavoro Artigianale nelle Immagini della eramica Greca tra VI e IV Secolo A.C.* Padua

Vivilakes, I., ed. (2007) *Stephanos: Volume Offered in Honor of Walter Puchner* (in Greek). Athens

Vogt-Spira, G. (1992) *Dramaturgie des Zufalls: Tyche und Handeln in der Komödie Menanders*. Munich

Von Möllendorff, P. (1995) *Grundlagen einer Ästhetik der Alten Komödie. Untersuchungen zu Aristophanes und Michail Bachtin*. Tübingen

(1996–1997) 'Aischylon hairêsomai – der 'neue Aischylos' in den *Fröschen* des Aristophanes', *Würzburger Jahrbücher für die Altertumswissenschaft* 21: 129–51

(2002) *Aristophanes*. Hildesheim, Zurich and New York

Walcot, P. (1987) 'Romantic love and true love: Greek attitudes to marriage', *Ancient Society* 18: 5–33

Wallace, R. (1994) 'The Athenian laws against slander' in G. Thür, ed., *Symposion 1993*, Cologne, 109–24

(2005) 'Law, Attic comedy, and the regulation of comic speech' in Gagarin and Cohen (2005) 357–73

Walsh, D. (2009) *Distorted Ideals in Greek Vase-Paintings: the World of Mythological Burlesque*. Cambridge

Walsh, P. A. (2008) 'Comedy and conflict: the modern reception of Aristophanes', Ph.D. thesis, Brown University

(2009), 'A study in reception: the British debates over Aristophanes' Politics and Influence', *Classical Receptions Journal* 1: 55–72

Walton, J. M. (1987) 'Revival: England' in Walton (1987) 329–54

(2006) *Found in Translation: Greek Drama in English.* Cambridge and New York

(2007) 'Good manners, decorum and the public peace: Greek drama and the censor' in Billiani (2007) 143–66

Walton, J. M. ed. (1987) *Living Greek Theatre: A Handbook of Classical Performance and Modern Production.* Westport, CT

Warmington, E. H., ed. (1935–1940) *Remains of Old Latin.* 4 vols., Cambridge, MA

Webster, T. B. L. (1948) 'South Italian vases and Attic drama', *Classical Quarterly* 42: 15–27

(1949) 'The masks of Greek comedy', *Bulletin of the John Rylands Library* 32: 97–133

(1970a) *Studies in Later Greek Comedy*, 2nd edn. Manchester and New York

(1970b) *Greek Theatre Production*, 2nd edn. London

(1973) 'Three notes on Menander', *Journal of Hellenic Studies* 93: 196–200

(1974) *An Introduction to Menander.* Manchester

(1978) *Monuments Illustrating Old and Middle Comedy*, 3rd edn revised and enlarged by J. R. Green. London (= *Bulletin of the Institute of Classical Studies* Suppl. 39)

(1995) *Monuments Illustrating New Comedy*, 3rd edn revised and enlarged by J. R. Green and A. Seeberg, 2 vols. London (= *Bulletin of the Institute of Classical Studies* Suppl. 50)

Wells, B., ed. (1992) *Agriculture in Ancient Greece.* Stockholm

Welsh, D. (1983) 'The chorus of Aristophanes' Babylonians', *Greek, Roman and Byzantine Studies* 24: 137–50

Werner, J. (1975) 'Aristophanes-Übersetzung und Aristophanes-Bearbeitung in Deutschland' in Newiger (1975) 459–85

West, M. L. (1979) 'The Prometheus trilogy', *Journal of Hellenic Studies* 99: 130–48

(1987) *Introduction to Greek Metre.* Oxford

Wetmore, K. J., Jr. (2002) *The Athenian Sun in an African Sky: Modern African Adaptations of Classical Greek Tragedy.* Jefferson, NC and London

Whitehead, D. (1977) *The Ideology of the Athenian Metic.* Cambridge

Whitman, C. H. (1964) *Aristophanes and the Comic Hero.* Cambridge, MA

Whittaker, M. (1935) 'The comic fragments in their relation to the structure of Old Attic Comedy', *Classical Quarterly* 29: 181–91

Wiles, D. (1984) 'Menander's *Dyskolos* and Demetrius of Phaleron's Dilemma', *Greece and Rome* 31: 170–80

(1989) 'Marriage and prostitution in classical New Comedy', *Themes in Drama* 11, Cambridge, 31–48

(1991) *The Masks of Menander: Sign and Meaning in Greek and Roman Performance.* Cambridge

(1997) *Tragedy in Athens: Performance Space and Theatrical Meaning.* Cambridge

Wilkins, J. (2000) *The Boastful Chef: The Discourse of Food in Greek Comedy.* Oxford

Willi, A., ed. (2002a) *The Language of Greek Comedy.* Oxford

(2002b) 'The language of Greek comedy: introduction and bibliographical sketch' in Willi (2002a) 1–32

(2002c) 'Languages on stage: Aristophanic language, cultural history, and Athenian identity' in Willi (2002a) 111–49

(2003a) *The Languages of Aristophanes: Aspects of Linguistic Variation in Classical Attic Greek.* Oxford

(2003b) 'New language for a new comedy: a linguistic approach to Aristophanes' Plutus', *Proceedings of the Cambridge Philological Society* 49: 40–73

(2008) *Sikelismos: Sprache, Literatur und Gesellschaft im griechischen Sizilien (8.-5. Jh. v. Chr.).* Basel

(2010a) 'The language of Old Comedy' in Dobrov (2010) 471–510

(2010b) 'Register variation' in Bakker (2010) 297–310

(2012) 'Challenging authority: Epicharmus between epic and rhetoric' in Bosher (2012) 56–75

Williams, R. (1977) *Marxism and Literature.* Oxford

Wilson, N. G. (1982) 'Two observations on Aristophanes' *Lysistrata*', *Greek, Roman and Byzantine Studies* 23: 157–63

(1996) *Scholars of Byzantium*, 2nd edn. London

(2007) *Aristophanea: Studies on the Text of Aristophanes.* Oxford

Wilson, P. (2000) *The Athenian Institution of the Khoregia: The Chorus, the City, and the Stage.* Cambridge

(2007a) '*Nikê*'s cosmetics: dramatic victory, the end of comedy, and beyond' in Kraus, Goldhill, Foley and Elsner (2007) 257–87

(2007b) 'Sicilian choruses' in Wilson (2007c) 351–77

(2008) 'Costing the Dionysia' in Revermann and Wilson (2008) 88–127

(2011) 'The glue of democracy? Tragedy, structure, and finance' in Carter (2011)18–43

Wilson, P. ed. (2007c) *The Greek Theatre and Festivals: Documentary Studies.* Oxford

Wilson, P. and P. Murray, eds. (2004) *Music and the Muses: the Culture of Mousikê in the Classical Athenian City.* Oxford

Winkler, J. J. (1990) 'Phallos politikos: representing the body politic in Athens', *Differences* 2: 29–45

Winkler, J. J. and F. Zeitlin, eds. (1990) *Nothing to Do with Dionysus? Athenian Drama in its Social Context.* Princeton, NJ

de Wit-Tak, T. (1968) 'The function of obscenity in Aristophanes' "Thesmophoriazusae" and "Ecclesiazusae"', *Mnemosyne* 21: 357–65

Wohl, V. (2002) *Love Among the Ruins: The Erotics of Democracy in Classical Athens.* Princeton, NJ

(2010) *Law's Cosmos: Juridical Discourse in Athenian Forensic Oratory.* Cambridge

Woolf, V. (1992) 'On not knowing Greek' in Bowlby (1992) 93–106

Worman, N. (2008) *Abusive Mouths in Classical Athens.* Cambridge

Wörrle, M. and P. Zanker, eds. (1995) *Stadtbild und Bürgerbild im Hellenismus.* Munich

Worthington, I., ed. (1994) *Persuasion: Greek Rhetoric in Action.* New York

(1996) *Voice into Text.* Leiden

Wright, E. O. (2005) *Approaches to Class Analysis.* Cambridge

Wright, J. (1974) *Dancing in Chains: The Stylistic Unity of the Comoedia Palliata.* Rome

Wright, M. (2007) 'Comedy and the Trojan War', *Classical Quarterly* 57: 412–31

Wright, W. (1931) *Cicero and the Theater.* Northampton, MA

Wrigley, A. (2007) 'Aristophanes revitalized! Music and spectacle on the academic stage' in Hall and Wrigley (2007) 136–54

Wycherley, R. E. (1957) *The Athenian Agora.* Vol. 3, Princeton, NJ

Wyse, W. (1904) *The Speeches of Isaeus.* Cambridge

Yaari, N. (2008) 'Aristophanes between Israelis and Palestinians' in Hardwick and Stray (2008) 287–300

Yunis, H. (1988) 'Law, politics, and the *graphe paranomon* in fourth-century Athens', *Greek, Roman and Byzantine Studies* 29: 361–82

Zacharia, K (1995), 'The marriage of tragedy and comedy in Euripides' *Ion*' in Jäkel and Timonen (1995) 45–65

Zagagi, N. (1979) 'Sostratos as a comic, over-active and impatient lover', *Zeitschrift für Papyrologie und Epigraphik* 36: 39–48

(1994) *The Comedy of Menander: Convention, Variation and Originality.* London

Zawistowski, W. (1937) 'The Polish theater after the war' in Dickinson (1937) 364–90

Zeitlin, F. I. (1981) 'Travesties of gender and genre in Aristophanes' *Thesmophoriazusae*' in Foley (1981) 169–217. Revised in Zeitlin (1996) 375–416

(1996) *Playing the Other: Gender and Society in Classical Greek Literature.* Chicago, IL

(2003), 'The Argive festival of Hera and Euripides' *Electra*' in J. Mossman (ed.), *Oxford Readings in Euripides.* Oxford, 261–84 (revised version of article originally published in *Transactions of the American Philological Association* 101 (1970) 645–69)

Zelnick-Abramovitz, R. (2002) 'Ploutos, the god of the oligarchs', *Scripta Classica Israelica* 21: 27–44

(2005) *Not Wholly Free: The Concept of Manumission and the Status of Manumitted Slaves in the Ancient Greek World.* Leiden

Zieliński, T. (1885) *Die Gliederung der altattischen Komödie.* Leipzig

Zimmermann, B. (1983) 'Utopisches und Utopie in den Komödien des Aristophanes', *Würzburger Jahrbücher für die Altertumswissenschaft* 9: 57–77

(1984) 'The parodoi of the Aristophanic comedies', *Studi Italiani di Filologia Classica.* 3rd series, 2: 13–24

(1997) 'Parodie dithyrambischer Dichtung in den Komödien des Aristophanes' in Thiercy and Menu (1997) 87–93

(1998) *Die griechische Komödie.* Darmstadt

Zimmermann, B. ed. (1995) *Griechisch-römische Komödie und Tragödie II.* Stuttgart (=*Drama* 5)

Zini, S. (1938) *Il linguaggio dei personaggi nelle commedie di Menandro.* Florence

Žižek, S. (2000) 'Class struggle or postmodernism? Yes please!' in Butler *et al.* (2000) 90–135

Zweig, B. (1992) 'The mute nude female characters in Aristophanes' plays' in Richlin (1992) 73–89

INDEX

actors, 116, 142, 392, 397, 418
adaptation, 414–16
Aeschines, 67
Aeschylus, 30, 39, 84, 86, 207, 280, 421
Afranius, 393
Agathon, 28
agôn, 45, 67, 322
Alcaeus (comic playwright), 75
Alexander the Great, 396
Alexandria, 172
Alexis (comic playwright), 61, 75, 77, 172, 301
  Demetrios, 409
  Karchêdonios, 410, 421
  Milesians, 66
Ameipsias (comic playwright), 210
Amphis (comic playwright), 75
Anaxagoras, 425
Anaxandrides (comic playwright), 61, 182, 300
Andronicus Callistus, 431
Antiphanes (comic playwright), 50, 75, 172, 182, 184, 217
  fr. 236 (unknown play), 149
  Omphalê, 65
  Poetry, 65, 147
Apollinarios of Laodicea, 394
Apollodorus (comic playwright)
  Epidicazomenê, 420
Apuleius, 394
Aratus, 418
Archilochus, 386
Archippus (comic playwright), 180, 296
Aristomenes (comic playwright)
  Dionysos askêtês (Tradesman Dionysus), 163

Aristophanes
  Acharnians, 27–8, 48, 55, 160, 161, 162, 164, 169, 173, 180, 183, 194–5, 208, 210, 212, 213, 217, 226, 227, 229, 230, 231, 237–8, 247, 263, 276, 277, 286, 294, 312–14, 330, 342, 343, 344, 346, 373, 380, 381, 384, 391, 404, 436, 437, 439
  Aeolosikôn, 73
  Assembly Women, 35, 61, 64, 73, 147, 160, 178, 193, 214–15, 217, 229, 243, 253, 254, 262, 264, 270–1, 273, 285, 299, 308–9, 312, 316, 344, 349
  Babylonians, 27, 54, 237, 294, 349
  Birds, 139, 161, 162, 180, 183, 194–5, 210–12, 213, 217, 230, 243, 263, 264, 284, 285, 286, 313, 323–4, 327–8, 396, 430, 437, 446–7
  Clouds, 47, 52, 102–4, 139, 147, 174, 183, 193–4, 197, 210, 212, 228, 230, 262, 264, 266, 276, 284, 295, 307, 328, 330, 342, 401, 429, 434, 436–7, 438, 441, 444
  Dionysos nauagos (Shipwrecked Dionysus), 163
  Frogs, 39, 139, 162, 164, 179, 181, 183, 189, 191–3, 212, 229, 230, 243, 265, 280, 284, 285, 296, 315–16, 349, 375, 377, 380, 384, 389, 390, 429, 436, 437, 444
  Fryers, 208
  Knights, 48, 51, 53–4, 165, 195, 210, 213, 216, 226, 228, 229, 248–50, 251, 262, 264, 284, 294–5, 314, 330, 342, 343, 346, 347, 380, 385, 395, 429, 430, 436, 437
  Kôkalos, 73

INDEX

Eupolis (comic playwright), 47, 50, 53, 63,
  73, 179, 180, 182, 280, 339
  Autolycus (I and II), 161
  Chrusoun Genos (Golden Generation),
    308
  Demes, 163, 285, 300, 428
  Kolakes (Flatterers), 161, 251
  Marikas, 47, 53, 295, 348
  Philoi, 161
  Poleis (Cities), 161, 349
  Taxiarchoi, 107, 163, 280
Euripides, 30, 39, 74, 259, 265, 277, 284,
  394
  (?) *Rhesus*, 30
  Alcestis, 41
  Andromeda, 308
  Bacchae, 281
  Cyclops, 34, 41, 227
  Electra, 45
  Helen, 308
  Ion, 40
  Orestes, 42, 302
  Telephus, 247, 256, 263

fabula palliata, 393, 404–22
fabula togata, 393
festivals, 259, 276, 306–20, 405
Fraenkel, Eduard, 407–9, 414–16
fragments, 49–52, 60–78
Frazer, James, 278
freedom of speech, 37, 293–5, 329–30, 334,
  402, 404
Freud, 196
Frischlin, Nicodemus, 436
function (linguistic), 173–4, 181–2

Gellius, 395, 401, 402, 412–14, 417
Gelon (Sicilian tyrant), 84
genre, 27–42
gods, 163, 275–86
Goethe, 439
Great(er) Dionysia (dramatic festival in
  Athens), 27, 44, 99–100, 108, 131, 278,
  292, 308

Harrison, Jane, 278
Heniochus (comic playwright), 299
Heracles, 163, 281
Hermippus (comic playwright), 47, 293,
  295
Hermogenes of Tarsus, 373, 383
Herodotus, 337
Hesiod, 207, 216

hetaira/courtesan (character type), 40, 66,
  67, 75, 147–67
Hieron I (Sicilian tyrant), 84, 91
Hieron II (Sicilian tyrant), 92
Homer, 31, 189, 309, 398, 401
  Iliad, 227, 276, 375
  Odyssey, 218, 225, 232, 374
  Homeric Hymn to Hermes, 225
Horace, 416
  Ars poetica, 71, 147, 402
  Satires, 386, 388
humour, 189–204
  paradigmatic *v.* syntacmatic, 173
Hutcheon, Linda, 414–16

Ion of Chios, 28
Isocrates, 67, 338, 425

Justinian, 428

Koraes, Adamantios, 440–1
Koun, Karolos, 442, 446

language, 168–85, 399
laughter, 189–204
lawcourts
  in Athens, 323
Lenaea (dramatic festival in Athens), 27, 44,
  131, 310–11, 314
Libanius, 381, 383, 400
Livy, 416
Lycurgus, 425
Lysias, 324, 325

Macedonia, 395
Machon (comic playwright), 172
masks, 28, 139–40, 149–53, 261
mêchanê (= stage crane), 136
Menander
  Adelphoi, 419
  Anatithemenê, 360
  and class, 250–2, 255–8, 349–51, 359–67
  and iconography, 116–25, 388–9, 397–8
  and intrigue-comedy, 75
  Aspis (The Shield), 38, 182, 198–202,
    204, 257, 269, 281, 283–4, 366–7, 375,
    380, 428
  Didumai, 360
  Dis Exapatôn, 408, 411–12, 419
  Dyscolus, 40, 58, 144, 158–60, 168–9,
    174, 183, 201–2, 218–20, 267, 268,
    269, 281, 283, 302, 306, 351, 355, 359,
    373, 375, 399, 419, 428

496

Cambridge Companions to . . .

AUTHORS

TOPICS

Printed in Great Britain
by Amazon

52766090R00294